A COVENANT WITH DEATH

A Covenant with Death

*Death in the Iron Age II
and Its Rhetorical Uses in Proto-Isaiah*

Christopher B. Hays

WILLIAM B. EERDMANS PUBLISHING COMPANY
GRAND RAPIDS, MICHIGAN / CAMBRIDGE, U.K.

© 2011 Mohr Siebeck Tübingen

Originally published 2011 by Mohr Siebeck Tübingen as
Death in the Iron Age II and in First Isaiah

This edition, with new title, published 2015 by
Wm. B. Eerdmans Publishing Co.
2140 Oak Industrial Drive N.E., Grand Rapids, Michigan 49505 /
P.O. Box 163, Cambridge CB3 9PU U.K.

Library of Congress Cataloging-in-Publication Data

Hays, Christopher B., 1973–   author.
    [Death in the Iron Age II and in First Isaiah]
A covenant with death : death in the Iron Age II and its rhetorical uses in proto-Isaiah /
Christopher B. Hays.
        pages   cm
Includes bibliographical references and index.
ISBN 978-0-8028-7311-8 (paperback)
1. Death in the Bible. 2. Bible. Isaiah, I-XXXIX — Criticism, interpretation, etc.
3. Iron age — Middle East. 4. Middle East — Antiquities. I. Title.
BS1199.D34H39 2011

224'.106 — dc23
2015019231

www.eerdmans.com

to Yvonne

Contents

List of Figures and Charts	xi
Foreword, *by Matthew J. Suriano*	xii
Preface	xv
Acknowledgments	xvi
Abbreviations	xviii

0. Introduction	**1**
0.1 Topic	1
0.2 Method	1
0.3 Historical context and mechanisms of influence (chs. 1–2)	3
0.4 ANE beliefs about death and their impact on Judah (chs. 1–4)	4
0.5 The rhetoric of death in Isaiah 1–39	7
1. Death and the Dead in Mesopotamia during the Iron Age II	**11**
1.1 Introduction	11
1.2 Historical sketch	11
1.3 Mechanisms of Mesopotamian influence	21
1.3.1 Linguistic contacts	23
1.3.2 The question of religious imposition	25
1.4 Death in Mesopotamia	34
1.4.1 Burial and mourning in Mesopotamia	35
1.4.2 The Mesopotamian dead	43
1.4.3 The Mesopotamian underworld and its deities	48
1.5 Conclusions	55
2. Death and the Dead in Egypt during the Iron Age II	**57**
2.1 Introduction	57
2.2 Historical sketch	58

2.3 Mechanisms of Egyptian influence — 60
2.4 Death in Egypt — 66
   2.4.1 Burial and mourning in Egypt — 67
   2.4.2 The Egyptian dead — 76
   2.4.3 The Egyptian underworld and its deities — 83
2.5 Conclusions — 89

3. **Death and the Dead in Syria-Palestine outside Israel and Judah** — 93
   3.1 Introduction — 93
   3.2 Bronze Age cults of the dead in inland Syria and Hatti — 95
   3.3 Ugarit — 98
      3.3.1 Ugarit and the Bible — 98
      3.3.2 The archaeology of death in Ugarit — 100
      3.3.3 Death in the Ugaritic texts — 104
         3.3.3.1 Burial and mourning — 105
         3.3.3.2 The Ugaritic dead — 105
            The Ugaritic cult of the dead up to the "Spronk synthesis" — 105
            The *rpum* (et al.) — 107
            The Ugaritic *marziḥu* — 115
            A "minimalist" backlash — 117
         3.3.3.3 The Ugaritic underworld and its deities — 122
   3.4 Between Ugarit and Israel — 127
   3.5 Conclusions — 131

4. **Death and the Dead in Iron II Israel and Judah and in the Old Testament** — 133
   4.1 Introduction — 133
   4.2 A brief history of modern scholarship — 135
      4.2.1 Early modern scholarship — 135
      4.2.2 The mid-century assertion of distinctiveness — 136
      4.2.3 A new flourishing of underworld and afterlife — 138
      4.2.4 "Minimalist" backlash, redux — 143
   4.3 The archaeology of death in ancient Judah — 147
   4.4 Death in the Hebrew Bible — 153
      4.4.1 Burial and mourning — 154
         4.4.1.1 Burial in the texts — 154
         4.4.1.2 Mourning — 162
         4.4.1.3 The *marzēaḥ* — 163
         4.4.1.4 The corpse — 165

    4.4.2 The Israelite dead 166
        4.4.2.1 The powers and cult of the dead 166
        4.4.2.2 The Rephaim 167
        4.4.2.3 Necromancy 168
        4.4.2.4 Summary 174
    4.4.3 The underworld and its deities 176
        4.4.3.1 Terms for and images of the underworld 176
        4.4.3.2 Underworld gods 179
            Molek and child sacrifice 180
        4.4.3.3 Demons 183
    4.4.4 Yahweh and the dead 184
  4.5 Historical conclusions 190
  4.6 The rhetoric of death in the Hebrew Bible 193
    4.6.1 Rhetoric and the Bible 193
    4.6.2 Uses of the rhetoric of death in the Hebrew Bible 196

5. **The Rhetoric of Death in Isaiah 1–39** 203
  5.1 Introduction 203
  5.2 Texts 203
    5.2.1 Threats of unhappy afterlife 203
        5.2.1.1 Isaiah 14:4–23: The tyrant in Sheol 203
            Reversal of royal funerary expectations 208
            The myth of Heˆleˉl 211
            The rhetoric in historical context 215
        5.2.1.2 Isaiah 30:27–33: A pyre for the king 222
        5.2.1.3 Isaiah 22:15–19: Shebna's tomb 232
        5.2.1.4 Isaiah 36:12: A hellish meal 249
    5.2.2 Comparisons of the living to the dead 253
        5.2.2.1 Isaiah 5:11–17: The nobility's parade to hell 253
        5.2.2.2 The *hôy*-oracles 258
        5.2.2.3 Isaiah 29:1–8: A "near-death experience" for Jerusalem 262
        5.2.2.4 Isaiah 8:16–9:6: Those who consult the dead are like them 270
    5.2.3 Other reactions to cults of the dead 279
        5.2.3.1 Isaiah 7:10–13: YHWH's sign from Sheol? 279
        5.2.3.2 Isaiah 19:1–15: Egypt will consult its ghosts in vain 281
        5.2.3.3 Isaiah 28:1–22: The covenant with Mut 288
            The Egyptian goddess Mut 294
            Competing proposals 303
            Exegesis 305
    5.2.4 Life's triumph over death 315

5.2.4.1 Isaiah 25:6–8: "He will swallow up Death forever"   318
5.2.4.2 Isaiah 26:11–21: "Your dead shall rise"   323
5.2.4.3 Isaiah 38:9–20: The Psalm of Hezekiah   337
5.2.4.4 Isaiah 37:4, 17: "The Living God"   345

6. Conclusions   347
  6.1 Death in the Ancient Near East during the Iron Age II   347
  6.2 The rhetoric of death in the Hebrew Bible   349
  6.3 Isaiah's rhetorical employment of death imagery   350
  6.4 The offer of life   352
  6.5 Implications   353
    6.5.1 "Foreign" influences   353
    6.5.2 The formation of the book of Isaiah   355
    6.5.3 Isaiah's role in the history of Judean religion   357
      6.5.3.1 Isaiah's condemnation of religious practices   357
      6.5.3.2 Isaiah and resurrection   358
    6.5.4 Isaiah as Judah's "Book of the Dead"?   359

Bibliography   363

Index of Sources   409

Index of Authors   430

Index of Subjects   439

List of Figures and Charts

Fig. 3.1	One of the underground tombs from the palace area in Ugarit	102
Fig. 3.2	The KTMW stele	129
Fig. 3.3	Detail from the sarcophagus of Ahiram of Byblos	130
Fig. 5.1	A Neo-Assyrian relief from the palace at Nineveh	225
Fig. 5.2	Reconstruction of an Egyptian tomb chapel from Deir el-Medina	237
Fig. 5.3	Wooden funerary stele, Egyptian, Third Intermediate Period	240
Fig. 5.4	Mut amulet from Iron II Lachish	293
Fig. 5.5	Lunette from the Victory Stele of Piye	297
Fig. 5.6	Statue of Mutemwia in the British Museum	298
Fig. 5.7	Ostracon: Ramesses II suckled by a goddess	309
Fig. 5.8	Goddess suckling a queen	310
Fig. 5.9	Blue-glazed amulet of Sekhmet-Mut suckling a king (Dynasty 22)	310
Chart 5.1	The *Hôy*-Oracles of Isaiah 1–33	259

Foreword

The 2011 publication of Christopher Hays' dissertation represented an important contribution to the study of death in the Hebrew Bible/Old Testament. As such, it found a prominent place among the growing number of works on this important topic. The study of death represents one of the more constructive outcomes of modern biblical scholarship. In this day and age, most research on the topic of death in the Bible is done outside of theological boundaries. That is, the principal questions are no longer driven by doctrines of soteriology or eschatology. Not that it is entirely void of theological concerns, but the historical-critical method has been one that works to root biblical interpretation in a solid foundation of culture and history. More broadly, the results are evident in historical and archaeological work on ancient Israel, as well as the linguistic advances made in our understanding of classical Hebrew. But the specific study of death brings its own unique challenges. Death is, and always has been, a sensitive topic. It is a subject that remains a constant question throughout humanity, and it is a problem that major world religions have confronted in systemic ways. Thus, it is necessary to set this volume against the backdrop of twentieth-century scholarship in order to understand its contribution to the study of death, in general, and Isaiah's rhetorical use of death, in particular.

The modern study of death, the dead, and the afterlife in biblical literature can certainly be traced back to Spinoza's rejection of the soul's immortality. The general trend continues today, as scholars are more attentive to the cultural world that produced the biblical texts. This is due, in no small part, to the ever-increasing amount of data that can be gleaned from the material remains of the ancient Near East. The results are manifest in two major approaches, which affect the way scholars analyze death in the Hebrew Bible. The first approach is the comparative analysis of biblical and ancient Near Eastern literature, otherwise known as "scripture in context." The second approach is the archaeological study of the ancient Levant, what was once popularly known as "biblical archaeology." The first approach has given scholars access to descriptions of the afterlife, forms of post-mortem existence (such as ghosts), and mantic interaction with the dead (necromancy). The second approach has shed important light on death and burial through the discovery of tombs and associated inscriptions from the Levant. These discoveries indicate the importance of the family in both life and death, and have underscored an ideal of immortality that was founded in memory rather than the transmigration of an incorruptible essence of being.

While both approaches offer productive insight into death and its conceptualization in biblical literature, they are not easily reconcilable. For example, the comparative approach often forefronts a mythology of death, seen in such notable examples as Tablet XII of Gilgamesh (and its Sumerian source), and Ishtar / Inanna's descent into the netherworld. But it is not always clear how to synthesize the data from mythological depictions of the netherworld and the dead with the archaeological remains that bear witness to cultural responses to death. Consequently, scholars frequently privilege one over the other in their particular research, following either a literary tack or an archaeological one. Hays, however, is able to draw expertly from both, and his synthesis provides an important perspective. The basis for this perspective is the rhetoric of death that Hays reconstructs in some of Isaiah's most difficult passages, a rhetoric that resonates within the mythology of death, but one that is carefully nuanced by the realia of mortuary remains. Moreover, the literary images of death, the dead, and the afterlife are drawn from multiple cultures, including Mesopotamia, Ugarit, and Egypt. In the case of Egypt, Hays' comparative study represents a necessary advancement. The contextual approach to biblical literature often neglects Egyptian sources, giving priority to cuneiform literature.

Hays is able to establish significant groundwork by demonstrating the role and extent of Egyptian culture in Isaiah's rhetoric of death. This is best exemplified in his exegesis of Isaiah 22:15–19, where he is able to interact with the archaeological remains of Jerusalem's Iron II cemetery in Silwan as well as Egyptian beliefs regarding the dead. The result is a new and innovative reading of Shebna's tomb. Another example that draws from both Egyptian and Ugaritic literature is his rereading of Isaiah 5:11–17, where he shows that the image of the dead is a key component in the choices that the prophet lays out before his audience. From here, Hays is able to show that the *hôy*-oracles of Isaiah 1–33 were formed from funerary laments. In other words, Hays' study moves beyond descriptive accounts of death in antiquity. What he offers is an exploration of the human response to mortality, and how the biblical writers utilized this response.

Finally, an important aspect of this book is that, in spite of its rich and complex contextual study, Hays is still able to emphasize the uniqueness of Isaiah's use of death imagery. While this imagery was influenced by the neighboring cultures of the Jerusalem prophet, at the same time the prophet's rhetoric of death emerged from his immediate environment. The rhetorical imagery is not some ethereal literary idea, nor was it culturally derivative; in proto-Isaiah, it was grounded in the realities of the Kingdom of Judah during the eighth and seventh centuries, set against the backdrop of the wider Near Eastern world. Within this setting, Hays is able to build his compelling conclusion that the dialectic of life-and-death, the "two ways," provides thematic structure for Isaiah. His further suggestion that

Isaiah was Judah's "Book of the Dead" is provocative and opens further avenues for future work.

This new edition of Christopher Hays' work, which Eerdmans has republished as *A Covenant with Death: Death in the Iron Age II and Its Rhetorical Uses in Proto-Isaiah*, provides us with a volume that is both accessible and affordable. The appearance of this edition is a welcome event in biblical studies and an important advancement in the ongoing work on death in the ancient world.

MATTHEW J. SURIANO

Preface

The present monograph is a significantly revised version of my Emory University dissertation. Although the structure and central theses have not changed in the three years since it was submitted, every piece of it has been polished and strengthened, and in some cases rewritten.

One tangible measure of this further work is that the bibliography grew by a third in revisions. This reflects additional research throughout, although chapter 2 on Egypt is notable for having been extensively re-researched with access to the Online Egyptological Bibliography at UCLA. New editions of Akkadian texts such as the "Evil Demons" incantation series and "Ishtar's Descent and Resurrection" also became available thanks to the State Archives of Assyria project, and they have been incorporated.

I am grateful for the feedback of the editors and reviewers of my work at *Vetus Testamentum* (on Isa 28), *Zeitschrift für die Alttestamentliche Wissenschaft* (on Isa 19 and 22), *Journal of Biblical Literature* (on ancient Near Eastern imagery of death and afterlife), *Journal of Ancient Egyptian Interconnections* (on the etymology of אוב), *Journal of Near Eastern Studies* (on Egyptian iconography), and *Religion Compass* (on recent research on Isaiah) – each of these served as drafts of sections of this book or allowed me to work on background issues. In many of those cases, the content of the articles does not overlap entirely with the discussions in this volume, but where they do overlap, the versions here supersede the periodical versions. Although this volume may be less accessible, it contains the most finished versions of my arguments. This is particularly pertinent in the case of § 5.2.3.3, on Isa 28, which is now much improved, even compared to the version that appeared in *Vetus Testamentum* in 2010.

Acknowledgments

My sense of indebtedness to those who made this project possible is such that I began planning these acknowledgments, and even taking notes for them, well before the dissertation on which it is based was complete. I have continued to be blessed by the support of many people through the process of editing it and bringing it to publication.

I could not have hoped for a wiser or more conscientious advisor than David Petersen. As befits a former president of his guild, he masterfully represented the profession and its standards while I worked to figure out my project's place within it. As a careful editor, he consistently challenged me to argue more clearly, and thereby strengthened my work immeasurably.

I was similarly blessed by the rest of the committee. Brent Strawn was a fantastic guide throughout my time at Emory, and remains a role model and friend. J. J. M. Roberts inspired me to undertake this project through his excellent seminars on Isaiah and ancient Near Eastern religion at Princeton Theological Seminary. Carol Newsom's creative genius also became an aspiration for me, and I researched significant parts of ch. 1 in one of her seminars.

I thank Mark Smith for accepting the manuscript, and for his detailed comments on it. Many of the insights I came to in my research would never have happened without the inspiration of my dear friend Joel LeMon, who encouraged me to pursue the iconographic and Egyptological aspects of this project; and who kindly read and commented on the whole manuscript. Others who read sections of the book and gave helpful feedback include Leslie Allen, Elizabeth Bloch-Smith, Jim Butler, John Goldingay, Jeremy Hutton, Martti Nissinen, Gay Robins, Matthew Schlimm and Elizabeth Waraksa. I am also indebted to Craig Melchert for his personal communication about Hittite texts, and to Betsy Bryan for helping me arrange a visit to the Mut Temple precinct and sharing some of her developing research on Mut with me.

My scholarly mentors beyond the scope of this project were numerous. Anyone who knows John H. Hayes' work will perceive his influence on me, and I aspire to his courageous intellectual independence. I also thank Gail O'Day for taking me under her wing as a teaching assistant and as her editorial assistant at the *Journal of Biblical Literature*, where I learned an immense amount. I am grateful to Billie Jean Collins for taking the time to work with me in Akkadian beyond my formal coursework. I also thank the faculty of Princeton Seminary who set me on this professional path, particularly my primary professors of Old Testament and Hebrew: Patrick Miller, C. L. Seow, Dennis Olson, Jacqueline Lapsley, and Eunny Lee.

I would like to thank Henning Ziebritzki, Lisa Laux, Tanja Mix, and the rest of the editorial staff at Mohr Siebeck for shepherding this volume through the editorial process and ensuring its quality in many ways.

Without various kinds of financial support, it would have been far more difficult to complete this book. I thank Fuller Seminary for the sabbatical leave in Fall 2010 during which I finished the revisions, and for summer funding to travel to Israel. I also thank Emory University for its Woodruff Fellowship and its summer research funding which allowed me to study in Germany and Israel; the Catholic Biblical Association for its Memorial Stipend; and the American Schools of Oriental Research and *Biblical Archaeology Review* for their funding of my participation in archaeological research. Finally, I was blessed to work for the Society of Biblical Literature at its main offices in Atlanta, and that experience was an education in itself. I thank Kent Richards in particular for his consistent mentoring and caring presence in my life.

I am indebted to the staffs at Emory's Pitts Theology Library and Woodruff Library for their outstanding efforts. The lengths to which both went to acquire needed materials amazed me. Particularly remarkable was the graciousness of Patrick Graham, who took seriously my requests and interests. David Bundy and the staff of Fuller's David Allan Hubbard Library have kindly helped me gather numerous other sources.

Numerous others at Fuller have helped me on this road. I thank my students Nathan Yearian and Andrew Giorgetti for compiling some of the indices herein. My patient research assistants have included Andrea Reinhardt, Michael Crosby, Renee Dutter, and Janna Gould. Furthermore, my students in seminars on Israelite Religion and Historiography of Ancient Israel, and in courses on Isaiah, Akkadian, Ugaritic, and Advanced Hebrew have become conversation partners as I have steadily worked on topics related to this book.

I also thank the pastors and churches that we have attended during these years, for ministering to me and my family, and for giving me opportunities to serve and teach: Rev. Gary Charles at Central Presbyterian Church in Atlanta; Revs. Andy Wilson and Lee Cook at La Crescenta Presbyterian; and Revs. Gary Dennis and Chuck Osburn at La Cañada Presbyterian.

Thus far I have thanked teachers, friends, financial supporters, bibliographical facilitators, and spiritual leaders. Penultimately, I must thank my parents, who have been all of these things to me over the years.

Absolutely foremost among those to whom I owe thanks is my beloved wife, Yvonne, whose love and care allowed me to finish this project, and who gave me Madeleine and Calvin, constant reminders of the joy of new life.

Abbreviations

AB	Anchor Bible
AcBib	Academia Biblica
ABD	Anchor Bible Dictionary
AfO	Archiv für Orientforschung
ANEP	Ancient Near East in Pictures
ANET	Ancient Near Eastern Texts
AnOr	Analecta orientalia
AOAT	Alter Orient und Altes Testament
BAR	Biblical Archaeology Review
BASOR	Bulletin of the American Schools of Oriental Research
BETL	Bibliotheca Ephemeridum Theologicarum Lovaniensium
BEvT	Beiträge zur evangelischen Theologie
BHS	Biblia Hebraica Stuttgartensia
Bib	Biblica
BibOr	Biblica et Orientalia
BJS	Brown Judaic Studies
BKAT	Biblischer Kommentar: Altes Testament
BO	Bibliotheca Orientalis
BT	The Bible Translator
BSac	Bibliotheca Sacra
BZ	Biblische Zeitschrift
BZAW	Beihefte zur ZAW
CAD	Assyrian Dictionary of the University of Chicago
CANE	Civilizations of the Ancient Near East
CAT	Cuneiform Alphabetic Texts (=KTU2)
CBQ	Catholic Biblical Quarterly
COS	The Context of Scripture
ConBOT	Coniectanea Biblica. Old Testament Series
DDD^2	Dictionary of Deities and Demons in the Bible (2nd ed.)
DJA	Dictionary of Judean Aramaic
DNWSI	Dictionary of Northwest Semitic Inscriptions
DUL	Dictionary of the Ugaritic Language
EBib	Études bibliques

EncJud	*Encyclopaedia Judaica* (New York: Macmillan, 1971–72)
ErIsr	*Eretz Israel*
ETL	*Ephemerides Theologicae Lovanienses*
FB	*Forschung zur Bibel*
FOTL	*The Forms of the Old Testament Literature*
FRLANT	*Forschungen zur Religion und Literatur des Alten und Neuen Testaments*
HALOT	*Hebrew and Aramaic Lexicon of the Old Testament*
HAR	*Hebrew Annual Review*
HI	*Hebrew Inscriptions* (Dobbs-Allsopp et al.)
HSM	*Harvard Semitic Monographs*
HTR	*Harvard Theological Review*
HUCA	*Hebrew Union College Annual*
HS	*Hebrew Studies*
IEJ	*Israel Exploration Journal*
JANER	*Journal of Ancient Near Eastern Religions*
JAOS	*Journal of the American Oriental Society*
JARCE	*Journal of the American Research Center in Cairo*
JBL	*Journal of Biblical Literature*
JCS	*Journal of Cuneiform Studies*
JEA	*Journal of Egyptian Archaeology*
JNES	*Journal of Near Eastern Studies*
JQR	*Jewish Quarterly Review*
JSNT	*Journal for the Study of the New Testament*
JSNTSup	Supplements to *JSNT*
JSOT	*Journal for the Study of the Old Testament*
JSOTSupp	Supplements to *JSOT*
JSS	*Journal of Semitic Studies*
KAI	*Kanaanäische und Aramäische Inschriften*
KAT	*Kommetar zum Alten Testament*
NCB	*New Century Bible Commentary*
NEA	*Near Eastern Archaeology*
NIB	*New Interpreter's Bible*
OBO	*Orbus Biblicus et Orientalis*
OEAE	*The Oxford Encyclopedia of Ancient Egypt*
Or	*Orientalia (NS)*
OTE	*Old Testament Essays*
OTG	*Old Testament Guides*
OTL	*Old Testament Library*
RA	*Revue d'assyriologie et d'archéologie orientale*
RB	*Revue biblique*
RdE	*Revue d'Égyptologie*
RlA	*Reallexikon der Assyriologie*
SAA	*State Archives of Assyria*

SAAB	State Archives of Assyria Bulletin
SAAS	State Archives of Assyria Studies
SBLDS	SBL Dissertation Series
SBLMS	SBL Monograph Series
SBLRBS	SBL Resources for Biblical Study
SBLSBS	SBL Sources for Biblical Study
SBLSymS	SBL Symposium Series
SBLTT	SBL Texts and Translations
SBT	Studies in Biblical Theology
Sem	*Semitica*
ST	*Studia theologica*
SubBi	Subsidia Biblica
TDOT	*Theological Dictionary of the Old Testament*
TQ	*Theologische Quartalschrift*
TUMSR	Trinity University Monograph Series in Religion
TynBul	*Tyndale Bulletin*
TZ	*Theologische Zeitschrift*
UF	*Ugarit-Forschungen*
VT	*Vetus Testamentum*
VTSup	*Vetus Testamentum* Supplements
WAW	SBL Writings from the Ancient Worlds
WBC	Word Biblical Commentary
WVDOG	Wissenschaftliche Veröffentlichung der Deutschen Orient-Gesellschaft
WW	*Word and World*
ZA	*Zeitschrift für Assyriologie*
ZAW	*Zeitschrift für die alttestamentliche Wissenschaft*
ZDPV	*Zeitschrift des deutschen Palästina-Vereins*

0. Introduction

0.1 Topic

The theme of death (and deliverance from death) is a dominant one in the early strata of the book of Isaiah, although it has not generally been recognized as such. Despite the repeated references to death in Isaiah 1–39 – more than a dozen prominent pericopae in chs. 5–38 alone[1] – no study exists that synthetically discusses the relevant passages in that corpus.

The primary question I have posed is how the imagery of death and its associated phenomena (including burial, the dead, the underworld, and ancestor cults) function rhetorically in the book. In order to bring this rhetoric into focus, I have laid out the book's ancient Near Eastern cultural context, so that the reader may better understand the thought-world out of which these texts emerged.

This study treats biblical texts as the complex ideological and literary products that they are, rather than assuming that they should express ideas identical to those of surrounding cultures, or that they should be completely opposed to them. The creativity of Isaiah and his early tradents makes the book especially rich subject matter – although this work should also shed light on many other books of the Hebrew Bible in which the theme of death and life is central (Psalms, Job, and Ecclesiastes come immediately to mind; see also § 4.6.2).

0.2 Method

In my view, rhetoric is most productively studied in its historical and cultural contexts. The focus of this book is on the text's meaning for its producers and its initial audiences. Prophetic oracles were first composed and uttered to persuade someone of something (or at least to pronounce a message) at a given place and time; this has been called the "rhetorical-historical situation."[2] It is in that sense that the book's method may be called rhetorical.

---

[1] The number would be much larger if each *hôy*-oracle (eighteen of them in Isa 1–33) were counted individually; see § 5.2.2.2. Insofar as religio-historical scholarship on death in ancient Israel has touched on Isaiah, it has been confined to a handful of passages.

[2] Brad E. Kelle, *Hosea 2: Metaphor and Rhetoric in Historical Perspective* (AB 20; Atlanta: SBL, 2005), 33, 27. I am sympathetic with Hans Barstad's comment that the emphasis on prophetic

For that reason, I draw heavily on historical and comparative data. As Laurent Pernot has written:

[R]hetoric is deployed in precisely datable political and institutional frameworks and ideological configurations. Rhetoric is anchored in society, and consequently it has a history that develops in relation to the general history of ancient societies.... . [R]hetoric is tied to historical settings, to social, political, and intellectual conditions, and ... it evolved with these conditions.[3]

In ch. 4, I expand on the idea of rhetoric as an historical phenomenon, and this perspective should not come as a surprise to scholars of the Hebrew Bible, especially of biblical prophetic literature. James Muilenburg observed years ago in his seminal presidential address to the Society of Biblical Literature: "The prophets do not speak *in abstracto*, but concretely."[4] That is to say, although the Hebrew prophets have spoken to many periods and peoples, they spoke first within specific historical contexts; and in crafting their messages, they worked with the cultural materials that their surroundings provided. Much of the work in these pages has therefore been to identify and describe the political, cultural, and religious contexts of the early strata of Isaiah.

I have described my understanding of the formation of the book of Isaiah in detail elsewhere;[5] for the purposes of introduction here, I simply note that I share in the critical consensus that chs. 1–39 are a layered and composite work when viewed as a whole. Although my research has implications for the formation of 1–39, its focus is on texts within those chapters that can be attributed to the prophet and his early tradents from the eighth century to the start of the Babylonian exile. This is what is meant by the shorthand "Proto-Isaiah" in the book's title. Other scholars call this part of the book "First Isaiah," which is fine insofar as these texts preceded the work of the second Isaiah, but it suggests a unity of composition which is not presupposed herein.

What distinguishes my view of Isaiah's formation from some others, in general, is that I see somewhat less necessity to posit tiny redactional accretions to explain shifts in imagery and form; I think that such complexities and seams in the text can often be more adequately understood as normal for certain ancient forms of literature. I have concluded that Isaiah's prophecies were probably first collected under Hezekiah just after Jerusalem weathered Sennacherib's siege in

---

books as literary creations of the Persian and even Hellenistic periods is "not only an unnecessary, but also an erroneous development." Barstad, "What Prophets Do. Reflections on Past Reality in the Book of Jeremiah," *Prophecy in the Book of Jeremiah* (eds. H. M. Barstad and R. G. Kratz; BZAW 388; Berlin: Walter de Gruyter, 2009). Indeed, it seems to me that this comment is even *more* relevant to Isaiah 1–39 than to Jeremiah.

[3] Laurent Pernot, *Rhetoric in Antiquity* (trans. W. E. Higgins; Washington, D.C.: Catholic University of America Press, 2005), x–xi, xii.

[4] James Muilenburg. "Form Criticism and Beyond," *JBL* 88 (1969): 6.

[5] Christopher B. Hays, "Isaiah" in *The Encyclopedia of the Bible* (Oxford: Oxford University Press), forthcoming.

701, and that much of what is now Isa 3–33 underwent a kind of double redaction, analogous to that that of the Deuteronomistic History[6] – i.e., once during the reign of Josiah of Judah,[7] and once more around the end of the Babylonian exile. I see little reason to date significant portions of chs. 2–39 in the fifth century BCE or later, and that is why Persian culture and religion are not given comparable treatment.[8]

More importantly, from a methodological standpoint, I find it important to understand the historical and cultural contexts of various periods *prior* to drawing conclusions about the date of texts. The reader will consistently see me weighing and analyzing each text in order to place it in its proper context, and these contexts are not all related to Isaiah of Jerusalem. However, the texts that I work with in this monograph are best explained as deriving from no later than the reign of Josiah.[9]

0.3 Historical Context and Mechanisms of Influence (chs. 1–2)

My goal in chs. 1–4 is to present the historical and religious context of Isa 1–39 in a way that is concise and accessible, yet thorough and well documented. Some aspects of Isaiah's context are already well digested and available from other sources; this is especially true of the political and historical context of the eighth and seventh centuries in Judah. In other important areas, however, the biblical scholar has considerably less previous scholarship with which to work.

One of those areas that needs further emphasis is the nature and degree of cultural and religious interaction between Judah and its imperial neighbors in the preexilic period, the Mesopotamians and Egyptians. The specific socio-historical conduits through which cultural influence worked were often overlooked or omitted in biblical studies in the past. This may be partly due to a very appropriate sense of reserve in the face of uncertainty, but it has seemed worthwhile to me

---

[6] Frank Moore Cross, "The Themes of the Book of Kings and the Structure of the Deuteronomistic History," in *Canaanite Myth and Hebrew Epic: Essays in the History of the Religion of Israel* (Cambridge, Mass.: Harvard University Press, 1973), 274–89; Richard D. Nelson, "The Double Redaction of the Deuteronomistic History: The Case is Still Compelling," *JSOT* 29 (2005): 319–37.

[7] This is consistent with the frequently-propounded idea that Isaiah underwent an "Anti-Assyrian redaction" – e.g., Hermann Barth, *Die Jesaja-Worte in der Josiazeit: Israel und Assur als Thema einer Produktiven Neuinterpretation der Jesajaüberlieferung* (WMANT 48; Neukirchen-Vluyn: Neukirchener Verlag, 1977) and Gerald T. Sheppard, "The Anti-Assyrian Redaction and the Canonical Context of Isaiah 1–39," *JBL* 104 (1985): 193–216 – although I do not always agree with those scholars about the specific contours of the redaction.

[8] The possibility of Persian influence on Judean beliefs as reflected in the Bible is discussed below, in the relevant portions of chs. 3 and 4.

[9] Possible exceptions include the passages in Isa 36 and 37, which are part of a Deuteronomistic section, and may thus derive from a redaction after the exile.

to lay out focused analyses of Judah's international connections during the eighth and seventh centuries. Thus, each of the first two chapters includes an analysis of *mechanisms of influence*[10] – Mesopotamian and Egyptian, respectively – on Israel and Judah.

In general, the finding here is in keeping with a growing sense of Israelite and Judean elites' connectedness with the cultures that surrounded them. To take just one example of that trend, Mark Smith's recent monograph *God in Translation*[11] demonstrates the ongoing cultural (and specifically religious/theological) contacts among Near Eastern cultures throughout ancient history. It would be an error to suppose that the international correspondence and mutual knowledge that are reflected in the Amarna Letters dissipated in the Iron Age simply because the great nations faded somewhat from their former dominance, or because a shift in writing technology made texts more perishable. Ithamar Singer has written that during the Hittite Empire, a "basic knowledge of foreign pantheons was not just an intellectual asset of Hittite theologians, but rather an essential requirement for the Hittite 'Foreign Office.' "[12] It seems to me that many scribes and religious experts in Iron Age Israel and Judah would have needed a similar level of cross-cultural expertise.[13]

No special section is devoted to the contacts between Mesopotamia and Egypt, although these are well established, and an awareness of the extensive trade and diplomatic exchange between the two powers may help to contextualize Judah's role as a small nation within the larger ancient Near Eastern milieu.[14]

0.4 ANE Beliefs About Death and Their Impact on Judah (chs. 1–4)

Death was among the focal points of cultural production – including both textual and material culture – in the ancient societies studied here, to the point that Jan

---

[10] See also Jeffrey Tigay's term "channels of transmission" in "On Evaluating Claims of Literary Borrowing," *The Tablet and the Scroll: Near Eastern Studies in Honor of William W. Hallo* (eds. M. E. Cohen, et al.; Bethesda, Md.: CDL Press, 1993), 250–55.

[11] Mark S. Smith, *God in Translation: Deities in Cross-Cultural Discourse in the Biblical World* (FAT 57; Tübingen: Mohr Siebeck, 2008).

[12] Itamar Singer, " 'The Thousand Gods of Hatti': The Limits of an Expanding Pantheon" in *Concepts of the Other in Near Eastern Religions*, eds. I. Alon, I. Gruenwald and I. Singer (IOS 14; Leiden: Brill, 1994), 93.

[13] Even at this writing, the recent discovery of a Neo-Assyrian treaty tablet in Tayinat, near the border of modern-day Turkey and Syria, continues to press the issue of cross-cultural religious knowledge, since the excavators argue that it was displayed in a temple. See further discussion below (§ 1.3).

[14] See Moshe Elat, "The Economic Relations of the Neo-Assyrian Empire with Egypt," *JAOS* 98 (1978): 20–34; Nadav Na'aman, "The Brook of Egypt and Assyrian Policy on the Border of Egypt," *Tel Aviv* 6 (1979): 68–90; Lisa A. Heidorn, "The Horses of Kush," *JNES* 56 (1997): 105–14.

0.4 ANE Beliefs About Death and Their Impact on Judah (chs. 1–4)

Assmann has made it the main argument of a recent monograph that "death is the origin and the center of culture."[15] Assmann's thesis suits his Egyptian materials better than it does the remnants of other ancient Near Eastern cultures, but there can be no doubt that the Assyrians, Babylonians, Hittites, Ugaritians, and other Levantine peoples also accorded death great prominence.

The resources for the study of death in the ancient Near East are extensive but unruly. Up to this point, the biblical scholar who intended to study that topic was left with three sorts of secondary sources:

(1) A rich assortment of scholarly monographs, articles, and dictionary entries on single civilizations or textual corpora, some of which are intentionally related to ancient Israel (itself conceived of in different ways by different authors), others not. It is these, along with the primary sources, that I have primarily marshaled in my discussion.

(2) Very broad surveys of death and/or afterlife in world religions or Western religions, which are often too thin and offer limited bibliographical resources for further study.[16] One of my secondary purposes has been to survey the literature for these topics thoroughly enough that an interested person may readily identify and follow the underlying scholarly conversations.

(3) Studies that are rich in detail and relevant to the biblicist but are colored, in my estimation, by various kinds of overt *Tendenzen* related to the monographs in which they appear.[17]

In the first two chapters, I have had to create my own syntheses of the practices and beliefs of Mesopotamia and Egypt, specifically during the Iron Age II (1000–586 BCE). For all the vast scholarly production that has recently attended death in the ancient world, I do not know of such a study that has been produced by Assyriologists or Egyptologists.[18]

---

[15] Jan Assmann, *Death and Salvation in Ancient Egypt* (trans. David Lorton; Ithaca, N.Y. Cornell University Press, 2005), 1.

[16] Two such volumes of good quality nevertheless illustrate different pitfalls: (1) Alan F. Segal's *Life After Death: A History of the Afterlife in Western Religion* (New York: Doubleday, 2004), which contains a sound but brief introduction to some of the issues surrounding afterlife in the First Temple period, but which also glosses over significant details and disagreements and has a bibliography that touches on only the major works while glossing over scholarly disputes. (2) *Death and Afterlife: Perspectives of World Religions*, edited by Hiroshi Obayashi (New York: Praeger, 1992). This volume includes brief contributions by eminent scholars in each field, but inevitably is not as focused as a single-authored work, and is again light on bibliography. (E.g., George E. Mendenhall's essay on death and afterlife in the Old Testament includes six footnotes.)

[17] In chs. 3 and 4, I discuss, as examples of this category, Brian B. Schmidt's *Israel's Beneficent Dead: Ancestor Cult and Necromancy in Ancient Israelite Religion and Tradition* (FAT 11; Tübingen: Mohr Siebeck, 1994) and Philip S. Johnston's *Shades of Sheol: Death and Afterlife in the Old Testament* (Downer's Grove, Ill.: InterVarsity Press, 2002). Another excellent volume that is pursuing a different agenda is Jon D. Levenson, *Resurrection and the Restoration of Israel* (New Haven: Yale University Press, 2006).

[18] In Assyriology, a hole has recently been filled with a very good monograph by Véronique

The restriction of the first two chapters to the Iron Age II is crucial, in that it limits topics that would otherwise explode the bounds of a monograph, let alone a chapter. Those chapters do not ignore longstanding cultural and religious trends surrounding death that were most clearly attested in other periods, but they also do not try to take much account of, for example, Early Dynastic burials in Mesopotamia or Seleucid-era texts from Egypt. They focus instead on the three centuries prior to the fall of Babylon, when Palestine was caught in a political crossfire between Mesopotamia and Egypt. The time frame with which these opening chapters interest themselves is still relatively broad, as it must be, given the conservatism and continuity of traditions.[19] There are only a few instances in which one can analyze diachronic religious developments for Judah's neighbors *within* the Iron Age II.

Ugaritologists have produced a number of studies of death and its attendant phenomena in Syria-Palestine, and have (with notable recent exceptions) been quick to draw conclusions about Iron-Age Israel based on Bronze-Age data. However, despite great scholarly efforts, the proper reconstruction of Ugaritic cults of the dead itself remains in dispute up to the present moment – a debate discussed in ch. 3.

Chapter 3 also surveys the scattered data from the Levant and Anatolia from the Late Bronze Age through the Iron Age in an attempt to bridge the gaps between Ugarit and Israel, and reflects on the methodological complexities in doing so. The aforementioned continuity of scribal traditions allows a limited freedom to "fill in blanks" with texts outside the period in question; for example, to assume that Ugaritic texts from the late second millennium and Sidonian inscriptions from the fifth century are relevant to understanding the religions of Iron Age Palestine in the intervening years. While the hazards of such a method are familiar, they are also inevitable. New data could fill out the picture of those religions, but they are unlikely to change it radically.

Building on those discussions, ch. 4 analyzes the religious situation in Judah during the monarchic period. Because this study is not primarily concerned with proving a thesis about the history of Israelite religion, none of the data is asked to conform to any particular hypothesis; it is simply context for understanding Isaiah. And indeed, I do not offer simple answers. Isaiah's Judah was a complex

---

van der Stede on the topic of death and afterlife (*Mourir au pays de deux fleuves: L'au delà Mésopotamien d'après les sources Sumériennes et Akkadiennes* [Lettres Orientales 12; Leuven: Peeters, 2007]). Still, I know of no independent study of specifically Neo-Assyrian beliefs about death. In Egyptology, there is a vast array of popular books, most of which focus on the more numerous and visually arresting archaeological remains from earlier periods than the Third Intermediate. A number of scholarly studies give brief attention to the Third Intermediate Period, but primarily focus on material culture rather than texts.

[19] An exception is made in the case of Egypt, where the classicizing tendencies of the Kushite and Saite dynasties are distinctive within a smaller time period.

religious and cultural *mélange*, so no neat model suffices to explain the backgrounds of Judean beliefs and practices related to death. In ch. 4, I try to lay out some of the diverse voices in that ancient theological conversation, and in § 6.5.3 I consider the implications of my study of Isaiah for the history of religion.

In my view, the best previous study of death in the ancient Near East is still that of Klaas Spronk, *Beatific Afterlife in Ancient Israel and in the Ancient Near East*, which is now 25 years old.[20] Even-handed and deeply engaged with the Ugaritic material, Spronk produced a necessary resource for a student of death and afterlife in the ancient world. In addition to taking account of the vast amount of scholarship of the past quarter-century, the present work offers three primary points of difference from Spronk: First, rather than focusing on "beatific afterlife" – a topic seemingly dictated by the interests of later Judaism and Christianity[21] – this work seeks to allow the ancient cultures' focal points to emerge with as little shaping by later categories as possible. Second, where Spronk's engagement with Egyptian materials is very limited, this study emphasizes their significance and influence. Lastly, Spronk allowed most questions about mechanisms of influence to remain latent. My assumption is that understanding the historical conditions under which cultural influence takes place is of paramount importance, not only in determining when such influence is plausible but also in assessing *how one text interacts with another*. Does it affirm it? Subvert its claims? Put a new spin on it? The "anxiety of (literary) influence" (to borrow Harold Bloom's phrase) ought to look rather different when the anxiety is felt by a Jerusalemite being harangued by a Neo-Assyrian besieger, than when it is felt by an American reading Shakespeare.

In the case of Isaiah, the influence of his context provoked a remarkable, epoch-making reaction. The prophet and his tradents gathered up these many threads of tradition in powerful ways; they spun them into dark and shocking images; but they also juxtaposed an image of a God who tore off the veil of death that was spread over the nations, introducing a bright era of new life.

0.5 The rhetoric of death in Isaiah 1–39

In my analysis of the theme of death and life, I found that Isaiah's rhetoric fell into a small number of categories:

(1) *Threats of unhappy afterlife* (Isa 14:4–23; 30:27–33; 22:15–19; 36:12): The employment of death as a punishment or negative outcome is surely as old as humankind. Isaiah not only foretold death for those who transgressed the will of

---

[20] Klaas Spronk, *Beatific Afterlife in Ancient Israel and in the Ancient Near East* (AOAT 219; Neukirchen-Vluyn: Neukirchener Verlag, 1986).
[21] Note Spronk's comments on the theological problems raised by existing views of the afterlife in the Old and New Testaments in Spronk (*Beatific Afterlife*, 2).

God, he often promised desecration of the burial, and suffering and unrest after death as well.

(2) *Comparisons of the living to the dead* (Isa 5:11–17, and the *hôy*-oracles as a whole; 8:16–22; 29:1–8): Isaiah was accustomed to portray the objects of his wrath as having abandoned not only YHWH, but also life itself; they were not merely foolish and apostate; they were as good as dead.

(3) *Condemnations of cults of the dead* (Isa 7:10–13; 19:1–15; 28:1–22): In this diverse set of texts, Isaiah condemns non-Yahwistic cultic practices by accusing them of being doomed, ineffectual, and ultimately death-seeking.

(4) *Life's triumph over death* (Isa 25:6–8; 26:11–21; 37:4, 17; 38:9–20): Isaiah's powerful but terrorizing rhetoric of death was balanced by a positive rhetoric of life. There are hints, in 9:1–6 and 29:5–8, of a promise that YHWH overcomes death, but it is in the four texts in this section, which are usually taken to derive from a period later than the career of Isaiah of Jerusalem, that the victory of life over death – and YHWH's identity as a God who offers life – is most emphatically asserted.

For each of these passages, ch. 5 inquires after the rhetorical-historical context, and analyzes the ways in which the text picks up and transforms ideas about death that were part of the ancient Near Eastern culture.

All of this exegetical work toward a broader portrait of Isaiah's purposes and methods has also yielded new insights at the level of details which will significantly affect the translations of certain passages, and also one's understanding of the historical and cultural backgrounds of Isaiah's prophecies. This came as something of a surprise, even to me. At the outset, I assumed that when it came to the translations and historical settings of individual passages, I would have to conclude, as H. W. F. Saggs once wrote, that I was "gleaning after the main harvest of distinguished predecessors," and could "dare hope for no more than to gather a few grains which they may have disregarded."[22] I thought that what was needed was primarily to gather up these fragments and assemble them. I have indeed done my share of gathering, but when the texts were considered from the perspective of Isaiah's rhetoric of death and life, new understandings emerged – most notably:

- In Isa 28:1–22, I argue that although the "covenant with Death" has rightly been taken to refer to a treaty with Egypt, the imagery can be explained as reflecting cultic rites specifically related to the Egyptian goddess Mut.[23]
- In Isa 22:15–19, I argue that the terms סכן, מצב, and מעמד refer to features of Shebna's tomb, bringing the oracle there into better focus.[24]

---

[22] H. W. F. Saggs, "'External Souls' in the Old Testament," *JSS* 19 (1974): 1.

[23] Aspects of this argument have been published (or will soon be published) as "The Covenant with Mut: A New Interpretation of Isaiah 28:1–22," *VT* 60 (2010): 212–40, and "The Egyptian Goddess Mut in Iron-Age Palestine: Further Data From Amulets and Onomastics," *JNES*, forthcoming.

- I argue that Isa 19:1–15 is a unified oracle that accurately reflects not only eighth-century geopolitics, but also Egyptian necromantic practices of the same period.[25]

Finally, I believe that the whole of this book helps restore an authentic coherence of vision to the passages discussed, and allows them to speak more clearly by placing them in a well-defined historical context. Death and life were much on the minds of Isaiah and his early tradents, and this study shows how they used those themes in their rhetoric.

---

[24] A version of this argument has been published as: "Refocusing Shebna's Tomb: A New Reading of Isa 22:15–19 in its Ancient Near Eastern Context," *ZAW*, 122 (2010): 558–75.

[25] Background work for this section appears in "Damming Egypt / Damning Egypt: The Paronomasia of *skr* and the Unity of Isa 19:1–15," *ZAW* 120 (2008): 612–16.

1. Death and the Dead in Mesopotamia during Iron Age II

1.1 Introduction

Assyria demands pride of place among the civilizations that form the backdrop for Isa 1–39.[1] This is due both to its stature as the imperial power whose political grasp on the Levant was strongest during the Iron Age II, and also to the large extent of its documentary corpus from that period, in contrast to the paltry textual remains of Israel's immediate neighbors. The Neo-Assyrians' significant points of cultural continuity with the briefer Neo-Babylonian Empire mean that Mesopotamian nations exercised hegemony over Israel and Judah up to the end of each kingdom.

1.2 Historical sketch

The broad geopolitical outlines of the rise and fall of the Neo-Assyrian Empire have been extensively covered,[2] so that only a brief sketch is necessary for the present purposes. After a flourishing under Tiglath-Pileser I (1115–1077), Assyria struggled for nearly a century and a half against the Aramean kingdoms in Syria and Mesopotamia, and to a lesser extent with Babylon. Aššur-dan (934–912) and his successors rebuilt Assyria's economic power and reconsolidated its hold on its immediate environs. However, it is Aššurnasirpal II (883–859) who is dubbed "the real founder of the final Neo-Assyrian empire" by

---

[1] "The activities of the Neo-Assyrian empire had a profound impact upon the book of Isaiah" (David L. Petersen, *The Prophetic Literature: An Introduction* [Louisville, Ky.: Westminster John Knox, 2002], 53).

[2] Marc Van de Mieroop, *A History of the Ancient Near East, ca. 3000–323 BC* (2nd ed.; Blackwell History of the Ancient World; Malden, Mass.: Blackwell, 2007), 229–69; Amélie Kuhrt, *The Ancient Near East*, vol. 1, *From c. 3000 B.C. to c. 1200 B.C.* (Routledge History of the Ancient World; London: Routledge, 1995), 473–46; H. W. F. Saggs, *The Might That Was Assyria* (London: Sidgwick & Jackson, 1984), 70–121; A. K. Grayson, "Assyrian Rule of Conquered Territory in Ancient West Asia," in *Civilizations of the Ancient Near East* (ed. Jack M. Sasson et al.; New York: Scribner, 1995), 1: 959–68; J. Maxwell Miller and John H. Hayes, *A History of Ancient Israel and Judah* (2nd ed.; Louisville, Ky.: Westminster John Knox, 2006), 234–38; John Bright, *A History of Israel* (4th ed.; Louisville, Ky: Westminster John Knox, 2000), 269–309.

H. W. F. Saggs.[3] He became the first Assyrian in two centuries to control the routes to the Mediterranean and received tribute from as far south as Tyre.[4] The Assyrian army was fast-moving, thanks to a system of highways connecting major points on the imperial grid,[5] and incorporated "many of the military improvements usually associated with much later periods."[6] The Assyrians were adept with diverse weaponry, incorporated mercenaries from conquered nations, and had an array of siege tactics at their disposal, as the remains of a huge Assyrian rampart built at Lachish show.[7] At its apex, Assyria theoretically could have raised an army of several hundred thousand troops,[8] and while this was almost surely never done in practice,[9] their military force was in most cases "simply overwhelming."[10]

Although Assyria had thus penetrated Israel's orbit, it took another century before its impact was significantly recorded by the biblical historians. Šalmaneser III (858–824) fortified his father's territorial advances, but Assyria suffered under its subsequent rulers, as Urartu, to its north, expanded into a distracting rival. Not accidentally, this period of Assyrian disarray and attention to the north coincides with the long and apparently successful reign of Jeroboam II in Israel.

It was only with the ascension of Tiglath-Pileser III (744–727), through a revolt in the capital city of Kalḫu, that Assyria regained its teeth and its interest in the West. By comparison with Assyria's deliberate and partly defensive expansion up to the second half of the eighth century, its explosion southward to Egypt over the ensuing seventy-five years is almost startling. Within five years of taking power, Tiglath-Pileser had reestablished Assyria's security against Babylon and Urartu and pushed into Syria-Palestine again in 738, exacting tribute from King Menahem of Israel, among others.

The renewed Assyrian aggression had a polarizing effect on the politics of the Levant; there was no middle ground for the smaller states. Tiring of Assyrian domination, Israel joined forces with what John H. Hayes has called a "Syro-

---

[3] Saggs, *Might That Was Assyria*, 72.

[4] Saggs, *Might That Was Assyria*, 74–75.

[5] Bustenay Oded, "Observations on Methods of Assyrian Rule in Transjordania after the Palestinian Campaign of Tiglath-Pileser III," *JNES* 29 (1970): 181–83.

[6] Ephraim Stern, *Archaeology of the Land of the Bible*, vol. 2, *The Assyrian, Babylonian and Persian Periods, 732–332 BCE* (Anchor Bible Reference Library; New York: Doubleday, 2001), 4.

[7] Stern, *Archaeology of the Land of the Bible*, 6; Van de Mieroop, *History of the Ancient Near East*, 230. On the significance of Lachish in Sennacherib's strategy, see David Ussishkin, "Sennacherib's Campaign to Philistia and Judah: Ekron, Lachish, and Jerusalem" in *Essays on Ancient Israel in its Near Eastern Context: A Tribute to Nadav Na'aman*, eds. Yairah Amit et al. (Winona Lake, Ind.: Eisenbrauns, 2006), 339–57.

[8] H. W. F. Saggs, "Assyrian Warfare in the Sargonid Period," *Iraq* 25 (1963): 165–70.

[9] Michael Mann, *The Sources of Social Power: Volume 1, A History of Power from the Beginning to AD 1760* (Cambridge: Cambridge University, 1986), 232–33.

[10] Bradley J. Parker, *The Mechanics of Empire: The Northern Frontier of Assyria as a Case Study in Imperial Dynamics* (Helsinki: Neo-Assyrian Text Corpus Project, 2001), 261.

Palestinian anti-Assyrian coalition,"[11] while Judah cast its lot with the empire. In the greatest historical conflict between the northern and southern kingdoms, the coalition attacked Judah in the Syro-Ephraimite War in 734, in order to replace Ahaz with a ruler more sympathetic to the coalition's goals. Judah weathered the assault, however, and Tiglath-Pileser wiped out the anti-Assyrian movement in his western campaign of 734–731. Israel's king, Pekah, was killed and replaced with Hoshea, whom Assyria supposed to be its puppet, with Israel its client state.

However, Hoshea withheld tribute in 725 – a move that constituted rebellion in the eyes of the Assyrians. Israel instead called on the support of Egypt, which was, as we shall note farther along, in no position to resist Assyria either. Although it took a few years for Assyria to free itself to return westward, when it did it crushed the rebellion without much trouble. Israel's capital city, Samaria, was besieged and sacked in 722–721 and its population largely fled or was deported, leading to an influx of northern refugees into Judah. Given that both Shalmaneser V (726–722) and Sargon II (721–705) are said to have overthrown Samaria in inscriptions,[12] the historical details are in dispute, but the larger outcomes are clear: Samaria became the Assyrian province of Samerina, while the political expediency of Judah's consistent submission to Assyria was confirmed. Sargon reports that he deported more than twenty-seven thousand Israelites,[13] and surely many others fled southward as refugees and were incorporated into Judean society.[14] At some point in the late eighth or early seventh centuries, the Assyrians also seem to have built a number of outposts throughout the South (identified archaeologically by architecture and pottery that mimic the styles of the home country), presumably to keep tabs on the affairs of the Levant and the Egyptian border.[15]

How were the Assyrians perceived in the Levant? The reasons for the Assyrians' interest in empire should not be misunderstood, although they are often

---

[11] Miller and Hayes, *History of Ancient Israel and Judah*, 374.

[12] For primary texts, see A. K. Grayson, *Assyrian and Babylonian Chronicles* (Texts from Cuneiform Sources; Locust Valley, N.Y.: J. J. Augustin, 1975), 72–73; *COS* 2, pp. 289, 292, 293, 295, 296; *ANET*, 286; See discussions and further bibliography in K. Lawson Younger, Jr., "The Fall of Samaria in Light of Recent Research," *CBQ* 61 (1999): 461–82; Hayim Tadmor, "The Campaigns of Sargon II of Assur: A Chronological-Historical Study," *JCS* 12 (1958): 22–40, 77–100; Miller and Hayes, *History of Ancient Israel*, 383–88; Bright, *History of Israel*, 275–76.

[13] *ANET*, 284–85; D. D. Luckenbill, *Ancient Records of Assyria and Babylonia* (2 vols.; Chicago: University of Chicago Press, 1926–27), vol. 2, par. 99 (*ANET*, 284–85). For a detailed study of the nature of the deportations from Israel, see K. Lawson Younger, Jr., "Recent Study on Sargon II, King of Assyria: Implications for Biblical Studies," in *Mesopotamia and the Bible: Comparative Explorations* (ed. Mark W. Chavalas and K. Lawson Younger, Jr.; Grand Rapids: Baker, 2002), 288–329. Assyrian administrative texts regarding deportations can be found in F. M. Fales and J. N. Postgate, *Imperial Administrative Records*, part 2 (SAA 11; Helsinki: Helsinki University Press, 1995), e.g., no. 167.

[14] See William M. Schniedewind, *How the Bible Became a Book: The Textualization of Ancient Israel* (Cambridge/New York: Cambridge University Press, 2004), 66, 69, 89.

[15] Jeffery A. Blakely and James W. Hardin, "Southwestern Judah in the Late Eighth Century B.C.E.," *BASOR* 326 (2006): 11–63, here 44.

portrayed in simplistic terms. Some scholars emphasize the Assyrians' militarism and violence,[16] while others (especially in recent years) perceive administrative practicality, a willingness to allow independence, and the benevolent imposition of a *pax Assyriaca* over the region.[17] Parpola is probably correct that the Assyrians' success was due to the tension between the "chilling fear" that they inspired, and the "numerous benefits" that allegiance to them could bring.[18]

If history has generally held a negative view of them, the Assyrians themselves bear much of the guilt – not only for their real depredations of other nations, but also because violence did in fact figure prominently in their iconography and propaganda. Their own inscriptions tell the story: Aššurnasirpal bragged, "I captured many troops alive: I cut off of some their arms and hands; I cut off of others their noses, ears, [and] extremities. I gouged out the eyes of many troops. I made one pile of the living and one of their heads. I hung the heads on trees around the city."[19] A Sennacherib inscription recounts: "With the bodies of their warriors I filled the plain, like grass. (Their) testicles I cut off, and tore out their privates like the seeds of cucumbers."[20] Tiglath-Pileser III said of a rebel king: "I impaled

---

[16] Theodore J. Lewis, " 'You Have Heard What the Kings of Assyria Have Done': Disarmament Passages vis-à-vis Assyrian Rhetoric of Intimidation" in *Isaiah's Vision of Peace in Biblical and Modern International Relations: Swords Into Plowshares* (eds. R. Cohen and R. Westbrook; New York: Palgrave Macmillan, 2008), 75–100; Erika Bleibtreu, "Grisly Assyrian Record of Torture and Death," *BAR* 17 (1991): 52–61, 75. A. Leo Oppenheim, "Neo-Assyrian and Neo-Babylonian Empires," in *Propaganda and Communication in World History*, vol. 1, *The Symbolic Instrument in Early Times* (ed. Harold D. Lasswell et al.; Honolulu: University of Hawaii Press, 1979), 111–44; Grayson, "Assyrian Rule of Conquered Territory"; K. Lawson Younger Jr., *Ancient Conquest Accounts: A Study in Ancient Near Eastern and Biblical History Writing* (JSOTSup 98; Sheffield: JSOT Press, 1990), 65–67; Bright, *History of Israel*, 241.

[17] See Frederick Mario Fales, "On *Pax Assyriaca* in the Eighth-Seventh Centuries BCE and Its Implications" in *Isaiah's Vision of Peace*, 17–35. Among Assyria's defenders is Saggs, who wrote, "[The Assyrians] have been maligned. Certainly they could be rough and tough to maintain order, but they were defenders of civilization, not barbarian destroyers" (*The Might That Was Assyria*, 2). Writes Parker, "By offering protection… the Assyrian oppressors soon became the protectors of those they oppressed" (*The Mechanics of Empire*, 259). Cf. Stephanie Dalley, "Recent Evidence from Assyrian Sources for Judaean History from Uzziah to Manasseh." *JSOT* 28 (2004): 387–401; Walter Mayer, "Sennacherib's Campaign of 701 BCE: The Assyrian View," trans. Julia Assante, in *'Like a Bird in a Cage': The Invasion of Sennacherib in 701 BCE* (ed. Lester L. Grabbe; JSOTSup 363; London: Sheffield Academic Press, 2003), 168–200. More recently, Fales has wearied of the whole conversation: "Le temps est … venu d'abandonner les interpretations moralisantes insistant sur le caractère belliqueux des Assyriens" (F. M. Fales, *Guerre et paix en Assyrie. Religion et imperialism* [Paris: Editions du Cerf, 2010], 229).

[18] Simo Parpola, "Assyria's Expansion in the 8th and 7th Centuries and Its Long-Term Repercussions in the West," in *Symbiosis, Symbolism and Power of the Past: Canaan, Ancient Israel, and Their Neighbors from the Late Bronze Age through Roman Palaestina*, eds. William G. Dever and Seymour Gitin (Winona Lake, Ind.: Eisenbrauns, 2003), 102.

[19] A. K. Grayson, *Assyrian Royal Inscriptions*, part 2, *From Tiglath-pileser I to Ashur-nasir-apli II* (Wiesbaden: Harrassowitz, 1976), 126. Full transcriptions of the Mesopotamian texts have been omitted in the interest of conciseness.

[20] Luckenbill, *Ancient Records of Assyria and Babylonia*, 2:254.

[him] before the gate of his city and exposed him to the gaze of his countrymen. His wife, his sons, his daughters, his possessions, the treasure of his palaces I despoiled."[21]

Neo-Assyrian treaties also contain graphic depictions of violence and death. The treaty of Aššur-nerari V with Mati'-ilu, king of Arpad, included a ritual of slitting a lamb's throat, meant to reflect the fate of the vassal king if he should rebel:

> This head is not the head of a spring lamb, it is the head of Mati'-ilu, it is the head of his sons, his magnates and the people of [his la]nd. If Mati'-ilu [should sin] against this treaty, then just as the head of this spring lamb is c[ut] off, and its knuckle placed in its mouth ... so may the head of Mati'-ilu be cut off, and his sons [and his nobles]... [22]

The text continues with similar curses reflecting the systematic dismemberment of the lamb.[23]

These texts were certainly propagandistic – they were intended to terrify anyone who would think of resisting Assyria – but there is little doubt that they also reflect real military practices.[24] As Eckart Frahm wrote, "recent scholarship ... has focused too little on the dark side of this remarkable state":

> [W]e should not forget, in our late discovery of the beauty of the artwork and our admiration for the administrative skills of the Assyrians, that their rulers, in order to achieve their goals – even such noble goals as establishing unity and order –, waged extremely aggressive wars, deported whole populations ... and killed large numbers of civilians.[25]

Nevertheless, cartoonish images of Assyria as *merely* rapacious and bloodthirsty (as in Byron's "The Destruction of Sennacherib," where the Assyrian king de-

---

[21] Hayim Tadmor, *The Inscriptions of Tiglath-Pileser III, King of Assyria: Critical Edition, with Introductions, Translations, and Commentary.* (Publications of the Israel Academy of Sciences and Humanities, Section of Humanities; Jerusalem: Israel Academy of Sciences and Humanities, 1994), 122–23.

[22] Simo Parpola and Kazuko Watanabe, eds., *Neo-Assyrian Treaties and Loyalty-Oaths* (SAA 2; Helsinki: Helsinki University Press, 1988), 9. There are no directions in the text about who would have read it, but since the terms are dictated by the Assyrians, it seems likely that their officials would have read it.

[23] Nor were such images limited to international relations; Neo-Assyrian legal contracts contain curses that the one who breaks the contract will have to burn his children before a deity (Morton Smith, "A Note on Burning Babies," *JAOS* 95 [1973]: 477–79, here 479). It must be noted that (1) this sort of curse is attested in only five texts; (2) there is no indication that it was carried out; and (3) it was not part of any regularized cult. See further discussion of child sacrifice in § 4.4.3.2 and § 5.2.1.2.

[24] See Seth Richardson, "Death and Dismemberment in Mesopotamia: Discorporation between the Body and the Body Politic" in *Performing Death: Social Analyses of Funerary Traditions in the Ancient Near East and Mediterranean Worlds* (ed. Nicola Lanieri; Oriental Institute Seminars 3; Chicago: University of Chicago Press, 2007), 189–208, here 198.

[25] Eckart Frahm, "Images of Assyria in Nineteenth- and Twentieth-Century Western Scholarship," in *Orientalism, Assyriology and the Bible* (ed. Steven W. Holloway; Hebrew Bible Monographs 10; Sheffield: Sheffield Phoenix, 2006), 92.

scends on Jerusalem "like a wolf on the fold"[26]) risk missing its similarities to modern empires. It was not through sheer aggression that Assyria built its massive empire. Instead, the portrait that has emerged in the past fifty years is of a nuanced and savvy administration that was bent on maximizing wealth and consolidating power more than wreaking havoc. If every nation had been content to bow at the emperor's feet and send the heavy tribute every year (which was Assyria's primary source of wealth from its empire[27]), it is doubtful that Assyria would ever have fought a battle.[28] This, of course, was not the case – not only because of the smaller nations' sense of pride or independence, but also because the tribute was a serious economic hardship that degraded the quality of life and led to suffering in vassal nations by sapping their resources.[29] That is likely the primary reason that nations "rebelled."

It may be, on the other hand, that Judah's royalty and trading classes profited to some extent from the increased trade brought by the Assyrian Empire.[30] Judah was known even in central Assyria as a major grain producer,[31] and its upper classes seem to have seen an upswing in wealth during the time of Hezekiah.[32] The same geography that made Judah a battleground also positioned it to benefit from commerce. The oracle in Isa 19:23–24 envisions that "there will be a highway from Egypt to Assyria, and the Assyrian will come into Egypt, and the Egyptian into Assyria ... On that day Israel will be the third with Egypt and Assyria, a blessing in the midst of the earth." Although this passage is often dated to a later period, its earliest form is quite plausibly rooted in the geopolitics of the eighth century, as has increasingly been recognized.[33] It is indeed understandable

---

[26] Less often noted is that Byron casts the Assyrians as worshipers of Baal in the third stanza of the poem!
[27] Susan Sherratt and Andrew Sherratt, "The Growth of the Mediterranean Economy in the Early First Millennium BC," *World Archaeology* 24 (1993): 361–78.
[28] Grayson, "Assyrian Rule of Conquered Territory," 961: "the Assyrians came to prefer psychological warfare whenever it was feasible"; Parpola and Watanabe, *Neo-Assyrian Treaties and Loyalty Oaths*, xxiii: "No doubt the Assyrian kings preferred 'expansion by treaties' to expansion by aggression. Waging war was costly and time-consuming, and wasted resources."
[29] See § 1.3 below; also Simo Parpola, "Assyria's Expansion in the 8th and 7th Centuries and Its Long-Term Repercussions in the West," *Symbiosis, Symbolism and Power of the Past: Canaan, Ancient Israel, and Their Neighbors from the Late Bronze Age through Roman Palaestina*, eds. William G. Dever and Seymour Gitin (Winona Lake, Ind.: Eisenbrauns, 2003), 101.
[30] Dalley sees Hezekian Judah as "a wealthy [nation] which had found ingenious ways to enrich itself" (Dalley, "Recent Evidence," 393).
[31] Avraham Faust and Ehud Weiss, "Judah, Philistia, and the Mediterranean World: Reconstructing the Economic System of the Seventh Century BCE," *BASOR* 338 (May 2005): 71–92.
[32] John S. Holladay, Jr., "Hezekiah's Tribute, Long-Distance Trade, and the Wealth of Nations ca. 1000–600 BCE: A New Perspective" in *Confronting the Past: Archaeological and Historical Essays on Ancient Israel in Honor of William G. Dever* (eds. Seymour Gitin et al.; Winona Lake, Ind.: Eisenbrauns, 2006), 309–31; Elizabeth Bloch-Smith, "Life in Judah from the Perspective of the Dead," *Near Eastern Archaeology* 65 (2002): 128–29; Dalley, "Recent Evidence," 393.
[33] The late dating has been assumed with "no adequate reasons," wrote Hans Wildberger

that a small nation should have aspired to be a world power along with the major neighboring empires.

The wealth of the Judean elite also would have led to intrasocietal tensions in Judah between those elites and rural farmers who may have felt the pinch more acutely; indeed it has recently been theorized that Josiah came to power as a puppet king after a revolt by the ʿām hāʾāreṣ ("the people of the land").[34] In any case, Stephanie Dalley has recently suggested that relations between Assyria and Judah were very warm during Hezekiah's reign – indeed familial, in that she believes Judean princesses were married to Tiglath-Pileser III and Sargon II. Among other supporting data, Judeans seem to have served as bodyguards for Sennacherib,[35] who also praised Hezekiah as "tough and strong" in an inscription, is an exceptional literary treatment for a foreign, rebel king.[36]

It is possible that a friendly history with Assyria helped to spare Jerusalem in 701 when it failed to pay its tribute and Sennacherib came to collect. The biblical (2 Kgs 18:13) and cuneiform accounts[37] agree that the campaign overwhelmed a number of Judean cities, with Sennacherib specifying forty-six.[38] Typically a rebel king would have at least been deposed, and often his city destroyed in such a case. The events of 701 are even more hotly contested than those of 722–721, and this is not the place to review the debates.[39] Second Kings states that Hezekiah sent word to Sennacherib trying to avert destruction, while the Assyrian inscription makes no mention of this. Sennacherib claimed that he received his

---

(*Isaiah 13–27: A Commentary* [Continental Commentaries; Minneapolis: Fortress, 1997], 279). See Alviero Niccacci, "Isaiah XVIII–XX from an Egyptological Perspective," *VT* 48 (1998): 214–238; J. J. M. Roberts, "Isaiah's Egyptian and Nubian Oracles," in *Israel's Prophets and Israel's Past: Essays on the Relationship of Prophetic Texts and Israelite History in Honor of John H. Hayes* (ed. Brad E. Kelle and Megan Bishop Moore; Library of Hebrew Bible/Old Testament Studies 446; New York: T& T Clark, 2006), 201–9, here 206; Sarah Israelit-Groll, "The Egyptian Background to Isaiah 19:18" in *Boundaries of the Ancient Near Eastern World: A Tribute to Cyrus H. Gordon*. Edited by Meir Lubetski et al. (JSOTSup 273. Sheffield: JSOT Press, 1998), 300–303.

[34] Christopher R. Seitz, *Theology in Conflict: Reactions to the Exile in the Book of Jeremiah* (BZAW 176; Berlin/New York: De Gruyter, 1989), 42–51; see also Schniedewind, *How the Bible Became a Book*, 107; J. Healy, "Am Ha'aretz," *ABD* 1:168–69.

[35] This is based on an interpretation of one of Sennacherib's reliefs from Nineveh (Dalley, "Recent Evidence," 391–92). Dalley does not explain, however, how a Judean could be distinguished iconographically from a Semite from the former kingdom of Israel.

[36] Akkadian *šepṣu mitru*; Dalley, "Recent Evidence," 392. The reading is in some dispute; *mitru* should perhaps be read *bēru*. See William R. Gallagher, *Sennacherib's Campaign to Judah: New Studies* (Studies in the History and Culture of the Ancient Near East 18; Leiden: Brill, 1999), 130 and n. 13.

[37] COS 2.119B.

[38] The violence of the campaign is confirmed by destruction layers in many Judean cities that are attributed to Assyrians (Stern, *Archaeology of the Land of the Bible*, 10).

[39] The most extensive attempt to make sense of the event in light of both literary and comparative concerns is Gallagher, *Sennacherib's Campaign to Judah*. While his conclusions will not convince all parties, his bibliography was very complete at that time.

tribute after a siege,[40] while the Bible is less clear on this point. The Bible does recount that Hezekiah gave the Assyrian king "all the silver that was found in the house of the LORD and in the treasuries of the king's house" and stripped the gold from the doors of the temple (2 Kgs 18:14–16), but this was prior to the siege according to the biblical narrative. The biblical and cuneiform texts record similar tribute amounts: thirty talents of gold in both cases, plus either three hundred (2 Kings) or eight hundred (Sennacherib) talents of silver. As has often been noted, Sennacherib claims only to have "shut [Hezekiah] up like a bird in a cage," which is not only a modest claim by Assyrian standards but one that is borrowed from an earlier inscription of Tiglath-Pileser III.[41] It is manifest that both the Assyrian and biblical texts serve ideological interests in this instance, and we are not likely to get any closer to the precise historical truth of the incident without further information coming to light.[42] It is not entirely clear whether Hezekiah was simply spared by Sennacherib because of a change of heart, or whether some combination of Egyptian military aid,[43] sickness among the Assyrian troops,[44] and/or divine intervention[45] caused the Assyrian king to

---

[40] COS 2.119B, ANET, 287–88, etc. Some scholars accept the Assyrian version of events as fact, e.g., Mayer, "Sennacherib's Campaign of 701 BCE." For a more balanced approach, see Younger, "Assyrian Involvement"; or W. W. Hallo, "Jerusalem under Hezekiah: An Assyriological Perspective," in *Jerusalem: Its Sanctity and Centrality to Judaism, Christianity, and Islam* (ed. Lee I. Levine; New York: Continuum, 1999), 35–50, esp. 38–43. For further bibliography, see Steven W. Holloway, *Aššur is King! Aššur is King! Religion in the Exercise of Power in the Neo-Assyrian Empire* (Culture and History of the Ancient Near East 10; Leiden: Brill, 2002), 4 n. 6.

[41] Hallo, "Jerusalem under Hezekiah," 39–40; Hayim Tadmor, "Sennacherib's Campaign to Judah," *Zion* 50 (1985): 65–80.

[42] On the ideological reshaping of Assyrian accounts, see Younger, "Assyrian Involvement," 247–54; Amélie Kuhrt, *The Ancient Near East* (Routledge History of the Ancient World; London: Routledge, 1995), 2:474–76. Regarding Sennacherib's siege, Kuhrt suggests that "both accounts are probably 'true' " (2:478), and Paul S. Evans seeks to harmonize the accounts with the theory that "Hezekiah reneged on surrendering the required payment of gold" (*The Invasion of Sennacherib in the Book of Kings: A Source-Critical and Rhetorical Study of 2 Kings 18–19* [Leiden: Brill, 2009], 192.)

[43] Evans cogently points out that Isaiah's consistent condemnations of Egyptian aid make it unlikely that this detail would have been included in the book of Isaiah unless it were historical; see *The Invasion of Sennacherib in the Book of Kings*, 192. The role of the Kushite force is described with conviction and detail by K. A. Kitchen, *On the Reliability of the Old Testament* (Grand Rapids: Eerdmans, 2003), 40–42, 50–51. For further recent discussion, see a trio of essays from *Jerusalem in Bible and Archaeology*, ed. Vaughn and Killebrew: Younger, "Assyrian Involvement"; J. J. M. Roberts, "Egypt, Assyria, Isaiah, and the Ashdod Affair: An Alternative Proposal" (265–83); James K. Hoffmeier, "Egypt's Role in the Events of 701 B.C. in Jerusalem" (219–34). See also Donald Redford, *Egypt, Canaan and Israel in Ancient Times* (Princeton: Princeton University Press, 1992), 353.

[44] Donald J. Wiseman suggests that it was a case of bacillary dysentery ("Medicine in the Old Testament World," in Bernard Palmer, ed., *Medicine and the Bible* [Exeter: Paternoster, 1986], 25). It is sometimes suggested that the divine slaughter in 2 Kgs 19:35 was the result of a rodent infestation among the Assyrians and that a scene from Herodotus's account of Sennacherib's campaign into Egypt preserves some version of this: "There came in the night a multitude of

return home in a hurry. It is certainly most surprising that Sennacherib would allow a rebel king to remain on the throne, when the whole point of the western campaign was to punish rebellious vassals.⁴⁶ Whatever other factors came into play, it is likely that Assyria did not deem Judah a highly profitable area to control, and so did not expend the energy to conquer it completely and turn it into a province.⁴⁷

Hezekiah's survival is reminiscent of another rebel king who was also anomalously left on his throne, Hanunu of Gaza. The Assyrian monarch in that instance, Tiglath-Pileser III, installed a gold image of himself in Hanunu's palace, "perhaps cast from Hanunu's own trade-gotten wealth."⁴⁸ It may be the case for both Hezekiah and Hanunu that "the economic networks they dominated rendered them more useful alive than flayed," but in both cases "[t]he lenient treatment ... may have come with a variety of unsubtle 'reminders' of Assyrian sovereignty ... intended to remind the wayward ruler that a sizable cut of his annual profits was earmarked for the Great King."⁴⁹ It was one thing to survive an Assyrian military campaign, but it is unthinkable that Sennacherib would have left Jerusalem without sending a strong message about imperial authority.

At all events, it is clear that Judah subsequently resumed its vassal status to Assyria, since the latter continued its southward expansion under Sennacherib

---

field-mice, which devoured all the quivers and bowstrings of the enemy and ate the thongs by which they managed their shields. Next morning they commenced their fight, and great multitudes fell, as they had no arms with which to defend themselves" (*Histories* 2.141). Needless to say, the difficulties of this theory far outweigh its explanatory power. For an assessment of the Greek material, see Brent A. Strawn, "Herodotus' *Histories* 2.141 and the Deliverance of Jerusalem: On Parallels, Sources, and Histories of Ancient Israel," in *Israel's Prophets and Israel's Past*, 210–38.

⁴⁵ Writes Baruch Halpern: "H(Dtr) portrays the plague in Sennacherib's camp as a miracle, as he or his source (a Hezekian dedication?) must have seen it. That something untoward did befall the beleaguerers – whether at Jerusalem or in the Philistine plain – is to be inferred from the fact that Hezekiah, alone among vassals besieged, forwarded his tribute to Assyria, rather than paying up on the spot" (*The First Historians: The Hebrew Bible and History* [San Francisco: Harper & Row, 1988], 247). Robert D. Bates has sought to prove that "[t]he only thing that could have interfered with Sennacherib's bringing a rebellious vassal to justice was a miraculous event completely outside of his control" ("Assyria and Rebellion in the Annals of Sennacherib: An Analysis of Sennacherib's Treatment of Hezekiah." *Near East Archaeological Society Bulletin* 44 [1999]: 57). H. H. Rowley was also in this camp: "Hezekiah's Reform and Rebellion," *Bulletin of the John Rylands Library* 44 (1962): 431.

⁴⁶ See A. R. Millard, "Sennacherib's Attack on Hezekiah," *TynBul* 36 (1985): 61–77; also Bates, "Assyria and Rebellion."

⁴⁷ Parker, *The Mechanics of Empire*, 25: "States in logistically difficult zones that maintained a friendly attitude towards the empire might get away with token tribute payments and the public acknowledgment of Assyrian authority." Parker helpfully describes the Assyrians' hybrid approach to empire, combining "low-cost/low-benefit" areas with "high-cost/high-benefit" areas. Presumably, in their "economy of force," the Assyrians had expended all they cared to.

⁴⁸ Holloway, *Aššur is King!*, 192.

⁴⁹ Holloway, *Aššur is King!*, 192–93; Holloway is speaking of Hanunu.

(704–681), which Esarhaddon (680–669) extended all the way across Egypt. It is hard to imagine that Assyria could have pressed so far south had they not been in firm control of Palestine. Although the biblical narrative seems to lose interest in Assyrian events after 701, an inscription of Esarhaddon[50] reveals that Manasseh of Judah was among the foreign kings compelled by him to bring building supplies to Nineveh for his palace,[51] and a long reign such as his (ca. 698–644) would not have been possible without the Assyrians' tolerance. Thus we can say that whereas Judah was not turned into a province as Israel had been, it was reduced to vassalship.

Decades later, when the Neo-Assyrian Empire began to collapse, Judah began to reassert its political independence. There are no records of Assyrian presence in Palestine after 645,[52] but Judah did not act immediately. Josiah made no moves regarding Assyria at all until his twelfth or eighteenth regnal year, that is, 628 or 622.[53] Assyria had already begun to crumble by then. Upon the death of Aššurbanipal in 627, revolt was everywhere. By 616, Babylon had mustered itself and begun to attack again in earnest. In 612, Nineveh fell, and the remnant of the Assyrians scattered.[54] Isaiah 14, probably composed upon the death of Sargon II in 705, must have sounded fresh again in 612 – "How you are cut down to the ground, you who laid the nations low ..." – and indeed it was probably re-framed at that time (see § 5.2.1.1).

Judah survived its imperial hegemon, but not by much. Assyria's disappearance left a power vacuum. For a short time Judah was able to enrich itself by reasserting control over northern territories and Palestinian trade routes, but Josiah's death, resulting from an encounter with the Egyptian pharaoh Neco II,[55] ended the last lengthy and successful reign in Judah. Soon enough, Babylon came calling. Judah had danced around Assyria for a century, but the same steps did not please the Babylonians as well. Perhaps there really were old loyalties

---

[50] *ANET*, 291.
[51] On the close (if coercive) relationship between Manasseh and the Assyrians, see Parpola, "Assyria's Expansion," 104.
[52] Stern, *Archaeology of the Land of the Bible*, 4.
[53] Chronicles records that Josiah began his reform in the twelfth year of his reign (2 Chr 34:3), while Kings has it in the eighteenth (2 Kgs 22:1). See further discussion below.
[54] Nebuchadnezzar II of Babylon (604–562) appears to have employed an Assyrian scribe or two at his court, as Babylonian documents from 603 and 600 have been found in the Neo-Assyrian dialect (John A. Brinkman, "Unfolding the Drama of the Assyrian Empire," in *Assyria 1995: Proceedings of the 10th Anniversary Symposium of the New-Assyrian Text Corups Project, Helsinki, September 7–11, 1995* [ed. S. Parpola and R. M. Whiting; Helsinki: Neo-Assyrian Text Corpus Project, 1997], 5). But overall, the one Mesopotamian power seems to have simply been swallowed up by the other, not to reemerge.
[55] The circumstances of Josiah's death are unclear: Chronicles (2 Chr 35:20–23) reports that he opposed the Egyptians militarily and died in battle, while the Kings account (2 Kgs 23:29) suggests the possibility that he merely went to meet with Neco and was murdered. See discussion and references in Miller and Hayes, *History of Ancient Israel and Judah*, 460–61 and nn. 28–29.

between Judah and Assyria that had earned the vassal exceptional leeway in the former times. Or, it may simply have been that the Neo-Babylonians were not interested in ruling far-flung city-states that did not produce large profits. Although they nominally took over the Neo-Assyrian provincial system, they governed it like strip miners rather than farmers:

> In contrast to the Assyrian kings, Nabopolassar and Nebuchadrezzar did not consider themselves rulers of the world and did not develop an imperial ideology like the Assyrian kings. The consequence was that they did not invest great resources in establishing their rule in the areas conquered. ... This policy led to a drastic decline throughout the Levant in economy and trade.[56]

The destruction of Jerusalem in 587 brought to a close a period of nearly two centuries in which Judah rode the rough seas of political change. It was this atmosphere of unrest that formed the backdrop for Isaiah's prophetic career.

1.3 Mechanisms of Mesopotamian influence

Assyria has been called "an empire of communications."[57] Letters and ambassadors shuttled between cities, and Jerusalem was one node in this network of information.[58] Some scholars have called attention to Assyria's intelligence-gathering operations, comparing their impact to that of "modern intelligence agencies such as the CIA, KGB or Mossad."[59] But information flowed out of Assyria as well; under these conditions, cultural influences traveled rapidly, as the archaeological record clearly shows. "Although they ruled for a relatively short time," remarks Ephraim Stern, "the Assyrians' impact on every aspect of Palestine's culture may be regarded as revolutionary: it brought an end to an age-old Israelite-Phoenician tradition and the introduction of the Mesopotamian-Assyrian one instead."[60]

---

[56] Oded Lipschits, *The Fall and Rise of Jerusalem: Judah under Babylonian Rule* (Winona Lake, Ind.: Eisenbrauns, 2005), 188; cf. D. S. Vanderhooft, *The Neo-Babylonian Empire and the Latter Prophets* (HSM 59; Atlanta: Scholars Press, 1999), 9–59.

[57] Simo Parpola, ed., *The Correspondence of Sargon II*, part 1, *Letters from Assyria and the West* (SAA 1; Helsinki: Helsinki University Press, 1987); cf. Oded, "Observations on Methods of Assyrian Rule," 177–86; also Kuhrt, *Ancient Near East*, 2:535. Bradley Parker describes the Assyrian Empire as a "network empire," meaning that it was composed of connected nodes rather than contiguous territories (*Mechanics of Empire*, 255). Although this is not the same as a "networked empire," it does emphasize the importance of communication among these sometimes far-flung areas.

[58] Jerusalem also, of course, would have conducted its own court business – indeed the majority of it – apart from Assyrian oversight.

[59] Peter Dubovský, *Hezekiah and the Assyrian Spies: Reconstruction of the Neo-Assyrian Intelligence Services and its Significance for 2 Kings 18–19* (BO 49; Rome: Editrice Pontificio Istituto Biblico, 2006), 253.

[60] Stern, *Archaeology of the Land of the Bible*, 19. See also Gabriel Barkay, "The Iron Age II–

Stern of course was remarking on trends in *material* culture, but textual scholars have looked for similar influence on intellectual culture. Despite extensive publications on such influences, Simo Parpola could write in 2000 that "Assyria's role in affecting long-term cultural development in the territories subject to its expansion, particularly in the field of *intellectual life*, has not received the attention it deserves."[61] Parpola associates the major onset of this influence with the policies of Tiglath-Pileser III starting in 745 BCE – close to the beginning of Isaiah's career.

Isaiah's role in advising the royal court about political events has always been perceived by scholars;[62] one assumes that the prophet was therefore informed to some degree about international affairs. Less often, however, is the question posed how Isaiah might have been affected culturally and religiously by his position at an intersection of so many foreign influences.

Assyrian influence on Judah (specifically the Jerusalem court and its attendant elites) could have come through multiple means – certainly through diplomatic contact,[63] and likely through trade, since Judah is known to have exported its grain far and wide to Assyrian provincial cities.[64] The "Judahite *sĕ'āh*" was used as a measure even in Nineveh itself, and Judean weights have been found in various neighboring countries, suggesting that they served as one of the basic units of measure for trade in the region.[65] Diplomatic and economic contacts were inevitable between an ancient Near Eastern state and its clients, and indeed the Assyrian system of mass deportations "may have produced a more effective exchange

---

III," *The Archaeology of Ancient Israel* (ed. Amnon Ben-Tor; New Haven: Yale University Press, 1992), 351–53.

[61] Parpola, "Assyria's Expansion," 99. Emphasis in original.

[62] Not only is this an obligatory facet of any recent critical commentary, but it has also generated a number of monographs from eminent scholars over the past century and more. For example, S. R. Driver, *Isaiah: His Life and Times* (New York: Fleming H. Revell, 1888); A. H. Sayce, *The Life and Times of Isaiah: As Illustrated by Contemporary Monuments* (Oxford: Horace Hart, 1889); Jean Steinmann, *Le Prophète Isaïe: Sa vie, son oeuvre et son temps* (2nd ed.; Lectio Divina 5; Paris: Cerf, 1955); Herbert Donner, *Israel unter den Völkern: Die Stellung der klassischen Propheten des 8. Jahrhunderts v. Chr. zur Aussenpolitik der Könige von Israel und Juda* (Leiden: Brill, 1964); Walter Dietrich, *Jesaja und die Politik* (BEvT: Theologische Abhandlungen 74; Munich: Kaiser, 1976); John H. Hayes and Stuart A. Irvine, *Isaiah, the Eighth Century Prophet: His Times and His Preaching* (Nashville: Abingdon, 1987); Scholastika Deck, *Die Gerichtsbotschaft Jesajas: Charakter und Begründung* (FB 67; Würzburg: Echter, 1991); Lewis, "You Have Heard What the Kings of Assyria Have Done."

[63] The similarities of Deuteronomy to Neo-Assyrian treaties has long been noted. See, e.g., Eckart Otto, *Das Deuteronomium: Politische Theologie und Rechtsreform in Juda und Assyrien* (BZAW 284; Berlin: De Gruyter, 1999).

[64] Judean weights have also been found all across Palestine, Philistia, and the Transjordanian states, leading Ephraim Stern to conclude that "during this period the Judaean weight served as the basic unit of measure for trade transactions among all these nations, as well as trade with Egypt" (Stern, *Archaeology of the Land of the Bible*, 191). See also Fales, "On *Pax Assyriaca*," 20.

[65] Faust and Weiss, "Judah, Philistia, and the Mediterranean World," 82–83.

of artistic ideas and methods of craftswork than had been produced by ordinary trading contacts."[66]

1.3.1 Linguistic contacts

The question of the linguistic medium of the transmission of ideas is complex and complicated, going well beyond the scope of this study, and so the issue can only be summarized briefly.[67] The fact that the Bible shows influence by Mesopotamian literature and culture is one of the cornerstones of critical biblical scholarship, and new studies emerge regularly that argue this in new and varied ways. For all this, the manner in which that influence worked is surprisingly unclear in many cases. In the first place, Neo-Assyrian influence is only one of three possible historical periods in which the influence of Mesopotamian cuneiform literature might have been felt in Palestine: The other two are (1) the Late Bronze Age, at which time we have the numerous Amarna letters and other documents to testify to a relatively widespread cuneiform scribal culture in the Levant – but it does not seem that this scribal culture survived the political and cultural upheavals of the transition to the Iron Age;[68] and (2) the period of the Babylonian exile, when the Judean elites taken to Babylon would have been exposed to cuneiform (at least those with Jehoiachin at the royal court), though one can only speculate how much of it they could have learned.

The theory of specifically Neo-Assyrian influence deserves special attention here since Isaiah 1–39 is so insistent about its own location in that period, and since one finds numerous recent studies that find it a particularly significant time for cultural and linguistic influence.[69] Still, even if one grants that Assyrian influ-

---

[66] W. S. Smith, *Interconnections in the Ancient Near East: A Study of the Relationships between the Arts of Egypt, the Aegean, and Western Asia* (New Haven: Yale University Press, 1965), 55.

[67] For a more thorough discussion, see Willliam Morrow, " 'To Set the Name' in the Deuteronomic Centralization Formula: A Case of Cultural Hybridity," *JSS* 55 (2010): 365–83.

[68] William Morrow, "Resistance and Hybridity in Late Bronze Age Canaan," *RB* 115 (2008), 321–39; Wayne Horowitz, Takayoshi Oshima, and Seth Sanders, *Cuneiform in Canaan: Cuneiform Sources from the Land of Israel in Ancient Times* (Jerusalem: Israel Exploration Society and The Hebrew University of Jerusalem, 2006), 19.

[69] In addition to the cogent studies on Neo-Assyrian rhetoric by Peter Machinist and Chaim Cohen cited elsewhere, significant recent studies of Neo-Assyrian influence on biblical law alone include Moshe Weinfeld, *Deuteronomy 1–11* (AB 5; New York: Doubleday, 1991); Eckart Otto, *Das Deuteronomium: Politische Theologie und Rechtsreform in Juda und Assyrien* (BZAW 284, Berlin 1999); Bernard M. Levinson, "Is the Covenant Code an Exilic Composition? A Response to John Van Seters," *In Search of Pre-Exilic Israel* (JSOTS 406; London: T & T Clark, 2004); David P. Wright, *Inventing God's Law: How the Covenant Code of the Bible Used and Revised the Laws of Hammurabi* (Oxford: Oxford University Press, 2009), 3. In Israelite religion, there is Baruch Levine, "Assyrian Ideology and Israelite Monotheism," *Iraq* 67 (2005): 411–427; and Shawn Zelig Aster, "The Image of Assyria in Isaiah 2:5–22: The Campaign Motif Revisited," *JAOS* 127 (2007): 249–78. One could go on listing supporters of Neo-Assyrian influence nearly indefinitely, but each case of influence or intertextuality must still be argued on its merits.

ence was strong in Isaiah's time, how did it take place, from a linguistic standpoint? Three basic theories exist:

The first theory is that some Judean scribes could read Akkadian cuneiform texts. In support of this idea, Bernard Levinson adduces a text from Sargon II that says he made "populations of the four quarters of the world with strange tongues and incompatible speech ... accept a single voice."[70]

The second theory is that any transference of ideas and phrases had to come through the medium of Aramaic. William Schniedewind has argued that the "single voice" or language that Sargon II advocated was not Akkadian, but Aramaic,[71] and there is indeed every reason to think that Aramaic was the administrative language of the Neo-Assyrian empire in the West by the seventh century.[72] Isaiah's time was near the tipping point where the shift from Akkadian to Aramaic becomes more clear, but the small number of cuneiform documents from Iron Age Judah suggests it may have already happened. A well-known comment in Isa 36:11 has Hezekiah's officials ask an Assyrian representative to speak in Aramaic rather than "Judean" (יהודית) during Sennacherib's siege of Jerusalem in 701. The question of this story's historical accuracy is discussed in more detail in § 5.2.1.4, but I take it to support two unsurprising facts: (1) that Aramaic was a common diplomatic language in Palestine by the very end of the eighth century, and (2) that the Assyrian empire had experts in its court who could converse in the languages of its client states. Linguistic connections were thus a two-way street. This story does not bear directly on the question of the Judeans' knowledge of Akkadian.

The third theory is that Judeans could understand and even speak some Akkadian, but without reading cuneiform. Akkadian loanwords (or whole phrases) in biblical texts lend support to the idea that Judeans knew some Akkadian. The recent analysis by Paul Mankowski identifies 80 likely loanwords from Akkadian to Hebrew, not counting multiple uses of the same word,[73] and Isaiah has more such loanwords (13) than any other biblical book.[74]

---

[70] Levinson has argued this (Levinson, "Is the Covenant Code an Exilic Composition?" 295–96), and I am sympathetic to his case. However, the number of cuneiform texts that have been discovered from Israel and Judah in the Neo-Assyrian Period stands at only 18 at this writing, and most of these are Assyrian administrative tablets, royal inscriptions, and cylinder seals, which are probably not reflective of indigenous competence (Horowitz et al., *Cuneiform in Canaan*, 20).

[71] William M. Schniedewind, "Aramaic, the Death of Written Hebrew, and Language Shift in the Persian Period," in *Margins of Writing, Origins of Culture* (ed. S. L. Sanders; Oriental Institute Seminars 2, Chicago 2006), 139.

[72] Hayim Tadmor, "On the Role of Aramaic in the Assyrian Empire," in *Near Eastern Studies Dedicated to H. I. H. Prince Takahito Mikasa on the Occasion of His Seventy-Fifth Birthday* (Bulletin of the Middle Eastern Culture Center in Japan 5. Wiesbaden: Harrassowitz, 1991), 419–26.

[73] Paul V. Mankowski, *Akkadian Loanwords in Biblical Hebrew* (Winona Lake, Ind.: Eisenbrauns, 2000), 168–70.

[74] Mankowski, *Akkadian Loanwords*, 174.

This final theory is the one that William Morrow has recently adopted; regarding the pun on Akkadian *šarru* ("king") and Hebrew *śar* ("commander") in Isa 10:8 – "Are not all my commanders [שׂרי] kings?" – he remarks that "one does not require a great deal of fluency to learn the word for 'king' in Akkadian."[75] Although I think that it would have been desirable for the Jerusalem court to have scribes who could read cuneiform,[76] and that certain scribes knew more than a few scattered words, this theory best fits the data that we have today, and is sufficient to account for the sort of influences that one sees in Isaiah.

One objection that is sometimes raised against theories of subtle or esoteric literary borrowings and linguistic wordplay is that most of the biblical author's (or prophet's) audience would not have understood the reference; but this is not a serious hindrance. As Morrow rightly warns:

> It is not to be assumed that most people would have understood the subversive associations ... In the pre-exilic period, literature like Deuteronomy was the province of a small, educated elite. Only a rather select group would have appreciated the bilingual pun ... But the insertion of such abstruse knowledge is hardly exceptional in ancient Near Eastern scribal practice. There are many examples in Mesopotamian literature of obscure references that would only make sense to the especially learned.[77]

In the case of Isaiah, not only is he never portrayed as speaking to the masses, if anything he is portrayed as a difficult and mysterious figure who is hard to understand (Isa 6:9).

In sum, the biblical text itself points strongly toward a knowledge of Akkadian. Whether or not Judean scribes were able to read cuneiform is less important for the purposes of Isaiah, where the correspondences with, for example, Assyrian imperial rhetoric tend to be looser and briefer (in contrast to biblical law). Again, the ability to understand Assyrian speech at a basic level would be sufficient to support the arguments made in ch. 5 about Isaiah's knowledge of it.

1.3.2 The question of religious imposition

The question of cultural influence depends even more on the degree of Assyria's interference in the cultures of its provinces and vassals than on language. How heavy was the empire's hand on outlying areas and client states? Did it impose Assyrian religious duties upon conquered states, or did the religions of those nations continue essentially independent of imperial impact?

Up to the 1970s, the leading scholarly position was that Assyria's imperial

---

[75] Morrow, "To Set the Name," 378.
[76] As Morrow himself remarks elsewhere, scribes certainly had enough motivation to become familiar with Akkadian – it was a matter of national security, if nothing else. See William Morrow, "Cuneiform Literacy and Deuteronomic Composition," *BO* 62 (2005): 210.
[77] Morrow, "To Set the Name," 382.

system imposed elements of its religion upon its subordinated states. While this perspective was never unanimous,[78] influential early British Assyriologists in particular generally perceived Assyrian religious imposition. The foremost among them "threw their reputations behind an image of Assyrian imperial expansionism that exploited the state pantheon as much as it exploited terror of military reprisal."[79] A. T. Olmstead said that the "whole organization" of the Assyrian provincial system "centered around the worship of Ashur, the deified state and reigning king."[80] With varying degrees of nuance, histories by the likes of W. F. Albright and Martin Noth adopted this perspective.[81] According to this view, the religious reforms of Hezekiah and Josiah were inherently decisions "to repudiate the official Assyrian cult."[82] Frank Moore Cross and David Noel Freedman argued, based on the Chronicler's chronology of the reform (2 Chr 34:3–7), that Josiah's cultic actions mirrored "the progressive decline of Assyrian authority."[83] Beginning from a proposed chronology of the last Assyrian kings offered by W. H. Dubberstein,[84] the two tried to show that Josiah's eighth, twelfth, and eighteenth regnal years corresponded precisely to the years of Neo-Assyrian kings' deaths, so that with the end of each reign, Josiah became more daring in his reforms.

In 1973–74, two dissertations were published that challenged the consensus, John McKay's *Religion in Judah under the Assyrians*[85] and Morton [Mordechai]

---

[78] Assyriologists such as George Smith and Ernest Renan dissented early on from the consensus position. The latter saw the Assyrians as "almost indifferent in matters of religion" and as an empire that respected "religious liberty" (Renan, *History of the People Israel* [London: Chapman and Hall, 1891], 3:11, 148–153). For a summary and bibliography of the study of Assyrian imposition before and around the turn of the 20th century, see Morton [Mordechai] Cogan, *Imperialism and Religion: Assyria, Judah and Israel in the Eighth and Seventh Centuries B.C.E.* (SBLMS 19; Missoula, Mont.: Scholars Press, 1974); also Lowell K. Handy, "Josiah in a New Light: Assyriology Touches the Reforming King" in *Orientalism, Assyriology and the Bible* (ed. Steven W. Holloway; Hebrew Bible Monographs 10; Sheffield: Sheffield Phoenix, 2006), 415–35.
[79] Holloway, *Aššur is King!*, 42.
[80] Cited in Cogan, *Imperialism and Religion*, 3.
[81] Two notable scholars of the period who doubted this dominant view were Hugo Gressman and Yehezkel Kaufmann. Kaufmann saw "the influence of foreign paganism" but not imposition. Proceeding from a staunchly biblicist position, he believed that the worship of foreign gods was only very infrequent in the northern and southern kingdoms, and that such interludes were "solely ... products of royal initiative" (*The Religion of Israel, From Its Beginnings to the Babylonian Exile* [trans. M. Greenberg; Chicago: University of Chicago Press, 1960], 141, cf. 286–87.)
[82] Bright, *History of Israel*, 318.
[83] F. M. Cross and D. N. Freedman, "Josiah's Revolt Against Assyria," *JNES* 12 (1953): 56.
[84] Their chronology runs as follows: Aššurbanipal, 669–633; Aššur-etel-ilani, 633–629; Sin-šumu-lišir, 629; Sin-šar-iškun 629–612. It has not been generally adopted. Aššurbanipal, for example, is usually thought to have ruled until 627. Brinkman, in his chronology, would not even hazard a guess about the dates of two kings after Aššurbanipal (see A. Leo Oppenheim, *Ancient Mesopotamia Portrait of a Dead Civilization* [rev. ed. by Erica Reiner; Chicago: University of Chicago Press, 1977], 346).
[85] John W. McKay, *Religion in Judah Under the Assyrians, 732–609 BC* (SBT, 2nd series, 26; Naperville, Ill.: Alec R. Allenson, 1973).

Cogan's *Imperialism and Religion*. The two drew similar conclusions, but Cogan's contribution has generally been viewed as more significant owing to his superior command of the Assyriological data. He granted that Assyria certainly practiced hegemony through theology, including the well-known ancient practice of confiscating the statues of enemies' gods. However, it could also show mercy to the gods of conquered lands, returning them to their places. Foreign leaders might plead for the return of their gods, and this was sometimes granted, usually with the condition that markers of Assyrian overlordship were inscribed on them. In any case, the loss of divine images "does not seem to have proved fatal to the native cults."[86] Uruk, for example, simply fashioned a new statue after the first one was taken. Nor did Assyria seem to have objected to this. "The transfer of the divine images to Assyria was but the formal aspect of the submission and did not imply the abrogation of the native cults."[87]

The key to Cogan's argument is the distinction between provinces and vassal states. In his view, these two sorts of territories were subject to very different treatment. In the provinces that were formally incorporated into Assyria, "Ashur became the recognized head of a pantheon that now encompassed new foreign gods."[88] The provinces owed support specifically for the provisioning of the Aššur temple, although there was no direct abrogation of previous cults. Vassal states fared better still; they "bore no cultic obligations whatsoever."[89] He grants that *adê* (succession) treaties imposed duties on vassals both in the name of the king and in the name of "Aššur, your god," but the first-person sections spoken by the vassal did not name Aššur as god.[90] Heavy taxation ("the yoke of Aššur") was imposed on vassals as well, but not specifically for religious purposes.

On the basis of this groundwork, Cogan's reading of the Deuteronomistic History could be straightforward: features of Judahite religion condemned as heterodox by the Deuteronomistic Historian were in no case Assyrian impositions, contrary to what earlier scholars had argued. For example, Ahaz's altar in 2 Kings 16 was based on Syrian influence and was used for Yahwistic, not imperial, purposes. Astral cults (2 Kgs 17:16; 21:3–5; 23:4; etc.) may have had Assyrian origins, but were mediated to Judah through Aramean syncretism: "[N]ew forms dressed up old Canaanite ritual."[91] Thus Cogan argued that Assyria did not impose cultic practices, and that the practices undertaken by Ahaz and Manasseh

---

[86] Cogan, *Imperialism and Religion*, 33.
[87] Cogan, *Imperialism and Religion*, 34
[88] Cogan, *Imperialism and Religion*, 112.
[89] Cogan, *Imperialism and Religion*, 112.
[90] Cogan, *Imperialism and Religion*, 46.
[91] Cogan, *Imperialism and Religion*, 87. Similarly, Cogan says that the cult of Molech may have been mostly divinatory rather than sacrificial, and that it seems to have been "at best ... [a] vestigial human sacrifice amidst 8th century B.C.E. Assyro-Aramean cultural traditions" (ibid., 83).

and battled by Hezekiah and Josiah were not even necessarily Assyrian in provenance.

However cogent Cogan's argument is in general, certain details deserve skepticism. Whether or not Assyrian religion was directly imposed, might a client king not rankle under the religious claims of his conqueror? For example, is one to believe that simply because it was the imperial representative and not the native who identified Aššur as king of the conquered land, Aššur's rule was not viewed as an "imposition"?

Another major entry in the conversation came in 1982, when Hermann Spieckermann countered Cogan and McKay.[92] Spieckermann's survey of the Assyrian evidence found a loss of confidence in seventh-century Assyria that led to superstition and increased interest in oracles, liver omens, astral phenomena, etc. His corresponding treatment of the biblical data argued that these same practices had a significant and direct influence on Judah. For example, he says that biblical references to Baal, Asherah, and the Host of Heaven can be identified with Assyrian deities. Assyrian religion, he says, was not only adopted voluntarily but also imposed by the empire. Unlike Cogan, he does not think there is any clear distinction between provinces and vassals with respect to religious imposition.[93] He closes by arguing that Josiah's reform was inspired by a form of "intolerant Yahwism" that reacted violently against Assyrian hegemony.

John Bright, while aware of the research of Cogan and McKay, struck a very similar balance to Spieckermann in the third edition of his *History of Israel*:

Not the least serious of the consequences of Ahaz' policy lay in the realm of religion. Though we are not told that Assyrian kings compelled their vassals to worship Assyria's gods, it is understandable that many a vassal should have felt it politic to do so. This apparently explains the innovations (II Kings 16:10–18) that Ahaz introduced in the Temple of Jerusalem. We are told that he was obliged to appear before Tiglath-Pileser in the new provincial capital of Damascus to give allegiance to him and, so it seems, to pay homage to the Assyrian gods at a bronze altar that stood there. A copy of this altar was then made and erected in the Temple for the king's use, the bronze altar already there having been set aside. ... Although Ahaz' hands were tied, it is certain that such measures were widely regarded as both humiliating and an insult to the national God. Yahweh no longer has full disposal of his house![94]

---

[92] Hermann Spieckermann, *Juda unter Assur in der Sargonidenzeit* (FRLANT 129; Göttingen: Vandenhoeck & Ruprecht, 1982).

[93] Simo Parpola has recently asserted his support of the idea of Assyrian religious imposition as well: "Assyria's Expansion," 100–101 n. 4.

[94] Bright, *History of Israel*, 276–77; Similar is Postgate's observation: "Incorporation into Assyria meant participating in the cult of its god; it need not have meant abandoning the worship of the local deity, but it would have affected the significance of that cult as a political statement..." (J. N. Postgate, "The Land of Assur and the Yoke of Assur," *World Archaeology* 23 [1992]: 252). Of course, Judah was never incorporated as a province, but neither did it enjoy the relative independence of a client state in this period. Postgate, dealing with an earlier period, does not adequately differentiate among the levels of incorporation in this instance.

1.3 Mechanisms of Mesopotamian influence

More support for the idea of Assyrian encroachment into vassals' religion may be forthcoming, as excavators at Tayinat (in present-day Turkey near the Syrian border) claim to have discovered a Neo-Assyrian treaty tablet that was elevated on a pedestal in the holy of holies of the temple there.[95] This claim has not yet undergone peer review, but it would lend support the existing theory that such treaties were displayed prominently in vassal capitals such as Jerusalem.[96]

In the end, the most serious point of contention between Spieckermann and Cogan concerns the real roots of the cultic practices mentioned in the Deuteronomistic History: were they essentially Assyrian or essentially indigenous to the Levant? Cogan tried to sidestep this question in a 1992 review article by writing that "it was a new cultural and technological *koinē*, Assyro-Aramean in derivation, that ultimately dominated the entire region."[97]

The latest and most extensive survey of the data is by Steven W. Holloway, who enumerates Assyrian imperial practices regarding religion under four categories: the destruction of temples (attested five times),[98] the destruction of divine images (twice),[99] the deportation of divine images (fifty-five times),[100] and the establishment of the "symbol of Aššur" in foreign temples, palaces, or lands (sixteen times).[101]

Holloway concluded that Assyria's religious imperialism was not typically violent or iconoclastic. It could even function in constructive diplomacy by subsidizing religious projects in conquered lands (only in its provinces, however – primarily Babylonia and Ḥarrān). (A smaller act of endorsement may be reflected in 2 Kgs 17:24–28, if the account of the Assyrians' restoration of a Yahwistic priest to Samaria is accurate.) The extant records indicate that destruction of cults was uncommon and was reserved for prominent cults in neighboring provinces (Muṣaṣir, Susa, and Babylon) that might be seen to compete seriously with that of Aššur. Such acts of destruction reflected "the grim determination of the Assyrians to communicate to the world at large that these three kingdoms had been cultically and politically nullified."[102]

---

[95] *The Independent*, October 15, 2010 (accessed electronically: http://www.independent.co.uk/news/science/archaeology/news/2700yearold-royal-loyalty-oath-discovered-in-turkey-2107830.html)

[96] Karen Radner, "Assyriche *ṭuppi adê* als Vorbild für Deuteronomium 28,20–44?" in *Die deuteronomistischen Geschichtswerke: Redaktions- und religionsgeschichtliche Perspektiven zur "Deuteronomismus"-Diskussion in Tora und Vorderen Propheten.* (eds. Markus Witte, Konrad Schmid, Doris Prechel and Jan Christian Gertz. Berlin: De Gruyter, 2006), 351–78.

[97] M. Cogan, "Judah under Assyrian Hegemony: A Re-examination of *Imperialism and Religion*," *JBL* 112 (1993): 412.

[98] Holloway, *Aššur is King!*, 109–11.

[99] Holloway, *Aššur is King!*, 118. It is possible, of course, that other acts of impiety against foreign gods took place but were thought to be better omitted from the annals.

[100] Holloway, *Aššur is King!*, 123–44.

[101] Holloway, *Aššur is King!*, 151–59.

[102] Holloway, *Aššur is King!*, 117.

Holloway concurred with Cogan that the removal of divine images ("godnapping," in Alasdair Livingstone's felicitous phrase) was usually described by the Assyrians in terms of "divine abandonment," not the defeat or death of a god. That is, it was not that the foreign gods had been defeated, but that they had abandoned their peoples to Assyrian might because of various wrongdoings. Holloway further concluded that the Assyrians did not aggressively enforce the suspension of local cult activity even if they captured the god's image and destroyed the temple. Other gods were not inherently dangerous, in their view, as long as the defeated knew that Aššur ruled the heavens just as Assyria ruled the earth.

In Holloway's view, the "symbol of Aššur" was a forceful reminder of the imperial god and king, and for this it seems to have marked "the extreme limits of effective Assyrian political control ... another act in the inimitable Assyrian theater of cruelty."[103] The symbol seems to have been used primarily as a means of administering loyalty oaths to vassals, and Holloway suggests that the numerous references in eighth-century inscriptions to the weapon or symbol of Aššur are shorthand for such oaths.[104] However, he thinks that they were used for little else; that is, they were not set up in cultic sites to be worshiped by the inhabitants of a region.[105] In short, Assyrian letters and administrative texts suggest that "the day-to-day functioning of temples outside of the ancient cult cities of Mesopotamia [was] of little concern to the Great Kings and their magnates."[106]

In contrast to his ambitious survey of the data, Holloway's conclusions are relatively modest. He avers that "[n]either administrative texts nor royal correspondence nor royal prophecies suggest that a cult of Aššur was established on foreign soil."[107] He also agrees with Cogan that dues for the cult of Aššur were characteristic of provinces but not client states.[108] Apart from that point, however, he thinks Cogan goes too far in trying to establish "policies" on the empire's part:

The empire lasted too long, covered too much space, encroached on and absorbed too many cultures and was guided by too many idiosyncratic kings; the imperial archive is at once too fragmentary, cryptic and blatantly propagandistic; and the boundaries of histori-

---

[103] Holloway, *Aššur is King!*, 163.
[104] Holloway, *Aššur is King!*, 176.
[105] Holloway, *Aššur is King!*, 177, 199.
[106] Holloway, *Aššur is King!*, 164.
[107] Holloway, *Aššur is King!*, 200.
[108] Postgate concurs: "Correspondence from the royal archives reveals an obligation on provincial governors to supply sheep offerings to the Assur Temple (and a failure of some governors to meet those obligations on time).... This is not tribute from a client state, but offerings from one part of the land to its central shrine" ("Royal Ideology in Sumer and Akkad," in *Civilizations of the Ancient Near East* [ed. Jack M. Sasson; New York: Scribner, 1995], 1:409–10).

cal epistemology are too provincial to encourage sweeping generalities and the construction of a monolithic "policy" binding the entire Neo-Assyrian world.[109]

More specifically:

To attempt to canvass three hundred years of Neo-Assyrian religious imperialism outside of Mesopotamia based on [a few] disparate citations is simply hubris, and signals scholarly self-deception in progress.... [T]he theory that the Assyrians made a hard-and-fast distinction between the religio-political treatment of client state and province is untenable."[110]

Instead of being guided by fixed policies, Holloway perceives an Assyrian Empire that, like the Roman Empire, responded to problems in an *ad hoc* manner and "followed the dictates of situational military and political expediency."[111] Based on this conclusion, it would be a methodological error to use a study of Assyrian religious imperialism to interpret the history of the divided kingdom. This is a valid objection; the references to the western provinces are too few, and the practices were too variable to form a foundation any firmer than that of the biblical account.

A different way to approach the problem would be to treat it as a matter of cultural hegemony rather than strictly political imposition. Because of the complex nature of a "*koinē* culture," such as that which prevailed in Palestine at least from 750 BCE until the exile, it is not clear that the disagreement over imposition needs to be sketched as starkly as has sometimes been done. The distinction between vassal and province could become fuzzy in the case of religion, and the issue is further clouded by the imbalance of power between Assyria and its satellites. On the one hand, conquered client states might well have been angered by the Assyrians' cultural and religious claims. One might compare the feelings of Americans, if, for example, China conquered the United States and, while permitting the exercise of existing religions, installed Chinese flags in all churches, synagogues, and mosques.

On the other hand, in ancient times as well as modern, it is the nature of colonial hegemony that it functions not only by force but by prestige.[112] The

---

[109] Holloway, *Aššur is King!*, 97.

[110] Holloway, *Aššur is King!*, 193, 198. This argument is also supported by Postgate, who wrote, "The form Assyrian control took varied: it did not emerge in a vacuum, and in each case it depended not only on the character of the central Assyrian government itself, but also on the political and social order in the lands absorbed. Both inside and outside Assyria the current realities were also tempered, and policies affected, by perceptions of precedents" ("Land of Assur," 247).

[111] Holloway, *Aššur is King!*, 214. See also Parker, *Mechanics of Empire*, 252.

[112] So Ngugi wa Thiong'o: "The economic and political dependence of this African neo-colonial bourgeoisie is reflected in its culture of apemanship and parrotry enforced on a restive population through police boots, barbed wire, a gowned clergy and judiciary; their ideas are spread by a corpus of state intellectuals, the academic and journalistic laureates of the neo-colonial establishment" (*Decolonizing the Mind: The Politics of Language in African Literature* [London: J. Currey, 1986], 2).

vassal may admire and embrace foreign ways. J. N. Postgate notes that Assyrian cultural influence is "plainly visible" in the material culture even in client states where it was not imposed, and he perceives the process as "one of active emulation: we should not see the client rulers as cowering in their citadels waiting to be irradiated with Assyrian influence, but absorbing the scene in Nineveh, fingering the tapestries and envying the silverware."[113] Simo Parpola goes into somewhat more detail:

[E]lites were the primary target group on which the Assyrians focused their attention in their efforts to assimilate a country. Pro-Assyrian foreign elites were the best possible medium to advance Assyrian interests in a country waiting to be annexed or already annexed. For this reason, foreign ambassadors and visitors to the Assyrian capital were lavishly entertained and honored at the royal court, while exiled princes and aristocratic youths sojourning or held at the court received a thorough education in Assyrian literature, science, and ways of life in general. The overall goal was to integrate all foreign elites as much as possible within the imperial elite and then to work on the masses through these elites.[114]

In ancient Palestine, imitation of Assyrian models can be seen in numerous aspects of material culture, from art to architecture.[115] So, for example, despite Cogan's insistence that Ahaz's altar and other changes to the temple were not, properly speaking, Assyrian *impositions*, they were in some way a result of emulation of foreign practices that were under Assyrian influence.

In sum, then, one should not draw bright lines between imposition and independence, or between religious and "secular" issues. The best formulation of the matter may be that of R. H. Lowery:

In lopsided social-political relationships, the line between force and persuasion is very thin. In such cases, "imitation" is very difficult to distinguish from "imposition." ... [R]esistance to Assyrian rituals – even when joined with a broader rejection of all "foreign" gods – was not "purely religious." As is always the case with religious controversy, a whole range of social, economic and political factors came into play. Purging Assyrian rituals from the Judean cult, regardless of the larger scope of the reform, was also rejection of the political, economic and cultural hegemony of the empire.[116]

As Lowery noted, most scholars now seem to have adopted Cogan's non-imposition perspective. This is sometimes taken too far, so that the Assyrian rulers

---

[113] Postgate, "Land of Assur," 259–60. As an example Postgate cites the "sheik's hall" at Tell Halaf. Of course, the elite structures of Jerusalem have long since been destroyed, but the changes mentioned in 2 Kgs 16:17–18 suggest similar mechanisms of influence even in more distant Judah.

[114] Parpola, "Assyria's Expansion," 101–2.

[115] Stern, *Archaeology of the Land of the Bible*, 14–41; Stern notes "the influence of the new Assyrian style on local artisans, who began to imitate it from then on and through later periods" (19). See also Othmar Keel and Christoph Uehlinger, *Gods, Goddesses and Images of God in Ancient Israel* (trans. Thomas H. Trapp; Minneapolis: Fortress, 1998), 287–98.

[116] R. H. Lowery, *The Reforming Kings: Cults and Society in First Temple Judah* (JSOTSup 120; Sheffield: JSOT Press, 1991), 140.

begin to look like Cyrus on a good day. Dalley, for example, intoned that "[r]eligious tolerance is a particular hallmark of Assyrian control."[117]

I believe it would be closer to the truth to say that the hallmark of Assyrian control was the concern for political control and stability – by any means necessary – in order to enrich the homeland.[118] Assyria had little room for ideals like "tolerance." It was a military state, playing Sparta to Babylon's more cultured Athens. It was in the political realm, not the religious, that Assyria most insisted on fidelity. Thus, by no means did Assyrians commonly practice iconoclasm of foreign gods or the like. However, they certainly recognized the potential of religion to undermine imperial ideology, and so they used theology ruthlessly to ensure their control.[119] This can be perceived both in the rhetoric of the *rab šāqeh* at the wall of Jerusalem in 701 (which Peter Machinist has convincingly argued is a relatively accurate reflection of Assyrian imperial rhetoric;[120] see § 5.2.1.4 below), and also in native Akkadian documents. In Jerusalem, the Assyrians encountered a theology that resisted their claims.

It hardly needs to be pointed out that Mesopotamian influence on elite Judeans would only have intensified during the Neo-Babylonian period. Although assessments vary regarding the nature and conditions of the Babylonian exile, there can be no doubt that it had a vast cultural impact on Judeans and on their Scriptures. It is difficult, furthermore, to distinguish between Assyrian and Babylonian influence, except in cases where one power or the other is named, or where a text can be dated with confidence. To mention only two examples, it has recently been argued that the story of the Tower of Babel (Genesis 11) actually accords better with Assyrian imperial propaganda of "one speech,"[121] and the taunt against the "king of Babylon" in Isaiah 14 is often taken to refer to the Assyrian king Sargon II (see § 5.2.1.1).[122] Because, however, the argument being

---

[117] Dalley, "Recent Evidence," 397. Similarly, Postgate says, "The Assyrian administration would have had nothing to do with the internal affairs of the client state" ("Land of Assur," 255) and then in the next breath speaks of the tribute tax and the stationing of Assyrian troops in strategically important cities and towns. These practices certainly would have been perceived as interference in "internal affairs" by the states in question.

[118] Grayson, "Assyrian Rule of Conquered Territory," 962: "[D]efense and greed were the primary motives for conquest." Suffice it to say that the Assyrians were not playing defense in Palestine.

[119] Grayson, "Assyrian Rule of Conquered Territory," 961; A. Leo Oppenheim, "Neo-Assyrian and Neo-Babylonian Empires," in *The Symbolic Instrument in Early Times* (ed. Harold D. Lasswell et al.; Propaganda and Communication in World History 1; Honolulu: University of Hawaii Press, 1979), esp. 133–34.

[120] Peter Machinist, "Assyria and Its Image in First Isaiah," *JAOS* 103 (1983): 719–37.

[121] Christoph Uehlinger, *Weltreich und "Eine Rede": Eine Neue Deutung der Sogenannten Turmbauerzählung (Gen 11, 1–9)* (OBO 101; Freiburg, Schweiz: Universitätsverlag, 1990). The older assumption of Babylonian influence is exemplified by, e.g., Nahum Sarna, *Understanding Genesis* (Heritage of Biblical Israel 1; New York: Jewish Theological Seminary, 1966), esp. 75–77.

[122] H. L. Ginsberg states: "In view of Sargon's notorious Babylonism, whose manifestations included a three years' residence in Babylon and the stressing of both his Babylonian titles and of

made in the chapters to come is related to the historical condition of subjugation by an imperial power, rather than to specific historical events, such distinctions are not of the first importance.

1.4 Death in Mesopotamia

Despite the importance of Mesopotamian ideas and practices regarding death and afterlife, there has been no recent synthetic survey in English, apart from encyclopedia entries.[123]

As the Neo-Assyrians were building the largest empire yet known to humankind, their literature suggests a simultaneous growth in their cultural production concerning the underworld. It is true that formal cults of the dead go back to very ancient times in Mesopotamia – at least the third millennium BCE,[124] but Thorkild Jacobsen observed that in first-millennium Mesopotamia, "[t]he ubiquity of the powers of sudden death led understandably to an increased interest in what these powers and their domain, the netherworld, were like; stories and descriptions of them became popular."[125] There was a flourishing of baroque portraits of the underworld and of protective spells against demons and the dead.[126] The

---

his benefactions to the inhabitants and temples of the southern metropolises in an account intended for foreigners (the Cyprus Stela), it would not be remarkable if Isaiah regarded Babylon (a city whose name was presumably far more familiar to him ... than Calah ... let alone Dur-Sharrukin, of which he probably never heard), as the center of the Assyrian empire" ("Reflexes of Sargon in Isaiah After 715 BCE," *JAOS* 88 [1968]: 49).

[123] One such monograph has recently appeared in French: Véronique van der Stede, *Mourir au pays de deux fleuves: L'au delà Mésopotamien d'après les sources Sumériennes et Akkadiennes* (Lettres Orientales 12; Leuven: Peeters, 2007).

[124] Andrew C. Cohen, *Death Rituals, Ideology, and the Development of Early Mesopotamian Kingship: Toward a New Understanding of Iraq's Royal Cementery of Ur* (Studies in Ancient Magic and Divination 7; Leiden: Brill, 2005); Akio Tsukimoto, *Untersuchungen zur Totenpflege (kispum) im alten Mesopotamien* (AOAT 216; Neukirchen-Vluyn: Neukirchener Verlag, 1985).

[125] Thorkild Jacobsen, *The Treasures of Darkness: A History of Mesopotamian Religion* (New Haven: Yale University Press, 1976), 228. For the magical texts pertaining to ghosts, Jo Ann Scurlock, "Magical Means of Dealing with Ghosts in Ancient Mesopotamia" (Ph.D. diss., University of Chicago, 1988), 5. For the most famous Neo-Assyrian description of the underworld, see Alasdair Livingstone, "The Underworld Vision of an Assyrian Prince" in *Court Poetry and Literary Miscellanea* (ed. Alasdair Livingstone; SAA 3; Helsinki: Helsinki University Press, 1989), 68–76. Jacobsen's claim that the Assyrian world, "barely livable before, had now collapsed and become rank jungle" – thanks to civil wars, foreign wars, challenges from the Arameans, floods, famines, etc. – rings somewhat hollow in a description of a period in which Assyria achieved its greatest empire, along with some of the most impressive artistic accomplishments of the ancient world. For a balanced critique of Jacobsen's descriptions of the Neo-Assyrians, see Frahm, "Images of Assyria," 87. Nevertheless, Jacobsen's specific observation about the netherworld is borne out by the present research.

[126] Scurlock, "Magical Means," *passim*.

Neo-Assyrian kings were even more reliant on divination and their guild of magical scholars than earlier Mesopotamian monarchs.[127] Offerings were made regularly to propitiate the dead in a cult of royal ancestors that was even more elaborate than those of earlier periods.[128]

In summarizing key aspects of the Assyrians' views of the underworld in the first half of the first millennium BCE, one should bear in mind A. Leo Oppenheim's caveat that the Mesopotamian evidence, despite its profusion, "usually covers only a restricted area and period, permitting but an occasional insight" into its relationship to "the over-all picture."[129] To some degree, the same could be said about the Mesopotamians' views of death. Our focus here is on the Neo-Assyrian period, a relatively well-attested time frame, but certain aspects of our picture are inevitably filled in by reference to the broader corpus of data. One should also bear in mind Jean Bottéro's comment that the Mesopotamian underworld, for all its organization and vigor, is also characterized also by the "incoherent and irrational" points that are typical of mythological systems.[130] Ancient Near Eastern religions had no "systematic theologies."

1.4.1 Burial and mourning in Mesopotamia

A Mesopotamian who died of natural causes would have been attended by his family and perhaps placed on a funerary bed apart from his own.[131] It is believed that a chair was placed to the left of the bed – this was a "soul chair" or "ghost throne" on which the spirit of the deceased could repose after it left the body and could receive funerary offerings.[132] These same chairs could be used in later rituals to summon the dead.[133]

---

[127] Simo Parpola, "Introduction," in *Letters from Assyrian and Babylonian Scholars* (SAA10; Helsinki: Helsinki University Press, 1993), xxvii.
[128] Miranda Bayliss, "The Cult of Dead Kin in Assyria and Babylonia," *Iraq* 35 (1973): 125; Tsukimoto, *Untersuchungen zur Totenpflege*, 107–15.
[129] Oppenheim, *Ancient Mesopotamia*, 334. cf. Jerold S. Cooper, "The Fate of Mankind: Death and Afterlife in Ancient Mesopotamia," in *Death and Afterlife: Perspectives of World Religions* (Contributions to the Study of Religion 33; Westport, Conn.: Greenwood, 1992), 19–33, here 20.
[130] Jean Bottéro, "Les morts et l'au-delà deans les rituels en accadien contre l'action des 'revenants,'" *ZA* 73 (1983): 153–203, here 203
[131] On burial practices, see Karen Rhea Nemet-Najat, *Daily Life in Ancient Mesopotamia* (Peabody, Mass.: Hendrickson, 2002), 142–43; also Jo Ann Scurlock, "Death and the Afterlife in Ancient Mesopotamian Thought," in *Civilizations of the Ancient Near East* (ed. Jack M. Sasson; New York: Scribner, 1995), 3:1886–87.
[132] See Jo Ann Scurlock, "Soul Emplacements in Ancient Mesopotamian Funerary Rituals," in *Magic and Divination in the Ancient World* (ed. Leda Ciraolo and Jonathan Seidel; Ancient Magic and Divination 2; Leiden: Brill, 2002), 1–6.
[133] Pirjo Lapinkivi, *The Neo-Assyrian Myth of Ištar's Descent and Resurrection* (SAACT 6; Helsinki: Neo-Assyrian Text Corpus Project, 2010), 87.

Upon a person's death, the mouth of the corpse was tied shut and the body washed. As in Egypt, the dead soul would have been supplied with various goods to ease its journey to the world of the dead. Mesopotamian rulers in the third millennium BCE were sometimes buried with sacrificed human servants,[134] but this practice finds no echoes in the first millennium. About 85 percent of existing graves from the period have provisions, most commonly food offerings. In some cases the food seems to have been burned. Indeed, there is evidence of burning atop graves, "sometimes in the form of a hearth which seemed to have been used on more than one occasion."[135]

Individual burial was the norm. The Mesopotamian dead were buried in various types of graves, and the diversity is particularly pronounced in the period being studied here.[136] Common people were likely to be buried directly in the earth in a communal graveyard, at best wrapped in a reed mat.[137] Slightly more elaborate were burials in clay pots, bowls and tubs, although the social differentiation of these types is not clear.[138] Royalty and individuals of high status could be buried in stone sarcophagi, sometimes of massive scale, and were usually interred in vaulted chambers beneath the house or palace. In general, elaborate burials seem to have increased in Assyria in the first millennium, although this may be attributable partly to accidents of preservation.[139]

Burial beneath the house was the norm for kings; this was already the case in the Ur III period.[140] Six vaulted tomb chambers were excavated underneath the Old Palace at Aššur, and these contained sarcophagi from three Assyrian rulers: Aššur-bel-kala, Aššurnasirpal II, and Šamši-Adad V.[141] There is another tomb at

---

[134] P. R. S. Moorey, *Ur 'of the Chaldees': A Revised and Updated Edition of Sir Leonard Woolley's Excavations at Ur* (Ithaca, N.Y.: Cornell University Press, 1982), 72–76; Samuel N. Kramer, "The Death of Ur-Nammu and His Descent to the Netherworld," *JCS* 21 (1969): 104–25, here 119.

[135] Heather Baker, "Neo-Babylonian Burials Revisited," in *The Archaeology of Death in the Ancient Near East* (ed. Stuart Campbell and Anthony Green; Oxbow Monograph 51; Oxford: Oxbow Books, 1995), 219.

[136] Baker, "Neo-Babylonian Burials Revisited," 220.

[137] Postgate notes that a limited number of intramural burials were found at Nippur in the early second millennium. Although he grants that it is possible these are so located in order to facilitate a mortuary cult, he thought it more likely that they may simply have been the work of "urban families without land of their own." See J. N. Postgate, "Archaeology and the Texts – Bridging the Gap," *ZA* 80 (1990): 228–40, esp. 230–34.

[138] Baker, "Neo-Babylonian Burials Revisited," 220; see also W. Orthmann, "Grab," *RlA*, 581–605.

[139] Arndt Haller, *Die Gräber und Grüfte von Assur* (WVDOG 65; Berlin: Gebr. Mann, 1954); see also Maurice Lambert's review of Haller, *RA* 50 (1956): 153–58.

[140] P. R. S. Moorey, "Where Did They Bury the Kings of the Third Dynasty of Ur?" *Iraq* 46 (1984): 1–18. There is also second-millennium evidence for the practice; see Nadav Na'aman, "Death Formulae and the Burial Place of the Kings of the House of David," *Biblica* 85 (2004): 249.

[141] Na'aman, "Death Formulae," 248.

Nimrud that is likely to be royal,[142] and four tombs of royal women were discovered in Kalḫu.[143] Contemporaneous inscriptions attest that Sennacherib was also buried at Aššur, and that Aššurbanipal built himself a mausoleum (*bīt kimaḫḫi*) there as well.[144] It was was viewed as a curse that Sargon II "was not b[uried] in his house" because he was killed while on a military campaign.[145]

It was long assumed that burial near the living was important for the care of the dead, or in case one needed to summon them for various sorts of help, and this was likely the preference.[146] However, a new study by Brian Brown argues that in fact a king might rule from one city while the cult of dead ancestors was maintained in another;[147] this is only logical since the Assyrian capital city was moved with some frequency. Brown makes a cogent case that when Aššurnasirpal II moved the capital from Aššur to Nimrud in the early ninth century, he constructed a wing of the new palace for the maintenance of a royal mortuary cult, complete with pipes for libation offerings to the dead (see below).[148] The king simultaneously adopted the idea of memorial orthostats (stelae) from Syria (§ 3.2), so that he could perform the *kispu* for his ancestors at a distance from their tombs. Presumably he continued to make provisions for the ancestors buried in Aššur as well, so that a version of the *kispu* would have been carried out there as well. Brown perceives that Aššurnasirpal would have been "at pains to stress continuity with the past."[149] Seth Richardson has argued that Aššurnasirpal built a large-scale "garden of ancestors" at the new capital for the royal mortuary cult (see further at § 4.4.1.1).[150]

---

[142] John McGinnis, "A Neo-Assyrian Text Describing a Royal Funeral," *SAAB* 1 (1987): 8. See also Walter Andrae, *Das Wiedererstandene Assur* (Sendschrift der Deutschen Orient-Gesellschaft; Leipzig: Hinrichs, 1938), 136–40. Three tombs at Assur have been identified, those of Aššur-bêl-kala (1074–1057), Aššurnasirpal II (883–859) and Šamši-Adad (823–811). A tomb inscription of Aššurbanipal (704–681) also survives from Aššur (see below), although the tomb itself was destroyed. Aššurbanipal ruled in Nineveh but apparently had his body returned to Aššur for burial. See Jean Bottéro, "Les inscriptions funéraires cuneiforms," in *La mort, les morts dans les sociétés anciennes* (ed. G. Gnoli and J. P. Vernant; Cambridge: Cambridge University Press, 1982), 382.

[143] Muayad S. B. Damerji, "Gräber Assyrischer Königinnen aus Nimrud," *Jahrbuch des Römisch-Germanischen Zentralmuseums* 45 (1998): 19–84.

[144] Na'aman, "Death Formulae," 248.

[145] Hayim Tadmor, Benno Landsberger, and Simo Parpola, "The Sin of Sargon and Sennacherib's Last Will," *SAAB* 3 (1989): 10–11, ll. 19–20.

[146] In the Neo-Assyrian period, "bei der 'Totenpflege' damals das Vorhandensein des wirklichen Grabes oder der Leiche wichtig und notwendig war" (Tsukimoto, *Untersuchungen zur Totenpflege*, 115).

[147] Brian Brown, "Kingship and Ancestral Cult in the Northwest Palace at Nimrud," *JANER* 10 (2010): 1–53. Brown shows that Tsukimoto's textual case for necessity of the corpse's proximity is based on spotty data.

[148] Brown, "Kingship and Ancestral Cult," 16.

[149] Brown, "Kingship and Ancestral Cult," 35.

[150] Seth Richardson, "An Assyrian Garden of Ancestors: Room I, Northwest Palace, Kalḫu," *SAAB* 13 (1999–2001): 145–216.

The integrity of the corpse was very important in royal burials, at least by the Neo-Assyrian period; the bodies of dead kings were not to be disturbed. A form of preservation of the body may have been practiced in Assyria as well; in one Neo-Assyrian funerary text for an unnamed king, the son who oversaw the burial says he laid his father to rest "in kingly oil" – a surprising detail that may be confirmed by classical historians such as Ctesias and Herodotus, who recorded similar customs for the Babylonians.[151]

Neo-Assyrian texts describing royal burials are few,[152] but a picture can still be supplied. Although all of the Mesopotamian royal tombs were plundered prior to their discovery, it appears from textual witnesses that Assyrian kings' grave goods could be almost as extensive as those of their Egyptian counterparts and may have included weapons, toiletry, jewelry,[153] sandals, and even (in the case of kings) full-size chariots to carry them to their destination. One Neo-Assyrian funerary text for an unnamed king lists numerous types of garments and animals (ten horses, thirty oxen and three hundred sheep).[154] It is not clear whether these were meant to be supplies for the afterlife, offerings for the underworld gods, or both, but animal skeletons have been found in other Mesopotamian tombs. The same text mentions silver sandals, which have been found in an Old Babylonian grave and may have been intended for the dead king to wear on his journey to the underworld. Nabonidus's inscriptions describe the burial of his mother in a "splendid colored and bejeweled robe."[155]

The mirror image of the concern for correct burial is found in the repeated Neo-Assyrian accounts of "anti-burial." Sargonid kings frequently claimed in their inscriptions to have violated the tombs of enemy dynasties, disinterring cadavers and strewing the bones of the royal ancestors, most notoriously Aššurbanipal's exposure of the dead Elamite kings:

The burial places of their early (and) later kings, who had not feared Aššur/Ištar, my lords, (and) who had made my royal predecessors tremble, I devastated, I destroyed (and) let them see the sun; their bones I removed to Assyria. I laid restlessness on their spirits. Food-offerings (to the dead) and water-libations I denied them.[156]

Aššurbanipal also remembered the unfaithfulness of a governor of Nippur for eleven years; by the time he was able to return and subdue the city, the governor

---

[151] See text and discussion in McGinnis, "Neo-Assyrian Text Describing a Royal Funeral," esp. 8–9.
[152] Oppenheim, *Ancient Mesopotamia*, 234; Piotr Michalowski, "The Death of Šulgi," *Orientalia* 46 (1977): 220; Moorey, "Where Did They Bury the Kings of the Third Dynasty of Ur?", 14.
[153] See Andrae, *Das Wiedererstandene Assur*, Tafel 11.
[154] McGinnis, "Neo-Assyrian Text Describing a Royal Funeral," 9–10.
[155] C. J. Gadd, "The Harran Inscriptions of Nabonidus," *Anatolian Studies* 8 (1958), 53; see discussion in D. J. Wiseman, *Nebuchadrezzar and Babylon* (Schweich Lectures 1983; Oxford: Oxford University Press, 1985), 114.
[156] *Annals*, col. 6, lines 70–76. See Maximilian Streck, *Assurbanipal und die letzten Assyrischen Könige bis zum Untergange Ninivehs* (1916; repr., Leipzig: Zentralantiquariat, 1975), 54–57.

had died, but Aššurbanipal forced his sons to take his bones and grind them up in one of the gates of Nineveh.[157] Seth Richardson recounts an even more graphic episode in which Aššurbanipal violated the corpse of a Babylonian ruler:

The corpse of Nabû-bēl-šumāti was originally packed in salt for transport to Nineveh. ... In forcing the brother of Nabû-bēl-šumāti to wear the dead king's head around his neck for display, he said of that corpse: "I made him more dead than he was before."[158]

The Babylonians' concern about such abuses was evident when Marduk-apla-iddina II, having been defeated by Sennacherib, unearthed the bones of his own ancestors and brought them with him as he fled.[159] Their status was akin to that of national gods, and the living and dead royalty were, at least by the late eighth century, seen as interdependent.

Despite the Assyrians' general concern for preservation of the body, there is some indication that cremation was an option when for whatever reason burial in the homeland was not possible. For example, at a newly unearthed Neo-Assyrian governor's palace in Ziyaret Tepe (in present-day Turkey), at least five cremation pits have been uncovered, in which burned human bones were accompanied by elite grave goods.[160] Since a contemporaneous text reports that Sargon II "was not buried according to the law," Hayim Tadmor has suggested that he too may have been cremated at the site of the foreign battle where he died.[161] Just how exceptional cremation was remains to be determined.[162]

---

[157] A. C. Piepkorn, *Historical Prism Inscriptions of Ashurbanipal*, vol. 1 (Assyriological Studies 5; Chicago: University of Chicago Press, 1933). See discussion in S. W. Cole, *Nippur in Late Assyrian Times (c. 755–612 BC)* (SAAS 4; Helsinki: Neo-Assyrian Text Corpus Project, 1996), 54, 77–78.

[158] Richardson, "Death and Dismemberment in Mesopotamia," 198. For the texts, see Riekele Borger *Beiträge zum Inschriftenwerk Aššurbanipals: Die Prismenklassen A, B, C = K, D, E, F, G, H, J und T sowie andere Inschriften* (Wiesbaden: Harrassowitz, 1996), 59–60 (Prism A VII 39–50).

[159] Elena Cassin, "Le Mort: Valeur et représentation en Mésopotamie Ancienne," in *La Mort, les morts dans les sociétés anciennes* (ed. G. Gnoli and J. P. Vernant; Cambridge/New York: Cambridge University Press, 1982), 355–72.

[160] This find apparently still awaits peer review and scholarly publication. Last accessed on Oct. 22, 2010: http://www.sciencedaily.com/releases/2008/10/081021094216.htm.

[161] His full comment is that Sargon was not buried according to the law "either because it fell into the hands of the enemy or because it was lost on the battlefield; alternatively it may have been cremated in the absence of the means of embalmment" (Tadmor et al., "The Sin of Sargon," 3–51).

[162] It is not clear how relevant is the exchange between Bilgamesh and Enkidu in the Sumerian composition "Bilgamesh and the Underworld," in which Bilgamesh asks about one burned to death, and Enkidu replies, "I did not see him... His ghost is not there; his smoke went up to the heavens." Alster has taken this to reflect a belief that burning brought about "a total annihilation of the body and soul" ("The Paradigmatic Character of Mesopotamian Heroes,"

In addition to the rites surrounding burial, ancient Mesopotamian custom called for up to seven days of mourning for the deceased.[163] Professional mourners (*kalû*) were employed,[164] as elsewhere, and family and friends were also expected to make known their laments – a responsibility significant enough that mourning was sometimes stipulated as a legal responsibility of adopted children. Many Mesopotamian literary laments for the dead were quite beautiful and poetic in character; notable among these is Gilgamesh's lament for Enkidu in *The Epic of Gilgamesh*.[165] The length and extent of mourning appear to have corresponded to the importance of the person, so that the entire country was expected to lament for kings and queens. Nabonidus's mother's death was said to have been "attended by the people of Babylon as well as by representatives from the entire empire from the border of Egypt to the Persian Gulf including kings, princes and governors."[166] This same text records the common practice of shaving the head, gashing the body, and (possibly – the text is broken) tearing the clothes as expressions of grief. After seven days and nights of mourning all the guests feasted before returning home.

The prospect of mourning seems to have been meant to comfort a person about the prospect of death. In *Gilgamesh*, when Shamash hears the protestations of Enkidu, who is under the threat of death, the god replies,

> ...Gilgamesh, the friend who is like a brother to you
> will lay you to rest on a great bed...
> Princes of the earth will kiss your feet.
> He will make the people of Uruk weep for you, mourn for you,
> will fill the proud people with woe,
> and he himself will neglect his appearance after you(r death).
> Clothed only in a lionskin, he will roam the open country.[167]

RA 68 [1974]: 59–60), but A. R. George points out that the unhappy souls of the burned (*etem qalî*) are elsewhere referred to as haunting the living. For text and discussion, see George, *The Babylonian Gilgamesh Epic: Introduction, Critical Edition, and Cuneiform Texts* (2 vols.; Oxford: Oxford University Press, 2003), 14, 776.

[163] See, for example, Gilgamesh X,iii in which Gilgamesh says that he wept over Enkidu "for six days and seven nights ... until a worm fell out his nose."

[164] Gonzalo Rubio, "Inanna and Dumuzi: A Sumerian Love Story," *JAOS* 121 (2001): 268–74; F. N. al-Rawi, "Two Old Akkadian Letters Concerning the Offices of *kala'um* and *nârum*," ZA 82 (1992): 180–85.

[165] Gilgamesh 8:2–91; George, *The Babylonian Gilgamesh Epic*, 651–57. One might mention also the "Assyrian Elegy" for a deceased wife, which reads, in Erica Reiner's elegant translation: "Why are you adrift, like a boat, in the midst of the river, your thwarts in pieces, your mooring rope cut?" (*Your Thwarts in Pieces, Your Mooring Rope Cut: Poetry from Babylonia and Assyria* [Ann Arbor: University of Michigan Press, 1985], 86–87).

[166] Wiseman, *Nebuchadrezzar and Babylon*, 114; for the text, see Gadd, "Harran Inscriptions of Nabonidus," 53.

[167] Gilgamesh, VII,iii. Cf. Stephanie Dalley, *Myths from Mesopotamia: Creation, the Flood, Gilgamesh, and Others* (Oxford: Oxford University Press, 1989), 87–8.

By contrast, a lack of mourning was seen as a curse for the deceased; the speaker of the Babylonian poem *Ludlul bēl nēmeqi*, approaching his death, has a chilling vision of what is to come:

My grave was open, my funerary goods ready,
Before I had died, lamentation for me was done.[168]

This accords with a general view that true death came only in being forgotten.[169] While Neo-Assyrian tombs were modest in comparison with their Egyptian counterparts, the scores of memorial stelae for kings and nobles unearthed between the city walls of Aššur attest to the intensity of this concern.[170]

Care of the dead continued after the burial and mourning. The Mesopotamians seem to have been the primary practitioners of the *kispu* rite, a form of libation and sacrifice for (or cultic feeding of) the dead. Texts from a range of times and places throughout Mesopotamian history attest to food and drink being set aside for this purpose, and it is attested architecturally and textually in clay libation pipes known as *arūtu*.[171]

The *kispu* was performed by an heir for the deceased paterfamilias, both when the spirit first entered the underworld and perhaps later at regular intervals. As reflected in the story "Gilgamesh, Enkidu and the Netherworld" (see discussion below), mortuary care was the single greatest factor in one's happiness in the afterlife. (There are a few references in texts scattered across disparate periods and regions that have been taken to reflect a "postmortem judgment of the dead" in Mesopotamian religious thought, but these have not added up to a convincing synthesis.[172]) The *kispu* could also be used in various rituals intended to dispel evil or appease harmful spirits, or to conjure a spirit for help.[173] Such help might include divinatory requests for information (i.e., necromancy; see below).

In one typical *kispu* text, the offerer invokes the "ghosts of my family ... my father, my grandfather, my mother, my grandmother, my brother, my sister, my family, kith and kin, as many as are asleep in the netherworld."[174] He asks them: "Hand over to Namtar, messenger of the netherworld, the evils present in my

---

[168] *Ludlul bēl nēmeqi* II.114–15. (Cf. Lambert, *Babylonian Wisdom Literature*, 46.)
[169] Jean Bottéro, *Religion in Ancient Mesopotamia* (Chicago: University of Chicago Press, 2001), 110.
[170] Walter Andrae, *Stelenreihen in Aššur* (Leipzig: German Orient Society, 1913). On the relative modesty of Neo-Assyrian royal tombs, see Michael Roaf, "Palaces and Temples in Ancient Mesopotamia," in *Civilizations of the Ancient Near East* (ed. Jack M. Sasson; New York: Scribner, 1995), 1:436.
[171] *CAD* A II:324. See Brown, "Kingship and Ancestral Cult," 16.
[172] Van der Stede, *Mourir au Pays de Deux Fleuves*, 92–108.
[173] Tsukimoto, *Untersuchungen zur Totenpflege*, 125–83.
[174] Benjamin R. Foster, *Before the Muses: An Anthology of Akkadian Literature*, 3rd ed. (Baltimore, MD: CDL Press, 2005), 658. Transliteration: Erich Ebeling, *Tod und Leben nach den Vorstellungen der Babylonier* (Berlin, Leipzig: Walter de Gruyter & Co., 1931), I:131–32.

body, flesh and sinews," so that he can lock them up securely. A final type of *kispu* was performed for the Annunaku, the gods of the underworld.[175]

One of the best-attested uses of the *kispu* is among royal families, in which cases it affirmed the continuity and authority of the royal family and could even be used by a usurper to assert his legitimacy.[176] Among the most famous *kispu* texts is the "Genealogy of the Hammurapi Dynasty," which seems to have been composed for Ammiṣaduqa of Babylon (r. 1646–1626 BCE), the great-grandson of Hammurapi. The text begins with a lengthy list invoking the names of Mesopotamian rulers; the list stretches back into the mists of history to the point that the earliest names are of dubious historicity.[177] The tablet closes by seeking to include any of the dead who might have been forgotten in a cultic feast, including:

... the dynasty not recorded on this tablet, and the soldier(s) who fell while on perilous campaigns for their lord, princes, princesses, all "persons" from East to West who have neither *pāqidu* nor *sāḫiru*, come ye, eat this, drink this, (and) bless Ammiṣaduqa the son of Ammiditana, the king of Babylon.[178]

J. J. Finkelstein, who published the text, called it "the invocation to an actual memorial service to the dead, the central action of which was the offering to the *eṭemmû* – the ghosts or spirits of the dead – of the *kispu*."[179] The inclusion of so many of the dead probably reflects the concern to avoid the wrath of the uncared-for dead. Mesopotamian kings, who by later periods were not generally thought to be divine during their lives, do seem to have been divinized in the afterlife (see discussion of the dead in § 1.4.2.).

The implementation of the *kispu* was not consistent throughout Mesopotamian history, but it is attested from the Old Babylonian through the Late Babylonian periods.[180] For example, in the Old Babylonian period it was performed monthly, at Mari twice monthly, while in the Middle Babylonian period there is no discernible schedule and it was performed *daily* at one point. In the Neo-Assyrian period, Aššurbanipal claimed in an inscription that he had reinstated the *kispu*; but this was a common sort of boast among kings – reinstituting traditions, whether or not they had ever been discontinued.[181] Akio Tsukimoto, whose

---

[175] Tsukimoto, *Untersuchungen zur Totenpflege*, 184–200.
[176] E.g., Nabonidus; *ANET*, 561. See discussion in Greenfield, "Un rite religieux araméen et ses parallèles," *RB* 80 (1973): 49.
[177] A comparable list of "ancestors" is found in other Akkadian documents from other dynasties, suggesting that it was essentially propagandistic; see J. J. Finkelstein, "The Genealogy of the Hammurapi Dynasty," *Journal of Cuneiform Studies* 20 (1966): 97–103, 116–17.
[178] Finkelstein, "Genealogy of the Hammurapi Dynasty," 97. In this context, the *pāqidu* is the caretaker for the dead; *sāḫiru* is less clear but appears to refer to an analogous or complementary role in the cult of the dead; see Finkelstein's discussion on p. 115.
[179] Finkelstein, "Genealogy of the Hammurapi Dynasty," 115.
[180] In addition to Tsukimoto, see Bayliss, "Cult of Dead Kin in Assyria," 115–25.

monograph stands as the authoritative statement on the topic, perceived that "Assurbanipal für die Verstorbenen die zum assyr. Königshof gehört hatten, Ehrfurcht bzw. Respektgefühl hatte."[182] In the Neo-Assyrian period, the king also brought *kispu* offerings on some feast days – as if to allow the dead to participate in the festivities.[183]

Tsukimoto concluded that the *kispu* generally emphasized social aspects of death. The term *pāqidu*, "caretaker," referred both to an adult who cared for a child, and a child who cared for the cult of dead parents. The postmortem duty of the *kispu* was deemed important enough that wills from Nuzi seek to assure that someone, even if it is not a biological heir, will attend to the care of the author's ghost.[184] Whether or not the living were thought to commune with the dead, the *kispu* strengthened bonds among living family, who might also share in the meal offered to the dead.[185] Depending on where it was performed, it could indicate either the care or the veneration of the dead, or both. And insofar as it was used both to care for the beloved departed and to protect oneself from their wrath, it evoked both the honor and the fear of the dead.

1.4.2 The Mesopotamian dead

Mesopotamian anthropology identified various parts of a person after death, each of which had different role and status. On a naturalistic level, these included the corpse (*pagru*) and the breath of life (*napištu*). This array extended mythologically to include the *eṭemmu* and the *zaqīqu* as parts of the soul. Only the dead had an *eṭemmu* (usually translated "ghost"), and it was "closely associated with the a person's physical remains."[186] The *eṭemmu* could be propitiated for help and could offer prophetic knowledge.[187] This may be why Assyrian tombs were placed

---

[181] This skepticism is grounded in the fact that there are records of provisioning the *kispum* during the reign of Esarhaddon, Aššurbanipal's father (Tsukimoto, *Untersuchungen zur Totenpflege*, 111).

[182] Tsukimoto, *Untersuchungen zur Totenpflege*, 112.

[183] Tsukimoto, *Untersuchungen zur Totenpflege*, 223–27.

[184] H. Rouillard and J. Tropper, "*Trpym*, rituels de guérison et culte de ancêtres d'après 1 Samuel XIX 11–17 et les textes parallèles d'Assur et de Nuzi," *VT* 37 (1987): 353–54; O. Loretz, "Die Teraphim als 'Ahnen-Götter-Figur(in)en' im Lichte der Texte aus Nuzi, Emar, und Ugarit: Anmerkungen zu *ilānū/ilh, ilhm/ʾihym* und DINGIR.ERÍN.MES/*ins ilm*," *UF* 24 (1992): 152–67.

[185] Karel van der Toorn, *Family Religion in Babylonia, Syria and Israel: Continuity and Change in the Forms of Religious Life* (Leiden: Brill, 1996), 48–52; Brown, "Kingship and Ancestral Cult," 16.

[186] Scurlock, "Death and the Afterlife," 1892; also Jean Bottéro, "La création de l'homme et sa nature dans le poeme d'Atrahasis," in *Societies and Languages of the Ancient Near East: Studies in Honour of I. M. Diakonoff* (Warminster: Aris & Phillips, 1982), 24–32. Van der Stede points out that the *eṭemmu* is closer to a "ghost" than a "soul" (*Mourir au pays de deux fleuves*, 16–25).

[187] See *ABL* 614, r. 4–6 in "eṭemmu," *CAD* E, 397.

close at hand, for example, underneath living quarters. However, the *eṭemmu* could also be a demonic force attacking the living and inflicting sickness, perceived to be such a frequent occurrence that "hand of a ghost" was a common medical diagnosis.[188] The *zaqīqu*, by contrast, was not an affliction; it was a spirit in the sense of a wispy apparition and is equated with "wind" (*šāru*) in lexical lists;[189] in the Gilgamesh epic, when Enkidu comes up from the netherworld as a ghost, he comes up through a hole "like a *zaqīqu*."[190] Aššurbanipal reported that the god Nabu sent a *zaqīqu* to him as a messenger,[191] a natural mission, since *zaqīqû* were thought to be more free from bodily constraints than *eṭemmû*. The term *zaqīqu* could also have a pejorative connotation, signifying "nothingness." Tiglath-Pileser I bragged that he sent "the arrogant enemies of Assyria to the pit, and considered them (as mere) *zaqīqu*."[192]

As the comments about the underworld may suggest, the dead were perceived paradoxically in Mesopotamian mythology. On the one hand, their status, comfort, and ability to provide for themselves were reduced; on the other hand, if angry they could be very powerful in tormenting the living: "The anger and resentment resulting from [the neglect of proper burial and mourning rites] turned an otherwise friendly ghost into a vicious demon."[193] It would therefore be a serious error to assume that Mesopotamian ghosts were weak and powerless simply because they required care.[194] It was not only the uncared-for dead who might have reason to be angry. "Equally vengeful were persons who had died violent and unhappy deaths, before they had had the opportunity to live out a normal life on earth."[195] In the Neo-Assyrian version of the myth of "Ištar's Descent," an angered Ištar threatens to break down the door of the underworld

---

[188] Jo Ann Scurlock, *Magico-Medical Means of Treating Ghost-Induced Illnesses in Ancient Mesopotamia* (Ancient Magic and Divination 3; Leiden: Brill/Styx, 2006); Jo Ann Scurlock and Burton Andersen, *Diagnoses in Assyrian and Babylonian Medicine: Ancient Sources, Translations, and Modern Medical Analyses* (Urbana and Chicago: University of Illinois Press, 2005); R. Campbell Thompson, "Assyrian Prescriptions for the 'Hand of the Ghost,'" *Journal of the Royal Asiatic Society of Great Britain and Ireland* (1929): 801–19.

[189] Lapinkivi, Ištar's Descent, 37. He points out that *zaqīqu* derives from *zâqu*, "to blow."

[190] Gilgamesh XII:87. George, *The Babylonian Gilgamesh Epic*, 194.

[191] James A. Craig, *Assyrian and Babylonian Religious Texts* (2 vols.; 1895–97; repr., Leipzig: Zentralantiquariat der Deutschen Demokratischen Republik, 1974), I.6:23.

[192] *CAD* Z, 59 (*AfO* 18 349:10). The claim was echoed in the Neo-Assyrian period by Tiglath-Pileser III.

[193] Scurlock, "Death and the Afterlife," 1890; cf. Bottéro, *Religion in Ancient Mesopotamia*, 110

[194] Jo Ann Scurlock, "Ghosts in the Ancient Near East: Weak or Powerful?" *HUCA* 68 (1997): 77–96. She is reacting against arguments like that of Brian B. Schmidt in *Israel's Beneficent Dead: Ancestor Cult and Necromancy in Ancient Israelite Tradition and Religion* (FAT 11; Tübingen: Mohr Siebeck, 1994).

[195] Scurlock, "Death and the Afterlife," 1890; cf. Bottéro, *Religion in Ancient Mesopotamia*, 109–10; Scurlock, "Ghosts in the Ancient Near East," 92–93.

and free the dead who are confined there; "I will raise up the dead to devour the living," she says. "The dead will outnumber the living."[196] In the interest of keeping the unhappy dead under control, there exist a great number of exorcism texts "devoted to symbolically burying or re-burying ... errant spirits."[197]

The perceived power of ghosts is underscored by the way in which certain Akkadian terms for the ghosts of the dead are preceded by the DINGIR determinative, marking them as divinized. The unburied or unhappy dead could "become part of the demonic world. ... Hence, *eṭemmu* (ghost) may become associated with the demonic *utukku*, and even be so designated."[198] Conversely, demons are usually seen as coming from the underworld. The Sumero-Akkadian incantation series "Evil Demons" (*Utukkū lemnūtu*) includes a great catalogue of demons, and in one section it includes words intended to protect against those who have died in tragic ways: the one who died in the steppe, the one killed by a weapon, the one mauled by a dog or lion or fell from a roof or date-palm, or who drowned. This series continues in this way:

> ...whether you are an unburied ghost,
> or the one who has no *pāqidu*,
> or the ghost who has no one to make a funerary offering
> or the ghost who has no one to pour out a water llibation;
> whether you are are one with no one to call (his) name...[199]

The same assumption about the provenance of demons is shared throughout multiple spell series. Scholars therefore tend to speak of these beings under a single heading.[200]

There were numerous demons with proper names in ancient Mesopotamia, many of them sickness demons who caused plague, fever, headache, etc. (Asakku, Aḫḫazu, Bennu, Rabiṣu, Shulak, Mukil-reš-lemutti, Muruṣ qaqqadi). There were

---

[196] Lapinkivi, *Ištar's Descent*, 29 (ll. 19–20). The threat echoes almost precisely the threat in the Middle Babylonian myth *Nergal and Ereškigal* by an angered Ereškigal: "I will raise up the dead, and they will devour the living./ I will make the dead outnumber the living." See Dalley, *Myths from Mesopotamia*, 173.

[197] Cooper, "Fate of Mankind," 27–28.

[198] Tzvi Abusch, "*eṭemmu*," *DDD*, 589. See also Scurlock, "Magical Means," 1; Bottéro, "Les morts et l'au-delà deans les rituels en accadien," 170–72.

[199] *Utukkū lemnūtu* 4:145′–49′. See Markham J. Geller, *Evil Demons: Canonical Utukkū Lemnūtu Incantations* (State Archives of Assyria Cuneiform Texts 5; Helsinki, Finland: Helsinki University Press, 2007), 207. Similarly, a tablet from a Neo-Assyrian copy of the apotropaic spell series "Ti'i" begins: "The evil spirit (*utukku*), the evil demon, the evil ghost (*eṭemmu*), the evil devil from the earth have come forth, from the underworld to the land they have come forth... ." See R. C. Thompson, *The Devils and Evil Spirits of Babylonia* (London: Luzac, 1903–4), vol. 2, Tablet CC. Thompson misread "etemmu" as "ekimmu."

[200] In "Death and the Afterlife," Scurlock uses "demon" and "ghost" almost interchangeably (see 1897). Similarly, Walter Farber treats "Demons and Ghosts" under one subheading in his article "Witchcraft, Magic and Divination in Ancient Mesopotamia," in *Civilizations of the Ancient Near East* (ed. Jack M. Sasson; New York: Scribner, 1995), 3:2059–70.

also demons of the night (Lilû, Ardat-lili, Lilitu), and the list goes on: Alû, Gallû, Namtar, Lamaštu, Pazazu, Samanum, Humbaba/Huwawa, etc.[201] In addition to these names, demons were also described in numerous metaphorical or mythological ways: as hags and robbers,[202] as storms, frost and floods,[203] and especially as animals. Animalistic descriptions of demons included images of dogs, snakes, birds, and bulls.[204] There was a particularly rich tradition relating the dead to birds. *Utukkū lemnūtu* describes a demon as one who "always flies around at night like a bird in the dark"[205] and "fly in dark places like a bird of the night."[206] In the same series, evil spirits are portrayed as "twittering below" (5:6) and crying out like an owl (5:9).[207] Another incantation series says of the prominent demon Lamaštu: "Her feet are those of an eagle; her hands mean decay."[208] Birds' feet were also characteristic of demons. The gatekeeper of the netherworld, too, is described with "the feet of a bird" in a Sumerian text, and of

---

[201] Marcel Leibovici, "Génies et démons en Babylonie," in *Génies, anges, et démons, Égypte, Babylone, Israel, Islam* (Sources orientales 8; Paris: Seuil, 1971), 85–111. On demons as agents of sickness and harm, see further Bottéro, "Les morts et l'au-delà deans les rituels en accadien," 161–69. Bottéro speaks of the "activité pathogène des *eṭimmu*" (164). See also the listings in Geller, *Evil Demons*, passim.

[202] E.g., the "Elegy for a Woman Dead in Childbirth": "While I lived with him who was my lover / Death was creeping stealthily into my bedroom" (Foster, *Before the Muses*, 949; Reiner, *Your Thwarts in Pieces*, 88–89.)

[203] In *Utukkū lemnūtu* the evil spirits are described as "huge storms ... released from heaven" (5:8), "harmful gales... the flood-storm... they walk on the right side of Adad" (16:17–18). This is only a representative sampling of phrases. See Geller, *Evil Demons*, 208, 251.

[204] This can be confirmed by a perusal of *CAD* under the relevant Akkadian terms; see also Geller, *Evil Demons*; for snakes, 6:174′; dogs, 6:176′. One Sumero-Akkadian incantation calls a *gallû*-demon "a goring ox (GUD/*alpu*), a powerful ghost"(Thompson, *Devils*, 1:69; CT 17, 14.iv.14ff.). The ferocity of the ox would have been seen by later Akkadian authors as comparable to that of the *ūmu*-demon (Chikako E. Watanabe, *Animal Symbolism in Mesopotamia: A Contextual Approach* [Vienna: Institut für Orientalistik der Universität Wien, 2002], 4). *Ašakki marṣūti*, XII.4. Thompson, *Devils*, 2:38–39; CT 17, plate 27. Note also that in the Neo-Babylonian version of the "Prayer of Lamentation to Ishtar" l.51, the one lamenting prays, "O angry wild ox (*rīmi*), let thy spirit be appeased" (*ANET*[6], 384). The demon who hauls Enkidu off to the underworld in the *Gilgamesh Epic* is also described with bird and bull attributes (George, *Babylonian Gilgamesh Epic*, 1:642–43; see also Stephanie Dalley, *Myths from Mesopotamia: Creation, the Flood, Gilgamesh, and Others* [Oxford: Oxford University Press, 1989], 89).

[205] *Utukkū lemnūtu* 8:19 (Geller, *Evil Demons*, 226). Cf. Farber, "Witchcraft, Magic and Divination," 1896.

[206] Thompson, *Devils*, 1:130; *Cuneiform Texts from Babylonian Tablets in the British Museum* (London: British Museum, 1903), vol. 16, plate 28.

[207] Geller, *Evil Demons*, 208; CT 16, plate 12. Note also *Utukkū lemnūtu*, and 4:176′ et pars., which adjure the spirit: "Fly up to heaven although you have no wings" (*Evil Demons*, 207).

[208] *Lamaštu* series, Tablet I. An amulet bearing Lamaštu's image and a Neo-Assyrian cuneiform text has been found in promixity to Lachish, but it seems most likely that it was dropped there by an Assyrian, so that it may not bear witness to knowledge of Lamaštu in Iron Age Judah. See Mordechai Cogan, "A Lamashtu Plaque from the Judaean Shephelah," *IEJ* 45 (1995): 155–61.

another demon it is said, "his right foot is a bird's claw."²⁰⁹ An incantation text found in a copy at Nineveh seeks to make a (demonized) headache fly away "like the bird of the open steppes."²¹⁰ This tendency toward birdlike characteristics could be compared with the Egyptian *ba*-bird and certain biblical portrayals of dead spirits; e.g., Isa 8:19; 29:4.

Apotropaic spells attest to the Mesopotamians' dread of the wrath of the dead. However, as powerful beings, Mesopotamian ghosts could also be useful to the living. In necromantic rites, ghosts could be summoned by the living to gain access to knowledge. "The existence of necromancy in Mesopotamia at least in certain periods can scarcely be denied," concluded Irving Finkel.²¹¹ The support for this claim is diverse. "The professions list known as Lu mentions in both second and first millennium versions the *ša eṭemmi* and the *mušēlu eṭemmi*,²¹² each term patently a necromancer."²¹³ Two further tablets published by Finkel include detailed necromantic rituals that promise to allow a person to converse with a ghost. One reads: "You will see the ghost: he will speak with you. You can look at the ghost: he will talk with you."²¹⁴

There is reason to think that such divinatory practices reached a peak under the Sargonids. While divination was certainly a long-standing practice in Mesopotamia, the caches of divinatory tablets from the libraries of Aššurbanipal and Esarhaddon are far more extensive than those from any other period.²¹⁵ "The codification of centuries of accumulated omina into vast compendia of ordered information ... was accomplished under the sponsorship of Sargonid kings," writes Holloway.²¹⁶ One of the most spectacular examples of this trend involves both divination and death – the "substitute king" (*šar pūḫi*) ritual, which is known to have been employed by Esarhaddon. It was used when an omen por-

---

²⁰⁹ *Mitteilung des Instituts für Orientforschung*, I:74 r.iv 43; cf. Thompson, *Devils*, 2:153. Note also the incantation series *Ṭi'i* ("Headache"), in which the supplicant hopes "that the Headache, like the dove to the cote, like the raven to heaven, like the bird of the open steppes, may fly away" (lines 140–44; cf. Thompson, *Devils*, 2:77).

²¹⁰ *Ṭi'i* IX.145. Thompson, *Devils*, 2 :76–77; CT 17, plate 22. Cf. *Utukkū lemnūtu* 1:34' (Geller, *Evil Demons*, 191).

²¹¹ Irving R. Finkel, "Necromancy in Ancient Mesopotamia," *AfO* 29 (1984): 3. For a contrary interpretation of the same data, see Frederick H. Cryer, *Divination in Ancient Israel and Its Near Eastern Environment: A Socio-Historical Investigation* (JSOTSup 142; Sheffield: Sheffield Academic Press, 1994), 181–83.

²¹² *mušēlu* = "one who raises"; see *CAD* M/2, 265: "necromancer" (Š ptc from *elû*).

²¹³ Finkel, "Necromancy in Ancient Mesopotamia," 1.

²¹⁴ The text is BM 36703 (Late Babylonian), lines 22b–23: "ɢɪᴅɪᴍ ta-ba-ri it-ti-k[a i-qab-bi]; ta-na-ṭal-ma it-t[i-ka i-dab-bu-ub]" (Finkel, "Necromancy in Ancient Mesopotamia," 10).

²¹⁵ Ivan Starr, "Introduction," in *Queries to the Sungod: Divination and Politics in Sargonid Assyria* (ed. Ivan Starr; SAA 4; Helsinki: Helsinki University Press, 1990), xiv.

²¹⁶ Holloway, *Aššur is King!*, 85; see also Erica Reiner, "First-Millennium Babylonian Literature," in *The Cambridge Ancient History*, part 2, *The Assyrian and Babylonian Empires and Other States of the Near East, from the Eighth to the Sixth Centuries BC* (2nd ed.; Cambridge: Cambridge University Press, 1991), 313.

tended serious misfortune for the real king; a substitute was crowned and "ruled" for one hundred days before being "killed, buried, and lamented."[217] This was thought to fool the fates, so that the substitute would bear the bad omen and the real king be spared.

Sargon and Sennacherib also are known to have consulted diviners, most famously the latter's effort to discover the reason for his father's death on the field of battle.[218] One text invokes the ghost of Sennacherib to justify a policy probably instituted by his son, Esarhaddon.[219] In one of Esarhaddon's letters, an exorcist cites the words of another royal ghost (the king's deceased queen) in support of the king's controversial choice of Aššurbanipal as his heir-apparent. Thus, it is "beyond doubt" that "summoning spirits of the dead to act as 'political witnesses' was not at all unthinkable at the Assyrian imperial court."[220] Indeed, Ivan Starr suggests that the only reason we do not have many primary divinatory texts from their reigns is that their archives have not yet been discovered.

It is debatable whether the pejorative term "superstitious," often applied to these late-Sargonid monarchs, is applicable;[221] but it is clear that the production and collection of divinatory and apotropaic texts regarding the dead reached a peak at that time.

1.4.3 The Mesopotamian underworld and its deities

The underworld goes by various proper names in Sumero-Akkadian literature: ^{d}Irkalla,[222] Arallû (see further at § 5.2.2.3), and Ganzer.[223] The last of these is a homophone for "flame" in Sumerian, and although the two words are usually

---

[217] Quoting a letter to Esarhaddon: Parpola, *Letters from Assyrian and Babylonian Scholars*, no. 280.
[218] Starr, "Introduction," xxx–xxxi; Livingstone, *Court Poetry*, 77–79.
[219] K.4730(+). See Tadmor, Landsberger, and Parpola, "The Sin of Sargon," 3–51.
[220] The text is LAS 132. The comment is from Simo Parpola, "Synthesis" in "Sin of Sargon and Sennacherib's Last Will," 45.
[221] See examples in Holloway, *Aššur is King!*, 78 n. 263. This view is no mere historical curiosity: In 1992, Jerold S. Cooper commented that "Esarhaddon was notoriously superstitious, or rather excruciatingly attentive to anything that might portend ill for him and his regime" ("Fate of Mankind," 22).
[222] Irkalla can also appear in phrases such as *šubat/bīt ^{d}Irkalla*, "the dwelling/house of Irkalla," leading some scholars to conclude that Irkalla is also the name of a deity, most likely Ereškigal. Wayne Horowitz, however, considers Irkalla the Akkadian phonetic equivalent of the Sumerian URUGAL/IRIGAL, "great city" (*Mesopotamian Cosmic Geography* [Winona Lake, Ind.: Eisenbrauns, 1998], 288). Irkalla is also equated in lexical lists with Sumerian names hilib/halib, kir$_5$, and lamhu (Lapinkivi, *Ištar's Descent*, 36).
[223] Ganzer is a Sumerian name (perhaps of Proto-Euphratic derivation; see A. R. George, "Sennacherib and the Tablet of Destinies," *Iraq* 48 [1986]: 133–46). Ganzer is sometimes portrayed as a palace or a gate; Dina Katz has theorized that there might have been a gate named Ganzer in Uruk that was used for funeral processions, but this remains in the realm of speculation (*The Image of the Netherworld in the Sumerian Sources* [Bethesda, Md.: CDL Press, 2003], 45–46).

written with different signs, it has been suggested that this reflects a very ancient tradition of a fiery afterlife, or at least a fiery passage into the underworld.[224]

Imagistically, it can be referred to simply as "the grave" (*naqbaru/qabru*),[225] "the pit" (BÙR/*ḫaštu*), or as a "house" (*bītu*) – sometimes a "house of darkness" (*bīt eṭuṭi/ekleti*), "house of dust" (*bīt epri*), "house of the dead" (*bīt mūti*), etc. It is also commonly conceptualized in geographical terms: it is frequently described as a "great city" (IRIGAL/URUGAL), or a "land" of various sorts: the lower land (*erṣetu šaplitu*), the wide or large land (*erṣetu rapaštu/rabītu*), the land of the dead, or the land without return (*erṣetu la târi*, or sometimes simply transliterated *kurnugû* from the Sumerian equivalent KUR.NU.GI₄.A). The preparation of grave goods emphasizes that the netherworld was seen as a distant land (*erṣetu rūqtu*) to which the deceased had to travel.

There are at least three distinct portrayals of the afterlife journey. The most commonly described route traversed demon-infested steppes to cross the Ḫubur River, then through the seven gates of the netherworld.[226] As more famously in Egypt, the underworld was often conceptualized as lying in the West, and ghosts might be banished through magical spells forcing them to travel back there.[227] Véronique van der Stede suggests that the underworld moved underground in mythical thought as the Mesopotamians' knowledge of the actual geography of outlying areas improved – that is to say, exploration taught them that the underworld was not just over the hills.[228] Thus, a second, less-common route was to go by boat down the rivers of the upper earth and across the *apsû*, the watery deep, until one reached the lower earth.[229] Finally, and least commonly, there is the motif of an afterlife ascent to heaven, attested primarily for Neo-Sumerian kings of the Ur III dynasty. Two tablets report the year when the king "ascended to heaven."[230]

Other passing references in Akkadian literature describe the route to and from the underworld as a crevasse, a stairway, a path, and "the door of the setting sun,"

---

[224] Lapinkivi, *Ištar's Descent*, 45. He notes that ganzer is also equated in lexical lists with terms for darkness, such as *kukkû*, *ekletu*, and *eṭūtu*. Niek Veldhuis cautions against any facile comparison to later images of hell ("Entering the Netherworld," *CDL Bulletin* 2003:6. Accessed electronically at http://cdli.ucla.edu/pubs/cdlb/2003/cdlb20030006.html).

[225] Bottéro, "Les morts et l'au-delà deans les rituels en accadien," 196.

[226] In reality, there was no ancient Mesopotamian city with seven walls; three was the maximum. It appears that the seven walls correspond to the seven layers of a ziggurat. For the detailed argument, see Lapinkivi, *The Neo-Assyrian Myth of Ištar's Descent*, 79–80.

[227] Bottéro, "Les morts et l'au-delà deans les rituels en accadien," 191.

[228] Van der Stede, *Mourir au pays de deux fleuves*, 38.

[229] Scurlock, "Death and the Afterlife," 1886–87; van der Stede, *Mourir au pays de deux fleuves*, 40.

[230] There is also a text from the ruler Šulgi that reads, "Whatever is acquired is destined to be lost; What mortal has ever reached the heavens," which, despite its pessimistic tone, reflects the same theology. See discussion and references at Lapinkivi, *Ištar's Descent*, 42.

reflecting Šamaš's role as psychopomp, a guide for the spirits of the dead (see below).[231]

In one Sumero-Akkadian myth, when the goddess Inanna/Ištar descends to the underworld, she is progressively stripped of her clothing at each of the seven gates – a process that was once thought to reflect a practice of burying the dead unclothed. However, the burials in the archaeological record do not support that theory – they show that people were generally buried clothed.[232] Instead, it is likely Ereškigal, queen of the netherworld in the story, insists that Ištar be stripped as a way of reducing her status and power. Her nakedness also probably reflects the bereft condition in which the *uncared-for* dead were thought to exist.

The Mesopotamian perception of the underworld was certainly negative in general. From the beginnings of Sumerian literature, one finds texts that portray it in relatively unpleasant terms. The underworld is a land of darkness.[233] The dead eat dust and clay there;[234] as attested in the myth of "Ningišzida's Boat-Ride to Hades":

The river of the Nether World carries no water,
no water is drunk from it.
The fields of the Nether World carry no grain,
no flour is milled from it.[235]

Sumerian descriptions of the underworld appear to have been closely linked with the nature of the grave itself, as attested in the story "Gilgamesh, Enkidu, and the Netherworld." In that tale, Enkidu has a dream about the world of the dead and reports it to Gilgamesh. He describes the underworld as dark and dusty, and its inhabitants are said to suffer if grave offerings are not provided by their descendants:

(G:) Did you see the way things are in the underworld?
(E:) If I tell you, my friend, if I tell you,
If I tell you the way things are in the netherworld,
You would sit down and weep, I would sit down and weep too.
My body you once touched, in which you rejoiced,
It will [never] come [back].
It is infested with lice, like an old garment,
It is filled with dust, like a crack (in parched ground).[236]

---

[231] Van der Stede, *Mourir au pays de deux fleuves*, 72–84.
[232] Lapinkivi, *Ištar's Descent*, 55–56.
[233] An alternate and less prominent tradition describes the underworld as illuminated by the sun-god Šamaš for part of the day (van der Stede, *Mourir au pays de deux fleuves*, 86).
[234] Already in the Sumerian "Descent of Ur-Nammu," the writer remarks: "Bitter is the food of the netherworld, brackish is the water of the Netherworld" (1.82). See Kramer, "Death of Ur-Nammu," 104–22.
[235] Thorkild Jacobsen and Samuel Noah Kramer, "Ningišzida's Boat-Ride to Hades," in *Wisdom, Gods, and Literature: Studies in Assyriology in Honour of W. G. Lambert* (ed. A. G. George and I. L. Finkel; Winona Lake, Ind.: Eisenbrauns, 2000). See also *Ur Namma A* 83.

Similarly, in "The Descent of Inanna," the underworld is portrayed rather simply, as dusty and without return. Inanna is instructed to pray, "O Father Enlil, do not let your daughter / be put to death in the underworld. / Do not let your bright silver / be covered with the dust of the underworld."[237]

By the second millennium, in "The Descent of Ištar," this picture is filled out with other unpleasant features:

> To the netherworld, land of [no return],
> Ishtar, daughter of Sin, was [determined] to go.
> Indeed, the daughter of Sin did set her mind
> To the dark house, seat of the netherworld (^{d}Irkalla),
> To the house which none leaves who enters,
> To the road whose journey has no return,
> To the house whose entrants are bereft of light,
> Where dust is their sustenance and clay their food.
> They see no light but dwell in darkness,
> They are clothed like birds (MUŠEN) in feather garments (ṣubat kappi),[238]
> And dust has gathered on the door and bolt.[239]

This description seems to have been accorded great esteem in the Sumero-Akkadian scribal tradition. By the Late Babylonian period, exactly parallel passages are found in the Standard Babylonian version of *The Epic of Gilgamesh*[240] and in "Nergal and Ereshkigal."[241] In each case, the description is *not* found in older, second-millennium versions. In short, the pericope above seems to have become an increasingly popular description of the world of the dead in Mesopotamia.

The increasingly detailed nature of these descriptions, along with the other information already surveyed, supports Jacobsen's observation about the growing fascination with the world of the dead in the first millennium. Furthermore, Scurlock notes in her study of Akkadian incantation texts intended to protect from ghosts that none comes from earlier than the Neo-Assyrian period, and nearly all come from Assyrian libraries.[242] This is not likely to be a mere accident of preservation. Additional support may come from the observation that the

---

[236] *The Epic of Gilgamesh* (trans. and ed. Benjamin R. Foster; New York: W. W. Norton, 2001), 138–41. Cf. George, *The Babylonian Gilgamesh Epic*, 732–35, 774.

[237] Diane Wolkstein and Samuel Noah Kramer, *Inanna: Queen of Heaven and Earth* (New York: Harper & Row, 1983), 54.

[238] Akk. *kappi* = "feathers" or "wings."

[239] Benjamin R. Foster, *From Distant Days: Myths, Tales, and Poetry of Ancient Mesopotamia* (Bethesda, Md.: CDL, 1995), 78–79.

[240] Tablet VII (Dalley, *Myths from Mesopotamia*, 89; Foster, *Epic of Gilgamesh*, 57–58).

[241] Dalley, *Myths from Mesopotamia*, 168.

[242] Scurlock, "Magical Means," 5. It seems to me that there may be a diachronic element here: Demons are a concern throughout Mesopotamian religious history, but it may be that the dead are associated with them as a harmful force only in the Neo-Assyrian period.

Anunnaki, once the title of all the great gods as a group, became by the late periods of Akkadian literature a term for specifically underworld gods.[243]

According to one Neo-Assyrian text, there were six hundred Anunnaki confined in the underworld,[244] and a large number of named deities could be included in a thorough treatment. For the present, however, we confine ourselves to major figures. Ereškigal ("Lady of the Great Earth") emerged in the Middle Babylonian period as queen of the underworld, and she continued in that role throughout the Neo-Assyrian/Neo-Babylonian period. The king of the Mesopotamian underworld by the first millennium was clearly Nergal, but he was in fact a later addition to it.[245] Originally a city deity, he was seduced by Ereškigal and thus came to rule alongside her. Like any proper king and queen, they were supported by the usual retinue of servants, such as a vizier/messenger, a porter/doorman, a throne-bearer, a boatman, a scribe, etc.[246]

Some of these characters figure in "The Underworld Vision of an Assyrian Prince,"[247] parade example of the baroque elaboration of mythological portrayals of the underworld in the Neo-Assyrian period. This text was preserved in a private archive in a house in the remains of Aššur (sacked in 612 BCE), and is *sui generis* within Akkadian literature.[248] Given its similarity to Egyptian ghost stories (§ 2.4.2), however, other examples are likely to have existed.

In the text, the prince Kummâ (or Kummay[249]), who may represent Aššurbanipal, has multiple highly detailed dreams of the underworld that linger over the terrifying attributes of the chthonic deities:

I saw Namtar,[250] the vizier of the underworld, who fashions the visceral omens; a man stood before him, while he held the hair of his head in his left hand, and wielded a dagger in the right [...]
Namtartu, his wife, had the head of a cherub, (her) hands and feet being human. Death had the head of a dragon, his hands were human, his feet [...]

---

[243] Burkhart Kienast, "Igigū und Anunnakū nach den Akkadischen Quellen," *Assyriological Studies* 16 (1965): 141–58; John F. Healey, "Malkū : MLKM : Anunnaki," *UF* 7 (1975): 235–38; Alasdair Livingstone, *Mystical and Mythological Explanatory Works of Assyrian and Babylonian Scholars* (Oxford: Clarendon, 1986), 135–36; Bottéro, "Les morts et l'au-delà deans les rituels en accadien," 200.
[244] KAR 307, l. 37; Livingstone, *Court Poetry*, 100.
[245] The Sumerian deity Ninazu seems to have been viewed as ruler of the underworld in the earliest periods.
[246] For further discussion of these figures, see van der Stede, *Mourir au pays de deux fleuves*, 63–71.
[247] Wolfram von Soden, "Die Unterweltsvision eines assyrischen Kronprinzen," *ZA* 43 (1936): 1–31; Livingstone, *Court Poetry*, 68–79.
[248] Seth Sanders remarks that "in 2,000 years of cuneiform literature, there are no other examples of the genre it represents." ("The First Tour of Hell: From Neo-Assyrian Propaganda to Early Jewish Revelation," *JANER* 9 [2009]: 151)
[249] See Sanders, "The First Tour of Hell," 157 n. 16.
[250] In Sumerian, NAM.TAR, a partiple meaning "he who decrees the fates."

1.4 Death in Mesopotamia

The Evil Genie had a human head and hands, was crowned with a tiara and had the feet of a bird.[251] With his left foot he was trampling on a *crocodile*. Alluhappu had a lion's[252] head, his four hands and feet (like) those of a human beings.

The Upholder of Evil had the head of a bird,[253] his wings (*akappu*) were spread out and he flew here and there; (his) hands and feet were human. Humut-tabal, the ferryman of the underworld had an Anzû head, his hands and feet [...]

The *Ghost* (GIDIM[=*eṭemmu*]) had an ox's (GUD) head, his four hands and feet were (like) those of human beings. The Evil Spirit (*utukku*) had a lion's head, (his) hands and feet were like those on Anzû. Šulak was a lion, standing constantly on his hind legs.

The Oath had a goat's head, (his) hands and feet were human. Nedu, the porter of the underworld, had a lion's head, and human hands, his feet were those of a bird. Total Evil had two heads, one was the head of a lion, the second was the head of [...].

[Muh]ra had three feet, the two front ones were those of a bird, the rear one was that of a bull (GUD.NITÁ[254]). He had fearsome and luminous splendor. Of two gods I did not know the names – one had the head, hands and feet of Anzû, in his left hand [...]

The other had a man's head, he was crowned with a tiara, carried in his right hand a mace, in his left hand, before him... . In all, fifteen gods were present."[255]

At the end of this scene, Kummâ sees Nergal enthroned in terrible splendor, and holding "two grim maces," one in each hand. Nergal draws his scepter to kill the prince, but relents when an adviser intercedes. Nergal settles for warning the prince: "Do not forget or neglect me! ... May this word be set like a thorn in your heart!" The consequence is that there be no peace in his reign, so that his sleep is disturbed by "distress, acts of violence, and rebellion."[256] The prince wakes up in terror, "like a man who has let blood, who roams alone in a reed thicket, whom a runner catches up with, so that his heart pounds."[257] The import of the vision appears to be that the prince should conscientiously maintain the cult of the underworld gods. If the vision is royal propaganda, as has often been supposed,[258] then it must be from late in the reign of Aššurbanipal, after the threat of instability from the succession was past, and when the cult of the underworld gods was already being conscientiously maintained.[259]

The sun god Šamaš, like Re in Egyptian myth and Šapšu at Ugarit, was thought to traverse the underworld at night and thus also had important underworld

---

[251] Here the orthography is ÉR.MUŠEN – literally, "weeping bird" or "lamentation-bird." Alasdair Livingstone guesses that this may be "an esoteric writing for *erû*" ("eagle"; *Court Poetry*, 71), but the songbird is the more likely referent, given the association of ÉR with mourning (ÉR=*dintu*, "tear").
[252] "Lion" is written as UR.MAḪ throughout this pericope.
[253] "Bird" is written as MUŠEN throughout this pericope.
[254] NITÁ = "male," thus "male ox."
[255] "The Netherworld Vision of an Assyrian Prince," r. 2–9; Livingstone, *Court Poetry*, 71–72.
[256] "The Netherworld Vision of an Assyrian Prince," r. 20, 28; Livingstone, *Court Poetry*, 72, 73.
[257] "The Netherworld Vision of an Assyrian Prince," r. 29; Livingstone, *Court Poetry*, 73.
[258] von Soden, "Die Unterweltsvision," 7.
[259] Sanders, "The First Tour of Hell," 164–65.

aspects. As one who spanned day and night, Šamaš seems to have had a gatekeeper's role, keeping the living and dead in their proper places and punishing the dead who afflicted the living without cause. According to a hymn in his honor, Šamaš "makes light the dark[ness for mankind a]bove and below ... Gods and netherworld gods rejoiced when you appeared... . The wandering dead, the vagrant spirit come before you."[260] Šamaš was also given the titles *šar eṭimmê* ("ruler of the ghosts") and *bēl mīti* ("lord of the dead").[261] One aspect of this role, attested in a ritual text from Kuyunjik, was to summon "a ghost of the darkness (*eṭemmi eṭūti*)" in a necromantic consultation;[262] this would have been seen as naturally within his purview.

Other gods with prominent chthonic aspects include Dumuzi/Tammuz, a mythical human king who was banished to the underworld by his wife, Inanna/Ištar. His epithet "the lord of the flocks" made him function in some contexts as the shepherd of the dead.[263] A final figure who deserves mention among underworld gods is the legendary king Gilgamesh, who seems to have assumed the status of a minor deity and received sacrifices in burial rituals.[264] There is also Maliku, who is equated with Nergal in both Old Babylonian and Neo-Assyrian god lists, but Maliku is more likely to be a Syrian deity (see § 3.3.3.3).[265]

In addition to deities with underworld aspects, there are others who are said to heal or save (esp. *balāṭu*, D stem) from death. Often these are given the Akkadian title *muballiṭ mīti*: "the one who heals/raises the dead," and they include Nabu, Ninlil, and Marduk, with attestations continuing into the Neo-Assyrian and Neo-Babylonian periods.[266] Alexander Heidel argues that phrases such as *muballiṭ mīti* are metaphorical and are intended to evoke only healing powers, but this interpretation is impossible in at least one text, from the fourth tablet of *Ludlul bēl nēmeqi*.[267]

---

[260] COS 1.117; W. G. Lambert, *Babylonian Wisdom Literature* (Oxford: Clarendon, 1960), 121–38; Bottéro, "Les morts et l'au-delà deans les rituels en accadien," 201–2.

[261] J. F. Healey, "The Sun Deity and the Underworld in Mesopotamia and Ugarit," in *Death in Mesopotamia: Papers Read at the XXVIe Rencontre Assyriologique Internationale* (ed. Bendt Alster; Mesopotamia 8; Copenhagen: Akademisk Forlag, 1980), 240.

[262] Finkel, "Necromancy in Ancient Mesopotamia," 5.

[263] Bottéro, "Les morts et l'au-delà deans les rituels en accadien," 193–96.

[264] If McGinnis's reading of the Neo-Assyrian funeral text is correct, "it would be first-hand evidence of the Neo-Assyrian kings sacrificing to the demi-god [Gilgamesh]. Ur-Nammu, too, made offerings to Gilgamesh (amongst others) at his arrival in the underworld, and the co-incidence of this, along with the fact that vessels, animals and textiles are also mentioned in the Ur-Nammu text strongly suggests a continuity of tradition, either in actual practice or in the literary transmission" (McGinnis, "Neo-Assyrian Text Describing a Royal Funeral," 7).

[265] John Day, *Molech: A God of Human Sacrifice in the Old Testament* (Cambridge: Cambridge University Press, 1989), 48–49.

[266] For a fuller accounting, see *CAD* B, 58: "*balāṭu*," 5a.

[267] Heidel, *The Gilgamesh Epic and Old Testament Parallels* (Chicago: The University of Chicago Press, 1946), 208.

bēli uballiṭanni ...
"The Lord gave me life... .
ša la ᵈMarduk mannu mitutašu uballiṭ
Who but Marduk restores his dead to life? ...
ᵈMarduk ina qabri bulluṭa ilī'i
Marduk can restore to life *from the grave.*" (*Ludlul* IV.4, 33, 35)²⁶⁸

This Babylonian text derives from the Kassite period (ca. 1600–1200 BCE), and it seems apparent that such resurrection imagery continued to be operative throughout the history of Babylon and Assyria.

It may help to clarify my use of terminology to note that there is no systematic distinction between "revivification" and "resurrection" prior to the evolution of the later Jewish and Christian doctrines of resurrection. One might distinguish between those who are restored to normal human life, only to die again (revivification) and those who are raised to beatific afterlife (resurrection?), but only on the basis of literary contexts. There is no distinction in terminology in any ancient Near Eastern language of the Bronze or Iron ages. Thus I prefer "revivification," but may sometimes use the terms interchangeably.

Although the afterlife could portend horror for an Assyrian, it seems to have been assumed in many cases that proper care could assure the deceased a relatively pleasant afterlife, or better. In the *Gilgamesh Epic*, Enkidu describes the afterlife of men with male offspring to care for them (as *pāqidû*):

> Gilgameš: Did you see the man with six sons?
> Enkidu: I saw him; Like a ploughman his heart rejoices.
> G: Did you see the man with seven sons?
> E: Among the junior deities he sits on a throne and listens to the proceedings.²⁶⁹

At a minimum, death might be faced with equanimity by the mighty, those who could feel confident about the survival of their memory and care. Thus, Sennacherib's tomb inscription identified the place as a "palace of sleep, tomb of repose, eternal residence, stable family dwelling."²⁷⁰ On the other hand, texts such as this are also susceptible to the same interpretation as those of the Egyptians – i.e., that their positive images are merely the reflection of their inhabitants' fears (§ 2.4.3–2.5).

1.5 Conclusions

Mesopotamian beliefs and practices related to death form an important background for those of Judah. Where there are similarities, one cannot discount the

---

²⁶⁸ Lambert, *Babylonian Wisdom Literature*, 58–59.
²⁶⁹ George, *Babylonian Gilgamesh Epic*, 734–35 (XII. 113–16).
²⁷⁰ Bottéro, "Les inscriptions funéraires cuneiforms," 382.

possibility of common traditions, but the most obvious point at which the Mesopotamian civilizations influenced Israel and Judah was in the monarchic and exilic periods, when both direct political intervention and elite emulation forged closer cultural connections.

In assessing the history of Mesopotamian religion, one is hampered by lacunae and is perhaps tempted to overstatement by accidents of preservation. Still, there is certainly enough data to draw conclusions. The natural lot of the dead was usually thought to be unhappy, and those who had suffered particularly unpleasant fates might be angry enough to attack the living. With proper care, however, the dead could also attain almost divine status in the netherworld; because they were dependent on the living for this care, they could be enlisted for help, including necromantic consultations. Because of the power of the dead, the Neo-Assyrians and Neo-Babylonians were deeply concerned with the integrity of the corpse, and its violation was viewed as a profound curse upon the house of its family.

The Mesopotamian underworld and its dead were portrayed in a vast array of mythological images. By the Neo-Assyrian period, there was a flourishing in the composition and collection of magical texts intended to protect the living from the dead; the prominence of the *kispu* mortuary meal-offering was reasserted by Sargonid kings (who also deliberately abrogated the mortuary cults of their enemies); and literary texts demonstrate an increasing complexity and a variety of depictions of the underworld. The sum total of the data does nothing to disprove Jacobsen's comment about the increasing fascination with the underworld in the Neo-Assyrian period.

One way in which that fascination manifested itself was in the terrorizing, propagandistic rhetoric of the Assyrians, which brought a startling array of images of torture, destruction, and death to the attention of vassals and client states. In this way and others, the empire's increasing power and the highly effective administrative and communications structures brought its ideas to Israel and Judah. The form and impact of that influence probably changed over time; it was neither entirely coercive nor entirely voluntary. The reception of those ideas in Judah by elites – who were motivated to understand the empire but simultaneously suspicious (or even frightened) of it – would have been similarly complex. Specific instances of that reception are discussed in chapters 4 and 5.

2. Death and the Dead in Egypt during the Iron Age II

2.1 Introduction

Ancient Egypt's practices and beliefs surrounding death are the most famous of any ancient civilization; its pyramids and mummies have become the stuff of popular culture, even in far-flung parts of the world. Some of our perception that the Egyptians were preoccupied with death may be due to the nature of archaeological preservation – i.e., the ability of tombs to preserve information while other spheres of culture have been largely lost – but the pervasiveness of death in the ancient Egyptian consciousness should not be underestimated. As Jan Assmann has written: "A comprehensive treatment of the theme of death can ... constitute an introduction to the essence of all of ancient Egyptian culture."[1] (Indeed, his magisterial monograph on the subject constitutes just such an introduction.) In any case, any discussion of ancient Egypt must deal with mortuary data, since it provides "the overwhelming majority of archaeological data" from most periods.[2]

Given Egypt's cultural prestige, it is not at all surprising that its burial practices were known beyond its borders and appear even in the Hebrew Bible (e.g., Gen 50:2). This chapter lays the groundwork for ch. 5, which in turn expands the number of likely references in the Bible to Egyptian afterlife beliefs and burial practices.

The focus of this study on Israel's Iron Age II does not neatly line up with a single period of Egyptian history; it comprises the latter part of the Third Intermediate Period and the beginning of the Late Period (the beginning of which is usually marked by Psamtik I's ascension to begin the Saite Twenty-sixth Dynasty in 664). In chapter 5, I argue that the period of the Kushite Twenty-fifth Dynasty (ca. 755–656) is the most relevant for understanding the passages I have delineated in Isa 1–39.

---

[1] Jan Assmann, *Death and Salvation in Ancient Egypt* (trans. D. Lorton; Ithaca, N.Y.: Cornell University Press, 2005), 2.
[2] Janet E. Richards, *Society and Death in Ancient Egypt: Mortuary Landscapes of the Middle Kingdom* (Cambridge: Cambridge University Press, 2005), 60.

2.2 Historical Sketch

In contrast to the troves of documents recovered from first-millennium Mesopotamia, Egyptian records from the Third Intermediate Period (roughly 1064–664)[3] are not as numerous, especially the monumental royal inscriptions and administrative texts that are so essential to an historian.[4] This state of affairs "continues to bedevil attempts to write a history of relations between the two regions [Egypt and western Asia] in the first third of the first millennium."[5] Much of what we know about Egyptian military activity in the period comes from Assyrian inscriptions and thus dates only to the very end of the Neo-Assyrian period, when the Mesopotamians' imperial reach finally extended into Egypt. Although this means that a precise chronology is exceedingly difficult to reconstruct, some broad outlines can be sketched with confidence.

The eleventh century BCE saw the end of the period of Ramesside rule over Egypt; with its dissolution, the local viziers and chieftains who had governed under the pharaohs became petty kings in their own right. Although this Third Intermediate Period was a time of disunion and unrest, the Egyptian kingdoms remained influential in international affairs. The Delta rulers were typically concerned about challenges from large powers in Palestine and thus worked to subvert them.[6] This would have ensured Egypt both "a buffer against invasion from Asia,"[7] and also the economic benefits of the limited vassalship of the Palestinian states. In general, the Palestinian kingdoms were more likely to view Egypt as an ally against northern powers, and the pharaohs tried to play that role. The Delta kingdoms never became expansionistic like Assyria, however. Thus the Palestinian campaign of Sheshonq in the 930s (noted in 1 Kgs 14:26, 2 Chr 2:2–12) would

---

[3] Regnal dates at the early end of this range (prior to about 800 BCE) are contested and might need to be lowered by about fifty years. For discussion, see Aidan Dodson, "Third Intermediate Period," in *The Oxford Encyclopedia of Ancient Egypt* (Oxford: Oxford University Press, 2001), 389. I have followed the chronology of K. A. Kitchen, *The Third Intermediate Period in Egypt, 1100–650 B.C.* (3rd ed.; Warminster: Aris & Phillips, 1996).

[4] Dodson, "Third Intermediate Period," 388–89: "There are a number of sources of data available for the study of this period, although far more scanty than those preserved from Ramesside times. ... For the latter part of the Third Intermediate Period, numerous private stelae record pious donations, and there are a series of statues of private individuals, both of which frequently mention contemporary monarchs and dates." Many of these texts are now compiled in Robert K. Ritner, *The Libyan Anarchy: Inscriptions from Egypt's Third Intermediate Period* (WAW 21; Atlanta: SBL, 2009).

[5] Donald B. Redford, *Egypt, Canaan and Israel in Ancient Times* (Princeton: Princeton University Press, 1992), 319.

[6] For a general survey of Egyptian military activity in Palestine in the Iron Age II, see Edward Lipiński, *On the Skirts of Canaan in the Iron Age: Historical and Topographical Researches* (OLA 153; Leuven: Peeters, 2006), 95–162.

[7] Redford, *Egypt, Canaan and Israel in Ancient Times*, 318, 337; idem, "Studies in Relations Between Palestine and Egypt During the First Millennium B.C.: II. The Twenty-Second Dynasty," *JAOS* 93 (1973): 14.

have been an exception; and even in that case, "there is no evidence that he made any real attempt to secure the territory he ravaged,"[8] although destruction layers and a fragment of a victory stele at Megiddo attest to his presence.

The "Libyan" kingdoms of the Delta were long content to hold their ground, and Egyptologist Donald Redford portrays these as increasingly provincial chiefdoms without international political ambitions.[9] In the latter half of the eighth century, however, Tefnakhte of Sais in the west Delta unified Lower Egypt and began to press southward. This threat roused the Kushite ruler, Piankhy, who drove back Tefnakhte's forces and eventually conquered the important city of Memphis in 728. Although the Delta would have been his for the taking, Piankhy returned to the Kushite capital of Napata after taking Memphis, leaving a power vacuum in the north.

Tefnakhte and his Libyan successors were only too happy to fill that vacuum in the Delta, but this Egyptian dynasty was a shadow of its former glory. The Delta dynasty continued to be in contact with Palestine, but they would have been little help to its rulers. Consider 1 Kgs 17:4:

[Hoshea, king of Samaria,] sent messengers to King So of Egypt,[10] and offered no tribute to the king of Assyria, as he had done year by year; therefore the king of Assyria confined him and imprisoned him. Then the king of Assyria invaded all the land and came to Samaria; for three years he besieged it.

Whatever the compositional history of this account, it gives an accurate portrayal of the balance of power in this period: the Egyptians, having received tribute from Israel, subsequently disappear from the story and are nowhere to be found when Assyria threatens. The well-known Assyrian campaigns of the late eighth century pressured the Delta rulers from the north, and even the powers of Palestine, which had traditionally dealt with the Delta-based kingdoms,[11] noticed the rise of Kush in the south (see Isa 18). Shabako succeeded Piankhy in 715, and a year later he pressed north for the reconquest of Egypt.

Thus, it was under Kushite rule (in 706) that Egypt extradited the fugitive king of Ashdod back to Assyria, against whom he had rebelled in 712.[12] But it was also the Kushites who came to the aid of Judah when Sennacherib campaigned to the

---

[8] Redford, "Studies in Relations between Palestine and Egypt," 11.
[9] Redford, "Studies in Relations between Palestine and Egypt," 14–15.
[10] This probably refers to Tefnakhte, with the "So" perhaps a distortion of "Sais" (J. Maxwell Miller and John H. Hayes, *A History of Ancient Israel and Judah* [2nd ed.; Louisville, Ky.: Westminster John Knox, 2006], 385). For a full review of the possibilities suggested for the name So, see Pnina Galpaz-Feller, "Is That So? (2 Kings XVII 4)," *RB* 107 (2000): 338–47.
[11] Redford, *Egypt, Canaan and Israel in Ancient Times*, 335.
[12] The extradition was concurrent with Shebitku's ascension to the throne in place of Shabako. See further J. J. M. Roberts, "Isaiah's Egyptian and Nubian Oracles," in *Israel's Prophets and Israel's Past: Essays on the Relationship of Prophetic Texts and Israelite History in Honor of John H. Hayes* (ed. B. E. Kelle and M. B. Moore; Library of Hebrew Bible/Old Testament Studies 446; New York: T&T Clark, 2006), 201–9.

doorstep of Hezekiah in Jerusalem in 701 (see below). It may have been that a tired Assyrian army was surprised by the initiative of the Kushites. The Assyrian *rab šaqeh* mocked the Jerusalemites for relying on the Egyptian pharaoh and calling the latter a "broken reed of a staff, which will pierce the hand of anyone who leans on it" (2 Kgs 18:21), but it is possible that the arrival of a Kushite army caused Sennacherib to rethink his siege (2 Kgs 19:7, 9 // Isa 37:9).[13]

The Kushites do seem to have been a more effective military force than their Delta peers. The Victory Stele of Piye, which recounts events from ca. 728, portrays a Kushite army that was skilled in field and siege warfare, and whose leaders possessed tactical acumen.[14] However, Egypt's interest in Palestine was still as a buffer zone, unlike Assyria's. Under the Kushite monarchs, as earlier, Egypt was content to keep the *status quo* in Palestine, hoping to maintain trading freedom and diplomatic hegemony without any great expenditure of military force. Under these circumstances, it is not hard to see why rulers in Israel and Judah were more inclined to seek Egyptian support than to become caught up in the sausage-grinder of Assyrian ambition.

In the long term, however, Egypt's halfhearted support did little good for Palestine against the might of Assyria; the buffer zone was breached, and Egypt itself came under attack in the early seventh century. Esarhaddon and his son Aššurbanipal, rightly viewing Egypt as a source of unrest in Palestine, campaigned southward in 674 and 667, respectively. These campaigns gave Assyria its largest geographical extent and drove the Kushites out of Memphis and Thebes and all the way back to Napata. In accordance with its imperial practice, Assyria installed Neco of Sais as a puppet ruler over Egypt.

Although Saite Egypt was initially a vassal, it remained in contact with Palestine, including Judah, and with the fading of Assyrian power in the late seventh century, it regained autonomy. However, it was again a disappointment to Judah in the face of the Babylonian onslaught of 587/586 (see Jer 37:5–7). In sum, Egypt was never a serious rival to the Mesopotamian empires, but its culture was always influential, even to its conquerors.

2.3 Mechanisms of Egyptian influence

Egypt has often been ignored in discussions of ancient Near Eastern backgrounds to biblical beliefs about death, but as various sections of chapter 5 will show, this is a very serious oversight in the case of Isaiah. The mechanisms of Egyptian influence during the eighth century are complex, incorporating both direct and

---

[13] See references and discussion of these events in § 1.2.
[14] Pnina Galpaz, "The Victory Stela of King Piye: The Biblical Perspective on War and Peace," *RB* 100 (1993): 399–414.

2.3 Mechanisms of Egyptian influence 61

indirect pathways. Egypt's hegemony in Palestine in the Late Bronze Age and Iron Age IA means that Egyptian culture was to some degree a part of Israel's "Canaanite" heritage. Carolyn Higginbotham has recently shown by her analysis of material culture that Egyptian influence spread through second-millennium BCE Palestine through both direct rule and elite emulation.[15]

In later periods, there was also extensive contact between Egypt and Israel throughout the monarchic periods of Israel and Judah. Sadly, there is nothing from first-millennium Egypt like the Amarna letters (ca. fourteenth century BCE) that would document the discourse between Palestinian states and Egyptian rulers. Nevertheless, both Assyrian and biblical texts demonstrate Palestine's recourse to Egypt in times of distress. For example, when the Philistine city of Ashdod led a revolt of smaller states in 713–711, Sargon II campaigned westward to put down the rebellion. Ashdod's king, Yamani, fled to Egypt for refuge, only to be extradited to Assyria by the Kushite pharaoh. This is recounted in one of Sargon's inscriptions[16] and alluded to in Isaiah 20:1. Another event attested in both biblical and Assyrian sources is the aforementioned Egyptian support of Judah against Sennacherib in 701.[17] At the battle of Eltekeh (west of Jerusalem near the Mediterranean coast), an Egyptian force seeking to stop Assyria's advance met Sennacherib's army. While the Assyrian king claimed a victory and specifically bragged of having taken prisoner Egyptian charioteers and princes, it is not clear that the battle was as successful as it might have been. The Assyrian campaign went no further after that, and Sennacherib returned home.

The (relative) harmony of biblical and extrabiblical sources concerning these and other events is enough to convince many scholars that the biblical primary history of the divided monarchy is generally reliable in its reporting of diplomatic contacts with Egypt. In this case, one would take quite seriously the numerous biblical references to such contacts, both in the histories (1 Kgs 3:1; 9:16; 10:28–29; 11:17–18, 40; 14:25; 2 Kgs 7:6; 17:4; etc.) and in prophetic texts.[18] The very significant biblical tradition of interchange with Egypt should not be overshadowed by the anti-Egyptian exodus traditions and prophetic oracles.[19] Even

---

[15] Carolyn R. Higginbotham, *Egyptianization and Elite Emulation in Ramesside Palestine: Governance and Accommodation on the Imperial Periphery* (Leiden: Brill, 2000). See also Amihai Mazar, *Archaeology of the Land of the Bible, 10,000–586 B.C.E.* (New York: Doubleday, 1990), 296–300. Some striking examples of what K. A. Kitchen called "a cosmopolitan age" are given in "High Society and Lower Ranks in Ramesside Egypt at Home and Abroad," *British Museum Studies in Ancient Egypt and Sudan* 6 (2006): 31–36.

[16] *COS* 118E.

[17] *COS* 119B; cf. 2 Kgs 19:9, Isa 37:9.

[18] For a general survey of the political backgrounds of Isaiah's oracles regarding Kush and Egypt, see Roberts, "Isaiah's Egyptian and Nubian Oracles."

[19] Mordechai Cogan, "The Other Egypt: A Welcome Asylum," in *Texts, Temples, and Traditions: A Tribute to Menahem Haran* (ed. M. V. Fox et al.; Winona Lake, Ind.: Eisenbrauns, 1996), 65–70. Cogan draws particular attention to the law of inclusion in Deut 23:4–9, which is relatively more welcoming toward Egyptians than some of Israel's Canaanite neighbors.

scholars who think that the biblical history shows signs of "heavy-handed editing"[20] and doubt that primary source materials were used by the Deuteronomistic Historian still perceive a general situation of contact between Judah and Egypt. "Given all the contact," wrote Redford, it would be "passing strange" if Judah's culture had been "wholly isolated from influences emanating from the closest major nation-state in the region."[21] There was extensive trade between Egypt and Phoenicia throughout the biblical period, which was only briefly hampered by the conquests of the Assyrians and Babylonians.[22] Redford believes that Egyptian influence on the "Hebrew kingdoms" would probably have come by sea through the coastal states, since overland travel meant passing through as many as nine individual fiefdoms. Pottery evidence suggests that Israel traded with Phoenicia beginning in the eleventh century BCE,[23] and a recent archaeological study of the Palestinian economy in the seventh century concluded that the many fish bones found in Judah suggest "intensive trade" with the seacoast, as do finds of imported wood, shells, and pottery.[24] Although it was militarily weakened at that time, Egypt was still wealthy and a source of desirable material goods for its trading partners; its cultural prestige remained high and its cultural influence significant.[25]

Redford has said various things about the actual level of interaction between Egypt and Israel, but his most prominent conclusion seems to be that "signs of Egyptian influence in the Bible, or specific borrowings by Israelite culture, are remarkably few and certainly do not pop out instantly."[26] John D. Currid laments that this conclusion has been so widely adopted in the biblical studies guild that the relationship between the Hebrew Bible and Egypt has become "a neglected subject."[27]

---

[20] Redford, *Egypt, Canaan and Israel in Ancient Times*, 320.
[21] Redford, *Egypt, Canaan and Israel in Ancient Times*, 365.
[22] Marc Van de Mieroop, *A History of the Ancient Near East, ca. 3000–323 BC* (2nd ed.; Blackwell History of the Ancient World; Malden, Mass.: Blackwell, 2007), 220–22; Ephraim Stern, *Archaeology of the Land of the Bible*, vol. 2, *The Assyrian, Babylonian and Persian Periods, 732–332 BCE* (Anchor Bible Reference Library; New York: Doubleday, 2001), 228–29.
[23] Mazar, *Archaeology of the Land of the Bible*, 514.
[24] Avraham Faust and Ehud Weiss, "Judah, Philistia, and the Mediterranean World: Reconstructing the Economic System of the Seventh Century BCE," *BASOR* 338 (May 2005): 71–92. See also John S. Holladay, Jr., "Judeans (and Phoenicians) in Egypt in the Late Seventh to Sixth Centuries B.C." in *Egypt, Israel, and the Ancient Mediterranean World: Studies in Honor of Donald B. Redford* (ed. G. N. Knoppers and A. Hirsch; Leiden: Brill, 2004), 405–38.
[25] Smith, *Interconnections in the Ancient Near East*, 52.
[26] Redford, *Egypt, Canaan and Israel in Ancient Times*, 365. The tone of Redford's comments in an essay written only a few years earlier are startlingly different; he allows not only for significant Egyptian influence on Israel but also emphasizes West Semitic cultural influence on Egypt: "The Relations between Egypt and Israel from El-Amarna to the Babylonian Conquest," in *Biblical Archaeology Today: Proceedings of the International Congress on Biblical Archaeology, Jerusalem, April 1984* (Jerusalem: Israel Exploration Society: 1985), 192–205.
[27] John D. Currid, *Ancient Egypt and the Old Testament* (Grand Rapids: Baker, 1997), 23–27.

2.3 Mechanisms of Egyptian influence

One problem with the effort to connect these worlds has been its focus on the exodus and on the period of Solomon and David, where the extrabiblical data are very scarce.[28] More positively, Redford has written that it was during the Egyptian Twenty-fourth to Twenty-sixth Dynasties that one might best look for Egyptian influence on the ancient Near East:

It is at that period, say between 725 and 525 B.C., that Egypt and the entire eastern Mediterranean ... found themselves thrown together in a cultural, an economic, and, more importantly, a spiritual community of interests. This period has never been adequately explored by scholars.[29]

The data presented here, while far from being the sort of ambitious study of cultural contacts that Redford envisioned, will emphatically support his thesis.

Iconographic studies by Othmar Keel and Christoph Uehlinger also suggest a later period for focus; they found that Judahite crafts during the Iron IIB era (ca. 925–725) give "evidence of an intense fascination with Egyptian power symbols."[30] This refers to symbols of *political* power, such as the royal *cartouche*; the situation with religious symbols was different. Judah was more resistant to the incorporation of religious iconography than Israel, but this trend too accelerated in Judah by the second half of the eighth century. This increase, Keel and Uehlinger wrote, "relates indirectly to the encroachment of the Assyrians and to the related fact that Judah established considerably closer ties with Egypt under Hezekiah ... when it faced the threat from the north."[31] In other words, Judean adoption of Egyptian religious motifs accelerated as the political relationship between the two nations grew warmer.

There even seem to have been similarities between Kushite and Judean religious innovations: P. Kyle McCarter, among others, has tentatively pointed to "a curious parallel" between Josiah's reforms and the Shabaka Stone (a.k.a. the "Memphite Theology") from the Egyptian 25th dynasty; the Shabaka Stone's

---

[28] The scanty exodus data are well known. On the period of the united monarchy, see, e.g, Paul S. Ash, *David, Solomon and Egypt: A Reassessment* (JSOTSup 297; Sheffield: Sheffield Academic Press, 1999).

[29] Redford, *Egypt, Canaan and Israel in Ancient Times*, 399–400. See also idem, "Studies in Relations between Palestine and Egypt," *passim*.

[30] Othmar Keel and Christoph Uehlinger, *Gods, Goddesses and Images of God in Ancient Israel* (trans. Thomas H. Trapp; Minneapolis: Fortress, 1998), 266.

[31] Keel and Uehlinger, *Gods, Goddesses and Images of God*, 272. See also John Strange, "Some Notes on Biblical and Egyptian Theology," in *Egypt, Israel, and the Ancient Mediterranean World* (Leiden: Brill, 2004), 347. As a specific example of Judean adoption of motifs usually thought of as Egyptian, one might note Strange's earlier argument that the lotus pattern on the walls and doors of Solomon's temple (1 Kgs 6:18–35) suggests that monarchic Jerusalem knew of Egyptian beliefs about the afterlife, since the lotus was an Egyptian symbol of resurrection (Strange, "The Idea of the Afterlife in Ancient Israel: Some Remarks on the Iconography of Solomon's Temple," *PEQ* 117 [1985]: 35–40). Of course, the status of this theory is tenuous since the temple has never been unearthed, and the texts in 1 Kings cannot be dated with certainty.

claim to be a copy of a worm-eaten scroll containing ancient theological precepts is akin to the discovery of the "book of the law in the house of the LORD" (2 Kgs 22:8–13).[32]

More specific to this study, Sarah Israelit-Groll opines that Isaiah "was acquainted with the Egyptian language and culture," as a part of his "deep sensitivity to and subtle conception of the international affairs of his time."[33] The linguistic case is even more difficult to make for Judean knowledge of Egyptian than for knowledge of Akkadian (§ 1.3.1), given that Egyptian is less closely related to Hebrew than Akkadian is. Then again, there was a long history of linguistic contact between Egypt and Palestine – in addition to the letters, inscriptions, and archaeological data from the Bronze Age, one could mention the "Report of Wenamun," the story of the travels of an Egyptian priest during the New Kingdom, which presumes that Wenamun had no trouble communicating with the court of Byblos and also found someone who understood Egyptian at another port of call. This suggests that multilingualism was characteristic of the courts of other major trading centers at that time.[34]

Iron Age Israel and Judah are of course at some remove from those Bronze Age coastal cities, but numerous amulets with hieroglyphic inscriptions have been found from all over Iron Age Palestine, including many Judean and Israelite cities.[35] It is not clear to what extent the wearers of these amulets understood the writing on them, and to what extent the writing was merely viewed as a kind of magic. However, given that there are a number of recognized Egyptian loanwords in Isaiah,[36] the same kind of (at least) fragmentary knowledge among court elites that is theorized for Akkadian may apply to Egyptian as well.

Beyond Isaiah's time, large lacunae in the epigraphic data make the seventh century hard to reconstruct, but from the material culture it appears that Egypt

---

[32] McCarter, "The Religious Reforms of Hezekiah and Josiah," in *Aspects of Monotheism: How God Is One: Symposium at the Smithsonian Institution, October 19, 1996, sponsored by the Resident Associate Program* (ed. Hershel Shanks and Jack Meinhardt; Washington, D.C.: Biblical Archaeology Society, 1997), 57–58. For the text of the Shabaka Stone, see *COS* 1.15 (and literature cited there) or Miriam Lichtheim, *Ancient Egyptian Literature: A Book of Readings* (3 vols.; Berkeley: University of California Press, 1973–80), 1:51–57.

[33] Sarah Israelit-Groll, "The Egyptian Background to Isaiah 19:18," in *Boundaries of the Ancient Near Eastern World: A Tribute to Cyrus H. Gordon* (eds. Meir Lubetski et al.; JSOTSup 273; Sheffield: JSOT Press, 1998), 300–303; here 300, 303.

[34] "The Report of Wenamun," *COS* 1.41; cf. W. S. Smith, *Interconnections in the Ancient Near East: A Study of the Relationships between the Arts of Egypt, the Aegean, and Western Asia* (New Haven: Yale University Press, 1965), 51.

[35] Christian Herrmann, *Ägyptische Amulette aus Palästina/Israel: Mit einem Ausblick auf ihre Rezeption durch das Alte Testament* (Freiburg, Schweiz: Universitätsverlag; Göttingen: Vandenhoeck & Ruprecht, 1994).

[36] See further at § 5.2.3.2; and also Christopher B. Hays, "Damming Egypt/Damning Egypt: The Paronomasia of *skr* and the Unity of Isa 19:1–15," *ZAW* 120 (2008): 612–16; and Christopher B. Hays and Joel M. LeMon, "The Dead and Their Images: An Egyptian Etymology for Hebrew ʾôb," *Journal of Ancient Egyptian Interconnections* 1 (2009): 1–4.

was even more of a force in Palestine during the hiatus between Assyrian and Babylonian control of the area (roughly 630–605).[37]

All this demonstrates that Israel and Judah's political contacts with Egypt brought cultural contacts in their wake. If this is apparent in material culture, one should look for knowledge of Egyptian culture and religion on the part of the eighth-century Hebrew prophets. Indeed, Alviero Niccacci has argued that nearly all of Isaiah 18–20 is the work of Isaiah ben Amoz, and that it reflects extensive knowledge not only of late-eighth-century geopolitics, but also of Egyptian culture and even phraseology.[38] Such knowledge can be found elsewhere in the Hebrew Bible. The universally observed similarity between Prov 22:17–24:22 and the Egyptian "Instruction of Amenemope" is perhaps the clearest instance of the relationship. "It can hardly be doubted," writes Miriam Lichtheim, "that the author of Proverbs was acquainted with the Egyptian work and borrowed from it."[39] Whereas Lichtheim assumes that this literary influence came during the Ramesside period, it is highly unlikely that such influence took place prior to the United Monarchy and the development of a specifically Israelite scribal culture. If one searches for another period in which such influence might have taken place, the time of Isaiah is again promising. In Prov 25:1, one reads, "*These, too, are proverbs of Solomon that the officials of King Hezekiah of Judah copied.*" This calls attention to the possibility that Judean scribes were working with such Egyptian wisdom traditions in the Neo-Assyrian period.[40] Furthermore, it is in this same period that Currid saw the "Nile-Curse" beginning to be employed by the biblical prophets, which suggests an understanding of the Nile's centrality in the Delta's economy.[41]

Although so many signs point to Egyptian cultural influence on Judah during the Neo-Assyrian period, one should not assume that it would always be as clear or as direct as it is in the case of "The Instruction of Amenemope." It is more often filtered or refracted through a native cultural lens so that it is less obvious. Twenty years ago, Klaas Spronk briefly reviewed theories about Egyptian influence on biblical texts relating to the afterlife, finding that in some cases the

---

[37] Stern, *Archaeology of the Land of the Bible*, 228–35; cf. Miller and Hayes, *A History of Ancient Israel*, 446–48; Kuhrt, *The Ancient Near East*, 2.643–44.

[38] Alviero Niccacci, "Isaiah XVIII–XX from an Egyptological Perspective," *VT* 48 (1998): 214–38.

[39] *COS* 1.47. There are those who argue other literary relationships, for example, biblical priority or a Semitic original preceding both texts. For a summary of some of the major positions, see William McKane, *Proverbs: A New Approach* (Philadelphia: Westminster, 1970), 371; or, more recently, Tremper Longman III, *Proverbs* (Grand Rapids: Baker Academic, 2006), 52–54.

[40] R. N. Whybray, "The Sage in the Israelite Court," in *The Sage in Israel and the Ancient Near East* (ed. J. G. Gammie and Leo G. Perdue; Winona Lake, Ind.: Eisenbrauns, 1990), 138.

[41] E.g., Isa 19:5–10; Ezek 30:12; Zech 10:11; Currid, *Ancient Egypt and the Old Testament*, 229–46.

biblical authors seemed to have adopted or modified Egyptian motifs, and in other cases they seemed to inveigh against them.[42] This picture accords well with our study in chapter 5, where we shall see that the references to Egyptian religion in the book of Isaiah have often been overlooked or misunderstood, and that their ideological relationships to Egyptian religion are complex.

2.4 Death in Egypt

This section is limited to surveying briefly the key themes in the Egyptian cults and mythologies surrounding death, and bringing into focus the points at which the Third Intermediate Period shows distinctive emphases or diverges from long-standing Egyptian traditions. While the Egyptian view of death distinguishes itself from those of its neighbors at a significant number of points, this chapter also argues against facile dichotomies between Egyptian views of death and those of Mesopotamians and Judeans.

Despite the large role that tombs have played in our understanding of ancient Egypt, the reader should not think that the antiquarian fascination with Egyptians' mortuary beliefs and practices is a modern phenomenon. No later than the Middle Kingdom, near the start of the second millennium BCE, Egyptian elites began to take an interest the tombs of their predecessors – they began to visit and even restore them.[43]

Given Egypt's massive cultural production surrounding death, no single perspective can account for all the diversity and richness of the data. Egyptian beliefs and practices not only changed over time but were complex and multivalent in any given period. As A. J. Spencer observed, "Egyptians did not necessarily hold a single view of the next world at any one time, but, because of their reluctance to abandon old ideas, were quite capable of maintaining two or more conflicting opinions at once."[44]

---

[42] Klaas Spronk, *Beatific Afterlife in Ancient Israel and in the Ancient Near East* (Alter Orient und Altes Testament 219; Neukirchen-Vluyn: Neukirchener Verlag, 1986), 86–95. Previously cited examples in influence include Ps 22:30's "going down to the dust" and bowing before YHWH, Ezekiel 37's resurrection of the dry bones, Job 19's view of posthumous judgment, and Isa 26:19's "radiant dew."

[43] Richards, *Society and Death in Ancient Egypt*, 50.

[44] A. J. Spencer, *Death in Ancient Egypt* (London: Penguin, 1982), 139; see also Assmann, *Death and Salvation*, 26–27.

2.4.1. Burial and mourning in Egypt

The New Kingdom text "The Instruction of Any" emphasizes the central position that the tomb occupied in Egyptian thought:

> Do not leave your house
> without knowing your place of rest... .
> Furnish your station in the valley [of the dead]
> the grave that shall conceal your corpse.[45]

For the ancient Egyptian, it seems that the need to prepare for death was "ever-present. ... The choice and preparation of one's tomb was one of the tasks befalling every mortal."[46] Those who kept death in mind were praised, which helps explain the scale of some Egyptian burials. Even among the nonroyal artisan class during the New Kingdom, a person might spend a year's salary on a decorated coffin, and half that on a funerary papyrus.[47] The tomb was the ultimate (i.e., both the last and highest) status symbol. C. H. Gordon remarked that to an Egyptian, proper burial "was more important than one's love for wife, children, and possessions," or even than "life, liberty and the pursuit of happiness."[48]

To an earlier generation of scholars, the Egyptian focus on death and funerary preparations seemed morbid, or even tragic; but this view has given way to a more rounded and appreciative view of their humanistic value.[49] As a very popu-

---

[45] *COS* 1.46; Lichtheim, *Ancient Egyptian Literature*, 2:138.

[46] Morenz, *Egyptian Religion*, 192–93.

[47] Edward Wente, "Funerary Beliefs of the Ancient Egyptians: An Interpretation of the Burials and the Texts," *Expedition* 24 (1982): 17–26. Whereas the land for an elite tomb was typically granted by the pharaoh and thus "reflected the owner's position in the hierarchy of the administration, the lavishness of the tomb reflected the individual's personal means," and "[t]he two aspects do not always correspond" (Kanawati, *The Tomb and Beyond*, 8).

[48] C. H. Gordon, "The Marriage and Death of Sinuhe," in J. H. Marks and R. M. Good, eds., *Love & Death in the Ancient Near East: Essays in Honor of Marvin H. Pope* (Guilford, Conn.: Four Quarters, 1987), 44.

[49] In Alan Gardiner's Frazier Lectures of 1935, he noted the Egyptians' "fanatical abhorrence of death" (*The Attitude of the Ancient Egyptians to Death and the Dead* [Frazer Lecture for 1935; Cambridge: Cambridge University Press, 1935], 6). In sum, Gardiner saw the Egyptians as "pathetic"; all their lavish preparations for the afterlife, both material and magical, only showed them to be "panic-stricken as to what might be done or might happen to them after their deaths" (Gardiner, *Attitude*, 20). There is surely an implicit critique here from the standpoint of the more dualistic anthropologies of later Western religions in which, despite the concern for proper burial, it is the fate of the soul that is most emphasized. A generation later, Siegfried Morenz would offer an eloquent apologia for Egypt's afterlife practices, seeking to emphasize the way in which the hope for life was integrated into Egypt's focus on death: "In spite of his intense awareness of death the Egyptian also made an active contribution to the affairs of this world," he wrote. "The Egyptian was not crushed by death, which he experienced so pervasively and to which he attached such negative connotations. Instead he was inspired by it to splendid creative accomplishments. To borrow a germane phrase: *hic gaudet mors succurrere vitae*" ("Here death rejoices to serve life") (*Egyptian Religion* [Ithaca, N.Y.: Cornell University Press, 1973], 197–98).

lar and long-lived Egyptian phrase put it: "the house of death counts for life." That is, "the tomb served life."[50] There was a social function as well: the tomb was "not only an eternal house for the deceased, but also a point of connection between the living and the dead."[51]

The cultural emphasis on burial can be found from the earliest dynastic periods onward, but with significant differences according to social rank, and with diachronic shifts in specific beliefs and practices. It could be said that Egyptian burials were characterized by their imposing architecture, lavish grave provisions, their efforts to preserve the body, and the inclusion of magical texts, although the nature and distribution of each of these elements changed over time.

The best-known type of Egyptian tomb architecture is the pyramid, but the most famous and imposing pyramids are the work of very early pharaohs, peaking in the fourth through sixth dynasties (ca. 2625–2170 BCE). The great pyramids integrated the burial-place of the pharaoh and the chapel at which his mortuary cult could be practiced (see below). Eventually, however, rulers came to see that the pyramids did not afford the corpse protection, since determined grave robbers could always penetrate their defenses. Thus, the pharaohs and other high officials began to separate their tombs from their mortuary chapels. The external structures of the tombs shrank, although they were still often capped by a pyramidion (a miniaturized pyramid), and the burial chambers were hidden away, cut into cliffs.[52] These "rock tombs" sometimes had chapels cut into the cliffs as well as burial chambers, but the massive pyramids that had characterized pharaonic burials in the early periods disappeared during the Middle and New Kingdoms.

To understand Egyptian mortuary religion in later periods, one could begin at the end of the Amarna period (1360–1340 BCE), which marked a major watershed. Among the effects of Akhenaten's reform had been to radically de-emphasize the netherworld. In Amarna solar religion, there was "only one realm: that of the here and now, of the reality lit up by the sun god."[53] However, "[w]hen Amarna religion failed and the traditional religion was restored, those aspects of it which Akhenaten had particularly persecuted and excluded were now placed center stage and elaborated on." Thus, the later periods became for Egypt a time

---

However, Lichtheim's scathingly negative assessment of the Coffin Texts (*AEL* I.131) as lacking in humility and reason, and instead as "grandiose," "petty," and "delusional," demonstrates how strangely these texts can still ring in modern Western ears.

[50] Assmann, *Death and Salvation*, 12–13. The quotation may be found in the Instruction of Djedefhor, among other places.

[51] Richards, *Society and Death in Ancient Egypt*, 62.

[52] Spencer, *Death in Ancient Egypt*, 227; Françoise Dunand and Roger Lichtenberg, *Les Momies et la Mort en Egypte* (Paris: Errance, 1998), 90.

[53] Assmann, *Death and Salvation*, 15. On Akhenaton's rejection of Osirian religion and the underworld, see Donald B. Redford, *Akhenaten: The Heretic King* (Princeton: Princeton University Press, 1984), 175–76.

of increased speculation about the netherworld, just as the first millennium was in Mesopotamia. Artistic portrayals of the underworld, which had been repressed amid the "deiconization" of the Amarna period, also saw a boom.[54]

After the power and glory of the Ramesside period, much of the Third Intermediate Period could be seen as a relatively dark age. During Isaiah of Jerusalem's prophetic career, however, there was a new flourishing of Egyptian burial practices. In the eighth century, when the Kushite (i.e., Nubian) kings ruled over Lower (Delta) Egypt for the first time, they came to admire and emulate classical Egyptian art, architecture, and religious practices.[55] The Twenty-fifth and Twenty-sixth (Saite) Dynasties (ca. 747–656) marked a zenith in "tourism to, restoration of, and commemoration in ancient cemeteries."[56] This trend was evident in tomb design:

> The deliberate revivalism of the period is seen in the careful copying of motifs and styles from all previous periods in Egyptian history. Massive tomb complexes were built at Thebes along the causeway of the Hatshepsut mortuary temple at Deir el-Bahri. Painted tombs and relief-decorated rock-cut tombs also reappear. These elaborate tombs continue into the Saite Period, along with great shaft tombs containing massive stone sarcophagi and great rock-cut catacombs.[57]

In this period, many high officials had monumental tombs constructed in the style of royalty.[58] (The classicizing tendency was also apparent in theological texts such as the aforementioned, pseudepigraphic "Memphite Theology," which claimed to be a copy of a text from a much older period.[59])

Egyptian mourning practices included smearing the dead and one's face with dust, baring and beating breasts, tearing of clothing, crouching low or other symbolic postures. Men and women are sometimes portrayed as grieving separately in tomb decorations.[60] In early periods, men were portrayed in iconography as stoic, but after the Amarna period they too could be depicted expressing

---

[54] Redford, *Akhenaten*, 225–27; Assmann, *Death and Salvation*, 251.

[55] John H. Taylor, *Death and the Afterlife in Ancient Egypt* (Chicago: University of Chicago Press, 2001), 154; Dunand and Lichtenberg, *Les Momies et la Mort en Egypte*, 93. This was not a matter of adopting a novel and exotic religion, of course; Delta Egypt had long ruled over Kush with an Egyptianized administration, including religious imposition. See discussion in K. Lawson Younger, Jr., *Ancient Conquest Accounts: A Study in Ancient Near Eastern and Biblical History Writing* (JSOTSup 98; Sheffield: JSOT Press, 1990), 175–89.

[56] Richards, *Society and Death in Ancient Egypt*, 52.

[57] Sue D'Auria, Peter Lacovara, and Catharine H. Roehrig. *Mummies & Magic: The Funerary Arts of Ancient Egypt* (Boston: Northeastern University Press, 1988), 24.

[58] Taylor, *Death and the Afterlife in Ancient Egypt*, 154; Dunand and Lichtenberg, *Les Momies et la Mort en Egypte*, 94. László Török points out that although the Egyptianization of tombs was complete among Kushite royalty, the same could not be said for the elite and middle classes (*The Kingdom of Kush: Handbook of the Napatan-Meroitic Civilization* [Leiden: Brill, 1997], 326–32).

[59] See above, n. 32.

[60] Kanawati, *The Tomb and Beyond*, 29.

pain and sadness.[61] The wealthy might have professional mourners hired for their funeral.[62]

Death was not an entirely somber occasion, however. Burial was accompanied by a feast at the tomb, and often dancing, and the deceased was invited into these festivities by means of the "Opening of the Mouth" ritual, which allowed the mummy to receive its protecting spirit (*ka*) and also food offerings.[63] The ritual meal was held on an offering table in the funerary chapel, in which relatives and mourners took part. This feast might include libations, incense offerings, and the sacrifice of cattle, and could be repeated intermittently. During the Middle Kingdom and the New Kingdom, the royal dead were mourned in a "Feast of the Valley" at Thebes, which "joined the living and the dead in common and bibulous festivities: the families of the dead, in the retinue of Amon, would come to visit this necropolis in the West."[64]

Herodotus cites the exhortation of one of these feasts: "Gaze here,[65] and drink and be merry; for when you die, such will you be."[66] Although one might doubt a Greek historian's account of ancient Egypt, Herodotus's account of Egypt has been praised as the "earliest example of *vergleichende Religionsgeschichte*" and as "little short of brilliant" for its time.[67] Indeed, there is reason to credit the accuracy of this particular detail, since banquet songs from the Middle Kingdom onward emphasize the same themes; for example, the "Song from the Tomb of King Intef":

> Hence rejoice in your heart!
> Forgetfulness profits you,
> Follow your heart as long as you live!
> Put myrrh on your head,
> Dress in fine linen,
> Anoint yourself with oils fit for a god,
> Heap up your joys,
> Let your heart not sink!
> Follow your heart and your happiness,
> Do your things on earth as your heart commands!
> When there comes to you that day of mourning,
> The Weary-hearted hears not their mourning,
> Wailing saves no man from the pit.[68]

---

[61] Assmann, *Death and Salvation*, 114.
[62] Taylor, *Death and the Afterlife in Ancient Egypt*, 188.
[63] Assmann, *Death and Salvation*, 310–16; Taylor, *Death and the Afterlife in Ancient Egypt*, 190.
[64] Morenz, *Egyptian Religion*, 194.
[65] Perhaps at a statue or portrait of the deceased, or even the mummy itself, if it had not yet been buried.
[66] Morenz, *Egyptian Religion*, 195.
[67] Alan B. Lloyd, *Herodotus, Book II, vol. I, Introduction* (Leiden: Brill, 1975), 170.
[68] Lichtheim, *Ancient Egyptian Literature*, 1:197. "The Weary-hearted" refers to Osiris.

In addition to the similarities to Isa 22:13 (especially to Herodotus's formulation, admittedly), one can find similar advice throughout Ecclesiastes.

Although archaeological data is still being assessed, there are also a number of bust portraits from Egypt that are now generally accepted to have been displayed in private homes for ancestor-cult purposes – so that the deceased could participate in family feasting – and it may even be that mummies were sometimes kept in nonroyal homes for the same purpose.[69]

Mummification, the preservation of the physical body, was the "distinguishing feature of Egyptian mortuary practice,"[70] though the ways it was carried out varied. Not only was the body itself treated and stuffed in various ways to make it appear as lifelike as possible, but wrappings, coverings, and sarcophagi might all be decorated to represent the decedent in living splendor. The ideal period of embalming and mourning was seventy days, as is attested in various texts from the Eighteenth Dynasty onward, but this seems to have been practiced only in very elite and elaborate cases.[71] The quality of the work varied not only by social class, but also by period; it was generally worse in later periods. But in any case, mummification was seen as central to the goal of overcoming death. Mummification was not merely a decorative or preservative art, but also one of the means of endowing the deceased with the powers necessary to reach the happy afterlife; in the Egyptians' phrase, the mummy was "filled with magic."[72]

In burial practices as in other ways, the Twenty-fifth and Twenty-sixth Dynasties were a locus of change, as a new type of anthropoid case was introduced in which the image of the deceased in mummified form and on a pedestal was painted onto the lid. Beaded funerary cloaks for the mummy also came into use at that time.[73]

Egyptian graves were provisioned with supplies in order that the deceased might in some way live happily in the hereafter. This would commonly have entailed the sort of food and drink found in graves throughout the ancient Near East, but in the case of royal and elite tombs, could also include furniture, jewels, weapons, games, and the wide apparatus of paraphernalia one would need to

---

[69] Barbara E. Borg, "The Dead as a Guest at Table? Continuity and Change in the Egyptian Cult of the Dead" in *Portraits and Masks: Burial Customs in Roman Egypt* (ed. Morris L. Bierbrier; London: British Museum Press, 1997), 26–32; Werner Kaiser, "Zur Buste als einer Darstellungsform ägyptischer Rundplastik," *Mitteilungen des Deutschen Archäologischen Instituts Kairo* 46 (1990): 269–85.

[70] Robert K. Ritner, "Magic," in *The Oxford Dictionary of Ancient Egypt* (ed. Donald B. Redford; New York: Oxford University Press, 2001), 334.

[71] Taylor, *Death and the Afterlife in Ancient Egypt*, 77. For a more detailed discussion of the texts and periods of mummification, see Arthur F. Shore, "Human and Divine Mummification" in *Studies in Pharaonic Religion and Society in Honour of J. Gwyn Griffiths* (ed. Alan B. Lloyd; London: Egypt Exploration Society, 1992), 226–35.

[72] Assmann, *Death and Salvation*, 33.

[73] Salima Ikram, *Death and Burial in Ancient Egypt* (Harlow: Longman, 2003), 101–2.

prepare bread, weave cloth, etc. At first such implements were full-sized, but in later periods they were miniaturized or even represented pictographically. Similarly, elite graves were supplied with staffs of servants represented by statuettes called *shabtis* – or *ushabtis* in later periods such as the Third Intermediate, when they were generally crude and mass-produced.[74] Nor were grave goods only of a practical nature; they also included amulets, "magic bricks" and other magical figurines, including (in later periods) fertility figurines. The provisioning of the tomb of Tutankhamun (1334–1325 BCE) was so extensive that "debate continues over whether so much could have been buried in each of the New Kingdom royal tombs."[75] His tomb included everything a boy king could want, from model ships to full-sized chariots.

It is commonly observed that the Egyptian envisaged the happy afterlife as "a continued corporeal existence."[76] Herman te Velde, however, has argued that that common idea is a modern misunderstanding: "This approach would leave the Egyptians little other motivation than the completely stupid idea that you can take it with you. But the matter is not so simple."[77] He uses the example of a folding chair from Tutankhamun's tomb that did not fold as a real chair would have: the chair was not actually intended for continued life, he argues, but was a symbol; models and images of food are perhaps better known examples of the same phenomenon. He concludes, "Just as the Egyptians when giving shape to their gods knew that the true nature and the true form of the gods was hidden, they also knew that the true nature and form of the life after death was hidden."[78] Spell 175 of the Book of the Dead poses a question that reflects such an agnosticism: "Atum, what does it mean, that I proceed there, the Land of Silence, which has no water and no air and is very deep and dark, and where all is lacking and one lives in quietness of heart?" It does indeed seem that the Egyptians were aware that the afterlife was a mystery into which their eyes could not quite see, as the discussion of pessimism below suggests (§ 2.4.3).

In any case, care of the dead continued after the funeral. "Tombs were intended to be visited by posterity,"[79] and mortuary stelae were placed in or outside Egyptian tombs in every period. They not only identified the one buried in the tomb; they also often bore prayers for the care of his or her ghost, or depicted the

---

[74] Ikram, *Death and Burial in Ancient Egypt*, 131.
[75] Leonard H. Lesko, "Death and Afterlife in Ancient Egyptian Thought," in *Civilizations of the Ancient Near East* (ed. Jack M. Sasson; Peabody, Mass.: Hendrickson, 2000), 1773.
[76] Morenz, *Egyptian Religion*, 190.
[77] He grants that "there will have been stupid people in the Egyptian culture as in ours"! Herman te Velde, "Commemoration in Ancient Egypt," in *Visible Religion: Annual For Religious Iconography, 1982, Volume I – Commemorative Figures: Papers Presented To Dr. Th. P. Van Baaren On The Occasion Of His Seventieth Birthday, May 13, 1982* (eds. H. G. Kippenberg, L. P. van den Bosch et al. E. J. Brill: Leiden, 1982), 138.
[78] Te Velde, "Commemoration in Ancient Egypt," 138.
[79] Assmann, *Death and Salvation*, 56.

deceased receiving bountiful food and drink offerings in the afterlife.[80] In the New Kingdom and into the Late Period, a particular genre appeared called the 3ḥ ikr n Rᶜ ("able spirit of Re") stela, which depicted the deceased with that rubric, indicating that he or she was powerful, righteous, and could expect to ride in the sun bark with the god Re. This was the closest a nonroyal person could come to divinization. In his seminal study on ancestor worship, R. J. Demarée concluded that these stelae "were an element of the house-cult for deceased relatives" and that "the worship of elders/ancestors definitely formed part of an ancestor cult in Ancient Egypt."[81] The importance of this cult can hardly be overemphasized; as a Late Period saying put it, "One lives, if his name is mentioned."[82] As in Mesopotamia, this was first and foremost portrayed as a duty of sons toward fathers,[83] and a rich man would provide for mortuary care in his will. As elsewhere, adoption was an option for the childless, to assure that there would be "one who pours water on his hands as a genuine eldest son."[84] A distinctive feature of the Kushite royal funerary cult was a comparable emphasis on the cult of the king's dead female kin.[85] False doors or stelae were used to symbolize a door through which the deceased could emerge to receive offerings.

If the sanctity of the tomb, the wholeness of the body, and the adequacy of provisions were the dead's sole hopes for the afterlife, then the prospects were bleak. Tombs were almost always robbed, and usually not long after the burial. Tomb robbery papyri from the Twentieth Dynasty, the last of the New Kingdom, show that the New Kingdom necropolis had already been thoroughly plundered.[86] Grave goods, including even coffins, were sometimes reused, and the corpse was often mutilated, perhaps in an attempt to render the deceased powerless.[87] Perhaps as a result of the awareness of robbers' depredations, Egyptians placed increasing emphasis on magical means of attaining the afterlife. This can be seen not only in the increasingly symbolic nature of grave goods, but also in

---

[80] Regina Hölzl, "Stela," in *Oxford Encyclopedia of Ancient Egypt* (Oxford: Oxford University Press, 2001), 3:319–24. Karl Martin, "Stele," in *Lexikon der Ägyptologie* (Wiesbaden, Otto Harrassowitz: 1986), 6:1–6.

[81] R. J. Demarée, *The 3ḥ ikr n Rᶜ-Stelae: On Ancestor Worship in Ancient Egypt* (Leiden: Nederlands Instituut voor het Nabije Oosten, 1983), 290. See also Alan R. Schulman, "Some Observations About the 3ḥ ikr n Rᶜ Stelae," BO 43 (1986): 347.

[82] Cited in Assmann, *Death and Salvation*, 39.

[83] Assmann, *Death and Salvation*, 41–52.

[84] Nicola Harrington, "Children and the Dead in New Kingdom Egypt" in *Current Research in Egyptology 2006: Proceedings of the Seventh Annual Symposium, University of Oxford, April 2006* (ed. Maria Cannata; Oxford: Oxbow, 2007), 55.

[85] Török, *Kingdom of Kush*, 329–30.

[86] E.g., the striking accounts of tomb-robbing from the Amherst Papyrus published in T. Eric Peet, *The Great Tomb-Robberies of the Twentieth Egyptian Dynasty* (Oxford: Clarendon, 1930) and Jean Capart et al., "New Light on the Ramesside Tomb-Robberies," JEA 22 (1936): 169–93.

[87] Ritner, "Magic," 336.

the rise of offering formulae in place of mortuary cults. While actual mortuary cults (akin to the aforementioned Mesopotamian *kispu*) were practiced – possibly over a long period for kings – they lasted at most a generation or two for non-royal individuals, and for any person they failed eventually. With offering formulae, any person visiting the chapel or burial site could speak a prayer to "supply" the deceased.[88] This preference for texts over physical preparation could be taken even further: As part of his case for the superiority of the scribal life, the author of the Ramesside-period Papyrus Chester Beatty IV opined; "Better is a book than a graven stela, than a solid tomb enclosure. [Books] act as chapels and tombs in the heart of him who speaks their name."[89]

The ancient Egyptian's magical repertoire for flourishing in the afterlife was by no means exhausted by goods and offerings. Funerary texts (or "underworld books") were series of magical spells placed with the mummified body and intended to aid the deceased in his quest for a happy afterlife. The nature of the spells varied, but they eventually included everything from keeping the body whole, to transforming the bearer into various animals (esp. birds, which symbolized the soul's freedom to leave the tomb), to proclamations of innocence from wrongdoing, to specific disavowals of certain negative fates that could await the dead in the afterlife, such as eating feces. The Pyramid Texts were the earliest exemplar, intended only for pharaohs in the Old Kingdom. In the Middle Kingdom, this gave rise to the Coffin Texts, which drew on some of the same material found in the Pyramid Texts,[90] but were used by elites other than the king. In the New Kingdom, the "Book of Going Forth by Day" (sometimes called simply "The Book of the Dead") appeared. While open to an even broader spectrum of society, this latter book became the most important afterlife text through the Ptolemaic period.[91] During the Third Intermediate Period, the "Book of Going Forth by Day" was even "used extensively in royal tombs, reversing the previous emphasis."[92] Due in part to its "extraordinary popularity," the book attained a relatively fixed, canonical form by the Saite Twenty-sixth Dynasty.[93]

The Third Intermediate Period might be said to be a high point in a long process that is generally referred to as the "democratization of death" in Egypt, although that process began after the Old Kingdom.[94] Democratization went

---

[88] Cf. Ritner, "Magic," 334.
[89] Kanawati, *The Tomb and Beyond*, 46.
[90] For the reuse and reinterpretation of older traditions in the underworld books, see Ritner, "Magic," 334.
[91] Taylor, *Death and the Afterlife in Ancient Egypt*, 198.
[92] Salima Ikram, *Death and Burial in Ancient Egypt* (Harlow, England: Longman, 2003), 45.
[93] Assmann, *Death and Salvation*, 204, 250.
[94] Note, for example, Hans Goedicke's discussion of the shifting formulae used in tomb inscriptions for passing from death to life, which reflect a decreased connection of the private funerary cult to ideas of kingship, and a shift instead to Osirian religion and a more individualistic focus: Goedicke, "The Egyptian Idea of Passing from Life to Death (An Interpretation)," *Orientalia* 24 (1955): 225–239.

hand in hand with elaboration, a phenomenon that Assmann connects to the brief "abolition of the afterlife" by Akhenaten: "When Amarna religion failed and the traditional religion was restored, those aspects of it which Akhenaten had particularly persecuted and excluded were now placed center stage and elaborated on."[95] Thus at that time, interest in and books about the afterlife "experienced an enormous upswing"[96] that continued into the later periods. This extended the attestation of afterlife beliefs not only to wider portion of social classes, but also to children. Whereas in earlier periods even elite children were generally not buried like adults, but rather in pits or under the floors of houses,[97] in the Third Intermediate period, one begins see to individual funerary monuments for the young.[98]

Nevertheless, when one tries to assess the place of the Third Intermediate Period in the long and rich history of Egyptian beliefs and practices regarding death, one encounters a problem familiar from the study of other regions: a decided incompleteness in the data. It has been noted that the number of Egyptian burials that have been excavated and recorded is only a small percentage of the total population of a given community in a given time. As Naguib Kanawati points out, for most of ancient Egyptian history, "owning any tomb, large or small, decorated or undecorated was ... a favor reserved for the royal family and administrative classes, [so that] we know almost nothing about the fate of populace, the larger portion of society."[99] Even where the unmarked graves of common people have been found, they have often been ignored – at best. Archaeologists, in their haste to excavate elite graves, regularly discarded surface burials of commoners without recording them, especially in the early period of modern Egyptological research.[100] Furthermore, even many elite individuals did not complete their tombs with inscriptions and decoration.[101] This means that the data sample for research is fairly limited. Furthermore, some aspects of Egyptian burial that might surprise us and complicate our ideas about their beliefs – such as the aforementioned burial practices for children – are not widely reported in mainstream publications.

Given the problems with the data, how accurate is the phrase "democratization of death"? It is possible that the middle and lower classes in Egypt held beliefs

---

[95] Assmann, *Death and Salvation*, 15.
[96] Assmann, *Death and Salvation*, 16.
[97] Richards, *Society and Death in Ancient Egypt*, 66; Naguib Kanawati, *The Tomb and Beyond: Burial Customs of Egyptian Officials* (Warminster, England: Aris & Phillips, 2001), 5; Harrington, "Children and the Dead in New Kingdom Egypt," 60–61.
[98] Harrington, "Children and the Dead in New Kingdom Egypt," 63.
[99] Kanawati, *The Tomb and Beyond*, 13.
[100] Richards, *Society and Death in Ancient Egypt*, 66–67.
[101] For example, Naguib Kanawati reports that only 60 of 884 tombs in El-Hawawish, a cemetery in use during the First Intermediate Kingdom and Middle Kingdom, had their walls plastered and decorated (Kanawati, *The Tomb and Beyond*, 13).

similar to those of the kings even during the Old Kingdom, and that our impression of democratization is only due to the fact that it is royal tombs and texts that have survived.[102] Nevertheless, as long as one bears in mind that one is speaking of a democratization of cultural production only, and that ancient beliefs are accessible only through that imperfect optic, then the problem becomes bearable. Indeed, in studying cultural diffusion across international lines, the widening of certain kinds of cultural production is precisely the point: the same elites who produced and consumed the materials are likely to have been involved in the kind of diplomacy and trade that would have resulted in cultural contacts. The distinctively Egyptian coffins of Late Bronze Age Egyptian soldiers in Palestine, which were copied by the Philistines, the Ammonites and others into the Iron Age, are only one example of cultural diffusion.[103]

2.4.2 The Egyptian dead

Since one of Isaiah's foremost characterizations of the Egyptians was as a people who consulted spirits and ghosts as gods (see § 5.2.3.2), a primary interest of this study is to determine whether such a claim had any historical reference or veracity between the eighth century and the exile. Did the Egyptians view their dead as powerful – in particular, as capable of supplying hidden knowledge – and, if so, how did they believe they could have access to their power?

Egyptian theological anthropology – that is, its view of the parts of the human soul – was still more complex than that of its neighbors. The *akh* (3ḫ) of a dead person was the powerful, divinized spirit of a deceased person, which was thought able to act in ways that the living could perceive. "Living individuals beset with problems could appeal to the *akh* of a relative to intercede against other *akh*s believed to be causing their grief or aiding their tormentors."[104] (We shall return shortly to these requests and the beliefs that undergirded them.) In addition, a person was thought to consist of numerous *kheperu* (ḫprw), or aspects of human existence, all of which needed to be preserved through eternity. These included the *ba*, *ka*, and *šuyt*,[105] though one could also mention "the name" and "the heart" as distinct aspect of the Egyptian personality.[106]

---

[102] So Schulman, "Some Observations," 312: "The fact that, in the Old Kingdom, they are not attested in the great religious literature with reference to private individuals is certainly due to the nature of the literature itself, the Pyramid Texts which, after all, is concerned with the dead king, not the dead commoner. Yet the cult of the dead commoner certainly flourished then as it did in all periods of Egyptian history."
[103] Stern, *Archaeology of the Land of the Bible*, 256.
[104] Lesko, "Death and Afterlife," 1764.
[105] Lesko, "Death and Afterlife," 1763–64; cf. Assmann, *Death and Salvation*, 14.
[106] Alan B. Lloyd, "Psychology and Society in the Ancient Egyptian Cult of the Dead" in *Religion and Philosophy in Ancient Egypt* (ed. James P. Allen et al.; Yale Egyptological Studies 3; New Haven, Conn.: Yale University, 1989), 120.

A few more words about each of the *kheperu* are in order. The *ba* (*b3*) was seen as active during life as well as after death, as is evident from "The Dispute between a Man and His *Ba*," from the Middle Kingdom.[107] In this wisdom dialogue debating the desirability of life, the *ba* is a sort of intellectual faculty or conscience. In death, the *ba* – often represented iconographically as a bird with a human head – was a significant feature of ancient Egyptian beliefs about the world of the dead. According to texts from the Middle Kingdom onward, the *ba*-bird was able to "leave the grave-shaft ... and provide the corpse, which remained in the depths, with every good thing."[108] This can be seen on illustrated papyri of the "Book of Going Forth by Day," in which the *ba* is shown rising up from the tomb or perching atop its owner.

Apart from the *ba*, the other aspects of the soul are difficult enough to define that one should not put much stock in any brief explanations.[109] The *ka* (*k3*) has been described as a person's "vital force."[110] With respect to the dead, it was the "vehicle of vindication" that ensured the person's social status.[111] It was often embodied as a statue or simply a bust of the deceased, which was believed to guarantee the person's survival even if the corpse was destroyed. The *ka*, even of common people, was represented as divine in hieroglyphic writing.[112] The *akh* was sometimes described as the union of the *ba* and the *ka*, both of which in turn depended on the preservation of the physical body,[113] which helps to explain the significance of mummification.

The "shadow" (*šwt*), was portrayed as a black silhouette of the deceased's earthly form. It was another aspect of the soul that a person sought to free by magical means. Finally, the name (*rn*) was part of the person's essence, and having it forgotten or destroyed meant total destruction; and the heart (*ỉb*) was the seat of the intellect.[114]

In Egypt, "the dead are called 'gods' from an early period on."[115] As in other ancient Near Eastern cultures, dead kings seem to have been the first who recorded the belief that they would be with the gods after death and would have

---

[107] Lichtheim, *Ancient Egyptian Literature*, 1:163–68.
[108] Keel, *The Symbolism of the Biblical World: Ancient Near Eastern Iconography and the Book of Psalms* (tr. Timothy J. Hallett; New York: Seabury Press, 1978), 65.
[109] Even Assmann despairs of a definition of the *ka*, for example: "For every attempt at a definition, contrary examples could be adduced" (*Death and Salvation*, 96).
[110] For discussion and literature, see Andrew A. Gordon, "The *ka* as an Animating Force," *Journal of the American Research Center in Egypt* 33 (1996): 31–35.
[111] Assmann, *Death and Salvation*, 97.
[112] Kanawati, *The Tomb and Beyond*, 20.
[113] Salima Ikram, "Afterlife Beliefs and Burial Customs" in *The Egyptian World* (ed. Toby Wilkinson; New York: Routledge, 2007), 342.
[114] Lloyd, "Psychology and Society in the Ancient Egyptian Cult of the Dead," 119.
[115] Erik Hornung, *Conceptions of God in Ancient Egypt: The One and the Many* (trans. J. Baines; Ithaca, N.Y.: Cornell University Press, 1982), 62.

divine powers. Unlike in other cultures, the dead king in Egypt was said actually to take the place of a named high god. For example, one of Pepi I's spells says that he has died only so that he may "take control as a god, as Osiris' replacement."[116] In later periods, consonant with the oft-noted "democratization of death," anyone could become "an Osiris" – or at least anyone who had access to the magical texts that promised such power (women were more often identified with Hathor[117]). The dead also identify with other gods, and they "occasionally depart from the normal usage and do not identify with specific deities" but with "god" (*ntr*) in general.[118] For example, Coffin Texts 411 reads, "'God' is my name. I do not forget it, this name of mine." The association of the dead with gods is another indication of their potential positive power.

Because the Egyptian portraits of death as deification or continued happy existence are more numerous and more detailed than in other cultures, it has sometimes been assumed that the Egyptian view of the dead is relatively distinctive. For example, Spencer asserted that "[t]he dead were not ... thought to be particularly malevolent, as is often the case in other cultures."[119] Similarly, Gardiner cautioned that "to fear death and to fear the dead are two very different things,"[120] and that Egyptians feared the first but not the second. However, I perceive only a difference of degree between Egypt and Mesopotamia, not a difference of kind. The Egyptians feared not only death, but in many cases the dead as well.[121] Demarée deduced from his study of funerary stelae a picture of the Egyptian dead that is highly reminiscent of Mesopotamia: in response to offerings, they were believed to serve the wishes of the living, including acting as intermediaries to the gods, but – particularly in the New Kingdom – they "had to be kept appeased ... in order to prevent them from becoming haunting spirits."[122] The Instruction of Any, from the New Kingdom, is clear on this point:

Satisfy the ancestral spirit; do what he wishes.
Keep yourself clear of what he abominates.
that you may remain unscathed by his many hurts.

---

[116] Pepi I's Spell 4 in James P. Allen, *The Ancient Egyptian Pyramid Texts* (SBL Writings from the Ancient World 23; Atlanta: Society of Biblical Literature, 2005), 100.
[117] Kanawati, *The Tomb and Beyond*, 43.
[118] Hornung, *Conceptions of God in Ancient Egypt*, 58–59.
[119] Spencer, *Death in Ancient Egypt*, 73.
[120] Gardiner, *Attitude of the Ancient Egyptians to Death*, 7; also John Barclay Burns, "Some Conceptions of the Afterlife in Ancient Egyptian Thought," *The Philosophical Journal, Glasgow* 9 (1972): 140.
[121] Even Gardiner's conscience required him to grant that the magical spells "do betray at least a certain degree of fear of the dead" (*Attitude of the Ancient Egyptians to Death*, 18).
[122] Demarée, *The 3ḥ ikr n Rꜥ-Stelae*, 280. Assmann contrasts the Egyptians' sense of control over the "border-crossings" between the realms of the living and the dead (*Death and Salvation*, 158–63). This seems to contradict the view of other scholars and may be more reflective of early periods than later ones.

2.4 Death in Egypt

Beware of every sort of damage.
The cow in the field was stolen?
It is he who does the like.
As for any loss from the threshing floor in the field –
"That is the ancestral spirit," one says.[123]

Positively, the deceased could also be "a protection to his children daily."[124] The literary dialogue "The Dispute of a Man with His *Ba*" says that "the one who is yonder [i.e., in the land of the dead] will be a living god, punishing the evildoer's crime."[125]

The point of strongest similarity between Egypt and Mesopotamia regarding fear of the dead is found in the Egyptian magical texts intended to protect against the dead. These have come down to us in collections of "everyday magic,"[126] that is, protective texts from private collections, not temples or royal settings. Thus, these spells serve as a complement to some of the books of the dead, which were initially more elite compositions. Concerns about "male dead (*mt*) or female dead" are pervasive in these spells; sicknesses and many other problems are blamed on them. For example, one spell seeks to prevent "any male dead, any female dead, any male opponent, any female opponent which is anywhere in the body of NN born of NN from killing him."[127]

Demons and the dead were arguably distinct entities, but in such spells they could be used in the very same contexts, a situation similar to that in Mesopotamia. Also similar was the inclusion of both these entities as part of the category of "gods."[128] "Some demons were emanations of human beings, either dead or alive," writes Dmitri Meeks.[129] They might be "either dangerous or beneficial to humans."[130] Nevertheless, it is possible to distinguish, at least linguistically, between the roaming dead (*mwt*) and spirits (*3ḫ*) on the one hand, and demons on the other.[131] There is no native Egyptian word for "demon," so they can be

---

[123] Cited in Assmann, *Death and Salvation*, 163. Cf. the similar quotation from a Tuthmosis III-era tomb on p. 219.

[124] Inscription from Theban Tomb 83, cited in Assmann, *Death and Salvation*, 216.

[125] Lichtheim, *Ancient Egyptian Literature*, 1:168.

[126] J. F. Borghouts, *Ancient Egyptian Magical Texts* (Nisaba 9; Leiden: Brill, 1978), vii. See also the Demotic magical papyri in Hans Dieter Betz, *The Greek Magical Papyri in Translation, Including the Demotic Spells* (2nd ed.; Chicago: University of Chicago Press, 1996), 199–200, 238–39. Writes Ritner: "Despite their late date, the practices of such Demotic papyri are not foreign, but the culmination of native beliefs and acts regarding the empowered dead. The role of dead as intercessor was certainly established by the Old Kingdom" (Robert K. Ritner, "Necromancy in Ancient Egypt," in *Magic and Divination in the Ancient World* [eds. Leda Ciraolo and Jonathan Seidel; Ancient Magic and Divination 2; Leiden: Brill, 2002], 90).

[127] Borghouts, *Ancient Egyptian Magical Texts*, 4. (Spell No. 8)

[128] Dmitri Meeks, "Demons," in *The Oxford Encyclopedia of Ancient Egypt* (ed. Donald B. Redford; New York: Oxford University Press, 2001), 375.

[129] Meeks, "Demons," 375.

[130] Meeks, "Demons," 376.

[131] Rita Lucarelli, "Demons (Benevolent and Malevolent)," *UCLA Encyclopedia of Egyptology* (2010), 2. Accessed electronically: *http://uee.ucla.edu/*.

identified only by their actions and context, and sometimes by the way their names are written in red ink.[132] (Demonic forces that are not manifestations of the dead but are associated with the underworld are discussed below, with underworld gods.)

In addition to spells, the power of the dead could be seen in various other genres. Tomb inscriptions warn of the vengeance of the inhabitant on grave robbers, and are precursors to the threats on later Sidonian coffins (§ 3.4). The tomb curse of Ankhmahor from Saqqara warns of *ius talionis*: "Anything that you might do against this tomb of mine ... the like shall be done against your property." If anyone defiles the tomb, "I will seize him like a goose, placing fear in him at seeing ghosts (*akhs*) upon the earth."[133] On the one hand, it could be argued that such threats were not taken very seriously, since tombs were regularly plundered anyway. On the other hand, the robbers' vandalizations of corpses and tombs may have been an attempt to "cripple the deceased's spirit by removing his magical system of empowered supplemental imagery."[134] Desecration of tombs and remains was also carried out for political and theological reasons, as for example in the cases of Hatshepsut and Akhenaten; but in any case the goal was to deny the victim the hoped-for powers and privileges of the afterlife. In the absence of these, one died the "second death."[135]

Perhaps the most striking indications of a common Egyptian belief in the power of the dead are the Letters to the Dead. While extant examples of the genre are not numerous, they point to a broader practice and a belief that "the dead were approachable and reproachable; they could be cajoled, and they could meddle in the affairs of the living."[136]

The Letters to the Dead proper are personal compositions from relatively common people, asking a deceased person either for help or to cease tormenting the living one.[137] For example, in one letter the living writer asks, "Let a healthy son be born to me, for you are an able spirit."[138] In another, a husband who has outlived his wife asks her to stop making him suffer: "What evil have I done to

---

[132] Kasia Szpakowska, "Demons in Ancient Egypt," *Religion Compass* 3 (2009): 799–805. Szpakowska suggests using the term "genii" for what Lucarelli would call benevolent or guardian demons.

[133] Ritner, "Magic," 335.

[134] Ritner, "Magic," 336.

[135] See, e.g., Aidan Dodson, "Death After Death in the Valley of the Kings," in *Death and Taxes in the Ancient Near East* (ed. Sara E. Orel; Lewiston, N.Y.: Edwin Mellen, 1992), 53–59.

[136] Lesko, "Death and Afterlife," 1765.

[137] Ritner, "Magic," 336: "Direct assistance of the deceased is promised in the rubrics of many spells in the Book of Going Forth by Day that might be performed by the living on behalf of dead relatives. Conversely, the custom of 'letters to the dead' comprises petitions from the living for assistance from the underworld."

[138] From the Chicago Jar Stand, l. 4; Alan H. Gardiner, "A New Letter to the Dead," *JEA* 16 (1930): 19–22; Sharon Ruth Keller, "Egyptian Letters to the Dead in Relation to the Old Testament and Other Near Eastern Sources" (Ph.D. diss., New York University, 1989), 144–57.

you that I should be in the bad state in which I am? What have I done to you? This (is what) you have done: you have put your hand on me."¹³⁹ In every case, the recipient of the letter is an immediate relative to the author.¹⁴⁰ Dreams played a role in the transmission of messages from the dead to the living, and it is possible that the Egyptians practiced a form of dream incubation by sleeping in the deceased's mortuary chapel.¹⁴¹

These letters appear to have been produced by professional scribes, an indication of at least a cottage industry surrounding necromancy.¹⁴² They are attested throughout Egyptian history through the Third Intermediate Period, with the largest number coming from the end of the Old Kingdom and the First Intermediate Period. It has been suggested that this is because normally human political systems do an adequate job of enforcing justice, but "when uncertain, revolutionary periods arrived ... the disinherited person needed to have recourse to supernatural influences to have any hope of gaining his/her rights."¹⁴³ That description fits the social situation of the Third Intermediate Period as well. Nearly half of the extant letters make at least passing reference to a kind of tribunal in the afterlife, at which the authors believed their dead kin could advocate for them.¹⁴⁴

Robert Ritner has argued in recent years that the idea of "necromancy" needs to be introduced into the Egyptological vocabulary.¹⁴⁵ He argues that questions in the Letters to the Dead – such as "Why is he injuring me?" "What about the maidservant, who is ill?" "What have I done against you?" – are not merely rhetorical questions. Instead, he says "the sender expected to receive a response through incubation, as indicated by the texts themselves: 'Please become a spirit for me [before] my eyes so that I may see you in a dream fighting on my behalf.'"¹⁴⁶ Even seemingly innocuous questions such as "What is your condition?" or "How are you?" were inquiries about how the sender could care for the spirit and thus invoke its help. Ritner goes on to point out that by the time of the Old Kingdom it was already established that dead pharaohs could speak from the beyond, and this is reinforced by canonical texts such as "The Teaching of Ame-

---

¹³⁹ From the Leiden Papyrus, ll. 1–3; Alan H. Gardiner and Kurt Sethe, *Egyptian Letters to the Dead, Mainly from the Old and Middle Kingdoms* (London: Egypt Exploration Society, 1928), 8, pl. VII; Keller, "Egyptian Letters to the Dead," 107–43.
¹⁴⁰ Michael O'Donoghue, "The 'Letters to the Dead' and Ancient Egyptian Religion," *Bulletin of the Australian Centre for Egyptology* 10 (1999): 97.
¹⁴¹ O'Donoghue, "Letters to the Dead," 101–2.
¹⁴² Kanawati, *The Tomb and Beyond*, 17.
¹⁴³ Max Guilmot, "Lettres aux morts dans l'Egypte ancienne," in *Revue de l'histoire des religions* 170 (1966): 7. Cited and translated in O'Donoghue, "Letters to the Dead," 93.
¹⁴⁴ O'Donoghue, "Letters to the Dead," 101.
¹⁴⁵ Ritner notes that neither the *Lexikon der Ägyptologie* nor the basic reference on Egyptian divination includes references to the practice (Ritner, "Necromancy in Ancient Egypt," 89).
¹⁴⁶ Ritner, "Necromancy in Ancient Egypt," 91.

nemhet I for his Son Sesostris"[147] (Middle Kingdom), in which the deceased king reveals his son's fate to him, and the lengthy Harris Papyrus[148] (New Kingdom), in which the dead king Ramesses III gives instruction to the whole population about what to do.

By the New Kingdom, it became very popular in Egypt to consult royal necromantic cults. An oracle of the dead king Amenhotep I (1427–1392) "dominated local religion and jurisprudence for well over a century. ... Questions were inscribed on ostraca, and many examples have survived."[149] The situation amounted to "truly 'institutionalized necromancy' sponsored by the state for public benefit."[150] Other deceased kings had similar cults, the likes of which continued into the common era. Even nonroyal persons who drowned in the Nile and mummified animals were later consulted in necromancy. Ritner concludes that the hindrance to the recognition of necromancy in Egypt is not so much its scarcity as its ubiquity: "the range of associated actions is simply too broad to warrant a restrictive designation."[151]

Egyptian ghost stories receive less attention in secondary literature, but they too attest to the concern for care of the tomb to assure the happiness of the deceased.[152] Like Letters to the Dead, the ghost story genre is sparsely attested,[153] but "gradually increased in popularity" in later Egyptian history. It is attested in the 25th dynasty text called "The Levitating Ghost," which is unfortunately very fragmentary.[154] The earliest exemplar, and one of the fullest, is "Khonsemhab and the Ghost," from the 19th dynasty. In it, Khonsemhab, a high priest of Amon-Re, is visited by the spirit of a dead priest. He says to the ghost, "[How badly you fare] without eating or drinking, without growing old or becoming young, without seeing sunlight or inhaling northerly breezes. Darkness is in your sight each day." And Khonsemhab promises, "I will have a sepulcher prepared

---

[147] Lichtheim, *Ancient Egyptian Literature*, 1:135–39. On this text as the first Egyptian "ghost story," see Christina Adams, "Shades of Meaning: The Significance of Manifestations of the Dead as Evidenced in Texts from the Old Kingdom to the Coptic Period," in *Current Research in Egyptology 2006: Proceedings of the Seventh Annual Symposium, University of Oxford, April 2006*, ed. Maria Cannata (Oxford: Oxbow, 2007), 6.

[148] Pierre Grandet, *Le papyrus Harris I (BM 9999)* (2 vols.; Bibliothèque d'Étude 109/1–2; Cairo: Imprimerie de l'Institut français d'archéologie orientale du Caire, 1994).

[149] Ritner, "Necromancy in Ancient Egypt," 93.

[150] Ritner, "Necromancy in Ancient Egypt," 94.

[151] Ritner, "Necromancy in Ancient Egypt," 95.

[152] Christina Adams, "Shades of Meaning: The Significance of Manifestations of the Dead as Evidenced in Texts from the Old Kingdom to the Coptic Period," in *Current Research in Egyptology 2006: Proceedings of the Seventh Annual Symposium, University of Oxford, April 2006*, ed. Maria Cannata. (Oxford: Oxbow, 2007), 1–20.

[153] Carolyn Thériault attributes this relative scarcity to the fact that "folklore is seldom committed to writing." ("The Literary Ghosts of Pharaonic Egypt," in *Death and Taxes in the Ancient Near East* [ed. Sara E. Orel; Lewiston, N.Y.: Edwin Mellen Press, 1992], 208.)

[154] Georges Posener, "Une nouvelle histoire de revenant," *RdE* 12 (1960): 75–82.

[anew] for you ... and you shall rest therein, and I will have done for you all that is done for one who is in [your position]."[155] The broken context makes it difficult to ascertain the main point of the story, but it appears to recount a reminder from the beyond about the care of the dead comparable to that of The Underworld Vision of an Assyrian Prince. Despite the similarities, however, there is not necessarily any influence between the two cultures' stories in this period.[156] The primary differences are that the Egyptian texts preserve the personality of a deceased person, whereas the Assyrian text the gods of the underworld represent the chthonic cult; and whereas the Assyrian text emphasizes the terrors of the underworld, the Egyptian stories focus on the plight of the dead, and portray a potential symbiosis between them and the living.

All in all, it is quite reasonable to speak of an Egyptian cult of the dead, and its extent will probably be recognized more over time.[157]

2.4.3 The Egyptian netherworld and its deities

Two primary myths underlay the Egyptian mythology of death: the first was the murder of Osiris, and the second was the journey of the solar bark through the sky.

In an ancient myth, Osiris was murdered by his brother Seth, who cut up the corpse and scattered its pieces. Isis gathered the pieces and reassembled them; and she joined a second sister, Nephthys, in mourning their brother. Horus then aids Osiris in a legal proceeding in which Seth is convicted and Osiris is vindicated. These plot details can be seen to correspond to various aspects of the funerary cult: the care of Isis, to the embalming; hers and Nephthys' mourning, to human mourning; the judgment of Seth, to the sacrifice of an ox at the tomb; and the vindication of Osiris, to the deceased's successful passing of the judgment of the dead (see below). In sum, Osiris's triumph over death potentially symbolized that of every person. The process of mummification was, from one perspective, a re-enactment of the myth of Osiris' regeneration.[158]

---

[155] Simpson, W. K., ed. *The Literature of Ancient Egypt*, 3rd ed. (New Haven & London: Yale University Press, 2003), 113. Original publication: Jürgen von Beckerath, "Zur Geschichte von Chonsemhab und dem Geist," *Zeitschrift für ägyptische Sprache und Altertumskunde* 119 (1992): 90–107.
[156] Adams, "Shades of Meaning," 7.
[157] Martin Fitzenreiter, "Zum Ahnenkult in Ägypten," *Göttinger Miszellen* 143 (1994): 51–72; Herman te Velde, "Commemoration in Ancient Egypt," in *Visible Religion: Annual For Religious Iconography, 1982, Volume I: Commemorative Figures: Papers Presented To Dr. Th. P. Van Baaren On The Occasion Of His Seventieth Birthday, May 13, 1982* (eds. H. G. Kippenberg, L. P. van den Bosch et al.; E. J. Brill: Leiden, 1982), 135–46.
[158] Shore, "Human and Divine Mummification." 226–35; Jan Assmann, "Death and Initiation in the Funerary Religion of Ancient Egypt" in *Religion and Philosophy in Ancient Egypt* (ed. James P. Allen et al. Yale Egyptological Studies 3; New Haven, Conn.: Yale University, 1989), 135–59.

In addition to becoming "an Osiris," the deceased was also often portrayed as riding through the netherworld in the sun god's boat, which traveled through the sky during the day and beneath the earth at night. Early Egyptian portrayals of the place of the dead had already emphasized the sky as the place where the deified pharaoh would reign,[159] but in the Middle Kingdom (as attested by the Coffin Texts) the afterlife in the sky is complemented by the underworld, and by the New Kingdom the idea of death as descent was more prominent than that of death as ascent. After the brief but stark discontinuity of Akhenaten's solar religion, this dualistic sky/underworld conception was systematized and elaborated. The netherworld was "minutely described in the New Kingdom underworld books. The dichotomy of sky and underworld for the afterlife, and also for the abode of the gods, is reflected endlessly in set phrases in New Kingdom texts."[160] The most famous of these texts was the aforementioned "Book of Going Forth by Day," but lesser-known texts multiplied the portrayals of the journey to the afterlife, and these tended to be richly illustrated: the "Amduat" ("The Guide to the Underworld");[161] the "Litany of Re"; the "Book of Gates"; the "Book of Caverns"; the "Books of Sky and Earth"; the "Book of the Night"; the "Book of Nut"; and other forms of these texts.[162] Eventually, they proliferated to the point that "Amduat" can be considered a genre. Although the initial flourishing of the genre dates to the Ramesside period, these books were taken up again with a passion during the Twenty-fifth and Twenty-sixth Dynasties.[163] The crypt of Taharqa at Karnak was "richly decorated with representations of solar and other rituals."[164]

The deceased's journey to the afterlife was itself believed to be treacherous. There was the risk that the sun god's boat would be swallowed by the great serpent Apophis. And as in Mesopotamian mythology, the passage to the underworld was treacherous; each gate of the underworld brought its own set of demonic guardians or genii:

---

[159] So Pepi's Spell 4 in the Pyramid Texts: "The sky's door has been opened to you, the Cool Waters' door has been made to pull open to you, and you will find the Sun standing waiting for you. He will take hold of your arm, lead you into the sky's dual shrines, and put you on Osiris' throne." Cited in Allen, *The Ancient Egyptian Pyramid Texts*, 100; cf. Hornung, *Conceptions of God in Ancient Egypt*, 227.

[160] Hornung, *Conceptions of God in Ancient Egypt*, 228. On the cosmological significance of such journeys, see S. J. Watson, "Death and Cosmology in Ancient Egypt," *JNSL* 17 (1991): 151–71. Watson remarks, "[W]hen it comes to man, his death and his resurrection abide the rules of the cosmos" (169).

[161] E. A. Wallis Budge, *The Egyptian Heaven and Hell* (London: Kegan, Paul, Trench, Trübner, 1905); Ina Hegenbarth-Reichardt, *Der Raum der Zeit: Eine Untersuchung zu den Altägyptischen Vorstellungen und Konzeptionen von Zeit und Raum Anhand des Unterweltbuches Amduat* (Wiesbaden: Harrassowitz, 2006).

[162] For a more complete accounting, see Erik Hornung, *The Ancient Egyptian Books of the Afterlife* (trans. David Lorton; Ithaca, N.Y.: Cornell University Press, 1999).

[163] Hornung, *Ancient Egyptian Books of the Afterlife*, 30, 56, 96, 113, 116, 123.

[164] Assmann, *Death and Salvation*, 206.

2.4 Death in Egypt

The underworld was full of evil demons, especially in the spaces between the living world and the Hall of Osiris, which gave access to the green fields of paradise. They guarded the gates, channels, crossings, and so on, which the dead had to pass to reach the hall. Unable to avoid them, the deceased had to persuade them to let him pass. He usually had to answer questions posed by the demons, who only let pass those who could prove that during life they had learned enough about the underworld to be allowed to travel in it.[165]

Also as in Mesopotamia, such guardian demons were commonly portrayed as fantastic, monstrous, composite beings made up of parts of different animals.[166] Other demons might be portrayed as disfigured humans and inflict sicknesses.[167] There appears to have been an increased interest in demonology in the Late Period, with new demonic figures arising that had not been attested earlier.[168]

Dead persons could also be found guilty in a final judgment, a complex tradition that can be discussed only briefly here.[169] The idea of judgment after death by some sort tribunal is as ancient as the Old Kingdom; by the Middle Kingdom a distinct mythological tradition emerged in which Osiris oversaw the weighing of the heart of the deceased to determine its righteousness by the measure of Maat (*mɜʿt*, "justice," both an abstract concept and a goddess). The god Thoth functioned as prosecutor; those who failed the inquisition would be drowned or devoured by the monster Ammut. Those who failed the judgment could also be portrayed as decapitated, bound, boiled in a cauldron, or burnt by snakes and other divine creatures spitting fire.[170] However, this punishment is always reserved for other people; not surprisingly, Ammut is never portrayed devouring the heart of the owner of a tomb. This traditional scene endured in Egyptian religious texts for thousands of years; in Kushite and Saite periods it was emblazoned in a band across the chests of sarcophagi.

---

[165] Meeks, "Demons," 377. These demons can be distinguished from wandering demons, which were messengers (and perhaps creations) of the gods, and which are not discussed here (see Lucarelli, "Demons," 3).

[166] Lucarelli, "Demons," 5. Another similarity is that Egyptian demons were said to travel in sevens; see Meeks, "Demons," 377. Cf. the ^d*Sibitti* (a traditional grouping of seven demons) of Mesopotamia (*CAD* S, 230–31).

[167] Demons are sometime portrayed "twisted with their head facing backwards, unable to see forward" (Szpakowska, "Demons in Ancient Egypt," 800). One spell warns that "he (the demon) will not go forth face forwards, limbs as sound limbs." See R. K. Ritner, "O. Gardiner 363: A Spell Against Night Terrors," *JARCE* 27 (1990): 25–41.

[168] Rita Lucarelli, "Demons in the Book of the Dead" in *Totenbuch-Forschungen: Gesammelte Beiträge des 2. Internationalen Totenbuch-Symposiums, Bonn, 25. bis 29. September 2005* (eds. Burkhard Backes, Irmtraut Munro und Simone Stöhr; Studien zum altägyptischen Totenbuch 11; Wiesbaden: Harrassowitz, 2006), 210.

[169] For fuller discussion and references to Egyptian texts, see Stephen G. J. Quirke, "Judgment of the Dead," in *Oxford Encyclopedia of Ancient Egypt* (ed. Donald B. Redford; Oxford: Oxford University Press, 2001), 2:211–14.

[170] Kanawati, *The Tomb and Beyond*, 36.

The goal of the deceased was to be found blameless, or, in the Egyptian phrase, "true of voice." To prepare him or her for the moment of judgment, the underworld books are full of protestations of innocence and purity ("negative confessions"), the lengthiest of which is found in the "Book of the Dead," Spell 125. It reads in part:

Hail to you, great god, Lord of Justice! ... Behold, I have come to you, I have brought you truth.... I have not done falsehood against men, I have not impoverished my associates.... I have done no evil.... I have not deprived the orphan of his property.... I have not calumniated a servant to his master, I have not caused pain, I have not made hungry, I have not made to weep, I have not killed, I have not commanded to kill.... I have not lessened the food-offerings in the temple, I have not destroyed the loaves of the gods.... I am pure, pure, pure, pure![171]

Such a text finds a Mesopotamian cognate not in any underworld text but in prayers for divine salvation such as the incantation series known as DINGIR.ŠÀ.DIB.BA ("Appeasing the heart of an angry god"), in which the supplicant addresses the god: "O one whose slave I am, what have I done? / I have not held back from [my god] the ox in the stall, / I have not held back from him the sheep in the pen, / I have not held back from him the valuables which I owed. / The food I found I did not eat to myself / The water I found I did not drink to myself."[172] For the Mesopotamian, therefore, one might conclude that the judgment took place before death – with death representing a guilty verdict.

If the journey to the Egyptian afterlife was long and dangerous, it was interesting enough to the Egyptians to be adapted into a board game called "Passage." According to Assmann, the game required two players, and its object was "to find oneself a passage through 30 fields of salutary or evil nature until one arrives in the vicinity of the god, who then grants sustenance (bread and water) and justification."[173]

Still other deities also played a role in the Egyptian mortuary cult – primarily as protectors of their devotees in the afterlife. The most prominent and traditional of these was Nut, a sky- and mother-goddess, who was frequently portrayed as a sheltering presence on coffins and in tombs; but other goddesses such as Mut and Neith also took on these same characteristics, especially in later periods. This is discussed further in the analysis of Isa 28:1–22 (§ 5.2.3.3).

Just as the myth of Osiris corresponded to the preparation of the body for burial, so the mythological journey of the deceased to the afterlife mirrored the

---

[171] Raymond O. Faulkner, *The Ancient Egyptian Book of the Dead: The Book of Going Forth by Day* (San Francisco: Chronicle Books, 1994), 29–30.
[172] W. G. Lambert, "DINGIR.ŠÀ.DIB.BA Incantations," *JNES* 33 (1974): 267–322. In this instance, of course, the issue seems to be cultic rather than moral rectitude. Biblical texts for comparison with the Egyptian "negative confession" include Deut 26:13–14; Job 23:12, 31:30; Ps 40:10–11; Jer 2:35 warns against such claims.
[173] Assmann, "Death and Initiation," 148.

journey of the mummy to the tomb by ritual procession.[174] The physical transportation of the body to the necropolis and tomb (the most prominent of which were on the west bank of the Nile) symbolized the deceased's journey to the "blessed West," and the body's preparation for burial by cleansing and magical provisioning symbolized the deceased's preparation for judgment. The grave-feast symbolized the deceased participation in eating, drinking, and celebrating, and part of it was left as an offering.[175]

Remarkably, there are few accounts or depictions of the final interment, when the mummy was placed in the sarcophagus, though the placement of some of the stone sarcophagus lids was a massive undertaking requiring (according to one Old Kingdom text) eighty men.[176] Such practical details were almost completely overwritten by the mythological journey. In the Egyptian phrasing, the successful attainment of the afterlife meant reaching the "Field of Reeds," a sunlit land of bounty which Assmann compares to the Greeks' Elysian Fields. The afterlife could also be called the "Field of Offerings," the "Isle of the Just," and (as in Mesopotamia) the "Great City,"[177] and a land from which "none comes back"[178] – although this last title is applied only late, beginning with the rather pessimistic Harper's Songs.[179] In more typical Egyptian theology, it was only the "place of destruction," the destination of souls found guilty in the judgment, that had "no escape."[180]

It has already been noted that the Egyptians were capable of holding together in their minds concepts that seem disparate, but in fact there is a logical connection between the idealized views of the afterlife presented in the many Egyptian materials and the contrasting picture painted in others – of a world that is "utterly deep, utterly dark, utterly endless,"[181] where one must walk upside down on the ceiling, eat excrement, and risk being torn limb from limb.[182] One Ramesside-period text paints a portrait that would be at home in Mesopotamia:

---

[174] Kinney, Lesley. "The Funerary Procession" in *Egyptian Art: Principles and Themes in Wall Scenes* (eds. Leonie Donovan and Kim McCorquodale; Prism Archaeological Series 6; Giza, Egypt: Prism, 2000), 157–70.
[175] Kinney, "The Funerary Procession," 163; See Assmann, *Death and Salvation*, 310–29.
[176] Kinney, "The Funerary Procession," 163. Perhaps this procedure is rarely reported because "[t]he casket is in the most secret place in the Netherworld, known only to Osiris himself and the Sun-god or the deceased, invisible and unknown to all others" (Erik Hornung, "Black Holes Viewed From Within: Hell in Ancient Egyptian Thought," *Diogenes* 42 [1994]: 147)?
[177] Assmann, *Death and Salvation*, 392.
[178] *ANET* 467 ("A Song of the Harper").
[179] Hornung, "Black Holes Viewed From Within: Hell in Ancient Egyptian Thought," 134.
[180] Hornung, "Black Holes Viewed From Within," 134.
[181] "Book of the Dead," Spell 175.
[182] See "Book of the Dead," chs. 51–52; also Borghouts, *Ancient Egyptian Magical Texts*, Spell 22; Paolo Xella, "Sur la Nourriture des Morts," in *Death in Mesopotamia: XXVIe Papers Read at the XXVIe Rencontre Assyriologique Internationale* (ed. B. Alster; Mesopotamia 8; Copenhagen: Akademisk Vorlag, 1980), 151–60.

> Those in the West are in difficulty, their condition is bad.
> How motionless is the one who has gone to them.
> He cannot describe his condition.
> He rests in his lonely place,
> and eternity is with him in darkness.[183]

Indeed, the Coffin Texts and the "Book of the Dead" could portray the underworld as a gated city[184] and as "The House of Darkness," ideas entirely familiar from Semitic texts.[185] Similar themes are found in a "lament of Isis":

> Where are you going, child of the Golden One,
> who, born yesterday, are going off today
> to those whose land lies in darkness,
> whose fields are sand,
> whose tombs serve silence,
> whose call is not heard?[186]

"If we wish to learn something about the experience of death in Egypt," wrote Assmann, "we must turn [positive] images [of the afterlife] inside out."[187] The positive images of death were not death itself but an existence *created* by humankind by means of its power over magic and the divine. To say that a happy afterlife was the natural state of death to an Egyptian would be like saying that a rose garden is the natural state of a field.

> [The happy afterlife] was the distant goal of countless efforts, without which death would be an absolute opposition: isolation, termination, end, disappearance, darkness, filth, defectiveness, distance from the divine, decomposition, dismemberment, dissolution, in short, all that constitutes the opposite of those radiant images of a transfigured existence. The Egyptian experience of death was not, overall, much different from that elsewhere in the world, except for the astonishing, and in this respect probably unique, attitude that the Egyptians assumed toward this experience, an attitude based on trust in the power of counterimages, or rather in the power of speech, of representation, and of ritual acts, to be able to make these counterimages real and to create a counterworld through the medium of symbols.[188]

One could go farther in emphasizing negative aspects of the Egyptian afterlife: Erik Hornung's article "Black Holes Viewed From Within: Hell in Ancient Egyptian Thought,"[189] which focuses on the post-Amarna guides to the underworld, is

---

[183] From the tomb of Nefersekheru. Cited in Assmann, *Death and Salvation*, 114.
[184] Assmann, *Death and Salvation*, 191.
[185] Assmann, *Death and Salvation*, 45.
[186] Papyrus New York Metropolitan Museum of Art 35.9.21, 7.1–4. Cited in Assmann, *Death and Salvation*, 118.
[187] Assmann, *Death and Salvation*, 18.
[188] Assmann, *Death and Salvation*, 18. On this tension, see also Burns, "Some Conceptions of the Afterlife," 140–49.
[189] *Diogenes* 42 (1994): 133–56.

a compendium of the horrors of the afterlife as the Egyptians perceived them. Those horrors were not surpassed by medieval Christian portrayals of hell. While this "dark side of death" could be construed as "a call to action,"[190] it seems that in first-millennium BCE Egypt, as in Mesopotamia, pessimism and skepticism about the happy afterlife increasingly crept into the cultural discourse.

Naguib Kanawati locates the first signs of skepticism much earlier, in the First Intermediate Period; he perceived that the Egyptians "were generally not less grieved by, or less fearful of, death than any other people of any time."[191] Still, there may be an argument for an increase in such thinking in the first millennium. Maya Müller perceived that, "starting around 1000 BCE, there is formulated the sad certainty that a deceased person loses individual consciousness and lingers on in a gloomy state of slumber."[192] Shannon Burkes has pointed out that while skepticism's roots in Egyptian culture are old, the Late Period was one "of distress, of inquiry, and ... of skepticism." In contrast to traditional beliefs, new texts "testify to the view that death had become omnipotent, and announce that the traditional mortuary religion is empty, because death is deprivation and ultimately, insensibility."[193] Traditional mortuary religion and expressions of the traditional beliefs about death continued unabated during this period, of course, but now they were increasingly caught in dialogue, and in a tension between hope and despair.

2.5 Conclusions

Ancient Egyptians lived a life permeated by death, a phenomenon that inspired artistic creativity unparalleled in its time. Egypt was a major exporter of material goods and cultural influence; and throughout the period of the Israelite monarchies, it was very much involved in the political affairs of Palestine as well.

Despite the magnificent richness of Egyptian beliefs and practices surrounding death, and the literature and art that attest to them, the differences between the Egyptians and Mesopotamians in this regard should not be overdrawn. The old judgment that Mesopotamian religion was "das Gegenstück der ägyptischen Religion,"[194] must be set aside. That is especially the case in the first millennium; perhaps international contacts accelerated processes of assimilation through cross-fertilization of religious ideas.

---

[190] Assmann, *Death and Salvation*, 19.
[191] Kanawati, *The Tomb and Beyond*, 46.
[192] Maya Müller, "Afterlife," in *Oxford Encyclopedia of Ancient Egypt* (ed. Donald B. Redford; Oxford: Oxford University Press, 2001), 36.
[193] Shannon Burkes, *Death in Qohelet and Egyptian Biographies of the Late Period* (SBLDS 170; Atlanta: Society of Biblical Literature, 1999), 233–34.
[194] Alfred Jeremias, *Hölle und Paradies bei den Babyloniern* (2nd ed.; Leipzig: Hinrichs, 1903), 3.

The shared traits of the Egyptian and Mesopotamian religion include:
1. the belief that the afterlife was unhappy and risky without ritual intervention, balanced by a hope for a happy afterlife with the proper intervention;
2. the employment of rituals by which the dead could be cared for;
3. a general concern for the integrity of the corpse;
4. a belief in the power of the dead to inflict harm but also to help those who cared for them, especially family;
5. an increasing pessimism about death in later periods; and
6. an increasing volume of cultural production surrounding death in the same periods.

However, the two religions cannot be equated and should not be conflated into a "common theology."[195] Distinctive features of the Egyptian approach to death include:

1. the monumental scale of its tombs and the nearly lifelong efforts that were associated with their construction and provisioning;[196]
2. the associated intellectual focus on death as the culmination of life;
3. the preservation of the body through mummification;
4. a particularly forceful denial of death's claims – that is, a particularly stubborn optimism about the deceased's prospects after death. This resulted in Egypt's incredibly well-developed descriptions of the afterlife, unique in their time.
5. Finally, the mythic models that lay beneath these expressions are also either unique in the ancient Near East (Osiris' murder) or at least unique in the extent of their development (the journey on the sun god's bark, which has analogies in Mesopotamia and Ugarit, but nothing to rival the afterlife books).

Egyptians aspired to self-sufficiency in the afterlife in a way that does not seem to have occurred in other nations. This tendency is apparent particularly in the proliferation of afterlife books. Such texts were intended to give the deceased the magical power to overcome death, and the result is that one who achieved the Field of Reeds could be called "a god who has rejuvenated *himself*."[197] By contrast, it seems that Mesopotamians and others, insofar as they hoped for a happy afterlife, referred those hopes exclusively to the care of others. Certainly, Egyptians also felt themselves dependent on care, and to some extent on the grace of

---

[195] Morton Smith, "The Common Theology of the Ancient Near East," *JBL* 71 (1952): 135–47.
[196] This is distinctive as far as we know for the Iron Age; for later periods, monumental tombs of comparable scale are known elsewhere in the Persian and Hellenistic periods.
[197] Assmann, *Death and Salvation*, 287.

2.5 Conclusions

the gods,[198] but their sense of authority over their own eternal fates is unmistakable.

Chapters 4 and 5 develop some ways in which Egyptian religion, and specifically its ideas about death, influenced the Hebrew Bible and Isa 1–39 in particular. In preparation for those detailed arguments, I would like to suggest two ways of thinking about Isaiah's rhetoric of death in light of Egyptian culture:

First, there is a synchronism between Isaiah's career and the resurgence of traditional mortuary religion in the Twenty-fifth and Twenty-sixth dynasties; insofar as Judah was in contact with Egypt in that period, this upswing in interest in the afterlife must have filtered across the cultural barriers.

Second, Burkes has attributed the Late Period's "high level of thought and creativity" about death to social and political conditions, that is, to the chaotic, uncertain, and distressing historical situation.[199] (Her argument is not unlike Thorkild Jacobsen's, which posited the upswing in Neo-Assyrian speculation about the world of the dead to the increasing violence of the period.) During the Late Period, Egypt was successively overrun by Persians and Greeks, and Isaiah certainly lived in an analogous period in Palestine, in which Israel and Judah were under constant threat from imperial powers, and wars were frequent. The data presented in these first two chapters suggest that the time was ripe in Isaiah's Judah for creative reflection on death.

---

[198] Assmann argues that Egyptian afterlife magic is not a form of Gnosticism (*Death and Salvation*, 404).

[199] Burkes, *Death in Qohelet*, 233; see her discussion of the historical and cultural context, pp. 209–32.

3. Death and the Dead in Syria-Palestine outside Israel and Judah

3.1 Introduction

In the effort to understand the religious and ideological world(s) in which Isa 1–39 took shape, Syro-Palestinian data would seem at first glance to be more relevant than what has already been surveyed, since the material derives from Judah's more immediate geographical and linguistic environment.[1] Unfortunately, moving closer to Judah geographically forces one to range more widely in time in order to compile a meaningful comparative corpus. The inscriptional sources from Iron II Palestine are severely limited in comparison with the extensive Mesopotamian and Egyptian records that have come down to us. Furthermore, the texts that have survived from the Iron Age in non-Israelite Palestine are almost entirely monumental or epistolary in nature, so religious data can be gleaned only from hints or by reference to architecture and iconography. Ephraim Stern has argued based on archaeological remains that the cults of Israel, Judah, Philistines, Ammonites, Moabites, and Edomites "were almost one and the same" apart from the name of the national deity, and that "all stemmed from the cult of the Phoenicians, thus continuing the older Canaanite model."[2] Such a claim, while indicative of the similarites among the closely-packed nations, goes beyond the probative power of the available data.

Because of these limitations, much of the weight of the discussion falls on Ugarit, a wealthy city-state on the coast of Palestine during the Late Bronze Age. The bulk of this chapter surveys the archaeological and textual records of Ugarit's beliefs and practices regarding death. It seems that Ugarit had a mythology of death nearly as elaborate as those of Egypt or Mesopotamia, with associated ritual practices. In these texts, the god of death does battle with the high god, divinized ancestors are summoned to help welcome a newly deceased king into the under-

---

[1] Shemaryahu Talmon, "The 'Comparative' Method in Biblical Interpretation: Principles and Problems," in *Congress Volume: Göttingen, 1977* (VTSup 29; Leiden: Brill, 1978), 320–56.

[2] Ephraim Stern, "The Phoenician Source of the Palestinian Cults at the End of the Iron Age," in *Symbiosis, Symbolism, and the Power of the Past: Canaan, Ancient Israel, and Their Neighbors from the Late Bronze Age through Roman Palaestina* (eds. W.G. Dever and Seymour Gitin; Winona Lake, Ind.: Eisenbrauns, 2003), 309–10.

world, and hopes for a happy afterlife are balanced against a more skeptical strain of thought.

There has been a significant dispute, however, about whether (or how much) the Ugaritic data indicates an active cult of dead ancestors. Therefore, in order to supply as much context as possible, this chapter also ventures into brief surveys of Hittite beliefs during Hatti's imperial period, and into the spottier data from Syro-Palestinian city-states in the second millennium (Ebla, Mari, Emar) and first millennium (Byblos, Sidon, Sam'al). These sources, in my view, lend weight to the common contention that Ugarit had a royal cult of the dead and a belief in a divinized afterlife.

In the wake of the discoveries at Ras Shamra some eighty years ago, discussions of Israelite religion and Ugaritic religion have rarely been conducted in isolation from each other. As a result, trying to separate the threads of the two conversations is difficult. However, I have done so here as much as possible in order to allow the evidence for each to be considered on its own merits. Therefore, I discuss the archaeology of Judean burials and the textual witnesses of the Hebrew Bible separately, in the next chapter.

This chapter does not summarize political and cultural interactions between Judah and its immediate neighbors, as did the previous chapter with Mesopotamia and Egypt. On the one hand, there *was no* direct historical contact between Israel or Judah and the second-millennium cultures surveyed here; any cultural influence would have to have been mediated, over centuries, through other Levantine entities. On the other hand, it is worth reiterating what the first chapter already established: it is well attested in archaeology and in biblical and extra-biblical texts that monarchic Israel and Judah had extensive contact with Phoenician and Syrian nations of the first millennium.[3] Those cultures inherited many aspects of Ugaritic religion; thus, one could well theorize a dissemination of religious ideas through that conduit, given Judah's extensive political and economic contacts.

At the outset, some definitions are in order. Emile Durkheim defined a cult of the dead as "repeated standardized practices oriented toward the dead at ritual locations associated with the dead."[4] In my view, this definition needs to be modified in two ways in order to be useful for the ancient Near Eastern data: first, the restriction to "ritual locations associated with the dead" should be removed, since the *kispu* mortuary cult could be conducted apart from cultic sites (§ 1.4.1), as in the case of its apotropaic applications; second, the stipulation should be

---

[3] In addition to the summary and documentation presented in chapters 1 and 2 above, see J. Maxwell Miller and John H. Hayes, *A History of Ancient Israel and Judah* (2nd ed.; Louisville, Ky.: Westminster John Knox, 2006), 209–14, 303–11, 329–35, 395–98, etc.; and Philip J. King, "The Eighth, the Greatest of Centuries?" *JBL* 108 (1989): 6.

[4] Emile Durkheim, *The Elementary Forms of the Religious Life: A Study in Religious Sociology* (trans. J. W. Swain; London: G. Allen & Unwin, 1915), 63.

added that some sort of divine power of the dead is presumed – otherwise the term "cult" loses its primary sense of "worship ... rendered to a divine being."[5] Thus, we might adapt Durkheim's definition to read: "repeated standardized practices oriented toward the divinized dead intended to influence them." Brian B. Schmidt has further recommended a distinction between "funerary" cult and "mortuary" cult, the former referring only to burial rituals, the latter to continuing activities intended to influence the dead on behalf of the living.[6] Although many scholars justifiably use the term "mortuary" more broadly,[7] I use it in the strict sense that Schmidt advocated. When I refer to "cults of the dead" or "death cults," I mean continuing care of the dead under the assumption of their power.

3.2 Bronze Age Cults of the dead in inland Syria and Hatti

So deeply controverted are the facts surrounding Ugaritic (and, by extension, Judean) death cults that it will be desirable to provide as much context as possible. We begin with a brief survey of Syro-Palestinian data from the third and second millennia.

Syrian Bronze Age architectural and textual data attest to cults of the dead.[8] For example, at Ebla a rich royal cemetery underneath a palace has been understood as having hosted a cult of ancestors.[9] One Eblaite text lists dead kings with the divine determinative, and others record sacrificial portions for the "divinized

---

[5] See *Oxford English Dictionary*, s.v. "cult." The same objection might be raised against the definition of Charles A. Kennedy in the *Anchor Bible Dictionary*: "Periodic rituals performed by the living on behalf of the dead members of the family. These rituals were conducted subsequent to and apart from funerals and usually included offerings at the grave site of food and drink which were intended for the well-being of the dead. These occasions were also social gatherings of heirs, relatives, and friends of the deceased, who in some cases was considered the host as well as the beneficiary of the memorial meal" ("Dead, Cult of the," *ABD* 2.105).

[6] Brian B. Schmidt, *Israel's Beneficent Dead: Ancestor Cult and Necromancy in Ancient Israelite Religion and Tradition* (FAT 11; Tübingen: Mohr Siebeck, 1994), 4–12.

[7] The *Oxford English Dictionary*'s primary definition of "mortuary" is: "Of or belonging to the burial of the dead." In other words, it can be used nearly synonymously with "funerary."

[8] It has even been argued that the *kispu* was imported to Mesopotamia from Syria in the third millennium; see Paolo Xella, "Culto Dinastico Tradizioni Amoree nei Rituali Ugaritici," *SEL* 5 (1988): 219–25. However, it is much more likely that earlier Sumerian rituals attested at Lagash propagated both (Schmidt, *Israel's Beneficent Dead*, 41–43).

[9] Paolo Matthiae, "Princely Cemetery and Ancestors Cult at Ebla During Middle Bronze II: A Proposal of Interpretations," *UF* 11 (1979): 563–69; idem, "New Discoveries at Ebla: The Excavations of the Western Palace and the Royal Necropolis of the Amorite Period," *BA* 47 (1984): 18–32, and further literature cited there. For a contrary assessment, see Wayne T. Pitard, "Tombs and Offerings: Archaeological Data and Comparative Methodology in the Study of Death in Israel," in *Sacred Time, Sacred Place: Archaeology and the Religion of Israel*, ed. Barry M. Gittlen (Winona Lake, Ind.: Eisenbrauns, 2002), 155–62. Pitard points out that the so-called "royal necropolis" in Ebla was based on only three royal graves, which were spaced over centuries; and he argues that the use of the "death-cult building" is far from clear.

father(s)" or "divinized king(s)."[10] Recent statuary finds have emboldened Paolo Matthiae in claiming that there was also a cult of dead queens.[11] At Mari a letter records the oracle of a prophet of Dagan demanding a "*kispu* for the ghost [*kispi ana iṭemmim*] of Yaḫdun-Lim,"[12] and in another letter Dagan is identified as "the lord of the dead" (*bēl pagrê*).[13] Still another letter instructs that a "sacrifice for the dead" (*niqî pagrai*) should be performed on a certain date.[14] From Emar come wills that seek to assure that nontraditional heirs (i.e., other than an eldest son) will perform care for "the gods and the dead/ghosts" of the testator.[15] Emar also furnishes further texts, more difficult to interpret, that seem to attest to offerings for deceased officials and cultic personnel.[16]

From fourteenth- and thirteenth-century Hatti come cuneiform texts describing one of the most elaborate royal burial rituals known in the ancient Near East outside Egypt.[17] The Hittite Royal Funerary Ritual (the brief native title is *Šalliš waštaiš*) lasted fourteen days and was distinguished by the cremation of the

---

[10] The interpretation of the Eblaite data is naturally dependent on the earlier interpretations of the Ugaritic data, which will be taken up below. The terms for "divinized father(s)" or "divinized king(s)" are DINGIR A-MU and DINGIR EN(-EN), respectively. For the former, see TM.75.G.2403 obv. I:16–II:5. For the latter, see TM.75.G.2398, TM.75.G.10088, etc. Other texts from Ebla suggest that even deceased queens might receive sacrifices, something not attested at Ugarit. For a fuller discussion, see Alfonso Archi, "Cult of Ancestors and Tutelary God at Ebla," in *Fucus: A Semitic/Afrasian Gathering in Remembrance of Albert Ehrman* (ed. Yoël L. Arbeitman; Amsterdam: John Benjamins, 1988), 103–12. Also Robert R. Stieglitz, "The Deified Kings of Ebla," in *Eblaitica 4* (eds. C. H. Gordon and G. A. Rendsburg; Winona Lake, Ind.: Eisenbrauns, 2002), 215–22.

[11] Marco Merola, "Royal Goddesses of a Bronze Age State," *Archaeology* 61 (2008): 9.

[12] ARM III 40:16.

[13] ARM X 63:15.

[14] ARM II 90:18, 22; see also ARM I 65:5; J.-M. Durand has stated that he believes these sacrifices were mortuary in character (ARMT XXVI:1 p. 612) and were celebrated particularly for the dead of the royal line (Bordreuil and Pardee, "Textes ougaritiques oubliés et transfuges," *Semitica* 41–42 [1993]: 25 n. 6).

[15] For citations and discussion, see Wayne T. Pitard, "Care of the Dead at Emar," in *Emar: The History, Religion and Culture of a Syrian Town in the Late Bronze Age* (ed. M. Chavalas; Bethesda, Md.: CDL, 1996), 123–40. See also Oswald Loretz, "Die Teraphim als 'Ahnen-Götter-Figur(in)en' im Lichte der Texte aus Nuzi, Emar, und Ugarit: Anmerkungen zu *ilānū/ilh, ilhm/ʔihym* und DINGIR.ERÍN.MES/*ins ilm*," *UF* 24 (1992): 152–67; and John Huehnergard, "Biblical Notes on Some New Akkadian Texts from Emar (Syria)," *CBQ* 47 (1985): 428–34. Pitard states cautiously that "these tablets cannot be used as independent evidence for a cult of the deified dead at Emar," but this seems unduly reserved. Pitard's concern is that the dead may not actually be perceived as powerful, but rather as needy (in which view he is influenced by Schmidt). We have already alluded to this issue in chapter 1, and it is taken up again below. Neediness and power are not mutually exclusive as regards the dead. In light of the larger picture of the dead in Mesopotamia and Egypt, the fact that the dead receive offerings alongside the gods suggests that they are perceived at least analogously, if not equally.

[16] The texts in question are *Emar* 6, 452 and 6, 359.

[17] The whole ritual comprised 3000–3500 lines. See Theo P. J. van den Hout, "Death, the Afterlife and Other Last Things: Anatolia," in *Religions of the Ancient World: A Guide* (ed. Sarah Iles Johnston; Cambridge, Mass.: Belknap Press of Harvard University Press, 2004), 483–85.

ruler's body on the night between the second and third days.[18] After the cremation, the ashes and bones were placed on a throne and moved to the royal mausoleum (called the "Stone House" or *ḫegur*-house), which was often carved into rocky outcroppings outside the main city of Hattuša.[19] As in Egypt, Hittite rulers "sometimes started planning and building their tombs already during their lives, at great expense."[20] During the rituals in the Stone House, the ruler was represented by a statue, and priests performed various rituals to prepare him or her for the afterlife, including offerings to effect reconciliation, and provisions of food and drink.[21] With such care, the king became divinized – "the king (or queen) became a god" was a common idiom for a royal death – and could anticipate "a very pleasant existence" in the afterlife.[22] Statues of deceased kings and queens continued to receive offerings in a mortuary cult.[23]

Other aspects of Hittite imperial mortuary religion will be familiar to readers familiar with Mesopotamian and Egyptian religion: the role of the sun god as royal psychopomp; the belief in an afterlife where food and drink are scarce; the fear of the uncared-for dead; and the practice of necromancy.[24]

The Hittite texts probably reflect certain long-standing traditions and older prototypes,[25] but Dominik Bonatz has argued that there was "an increasing importance of the cult for the deceased kings and their ancestors towards the end of the Hittite Empire period."[26] Most of the extant texts are from palace and temple,

---

[18] Alexei Kassian, Andrej Korolëv, and Andrej Sidel'tsev, *Hittite Funerary Ritual: šalliš waštaiš* (Münster: Ugarit-Verlag, 2002).

[19] Van den Hout, "Death, the Afterlife and Other Last Things," 484. Van den Hout elsewhere clarifies that the two terms are not synonymous; the "(Divine) Stone House" is the actual royal tomb, whereas *ḫegur* derives from a term for a mountain peak that came to refer to stone monuments and buildings of various kinds. Van den Hout, "The (Divine) Stone House and Ḫegur Reconsidered," in *Recent Developments in Hittite Archaeology and History: Papers in Memory of Hans G. Güterbock*. Eds. K. A. Yener and H. A. Hoffner Jr. (Winona Lake: Eisenbrauns, 2002), 73–91.

[20] Van den Hout, "Death, the Afterlife and Other Last Things," 484.

[21] Van den Hout, "Death, the Afterlife and Other Last Things," 484.

[22] Harry A. Hoffner, "The Royal Cult in Hatti," in *Text, Artifact, Image: Revealing Ancient Israelite Religion* (eds. Gary M. Beckman and Theodore J. Lewis; BJS 346; Providence: Brown Judaic Studies, 2006), 144–51. As Hoffner points out, the Hittite king may already have been viewed as divine during his life, in the manner of Egyptian pharaohs. A royal prayer addresses the sun god, asking "let me ascend to my divine fate, to the gods of heaven, and free me from among the (ghosts of the) dead" (KBo XV 2 rev 14'–19'). However, Hittite kings and queens never receive the divine determinative, surprisingly. See Theo P. J. van den Hout, "Death as a Privilege: The Hittite Royal Funerary Ritual," in *Hidden Futures: Death and Immortality in Ancient Egypt, Anatolia, the Classical, Biblical and Arabic-Islamic World* (ed. J. M. Bremmer, Th. P. J. van den Hout, and R. Peters; Amsterdam: Amsterdam University Press, 1994), 46.

[23] Dominik Bonatz, "Syro-Hittite Funerary Monuments: A Phenomenon of Tradition or Innovation?" in *Essays on Syria in the Iron Age* (ed. G. Bunnens; Louvain: Peeters, 2000), 198.

[24] Van den Hout, "Death as a Privilege," 37–76.

[25] Kassian et al., *Hittite Funerary Ritual*, 13.

[26] Bonatz, "Syro-Hittite Funerary Monuments," 201.

giving little insight into the beliefs of the rest of the society, although there are oracular inquiries directed to the souls of the angry dead, not all of whom were royal.[27] Therefore it appears that the Hittite dead in general, like the Egyptian dead, were thought to live on after the death of the body[28] – and that they were prone to need to be appeased.

Hittite mortuary chapels, like Egyptian mortuary chapels, were not burial sites. No remains have been found with the stelae discussed above. The Royal Funerary Ritual describes the cremation of the body, and indeed a number of cremation burials have been found in Bronze Age Anatolia. Extramural inhumation of the body (i.e., away from human settlements) seems to have been more common during the period of the Empire, however. By contrast, one finds large-scale cremation cemeteries in Iron Age Neo-Hittite cities such as Carchemish and Hamath, so that cremation seems to have been increasingly the norm.[29]

These data set a larger cultural context that shapes one's interpretation of Ugaritic and Judean data. In conjunction with the Mesopotamian and Egyptian data, they should establish the expectation of a belief in a supernatural afterlife, at least for royalty, and the existence of cults of the dead.[30]

3.3 Ugarit

3.3.1 Ugarit and the Bible

Ugarit, a Bronze Age city-state on the northern coast of Palestine, has become a flashpoint of controversy, generating both heat and light. Its culture has been studied out of proportion to its historical stature, largely because of the significance of Ugaritic religion for the reconstruction of West Semitic religion in general, and specifically Israelite religion and its "Canaanite" context.

The contribution of the Ugaritic data to the study of the Hebrew Bible is unquestionable; scarcely any part of the Bible has been untouched by the discoveries from Ras Shamra. Methodological difficulties remain, however. Ugaritic

---

[27] I am indebted to Craig Melchert for drawing my attention to these texts. See, e.g., Theo van den Hout, *The Purity of Kingship: An Edition of CHT 569 and Related Hittite Oracle Inquiries of Tuthaliya IV* (Leiden: Brill, 1998); 187. The text in question is KUB 22.35.

[28] See also KUB 43.60 i 26–28, which reads, in Melchert's translation: "The soul is great. The soul is great. Whose soul is great? The mortal('s) soul is great. What road does it have? It has the great road."

[29] Charles Allen Burney, "Burial Customs" and "Cremation" in *Historical Dictionary of the Hittites* (Lanham, Md.: Scarecrow Press, 2004).

[30] Brian B. Schmidt, exceptionally, dismisses the Ebla, Nuzi, and Emar evidence and argues that the Mari mortuary rituals "do not necessarily signify the belief in the dead's supernatural beneficence" (*Israel's Beneficent Dead*, 41; also 14–46; 122–31). This mirrors facets of his arguments about Ugarit and Israel/Judah; see further discussion below.

religion was long taken as nearly equivalent to "Canaanite religion" as described in the Bible.³¹ This use of the term "Canaanite" is problematic.³² The area the Bible describes as "Canaan" encompassed a much more extensive and diverse area than Ugarit, including southern Palestinian nations with religions unlike that of Ugarit.³³ Indeed, Ugaritians themselves sometimes referred to "Canaanites" among foreigners.³⁴ Therefore I avoid the term "Canaanite"; when a broader category is needed, I prefer "Syro-Palestinian."

Ugaritic religion has been taken not only as a foil to biblical Yahwism but also as a complement to it. Many scholars have worked under the assumption that, as H. L. Ginsberg once put it, "the Hebrew Bible and the Ugaritic texts are to be regarded as one literature."³⁵ As a pinnacle of this phenomenon, one could take *Ras Shamra Parallels* (*RSP*), a three-volume encyclopedia of perceived linguistic (primarily lexical) similarities between Ugaritic and biblical texts. Although edited by Loren R. Fisher and Stan Rummel, it especially showcased the work of Mitchell Dahood.³⁶ For many readers, studies like *RSP* raised "the specter of pan-Ugaritism"³⁷ (a reference to the earlier excesses of "pan-Babylonism"), and Dahood in particular has become synonymous with overambitious comparison.

---

³¹ To list just a few examples from across the decades, from authors who use the terms "Canaan" and "Canaanite" with varying levels of self-consciousness: Charles Virolleaud, *Légendes de Babylone et de Canaan* (Orient ancien illustré 1; Paris, Dépôt: A. Maisonneuve, 1949); M. D. Coogan, ed., *Stories from Ancient Canaan* (Philadelphia: Westminster, 1978); G. del Olmo Lete, *Mitos y Leyendas de Canaan: Según la Tradición de Ugarit* (Madrid: Ediciones Cristiandad; Valencia: Institución San Jerónimo, 1981); G. R. Driver, *Canaanite Myths and Legends* (Edinburgh: T & T Clark, 1956). There are many reasons for this conclusion, not least of which is the identification of Ugarit's chief god, Baal, with the "Baals" who epitomize apostasy from YHWH in the Hebrew Bible.

³² For a fuller discussion, see Mark S. Smith, *The Origins of Biblical Monotheism: Israel's Polytheistic Background and the Ugaritic Texts* (Oxford: Oxford University Press, 2001), 14–18.

³³ E.g., Moab, Edom, Ammon; see Patrick D. Miller, *The Religion of Ancient Israel* (Library of Ancient Israel; Lousiville, Ky., Westminster John Knox, 2000), 4; André Lemaire, "Déesses et dieux de Syrie-Palestine d'après les inscriptions (c 1000–500 av. n. è.)," in Walter Dietrich and Martin A. Klopfenstein, eds., *Gott Allein? JHWH-Verehrung und biblischer Monotheismus im Kontext der israelitischen und altorientalische Religionsgeschichte* (OBO 139; Göttingen: Vandenhoeck & Ruprecht, 1994), 127–58.

³⁴ Smith, *Origins of Biblical Monotheism*, 14–15.

³⁵ H. L. Ginsberg, "The Ugaritic Texts and Textual Criticism," *JBL* 62 (1943): 109. Kathleen Kenyon theorized, from a more historical perspective, that "Canaanite" culture had its origins "in the coastal Syrian area centered on Byblos." See Kenyon, "Palestine in the Middle Bronze Age," in *Cambridge Ancient History*, II/3 (rev. ed.; Cambridge: Cambridge University Press, 1966), 11, 38.

³⁶ Loren R. Fisher and Stan Rummel, eds., *Ras Shamra Parallels* (3 vols.; AnOr 49–51; Rome: Pontificium Institutum Biblicum, 1972–81).

³⁷ J. C. de Moor and P. van der Lugt, "The Spectre of Pan-Ugaritism," *BO* 31 (1974): 3–26. This is of course part of a larger conversation about the use of comparative data in biblical studies. One might also mention Samuel Sandmel, "Parallelomania," *JBL* 81 (1962): 1–13, a similar reaction in New Testament studies.

The retrenchment of recent years, acknowledging the distance and the differences among Ugarit, Canaan, and Israel, has been salutary.[38]

In spite of the methodological problems, any reconstruction of the religions of Palestine in the first millennium must deal thoroughly with the Ugaritic data; although Ugarit is not the equivalent of Israel, Judah, or "Canaan," it forms a crucial piece of their cultural matrix, and there remain specific shared features of Ugaritic and Israelite religion.[39]

3.3.2 The archaeology of death in Ugarit

Ugarit's tombs are distinctive in the archaeological record of ancient Syria-Palestine in that they are intramural; that is, they were built within the city, beneath homes. Not every home had its own tomb, but rather it appears in many cases that multiple homes shared a tomb. This may reflect that not only nuclear families but whole clans would bury their dead together.[40] A number of large, luxurious, high-status tombs have been found in Ugarit; by contrast, no common or rural burials from the area of Ugarit have been published – but this is a common lacuna in the archaeology of the ancient Near East.

The first excavations at Minet el-Beida, the site of Ugarit's port, helped to make the "cult of the dead" a primary topic of discussion. Its popularity owes much to certain findings of Claude Schaeffer, who oversaw the initial dig.[41] In his initial reports, Schaeffer wrongly concluded that the area was a huge necropolis.[42] His error resulted from not realizing that the common tombs in Ugarit were built beneath homes, unlike any other site in Syria. Because Schaeffer assumed that the above-ground structures would not be homes, he interpreted them, and all their associated architectural features, as part of massive tombs for the dead

---

[38] Regarding cults of the dead specifically, see discussion below. For general discussion, see P. C. Craigie, "Ugarit, Canaan and Israel," *TynBul* 34 (1983): 145–67. Wrote O. Keel and C. Uehlinger: "[T]rying to make sense of the symbol system of ninth- or seventh-century Palestine with the aid of texts from Ugarit is extremely problematic. Frequently, these can offer nothing more than 'parallels,' a situation which increases the likelihood that someone will try to use them to fill in details. They are not primary sources for the religious history of Canaan and Israel" (*Gods, Goddesses and Images of God in Ancient Israel* [trans. T. Trapp; Minneapolis: Fortress, 1998], 396). See also Smith, *Origins of Biblical Monotheism*, 16.

[39] For additional examples and discussion of methodology, see Mark S. Smith, "Recent Study of Israelite Religion in Light of the Ugaritic Texts," in *Ugarit at Seventy-Five* (edited by K. Lawson Younger Jr.; Winona Lake, Ind.: Eisenbrauns, 2007), 1–25.

[40] Jean-François Salles, "Rituel mortuaire et rituel social à Ras Shamra/Ougarit," in *The Archaeology of Death in the Ancient Near East* (ed. Stuart Campbell and Anthony Green; Oxbow Monographs 51; Oxford: Oxbow Books, 1995), 173, 175.

[41] Claude F. A. Schaeffer, *Ugaritica: Études Relatives aux Découvertes de Ras Shamra*, Première série (Mission de Ras Shamra 1; Paris, P. Guethner, 1939).

[42] Wayne T. Pitard, "The 'Libation Installations' of the Tombs of Ugarit," *BA* 57 (1994): 20–37.

who were buried underneath. He explained these features by reference to then-current understandings of Mycenaean tombs, which were the closest analogues available to him.⁴³ Thus, gutter systems became libation channels for pouring offerings for the dead into the tombs; holes in tomb ceilings became a way to insert offerings. (Wayne Pitard has demonstrated that the gutters did not originally drain into the tombs, but rather away from them and that many of the ceiling holes were made by looters after the city ceased to be inhabited.⁴⁴) Storage jars beside the doors to tombs became receptacles for mortuary offerings, and tables for pressing olive oil became the so-called libation tables.

Although Schaeffer eventually realized his mistake, and although he mentioned the correct interpretation in later publications, he never systematically republished his initial findings, and so the misconceptions were allowed to survive, especially among nonarchaeologists. Even though it became widely understood that the structures atop the tombs were homes, the death-cult interpretation of the associated paraphernalia stuck. Klaas Spronk, in his watershed 1986 monograph (see § 3.3.3.2.1 below), followed Schaeffer's initial interpretations, commenting that Ugaritic houses show "a more than usual emphasis on repeated offering to the dead."⁴⁵ As late as 1989, Theodore Lewis also used Schaeffer's early findings and diagrams in arguing for a cult of the dead at Ugarit.⁴⁶ Some years

---

⁴³ G. del Olmo Lete sees the cults of the deified kings as "yet another element in the area of cultural similarity between Greeks and Semites" (*Canaanite Religion: According to the Liturgical Texts of Ugarit* [tr. W. G. E. Watson; Winona Lake, Ind.: Eisenbrauns, 2004], 326). The scholarly debate regarding the Mycenean cult of the dead is no more settled today than that regarding the Ugaritic cult of the dead. See Chrysanthi Gallou, *The Mycenean Cult of the Dead* (BAR International Series 1372; Oxford: Archaeopress, 2005). Gallou finds a movement of growing skepticism toward the Mycenaean cult of the dead (which began much earlier than the skepticism toward that of Ugarit). She, however, renews the arguments for it based on both tomb architecture and art, particularly funerary iconography (pp. 16–18). Of particular relevance to Isaiah's time, one Hellenistic scholar "concluded that cult of the dead and heroic cult was practiced undeniably *only in eighth-century* Greece" (p. 19, emphasis added), and Walter Burkert has argued that the eighth century was a time of particular cultural influence of the Orient on Greece (*The Orientalizing Revolution: Near Eastern Influence on Greek Culture in the Early Archaic Age* [Cambridge, Mass.: Harvard University Press, 1992], 8, 128–29). See also Glen Markoe, "The Emergence of Orientalizing in Greek Art: Some Observations on the Interchange between Greeks and Phoenicians in the Eighth and Seventh Centuries B.C.," *BASOR* 301 (1996): 47–67. Could it be that contact with (and emulation of) the Syro-Palestinian seacoast was the impetus for a particular surge in death cults' popularity in Greece during that period? (For a different view, see C. H. Gordon, *Before the Bible: The Common Background of Greek and Hebrew Civilisations* [London: Collins, 1962], which perceives common roots for the two civilizations in second-millennium "Eastern Mediterranean culture," visible primarily in Ugaritic remains.)

⁴⁴ Pitard, "'Libation Installations,'" 22–33.

⁴⁵ Klaas Spronk, *Beatific Afterlife in Ancient Israel and in the Ancient Near East* (AOAT 219; Neukirchen-Vluyn: Neukirchener Verlag, 1986), 144.

⁴⁶ Theodore J. Lewis, *Cults of the Dead in Ancient Israel and Ugarit* (HSM 39; Atlanta: Scholars Press, 1989), 97–98. See also J. W. Ribar, "Death Cult Practices in Ancient Palestine" (Ph.D. diss., University of Michigan, 1973), 47–50.

Fig. 3.1 One of the underground tombs from the palace area in Ugarit, showing the unblocked doorway, wall niches, and floor hole. Photo courtesy of Rudy Dornemann. From Sophie Marchegay, "The Tombs", *NEA* 63 (2000): 209.

later, after the publication of Pitard's article, he wrote that he had been "duped."[47]

It does not seem to me, however, that the cultic interpretation of the tombs should be so quickly dismissed. There remain at least three possible critical responses to Pitard. First, certain features of the tombs that he did not discuss

---

[47] Theodore J. Lewis, "How Far Can Texts Take Us? Evaluating Textual Sources for Reconstructing Ancient Israelite Beliefs about the Dead," in *Sacred Time, Sacred Place: Archaeology and the Religion of Israel* (ed. Barry M. Gittlen; Winona Lake, Ind.: Eisenbrauns, 2002), 169–217. In fact, it would appear that some scholars simply are not convinced by Pitard's revision of the data: R. E. Friedman and S. D. Overton, "Death and Afterlife: The Biblical Silence," in *Judaism in Late Antiquity, Part 4, Death, Life-after-Death, Resurrection and the World to Come in the Judaisms of Antiquity* (ed. Alan J. Avery-Peck and Jacob Neusner; Handbuch der Orientalistik 55; Leiden: Brill, 2000), 38.

remain as possible witnesses to a cult of the dead. J. David Schloen mentions wall cavities that, by analogy with tombs at Ur, seem to have been intended to hold images of household gods or ancestor figurines; holes for wooden altar installations in the tombs; and also pottery bowls that likely held food offerings.[48] Most significantly, Pitard entirely omitted discussion of one of the key features that Schaeffer thought was relevant to the cult of the dead: "Les Myceniens avaient l'habitude de murer les portes de leurs tombes. Cela nous n'avons pu l'observer avec certitude dans aucune des grandes tombes d'Ugarit."[49] Of course, the absence of sealed doors constitutes an argument *ex silentio* – but if the doors were indeed left unsealed, it would have given easy access to the tombs in a way that might not have been necessary for infrequent burials.[50] J. W. Ribar suggested just such a "'walk-in' death cult" interpretation of Tomb 103 at Samaria.[51] Presumably, Ribar meant that a mortuary cult could easily have been practiced in the tombs. Jean-François Salles has further pointed to holes in the floors of the tombs that he believes were intended as portals for the spirits of the dead to go to and from the underworld. Indeed, he argues that since no human remains were found in the "tombs," one could go so far as to interpret them instead as funerary chapels.[52]

Second, Pitard was not able to exclude the possibility that *some* of the archaeological features he did discuss could still indicate a cult of the dead. For example, some of the ceiling holes seem to have been part of the original architecture and thus *would* have allowed access from the home above. He also granted that the storejars by the entrance to Tomb IV may have been cultic in nature. Furthermore, although the "tomb windows," into which offerings could be inserted, do not seem to have been accessible from the rooms above, they *do* seem to have been left open on purpose, and thus to have given access to the tomb. Pitard concluded that they "would have functioned only during rituals taking place inside the tomb, which most likely were performed only on the occasion of burials."[53] But this conclusion about the frequency of ritual actions toward the dead is quite uncertain for the reasons outlined above.

Third, the existence of cults of the dead does not necessarily depend on architectural features. For example, as one recent study showed, libation offerings in

---

[48] J. David Schloen, *The House of the Father as Fact and Symbol: Patrimonialism in Ugarit and the Ancient Near East* (Winona Lake, Ind.: Eisenbrauns, 2001), 346.

[49] "The Mycenians had the custom of walling up the doors of their tombs. We have not observed this with certitude in any of the great tombs of Ugarit." Schaeffer, *Ugaritica*, 79.

[50] Ugaritic tombs were often shared by two or three homes, as in the Centre de la Ville and the Ville Sud (Salles, "Rituel mortuaire et rituel social," 175; Schloen, *House of the Father*, 346); even so, how many deaths could one expect in a year among a few families?

[51] Ribar, "Death Cult Practices in Ancient Palestine," 62.

[52] Salles, "Rituel mortuaire et rituel social," 176–77. Although Salles' essay appeared at least a year after Pitard's critique of Schaeffer, it does not appear that Salles had the chance to take it into account.

[53] Pitard, "'Libation Installations,'" 29.

the ancient world typically did not require any permanent receptacle.[54] They could be poured directly on a grave, into a portable vessel, or on the ground. The pouring of offerings directly on the ground appears to be related in *CAT* 1.3 iii 15–22 (line 16: *sk.šlm.lkbd.arṣ*: "pour a peace-offering into the midst of the earth").[55] In conjunction with mortuary libation practices and structures that have been reported in Palestine,[56] Mesopotamia,[57] and Greece,[58] ideally the Ugaritic tombs deserve another firsthand look. Unfortunately, flaws in the initial excavation may make this impossible: "The LB tombs at Ras Shamra and elsewhere, including Palestine, were so poorly excavated and their contents so badly recorded that they can be understood only in light of pertinent texts."[59]

In conclusion, a number of possible indications of a cult of the dead at Ugarit survive Pitard's critique; and in any case, such cults cannot be disproved by archaeological data alone. At the very least, the unusual (for Syria) proximity of Ugarit's tombs to its homes suggests that its beliefs and rituals should not be too quickly equated with those of other cultures. There remain reasons to think that Ugaritians purposely allowed access to the tombs for cultic purposes.

3.3.3 Death in the Ugaritic texts

From the earliest publications on Ras Shamra in the 1930s up to the 1980s, an assortment of scholars assembled data supporting the idea that Ugarit was home to an elaborate ancestor cult and highly developed imagery of the dead and their powers. That view was largely uncontested. In the 1980s and 1990s, however, a smaller number of scholars, many of them very prominent, called into question the validity of that extensive synthesis. It would appear today that these objections, while salutary, will have succeeded only in reducing the scale and scope of their object; the Ugaritic death cult lives on.

---

[54] Amy M. Fisher, "Pour Forth the Sparkling Chalice: An Examination of Libation Practices in the Levant" (Honors thesis, Macalester College, 2007).

[55] See also parallels at *CAT* 1.1 ii 19–25; 1.3 iv 8–14, 28–31.

[56] Elizabeth Bloch-Smith, *Judahite Burial Practices and Beliefs About the Dead* (JSOTSup 123; Sheffield: JSOT Press, 1992), 143; Ribar, "Death Cult Practices in Ancient Palestine," 47–50.

[57] The Akkadian term *arūtu* refers to a libation-pipe. Cf. *CAD* A/II, 324b.

[58] E.g., Pausanius 10.4.7; see also *Encyclopedia of Ancient Greece* (ed. Nigel Wilson; London: Routledge, 2005), 134–35; Gallou, *Mycenean Cult of the Dead*; Joseph Rykwert, *The Dancing Column: On Order in Architecture* (Cambridge, Mass.: MIT Press, 1996), 320; William Bell Dinsmoor, *The Architecture of Ancient Greece: An Account of Its Historic Development* (3rd rev. ed.; London: B. T. Batsford, 1950), 65; L. B. Patton, *Spiritism and the Cult of the Dead in Antiquity* (New York: Macmillan, 1921), 140–41; J. G. Frazer, *Pausanius' Description of Greece* (London: Macmillan, 1898), 227–28.

[59] Philip J. King and Lawrence E. Stager, *Life in Biblical Israel* (Library of Ancient Israel; Louisville: Westminster John Knox, 2001), 376.

3.3.3.1 Burial and mourning

Mourning in Ugarit seems to have taken forms familiar from other cultures, if the Baal Cycle is any indication:[60] Upon Baal's death, El and Anat both wail (ṣḥ), put on a specific type of clothing (*mizrt*), and gash their faces, arms, and torsos (see *CAT* 1.5 vi:14–1.6 i:7). El further puts dust on his head. In the Kirta epic, the eponymous king retires to his room, weeping, after the death of his entire family (*CAT* 1.14 i:26–35). It is not clear whether the ensuing sacrifice on the rooftops (1.14 ii:19–24) is related to the deaths[61] or is simply part of an effort to elicit a better fate from the gods. As for specifically royal funerary practices, the command to mourn over the throne and footstool of the dead king (*CAT* 1.161:13–14) suggests that a chair served as a placeholder for the deceased's spirit, as in Mesopotamian and Hittite funerals.

3.3.3.2 The Ugaritic dead

The Ugaritic cult of the dead up to the "Spronk synthesis"

In the same year that Schaeffer published his analysis of Ugarit's tombs, he published a synthetic study of Ugaritic texts, of which one chapter was entitled "Fertility Cult and Cult of the Dead at Ugarit."[62] He argued that the aforementioned text from the Baal Cycle, which speaks of pouring libations "into the midst of earth," reflected a ritual intended to secure the goodwill of "Aliyan, son of Baal" and thereby to ensure the fertility of the trees and fields.[63] Schaeffer compared this ritual with the Greek myth of the Danaids, who killed their husbands and were sentenced by the gods to pour water into a bottomless pot. He suggested that that task was not originally a Sisyphean punishment, but was intended to provide care for the deceased husbands.[64]

Because many of the key texts were not available in wide publication until the 1960s and 1970s (e.g., *CAT* 1.20–22 and 1.161; see below), Schaeffer's theory initially seems to have elicited little reaction. However, in the wake of new publications, in the 1970s and 1980s the study of the Ugaritic cult of the dead was taken up enthusiastically by a number of scholars. Johannes C. de Moor (1972)

---

[60] The question of whether the actions of the gods reflect the ritual actions of humankind is a crucial one in interpreting Ugaritic religion. Jack M. Sasson has called for greater methodological rigor in interpreting the Ugaritic stories ("Literary Criticism, Folklore Scholarship, and Ugaritic Literature," in *Ugarit in Retrospect: Fifty Years of Ugarit and Ugaritic* [ed. Gordon D. Young; Winona Lake, Ind.: Eisenbrauns, 1981], 81–98). In this case, the extensive comparative data on mourning allow one safely to draw conclusions.

[61] This conclusion is tempting in light of the collocation in Jer 19:10–13 of rooftop sacrifice with the Tophet cult of human sacrifice (see § 4.4.3.2.1).

[62] Chapter 3 in Claude F. A. Schaeffer, *The Cuneiform Texts of Ras Shamra-Ugarit* (Schweich Lectures; London: Oxford University Press, 1939).

[63] Schaeffer, *Cuneiform Texts of Ras Shamra-Ugarit*, 46. (CAT 1.3 iii 16)

[64] Schaeffer, *Cuneiform Texts of Ras Shamra-Ugarit*, 53.

theorized that "communion with the dead," including the pouring of libations, was a major feature of the Ugaritic "New Year's festival."[65] Jonas C. Greenfield[66] and especially Marvin H. Pope[67] were also in the vanguard of the movement.

The work of that entire generation of Ugaritologists is meticulously compiled in Klaas Spronk's *Beatific Afterlife in Ancient Israel and in the Ancient Near East* (1986), initially a dissertation written under de Moor. As the title suggests, Spronk's own interests led him to other matters, but en route his survey still represents the most ambitious attempt to argue for widespread cults of the dead throughout the ancient Near East. Given Spronk's intellectual heritage, it is not surprising that his work on the Ugaritic texts was particularly thorough, if perhaps *too* far-reaching.[68] I have cited his forebears occasionally in what follows, but a fuller sense of the literature is best gained by reading the relevant passages in *Beatific Afterlife*. Thus, "Spronk" becomes, for the sake of simplicity, a metonym for the accumulated views of the previous generation.

Spronk was followed three years later by Lewis, whose *Cults of the Dead in Ugarit and Israel* (1989) is a more limited but also more judicious treatment of the Ugaritic texts. Lewis implicitly restricted the scope of his study by focusing less on the epic/mythical texts (which had made the strongest first impression on the field) and more on ritual texts,[69] perhaps because these were taken to be more reliable indicators of actual Ugaritic(/"Canaanite") practices.[70] While Lewis disagreed with Spronk on certain details, his work reinforced many of Spronk's

---

[65] J. C. de Moor, *New Year with Canaanites and Israelites* (Kampen: Kok, 1972), 8; idem, "Rapi'uma – Rephaim," *ZAW* 88 (1976): 331.

[66] J. C. Greenfield, "Un rite religieux araméen et ses parallèles," *RB* 80 (1973): 47.

[67] Further discussion and literature at § 4.2.3. See M. H. Pope, "Notes on the Rephaim Texts from Ugarit," in *Essays on the Ancient Near East in Memory of Jacob Joel Finkelstein* (ed. M. de Jong Ellis; Memoirs of the Connecticut Academy of Arts and Sciences 19; Hamden, CT: Archon Books, 1977), 163–82; idem, "The Cult of the Dead at Ugarit," in *Ugarit in Retrospect: Fifty Years of Ugarit and Ugaritic* (ed. G. D. Young; Winona Lake, Ind.: Eisenbrauns, 1981), 159–79; idem, "Le mrzḥ à Ougarit et ailleurs," *Annales Archéologiques Arabes Syriennes* 29–30 (1979–80): 141–43: "la nature essentielle du *marzeaḥ* [est] comme banquet pour les morts aussi bien que pour les vivants" (143). Much the same summary is given by Michael C. Astour in "The Nether World and Its Denizens at Ugarit," in *Death in Mesopotamia: Papers Read at the XXVIe Rencontre Assyriologique Internationale* (ed. Bendt Alster; Mesopotamia 8; Copenhagen: Akademisk Forlag, 1980), 227–38.

[68] For a critical view of the book, see Mark S. Smith and Elizabeth Bloch-Smith, "Death and Afterlife in Ugarit and Israel," *JAOS* 108 (1988): 277–84. Another ambitious synthesis and systematization of Ugaritic beliefs was undertaken by Massimo Baldacci, a student of Dahood's: *Il Libro dei morti dell'antica Ugarit: Le più antiche testimonianze sull'Aldilà prima della Bibbia* (Casale Monferrato: Edizioni Piemme, 1998).

[69] Lewis's *Cults of the Dead* focuses on four key texts: the Ugaritic Funerary Text (*CAT* 1.161 = RS 34.126), the Ugaritic King List (*CAT* 1.113 = RS 24.257), the Duties of an Ideal Son (*CAT* 1.17.1.26–34), and the Dagan Stelae (*CAT* 6.13–14).

[70] On this topic, see Sasson, "Literary Criticism, Folklore Scholarship and Ugaritic Literature."

essential conclusions about the Ugaritians' view of death and the dead. The following sections summarize and assess the arguments about key issues.

The rpum (et al.)

Two key Ugaritic terms for the dead are *mt* and *rpum* (cognate with Hebrew מֵת and רְפָאִים). As in Hebrew, the etymology of the latter term is not settled (see § 4.4.2.2), but an older theory – that the term is derived from the Semitic root *rph*, "sink down, be weak" – has largely been set aside in favor of a derivation from the root *rpʾ*, "heal."[71] Thus, the typical understanding is that the dead were seen as supernatural "healers" or helpers of the living.[72]

The *rpum* appear some fifty times in the Ugaritic literature, in a number of contexts. A passage from the Baal Cycle illustrates the potential interpretive problems:

špš . rpim . tḥtk	Šapšu, you rule the Rapaʾuma,
špš . tḥtk . ilnym	Šapšu, you rule the divine ones.
ʿdk . ilm	The gods are your company;
hn . mtm . ʿdk	even the dead are your company. (*CAT* 1.6 vi:45–47)

The interpretation of the passage depends greatly on the translation of the word *mt*, which can mean either "dead (person)" or "man." Schmidt argues that the parallelism of the second couplet comprises a merismus (gods/men),[73] but the synonymous parallelism of the couplets does not support such an interpretation. Both the *rpim* and the *mtm* are parallel to divine beings (*ilnym, ilm*).[74] Schmidt would prefer to see the *rpum* as only semidivine, or perhaps only heroic; but while a few unclear occurrences may point to a second sense of the *rpum* as a class of warriors[75] or a mytho-historical tribe (as in the Hebrew Bible; e.g., Deut 3:11–14), Spronk is probably right that in general "*rpʾm* is a name for the deified royal ancestors who are called up from the netherworld, where they live like shades."[76]

---

[71] Theodore J. Lewis, "Toward a Literary Translation of the Rapiuma Texts," in *Ugarit, Religion and Culture: Essays Presented in Honour of Professor John C. L. Gibson* (ed. N. Wyatt et al.; Ugaritisch-biblische Literatur 12; Münster: Ugarit-Verlag, 1996), 118. Schmidt tentatively suggests translating *rpum* as "Great Ones," based on a theorized cognate relationship between *rpʾ* and Akk. *rabāʾum* (*Israel's Beneficent Dead*, 92–93). The root *rpʾ* is rare in Ugaritic outside references to the *rpum*, but it does exist; see *CAT* 1.114:28.

[72] De Moor, "Rapiʾuma – Rephaim," 323–45; André Caquot, "Les Rephaim Ougaritiques," *Syria* 37 (1960): 72–93.

[73] Schmidt, *Israel's Beneficent Dead*, 87.

[74] Tromp, *Primitive Conceptions*, 177; Theodore J. Lewis, "Dead," *DDD*², 227.

[75] Schmidt (*Israel's Beneficent Dead*, 89–90) cites 4.232:8, 33 in this regard. However, the phrase there is *bn rpiyn*, which may shed very little light on the *rpum* proper. This could just as easily be a group of humans under the divine patronage of the *rpum*.

[76] Spronk, *Beatific Afterlife*, 195. In the Hebrew Bible, the Rephaim frequently appear in parallel with "the dead" and in other underworld contexts (e.g., Ps 88:10; Isa 14:9; see § 4.4.2.2 below).

This conclusion draws further support from the occurrences of forms of *rpʾ* as a theophoric element in personal names.[77]

A number of texts enumerate among the gods the *ilib*, usually taken to mean "the divine ancestor."[78] Two texts from the royal cult affirm the hypothesis that at least the kings of Ugarit were thought to have been divinized after death.[79] The first of these is the "Ugaritic King List" (*CAT* 1.113), of which the reverse is a list of royal ancestors preceded by the word *ʾil*, "god," for example, *ʾil nqmd*.[80] Considerable controversy surrounded the understanding of *ʾil* in the titles of the ancestors – some scholars, such as Schmidt, argued that it simply means "the god of RN"[81] or simply withheld judgment – but the 1998 publication of a syllabic version of the king list (RS 94.2518) using the Sumero-Akkadian divine determinative (i.e., reading DINGIR RN instead of *ʾil* RN) erased doubts about the divinization of dead kings, even among skeptics.[82] Dennis Pardee has also noted that there are check marks on both texts that seem to indicate their sacrificial usage, making it probable that they were associated with a *kispu*-type ritual. Presumably the marks were used to indicate the fulfillment of offerings for each divinized king.[83] Thus, one must understand a name such as the aforementioned *ʾil nqmd* to mean "the divine Niqmaddu," and so forth.[84] Not surprisingly, Lewis deemed *CAT* 1.113 "a most important piece of evidence for the existence of a cult of the dead at Ugarit."[85]

The second text attesting to the divinization of royal dead is *CAT* 1.161, sometimes known as the "Liturgy of the Shades," or simply as the "Ugaritic Royal Funerary Text." This document is entitled *spr dbḥ ẓlm*, "document of the sacrifice

---

[77] Frauke Grøndahl, *Die Personennamen der Texte aus Ugarit* (Studia Pohl 1; Rome: Pontifical Biblical Institute, 1967), 180.

[78] 1.47:2; 1.118:1; etc. See discussion of 1.17 i:26 below.

[79] See discussion by N. Wyatt, "The Religion of Ugarit: An Overview," in *Handbook of Ugaritic Studies* (ed. W. G. E. Watson and N. Wyatt; Leiden: Brill, 1999), 560–62. Indeed, Wyatt has more recently suggested that the king "somehow shared in the ontology of the divine realm" even while *living* ("The Religious Role of the King at Ugarit," *UF* 37 [2005]: 695–727).

[80] The obverse is fragmentary, but appears to indicate a musical ritual involving drum and pipes.

[81] Schmidt, *Israel's Beneficent Dead*, 69–70.

[82] D. Arnaud, "Prolégomènes à la rédaction d'une histoire d'Ougarit II: Les bordereaux des rois divinizés," *Studi Miceni ed Egeo-Anatolici* 41 (1998): 153–73; Dennis Pardee, *Ritual and Cult at Ugarit* (WAW 10; Atlanta: Society of Biblical Literature 2002), 199. In addition to the data unique to the Akkadian tablet, Pardee grants that it is *prima facie* unlikely that each king in a dynasty would have a different god and that a text intended to honor all these different gods would leave them all unnamed (*Ritual and Cult at Ugarit*, 195).

[83] Similar marks are found by the names of the kings in the Akkadian "Genealogy of the Hammurapi Dynasty" (see § 1.4.1 above).

[84] Pardee, *Ritual and Cult at Ugarit*, 200. Pardee worries about the use of the unusual "genitive of identification," but it may also be an appositional nominative; and furthermore the phrase can be understood as a simple calque of the Akkadian.

[85] Lewis, *Cults of the Dead*, 49.

of the shades."[86] It includes a partial list of deceased rulers of Ugarit, and appears to have been written either for the thirteenth-century king Niqmaddu III in anticipation of his death, or for his heir, 'Ammurapi. In it, the *rpim qdmym* ("ancient Rephaim") are summoned, some by name. The text calls for mourning over the throne (*ks'*) and footstool of the king. Next, the sun god, Šapšu, is summoned and instructed to order the deceased king to follow the Rephaim and "descend into the earth and lower (himself) into the dust." Numerous sacrifices are then commanded, and the text closes with prayers of well-being for the new king, 'Ammurapi, for his queen, for their household, and for the city.

The funerary ritual reflected in *CAT* 1.161 is seemingly intended to assure the descent of Niqmaddu to his place among the royal dead. At a minimum, the liturgy establishes that Ugaritians understood their dead kings to be divinized and to "participate" in cultic activities. Although it is not stated in the text, the kings seem to have functioned as guarantors of the royal succession and protectors of the city – an inference from the closing lines, which invoke blessings for the new king and queen, and for Ugarit. Thus, the ritual seems to function similarly to the *kispu*; although it is not clear that the offerings (lines 27–30) are intended for the dead kings, the kings are named for a second time immediately beforehand (lines 23–26). Spronk perceived that "all deceased members of the dynasty of Ugarit are invoked. The ancestors receive sacrifices: they are believed to bless the living king in return."[87] The invocation of the dead ancestors and the request for blessing are structurally parallel to the Mesopotamian "Genealogy of the Hammurapi Dynasty" (see § 1.4.1).[88]

---

[86] The understanding of the term *zlm* is controverted; thankfully, it is not of first importance to the reconstruction of the Ugaritic cult of the dead, since it does not occur in the other texts under discussion. My translation understands *zl* as "shade," which occurs a number of times in Ugaritic, including in the phrase *zlmt* ("shadow of death," *CAT* 1.4 vii:55; cf. Ps 23:4). Further support for this theory is found in the Akk. title *mušêli șilli*, "raiser of shades," which occurs in a lexical list shortly after *mušêli eṭimmi*, "raiser of ghosts" (Jean Bottéro, "La mythologie de la mort en Mésopotamie ancienne," in *Death in Mesopotamia*, 45 n. 28). "Shadow" carries the connotation of protection in numerous Semitic languages (Ps 91:1; etc.); thus, the "shades" may also be viewed "protectors" of the dynasty in this case. There are two other major possibilities that have been advanced for *zlm*: (1) that it is from a root of the same spelling, cognate with Akk. *ṣalāmu*, "to be dark," thus a "nocturnal sacrifice" (Lewis, *Cults of the Dead*, 7, 10–12); or (2) that it means "statue," cognate with Akk. *ṣalmu*. There are indeed a number of Mesopotamian and Hittite rituals in which a dead king is symbolized by a statue, and the reference to the throne in *CAT* 1.161:20 particularly sounds like the Hittite Royal Funerary Ritual. However, such a word for "statue" is not otherwise attested in Ugaritic. In any case, none of these conclusions, if adopted, would greatly alter one's understanding of the text as a whole. For a fuller survey of the proponents of each theory, see Schmidt, *Israel's Beneficent Dead*, 109–10.

[87] Spronk, *Beatific Afterlife*, 191.

[88] See also B. A. Levine and J. M. de Tarragon, "Dead Kings and Rephaim: The Patrons of the Ugaritic Dynasty," *JAOS* 104 (1984): 649–59

Lewis argues that *CAT* 1.161 depicts "only part of a seemingly elaborate cult of the dead in ancient Ugarit."[89] He imagines a ritual stretching over seven days,[90] as is the case with a number of instances of mourning in the Hebrew Bible.[91] In line with his assumption that this is a *kispu*, he describes the heir 'Ammurapi as a *paqidu*, "caretaker," a role attested in the Mesopotamian mortuary cult (§ 1.4.1), but not actually given by the text.[92]

Up to this point, Spronk and Lewis are in agreement, but Spronk's treatment becomes more ambitious. The first major point on which they diverge needs only brief mention because it has not fared well in the discussion of the Ugaritic death cult subsequent to Spronk's work. The passage in question occurs in the Aqhat epic (*CAT* 1.17 i:26–34, cf. ii:1–8, ii:16–23). In it, Baal asks El to grant Dan'el a son to perform various duties for him:

> ... so that his son might be in the house,
> A descendant within his palace;
> Someone to set up the stela (*skn*) of his divine ancestor (*ilibh*),
> in the sanctuary the votive emblem of his clan;
> To send up from the earth his smoke,
> From the dust the protector of his place;
> To shut up the jaws of his detractors,
> to drive out anyone who would do him in;
> To take his hand when he is drunk;
> to bear him up [when] he is full of wine;
> To eat his spelt-offering in the temple of Baal,
> his portion in the temple of El;
> To resurface his roof on a [mud]dy day,
> to wash his outfit on a muddy day.[93]

Pope and others dubbed this text "The Duties of an Ideal Son," and concluded that it describes mortuary rites – an understandable reading in light of the references to sacrifices and stelae, and also to mud (Ug. *ṭiṭ*), a widely recognized component of underworld imagery. Pope thought that a number of these were duties of the ideal son in the role of a caretaker of his deceased ancestors,[94] albeit

---

[89] Lewis, *Cults of the Dead*, 31.
[90] On the basis of the sevenfold offerings at the end of the text. Lewis, *Cults of the Dead*, 96.
[91] E.g., Gen 50:10; 1 Sam 31:13; 1 Chr 10:12; Jdt 16:24; Sir 22:12.
[92] Lewis, *Cults of the Dead*, 34–35. Pitard is surprised that not all the ancestors are named, if it truly is a sacrifice for the ancestors, but Lewis and Spronk think they are included in the more general invocations.
[93] After Pardee's translation in *COS* 1.103.
[94] Pope, "Cult of the Dead at Ugarit," 226–28; see also R. R. Wilson, *Genealogy and History in the Biblical World* (New Haven: Yale University Press, 1977), 121 n. 182, who perceived that "mortuary rites" performed by a son for a father were in view here. This view finds some support in Egyptian texts that delineate mortuary responsibilities, such as the Coffin Text in which a son says to a deceased father, "I ... am here as an advocate in the tribunal of men, / setting up your boundary stone, holding together your despondent ones, / and serving as your image on earth, /

expressed mostly in metaphorical terms. W. F. Albright suggested that the "smoke" (*qṭrh*) in line 28 represents the soul of the father, in parallel with *ḏmr*, the "protector" summoned from the dust in the next line.[95] Pope also believed that the phrase "full of wine" indicated a drunken funerary banquet.[96] Following these interpretations, Spronk concluded that when the tablets are arranged properly, the epic recounts "the tragedy of Daniel who longed for a son to take care of the ancestor-cult after his death, but who is now forced to perform similar rituals himself with regard to his son."[97] However, Dan'el asked Baal for a son to help him *while he is living*, not after he is dead. It is also not clear why many of the duties should be presented metaphorically. Lewis concludes that only *nṣb skn ilibh* in line 26 ("one who sets up the stele of his divine ancestor") pertains to mortuary duties.[98] Given the lack of clear support from other texts for the idea that the rest of the duties are mortuary in nature, it is probably better not to assume that they are. Therefore the text makes only a minor contribution to one's understanding of the cult of the dead, by attesting the use of mortuary stelae to represent ancestors.

Given the prominence of the *rpum* in reconstructions of Ugaritic beliefs about the dead, the "Rapiuma texts" (*CAT* 1.20–22) are significant; unfortunately they have also proved very difficult to interpret. The first tablet (1.20) begins: [*rp*]*um* . *tdbḥn* – an invitation to the *rpum* to do something, variously interpreted as "take part in sacrifice,"[99] "sacrifice,"[100] or "feast."[101] The text is broken, but at the end of lines 1–3, the terms *rpum*, *'ilnym*, and *mtmtm* are clearly parallel. The last term, *mtmtm*, has proved especially tricky to interpret, although a construct chain ("men of the dead"/"dead men") seems likely, thus one has a wordplay on the two senses of *mt*.[102]

---

while your gateway is secured by means of that which I do" (Adriaan de Buck, *The Egyptian Coffin Texts* [7 vols.; Chicago: University of Chicago Press, 1935–61], 1.175–76; cited in Jan Assmann, *Death and Salvation in Ancient Egypt* [trans. D. Lorton; Ithaca, N.Y.: Cornell University Press, 2005], 47).

[95] W. F. Albright, "The 'Natural Force' of Moses in the Light of Ugaritic," *BASOR* 94 (1944): 35. However, see Lewis, *Cults of the Dead*, 59–65; he prefers "song." Both roots ("protect" and "sing") are attested for *ḏmr* in Ugaritic.

[96] Pope, "Cult of the Dead at Ugarit," 228.

[97] Spronk, *Beatific Afterlife*, 161.

[98] Pardee initially objected that *ilib* in line 26 simply means "god of the father," i.e., a clan deity (*COS* 1.103 n. 6). The later revelation of the syllabic version of *CAT* 1.113, with its divinized King List, favors Lewis's interpretation. However, Pardee has since modified his stance to argue that *ilib* is "the ancestral head of 'Ilu's family," i.e., a sort of Ur-deity or "primeval cause" (*Ritual and Cult at Ugarit*, 280).

[99] J. C. de Moor, *A Cuneiform Anthology of Religious Texts from Ugarit* (Leiden: Brill, 1987), 287.

[100] Del Olmo Lete, *Mitos y Leyendas*, 417.

[101] Lewis, *Ugaritic Narrative Poetry* (ed. Simon B. Parker; WAW 9; Atlanta: Scholars Press, 1997), 197.

[102] Lewis (*Ugaritic Narrative Poetry*, 197) translates "the ancient dead," perhaps reflecting the

rp]um ¹⁰³ . tdbḥn   The Rephaim shall feast
š]bʿd . ilnym   the spirits [sev]enfold
] kmtmtm   [ ] like the ancient dead.¹⁰⁴

As Nick Wyatt remarked: "whatever the precise nuance, *ilnym* and *mtmtm* refer to the *rpum*."¹⁰⁵ It is probably the same figures who are invited to drink in line 7. Thus, the divinized dead are summoned to a sort of banquet. These are generally thought to be related to the Aqhat legend, both because *CAT* 1.21–22 are by the same scribal hand as the Aqhat tablets (*CAT* 1.17–19), and because in the Aqhat story Dan'el is repeatedly referred to as *mt rpi*, "man of the Rapiu." If they are to be appended to the foregoing narrative, then these texts tell of Dan'el summoning the *rpum* to a mortuary banquet for his dead son.¹⁰⁶

The question is: How many other references to the *rpum* are there in these so-called Rapi'uma texts? Spronk associates numerous other entities in *CAT* 1.20–22 with the *rpum*, so that all of the following become names for the divinized dead: *'ilm* (1.20 i:1, etc.), *aḥm* ("brothers," 1.22 i:5), *ǵzrm* ("heroes," 1.22 i:7) *mlkm* ("(dead) kings," 1.22 i:10),¹⁰⁷ *zbl* ("prince", 1.22 i:10), *ʿllmy* ("whose child?", i.e., uncared-for spirits, 1.22 i:10, 1.161:7), and *ʿbrm* ("those who cross over," 1.22 i:15). These equations in turn lead to an ever-widening array of texts that supposedly refer to the divinized dead under various other names: *šmym* ("those-of-heaven," 1.19 iv:24), *dʾiy* ("kite," 1.108:8), *ḏmr* ("protector," 1.17 i:28), *ḥl mlk* ("host of Malik," 1.41:48; 1.87:52), *qbṣ dtn* ("community of Ditan," 1.15 iii:4, 15), *ilm kbkbm* ("star-gods," 1.43:2–3), and *gtrm* (1.43:9, 17). He sometimes achieves these identifications by reconstructing references to the *rpum* in

---

understanding, "the dead(est) of the dead" (so also Spronk, *Beatific Afterlife*, 164). Del Olmo Lete, reading *km tmtm*, translates, "when you die." A minority contradictory view is expressed by Conrad L'Heureux, who argues for the reading *amtm* and denies that the *rpum* are the dead (*Rank among the Canaanite Gods: El, Baʿal, and the Repha'im* (Missoula, Mont.: Scholars Press, 1979), 130–31.

¹⁰³ The term *rpum* may be restored here with some confidence, on the basis of its occurrences in parallelism with *ilnym* in other passages, e.g., 1.21:3–4.

¹⁰⁴ Cf. Lewis's translation, *Ugaritic Narrative Poetry*, 197.

¹⁰⁵ N. Wyatt, *Religious Texts from Ugarit* (2nd ed.; Sheffield: Sheffield Academic Press, 2002), 315.

¹⁰⁶ Others, however, assume that it is El, because of his banquet for the gods in *CAT* 1.114 (see below). In that case, since 1.114 has rather little reference to the dead or the underworld, the relationship of the Rephaim texts to the cult of the dead would be much more tenuous, relying only on the terms *rpum*, *mtmtm* and *mrzʿy* (cf. 1.21:5, 9).

¹⁰⁷ See J.F. Healey, "Malku : MLKM : Annunaki," *UF* 7 (1975): 235–58 and idem, "MLKM/RPUM and the Kispum," *UF* 10 (1978): 89–91. In the first article, based primarily on a syllabic god list from Ugarit, Healey concluded that the *mlkm* in Ugarit "probably represent a ... group of spiritual or demonic powers" (238). Although akin to the Annunaki of the Mesopotamian netherworld, they were not yet formally identified with the gods of the underworld. The second article argues that the *mlkm* and the *rpum* refer to the same group of people, exclusively dead kings (91).

3.3 Ugarit

texts where they are not otherwise mentioned.[108] Another of his procedures is to note that the *rpum* may be portrayed as "fluttering" like birds,[109] and then to hunt for other occurrences of bird imagery that can be incorporated into the understanding of the *rpum*. The reason for the multiplicity of names, in Spronk's view, is that each captures a different aspect of the dead, e.g.: "Whereas *rp'um* is an indication of the deified dead as 'healers,' *mlkm* may have denoted their state as kings in the netherworld."[110] Without examples of the two terms in parallel usage, however, such equations are problematic. The same methodological flaws plague his discussion of the leaders of the *rpum*.[111] Spronk's net is probably cast too wide. In a polytheistic culture, why is it necessary for one group of divine beings to be so ubiquitous? More likely there were various groups of semidivinities, as in Mesopotamian and Egyptian demonology. It seems better not to read the *rpum* into texts where they are not found, but rather to assume that divine beings by other names are just that.

Spronk's argument about the resurrection of the dead at Ugarit is also tenuous. The best support for it comes from the Aqhat epic: When Anat tries to acquire Aqhat's bow, she famously says, "Ask for life, and I will give it to you / For immortality, and I'll make it yours" (*CAT* 1.17 vi:26–28). She continues: "I'll make you count the years with Baal / with the sons of the El will you count months" (lines 28–29). She seems to compare this offer of life to one made by Baal:

---

[108] For example, compare Spronk's reconstruction of 1.108:17 (*Beatific Afterlife*, 179) with the text in *CAT*, where the word *rpum* is missing entirely.

[109] Spronk understands the occurrences of *ndd* for *rpum* (e.g., *CAT* 1.20 i:2 and 1.21:4) as an image of the dead "fluttering" like startled birds. DUL ("go, move, launch") and other translators offer more sober translations. There is truth to the idea that the dead are frequently portrayed as birds; see Christopher B. Hays, "Chirps from the Dust: The Affliction of Nebuchadnezzar in Daniel 4:30 in Its Ancient Near Eastern Context," *JBL* 126 (2007): *passim*.

[110] Spronk, *Beatific Afterlife*, 188.

[111] Spronk, like a number of others, assumes that Baal is the leader of the *rpum*, based on his title *rpu bʻl* in *CAT* 1.22 i:8. However, it is not so clear that the god *rpu mlk ʻlm* named in 1.108:1 is the same. Rapiu, who appears as early as Mari, is generally taken to be a distinct deity and may in fact be independent of the *rpum* (Simon B. Parker, "The Ugaritic Deity Rapi'u," *UF* 4 [1972]: 97–104). The problem is compounded when Spronk uses one conjecture to prove another, as when he judges that the parallel double deities in 1.108:2, Gathar-and-Yaqar (*gtr.w yqr*), are both among "the famous ancestors of the dynasty of Ugarit," who are summoned from the netherworld along with Baal and Ditan (1:15 iii:4, 15). The parallel phrases *rpi.arṣ // qbṣ.ddn* (e.g., 1.161:2–3) do make it likely that Didanu (or Ditanu) was perceived as a heroic, semi-divine ancestor. However, Spronk takes the phrase *adn ilm.rbm* ("Lord of the Great Gods"), which occurs alongside Ditanu in 1.124, to refer to Baal and thus connects the entire text to the cult of the dead, so that it becomes a ritual in which the healing powers of the *rpum* are invoked (Spronk, *Beatific Afterlife*, 193–95). This is too ambitious; a reasonable position would be to limit the conversation about the powers of the dead to texts including certain important keywords such as *rpum*, *ilm arṣ*, and *mt*. It is quite possible to talk about healing and judging (or about Baal) without any reference to cults of the dead.

kbʿl.kyḥwy.yʿšr
As Baal, when he revives, invites to a feast
ḥwy.yʿšr.wyšqynh
He invites the living one to a feast and offers him drink...
ap ank.aḥwy aqht ġzr
So I will give life to noble Aqhat. (lines 30–33)[112]

A recently published seal from Tell Afis may attest a similar conviction, since it bears the name bʿlḥww, arguably to be translated "Baal gives life."[113] These texts reflect the fact that, like their congeners elsewhere (see §§ 1.4.3, 4.4.4), Ugaritic deities could be said to give or restore life.

Sponk, however, goes somewhat further. Combining this Aqhat passage with the idea that the dying and rising episodes in the Baal Cycle (see above) reflect a yearly cycle, he reconstructs a Ugaritic festival at which Baal's revivification and that of the *rpum* were celebrated. Such a festival, however, is only a conjecture, and his other primary example is not instructive.[114] Anat's promise to Aqhat appears to indicate simply the idea of feasting with the gods in the mortuary cult, as is attested in, e.g., the Panammuwa inscription (§ 3.4).[115] It is telling that Aqhat

---

[112] The translation is mine; for similar views, see DUL 188 (ʿšr), 379 (ḥwy), 840 (šqy); Parker, *Ugaritic Narrative Poetry*, 61; H. L. Ginsberg, *ANET*, 151. Other views include that of Pardee, who sees the revived one as "like Baʿlu (who), when he comes (back) to life, feasts: / they give a feast to the living one, give him drink" (*COS* 1.103; p. 347). Clearly this turns on Pardee's interpretation of the Ugaritic cult of the dead, which is discussed below. It is not clear how he derives a plural translation ("they give a feast") from the second occurrence of yʿšr, unless he deems it an impersonal construction. This seems to me an unnecessary move. Another conflicting view, that Baal "is served" by those whom he revives, has been espoused by K. van der Toorn ("Funerary Rituals and Beatific Afterlife in Ugaritic Texts and in the Bible," *BO* 48 [1991]: 46) and de Moor (*Cuneiform Anthology of Religious Texts from Ugarit*, 238)

[113] See M. G. Amadasi Guzzo, "Une Empreinte de sceau de Tell Afis," *Or* 70 (2003): 318–24; K. Lawson Younger, "Some of What's New in Old Aramaic Epigraphy," *NEA* 70 (2007): 140. This translation is not without problems, but the spelling would be normal in Phoenician.

[114] Much of Sponk's argument hangs on *CAT* 1.22 i:6–7, where he reads: ṯm.ytbš.šm.ʾil.mtm / yṯ(!)bš.brkn.šm.ʾil.ġzrm ("the name of El revivified the dead; / the blessings of the name of El revivified the heroes"). On this basis, he argues that the Rephaim "are revivified with Baal to take part in the New Year's festival celebrating Baal's return to life" (Sponk, *Beatific Afterlife*, 195; cf. 155–56, 205). In twice reading yṯbš, he assumes that there exists an Ugaritic cognate of the Š-stem of the Akk. verb bašû, "to bring into being, create." Sponk cites de Moor on this point. They seem to have changed their mind a year later when, in another publication, they called the form a D-stem of ṯbš and translated it "give substance" (*Cuneiform Anthology of Religious Texts from Ugarit*,175). However, this philological proposal is problematic. Neither root has any other attestation in Ugaritic or any other West Semitic language. And in any case, in the second line above (line 7), the text reads yʿbš, rather than yṯbš (Wyatt, *Religious Texts from Ugarit*, 321 n. 37). Indeed, Pitard corrects line 7 to yʿbš ("A New Edition of the Rapiʾuma Texts," *BASOR* 285 [1992]: 56–57), and he is followed by Lewis (*Ugaritic Narrative Poetry*, 203). The root ʿbš is itself scarcely understood (DUL offers: "?", and neither Wyatt nor Lewis translates it). In sum, this passage is an exceedingly shaky foundation on which to found a theory. See critique by Smith and Bloch-Smith, "Death and Afterlife in Ugarit and Israel," 279.

[115] This theme is commonly attested from the Middle Kingdom onward in Egypt, which was

himself is not impressed by the offer; he seems to sense that participation in the cult of the dead is not the same as true eternal life or resurrection. Aqhat's comment may represent a skeptical tendency in Ugaritic thought, but it may also point to a significant theological distinction. The Ugaritic dead were no more truly restored to life by the cult of the dead than Mesopotamian ghosts were by the *kispu*.

A final question about the Ugaritic *rpum*: Who could aspire to become one, and to feast with the gods? Although it now seems assured that at least dead kings could be called gods in Ugarit, the question of the divinization of nonroyal dead is not clearly answered by the extant Ugaritic texts. Lewis finds it most likely that any dead person could become an *ʾilu*, not only royalty, based on the aforementioned Baal Cycle text 1.6 vi.46–47, which uses *ilm* and *mtm* in parallel fashion.[116] Also supporting a broader interpretation of *mtm* as "divinized dead" are the numerous ritual texts in which the *ʾināšū ʾilīma* ("people of the gods"/"divine people") receive offerings.[117] On the one hand, based on the extant textual corpus, it seems safer to conclude with Spronk that "only a limited number of persons share in the blessing of belonging to the *rpʾum*."[118] If terms such as *mlkm* ("kings") and *ģzrm* ("heroes") indeed refer to the *rpum*, then they seem to describe the *rpum* as an elite class.[119] On the other hand, one can hardly expect proof of the divinity of the common Ugaritic dead, given the almost exclusively elite provenance of the surviving texts. It seems at least possible – and I find it probable – that a "democratization of death" took place in the West Semitic context as it did in Egypt, as "elite emulation" took its course.[120]

The Ugaritic marziḥu

An aspect of Ugaritic culture closely linked to the *rpum* is the *marziḥu* (*mrzʿ* or *mrzḥ*). At a material level, the *marziḥu* was an association that owned real estate,

---

certainly influential along the Syro-Palestinian seacoast while Ugarit was flourishing. As one representative stele reads: "May he have a superfluity of offerings and food ... on all the festivals. ... May he sit at the right of Osiris, at the head of the illustrious nobles." Stela of the Sealbearer Meri (Louvre C3), from the ninth year Senworset I, cited in Assmann, *Death and Salvation*, 225.

[116] Lewis, "Dead," 226–27.

[117] *CAT* 1.39:22; 1:41:5, 27, 40; 1.46:8; 1.105:26; 1.106:2, 7; 1.112:5, 1.132:14–15, 21, 24; 1.134:4; 1.171:5. See discussion in O. Loretz, "Die Teraphim als 'Ahnen-Götter-Figur(in)en' im Lichte der Texte aus Nuzi, Emar, und Ugarit," *UF* 24 (1992): 164–68; Pardee, *Ritual and Cult at Ugarit*, 280. For contradictory theories, see DUL, 84, s.v. "inš."

[118] Spronk, *Beatific Afterlife*, 173.

[119] If the name Didanu were also derived from an ancient class of elite chariot warriors, as is sometimes theorized, this would support the same elite interpretation. John Gray went so far as to see both the *rpi arṣ* and the *qbṣ dtn* as groups of elite (living) humans ("The Rephaim," *PEQ* 81 [1949]: 127–39; idem, "DTN and RPʾUM in Ancient Ugarit," *PEQ* 84 [1952]: 39–40).

[120] Schloen (*House of the Father*, 347) argues that archaeology of Ugaritic tombs suggests "the ongoing participation of deceased ancestors in the life of agrarian households."

including houses (*CAT* 3.9:4), storehouses (3.9:5) and vineyards (4.642:3, RS 18.01:5), all of which could be rented, presumably for banqueting or festivals.[121] The contract in *CAT* 3.9 suggests that it was collectively owned by "members" (*mt mrzḥ*).[122] The term *marziḥu* also applied to banqueting functions held at the property.

The ritual and mythological significance of the *mrzḥ* is in dispute, however. In one of the *rpum* texts (*CAT* 1.21), the *rpum* are invited to a *marziḥu*[123] that involved sacrificing and banqueting, so it has often been assumed that the *marziḥu* is inherently linked to the cult of the dead, especially in light of the association of the Hebrew *marzēaḥ* with mourning practices in Jer 16:5–7.[124] (On the biblical *marzēaḥ*, see § 4.4.1.3 below)

In 1960, André Caquot was among the first to make the broad connections among the Ugaritic *mrzḥ*, the Mesopotamian/Syrian *kispu*, and the sacrifice for the spirit of Panammuwa in *KAI* 214 (§ 3.4).[125] Greenfield followed,[126] and Pope enthusiastically agreed, consolidating some earlier comments in a 1980 article which adjudged: "Despite unfounded skepticism in some quarters, there is scant reason to doubt that the West Semitic Marzeaḥ was a feast for and with the departed ancestors."[127] According to Pope, the Ugaritic Rephaim were "the spirits, ghosts, or shades of the departed deified ancestors who are wined and dined in communal meals with the family, the revered ancestors and the great gods. This funeral feast, corresponding to the Mesopotamian kispu, was ... the Marzeaḥ of the Bible."[128] Spronk offered the somewhat more nuanced view that *mrzḥ* was "a cultic society in which communion with the dead *could* be practised."[129]

As with the *rpum*, the *marziḥu* is prone to expand in the minds of scholars without methodological controls. *CAT* 1.114 mentions a feast for the gods hosted by El at which he encourages them to get drunk and then leads the way himself, to the point that, in lines 21–22:

b ḥrih w tnth . ql. il . km mt	He has fallen into his own dung and urine like a dead man;
il . k yrdm . arṣ	El is like those who descend into the earth

---

[121] Patrick D. Miller, "The Mrzḥ Text," in *The Claremont Ras Shamra Tablets* (ed. L. R. Fisher; AnOr 48; Rome: Pontifical Biblical Institute, 1971), 37–48.
[122] Also attested in an Akkadian text as *amil marzihi* (RS 14.14).
[123] The term used in *CAT* 1.21:1 (and restored in line 9) is *mrzʿy*, but there is scarcely any disagreement that it is equivalent to *mrzḥ*.
[124] Pope, "Cult of the Dead at Ugarit," *passim*.
[125] Caquot, "Les Rephaim Ougaritiques," 93.
[126] Greenfield, "Un rite religieux araméen," 47.
[127] Pope, "Cult of the Dead at Ugarit," 242; see also idem, "Le mrzḥ à Ougarit," 141–43: "la nature essentielle du *marzeah* [est] comme banquet pour les morts aussi bien que pour les vivants" (143). Much the same summary is given by Astour in "Nether World and Its Denizens at Ugarit," 227–38.
[128] Pope, "Cult of the Dead at Ugarit," 241.
[129] Spronk, *Beatific Afterlife*, 202, emphasis added.

Although this text makes no mention of the *rpum* or other mythological aspects of the dead, this passage is used to connect it, too, to the cult of the dead. "This could also explain why the drunken El is compared to the dead," wrote Spronk. "If the communion of the living with the dead was experienced as a reality, the participants could change roles. The living were like the dead and the dead were brought to life."[130] Also from this text Spronk and his forebears concluded that the *marziḥu* typically involved drunkenness like the Greek *thiasos*.[131] Against these synthetic conclusions, it needs to be clarified that (1) neither the *rpum* nor the dead are among the attendees; only the *ilm* are mentioned, along with certain gods of the pantheon (Anat, Athtart); (2) the feast in 1.114 is initially called a *ṣd* ("feast," line 2), and only later is El portrayed "in his *mrzḥ*" (line 15); and (3) although the *marziḥu* may have typically owned vineyards, there is no other mention of drunkenness at a *marziḥu* in the Ugaritic texts, nor is there any clear reference anywhere to sexual practices associated with it.

The best conclusion one can draw is that the cult of the dead was a significant but not necessary facet of the *marziḥu*; it was also possible to "commune" with other divine beings at such an institution.[132] (The *marzēḥāʾ* in Nabatean religion seems to have been quite analogous in this respect, judging from later Aramaic texts and archaeological data.[133]) Drinking was a feature of many religious rituals in the ancient Near East; it was not uniquely associated with the cult of the dead.

A "minimalist" backlash

Spronk's monograph stands as an impressive synthesis of the work of a whole generation of Ugaritologists. However, it very quickly came under critique for the ambitiousness of its claims. I have already referred to the review article of Mark S. Smith and Elizabeth Bloch-Smith, which objected to Spronk's reconstruction of a New Year's revivification festival, to the large number of other terms he thought referred to the *rpum*, and to his tendency to correlate Ugarit

---

[130] Spronk, *Beatific Afterlife*, 202.

[131] Spronk, *Beatific Afterlife*, 202. See Pope's extensive comparative essay on the Ugaritic *mrzḥ* and other mortuary/funerary banquets, drawing largely from Greco-Roman and rabbinic writings, in *Song of Songs: A New Translation with Commentary* (Anchor Bible 7C; New York: Doubleday, 1977), 210–29. In light of rabbinic and Hellenistic portrayals of funerary banquets, Pope further theorized sexual connotations for the *mrzḥ*. Spronk picks up this theme and ties it in with the *mrzḥ*'s (speculative) link to New Year's Festival (following de Moor's *New Year with Canaanites and Israelites*).

[132] Dennis Pardee, "*Marzihu, Kispu*, and the Ugaritic Funerary Cult: A Minimalist View," in *Ugarit, Religion and Culture: Essays Presented in Honour of Professor John C. L. Gibson* (ed. N. Wyatt et al; Ugaritisch-biblische Literatur 12; Münster: Ugarit-Verlag, 1996), 278.

[133] John F. Healey, *The Religion of the Nabataeans: A Conspectus* (Leiden: Brill, 2001), 165–75. For archaeological evidence of other cultic sites perhaps related to funerary/mortuary feasting, see Manfred Bietak, "Temple or 'Bêt Marzeaḥ'?" in *Symbiosis, Symbolism and Power of the Past*, 155–68.

and Israel too closely.[134] Those cautions did not go far enough for other scholars, however. The middle of the 1990s saw a wave of "minimalist" interpretations of the cult of the dead that sought to rein in the excesses of "maximalists" such as Spronk. Pitard, who had compared the Ugaritic Funerary Text to the *kispu* in an earlier article on *CAT* 1.161,[135] later arrived at a much more skeptical position. His aforementioned revision of the archaeological data (see § 3.3.2) was among the first serious challenges to the consensus. In that article's summary, he wrote that without the support of material culture,

> none of these literary sources provide unambiguous evidence for the practice of giving regular water/food offerings to the dead at Ugarit. Although this cannot be taken as a sure indicator that such offerings were not regularly made, it is now clear that one must be very cautious about discussing such activities at Ugarit. There is simply less evidence about Ugaritic funerary practices and beliefs concerning afterlife than has been generally supposed.[136]

Pitard followed this article with a similarly negative assessment of the value of the burial data from Israel, Judah, and Ebla for proving cults of the dead in those locales.[137] While he saw significant parallels between Ugaritic and biblical mourning rites and did not rule out cults of the dead, he judged that the Ugaritic texts are "more ambiguous and impenetrable than earlier thought."[138] "We as scholars need to be more careful than we often are in how we interpret archaeological evidence," he concluded.

Pardee has been extraordinarily cautious in his treatment of the texts, and the minimalist/maximalist framing is his coinage.[139] Writing in 1996, he sought to disentangle the threads of texts that had been woven together by Pope, Spronk, et al. into the tapestry that was the "Ugaritic cult of the dead." Although the discovery of RS 94.2158 changed Pardee's view of the occurrence of a royal mortuary cult – he now acknowledges the *kispu* aspect of the King List and would seem to be edging away from some of his earlier "minimalism"[140] – some of his earlier cautions remain pertinent. Perhaps most significantly, Pardee sought to reduce the fund of terms that refer to the dead. There are only three terms that he accepts as referring to the Ugaritic dead: *rpum* ("shades"), *mlkm* ("deceased kings"), and

---

[134] Smith and Bloch-Smith, "Death and Afterlife in Ugarit and Israel."
[135] Wayne T. Pitard, "The Ugaritic Funerary Text RS 34.126," *BASOR* 232 (1978): 65–75.
[136] Pitard, "'Libation Installations,'" 34–35.
[137] Wayne T. Pitard, "Tombs and Offerings: Archaeological Data and Comparative Methodology in the Study of Death in Israel," in *Sacred Time, Sacred Place: Archaeology and the Religion of Israel* (ed. Barry M. Gittlen; Winona Lake, Ind.: Eisenbrauns, 2002), 145–68.
[138] Pitard, "Tombs and Offerings," 147.
[139] The transference of the term "minimalist" from the debate over the history of Israel seems appropriate in light of the apparent influence of Philip R. Davies's *In Search of Ancient Israel* (JSOTSup 148; Sheffield: Sheffield Academic Press, 1995) on Pardee's understanding of "the cult of the dead" as a scholarly construct.
[140] Pardee, *Ritual and Cult at Ugarit*, 199–201.

inš ilm (reflecting whatever part of the human race is divinized). Although one would expect at least the *mlkm* in royal ritual texts, only *rpum* is ever found "in the texts reflecting the regular Ugaritic cult."[141]

In regard to the *marziḥu*,[142] Pardee did not think that any of the data from Ugarit justify "a connection between the *marziḥu* and the mortuary cult."[143] The primary feature of the *marziḥu* was drinking, not cultic activities; the accounts of divinities at a *marziḥu* were simply projections of the human sphere onto the divine.[144] Similarly, he argues that there was no essential connection between the *rpum* and the *marziḥu*; the Rapiuma Texts are merely a singular literary invention, and the assumption that the *marziḥu* was the regular meeting place of the dead ancestors is "maximalism at its worst."[145]

Roughly concurrent with the work of Pitard and Pardee was Schmidt's *Israel's Beneficent Dead*, published in 1994 as an enlarged version of an Oxford dissertation. On the one hand, Schmidt's survey of the ancient Near Eastern evidence regarding death cults is admirably thorough. He also helpfully advocates for clear use of terminology for the rituals in question; he insists particularly on the funerary-versus-mortuary distinction already mentioned. On the other hand, his entire study is controlled by a questionable thesis: that death-cult practices came to Judah only under the Neo-Assyrians and that therefore any account of them in Israel or Judah prior to the Neo-Assyrian period is a literary invention under Mesopotamian influence. Quite apart from the way in which this theory would flatten the complex compositional history of the Hebrew Bible, Schmidt does not seem to have persuaded many of his peers that the Syro-Palestinian material is bereft of evidence for cults of the dead.

One of Schmidt's central and repeated arguments is that texts referring to the care and feeding of the dead reflect the neediness and powerlessness of the dead rather than a concern to propitiate them, under the assumption of their power. Jo Ann Scurlock has refuted this argument.[146] "[C]ontra Schmidt," she writes:

---

[141] Pardee, "Minimalist View," 284. It is not clear why Pardee excludes *CAT* 1.39, which in his own translation reflects sacrifices for the *inš ilm* (Pardee, *Ritual and Cult at Ugarit*, 69). See del Olmo Lete's interpretation below.

[142] Pardee, "Minimalist View," 278 n. 6; cf. Schmidt, *Israel's Beneficent Dead*, 62–66; Pardee calls into question *CAT*'s reading *mrzʿy* in the Rapiʾuma text 1.21:1 and argues that there are phonological problems in equating *mrzʿy* with *mrzḥ*. However, this might be understood as a sort of "reverse loan" from Akkadian, since syllabic equivalents of *mrzḥ* naturally do not include the *ḥ*: e.g., *bît amil* ᵐ*mar-za-i* (RS 15.70, 15.80). John Huehnergard attributes this to an "intervocalic voicing of /ḥ/ to [ʾ]"(*Ugaritic Vocabulary in Syllabic Transcription* [HSS 32; Atlanta: Scholars Press, 1987], 178); cf. Sponk, *Beatific Afterlife*, 197.

[143] Pardee, "Minimalist View," 277.

[144] Pardee, "Minimalist View," 278.

[145] Pardee, "Minimalist View," 279.

[146] Jo Ann Scurlock, "Ghosts in the Ancient Near East: Weak or Powerful?" *HUCA* 68 (1997): 77–96.

the need of the dead for "care and feeding" does not imply that they "have no power to affect the living in a beneficial (or, one might add, harmful) way." To a polytheist, to say that a spirit needs to be fed, clothed, and washed is to imply, not that he is useless to mankind, but on the contrary that mankind is thereby given the opportunity to enlist him as a friend, and conversely that, once a relationship has been established, it is necessary to keep providing for him lest he become angry. ... It by no means followed that there was no point in seeking their assistance or that there was no reason to fear their wrath.[147]

This is supported by the Mesopotamian *kispu* (§ 1.4.1) and the Egyptian Letters to the Dead (§ 2.4.2), in which the living concerned themselves with the perceived needs of the dead in the hope of enlisting their active help. In other words, a text such as CAT 1.161, which calls for blessings for the *rpum*, does so not primarily out of concern for their (diminished) well-being, but out of the assumption that they have the power to affect the lot of the living – for good or ill.

Another fundamental flaw in Schmidt's argument was revealed when the aforementioned syllabic version of the King List was published, confirming the divinization of dead kings. This datum not only undercuts his contention that CAT 1.113 names a single dynastic god who is associated successively with a number of dead kings; it also invalidates his finding of "the absence of the explicit deification of dead kings at Ugarit."[148] Schmidt perceived the "crucial" nature of this point,[149] and it now clearly works against his argument.

In the end, Schmidt is swimming in a sea of contradictory data.[150] In fact, his book is that rare one that might convince readers of the *opposite* of its thesis owing to the essential honesty and thoroughness of its presentation. This negative summary may seem unfair to a work of such impressive industry and depth of detail as Schmidt's, but he is now often the only dissenting voice cited in this conversation. To my knowledge, he is the only major scholar presently arguing in a categorical way against the Ugaritic belief in the power of the dead.

Despite the reservations expressed by Schmidt, Pardee, and Pitard, it does not seem likely that the Ugaritic cult of the dead will be reduced to the small scale that they would prefer. A recent major synthesis such as G. del Olmo Lete's *Canaanite*

---

[147] Scurlock, "Ghosts in the Ancient Near East," 83. Lewis also criticizes Schmidt for basing his assertion (that care and feeding of the dead logically implies their weakness) on studies of African cults. Lewis warns against "importing definitions and comparisons from cultures that are too far afield," both in space and time, and (drawing on Scurlock) he cogently cites a number of Egyptian and Mesopotamian inscriptions that attest to offerings intended to elicit a certain favor from a ghost (Lewis, "How Far Can Texts Take Us?" 191). See further: Jean Bottéro, "Les morts et l'au-delà dans les rituels en accadien contre l'action des 'revenants,' " *ZA* 73 (1983): 153–203, esp. 169–74.

[148] Schmidt, *Israel's Beneficent Dead*, 113; cf. 67–71.

[149] Schmidt, *Israel's Beneficent Dead*, 113.

[150] His conclusion that the dead in Syria-Palestine were believed to have no powers was deemed "unpersuasive" by Mark Smith (Smith review, *CBQ* 58 [1996]: 724–25) and "quelque peu forcée" by André Lemaire (review in *JNES* 58 [1999]: 217–19), and these are only representative comments.

Religion (revised 1997) not only declined to follow their skepticism regarding the texts already prominent in the conversation, but consolidated the scholarship on a number of *additional* texts, creating a still more complex reconstruction of the royal cult of the dead that involved a garden that served as a royal pantheon, and necromantic consultations.[151] Nick Wyatt is another active scholar of Ugarit who is essentially positive on the main points of the cult of the dead.[152]

The controversy has recently flared up again in two lengthy articles in the past two volumes of *Ugarit-Forschungen*, in which (with enough patience on the part of the reader) the root of the disagreement becomes quite clear: it is an issue of comparative methodology. Del Olmo Lete protests: "my position is ... solidly based on the 'royal ideology,' on the significance of the ancestor cult in the whole Ancient Near East and on the unique importance of the king as supreme officiant."[153] He objects to what he perceives as Pardee's willful ignorance about many hypothetical matters.[154] Pardee, for his part, clarifies that he does think there was both a funerary and a mortuary cult at Ugarit,[155] but adds that he prefers not to say too much about them while "awaiting the discovery of texts that would allow us to learn the real frequency of the rite (or rites) and the details thereof."[156] He protests that del Olmo Lete "knew before he began examining the texts what they would say,"[157] and that his model abolishes the specificity of Ugaritic religion. In the end, Pardee's reading is more careful and better substantiated, but it seems quite likely that a number of details of the ancestor cult need to be filled in the manner of del Olmo Lete.

---

[151] Among the texts to which del Olmo Lete draws new attention is *CAT* 1.39, a ritual text including sacrifices to the *inš ilm* on "the night of Šapšu *pgr*" (on *pgr* as a sacrifice for the dead, see § 3.3.3.3). Del Olmo Lete also reaffirms existing theories about the "month of *gn*" as referring to a "garden" that functioned as a royal pantheon. The tablet *CAT* 1.106 gives instructions for a ritual stretching over twenty-five days that, in del Olmo Lete's view, takes place largely in the royal mausoleum (see further at § 4.4.1.1). This text, which has affinities also with other rituals of the same month, culminates with "a giving of reply" (*CAT* 1.106:31; *Canaanite Religion*, 232. The similar texts include *CAT* 1.105 and 1.112). This leads del Olmo Lete to conclude, "The cult of the royal dead ... goes in two directions – offering and reply – and supposes constant communication between 'the living' and 'the dead.'" He also finds necromantic aspects in *CAT* 1.41:46, 1.87:49–50, 1.104 and 1.124 (*Canaanite Religion*, 246). This emphasis on the necromantic aspects of the cult of the dead is a distinctive point of del Olmo Lete's treatment. Like Spronk and de Moor's New Year's festival, del Olmo Lete's royal funerary cult is an ambitious synthesis. Whether or not future scholarship follows him in the details of his argument, it will be hard to ignore its cumulative force.

[152] See Wyatt, "Religion of Ugarit", 560–61, 576–77; and *Religious Texts from Ugarit* 430–31.

[153] G. del Olmo Lete, "The Ugaritic Ritual Texts: A New Edition and Commentary; A Critical Assessment," *UF* 36 (2004): 645.

[154] Del Olmo Lete, "Critical Assessment," 543.

[155] Dennis Pardee, "G. del Olmo Lete's Views on Ugaritic Epigraphy and Religion," *UF* 37 (2005): 791–92.

[156] Pardee, "G. del Olmo Lete's Views," 802.

[157] Pardee, "G. del Olmo Lete's Views," 787.

In a related vein, some have tried to argue against an Ugaritic belief in a supernatural afterlife based on the culture's pessimistic traditions, especially as epitomized by the oft-cited confession of Aqhat: "The death of everyman I shall die / Like all mortals, I shall die"; *CAT* 1.17 vi.34–38). Such traditions hardly preclude a widespread belief in afterlife. Similar sorts of pessimistic literature are well known to have come from Mesopotamia ("Dialogue between a Man and His God," Gilgamesh's quest for eternal life, etc.), Egypt ("A Dispute between a Man and His *Ba*," the Harper's Songs, etc.) and Israel (Ecclesiastes, Job).[158] It is not at all surprising that Ugarit should have preserved contrasting traditions as well.

3.3.3.3 The Ugaritic underworld and its deities

In Ugaritic myth, the god Mot ("Death") is a spectacular figure but also a mysterious one. He is known primarily from his horrifying turn in the Baal Cycle, in which he is provoked to conflict by Baal's boasting. Mot initially defeats and swallows up the mighty Baal. Indeed, Mot's foremost characteristic in the text is his prodigious appetite and huge, devouring maw. He warns Baal:

"My throat consumes in heaps;
    yes indeed, I eat by double handfuls
And my seven portions are in a bowl
    and they mix (into my) cup a (whole) river."[159]

Mot is also described as being able to stretch "[one lip to] the earth, (the other) lip to the heavens ... (his) tongue to the stars."[160] A very similar account with slightly different details is found in *CAT* 1.133. The image of Death as swallowing finds some cognates in the myths of Egypt (in the underworld serpent Apophis; see § 2.4.3) and Israel (see §§ 4.4.3.2; 5.2.2.1; 5.2.4.1).

After Baal is swallowed up and seemingly killed, his sister Anat comes and kills Mot – she splits, pulverizes, and roasts him, then sows him into the field like grain (*CAT* 1.6 ii.30–35)[161] – at which point Baal is freed and returns to life. Then Mot himself also returns for a final battle against Baal, at the end of which Mot capitulates. This account of martial conflict between a god of death and another god is essentially *sui generis* in the ancient Near East, although certain aspects similar to it may be noted in the Hurrian Kumarbi myths and in a few biblical texts.[162]

---

[158] On Egypt and Israel, see Shannon Burkes, *Death in Qohelet and Egyptian Biographies of the Late Period* (SBLDS 170; Atlanta: Society of Biblical Literature, 1999), 45–80, 157–69.

[159] CAT 1.5 i 18–22: npš.blt / ḥmr.p imt.b klat / ydy.ilḥm.hm.šbʿ / ydty.b sʿ.hm.ks.ymsk / nhr.kl

[160] CAT 1.5 ii 2–3: [špt.l a]rṣ. špt.l šmm / [yšt.]lšn l kbkbm ...

[161] Agricultural interpretations of this passage are common, but John F. Healey cogently argues against these ("Mot," *DDD*², 599–600). The agricultural metaphor simply describes the destruction of Mot; his flesh is eaten by birds, a common ancient curse; cf. Gen 40:19; 1 Sam 17:44; 1 Kgs 21:24; Jer 7:33; etc.

In the Baal Cycle, Mot is referred to as a "beloved of El" (*ydd il*, *CAT* 1.4 vii:46) and elsewhere as a *bn ilm* ("son of El/god[s]," *CAT* 1.6 vi:26–27), but his battle with Baal probably should not be understood as a sibling rivalry. His status as a *bn ilm* more likely refers to his divinity, just as Heb. בן need not reflect literal sonship. Having said that, it is not clear that Mot was a god like other gods. His name is attested neither in cultic texts, nor in pantheon lists, nor in theophoric elements in the Ugaritic onomasticon – this makes him "the only major deity mentioned in [the Baal Cycle] to be totally absent" from these contexts.[163] In short, it appears that he received no offerings, unlike other ancient Near Eastern gods of the underworld, such as the Annunaki, Šamaš, Dagan, and Osiris. For this reason, it has been suggested that Mot simply represents death personified or even that the name Mot is an epithet of some other god.[164]

Mot has certain key aspects in common with demons, being a feared and harmful divine figure without a cult.[165] There are two further texts (*CAT* 1.23, 1.127) that would strengthen the case for Mot's demonic aspect, if the Ugaritic word *mt* in each is to be interpreted as a divine name.[166] Unfortunately, the word for "man, warrior" is spelled the same way. Thus, for example, the liver omen in *CAT* 1.127:29 contains the protasis "if *mt* attacks the city…", leaving open either possibility. Similarly, in *CAT* 1.23:8, a figure with the name *mt.w-šr* takes his place at a banquet of the gods. Insofar as he carries "in his hand a staff of bereavement, in his hand a staff of widowhood" (1.23:8–9), *mt.w-šr* has often been taken to mean something like "Death-and-Evil."[167] More recently, there seems to have been a scholarly movement to banish Death here, in favor of the translation "Warrior-Prince"[168] or "lord-and-master";[169] however, in his recent monograph on the text, Mark S. Smith translates "Death the Ruler."[170] Since

---

[162] For the Kumarbi myths, see Harry A. Hofner, *Hittite Myths*, 2nd ed. (SBLWAW 2; Atlanta: SBL, 1998), 40–45. For biblical examples, see, e.g., Isa 25:8. See also the survey of possibilities by John Day, *Yahweh and the Gods and Goddesses of Canaan* (Sheffield: Sheffield Academic Press, 2000), 184–97. Mark S. Smith believes that the Baal Cycle's battle between Baal and Mot is a burst of Ugaritic literary creativity that did not become part of the larger West Semitic cultural tradition (*Origins of Biblical Monotheism*, 130–31).

[163] Astour, "Netherworld and Its Denizens at Ugarit," 231. See also Paul Layton Watson, *Mot, the God of Death, at Ugarit and in the Old Testament* (Ph.D diss., Yale Univ., 1970).

[164] Healey, *DDD*^{2}, 598–599.

[165] Mark Smith considers Mot a "peripheral deity," like, for example, Tiamat or Yamm – a group that characteristically poses a threat and receives no cult (*The Origins of Biblical Monotheism*, 27–31). Demons are of course not always harmful (e.g., the Mesopotamian Pazazu has an apotropaic function), but I am speaking of the majority of cases.

[166] J. F. Healey, "Mot," *DDD*^{2}, 600.

[167] De Moor, *Cuneiform Anthology of Religious Texts from Ugarit*, 120 n. 15.

[168] Dennis Pardee, *COS* 1.87 n. 13.

[169] Wyatt, *Religious Texts from Ugarit*, 326 n. 10. See also discussion by Pardee, *COS* 1.276 n. 13.

[170] Mark S. Smith, *The Rituals and Myths of the Feast of the Goodly Gods of KTU/CAT 1.23: Royal Constructions of Opposition, Intersection, Integration, and Domination* (Resources for Biblical Study 51; Leiden/Boston: Brill, 2006), 19, 40–43.

"Death the Ruler" is pruned, bound, and felled like a vine in lines 9–11 – evocative of the grinding and sowing of Mot in the Baal Cycle – it seems that this text too relates the victory of the "beneficial gods" over the forces of death and chaos.[171]

Finally, Mot is named in a personal letter (*CAT* 2.10); in describing a plague on crops, the author says, "the hand of the gods is here, very strong, like Mot."[172] Despite these additional texts, Mot remains enigmatic: as an antagonistic and adversarial figure, he stands closer to the realm of demons than that of gods. If indeed Mot played a demonic role, the difficulties in defining him may be because the the demonology reflected in the Ugaritic texts is somewhat muted. Demons are attested in only a handful of apotropaic texts (and perhaps elsewhere as servants of the major gods); they do not seem to be connected with the dead.[173]

Other deities are also associated with the underworld at Ugarit: Šapšu, the sun-goddess, seems to function as a guide to the afterlife for the deceased king in *CAT* 1.161, as in the Hittite Funerary Texts, and not unlike the way the sun god's bark carried the deceased in Egyptian mythology.[174] The Baal Cycle reflects a similar role, when, at Anat's request, Šapšu carries the dead Baal to the tomb and buries him with the "divinities of the underworld" (*b ḥrt ilm arṣ*; *CAT* 1.6 i:13–18).[175] Later in the same myth, as noted above, the Rapiuma are placed under her control.[176] Theodore Lewis concluded that Šapšu "plays a most important role in the underworld and in the cult of the dead,"[177] in part by "making sure that the libations and offerings reach the deceased."[178] He saw the role of Mesopotamian Šamaš as an important mythological cognate. Šamaš has titles such as *sar/bēl*

---

[171] Smith, *Feast of the Goodly Gods*, 158–59. A final text, *CAT* 1.82, includes a reference to Mot in line 5, but the context is difficult to interpret. The text may be an apotropaic incantation including protection against Mot, although de Moor and Spronk perceive a reference to a covenant with Mot: "More on Demons in Ugarit (KTU 1.82)," *UF* 16 (1984): 239–40.

[172] *yd / ilm.p.kmtmt / ʿz.mid*

[173] See Paolo Xella, "Death and Afterlife in Canaanite and Hebrew Thought," in *Civilizations of the Ancient Near East* (ed. Jack M. Sasson; New York: Scribner, 1995), 3:2062; J. C. de Moor deems the *rpum* "benevolent demons," a characterization that may help define their function as lesser deities ("Demons in Canaan," *JEOL* 27 [1981–82]: 106–19.

[174] Here one might follow Lewis's interpretation regarding the word *išḥn* in 1.161:18. Formerly translated as "Burn hot!" from the root *šḥn*, it is instead taken by him from the root *šḥḥ*, "to bow down, sink down" (Lewis, *Cults of the Dead*, 22–23). Pitard takes *išḥn* as a G cohortative: "Let me be warm": "If this is the correct understanding of the verb, then the prayer is rather asking for Sapšu's presence in the netherworld" ("Ugaritic Funerary Text, 71). In fact, Šapšu's role may not be so different whether she is descending with the dead king or lighting his way.

[175] For *arṣ* = "underworld," see *DUL*, 107–8.

[176] *CAT* 1.6 vi:45–46: *špš tḥtk rpʾim* (O Šapšu, the Rapiuma are under you") On this contested passage, see further below. Also J. F. Healey, "The Sun Deity and the Underworld in Mesopotamia and Ugarit," in *Death in Mesopotamia*, 239–42.

[177] Lewis, *Cults of the Dead*, 35.

[178] Lewis, *Cults of the Dead*, 38.

eṭimmî ("ruler/lord of ghosts") and bēl mītî ("lord of the dead"). Although the idea of a nightly descent into the netherworld by Šapšu is scarcely attested at Ugarit, Lewis assumed that she does just that, as the Egyptian Re and the Mesopotamian sun deities do.[179] Šapšu's commerce with the dead may also have led to the perception that she played a role in healing.[180]

Dagan seems to have held a prominent place in Ugaritic religion, but his precise roles and aspects are less than clear. He may have received funerary offerings or conveyed them to the dead,[181] as at Mari.[182] The texts in question are a pair of stelae (*CAT* 6.13–14) with inscriptions incorporating Dagan and the term *pgr*, cognate with the Akkadian *pagru* and Biblical Hebrew פגר (both "corpse").[183] The stelae in question read:

skn . d šʿlyt	The stela which Taryelli
tryl . l dgn . pgr	dedicated to Dagan of the dead:
[š] w alp l akl	A sheep and an ox for the food offering.

and

pgr . d šʿlyt	The *pgr* which Uzzeni
ʿzn . l dgn . bʿlh	dedicated to Dagan, his lord:
[š w a]lp b mḥrṯt	A sheep and an ox for the [offering?].[184]

Is *pgr* here a technical term for a type of sacrifice *for the dead*, in which case the stelae support the existence of a mortuary cult?[185] Or does it simply mean the "corpse (of the sacrificed animal)," in which case there may be no association with the cult of the dead? It is hard to be certain. Even so, the identification of

---

[179] Lewis, *Cults of the Dead*, 46.

[180] Steve A. Wiggins, "Shapsh, Lamp of the Gods," *Ugarit, Religion and Culture: Proceedings of the International Colloquium on Ugarit, Religion and Culture: Edinburgh, July 1994: Essays Presented in Honour of Professor John C. L. Gibson* (eds. N. Wyatt, W. G. E. Watson and J. B. Lloyd; Ugaritisch-Biblische Literatur, Band 12. Munster: Ugarit Verlag), 338–46. The basis of the argument is her role in the snakebite texts CAT 1.100 and 1.107.

[181] Dagan is accorded a high place in pantheon lists and may have been the object of one of the two primary temples in Ugarit (the other belonging to Baal). Baal is called *bn dgn* ("son of Dagan"), but Dagan's aspects and relationships to other gods are not clear; see Healey, *DDD*², "Dagon." In support of Dagan's having an original underworld aspect in Mesopotamia, see J. J. M. Roberts, *The Earliest Semitic Pantheon: A Study of the Semitic Deities Attested in Mesopotamia before Ur III* (Baltimore: Johns Hopkins University Press, 1972), 18–19.

[182] On Dagan as recipient of funerary offerings at Mari, see ARM III 40, II 90; on Dagan as *bel pagrê*, see ARM X 63:15.

[183] René Dussaud, "Deux steles de Ras Shamra portent une dédicace au dieu Dagon," *Syria* 16 (1935): 177–80, pl. XXXI; also Claude F. A. Schaeffer, "Les fouilles de Ras Shamra," *Syria* 16 (1935): 155–56. See also DUL, 665: pgr = "body, corpse" as a "funerary offering."

[184] I have largely followed the restorations and translations of Lewis, *Cults of the Dead*, 75. However, DUL (537–38) takes *mḥrtt* to mean "(farm) work" (from ḥ-r-ṯ). Healey read *mḥrm*(!), "for total dedication" ("The Ugaritic Dead," 30).

[185] J. H. Ebach, "PGR = (Toten-)opfer? Ein Vorschlag zum Verständnis von Ez. 43,7.9," *UF* 3 (1971): 365–368.

Dagan as *bēl pagrê* at Mari, along with Šapšu's association with the *pgr* (*CAT* 1.102:12) may suggest that there is a relationship to the cult of the dead here.[186] Spronk is probably correct that "the *pgr*-offering was a special sacrifice for deities with an underworld character."[187] It is not clear, however, what effect the *pgr*-sacrifices were intended to have.

Rešeph, a god widely worshiped throughout the ancient Near East and Mediterranean, was a god of battle and sickness at Ugarit, whose "arrows brought plague and pestilence."[188] He also had an underworld aspect as the gatekeeper of the netherworld in an Ugaritic ritual text,[189] and he is identified in bilingual god lists with Nergal, a primary Mesopotamia chthonic god.[190]

Finally, there is the lightly attested *mlk* (Maliku? "King [of the underworld]"?), known from two snake charms (*CAT* 1.100, 1.107), a record of cultic rations (RS 1986.2235:17′),[191] and as a theophoric element in Ugaritic personal names.[192] One can theorize an underworld aspect of *mlk* since in both Old Babylonian and Neo-Assyrian god lists, ^{d}Maliku is held to be equivalent of ^{d}Nergal.[193] (On the relationship of this deity to the biblical Molek, see § 4.4.3.2.1)

There is relatively little description of the underworld itself in Ugaritic texts.[194] Here again, nearly all the direct information comes from the Baal Cycle. The entrance to Mot's home is at the base of two mountains with obscure names, *trġzz* and *trmg*. In *CAT* 1.4 viii 1–14, Baal sends his messengers to Mot, telling them to lift up the two mountains and then descend to Mot's "capital city," which goes by three names: *hmry*,[195] *mk*, and *ḥḥ*, which seem to reflect three aspects of

---

[186] Roberts, *Earliest Semitic Pantheon*, 19; W. F. Albright, *Archaeology and the Religion of Israel* (5th ed., Garden City, NY: Doubleday, 1969), 103.

[187] He goes too far when he claims, however, that "the *pgr*-offering is meant as a substitute for the one who offers it to Dagan or to Shapash: to be rescued from death a substitute is offered." (Spronk, *Beatific Afterlife*, 151).

[188] Day, *Yahweh and the Gods and Goddesses of Canaan*, 197. For very extensive bibliography on Rešeph, see ibid. n. 34.

[189] *CAT* 1.78:3–4: *špš tġrh ršp* ("Šapšu, Rešeph is her gatekeeper").

[190] Paolo Xella, "Resheph," *DDD²*, 701.

[191] Dennis Pardee, "A New Datum for the Meaning of the Divine Name Milkashtart," in *Ascribe to the Lord: Biblical and Other Studies in Memory of Peter C. Craigie* (eds. L. Eslinger and G. Taylor; Journal for the Study of the Old Testament, Supplement Series 67; Sheffield: Sheffield Academic Press, 1988), 55–68.

[192] There is also the reference to *rpu . mlk . ʿlm* ("Rapiu, eternal king") – is this connected to the references to a god Maliku? See Hans-Peter Müller, "Malik," *DDD²*, 540.

[193] John Day, *Molech: A God of Human Sacrifice in the Old Testament* (Cambridge: Cambridge University Press, 1989), 48–49; Müller, "Malik," 539–40. The infrequency of the Akk. Maliku, and its attestation in PNs at Ebla and Mari, suggests that the god was more at home in Syria than in Mesopotamia.

[194] On the Ugaritic underworld, see John F. Healey, "Das Land ohne Wiederkehr: Die Unterwelt im antiken Ugarit und im Alten Testament" (trans. H. Niehr), *TQ* 177 (1997): 94–104. Also Astour, "Nether World and Its Denizens at Ugarit."

[195] Likely related to *mhmrt*, the gullet of Mot (1.5 i 7–8); cf. DUL, Pardee *COS* 1.86 n. 215.

the underworld: "cesspool/muddy pit," "sinking down/collapsing,"[196] and "mire/hole." As in every ancient Near Eastern culture, the netherworld is describable at the most basic level as similar to the conditions of the grave: it is dirty, and it is located down below. Its inhabitants are called "sons of darkness" (*bn ẓlmt*; 1.4 vii:55), so presumably it is dark, as in Mesopotamia. In addition to lying at the edge of the earth, the netherworld could also be described as under the earth. Indeed, the Ugaritic word *arṣ* means both "earth" and "underworld" (e.g., 1.161:21; 1.5 vi:10; and frequently in the Baal Cycle).

Apart from this passage and its direct parallels in the Baal Cycle, however, there is practically no description of the Ugaritic underworld to compare with the extensive treatments in the Mesopotamian and Egyptian literature. Even in the Baal Cycle, the text has much more to say about "the pastureland, the beauty on the edge of death's realm" (*CAT* 1.5 vi:6–7) – perhaps analogous to the Egyptian "Field of Reeds" (see § 2.4.3), and the Greeks' Elysian Fields[197] – than about death's realm itself. Despite the significance of death in the Aqhat and Kirta epics, and in cultic text such as the "Liturgy for the Shades" (*CAT* 1.161), in none of these contexts has any fully developed mythology about the underworld (or about Mot, for that matter) survived. Recalling the flourishing of such mythology in later periods in Assyria and Egypt, one wonders whether perhaps a diachronic element is in play here; Ugarit had disappeared long before the first millennium, when Thorkild Jacobsen perceived an increased interest in the underworld (see § 1.4).

3.4 Between Ugarit and Israel

In assessing the relationship between the beliefs and practices of Ugarit and those of ancient Israel and Judah, one is not confined entirely to speculation. The intervening period saw changes in burial practices, as cremation burials in urns and stone funerary stelae that showed the deceased receiving offerings increased in popularity in first-millennium Syria.[198]

---

[196] DUL offers "large puddle, bog" for *mk* but with no apparent support apart from parallelism with *hmry* and *ḥḥ*. Instead, it apparently derives from the root *m-k-k*.

[197] Cf. Baruch Margalit, *A Matter of 'Life' and 'Death': A Study of the Baal-Mot Epic (CTA 4–5–6)* (AOAT 206; Kevelaer: Butzon & Bercker, 1980), 125–28. For the opposing view, see Spronk, *Beatific Afterlife*, 204; also Marjo C. A. Korpel, *A Rift in the Clouds: Ugaritic and Hebrew Descriptions of the Divine* (Münster: Ugarit-Verlag, 1990), 349. It does not make sense to say, as Spronk does, that these phrases are euphemisms intended to "avoid describing the horror awaiting" Baal in the underworld (*Beatific Afterlilfe*, 204 n. 3). Simply because the dead needed care and could become angry and dangerous does not mean that the underworld was uniformly horrifying. The very point of proper care for the dead was to avoid the horrors of the afterlife (see § 2.4.3).

[198] Peter M. M. G. Akkermans and Glenn M. Schwartz, *The Archaeology of Syria: From Com-*

From primarily the 9th and early 8th centuries BCE, a number of Neo-Hittite (i.e. Syro-Hittite) mortuary stelae reflect an expectation of care and enjoyment for the afterlife.[199] These stelae, found in dozens of towns,[200] attest the continuing practice of cults of the dead, and perhaps also to its democratization.

In one Syro-Hittite exemplar that has recently come to light, the KTMW stele from Zinçirli, the commissioner calls for mortuary banquets "for my soul that is in this stele" (*lnbšy . zy . bnṣb . zn*).[201] The novelty here is not the soul's survival apart from the body – a belief of great anquity in Anatolia – but rather the statement that that "the soul ... has been transferred to the mortuary stone."[202] This might be viewed as an adaptation of the longstanding Hittite belief, or perhaps as an effect of the influence of Egyptian beliefs and practices (§ 2.4.1), thus emphasizing again the large amount of interpenetration among cultures. Bonatz notes that despite the significant cultural continuity between the Hittite Empire and the Neo-Hittite states, the intervening "Dark Age" allowed for significant innovation as well.[203]

The archaeological context of the KTMW stele has been interpreted as a "mortuary chapel," and indeed its discovery *in situ* has helped to strengthen the identification of a number of Syro-Hittite cultic spaces as mortuary chapels.[204] Mortuary monuments appear to have proliferated among nonroyal elites beginning in the ninth century BCE, just as the Neo-Hittite states were becoming more centralized and then absorbed into the Assyrian empire.[205] This "self-assertion" and emulation of royal practices by nonroyal individuals has been remarked upon, but not fully explained;[206] it is perhaps significant to the present research that Judah in the eighth century was in a very similar situation: under

---

plex Hunter-Gatherers to Early Urban Societies (ca. 16,000–300 BC) (Cambridge: Cambridge University Press, 2003), 394–95.

[199] J. David Hawkins, "Late Hittite Funerary Monuments" in *Death in Mesopotamia* (ed. B. Alster; Mesopotamia 8. Copenhagen: Akademisk Forlag, 1980), 213–26; *idem*, "More Late Hittite Funerary Monuments" in *Anatolia and the Ancient Near East: Studies in Honor of Tahsin Özgüç* (Ankara, 1989), 189–197; Dominik Bonatz, *Das syro-hethitische Grabdenkmal: Untersuchungen zur Entstehung einer neuen Bildgattung in der Eisenzeit im nordsyrisch-südostanatolischen Raum* (Mainz: von Zabern, 2000).

[200] See Bonatz, "Syro-Hittite Funerary Monuments," 208–9.

[201] See Dennis Pardee, "A New Aramaic Inscription From Zincirli," *BASOR* 356 (2009): 51–71. His translation of the relevant section reads: "I am KTMW, servant of Panamuwa, who commissioned for myself this stele while still living. I placed it in my eternal chamber (?) and established a feast (at) this chamber(?): a bull for Hadad ... a ram for Šamš, a ram for Hadad of the Vineyards, and a ram for my 'soul' that (will be) in this stele."

[202] Quotation from interview with David Schloen by John Noble Wilford, "Found: An Ancient Monument to the Soul," *The New York Times*, Nov. 18, 2008. Accessed at *http://www.nytimes.com/2008/11/18/science/18soul.html*.

[203] Bonatz, "Syro-Hittite Funerary Monuments," 205–10.

[204] Eudora J. Struble and Virginia Rimmer Herrmann, "An Eternal Feast at Sam'al: The New Iron Age Mortuary Stele from Zincirli in Context," *BASOR* 356 (2009); 15–49.

[205] Bonatz, *Das syro-hethitische Grabdenkmal*, 161–79.

[206] Struble and Herrmann, "An Eternal Feast at Sam'al," 41–42.

3.4 Between Ugarit and Israel 129

Fig 3.2 The KTMW stele, discovered at Zincirli, portrays an official receiving mortuary offerings and expresses the belief that his soul is "in this stele." Courtesy of the Neubauer Expedition to Zincirli of the University of Chicago.

pressure from the Assyrian empire and newly centralized (particularly under Hezekiah). Perhaps the urbanization and re-establishment of international contacts on the periphery of the Assyrian empire allowed an elite trading class to arise. That class would have been important to local rulers for enriching the state and raising tribute for the empire, which would have made it unwise for rulers to squelch their aspirations for the afterlife.

Other data point to the continuity of beliefs like those of Ugarit. One might mention the well-known sarcophagus of Ahiram of Byblos (Fig. 3.2., also *ANEP*, pls. 631, 633), from the early tenth century BCE. On it women are depicted in mourning at the ends of the coffin, and the deceased king is portrayed sitting on a throne receiving funerary offerings – a scene reminiscent of the Ugaritic (and Hittite) Royal Funerary Rituals. The inscription (*KAI* 1) warns against disturbing

Fig. 3.3 Detail from the sarcophagus of Ahiram of Byblos.

the burial, a common concern known also from eighth- and seventh-century Aramaic inscriptions.[207]

Perhaps the clearest piece of evidence for actual hope of a divinized afterlife among royalty in first-millennium Syria-Palestine is an inscription by Panammuwa, king of the Aramean state of Sam'al in the eighth century. In the text written on his sarcophagus, he instructs whichever of his sons inherits the throne to make sacrifices and say to Hadad: "May the soul [*nbš*] of Panammuwa eat with you, and may the soul [*nbš*] of Panammuwa drink with you."[208]

As noted above, the idea of feasting with the gods in a cultic festival is also well attested in Egypt from the second millennium onward, and to a lesser extent in Ugarit. It is not clear whether Panammuwa's participation in a divine banquet reflects a belief in other divine powers of the dead, but it is likely in light of the portrayals of the necromantic powers of deceased Egyptian pharaohs (§ 2.4.2).

The excavations of the primary necropolis of Iron Age Tyre since 1990 have provided a clearer picture of Phoenician burial practices at that time. Cremation of bodies was "absolutely dominant,"[209] with the remains buried in one or two jars (the bones being separated from the ashes in the latter case). There is consistent evidence of food and drink offering associated with the burials, sometimes

---

[207] *KAI* 215 (Panammuwa; see below), 225 (Sinzeribni), and 226 (Si'gabbar).

[208] תאכל נבש פנמו עמך ותשתי נבש פנמו עמך (*KAI* 214:17, p. 39; *COS* 2.36). See J. C. Greenfield, "Un rite religieux araméen et ses parallèles," *RB* 80 (1973): 46–52; Smith and Bloch-Smith, "Death and Afterlife," 279.

[209] María Eugenia Aubet, "The Phoenician Cemetery of Tyre," *NEA* 73 (2010): 145.

with the crockery having been ritually smashed. The cemetery's excavator, María Eugenia Aubet, connects these remains with the practice of a cultic meal akin to the *marziḥu*.[210] Grave goods were few, but included some foreign luxury items such as Egyptian scarabs. Some graves were marked by a standing stone or wood stela, but social stratification was generally masked by an "egalitarian ideology,"[211] a tendency toward uniformity in burial.

Later Phoenician royal burials are more exceptional, and the inscriptions from their sarcophagi attest to the importance of the integrity of the corpse and the hope of a place among the divinized dead. A text on the sarcophagus of Tabnit of Sidon from the fifth century admonishes anyone who finds it: "If you open my cover and disturb me, may you not have ... a resting-place with the Rephaim."[212] The same curse is invoked in the sarcophagus inscription of his son ʾEshmunʿazor, and that text adds a *ius talionis* flourish in its curses against desecration: "let [the one who disturbs the remains] not be buried in a grave."[213] The influence of Egyptian burial arts is apparent both from the sarcophagi and from the fact that at least Tabnit's body was embalmed.[214]

Finally, an Aramaic letter may attest a curse to an unhappy afterlife (and perhaps also necromantic practices) among Jewish communities in approximately the same time period, although its broken state makes interpretation difficult.[215]

3.5 Conclusions

In sum, the Ugaritic evidence strongly suggests that at least kings in Ugarit anticipated a divinized afterlife and that living royalty (like their peers in Mesopotamia) hoped for the blessing of their dead ancestors and took ritual steps to assure it. The Ugaritic cult of the dead shared certain features with those of Mesopotamia in particular. The Ugaritic Royal Funerary Text and King List suggest a royal cult of dead kin similar to the Mesopotamian *kispu*, with their

---

[210] Aubet, "The Phoenician Cemetery of Tyre,"153.
[211] Aubet, "The Phoenician Cemetery of Tyre," 154–55.
[212] אם פתח תפתח עלתי ורגז תרגז אל יכון לך... משכב את רפאם (*KAI* 1.13, p. 3; cf. *COS* 2.56). *KAI* 1.9A:5 uses רגז in a similar way, as does 1 Sam 28:15 (see discussion in ch. 4).
[213] אל יקבר בקבר (*KAI* 1.14, p. 3; cf. *COS* 2.57).
[214] Edouard Lipiński, "Phoenician Cult Expressions in the Persian Period," in *Symbiosis, Symbolism and Power of the Past*, 298.
[215] A. E. Cowley, *Aramaic Papyri of the Fifth Century B.C.* (Oxford: Clarendon, 1923), text no. 71, line 15: וגרמיך לא יחתון שאול וטללך : "Your bones shall not go down to Sheol, nor your shade ... ." The passage that may refer to necromancy is very broken: "... his body to its grave (קברה), and ... and they shall speak to him and he shall answer (...)[...]ויאמרון לה ליעני..." (lines 29–31) This last fragmentary phrase is very reminiscent of Mesopotamian necromantic texts; see § 1.4.2.

systematic invocation of ancestors and request for their blessings. This invocation could have been connected to a royal necromantic cult as well. The sun deity also played the role of psychopomp in Ugarit, as in Mesopotamia and Egypt.

Beyond these similarities, Ugaritians do seem to have developed a distinctive array of terminology to describe the dead, and the extant textual corpus suggests that they did not hold as fearful an attitude toward the dead as did the Mesopotamians. Furthermore, Ugarit's tombs are unique in Syria-Palestine for their proximity to homes.

First-millennium inscriptions and reliefs from Phoenicia and Aram also attest to a royal hope for a divinized afterlife and cults of the dead in Syria-Palestine. Although they do not specifically indicate belief in the divine power of the dead or shed any light on mythological portrayals of the dead, they do little to contradict the impression of continuity between the beliefs and practices of Ugarit and those of later Palestinian cultures.

It is hard to escape the feeling, reading the nonbiblical Syro-Palestinian corpus from the Late Bronze and Iron Ages, that one is getting only tiny glimpses of the whole array of mythology and ritual that surrounded death in these cultures. So much of what is attested here finds cognates in Egypt or Mespotamia or both, and one very much suspects that the richness and diversity of beliefs and practices was similar to that which one finds those better-attested cultures. It is important to acknowledge difference and distinctiveness at the same time, but because of the paucity of Syro-Palestinian data, the scholar should not be at all surprised to find hints and pieces of these other cultures within the Bible, whether these similarities were mediated by Levantine intermediaries or resulted from direct contact. One should also not be surprised to see what appear to be texts that synthesize religious motifs in new ways. These may be the work of the creative literary mind on the part of a biblical author, or may simply reflect historical cultural syntheses that are unattested outside the Bible.

4. Death and the Dead in Iron II Israel and Judah and in the Old Testament

4.1 Introduction

In a study of Israelite religion, the religions of other ancient Near Eastern nations serve as context; in a study of a particular biblical book's use of the imagery of death, Israelite religion itself is context. Isaiah's message, however influential it would later become, is not a simple mirror of its religious milieu. In fact, it is safe to say that Isaiah was frequently opposed to the religious (as well as political) views of his contemporaries – what else can it mean that he called them deaf and blind (Isa 6:9)?

To be sure, the religious milieu of Judah in Isaiah's time would have been quite complex. The picture of "orthodoxy" that one might derive from a flat reading of the legal collections was almost certainly never achieved in practice and was probably never even attempted until at least the reign of Hezekiah, if not that of Josiah. Religious diversity of various kinds would have existed, which would have been partially explicable by reference to such categories as "national" versus "familial," or "elite" versus "common."[1] Like any nation, Israel and Judah had certain cultural heritages that preexisted their statehood. Since Israel was a nation of seemingly complex origin, these heritages derived not only from their immediate region but probably also from a broader swath of the ancient Near East. Furthermore, Israelite and Judean religion was also subject to numerous foreign influences throughout the monarchic period. Even as "reforming" kings tried to exercise a certain amount of "centripetal" force to unify their country, "centrifugal" religious forces (especially the familiar pressures of elite emulation) undermined them, as did the inertia of conflicting, ancient traditions.

With regard to death and its attendant beliefs and practices, historians have

---

[1] Rainer Albertz, *A History of Israelite Religion in the Old Testament Period* (2 vols.; trans. J. Bowden; Louisville, Ky.: Westminster John Knox, 1994), *passim*; Patrick D. Miller, *The Religion of Ancient Israel* (Library of Ancient Israel; Louisville, Ky.: Westminster John Knox, 2000), 62–105; Erhard S. Gerstenberger, *Theologies in the Old Testament* (trans. J. Bowden; Minneapolis: Fortress, 2002), *passim*. See further discussion: Christopher B. Hays, "Religio-Historical Approaches: Monotheism, Method, and Mortality," in *Method Matters: Essays on the Interpretation of the Hebrew Bible in Honor of David L. Petersen* (Atlanta: SBL, 2009), 169–93.

convincingly shown that Israel's religion was only a different species, with a few unique characteristics, but not a different genus from that of its neighbors. Even in the sometimes heavily edited text of the Hebrew Bible, it is quite possible to discern a society that, as a matter of course, worshiped chthonic gods, cared for its dead, practiced necromancy, knew very well about the religions and mythologies of its neighbors (at least at upper levels of society), and was often inclined to try them out, especially when YHWH did not seem to answer to the usual means. These are only selected examples; the issues are discussed below in greater detail.

One terminological clarification may be necessary: The terms "Israel" and "Israelite" are widely applied to the nation(s) and culture(s) that gave rise to the Bible, especially in discussions of the preexilic period; however, textual and archaeological data from the northern kingdom (Israel proper) regarding death and burial are exceedingly scant.[2] There are two rock-cut caves in the Omride compound at Samaria that have been identified as tombs by Norma Franklin, but this identification is hotly disputed.[3] The subterranean rooms under the palace at Samaria have similarities to both Ugaritic and Assyrian intramural tombs, and so if they were to be conclusively identified as tombs, they would transform our understanding of cults of the dead in Israel, but I omit them from my discussions for the time, pending a more conclusive analysis of the data.

As far as the texts go, it is possible that the accounts of the burials of northern kings are accurate indications of Israelite practice; or that Amos's references to the *marzeaḥ* and Sheol reflect the religion of the northerners to whom he was speaking; or that the account of Elisha raising a boy from the dead points to a distinctive northern belief; but it is a safer assumption that they were meaningful to the culture that eventually collected them as the Scriptures we know – that is, Judah. Therefore, this chapter is in reality almost entirely a discussion of *Judean* beliefs and practices, and my use of terminology will reflect that where applicable.[4] I do occasionally use the term "Israelite" to refer to phenomena that seem to be relevant to both kingdoms.

---

[2] The title of Elizabeth Bloch-Smith's *Judahite Burial Practices and Beliefs about the Dead* (JSOTSup 123; Sheffield: Sheffield Academic Press, 1992) is significant in this regard: as she writes, the "paucity of recovered burials currently precludes generalizing about burial practices from the kingdom of Israel."

[3] The debate is found in these articles (in order of appearance): Norma Franklin, "Lost Tombs of the Israelite Kings: Century-Old Excavation Report Yields Startling New Discovery," *BAR* 33:4 (2007): 26–35; David Ussishkin, "The Disappearance of Two Royal Burials." *BAR* 33:6 (2007): 68–70; *idem*, "Megiddo and Samaria: A Rejoinder to Norma Franklin," *BASOR* 348 (2007): 49–70; Norma Franklin, "Don't Be So Quick to be Disappointed, David Ussishkin," *BAR* 34:2 (2008): 70–71.

[4] I do not overlook the work of Gary Rendsburg in identifying "Israelian Hebrew" in biblical texts, which, he has argued, accounts for 24–30 percent of the Hebrew Bible ("A Comprehensive Guide to Israelian Hebrew: Grammar and Lexicon," *Orient* 38 [2003]: 5–35). However, the assumption that what is preserved in the Bible was relevant to Judah is more secure than the assumption that it reflects Israelite (northern) realities.

4.2 A brief history of modern scholarship

In 1995, Joseph Blenkinsopp could treat the matter of cults of the dead in Isaiah's period as a settled issue: "Since we now have competent recent studies of death cults and ancestor cults in Iron Age Israel, it will not be necessary to spend much time in establishing their existence."[5] This conclusion can no longer be so briefly asserted.[6] In a witty summary of scholarly reconstructions of Israelite and Judean attitudes toward the dead during the tenth to sixth centuries BCE, Elizabeth Bloch-Smith remarked, "Initially the dead were attributed an active role, only later to be consigned to Sheol. They were again resurrected and at present are being stripped of their powers."[7]

As Bloch-Smith's comment indicates, the topic of beliefs about the dead in ancient Israel is a well-plowed field. Although I do not wish to harrow the ground continually (Isa 28:24), in what follows I would like to elaborate on her terse outline, bring the history of scholarship up to date, and offer a fresh assessment of the primary data.

4.2.1 Early modern scholarship

Scholars in comparative religion had long theorized that Israelite religion included veneration of the dead. In particular, the turn of the twentieth century saw great interest in cults of the dead and their relevance to ancient Israel. Spronk's extensive review of research from the nineteenth and early twentieth centuries demonstrated that the survival of the soul (נפש) was widely accepted by scholars of religion working from an anthropological perspective at that time. In general, they looked for worship of the dead in the Old Testament, since it was believed that this was a common feature of "natural religion."[8] The description of the dead as weak in the Old Testament was chalked up to a Yahwistic critique of folk religion.[9]

---

[5] Joseph Blenkinsopp, "Deuteronomy and the Politics of Post-Mortem Existence," *VT* 45 (1995): 2.

[6] Even at the time of its publication, Blenkinsopp's comment did not, of course, reflect a unanimous consensus. As late as 1996, Jerome Neyrey could state flatly in his article on "Eternal life" in the *Harper Collins Bible Dictionary* (San Francisco: HarperOne, 1996) that "in ancient Israel there was no belief in a life after death" (310).

[7] Elizabeth Bloch-Smith, "Death in the Life of Israel," in *Sacred Time, Sacred Place: Archaeology and the Religion of Israel* (ed. Barry M. Gittlen; Winona Lake, Ind.: Eisenbrauns, 2002), 139.

[8] Klaas Spronk, *Beatific Afterlife in Ancient Israel and in the Ancient Near East* (Alter Orient und Altes Testament 219; Neukirchen-Vluyn: Neukirchener Verlag, 1986), 28. Proof that Israel originally worshiped the dead was supposed to be found in the plural term אלהים, supposedly representing the plurality of the dead spirits. See also J. W. Ribar, "Death-Cult Practices in Ancient Palestine" (Ph.D. diss., University of Michigan, 1973), 4–6.

[9] Adolphe Lods, *La croyance à la vie future et le culte des morts dans l'antiquité Israélite* (Paris: Fischbacher, 1906); Spronk, *Beatific Afterlife*, 38. Lods pointed out that not only was the cult of

4.2.2 The mid-century assertion of distinctiveness

Around the middle of the twentieth century, these comparative approaches, and especially the discoveries at Ugarit, brought new interest in ideas about death in Israel. Some of this interest took the form of theological treatises that tried to describe an "Israelite attitude toward death," which tended to center on the opposition between YHWH as a god of life and the various forces and regions that were associated with chaos and death.[10] Most of these studies made use of comparative data in different ways, even while seeking to isolate Israel's own distinctive character.

Another movement of the period was a more explicit reaction "against the hegemony of the comparative method,"[11] as Brevard S. Childs put it. There was a new vigor on the part of those who emphasized Israel's uniqueness in the ancient Near East. Yehezkel Kaufmann and George Ernest Wright were among the historian-theologians dissatisfied by the comparativists' assumption that Israel's religion was basically like those of its neighbors. Kaufmann criticized the "deeply ingrained habit" of scholars of religion to found their interpretations on the "testimony of obscure passages, on ingenious combinations of isolated 'hints' and 'clues' scattered here and here."[12] Not only did Israelites not practice "pagan religion," he said, but the biblical authors did not even understand it. Similarly, Wright argued that the Old Testament, far from reflecting polytheism or other common traits of ancient Near Eastern religion, was primarily a long diatribe against its religious environment. Wright perceived "elements of Israel's faith which distinguish it sharply from the religions of its environment."[13] Indeed, the world of the Old Testament was "a totally different religious atmosphere"[14]– not

---

the dead a feature of family religion, but that dead from beyond the family were also feared; he assumed that Israelites also practiced such a cult, as an adoption of Canaanite practices.

[10] Johannes Pedersen, *Israel: Its Life and Culture* (London: Oxford University Press, 1926–40), 453–96; Christoph Barth, *Die Errettung vom Tode in den individuellen Klage- und Dankliedern des Alten Testaments* (Zollikon: Evangelischer Verlag, 1947); A. R. Johnson, *The Vitality of the Individual in the Thought of Ancient Israel* (Cardiff: University of Wales Press, 1949); Ludwig Köhler, *Hebrew Man* (trans. Peter R. Ackroyd; New York: Abingdon, 1956), 91–96; Robert Martin-Achard, *De la mort à la résurrection: D'après l'Ancien Testament* (Neuchâtel: Delachaux & Niestlé, 1956); Ludwig Wächter, *Der Tod im Alten Testament* (Stuttgart: Calwer, 1967); Hans Walter Wolff, *Anthropology of the Old Testament* (trans. Margaret Kohl; Philadelphia: Fortress, 1974), 99–118. See discussion of this period in Brevard S. Childs, "Death and Dying in Old Testament Theology," in *Love & Death in the Ancient Near East: Essays in Honor of Marvin H. Pope* (ed. J. H. Marks and R. M. Good; Guilford, Conn.: Four Quarters, 1987), 89–91.

[11] Childs, "Death and Dying in Old Testament Theology," 90.

[12] Yehezkel Kaufmann, *The Religion of Israel, from Its Beginnings to the Babylonian Exile* (trans. Moshe Greenberg; Chicago: University of Chicago Press, 1960), 3.

[13] George Ernest Wright, *The Old Testament Against Its Environment* (SBT 2; London: SCM, 1957), 16.

[14] Wright, *Old Testament Against Its Environment*, 20.

because of different intellectual development but because of the experience of a God who is radically Other. (The influence of Barthian dialectical theology is evident here.) In his study of the religious and cultural institutions of the Old Testament, Roland de Vaux commented: "On a voulu interpréter ces rites funèbres comme des manifestations d'un culte des morts ... [mais l]'Ancien Testament ne fournit à ces opinions aucune base solide."[15]

It is not as if this viewpoint was endemic to mid-century theologians. A more even-handed assessment was rendered by Gerhard von Rad:

> Like most nations who were still unsophisticated in religion, the first datum, or at least the obvious thing to do, for Israel as well, was to confer a positive sacral value on the dead and on the grave. There was no doubt that the dead lived on – especially so if this was assured by means of rites. Thus the dead man was merely changed, and represented, to a higher degree than while living in the body, a power which had to be reckoned with in a very real way. In consequence, it was of prime importance to regulate the relationship of the living to these dead. The dead could of course do harm. But use could also be made of their higher knowledge. How close Israel stood to these ideas may be seen from the fact that the age of Deuteronomy and Isaiah was still exposed to the temptation to consult the dead (Is. viii. 19; Deut. xviii. 11). And on one occasion when such a spirit was conjured up, it is still actually designated אלהים (1 Sam. xxviii. 13). Even if we take the view that this is all just a matter of the survival of rudiments, a degraded and outlawed hole-and-corner cult, it would still be quite wrong on the one hand to set too little store on the temptation which emanated from this sphere, or, on the other, to underestimate the power of self-restraint which Israel had to call into being in order to renounce all sacral communion with her dead... . It is of course questionable whether the designation "cult of the dead" is not too honorific a one for such isolated practices. Did these paltry actions towards a dead man really still count as a cult in the real sense of the term? Nevertheless they did express a sacral relationship with the dead which was absolutely incompatible with Jahwism.[16]

Von Rad recognized that the cult of the dead was practiced in Israel even under the monarchy, and at the highest and most central parts of society. Perhaps more important, he recognized, at least to a degree, the complexity of the religious situation in ancient Israel. The remaining question, as we shall see presently, is whether von Rad was correct that "[a]s far as we can see back into the history, Jahwism turned with a special intolerance against all forms of the cult of the dead."[17]

Framed another way, the question is whether the Bible accurately reflects Israelite religion, especially that of the preexilic period. The theologians were correct that *if* the Mosaic law (a) reflected early Israelite religion and (b) was in fact normative for all of society, then there is room only for "paltry, isolated

---

[15] Roland de Vaux, O.P. *Les institutions de l'Ancien Testament,* vol. 1 (Paris: Éditions du Cerf, 1958), 100. "People have wanted to interpret these funerary rites as manifestations of a cult of the dead ... but the Old Testament does not furnish any solid foundation for these opinions."

[16] Gerhard von Rad, *Old Testament Theology,* vol. 1, *The Theology of Israel's Historical Traditions* (Louisville: Westminster John Knox, 2001), 276–77 (German orig., 1957).

[17] Von Rad, *Old Testament Theology,* 1:276.

actions" at the fringes. Therefore, in different ways both the source critics around the turn of the twentieth century and the more recent scholarship calling into question the historicity of the biblical primary histories have opened up room to question the orthodoxies of Deuteronomism and the prophets, including their prohibitions of cults of the dead.

4.2.3 A new flourishing of underworld and afterlife

Between those movements – that is, in the second quarter of the twentieth century – the study of Israelite cults of the dead was not entirely moribund,[18] but it seems to have been W. F. Albright's "The High Place in Ancient Palestine" (1956) that reopened the conversation in earnest.[19] Working from an assortment of cairns and stelae from Ebla, Byblos, Hazor, and elsewhere, and from the idea that Hebrew במה might be connected to Arabic *buhmatum* (which can mean both "mass of rock" and "great man, hero"), Albright concluded that the high places attested in the Hebrew Bible might well have been used for sacrifices to ancestors. He saw "a much greater significance for popular Israelite belief in life after death and the cult of the dead than has hitherto appeared prudent to admit."[20] The condemnations of the prophets (and, one might add, DtrH) were due to "conservative Yahwist reaction against objectionable funerary beliefs and practices."[21] The oft-cited dissertation of J. W. Ribar (1973) was critical of Albright's study of the high places, calling it inferential and inconclusive; but at the same time Ribar judged that the "impressive" volume of comparative data amassed by Albright lent the idea of an Israelite ancestor cult "a kind of *a priori* credibility."[22] Ribar set out to bolster Albright's theory by drawing on Syro-Palestinian tomb archaeology. While "[s]tructural evidence for death cult activities at burial sites in Iron Age Palestine" was "scanty, at best," there was "a renewed vogue in elaborate rock-cut chapels" between the eighth and sixth centuries BCE, leading Ribar to conclude that "death cult offerings similar to those proposed for the Bronze Age were practiced to some extent, at least, toward the end of Iron II."[23]

---

[18] For example, one could point to Otto Eissfeldt's *Molk als Opferbegriff im Punischen und Hebräischen und das Ende des Gottes Moloch* (Beiträge zur Religionsgeschichte des Altertums 3; Halle: Max Niemeyer, 1935).
[19] W. F. Albright, "The High Place in Ancient Palestine," in *Volume du Congrès: Strasbourg 1956* (VTSup 4; Leiden, Brill, 1957), 242–58.
[20] W. F. Albright, *Archaeology and the Religion of Israel* (5th ed., Garden City, N.Y.: Doubleday, 1969), 103.
[21] Albright, "The High Place in Ancient Palestine," 257.
[22] Ribar, "Death-Cult Practices," 33.
[23] Ribar, "Death-Cult Practices," 63. Spronk added to the discussion a temple in Iron Age Gozan (Tell Halaf) and a grave at Megiddo that appears to have been equipped for ritual feeding (Spronk, *Beatific Afterlife*, 139). He further notes graves at Middle Bronze Jericho in which the arms of the corpses had been removed, which he takes to have been an attempt to render them harmless.

The end of the 1960s and beginning of the 1970s brought great ferment to the study of death in the ancient Near East in general. Whereas the matter of cults of the dead was reopened by Albright, Nicholas J. Tromp's monograph *Primitive Conceptions of Death and the Netherworld in the Old Testament*[24] marked the most ambitious comparison of Ugaritic and Israelite *mythology* of death to that point. Tromp analyzed the deity, place, and imagery associated with death in Ugaritic texts and in the Hebrew Bible, concluding that mythological reflection on death was "not a peripheral phenomenon in Hebrew thought,"[25] but that it must have been "popular custom [that] kept up the ancient mythological traditions."[26] It was a limited investigation, however, with only thirteen pages devoted to Ugaritic evidence and practically none to any other comparative data.

Around the same time, Mitchell Dahood startled the field with the first volume of his Psalms commentary, which took up another of Albright's suggestions, that "we must be careful not to explain away passages in the Psalms and other poetic literature which suggest a more positive approach [to the existence of the afterlife]."[27] Dahood was inspired by Ugaritic texts like Aqhat:

Ask for life (*ḥym*) and I will give it to you
    immortality (*blmt*) and I will bestow it upon you
I will make you number the years like Baal,
    like the gods you will number months. (CAT 1.17 vi:27–29)

In light of this and other Ugaritic texts, Dahood believed he could identify references to the afterlife all over the Psalter. For example, as in the text above, he reads most instances of חיים as referring to "life eternal" – and indeed, there are places where this is a plausible suggestion, for example, Ps 21:5: "He asked you for life; you gave it to him – length of days forever and ever."[28] Elsewhere Dahood found references to the judgment of souls and beatific visions, not only in the Psalter but beyond, especially in Proverbs. Dahood concluded that the view that Israel did not know "of a faith in any resurrection ... will not survive serious scrutiny."[29]

Dahood's commentary inspired a vociferous response, much of it negative.[30] Scholars had become accustomed to thinking that beatific afterlife and

---

[24] Nicholas J. Tromp, *Primitive Conceptions of Death and the Netherworld in the Old Testament* (BibOr 21; Rome: Pontifical Biblical Institute, 1969).
[25] Tromp, *Primitive Conceptions of Death*, 211.
[26] Tromp, *Primitive Conceptions of Death*, 213.
[27] Albright, "High Place," 257.
[28] Mitchell J. Dahood, *Psalms: Introduction, Translation, and Notes* (3 vols.; AB 16, 17, 17A; Garden City, N.Y.: Doubleday, 1966–70), 3:xlvi. See also Ps 23:6.
[29] Dahood, *Psalms*, 1: xxxvi.
[30] A full critique is given by Bruce Vawter: "Intimations of Immortality and the Old Testament," *JBL* 91 (1972): 158–71; Tromp (in *Primitive Conceptions of Death*) also expressed skepticism about a number of Dahood's readings and theories. Some representative comments from book reviews: "[T]he subtlety of some of these allusions escapes the reader" (John L. McKenzie,

resurrection were late developments in Judaism, perhaps under the influence of Persian religion.[31] Its early presence in Egyptian religion and its occasional hints in Mesopotamian religion should have made it at least a possibility to be entertained, but as of 1970 neither Albright's cult of the dead nor Dahood's beatific afterlife had been much debated in the literature.

In the wake of the pioneering studies of Albright, Tromp, and Dahood, the 1970s and '80s became a heyday for theories about the dead in the Hebrew Bible. In 1973, H. C. Brichto published a lengthy article that is usually seen as a watershed in the discussion. Building on Albright and on earlier sociological theory, Brichto posited that kin, cult, land, and afterlife formed a single massive biblical thought-complex that ran deep but had gone mostly unnoticed.

Brichto argued that the dead were in fact the "constituent principle of the ancient family. Not generation, nor natural affection, nor the intrinsic power of the paterfamilias, but the religion of the dead ancestors 'caused the family to form a single body, both in this life and the next.'"[32] The land, the family inheritance on which the dead were buried, was the connection between generations; to lose the land was to lose the link to the dead.[33] In Brichto's view, Abraham's concern to secure a burial place shows that proper sepulture was linked to happiness in the afterlife. "The condition of the dead in this afterlife is, in a vague but significant way, connected with proper burial upon the ancestral land and with the continuation on that land of the dead's proper progeny."[34] He found evidence of this *in nuce* all over the Old Testament. For example, the fifth commandment's language of "honoring father and mother" (Exod 20:12 | Deut 5:16) suggests mortuary ritual (cf. also Prov 20:20; 24:20; 30:11).[35] Furthermore, Deut 26:14 implicitly

---

CBQ 31 [1969]: 81); "[M]any of Dahood's suggestions seem arbitrary or unnecessary" (Francis I. Andersen, *JBL* 88 [1969]: 208); "the author is too zealous in [seeking out references to the afterlife]" (B. K. Waltke, *BSac* 123 [1966]: 176); "Dahood comes up with some really wild interpretations, many of which concern very important theological matters (like the question to what extent the concept of immortality is present in the Psalter)" (D. A. Robertson, *JBL* 85 [1966]: 484).

[31] This view has recently been argued by, e.g., Bernhard Lang, "Life after Death in the Prophetic Promise," in *Congress Volume: Jerusalem 1986* (ed. J. A. Emerton; VTSup 40; Leiden: Brill, 1988); also John Day, "The Development of the Belief in Life after Death in Ancient Israel," in *After the Exile: Essays in Honor of Rex Mason* (ed. John Barton and David J. Reimer; Macon, Ga.: Mercer University Press, 1996), 241–43. For discussion, see § 5.2.4.2.

[32] Herbert Chanan Brichto, "Kin, Cult, Land and Afterlife – A Biblical Complex," *HUCA* 44 (1973): 5.

[33] Karel van der Toorn follows Brichto closely on many of these points: *Family Religion in Babylonia, Syria and Israel: Continuity and Change in the Forms of Religious Life* (Leiden: Brill, 1996), 206–35. See now also Francesca Stavrakopoulou, *Land of Our Fathers: The Roles of Ancestor Veneration in Biblical Land Claims* (LHBOTS 473; London: T & T Clark, 2010).

[34] Brichto, "Kin, Cult, Land and Afterlife," 23.

[35] This suggestion goes back at least to the seventeenth century, when John Marsham connected the fifth commandment to similar instructions for mortuary care in Egypt on the basis of Porphyry's portrayal (*Canon Chronicus Aegyptiacus, Ebraicus, Graecus & Disquisitiones* [Lon-

allows most food offerings to the dead by barring only a specific type.[36] The *teraphim* were ancestor figurines, he wrote, and they seem to have been allowed prior to the Josianic reform (2 Kgs 23:24).

The combination of Isa 14 and 1 Sam 28, Brichto thought, "would seem to be enough to guarantee that the afterlife was an unchallenged reality for biblical Israel."[37] Israel excluded such practices as necromancy not because they were seen as superstitious but because they were seen as potentially effective. They represented "recourse to a category of human wisdom whose very efficaciousness tempts man to pursue his goals without reference to the norms of God."[38] The evidence, Brichto wrote, "testifies overwhelmingly to a belief on the part of biblical Israel in an afterlife, an afterlife in which the dead, though apparently deprived of material substance, retain such personality characteristics as form, memory, consciousness and even knowledge of what happens to their descendants in the land of the living. They remain very much concerned about the fortunes of their descendants, for they are dependent on them, on their continued existence on the family land, on their performance of memorial rites, for a felicitous condition in the afterlife."[39] Thus, while Israelite religion rejected certain aspects of neighboring nations' beliefs and practices, it also carried on numerous others.[40]

Another major force in the study of death in Ugarit and Israel in this period was Marvin Pope, who in addition to exploring allusions in Job and Song of Songs,[41] published studies on the Rephaim,[42] the *marzēaḥ*,[43] the cult of the dead in general,[44] and Mot[45] (see also § 3.3.3.2).

---

don, 1672]). See discussion in Jan Assmann, *Death and Salvation in Ancient Egypt* (trans. David Lorton; Ithaca, N.Y.: Cornell University Press, 2005), 84–85.

[36] Brichto, "Kin, Cult, Land and Afterlife," 29.
[37] Brichto, "Kin, Cult, Land and Afterlife," 6.
[38] Brichto, "Kin, Cult, Land and Afterlife," 8.
[39] Brichto, "Kin, Cult, Land and Afterlife," 48.
[40] A study by Stephen L. Cook finds similar connections among kin, cult, and afterlife in the Bible, but additionally supports them by comparison with African religions and family structures: "Funerary Practices and Afterlife Expectations in Ancient Israel," *Religion Compass* 1 (2007): 1–24.
[41] Marvin Pope, *Job: Introduction, Translation, and Notes* (AB 15, 2nd ed.; Garden City, N.Y.: Doubleday, 1965); idem, *Song of Songs: A New Translation with Introduction and Commentary* (AB 7C; Garden City, N.Y.: Doubleday, 1977).
[42] Marvin Pope, "Notes on the Rephaim Texts from Ugarit," in *Essays on the Ancient Near East in Memory of Jacob Joel Finkelstein* (ed. M. de Jong Ellis; Memoirs of the Connecticut Academy of Arts and Sciences 19; Hamden, Conn.: Archon Books, 1977), 163–82.
[43] Marvin Pope, "Le *mrzḥ* à Ougarit et ailleurs," *Annales Archéologiques Arabes Syriennes* 29–30 (1979–80): 141–43.
[44] Marvin Pope, "The Cult of the Dead at Ugarit" in *Ugaritic in Retrospect: Fifty Years of Ugarit and Ugaritic* (ed. G. D. Young; Winona Lake, Ind.: Eisenbrauns, 1981), 159–79. Reprinted in *Probative Pontificating in Ugaritic and Biblical Literature: Collected Essays* (ed. Mark S. Smith; Münster: Ugarit-Verlag, 1994), 225–50.
[45] Marvin Pope, "Mot," in the Supplement to *The Interpreter's Dictionary of the Bible* (ed. George Arthur Buttrick, et al.; New York: Abingdon Press, 1976), 607–8.

Pope directed G. C. Heider's dissertation on Molek, which identified the endurance of nominally foreign practices in Israelite religion.[46] On the basis of the references in Lev 18:21 and 20:2–5, 2 Kgs 23:20; and Jer 32:35 to child sacrifices to Molek, and the association with the Ugaritic *Malīku* (see §§ 3.3.3.3; 4.4.3.2), Heider concluded that "both the extra-biblical and biblical evidence suggests that the cult [of Molek] is to be considered within the Israelite practice of the 'cult of the dead.'"[47] More specifically, "the cult of Molek was Canaanite in origin, well-established by the time of Ahaz, and was practiced at least at Jerusalem until the fall of the city in 587/6 B.C., with the exception of the reign of Josiah and possibly of Hezekiah."[48]

This multiplicity of focused studies set the stage for the works of Klaas Spronk and Theodore J. Lewis; their treatments of the Ugaritic data have already been summarized in chapter 3, but a few words are in order about their conclusions regarding Israelite religion.

Spronk clearly theorizes a connection between Israelite religion and its "Canaanite" precursors. He grants that "[c]lear evidence of a cult of the dead practiced by Israelites is scarce,"[49] but he finds such a cult referred to in Pss 16:3 and 106:28 (the cult of Baal Peor, not YHWH). In addition, combining the reference in Ezek 43:7–8 to defilement of the temple by the corpses of kings with the burial of Manasseh and Amon near the temple (2 Kgs 21:18, 26), he concludes that the royal cult of the dead was practiced by some Judean royalty who had special "sympathy for the Canaanite religion."[50]

Regarding the power of the dead, Spronk distinguishes between positive and malign powers. He perceives "no clear reference to the malign influences of unhappy spirits of the dead" in Judean literature until the intertestamental period, but thinks that it can be inferred from the Hebrew Bible.[51] As for the helpful powers of the dead, he argues that "ancient Israelite necromancy did not differ from the common ancient Near Eastern practices."[52] Despite the condemnations of necromancy as incompatible with Yahwism, it survived as "an under-current of the ancient religion of Israel next to the mainstream of Yahwism." Despite the references to royal necromancy, it was "usually connected with common people."[53] This last point deserves scrutiny, since it seems to owe more to received ideas about the roots of Israelite folk religion than it does to the data. The biblical

---

[46] George C. Heider, *The Cult of Molek: A Reassessment* (JSOTSup 43; Sheffield: JSOT Press, 1985).
[47] Heider, *Cult of Molek*, 383.
[48] Heider, *Cult of Molek*, 405.
[49] Spronk, *Beatific Afterlife*, 249.
[50] Spronk, *Beatific Afterlife*, 250.
[51] Spronk, *Beatific Afterlife*, 251.
[52] Spronk, *Beatific Afterlife*, 256.
[53] Spronk, *Beatific Afterlife*, 257.

texts bear little direct witness to popular religion, and a dearth of excavated common graves means that archaeology is largely mute on the topic as well.[54]

Lewis also concludes that the cult of the dead had "a lasting appeal in certain forms of 'popular religion,'"[55] and he lays special weight on the legal and prophetic condemnations of necromancy and death cult practices as signs of "an ongoing battle in ancient Israel to resist cults of the dead."[56] He notes that the remaining references to such cults are all the more significant, since it has survived in spite of the work of editors unsympathetic to such practices and beliefs.[57]

4.2.4 "Minimalist" backlash, redux

If the latter half of the 1980s saw a number of attempts to correlate biblical and extrabiblical data in support of a cult of the dead (Heider, Spronk, Lewis), it also saw the beginnings of a backlash. Even John F. Healey, who was certainly interested in Ugaritic mythology and cult surrounding death, warned against "overenthusiastic comparativism" in a 1986 article.[58] Two book-length critiques of the idea of an Israelite cult of the dead deriving from an indigenous Syro-Palestinian tradition eventually followed: Brian Schmidt's *Israel's Beneficent Dead* (1994) and Phillip Johnston's *Shades of Sheol* (2002). Each of these is controlled by a biblical studies agenda, although their agendas are very different.

Johnston's approach to the biblical text is more credulous than most. In sequentially addressing each of the issues regarding the dead and death cults, Johnston tends to summarize the Bible's own point of view in a synthetic (and often synchronic) way. For example, if 1 Sam 15 says that necromancy was outlawed in Saul's time, then Johnston concludes that it was nearly unheard-of in Israel then.[59] If the received form of the biblical text does not pay much attention to the spirits of the dead, then he concludes that the dead were not of much interest or concern to the ancient Israelites.[60] With its emphasis on Israelite distinctiveness, *Shades of Sheol* is something of a throwback. Although the book dutifully notes the extensive catalogue of comparative data, it does not, in the end, take it very seriously. The same might can be said about the large number of

---

[54] Elizabeth M. Bloch-Smith, *Judahite Burial Practices*, 149.
[55] Theodore J. Lewis, *Cults of the Dead in Ancient Israel and Ugarit* (HSM 39; Atlanta: Scholars Press, 1989), 174.
[56] Lewis, *Cults of the Dead*, 174.
[57] Lewis, *Cults of the Dead*, 176.
[58] John F. Healey, "The Ugaritic Dead: Some Live Issues," *UF* 18 (1986): 31.
[59] Philip S. Johnston, *Shades of Sheol: Death and Afterlife in the Old Testament* (Downers Grove, Ill.: InterVarsity, 2002), 154–58; Johnston argued that the location of the baʿălat ʾôb in Endor suggests that there were no necromancers to be found in Israel; but it is more likely merely due to the site's relative proximity to Gilboa, where the Israelites are said to have been encamped.
[60] E.g., Johnston, *Shades of Sheol*, 149, 166, 195.

biblical allusions to the powers of the dead and associated cultic practices that have been proposed (see above). For example, Johnston's summary of references to ancestor worship simply repeats the mantra "unconvincing ... unconvincing."[61] It is true that any one of these references, taken alone, proves little, and that many could potentially be explained away. At some point, however, the mass of these references, in conjunction with the aforementioned legal prohibitions, ought to force one to reassess the larger picture. It would be very hard for the references to the powers and importance of the dead to be completely convincing to a skeptic if they have been systematically excluded.

Some reviews of Johnston have been rather dismissive of its contribution,[62] but for the reader who wants a summary of Judean theology as it came to be, especially under the influence of Deuteronomism, *Shades of Sheol* is a useful book.[63] In any case, for the purposes of this study, which seeks to get at the theologies and ideologies of Isaiah's historical period prior to the major redactions of the text, a "final-form" reading such as Johnston's is not helpful.

It is equally difficult to engage Schmidt's *Israel's Beneficent Dead*, but for different reasons. Although the historical development of the biblical text is a primary interest of the study, Schmidt argues that all references to the cult of the dead early in the Hebrew Bible's narrative are late retrojections of Mesopotamian practices by Deuteronomistic scribes and do not reflect any indigenous Syro-Palestinian cult of the dead. Thus, in his own words, terms such as Canaanite, Hittite, Amorite do not "correspond to any specific political or ethnic entity known from the extrabiblical texts ... [they] functioned instead as ideological symbols for the indigenous non-Israelite inhabitants of Palestine."[64] Naturally, this means that Schmidt's book is subject to the conclusions of the vast debate over the history of Israel. As Lewis wrote, Schmidt's thesis is "primarily a literary one that argues that the biblical text is a fictitious construct that reflects Dtr's reimaging of Israelite religion out of whole cloth."[65] Lewis rightly objects that it is

---

[61] Johnston, *Shades of Sheol*, 194.

[62] For example, Theodore J. Lewis ("How Far Can Texts Take Us? Evaluating Textual Sources for Reconstructing Ancient Israelite Beliefs about the Dead," in *Sacred Time, Sacred Place*, 189) implies that Johnston is not especially "credible" or "astute."

[63] The numerous and positive citations of *Shades of Sheol* by Jon D. Levenson in *Resurrection and the Restoration of Israel: The Ultimate Victory of the God of Life* (New Haven: Yale University Press, 2006) suggest that it will be part of the conversation in years to come. However, there are briefer summaries of the "mainstream" of Hebrew Bible theology that simply leave out most of the contradictory data, rather than trying to explain it away; see, e.g., John Jarick, "Questioning Sheol" in *Resurrection* (ed. Stanley E. Porter et al.; JSNTSup 186; Sheffield: Sheffield Academic Press, 1999), 22–32.

[64] Brian B. Schmidt, *Israel's Beneficent Dead: Ancestor Cult and Necromancy in Ancient Israelite Religion and Tradition* (FAT 11; Tübingen: Mohr Siebeck, 1994), 139. Clearly, Schmidt's argument threatens to dredge up again the "minimalist-maximalist" debate about the history of Israel.

[65] Lewis, "How Far Can Texts Take Us?," 201–2.

hard to imagine an archaeologist or anthropologist who works on the period reaching Schmidt's conclusions.[66]

Because of the perception that much of the biblical canon, from the Tetrateuch to the prophets, underwent Deuteronomistic redactions, it is all too easy for Schmidt to assign nearly every reference to cults of the dead to Deuteronomistic editors. In the case of certain crucial Isaianic texts, he perceives largely the work of "a post-Isaianic redactor with a dtr orientation."[67] A more detailed analysis of these texts follows in the next chapter, which supports the recent critique of Schmidt's (and others') impulse toward "pan-Deuteronomism."[68] For now, it must suffice to say that Schmidt's reasoning becomes circular: Once he has decided that a concern about foreign death cults is a feature of Dtr, he can assign any such references to a late period and thus reinforce his thesis. The only check on his theory is the extrabiblical comparative data – which explains why, as demonstrated above, he argued so hard for the absence of Syro-Palestinian cults of the dead: their existence complicates the assumption that such cults were only a late concern in Israel and Judah.

Nevertheless, I believe there is something accurate in Schmidt's perception: The argument of the present study is that the Neo-Assyrian period in Judah *did* in fact see an increasing focus on the dead and their powers. Indeed, there is a growing consensus on that point.[69] However, Schmidt oversimplifies the reasons; and he therefore errs in trying to overturn one hundred years' worth of scholarship in order to make his case.

Rainer Albertz's treatment of the topic of Israelite veneration of the dead is also rather limited. He dispenses with the topic in a terse, two-page excursus,[70] concluding as follows: "The personal relationship to the God of the fathers had reduced the significance of divinized ancestors to remnants, for example to the sphere of safeguarding family continuity, oracles, and perhaps also healing functions."[71] But what important functions those are! Albertz later observes, "The

---

[66] Of course, Schmidt's thesis, if correct, would invalidate most studies of "Israelite religion" to date, and that may give reviewers a reason not to like it. However, it also reflects the book's minority stance.

[67] Schmidt, *Israel's Beneficent Dead*, 164. In fact, it would be hard to distinguish between Mesopotamian influence on a late-eighth-century prophet and on Deuteronomistic redactors. Both would have been under distinct cultural pressure from Mesopotamia.

[68] This problem is addressed by, for example, many of the essays in *Those Elusive Deuteronomists: The Phenomenon of Pan-Deuteronomism* (ed. L. S. Schearing and S. L. McKenzie; JSOTSup 268; Sheffield: Sheffield Academic Press, 1999).

[69] See, e.g., Blenkinsopp, "Deuteronomy and the Politics of Post-Mortem Existence," 1–16; Mary Douglas, "One God, No Ancestors, in a World Renewed," in *Jacob's Tears: The Priestly Work of Reconciliation* (Oxford: Oxford University Press, 2004), 176–95.

[70] Albertz, *History of Israelite Religion*, 1:36–39, but cf. 1:189, where he writes that "The Assyrian and Babylonian practice of resorting to oracles and conjurations of the dead ... seems to have been particularly attractive" in Israel.

[71] Albertz, *History of Israelite Religion*, 1:39.

Assyrian and Babylonian practice of resorting to oracles and conjurations of the dead ... seems to have been particularly attractive [during the Neo-Assyrian period]," and some connection between this attraction and an earlier Syro-Palestinian tradition of necromantic consultations seems likely. In any case, he would agree that cults of the dead held a special attraction around Isaiah's time.

The most plausible reconstruction to date of the relationship between Yahwism and Israelite cults of the dead is offered by Mark S. Smith and Elizabeth Bloch-Smith. In their aforementioned review of Spronk's *Beatific Afterlife*, in addition to their comments about Spronk's treatment of the Ugaritic material, they criticized him for failing to account for the "cultural, temporal and geographical discontinuities between Ugarit and Israel."[72] While they do not disagree entirely with Spronk,[73] they deemed his biblical exegesis insufficiently diachronically nuanced.[74] The Smiths perceive a development in views toward necromancy and care of the dead, arguing that only necromancy was negatively viewed early on, while care and veneration of the dead were probably widely practiced until the reforms of the seventh century. They have elaborated on this model in their individual writings; Smith agreed with Spronk that "the practices in the Bible concerning the dead belonged to Israel's Canaanite heritage,"[75] but he specifies that "the only practice associated with the dead that was possibly forbidden prior to the seventh century was necromancy."[76]

Bloch-Smith elaborates further, relating the banning of necromancy to the fall of the north and the concomitant integration of cultic personnel into the Jerusalem temple. With such a surplus of priests, the Yahwists could not afford to be challenged by necromancy, plus the fall of the North "necessitated a theological response."[77] Presumably this means that the Jerusalem priests needed to assert their status as the preeminent religious authorities, given the influx of northern religious professionals. Based on the relatively consistent archaeological record regarding burials (see below), Bloch-Smith saw "little or no change in attitude or practices among the inhabitants of Judah towards the dead throughout the Iron

---

[72] Mark S. Smith and Elizabeth Bloch-Smith, "Death and Afterlife in Ugarit and Israel," *JAOS* 108 (1988): 279. See also Karel van der Toorn, "Funerary Rituals and Beatific Afterlife in Ugaritic Texts and the Bible," *BO* 48 (1991): 40–66.

[73] They agree that there is a pre-Israelite Syro-Palestinian cult of the dead, and they grant that although Spronk had not proved it, there is a possibility that Israelite views were like those of the Hadad inscription (KAI 214), and that the idea of eating and drinking with God eventually evolved into the idea of being with God in heaven forever, that is, beatific afterlife. Following Dahood, they suggest Ps 21:3–5 as a locus for this belief.

[74] Bloch-Smith (*Judahite Burial Practices*, 17) applies this critique to both Spronk and Lewis.

[75] Mark S. Smith, *The Early History of God: Yahweh and the Other Deities in Ancient Israel* (2nd ed.; Biblical Resource Series; Grand Rapids: Eerdmans, 2002), 162; cf. idem, *The Origins of Biblical Monotheism: Israel's Polytheistic Background and the Ugaritic Texts* (Oxford: Oxford University Press, 2001), 68–70.

[76] Smith, *Early History of God*, 163.

[77] Bloch-Smith, *Judahite Burial Practices*, 131.

Age. Rather the [Dtr and Holiness Code] legislation reflects a policy change initiated in the eighth and seventh centuries BCE by the palace and Jerusalem Temple Yahwistic cult authorities."[78]

Changes in (or new regulations of) Judean practices toward the dead might not be immediately reflected in archaeological remains, however. It is not clear that funerary provisioning was banned, since it posed little threat to the prophets and priests who spoke for YHWH; it was mortuary rituals that reflected reliance on the dead instead of YHWH. Moreover, it is not clear that mortuary rituals required any permanent architectural features (see § 3.3.2), nor even where they were carried out. This would make them difficult to trace in the archaeological record. Like other cultic practices, the cult of the dead may have been carried out in private homes[79] – especially since Iron Age Judean tombs were placed outside of settled areas.

Therefore archaeology alone cannot determine anything conclusive about Judean mortuary religion toward the end of the monarchic period. With the various theories in mind, we turn to survey the archaeology and texts relating to Israelite and Judean practices and beliefs surrounding death.

4.3 The archaeology of death in ancient Judah

Among the handful of archaeological studies of burial in ancient Judah,[80] Bloch-Smith's is the most complete.[81] She began with the thesis that "the form of burial was determined not by theological considerations alone, but by numerous other factors, both cultural and geological."[82] Indeed, she found a very high correlation between burial types and cultural groups;[83] for example, Egyptians used pit burials, cist graves, and anthropoid coffins; the Assyrians used bathtub coffins; Phoenicians cremated and buried their dead; and the "indigenous highland popula-

---

[78] Bloch-Smith, *Judahite Burial Practices*, 132.
[79] Miller, *Religion of Ancient Israel*, 71–73; Albertz, *History of Israelite Religion*, 1:186–95; Oded Borowski, *Daily Life in Biblical Israel* (Atlanta: Society of Biblical Literature, 2003), 54.
[80] Previous studies include J. R. Abercrombie, "Palestinian Burial Practices from 1200 to 600 BCE" (Ph.D. diss., University of Pennsylvania, 1979); Stanislao Loffreda, "The Late Chronology of Some Rock-Cut Tombs of the Selwan Necropolis, Jerusalem," *SBFLA* 23 (1973): 7–36; idem, "Iron Age Rock-Cut Tombs in Palestine," *SBFLA* 18 (1968): 244–287; Ribar, "Death Cult Practices." See further Bloch-Smith, *Judahite Burial Practices*, 16 n. 1. Since the publication of Bloch-Smith's book, one might mention Rachel S. Hallote, *Death, Burial, and Afterlife in the Biblical World: How the Israelites and Their Neighbors Treated the Dead* (Chicago: Ivan R. Dee, 2001), which is more popular in nature.
[81] Philip J. King, reviewing the book in *CBQ* 56 (1994): 748–49, wrote, "I know of no other place [such an excellent synthesis] can be found."
[82] Bloch-Smith, *Judahite Burial Practices*, 18.
[83] Bloch-Smith, *Judahite Burial Practices*, 55.

tion" used caves as tombs.[84] The bench tomb became "the characteristic Judahite form of burial"[85] – although only for elites. The rock-cut bench tombs that have been discovered in Jerusalem thus far would have served only 1.5% of the population during the monarchic period.[86] It is nearly certain that not all such tombs from the period have been discovered, but even a multiple of that percentage would make burial in a bench tomb a minority practice for the elite.

Common people, as in Egypt and elsewhere, tended to bury their dead in simple pit graves, perhaps in a field owned by the family (as attested textually in, e.g., 2 Kgs 23:6; Jer 26:23; 31:39–40). Pit graves become nearly "invisible" to archaeology, although some have been excavated in such places as Lachish, Jerusalem, and Megiddo.[87]

That is not to say that all areas showed uniform burial types in a given period. Certain larger cities such as Azor, Lachish, and Jerusalem "displayed an unusually large variety of burial types not otherwise found together. This diversity suggests that they were cosmopolitan centers where different cultural groups co-existed and interred their dead."[88]

Early in the biblical period, cave tombs were more popular and were sometimes found at the same sites as bench tombs,[89] but during the course of the Iron Age II (1000–586 BCE), inhabitants of Judah increasingly buried their dead in bench tombs. Bloch-Smith theorized that, if burial in bench tombs was not a cultural choice, it may have been "adopted as a more elaborate or fashionable version of family burial in caves."[90] In any case, by the late eighth century, Judah's elites showed "virtually exclusive use" of the bench tomb.[91] Such tombs

---

[84] For example, the second half of the eighth century saw "the introduction of bathtub coffin burials in the territory of the former northern kingdom," reflecting the influx of Assyrians (Bloch-Smith, *Judahite Burial Practices*, 63).

[85] Elizabeth M. Bloch-Smith, "The Cult of the Dead in Judah: Interpreting the Material Remains," *JBL* 111 (1992): 216.

[86] Gabriel Barkay, "The Cemeteries of Jerusalem in the Days of the First Temple Period" in *Jerusalem in the Days of the First Temple* (eds. D. Amit and R. Goren; Jerusalem, 1990), 103 (Hebrew).

[87] Bloch-Smith, *Judahite Burial Practices*, 25–29.

[88] Bloch-Smith, *Judahite Burial Practices*, 55; cf. Amihai Mazar, *Archaeology of the Land of the Bible, 10,000–586 B.C.E.* (ABRL; New York: Doubleday, 1990), 525. Notably, most of the remains in the tombs in question have not been analyzed for ethno-cultural origin; in other words, if a member of one cultural group chose to be buried in the style of another cultural group, the archaeological record, as it is presently read, would not reveal it.

[89] Bloch-Smith, *Judahite Burial Practices*, 60–62. See also Mazar, *Archaeology of the Land of the Bible*, 520–21. Raz Kletter has pointed out the surprising absence of Iron I tombs by comparison with Late Bronze and Iron II tombs ("People without Burials? The Lack of Iron I Burials in the Central Highlands of Palestine," *IEJ* 52 [2002]: 28–48). Although the reasons for the shortage are not clear, Kletter's hypothetical factors included the tendency of a poorer, egalitarian society toward simple burials, or a cultural preference against burial altogether.

[90] Bloch-Smith, *Judahite Burial Practices*, 58.

[91] Bloch-Smith, "Cult of the Dead in Judah," 216.

would have been found or cut out of tell slopes or wadi cliffs near the cities. The typical structure of a bench tomb was as follows:

[A] doorway in a rock-cut façade opened into an approximately five meter square chamber with waist-high benches arranged around the perimeter of the room. Occasionally, additional chambers with benches were added. On the benches, individuals reposed, extended on their backs, with their heads on stone pillows or headrests when provided. ... When space was required for an additional burial, a previous burial and at least some of the mortuary provisions were moved to a repository pit carved inside the tomb.[92]

A family tomb was a symbol of the family's endurance and hoped-for permanence, and it may even have been a marker of the family's property.[93] It was not, however, viewed as an opportunity for artistic self-expression: Judean burials generally showed little variation in style, except in their relative wealth and fineness. Tombs showed a particular flourishing around the time of Isaiah of Jerusalem, since "[i]n the late eighth century, Judah reached the height of its power and prosperity."[94]

The prosperity of the period did not make it an especially peaceful or happy time, and such changes in tomb architecture likely marked an ideological struggle. Indeed, Avraham Faust and Shlomo Bunimovitz have argued that the rise in popularity of the rock-cut tomb was a reaction to rising social pressures:

Accelerated urbanisation, growing population density and social inequalities, evolving trade and mass production, and increased hired labour, along with external political and military pressures, all led to the disintegration of lineages and extended families in the urban sector and to growing insecurity.[95]

In this atmosphere of change and insecurity, the rock-cut tomb was, in their view, "an attempt to immortalize the *bet ʾab* in stone."[96] To put it in contemporary terms, it was an assertion of "family values" over against the forces of "modernization."

That modernization can be seen in the same period, as other rock-cut tombs went in the other direction, towards increasing individuation. The archaeological record preserves a handful of particularly rich tenth- and ninth-century tombs, with a further spread in the eighth and seventh centuries.[97] The elite tombs at

---

[92] Bloch-Smith, "Cult of the Dead in Judah," 217.
[93] Amos Kloner, "Iron Age Burial Caves in Jerusalem and Its Vicinity," *Bulletin of the Anglo-Israel Archaeological Society* 19–20 (2004): 113; Avraham Faust and Shlomo Bunimovitz, "The Judahite Rock-Cut Tomb: Family Response at a Time of Change," *IEJ* 58 (2008): 155.
[94] Nadav Na'aman, " 'Let Other Kingdoms Struggle with the Great Powers – You, Judah, Pay the Tribute and Hope for the Best': The Foreign Policy of the Kings of Judah in the Ninth-Eighth Centuries BCE," in *Isaiah's Vision of Peace in Biblical and Modern International Relations: Swords Into Plowshares* (eds. R. Cohen and R. Westbrook; New York: Palgrave Macmillan, 2008), 55–73.
[95] Faust and Bunimovitz, "The Judahite Rock-Cut Tomb," 162.
[96] Faust and Bunimovitz, "The Judahite Rock-Cut Tomb," 151.
[97] Elizabeth Bloch-Smith, "Life in Judah from the Perspective of the Dead," *NEA* 65 (2002):

Silwan were marked by a "total absence of bone repositories," such as would have been present in group or family tombs;[98] this reflects the hope that one's bones would not be swept away but would lie undisturbed indefinitely. Again, such changes reflect shifts in social structure and ideology in the eighth century, with some of the clan and family ties that had characterized the society straining and breaking.[99]

Other aspects of burial did not change much; for example, grave provisioning was practiced consistently by Judahites throughout the period. The dead were generally supplied with goods, the most ubiquitous being pottery jars and bowls indicating that food and drink were provided for the dead.[100] Other goods included travel gear, food, jewelry and amulets, and assorted household items.[101] Various clasps found among the remains indicate that the dead were clothed and wrapped in cloaks. A final type of grave provision, figurines, is poorly understood, but these too may indicate funerary or mortuary practices that are incompatible with the biblical portrait. The practice of provisioning graves, wrote Bloch-Smith, "continued unchanged in Judah throughout the Iron Age. Any historical reconstruction must account for this absence of change in spite of biblical legislation aimed at suppressing aspects of the cult of the dead."[102]

120–23, 128–29. Hallote perceives a lack of emphasis on individuality in Israelite burials (*Death, Burial, and the Afterlife*, 91); this comment presumably refers to the rule to which these few wealthy tombs were exceptions.

[98] David Ussishkin, *The Village of Silwan: The Necropolis from the Period of the Judean Kingdom* (Jerusalem: Yad Ben-Tzvi and the Society for the Exploration of the Land of Israel and Her Antiquities, 1986), 303.

[99] See Baruch Halpern, "Sybil, or the Two Nations? Archaism, Kinship, Alienation, and the Elite Redefinition of Traditional Culture in Judah in the 8th–7th Centuries BCE" in *The Study of the Ancient Near East in the Twenty-First Century: The William Foxwell Albright Centennial Conference* (eds. J. S. Cooper and G. M. Schwartz; Winona Lake, Ind.: Eisenbrauns, 1996), 291–338. But see also the critique of certain aspects of Halpern's use of archaeological data by Alexander Fantalkin, "The Appearance of Rock-Cut Bench Tombs in Iron Age Judah as a Reflection of State Formation," in *Bene Israel: Studies in the Archaeology of Israel and the Levant During the Bronze and Iron Ages in Honour of Israel Finkelstein* (eds. A. Fantalkin and A. Yassur-Landau; Culture and History of the Ancient Near East Series 31; Leiden: Brill, 2008), 17–44.

[100] Bloch-Smith, *Judahite Burial Practices*, 108.

[101] Hélène Nutkowicz, *L'Homme face à la mort au royaume de Juda: Rites, pratiques, et repésentations* (Paris: Éditions du Cerf, 2006), 127–99.

[102] Bloch-Smith, "Cult of the Dead in Judah," 219. There is much debate about their meaning, and they came in many types. There are Bes figurines, presumed to have functioned as protection for children and the dead. Female figurines became increasingly common in Judean burials at the end of the preexilic period, and their significance is particularly hard to determine; it is not even clear whether they were meant to represent humans or goddesses. Some connection to fertility and lactation is commonly theorized, and they are also frequently connected with Asherah. Are they signs of heterodox practices? Other types of models are found too sporadically to bear much weight in reconstructions of Judean religion; however, the set as a whole reinforces the idea that the religious landscape in the preexilic period was more complex than some parts of the biblical text suggest (and exactly as complex as other parts suggest, such as 1 Kgs 11:4–8). See also Karel van der Toorn, "Israelite Figurines: A View from the Texts," in *Sacred Time, Sacred Place*, 45–62.

4.3 *The archaeology of death in ancient Judah* 151

Tomb inscriptions from Judah are similar in certain ways to those of the Egyptians and Phoenicians (see §§ 2.4.1; 3.4). They tend to identify the tomb's owner and seek to ward off robbers. A particularly clear reflection of the concern about the integrity of the burial is shown by the contemporaneous Tomb of the Royal Steward inscription at the Silwan cemetery, which tells potential robbers that there is "no silver and no gold, only his bones and the bones of his slave-wife with him. Cursed be the man who will open this."[103] Another Silwan tomb from roughly the same period bore a similar, albeit broken, warning.[104] Inscriptions found on the walls of tombs at Khirbet Beit Lei include supplications for divine help, but they typically are taken to have been added later, perhaps by persons hiding in the tombs, rather than being related to the burials.[105]

There is also an unusual late-eighth-century tomb inscription from Khirbet el-Qôm (No. 3), which could be taken as evidence of a hope for divine intervention in the afterlife.[106] The transcription and translation of Roberts *et al.* reflects the views of a number of recent epigraphers:

1. *'ryhw . h'šr . ktbh*   Uriah the rich commissioned it.
2. *brk . 'ryhw . lyhwh*   Blessed was Uriah by YHWH,
3. *wmṣryh l'šrth hwš' lh*   and from his enemies by his Asherah he has delivered him.[107]

There have, however, been numerous reconstructions of the third line. The text is broken, scratched, and partly written over, making it extraordinarily difficult to

---

[103] Silwan Tomb 35, longer inscription. See Hebrew text at § 5.2.1.3. *HI*, 507–10; Ussishkin, *Village of Silwan*, 173–84, 221–26. It is probable that the disavowal of silver and gold was very specifically intended to dissuade tomb robbers on practical grounds, since (at least in Egypt, but surely in Palestine as well) such robbers preferred fungible metals to other artifacts that were more difficult to convert to wealth (Richards, *Society and Death in Ancient Egypt*, 68).

[104] Silwan Tomb 34: "*[z't] qbrt z[... / ...] 'šr yp[tḥ ...]*": "[This is] the tomb of ... whoever ope[ns] (this tomb) ...." *HI*, 510–11; Ussishkin, *Village of Silwan*, 165–72, 217–20.

[105] *HI*, 130–32; F. M. Cross, Jr., "The Cave Inscriptions from Khirbet Beit Lei," in *Near Eastern Archaeology in the Twentieth Century: Essays in Honor of Nelson Glueck* (ed. J. A. Sanders; Garden City, N.Y.: Doubleday, 1970), 299–306.

[106] Spronk, *Beatific Afterlife*, 307–10.

[107] *HI*, 408–14. I omit comment here on ll. 4–6, which may be part of a separate inscription and in any case raise different and more complex issues. Similar are the readings of Judith Hadley, "The Khirbet el-Qom Inscription," *VT* 37 (1987): 50–62; and Patrick Miller, "Psalms and Inscriptions," in *Congress Volume: Vienna 1980* (VTSup 32; Leiden: Brill, 1981), 311–32. See also Andre Lemaire, "Les inscriptions de Khirbet el-Qôm et l'Ashérah de YHWH," *RB* 84 (1977): 595–608, and Joseph Naveh, "Graffiti and Dedications," *BASOR* 235 (1979): 27–30. The excavator, William Dever, initially took it to be merely another simple warning against desecration:
'ryhw hqṣb ktbh.   Belonging to Uriyahu. Be careful of his inscription!
brk. 'ryhw. lyhwh   Blessed be Uriyahu by YHWH.
wm'rr yd l'šr thhwš 'lh And cursed shall be the hand of whoever (defaces it)!
See William G. Dever, "Iron Age Epigraphic Material from the Area of Khirbet el-Kôm," *HUCA* 40–41 (1970): 139–204; cf. Dever, "Khirbet el-Qôm," in *The Encyclopedia of Archaeological Excavations in the Holy Land* (ed. Michael Avi-Yonah; Englewood Cliffs, N.J.: Prentice-Hall, 1978), 4:976.

decipher.[108] Practically every West Semitic epigrapher has published on the inscription over the past forty years, as have not a few biblical scholars.[109] Spronk read it as wmmṣr dyh hl꜄: "[May YHWH deliver him] from the distress, as much as comes to him over there" – with "over there" referring to the afterlife.[110] That reading is unique and has found no support among the many others scholars who have examined the text; the near-consensus opinion is now that the final two lines refer to the blessings of YHWH and Asherah (brk. ʾryhw. lyhwh ... wlʾšrth). Ziony Zevit notes that the inscription is atypical for a Judean tomb inscription, and compares it to the Zakkur stele, which recounts a past act of divine salvation, but "in the liturgical language of a thanksgiving psalm."[111]

Nevertheless, it is not unlikely that Uriyahu hoped for protection and blessing in the afterlife; the matter does not depend on Spronk's reading. The inscription, as it is reconstructed, is very similar to the Kuntillet ʾAjrud inscriptions (Nos. 1–3), which *invoke* blessings (e.g. No. 3:5–7: brktk lyhwh tmn w lʾšrth, "I bless you by YHWH of Teman and by (his?) Asherah"). It is quite possible to understand brk in line 2 of the inscription as a passive participle ("Blessed be Uriyahu by YHWH...," or as an imperative ("Bless Uriyahu by YHWH..."), rather than as a perfective form ("Uriyahu was blessed..."), as the translation by Roberts et al. suggests.[112] Either of the first two interpretations of brk allows for the understanding that Uriyahu was asking for blessings and salvation in the afterlife instead of giving thanks for past blessings. Although tomb inscriptions from Egypt, for example, frequently gave thanks for a deity's past help during the deceased's lifetime (see § 5.2.3.3), I think that the ʾAjrud comparison suggests a future outlook.[113]

---

[108] William H. Shea thinks it was written over by Oniyahu, whose name appears beneath the original inscription. Shea takes him to have been an illiterate Egyptian servant of Uriyahu: "The Khirbet el-Qom Tomb Inscription Again," VT 40 (1990): 115.

[109] For a more detailed *Forschungsgeschichte* than what is offered here, see HI, 408–14.

[110] Spronk, *Beatific Afterlife*, 308.

[111] Ziony Zevit, *The Religions of Ancient Israel: A Synthesis of Parallactic Approaches* (London: Continuum, 2001), 368.

[112] Patrick Miller takes the perfective view – "Blessed is Uriyahu by YHWH / Yea, from his adversaries by his asherah he has saved him" ("Psalms and Inscriptions," in *Congress Volume: Vienna 1980* [VTSup 32; Leiden: Brill, 1981], 317–19) – as does Hadley, "The Khirbet el-Qom Inscription," 51; Sandra Landis Gogel, *A Grammar of Epigraphic Hebrew* (SBLRBSz 23; Atlanta: Scholars Press, 1998), 412. M. P. O'Connor takes the imperative view: "May you bless Uriah, O YHWH, / And from his enemies, O Asherata, save him" ("The Poetic Inscription from Khirbet el-Qôm," VT 37 [1987]: 228).

[113] One's conclusion depends in part on debatable grammatical features. At least three grammatical considerations are in play here: first, the understanding of the *l*-prepositions attached to YHWH and ʾǎšērâ, which O'Connor takes as vocative, a phenomenon well known in Ugaritic but scarcely attested in Hebrew (and not recognized in epigraphic Hebrew by Gogel, *Grammar of Epigraphic Hebrew*, 216). See also Patrick D. Miller, Jr., "Vocative Lamed in the Psalter: A Reconsideration," UF 11 (1979): 617–37. Zevit translates "for the sake of Asheratah save him!," which solves the grammar problem at the expense of his having to posit a compli-

If the afterlife is in view, then the request for protection from "enemies" in l. 3 might refer to the demonic forces that make the journey to the afterlife treacherous in the Egyptian Books of the Dead (see § 2.4).[114] Still, the Khirbet el-Qôm inscription alone is not a powerful piece of evidence for afterlife in ancient Israel; it is only one piece of evidence in a larger picture.

In the effort to sketch the cultural context of Isaiah's death imagery, one is hindered by the fact that the archaeological record may not accord with the biblical record at important points. It is incorrect to allow either archaeology or text to override the witness of the other; thus Bloch-Smith is quite right to use both in a complementary fashion.[115] Ian Hodder and Scott Hutson note that, particularly in the case of burial practices,

the notion that material culture is an *indirect* reflection of human society becomes clear. ... material culture and society mutually constitute each other within historically and culturally specific sets of ideas, beliefs and meanings. Thus, the relation between burial and society clearly depends on attitudes to death.[116]

The "ideas, beliefs and meanings" of ancient Judah are most readily accessible in its texts, challenging though they may be to interpret. Thus, in order to assess the other constituent of this complex, I turn to the Hebrew Bible.

4.4 Death in the Hebrew Bible

In its diverse references to death, the Hebrew Bible reflects its lengthy period of production. With respect to beliefs and practices, it contains some proscription, much description, but an almost total lack of prescription. Still, as long as the reader does not expect systematic theology from the text, a rich picture does emerge.

---

cated relationship between YHWH and Asherah wherein the goddess could not save because she was not a healing goddess, so that the supplicant had to pray in her name to another god (*Religions*, 369). Second, the *h* on the end of Asherah's name must be construed as a double-feminine marker, according to O'Connor (following Ziony Zevit, "The Khirbet el-Qom Inscription Mentioning a Goddess," *BASOR* 255 [1984]: 45–46), whereas it is more easily understood as a possessive by Miller ("Psalms and Inscriptions"). Against Miller's understanding is the problem of word order: Why should *wmṣryh* precede *l'šrth*? The phrase "by his *ʾăšērâ* he has saved him" introduces an unusual instrumental use of *lamed*. If the preposition is treated more normally, then *wmṣryh* seems to interrupt the syntax, as Gogel shows by flipping it and *wmṣryh* in her translation.

[114] S. Mittman has pointed out two Aramaic inscriptions from fifth-/fourth-century Egypt (*KAI* 267:1 and 269:1) that are similar to Khirbet el-Qom No. 3 (Mittman, "Die Grabinschrift des Sängers Uriahu," *ZDPV* 97 [1981]: 148).

[115] Bloch-Smith, *Judahite Burial Practices*, 17–19.

[116] Ian Hodder and Scott Hutson, *Reading the Past: Current Approaches to Interpretation in Archaeology* (3rd ed.; Cambridge: Cambridge University Press, 2003), 3.

4.4.1 Burial and mourning

4.4.1.1 Burial in the texts

The only prescription about burial in the Torah is that the one who is executed and hung on a tree must be buried the same day (Deut 21:23). It is only a slight exaggeration to say that the Bible's descriptions of Egyptian burials (Gen 50:2–3, 26) tell us more about those practices than they ever do about Israelite practices! Perhaps the most striking omission is the lack of any mention at all of tomb provisioning, given that it was practiced consistently in Judah throughout the biblical period.[117] One is left with numerous narrative accounts of burials, and although there is no need to reproduce Bloch-Smith's capable survey,[118] a brief overview is in order.

In general, the narrative of Genesis–2 Kings (and Chronicles) displays a strong interest in burials; and on the whole, the biblical authors seem to have been relatively cognizant of the diachronic shifts and cultural differences in customs. The lengthy account of Abraham's acquisition of a burial cave at Machpelah in Gen 23 is compatible with premonarchic practice in the Levant and may preserve some memory of older burial practices known to the author.[119] Abraham, Sarah, Isaac, Rebekah, Jacob, and Leah are all said to have been buried in this same cave (Gen 49:29–33), reflecting the custom of successive familial burials in one tomb.

By contrast, when Rachel died in childbirth while traveling, Jacob did not return her to the family tomb, but erected a pillar (מצבה) at her grave (Gen 35:20).[120] Erecting burial markers over inhumation graves was sometimes practiced by the Egyptians, Phoenicians, and Arameans, but there is no evidence for the practice in ancient Israel.[121] *Maṣṣēbôt*, or "standing stones," are known from cultic sites,[122] but none has been found in Israel or Judah that marks a grave.

---

[117] Bloch-Smith ("Cult of the Dead in Judah," 218) suggests that the reference to the ghost of Samuel wearing a robe (מעיל) in 1 Sam 28:14 is a reflection of the burial practice of wrapping the corpse in a cloak. However, Robert Alter points out that the robe is a characteristic of Saul throughout his life (cf. 1 Sam 2:19; 15:27) and is probably mentioned in 28:14 to "clinch the identification" of the prophet (*The David Story: A Translation with Commentary of 1 and 2 Samuel* [New York: W. W. Norton, 1999], 175.)

[118] Bloch-Smith, *Judahite Burial Practices*, 114–19.

[119] K. A. Kitchen goes so far as to argue that the account is potentially accurate (*On the Reliability of the Old Testament* [Grand Rapids: Eerdmans, 2003], 326–28).

[120] Benjamin D. Cox and Susan Ackerman have argued that it may have been normal practice in ancient Israel and elsewhere not to bury women who died in childbirth in a family tomb, in that they were automatically part of the "unhappy dead." ("Rachel's Tomb," *JBL* 128 [2009]: 135–48).

[121] Carl F. Graesser, "Standing Stones in Ancient Palestine," *BA* 35 (1972): 34–63, here 39–41; Bloch-Smith, *Judahite Burial Practices*, 103.

[122] Cf. Gen 28:17–18, Exod 24:4; Graesser, "Standing Stones in Ancient Palestine," 44–56; Philip J. King and Lawrence E. Stager, *Life in Biblical Israel* (Library of Ancient Israel; Louisville, Ky.: Westminster John Knox, 2001), 320–22.

(Then again, the likelihood of identifying such a burial would be small.) Although Albright's argument about the high places and the ancestor cult has come under stern criticism,[123] Bloch-Smith and Karel van der Toorn still think that stelae may have marked cult-of-the-dead locations.[124]

The biblical authors knew of the Egyptian practice of mummification and reported that it was carried out for the remains of both Jacob and Joseph (Gen 50:2, 26), as certainly would have been done for a high-ranking official and his kin. The forty-day embalming process and seventy-day mourning period (Gen 50:3) accord well with the independent Egyptian data;[125] indeed, "modern experiments have shown that optimum results in mummification are achieved after a maximum of forty days."[126] Given the longevity of the custom of mummification in Egyptian history, these details shed no light on the historicity of the accounts, but again, they do emphasize that the authors were conversant with the burial customs of other cultures.[127]

The Pentateuch also records the burial places of Miriam and Aaron. Quite exceptionally, Deut 34:5–6 seems to say that YHWH himself buried Moses, so that "no one knows where his grave is, to this day" – a somewhat mysterious omission.

---

[123] Summary by Lewis in *Cults of the Dead*, 140–41. For a critique, see W. Boyd Barrick, "The Funerary Character of 'High Places' in Ancient Palestine: A Reassessment," *VT* 25 (1975): 265–95.

[124] Bloch-Smith, *Judahite Burial Practices*, 113. Van der Toorn thinks that Albright's claims about the *bāmôt* as locations of ancestor worship needs to be salvaged (*Family Religion*, 220–22). In general, the conversation surrounding *maṣṣēbôt* has come to center not on ancestor cults but on Israelite aniconism; that is, do Israelite standing stones symbolize god(s), and if so, which one(s)? The key study is Tryggve N. D. Mettinger's *No Graven Image? Israelite Aniconism in its Ancient Near Eastern Context* (ConBOT 42; Stockholm: Almqvist & Wiksell International, 1995). A recent assessment by Bloch-Smith winnows the archaeological data: "Will the Real Massebot Please Stand Up: Cases of Real and Mistakenly Identified Standing Stones in Ancient Israel," in *Text, Artifact, Image: Revealing Ancient Israelite Religion* (ed. Gary M. Beckman and Theodore J. Lewis; Brown Judaic Studies 346; Providence: Brown Judaic Studies, 2006), 64–79.

[125] According to John H. Taylor, the ideal seventy-day period of embalming mentioned in various Egyptian texts "is perhaps to be understood as the length of time during which mourning for the deceased took place, within which period the body was embalmed. Only for an elaborate mummification would seventy days be required" (*Death and the Afterlife in Ancient Egypt* [Chicago: University of Chicago Press, 2001], 77).

[126] Ann Rosalie David, "Mummification," in *The Oxford Encyclopedia of Ancient Egypt* (Oxford: Oxford University Press, 2001), 2:443. Of course, the number 40 was also a traditional one in biblical literature; see J. Vergote, *Joseph en Égypte: Genèse chap. 37–50 à la lumière des études égyptologiques récentes* (Louvain: University of Louvain, 1959), 200; see also S. McEvenue, "A Source-Critical Problem in Nm 14,26–38," *Bib* 50 (1969): 455.

[127] Pnina Galpaz-Feller suggests that additional information about the Egyptian burial practices related in Genesis was suppressed since it could be understood to suggest that Jacob and Joseph had embraced Egyptian religion. See Galpaz-Feller, "'And the Physicians Embalmed Him' (Gen 50,2)," *ZAW* 118 (2006): 209–17. Vergote's concern with whether or not Egyptian "physicians" (cf. רֹפְאִים, Gen 50:2) concerned themselves with mummifications seems beside the point; clearly Hebrew had no native word for an "embalmer"; must one expect a calque of the Egyptian technical term (*wty*)? (Vergote, *Joseph en Égypte*, 197–200).

The burial accounts of the Pentateuch are often taken to be relatively late literary fictions. If so, then the authors were careful to portray the burials in historically plausible ways, which suggests a sensitivity to diachronic and international differences in culture. Donald B. Redford wrote that the Joseph story does reflect a certain volume of accurate knowledge about Egypt – specifically, Kushite or Saite Egypt. In other words, he suggests a somewhat detailed knowledge of Egyptian burial practices in precisely the time of Isaiah and his earliest tradents.[128] This accords well with my argument in chapter 5 that various texts in Isa 1–39 reflect knowledge of Egyptian culture.

The Deuteronomistic History twice records the death and burial of Joshua (Josh 24:29; Judg 2:8), and the burial places of Gideon and all the judges after him are also noted. Certain burials figure prominently in the plot of the narrative; for example, the secondary burial of Saul and Jonathan in their family tomb is said to restore divine favor to Israel: "After that, God heeded the pleas for the land" (2 Sam 21:14).

Burial practices around the time of Isaiah (during Iron IIB, roughly speaking) are of special interest here. The burials of Israelite and Judean kings are routinely recorded in the historical books; in 1–2 Kings, the recurrent phrase "he lay down with his fathers" (וישכב עם־אבותיו) reflects a peaceful death and normal burial.[129] Most kings are said to be buried in their capital cities, e.g.: David and Solomon in the City of David (1 Kgs 2:10; 11:43), Omri in Samaria (1 Kgs 16:28). Even kings slain in battle were returned by chariot to Jerusalem and buried there, if at all possible (e.g., Ahaziah in 2 Kgs 9:28; Josiah in 2 Kgs 23:30).

There is significant archaeological debate regarding the location of the "City of David" burial ground. Theories abound,[130] and finding it was deemed "the capital problem of Hebrew archaeology" more than a hundred years ago,[131] yet it has still never been conclusively identified. The issue is complicated by the fact that many of the Iron Age tombs in Jerusalem have been damaged by quarrying, or refas-

---

[128] Donald B. Redford, *Egypt, Canaan, and Israel in Ancient Times* (Princeton: Princeton University Press, 1992), 422–29; see also idem, *A Study of the Biblical Story of Joseph (Genesis 37–50)* (Leiden: Brill, 1970), 240–41.

[129] G. R. Driver, "Plurisma Mortis Image," in *Studies and Essays in Honor of Abraham A. Neuman* (eds. M. Ben-Horin et al.; E. J. Brill: Leiden, 1962), 141; Bloch-Smith, *Judahite Burial Practices*, 110; Ludwig Wächter, *Der Tod im Alten Testament* (Arbeiten zur Theologie II/8; Stuttgart: Calwer, 1967), 71–72; K. J. Illman, *Old Testament Formulas About Death* (RIAAF 48; Åbo, Finland: Åbo Akademi, 1979), 44–47; Baruch Halpern and David S. Vanderhooft, "The Editions of Kings in the 7th–6th Centuries. B.C.E.," *HUCA* 62 (1991): 179–244.

[130] A helpful summary is given in L. Y. Rahmani, "Ancient Jerusalem's Funerary Customs and Tombs, Part Two," *BA* 44 (1981): 232–33. On earlier efforts, see J. Simons, *Jerusalem in the Old Testament: Researches and Theories* (Leiden: Brill, 1952), 194–225; S. Yeivin, "The Sepulchers of the Kings of the House of David," *JNES* 7 (1948): 30–45. For a brief and recent assessment, see David Tarler and Jane M. Cahill, "David, City of," *ABD* 2:64–65.

[131] Charles Clermont-Ganneau, in a letter to the Academie des Inscriptions et Belles-Lettres, Aug. 13, 1897. Cited in Simons, *Jerusalem in the Old Testament*, 213.

hioned and re-used in later periods.[132] Nearly every location in Jerusalem where rock-cut Iron Age tombs are preserved has been proposed for the royal mausoleum, and Jeffrey Zorn has recently added complexity by suggesting that David might have re-used the Bronze Age tombs of the prior dynasty.[133] In any case, the data from Mesopotamia (§ 1.4.1) and Ugarit (§ 3.3.2) indicate that burial under or near the royal palace would have been the norm.

Ezekiel 43 strongly suggests that, just as an unnamed prophet was buried in the Bethel sanctuary (2 Kgs 23:15–18), so at least some Judean kings were buried in or adjacent to the Jerusalem temple:

> He said to me: Mortal, this is the place of my throne and the place for the soles of my feet, where I will reside among the people of Israel forever. The house of Israel shall no more defile my holy name, neither they nor their kings, by their whoring, and by the corpses[134] of their kings at their death. When they placed their threshold by my threshold and their doorposts beside my doorposts, with only a wall between me and them, they were defiling my holy name by their abominations that they committed; therefore I have consumed them in my anger. Now let them put away their idolatry and the corpses of their kings far from me, and I will reside among them forever.

Although the "abominations" are unspecified here, the context suggests that a mortuary cult may be in view; as in Neo-Assyrian burials, such practices would have been facilitated by the proximity of the corpse (§ 1.4.1). Perhaps the burial of kings in the temple is also what is reflected in the enigmatic aspiration to "dwell in the house of YHWH forever" in Ps 23:6.

Most of the kings up to Ahaz are said to have been "buried in the city of David," but this formula abruptly disappears after that point. It may be that at this late period the original royal necropolis was full, and that, unlike other dead, kings' bones were not cleared aside to make room. Bloch-Smith thinks that the burial of Hezekiah במעלה קברי בני דויד (2 Chr 32:33) should be translated "on the ascent to

---

[132] Simons, *Jerusalem in the Old Testament*, 196–98, 216–19; Rahmani, "Ancient Jerusalem's Funerary Customs," 232–33.

[133] For discussion and further literature: Jeffrey R. Zorn, "The Burials of the Judean Kings: Sociohistorical Considerations and Suggestions," in *"I Will Speak of the Riddles of Ancient Times": Archaeological and Historical Studies in Honor of Amihai Mazar on the Occasion of His Sixtieth Birthday* (eds. A.M. Maier and P. de Miroschedji; Winona Lake, Ind.: Eisenbrauns, 2006), 801–20. Zorn champions again the location suggested by Raymond Weill, *Cité de David: Campagne de 1913–14* (Paris: Geuthner, 1920).

[134] It is possible that the Hebrew פגר here refers not to "corpses" but to stelae – see Neiman, David. "PGR: A Canaanite Cult-Object in the Old Testament," *JBL* 67 (1948): 55–60; Walther Zimmerli, *Ezekiel* (trans. J.D. Martin; Philadelphia): Fortress, 1979, 2:417–18. However, this requires special pleading for an unusual definition found only here (and perhaps in Lev 26:30); furthermore, in Ezek 6:5 פגרי clearly means "corpses." Zimmerli's case is based on two very uncertain "facts": the location of the City of David burial grounds, and the meaning of *pgr* at Ugarit (see § 3.3.3.3). As Zimmerli grants, at least the burials in the Garden of Uzza seem to be close to the temple. Whether corpses or stelae are in view, Ezek 43 would be a reference to a royal mortuary cult in either case.

the Davidic tombs" (so already NRSV), which also could reflect a lack of space in the City of David. In general, the problem of burial space is reflected in the archaeological record of burial grounds expanding outward from Jerusalem over the course of the Iron Age,[135] and also in Jer 7:32: "they will bury in Topheth until there is no room."

Nadav Na'aman has argued that the place of the Judean kings' burials moved for religious reasons. It is written in 2 Kgs 21:18, 26 that Manasseh and his son Amon they were buried in "the garden of Uzza." Na'aman asserts that this is the same as the "garden of the king" in 2 Kgs 25:4; Jer 39:4; 52:7 and Neh 3:15, and that it was established by Hezekiah as a royal burial grounds outside the City of David in contrast to the earlier royal tombs near the palace; he views this as part of Hezekiah's reform program (2 Kgs 18:4, 22) and as a response to the priestly revulsion at the proximity of royal burials to the temple that is reflected in Ezekiel 43, above.[136] Although he views the purity laws of the Pentateuch as "late and irrelevant to the discussion," he perceives a more generalized "late First Temple priestly opposition to the practice of burial within the palace."[137]

However, Francesca Stavrakopoulou doubts that there was any such reform on Hezekiah's part.[138] She suggests that a garden for mortuary practices may have long been a part of the Judean royal compound, in light of the gardens that likely functioned as royal mausoleums or rituals areas in Ebla[139] and Ugarit (CAT 1.106:23–23)[140] – del Olmo Lete's *Dictionary of the Ugaritic Language* has gone so far as to list "cemetery; (royal) pantheon" as another definition for Ugaritic *gn*, which usually means "garden" as in Hebrew.[141] The Ugaritic tombs at the palace do appear to have been accessible from a nearby garden and may well have been used for mortuary rituals.[142] Furthermore, Seth Richardson has also recently

---

[135] Bloch-Smith, *Judahite Burial Practices*, 138–39.
[136] Nadav Na'aman, "Death Formulae and the Burial Place of the Kings of the House of David," *Bib* 85 (2004): 245–54. So also Schmidt, *Israel's Beneficent Dead*, 250–54.
[137] Na'aman, "Death Formulae," 252.
[138] Francesca Stavrakopoulou, "Exploring the Garden of Uzza: Death, Burial and Ideologies of Kingship," *Bib* 87 (2006): 1–21; cf. *idem*, *King Manasseh and Child Sacrifice: Biblical Distortions of Historical Realities* (BZAW 338; Berlin: Walter de Gruyter, 2004).
[139] Paolo Xella, "Gunu(m)^(ki) dans les texts d'Ebla," *Nouvelles Assyriologiques brèves et utilitaires* 89 (1995): 80–81; Paolo Matthiae, "Princely Cemetery and Ancestors Cult at Ebla during the Middle Bronze II: A Proposal of Interpretation," *UF* 11 (1979): 563–69.
[140] Paolo Xella, "Aspekte Religiöser Vorstellungen in Syrien nach den Ebla- und Ugarit-Texte," *UF* 15 (1983): 279–90; Gregorio del Olmo Lete, "GN, el cementerio regio de Ugarit," *SEL* 3 (1986): 62–64; idem, *Canaanite Religion According to the Liturgical Texts of Ugarit* (trans. W. G. E. Watson; Winona Lake, Ind.: Eisenbrauns, 2004), 232.
[141] DUL, 302.
[142] Ksenia Starodoub-Scharr, "The Royal Garden in the Great Royal Palace of Ugarit: To the Interpretation of the Sacral Aspect of the Royalty in the Ancient Palestine and Syria," in *Proceedings of the Twelfth World Congress of Jewish Studies. Division A: The Bible and Its World* (ed. R. Margolin; Jerusalem: World Union of Jewish Studies, 1999), 253*–268*.

argued that Aššurnasirpal II maintained a "garden of ancestors" at Kalḫu, in which he conducted a "venerative royal cult to ancestors ... on a grand scale."[143] He views this as an attempt to overcome the problem caused by moving the capital away from the royal tombs (§ 1.4.1). Zorn suggests that Judean kings were emulating Mesopotamian models by being buried in gardens, and mentions Manasseh's imprisonment in Babylon reported in 2 Chr 23:11 as a possible mechanism of influence.[144]

Stavrakopoulou goes on to argue that the references to Manasseh and Amon's burials in "the garden of Uzza" are part of the Deuteronomistic polemic against them – that is, the historians describe them as having been buried in a garden where condemned mortuary rituals were conducted as another detail describing his apostasy (cf. 2 Kgs 21:1–18). Thus, although there probably was a mortuary garden in the Judean palace-temple complex, the "garden of Uzza" as such is the late invention of a retrospective historian, and likely is a reference to Uzziah's burial in a field (because of his leprosy; reported in 2 Chr 26:23, but not in 2 Kgs 15:7). In this way, these "bad kings," Manasseh and Amon, are condemned to burial apart from their forebears.

There is something to be said for Stavrakopoulou's theory about the historians' characterization of Manasseh and Amon, and the data she adduces about mortuary gardens is very useful. However, she does not adequately explain why none of the subsequent kings is said to be buried in the City of David.

The best explanation of the disappearance of the "City of David" in burial formulae is probably a combination of literary-ideological shaping of the text and historical change. I find speculative the claim that Hezekiah established a new royal burial ground; however, it does not seem to me that Dtr's reports of royal burials are generally literary fictions. Therefore, I think the argument about a lack of space is more promising; the account of Josiah's burial best fits this theory. He is said to have been buried "in his (own?) tomb" (בקברתו; 2 Kgs 23:30), and the City of David is not mentioned. This may well be intended to emphasize that Josiah had a proper burial in an individual tomb despite the fact that he was not buried in the City of David.

By comparison with the notices in Kings, Chronicles is more selective and detailed about burial information and differs from Kings in its reports about several rulers, denying them placement in the royal tombs on the basis of impurity due to sickness (e.g., Jehoram in 2 Chr 21:20; Uzziah in 26:23) or wrongdoing (Ahaz in 28:27).

Most royal burials seem to have followed the tradition of allowing the body to decompose, but the burial of Asa (2 Chr 16:14) deserves special mention. It is said

---

[143] Seth Richardson, "An Assyrian Garden of Ancestors: Room I, Northwest Palace, Kalḫu." *SAAB* 13 (1999–2001): 145–216.

[144] Zorn, "The Burials of the Judean Kings," 814–15.

that he was buried "in the tomb that he had hewn out for himself in the city of David. They laid him on a bier that had been filled with various kinds of spices prepared by the perfumer's art; and they made an exceedingly great fire." The last phrase in the verse, עד־למאד, does not mean "in his honor" (so NRSV, Tanakh, NIV) but rather intensifies the massiveness of the fire.[145] The plain sense of this text is that Asa was cremated, despite efforts to deny it on the part of many scholars.[146]

Some aspects of Judean royal burial remain mysterious. For a number of kings who were murdered, no burial information is noted.[147] (Perhaps this is because the murdered were counted among the unhappy dead and so were not buried with the other kings.) And unlike the women of the Genesis narratives, "there is no indication that other family members were buried with" kings of Israel or Judah,[148] although a few nonroyal burials in other places are recorded (2 Sam 3:32; 4:12; 17:23; 19:38; 1 Kgs 2:34).

---

[145] עד־למאד has the same sense as the much more common עד־מאד, but with the proliferation of the *lamed* that is so typical of late biblical Hebrew. See Robert Polzin, *Late Biblical Hebrew: Toward an Historical Typology of Biblical Hebrew Prose* (HSM 12; Missoula, Mont.: Scholars Press for the Harvard Semitic Museum, 1976).

[146] Among those who would dispute this reading are Hallote, *Death, Burial, and Afterlife*, 52; Roland de Vaux, *Ancient Israel: Its Life and Institutions* (trans. John McHugh; New York: McGraw-Hill, 1961), 57; and Bloch-Smith, *Judahite Burial Practices*, 119. It is true that in many cases burning was prescribed as divine judgment (Gen 19:24; Amos 2:2, 5), and (similarly) as a way to purify evil (Gen 38:24; Lev 20:14; 21:9; Num 16:35). Asa is recorded in the histories as a successful (2 Kgs 15:11) and long-lived king, but he was also diseased (15:23). On the one hand, Chronicles might have added this detail out of a concern for the purity of the royal necropolis, that is, to allow kings to rest in the royal tombs without contaminating them. On the other hand, Chronicles' assessment of Asa adds negative elements not present in Kings, including oppression and consultation of doctors (or perhaps the Rephaim) rather than YHWH (2 Chr 16:10, 12). It is commonly observed that רפאים in 2 Chr 16:12 might be pointed either way; doctors are a rare sight in the Hebrew Bible, whereas the dead spirits are sought (דרש) for help in Isa 8:19; 19:3. See M. Jastrow, "Rō'ēh and ḥōzēh in the Old Testament," *JBL* 28 (1909): 49–50, n. 23. The emendation to רְפָאִים was noted and proposed by W. Rudolph in BHS. Therefore the burning might also be a sort of punishment. It is not impossible that Asa (or his family) might have emulated the burial practices of wealthy, influential neighbors. While perhaps exceptional for Judah, cremation was quite common in the coastland and was occasionally carried out by the Mesopotamians as well. For coastal Palestine, see Bloch-Smith, *Judahite Burial Practices*, 59. For the Neo-Assyrians, see Alexander Heidel, *The Gilgamesh Epic and Old Testament Parallels* (Chicago: University of Chicago Press, 1963), 163–64. The cremation of Saul and Jonathan (1 Sam 31:11–13) is worthy of mention here; although surely serving a rhetorical and theological purpose in their present place in the narrative, it reflects the author's awareness of cremation as a possible burial practice. Jeremiah 34:5 and 2 Chr 21:19 both refer to fires at the burials of kings, but do not clarify matters; some of the modern translations are overly exegetical. Amos 6:9–10 seems to testify to some sort of burning in the northern kingdom as well, but its nature is not clear either. The burning of the Assyrian king in Isa 30:33 is addressed in § 5.2.1.2.

[147] "Nadab, Elah, Zimri, Ahaziah, Zechariah and all subsequent kings" (Bloch-Smith, *Judahite Burial Practices*, 116).

[148] Bloch-Smith, *Judahite Burial Practices*, 116.

Whereas there is little instruction about how to bury the dead in the Hebrew Bible, it is quite clear throughout that the *lack* of proper sepulture and mourning is viewed as a horrible fate, as in the curse of Deut 28:26: "Your corpses shall be food for every bird of the air and the beasts of the earth, and there shall be no one to frighten them away" (cf. also 1 Kgs 13:22; 14:11–13; 2 Kgs 9:10; Ps 79:3; Eccl 6:3; Ezek 29:5). The threat of exposure is a particularly persistent theme in Isaiah and Jeremiah: "Human corpses shall fall like dung upon the open field, like sheaves behind the reaper, and no one shall gather them" (Jer 9:22; cf. 7:33; 8:1–2; 14:16; 16:4; 19:7; 22:18; 26:23; 36:30; Isa 14:19–20). There is also a phenomenon of burning kings (or their remains), probably as punishment for political "rebellion" (Amos 2:1; Isa 30:33), which reflects historical practices known in Egypt and Assyria (see §§ 5.2.1.2; 1.2.3.1), and which is certainly distinct from cremation. The Isaiah passages and possible reasons for this emphasis will be addressed in the next chapter. In light of the other ancient Near Eastern cultures already surveyed, the Bible's focus on the need for proper burial is what one would expect.

One might close this discussion of burial in the Bible with reference to a cogent recent study by Saul Olyan, which outlines a "hierarchy of burial types, from most desirable to least":[149]

1. honorable burial in the family tomb;
2. honorable interment in a substitute for the family tomb (e.g., Abner in 2 Sam 3);
3. honorable burial in someone else's family tomb (e.g., the disobedient man of God in 1 Kgs 13);
4. dishonorable forms of interment (e.g., the burial of Absalom in a pit covered with stones in 2 Sam 18);
5. nonburial (both of these last two types frequently occur with forms of שלך, "throw away").

This is a helpful list, and apart from the fact that instances of the second and third types of burials may not be numerous enough to derive a rule therefrom, I would make only one adjustment, subdividing non-burial into simple non-burial (abandonment of the corpse) and "anti-burial," i.e., violation of the corpse and/or exposure of the remains.[150] The latter was discernably worse in the ancient Near Eastern world (see § 4.6.2).

---

[149] Saul M. Olyan, "Some Neglected Aspects of Israelite Interment Ideology," *JBL* 124 (2005): 603–7.

[150] In addition to the passages cited above, see Jezebel's destruction in 2 Kgs 9:33–37, Josiah's burning of remains in 2 Kgs 23:16–20.

4.4.1.2 Mourning

Israelite and Judean customs of mourning and lamentation appear, from the biblical text, to have been very similar to those of their neighbors.[151] A great number of terms are used to refer to mourning in the Hebrew Bible (אבל, ספד, נהה, שחח, קדר, הילֿיל, and אניה – not all of which are limited to mourning the dead), but a coherent picture nevertheless emerges. At the death of a prominent person, a whole family (Zech 12:12) or tribe (Num 20:29) might gather. Indeed, allowing for hyperbole and the legendary character of certain texts, a whole nation might be said to gather (Gen 50:10; Deut 34:8; 1 Sam 25:1; 1 Kgs 14:18)[152] – more likely a maximum turnout would have included *representatives* from the whole nation, as the Neo-Babylonian king Nabonidus described in the case of his mother's burial (§ 1.4.1). Indeed, large numbers of mourners helped to mark a successful life, since lack of mourning was seen as a curse (Job 27:13; Ps 78:64; Jer 16:4; 25:33).

Vocal weeping and wailing (e.g., Jer 4:8) were central to mourning. Professional mourners seem to have been employed in some cases: "Call for the mourning women to come; send for the skilled women to come; let them quickly raise a dirge over us, so that our eyes may run down with tears" (Jer 9:16–17; cf. Amos 5:16).[153] There also are other signs that lament may have been formalized, such as the reference to the *qînâ*-form in Ezek 19:14: קינה היא ותהי קינה, "this is a lamentation, and it shall be (used as) a lamentation" (see also 27:2, 32; 28:12; 32:2, 16; Amos 5:1; 2 Chr 35:25, etc.).[154] The cry *hôy* (Jer 22:18; 34:5; Amos 5:16) also seems to have been typical of laments, although this sense was lost in later periods.[155] (I present a much fuller discussion of the *hôy*-oracle form in § 5.2.2.2.) A para-canonical written text of laments is referred to in 2 Chr 35:24, but no such text survived.

Mourning was accompanied by physical manifestations, which included a bowed posture (Ps 35:13); shaving of the head or disheveling of the hair (Ezek 27:31; Amos 8:9); the tearing of garments (Gen 37:34; 2 Sam 1:11; Joel 2:12); the donning of sackcloth or other specific "mourning garments" (2 Sam 14:2; Jer 4:8; 6:26; Joel 1:8); and the smearing of ashes on the body (Jer 6:26; Job 2:8). All of these are described by Olyan as processes of self-debasement through which "[t]he mourner parallels the spirit of the dead through his physical appearance."[156] In other words, by making oneself low, dusty, etc., one expressed one's

---

[151] Nutkowicz, *L'Homme face à la mort*, 27–61.

[152] For the texts cited here that refer to Israel's premonarchical period, the assumption is not that they necessarily present accurate historical events in each case, but that they at least reflect the practices and assumptions of later periods.

[153] See further Olyan, *Biblical Mourning*, 49–51.

[154] Karl Budde, "Das hebräische Klagelied," *ZAW* 2 (1882): 1–52; W. Randall Garr, "The *qinah*: A Study of Poetic Meter, Syntax and Style," *ZAW* 95 (1983): 54–75.

[155] Waldemar Janzen, *Mourning Cry and Woe-Oracle* (BZAW 125; Berlin: De Gruyter, 1972).

[156] Saul M. Olyan, *Biblical Mourning: Ritual and Social Dimensions* (Oxford: Oxford University Press, 2004), 43.

link to the dead. There were certain limitations on outward expressions of mourning, however: for example, gashing flesh (known also from the Baal Cycle text cited above) is portrayed as a foreign practice in Jer 49:3 and is specifically prohibited (Lev 19:28; Deut 14:1).[157] Mourning might also be accompanied by fasting (2 Sam 12:23; Ps 35:13).

It is not clear what a traditional period of mourning would have been; many references do not specify a length of time (Gen 27:41; 37:34; 2 Sam 13:37; 14:2; 1 Chr 7:22; Isa 60:20; 1 Macc 9:20; 13:26). When a length is specified, it may be one or two days (Sir 38:17), seven days (Gen 50:10; Sir 22:12), or up to thirty days (Num 20:29; Deut 34:8).

On the one hand, there do not seem to have been great changes in Israelites' personal mourning practices over time. On the other hand, specific public mourning festivals are reported to have arisen in specific periods to honor certain people such as Josiah (2 Chr 35:24–25) and Jephthah's daughter (Judg 11:39–40). Zechariah 7:3–5 refers to a custom of mourning in the fifth and seventh months, almost certainly related to the destruction of Jerusalem in the fifth month.

4.4.1.3 The marzēaḥ

Although the data are less than conclusive, it appears that there were some dedicated spaces for mourning and the cultic functions associated with burials. Ecclesiastes 7:2, 4 mentions a "house of mourning" (בית־אבל), and Judah seems to have had venues akin to the Ugaritic *marziḥu* (see § 3.3.3.2.3), in which funerary feasting could take place. Archaeological remains suggest that a cult of the dead involving feasting was indigenous to Palestine prior to the Israelites, and it is likely to have endured.[158]

The Hebrew term apparently referring to such feasts, *marzēaḥ*, is attested twice in the Bible. Jeremiah 16 clearly places the *marzēaḥ* in a mourning context:

They shall die of deadly diseases. They shall not be lamented, nor shall they be buried; they shall become like dung on the surface of the ground. They shall perish by the sword and by famine, and their dead bodies shall become food for the birds of the air and for the wild animals of the earth. For thus says the LORD: Do not enter the house of mourning (בית מרזח), or go to lament, or bemoan them; for I have taken away my peace from this people, says the LORD, my steadfast love and mercy. Both great and small shall die in this land; they shall not be buried, and no one shall lament for them; there shall be no gashing, no shaving

---

[157] Deuteronomy 14:1 also forbids shaving the temples. Olyan suggests that these prohibitions are based on the need to transition rapidly out of mourning at the end of the prescribed period: "laceration and shaving are not easily reversible" (*Biblical Mourning*, 146)

[158] Manfred Bietak has identified Bronze Age archaeological remains near to burial sites in at least three locations in and around ancient Israel, most significantly the so-called "Fosse Temple" at Lachish. Manfred Bietak, "Temple or 'Bêt Marzeaḥ'?" in in *Symbiosis, Symbolism and Power of the Past*, 155–68.

of the head for them. No one shall break bread for the mourner, to offer comfort for the dead; nor shall anyone give them the cup of consolation to drink for their fathers or their mothers. (Jer 16:4–7)

Could this be the same institution as the Ugaritic *marziḥu*? On the one hand, Jer 16:8's reference to the "house of feasting" (בית משתה) does not refer to the same location as the house of the *marzēaḥ* – the ensuing verse makes it clear that the feasting in view there is a joyful wedding celebration (these two houses also seem to be separate in Eccl 7:2). It functions as the other half of a merismus with the sadness of the house of the *marzēaḥ*. On the other hand, Jer 16:7's reference to the "cup (כוס) of consolation" is clearly to a cup used for wine in a mourning context.[159]

The reference to the *marzēaḥ* in Amos 6:7 is the only other reference in the Hebrew Bible. Following descriptions of people feasting, lounging, playing music, and drinking, it reads: "Therefore they shall now be the first to go into exile, and the *marzēaḥ* of the loungers (מרזח סרוחים) shall cease." It is tempting to say that it is merely the excesses of the wealthy that are condemned; however, the passage continues with a threat of death to the fortresses of the northern kingdom (6:9: "If ten people remain in one house, they shall die"). It seems more likely that 6:7 is a deliberate mischaracterization of the banquets of the wealthy as funerary feasts – i.e., the prophet threatens that death is coming, although the participants do not perceive it. This warning of impending but unforeseen doom for the comfortable is a central aspect of Amos's message (e.g., 4:11–12; 5:18–24).

Other possible biblical references to a *marzēaḥ* have been proposed over the years. In his study of ten proposed instances, John McLaughlin concluded that four were probable (Amos 4:1; Hos 4:16–19; Isa 28:7–8[22]; and Ezek 39:17–20).[160] His criteria, based on the extrabiblical data, were (1) extensive alcohol consumption, (2) by members of the upper class, (3) in a religious context.[161] I would not say that Ezek 39:17–20 is a *marzēaḥ* per se, but rather a very loose literary adaptation of it (Isaiah also adapts *marzēaḥ* imagery to his own purposes; see §§ 5.2.2.1; 5.2.3.3). However, McLaughlin was right to argue that references to the *marzēaḥ* are more widespread than the term itself. He was also

---

[159] For כוס as a wine cup, see Ps 75:9; Jer 25:15; 51:7; Lam 4:21; Ezek 23:22–23; Hab 2:16. The wine cup is frequently portrayed as an instrument of wrath and judgment; this might be understood a case of *ius talionis* against the wealthy who indulge too much at the expense of others. One might wonder whether YHWH's cult, as it was envisioned by the prophets, was a relatively teetotaling cult by comparison with those of other ancient Near Eastern deities. However, see Ps 116:13; Gen 40:11–13.

[160] The others were Amos 2:7c–8; Hos 9:1–6; Isa 5:11–13; 28:1–4; 56:9–57:13; and Ezek 8:7–13. John L. McLaughlin, *The Marzēaḥ in the Prophetic Literature: References and Allusions in Light of the Extra-Biblical Evidence* (VTSup 86; Leiden: Brill, 2001).

[161] McLaughlin, *Marzēaḥ in the Prophetic Literature*, 9–79.

4.4 Death in the Hebrew Bible 165

justified in following the lead of Ugaritologists in concluding that the *marzēaḥ* (like the *marziḥu*) was a cultic banquet that could be dedicated to any deity. Marvin Pope and others have reached analogous conclusions through a broader analysis that includes references to the similar *thiasos* in later Greek sources.[162]

Since the *marzēaḥ* is implicitly condemned in both its biblical attestations, it may well have been viewed by Yahwistic prophets as inappropriate and as a threat to YHWH's worship. We have no other information about the biblical *marzēaḥ*, however, so it is not clear whether it would have been funerary or mortuary in nature. However, Isaiah's condemnations of necromancy seem to presuppose an ongoing cult of the dead, whether in the context of feasting or family religion.

4.4.1.4 The corpse

Information about the status of dead bodies in Israelite religion is complex. On the one hand, corpses were perceived as ritually impure; but on the other hand there are intimations that they were thought to have supernatural powers.

The Priestly legislation is particularly concerned about defilement of the living by the dead – any person is made ritually unclean for seven days by contact with a human corpse (Num 19:11–16; 31:19), making it "the most powerful impurity."[163] Even the one who touches a person defiled by a corpse is unclean for a day (Num 31:22)! And the impurity extends beyond human corpses to animal corpses; the one who touches a dead lizard is also impure for a day (Lev 11:31). In keeping with the phenomenon of gradations of holiness, priests are allowed to handle the corpse only of close relatives (Lev 21:1–2), and the high priest is not allowed any contact at all with the dead (Lev 21:10–11).[164] Ezekiel and Haggai also show awareness of defilement by dead bodies (Ezek 6:5; 44:25; Hag 2:13–14), but the theme is absent from the Covenant Code and the Deuteronomic Code. Not surprisingly, then, the concern about corpse defilement is most likely to occur in works influenced by Priestly ideas.

The potential power of bones is seen most vividly in the resurrection miracle of Elisha's bones (2 Kgs 13:21), but also in the desire of the prophet from Bethel to

---

[162] Pope, *Song of Songs*, 221–28. So also Lorena Miralles Maciá, *Marzeah y Thíasos: Una Institución Convival en el Oriente Próximo Antiguo y el Mediterráneo* (Anejos 20; Madrid: Publicaciones Universidad Complutense de Madrid, 2007), 263–64.

[163] David P. Wright, *The Disposal of Impurity: Elimination Rites in the Bible and in Hittite and Mesopotamian Literature* (SBLDS 101; Atlanta: Scholars Press, 1987), 115.

[164] On gradations of holiness, see Menahem Haran, *Temples and Temple-Service in Ancient Israel: An Inquiry into the Character of Cult Phenomena and the Historical Setting of the Priestly School* (Winona Lake, Ind.: Eisenbrauns, 1985), 149–259; also Philip Peter Jenson, *Graded Holiness: A Key to the Priestly Conception of the World* (JSOTSup 106; Sheffield: JSOT Press, 1992). On the ritual purity of priests, see, e.g., Jonathan Klawans, "Pure Violence: Sacrifice and Defilement in Ancient Israel," *HTR* 94 (2001): 133–55.

be buried with the bones of the unnamed man of God (1 Kgs 13:30). Furthermore, the Bible's interest in the remains of Joseph (Gen 50:25; Exod 13:19) and Saul (2 Sam 21:12–14) might be simply a reflection of the preference for burial with one's family, but it also might be evidence of similar beliefs about the power of bones that have been obscured in the present form of the text.

4.4.2 The Israelite dead

4.4.2.1 The powers and cult of the dead

The biblical literature is distinguished from its cultural congeners by its polemic against the power of the dead. The dead, it is said, do not praise (Ps 30:10; 88:10; etc.); instead they "go down into silence" (Ps 115:17). They know nothing (Eccl 9:5, 10) and sit in darkness (Lam 3:6). Whereas these ideas can be inferred from pessimistic texts in Mesopotamia and even Egypt, in Israel and Judah it is the majority witness of the extant texts.

Many treatments of the Israelite dead assume that these statements were normative.[165] However, many of the texts that assert the weakness and insubstantiality of the dead are susceptible to doubt: do they really reflect typical beliefs? In prayer contexts, such descriptions typically are part of the psalmists' exhortations to God to save; they try to motivate YHWH with the need for praise. And the assertion that the dead do not praise YHWH does not necessarily mean that they have no power. Furthermore, Ecclesiastes' theology is exceptional in many ways; the book's despairing view of the afterlife must be attributed to its broadly pessimistic outlook. In no historical period was the book's theology normative (as far as one can tell), and in the (probably) late context of its composition, brighter expectations for the afterlife would have been flourishing already.[166]

As noted above in the discussion of Dahood's commentary, there are certainly psalms that, if they do not express hope in an "eternal life," it is difficult to know what they *could* mean: "He asked you for life; you gave it to him – length of days forever and ever" (ארך ימים לעולם ועד; Ps 21:4, cf. 16:9–10).[167] Dahood's thesis can be maintained, at least in a moderated form in which the hope for beatific afterlife is only royal (by analogy with the situation at Ugarit, Egypt, and

---

[165] See recently Schmidt, *Israel's Beneficent Dead*, 267–73; Johnston, *Shades of Sheol*, 141–42, 193–95; Jarick, "Questioning Sheol," 22–32.

[166] Emile Puech, *La croyance des Esséniens en la vie future: Immortalité, résurrection, vie éternelle? Histoire d'une croyance dans le Judaïsme ancien* (Paris: Librairie Lecoffre, 1993), 137–199.

[167] John J. Collins objects that "this is an exceptional passage, and there is little evidence to suggest that the immortality of the king was commonly accepted in Israel": "Death, the Afterlife and Other Last Things: Israel," in *Religions of the Ancient World: A Guide* (ed. Sarah Iles Johnston; Cambridge, Mass.: Belknap Press of Harvard University Press, 2004), 481.

Hatti).¹⁶⁸ On that basis, Healey has posited a "democratization of the afterlife" in Israel and Judah, such as took place earlier in Egypt (see § 2.4.1).¹⁶⁹

Eternal life or beatific afterlife could theoretically be distinct from divinization or active power in the world of the living, but this is unlikely by comparison with other ancient Near Eastern cultures. Instead, the view that the dead were seen as divinized or active by ancient Israelites requires the argument that the biblical text has largely been purged of such references.

4.4.2.2 The Rephaim

The numerous references to the Rephaim (רפאים) attest that Israel clearly knew of the common Syro-Palestinian belief in a group of supernatural dead (see §§ 3.3.3.2; 3.4).¹⁷⁰ The etymology of the Hebrew term is subject to much the same questions as that of the Ugaritic *rāpiʾūma*. Nearly all of the biblical occurrences (and all of the plural ones) take it from the root רפא, "to heal,"¹⁷¹ but the pointing is not the Qal active participle that one would expect (רֹפְאִים). It may be that the Masoretic pointing reflects a perpetual *qere* as if רפאים were from the root רפה, "to sink down, be weak," deliberately obfuscating the meaning.¹⁷²

More clearly than the Ugaritic *rāpiʾūma*, the Hebrew Rephaim fall into two categories: They are sometimes reckoned as a mythic ancient tribe (Gen 14:5; 15:20; Deut 2:11) of giants (Deut 3:11), and at other times the term refers to the assembled dead. This group of the dead is sometimes royal in nature (Isa 14:9), but in most cases their rank is not specified, so that they may include any and all of the dead: "[the strange woman's] house leads down to death and her paths to the רפאים" (Prov 2:18; cf. Job 26:5; Ps 88:10; etc.). Scholars commonly posit a connection between these two uses – generally, that the ancient term for the mighty dead seemed natural to apply to a defunct tribe of giants¹⁷³ – although others have argued that the term originally referred to human rulers who were thought to be divinized at death, and that the term was eventually "democratized" to include all the dead.¹⁷⁴

---

¹⁶⁸ Such a position is argued by John F. Healey, "The Immortality of the King: Ugarit and the Psalms," *Or* 53 (1984): 245–54.

¹⁶⁹ Healey, "Immortality of the King," 254. On the democratization of the royal psalms in general, see Sigmund Mowinckel, *The Psalms in Israel's Worship* (trans. D. R. Ap-Thomas; 2 vols.; Oxford: Basil Blackwell, 1962; repr., Grand Rapids: Eerdmans, 2004), 1:78–80.

¹⁷⁰ Mark S. Smith, "Rephaim," ABD 5:674–76.

¹⁷¹ The notable exception is the reference to the giant warriors slain by David in 2 Sam 21:20, 22, who were said to be "born to the הרפה"; interestingly, the parallels in 1 Chr 20:4, 6, 8 use רפא.

¹⁷² J. C. de Moor, "Rapi'uma – Rephaim," *ZAW* 88 (1976): 340.

¹⁷³ Day, "Development of the Belief in Life after Death," 232–33; Simon B. Parker, "The Ugaritic Deity Rap'iu," *UF* 4 (1972): 103.

¹⁷⁴ Conrad L'Heureux, "The Ugaritic and Biblical Rephaim," *HTR* 67 (1974): 263–74; John Gray, "The Rephaim," *PEQ* 81 (1949): 138–39.

A text such as Ezek 32:17–32 capitalizes on both senses of the Rephaim, although the term is not used. It associates the mighty ones of the past with the fallen warriors (גבורים) of Israel's imperial enemies within recent memory, such as Assyrians, Egyptians, Edomites, and Sidonians. Still, none of the biblical occurrences of the term רפאים attests to the power of the dead.

YHWH is frequently called a healer in the Hebrew Bible (e.g., Deut 32:39), which has led a number of scholars to suggest that this is another instance of YHWH's adoption of Baalistic powers and characteristics (since Baal bears the epithet *rpu bʿl* in Ugaritic texts and may have been viewed as the "leader" of the *rāpiʾūma*). The strongest example suggesting that YHWH assumed Baal's role is Hos 11:2–3 ("they kept sacrificing to the Baals ... they did not know that it was I who healed them").[175] Healing was a prominent divine function throughout the ancient Near East,[176] however; texts such has this do not provide a firm foundation for arguments in favor of an Israelite belief in the power of the Rephaim or the cult of the dead. Certain other texts sometimes thought to reflect the powers of the dead can be excluded as well.[177]

Thus far, apart from these scattered and contestable references, the dead do not appear very active in the Hebrew Bible. The etymology of רפאים from רפא straightforwardly indicates that the Hebrew term had its roots in a belief in the powerful dead; but these powers are not reflected very often in the biblical text.[178] In particular, the fear of the wrath of the dead that was prevalent in Mesopotamia seems to have been as muted in Israel and Judah as it was in Ugarit.

4.4.2.3 Necromancy

The exception to the apparent weakness of the dead in the Hebrew Bible is necromancy; the idea that the dead are a source of divinatory knowledge is richly attested. Furthermore, in extrabiblical inscriptions, the occurrences of familial

---

[175] De Moor, "Rapiuma – Rephaim," 337.
[176] M. L. Brown, "רפא," *TDOT* 13:596, 601.
[177] For example: (1) B. Halevi argued that the admonition of Lev 19:32 (מפני שיבה תקום והדרת פני זקן ויראת מאלהיך) should be translated "You shall rise before the aged, and defer to the old; and you shall fear your divine ancestors" (B. Halevi, "'qbwt nwspym lpwlhn ʾbwt" (in Hebrew), *Beth Mikra* 64 (1975): 101–17, cited in Bloch-Smith, *Judahite Burial Practices*, 126–27). Halevi's argument is undercut by the fact that the text follows immediately after the emphasis on the sanctuary of YHWH and the prohibition of necromancy. Thus, the verse should be translated, "you shall fear your god," as it usually is. (2) David's order to cut off the hands and feet of the murderers of Ishbosheth could reflect a concern to rob the dead of their powers in case of retribution, but since they had cut off Ishbosheth's head, it is also possible that it is a simple case of *ius talionis*: one violation of a corpse deserves another.
[178] De Moor, "Rapiʾuma – Rephaim," 341–42. William J. Horwitz theorized that the power of the Rephaim was simply forgotten, even before the biblical period ("The Significance of the Rephaim," *JNSL* 7 [1979]: 37–43), but the data laid out throughout this chapter make that theory unlikely.

terms in place of the theophoric element in personal names – e.g., אבאל ("my father is El/a god") or אחאל ("my brother is El/a god")[179] – suggests the possibility of divination by means of ancestors. (Such names also recall the divinized ancestor *ilib* from the Ugaritic texts; see § 3.3.3.2)

Necromantic practices are banned or condemned in various strata of biblical literature, including the Holiness Code (Lev 19:31; 20:6, 27), the Deuteronomic Code (Deut 18:11) and Deuteronomistic History (2 Kgs 21:6), and Chronicles (1 Chr 10:13–14). This assortment of texts does not necessarily prove Bloch-Smith's thesis that necromancy was legal until the fall of the northern kingdom, but it at least reflects an increased concern about necromancy in the Neo-Assyrian period and thereafter.[180]

The story of Saul and the necromancer in 1 Sam 28 has become the touchstone in the study of Israelite necromancy, and studies of it abound.[181] Its import can be summed up quite briefly, however: it reflects a straightforward belief in the efficacy of necromancy. Lewis expressed surprise that such an account has survived,[182] but it is very much in keeping with the henotheism of much of the Hebrew Bible.[183] That is, for the most part, biblical authors acknowledged other supernatural powers, but they asserted that one was not to worship them. The text's primary concern seems to be to portray Saul negatively for his religious transgression, not to argue against the effectiveness of necromancy.[184] Efforts to explain away the event as a hallucination (since Saul had not eaten and was perhaps half-mad),[185] the work of a deceiving spirit,[186] or an aberration (because

---

[179] F. M. Cross, *From Epic to Canon: History and Literature in Ancient Israel* (Baltimore: Johns Hopkins University Press, 1998), 6; van der Toorn, *Family Religion*, 229. Of course, these names could also be understood as "El is my father" and "El is my brother."

[180] For the association of the Holiness Code with Deuteronomic interests, see Israel Knohl, *Sanctuary of Silence: The Priestly Torah and the Holiness School* (Minneapolis: Fortress Press, 1994), 199–224, esp. 212.

[181] In addition to the treatments in each of the monographs on biblical cults of the dead cited here, see Joseph Blenkinsopp, "Saul and the Mistress of the Spirits (1 Samuel 28.3–25)," in *Sense and Sensitivity* (London: Sheffield Academic Press, 2002), 49–62; George E. Mendenhall, "From Witchcraft to Justice: Death and Afterlife in the Old Testament," in *Death and Afterlife* (Westport, Conn.: Greenwood, 1992), 67–81; and Bill T. Arnold, "Necromancy and Cleromancy in 1 and 2 Samuel," *CBQ* 66 (2004): 199–213.

[182] Lewis, *Cults of the Dead*, 117.

[183] Smith, *Origins of Biblical Monotheism*, 78, 154–55.

[184] This observation is in accordance with the cogent argument by Meir Sternberg about the narrator's purposes regarding Saul in *The Poetics of Biblical Narrative: Ideological Literature and the Drama of Reading* (Bloomington, Ind.: Indiana University Press, 1985), 482–515. In a similar vein, see Blenkinsopp, "Saul and the Mistress of the Spirits."

[185] E.g., Heidel, *Gilgamesh Epic*, 189–90

[186] This line of interpretation goes back to the patristic period. See discussion and citations in Bill T. Arnold, "Soul-Searching Questions about 1 Samuel 28," in *What about the Soul? Neuroscience and Christian Anthropology* (ed. Joel B. Green; Nashville: Abingdon, 2004), 77.

the woman who summons him is startled)[187] ring hollow. Samuel is summoned, and his ghost rises. He is asked about the future, and his prediction is correct. If the story's author was at all concerned about the credulity of his readers, then it seems safe to say that at whatever time period the story was written (and compiled), such necromantic practices were known in Judah. It is also likely that they were viewed negatively by the author, since the episode is part of the account of Saul's destruction. The most likely period in which those conditions obtained was in the late seventh century, during the reign of Josiah (note his abolishment of necromancy among his reforms in 2 Kgs 23:24) – the same period in which the first edition of the Deuteronomistic History was probably produced.

The terminology surrounding necromancy raises significant critical issues. The woman whom Saul consults is called a בעלת־אוב, a "mistress" of something. The nature of the אוב, and also that of the associated term ידעני, have been a source of consternation, but I will propose a new interpretation here based on an Egyptian etymology.[188] There are three common interpretations of אוב:[189]

(1) It is a spirit of a dead person that can be consulted for necromantic purposes.[190] In Isa 19:3 the אבות are classified with the אטים, which, although a *hapax legomenon* in the Bible, is almost certainly cognate with the Mesopotamian *etemmû* ("ghosts"). Furthermore, Lev 20:27 condemns any person "who has in them an אוב," almost certainly referring to one who channels a spirit of the dead. In this case, the term has been related to אָב, "father," and thus to the ancestor cult. The two words have the same consonantal spelling in the plural (אבות), and the Canaanite vowel shift ā 〉 ō and/or a consistent scribal emendation to differentiate the two words might account for the different vocalizations. (A different etymology was offered by Albright, who theorized that אוב means "revenant/ one-who-returns," based on Arabic *ʾāba*, "to return";[191] however, this finds no support from any ancient Semitic cognate. Given the disfavor into which Arabic etymologies have generally fallen of late, Albright's theory has won a remarkable

---

[187] Joyce G. Baldwin, *1 and 2 Samuel: An Introduction and Commentary* (Leicester: Inter-Varsity, 1988), 159.

[188] See also Christopher B. Hays and Joel M. LeMon, "The Dead and Their Images: An Egyptian Etymology for Hebrew *ʾôb*," *Journal of Ancient Egyptian Interconnections* 1 (2009): 1–4.

[189] See Blenkinsopp, "Deuteronomy and the Politics of Post-Mortem Existence," 1–16.

[190] Spronk, *Beatific Afterlife*, 253–54; M. Dietrich, O. Loretz, and J. Sanmartin, "Ugaritisch ILIB und hebräisch *ʾ(W)B* 'Totengeist,' " *UF* 6 (1974): 450–451; Hedwige Rouillard and Josep Tropper, "*Trpym*, rituels de guérison et culte des ancêtres d'après 1 Samuel XIX 11–17 et les textes parallèles d'Assur et de Nuzi," *VT* 37 (1987): 340–61; J. Lust, "On Wizards and Prophets," in *Studies on Prophecy: A Collection of Twelve Papers* (VTSup 26; Leiden: Brill, 1974), 135; Hans-Peter Müller, "Das Wort von Totengeistern (Jes 8,19f.)," *WO* 8 (1975–76): 65–76; Lods, *La croyance à la vie future*, 248. Albright quite plausibly suggested restoring אבות for אָבוֹת in Job 8:8–10: *Yahweh and the Gods of Canaan: A Historical Analysis of Two Contrasting Faiths* (Garden City, N.Y.: Doubleday, 1968), 142;

[191] Albright, *Archaeology and the Religion of Israel* (5th ed.; Garden City, N.Y.: Doubleday, 1969), 202 n. 32.

4.4 Death in the Hebrew Bible   171

amount of support in recent years[192] – which in my view reflects the weakness of the other proposed etymologies.)

(2) It is a piece of equipment used in such consultations. A list in 2 Kgs 23:24 includes the אוב and ידעני among cultic objects that Josiah removed. The most widely accepted form of the "object" theory is the contention that it is cognate with Akkadian *apu*, "pit," which is attested in a few necromantic texts, and also with Hittite *a-a-pi*.[193] However, the supporting theory that Ugaritic *ʾPb* should be understood as "god of the pit" has not found acceptance,[194] nor do any of the references in Hebrew necessitate the interpretation "pit." Perhaps most importantly, in distinction from Hebrew אבות, there seems to be no instance in which *apu* or cognates refer to spirits of the dead; the *apu* is only a pit in which they can be summoned.

(3) It is a technical term for a necromantic diviner (so NRSV, NIV: "medium"), in which case the title in 1 Sam 28 would be pleonastic ("mistress of a necromancer"?). I do not find any passages that necessitate the interpretation "medium" or "necromancer."[195]

Given that both of the first two interpretations of אבות/אוב seem possible, and that the etymology remains unclear, I would like to suggest a new explanation for the term, based on the Egyptian cognate *3bwt*, "family, household, image."[196] Not only is the spelling of the term identical with the Hebrew plural, *3bwt* also has a range of meanings that meshes well with the range of biblical uses, since it may denote both a dead ancestor and a cult image. It is of interest that in Isa 19:3 the Egyptians are said to consult "their אבות": could it be that instead of this being a formulaic (Deuteronomistic) indictment, as Schmidt thought,[197] it is the one instance that reveals the provenance of a term that later became standardized? (See further discussion in § 5.2.3.2.)

The typical translation of *3bwt* in early Egyptian texts, as given in the *Wörterbuch der Ägyptischen Sprache* is "family," or sometimes "household." In the Cof-

---

[192] E.g., Lewis, *Cults of the Dead*, 56, 113 n. 36; Schmidt, *Israel's Beneficent Dead*, 151. For critique, see Lust, "On Wizards and Prophets," 135.

[193] Harry A. Hoffner, "Second Millennium Antecedents to the Hebrew ʾÔb," *JBL* 86 (1967): 385–401; Maurice Vieyra, "Les Noms du 'Mundus' en Hittite et en Assyrien et la Pythonisse d'Endor," *Revue Hittite et Asianique* 19 (1961): 47–55; Hoffner, "אוב," *TDOT* 1:130–34. Other possibilities include a bag (Job 32:19) and a "whirring stick" (H. Schmidt, "âwb," in *Vom Alten Testament: Festschrift K. Marti* [BZAW 41; Giessen: Töpelmann, 1925], 253–54).

[194] Lust, "On Wizards and Prophets," 136–37; Dietrich, Loretz, and Sanmartin, "Ugaritisch *ILIB*," 450–51.

[195] The possible etymological connection between ידעני and Akk. *mūdū*, "scholar" (P. Jensen, "Akkadisch *mudū*," *ZA* 35 [1924]: 124–32; *AHw*, 666a; *HALOT*, 393) is too tenuous as a basis to define both Hebrew terms.

[196] There are of course numerous Egyptian loanwords (or cognates) in the Hebrew Bible. See, e.g., Thomas Lambdin, "Egyptian Loan Words in the Old Testament," *JAOS* 73 (1953): 145–55. Also see discussion of likely Judean familiarity with Egyptian culture in § 2.3 and § 5.2.3.2.

[197] Schmidt, *Israel's Beneficent Dead*, 157.

fin Texts, the deceased aspires to be reunited with "the *3bwt*, the father, the mother, the parents ... the in-laws, the children, the spouses, the concubines, the servants ... everything that returns to a man in the necropolis."[198] Because the term can refer to the living and the dead alike, a phrase from the Coffin Texts such as *wrw nw 3bwt* can sometimes also be translated "the nearest ancestors."[199] Dmitri Meeks has adduced a number of examples, largely from funerary inscriptions, in which the translation "family" does not quite fit; he suggests "domestic servants,"[200] but in my estimation, the translation "dead ancestors" fits a number of these occurrences better. For example, in Coffin Texts Spell 149, the deceased is given the power to become a falcon and destroy his enemy: "I have repulsed my enemy; I have crushed his *3bwt*; I have thrown down his house."[201] This would seem to reflect the power of the enemy's dead kin to fight on his behalf in the afterlife (as also in the Letters to the Dead; cf. § 2.4.2).

Furthermore, Stele BM 159 reads, "I was a great one in his village, a rich man in his house, a lofty pillar for his *3bwt*," perhaps attesting to his support and care of his dead kin. There is also the formulaic affirmation, common in autobiographical documents that the author was "kind to his *3bwt*."[202] It seems natural that a person who desired care for himself or herself in the afterlife, should in preparation assert that he or she had always been concerned for the well-being of the dead. Striking, too, is the assertion of Seti I concerning his father Ramses I: "I did not banish his *3bwt* from before me, but I reunited the survivors for a royal meal."[203] The "royal meal" here would appear to be a sort of *kispu* meal, in which the dead king is summoned. If so, then Seti was describing his mortuary care of his dead father.

If this is correct, then it also suggests a connection with the late Egyptian term of the same root (*3b*)[204] and spelling, *3bwt*, "form," which can be used interchangeably with *tit*, "image."[205] In some texts, sacrificial animals are identified as the *3bwt* ("images") of the enemies of the gods. Insofar as these terms can appear with the "mummiform effigy" determinative, designating the "form" of a person, it seems possible that *3bwt* might also signify a statue of a deified ancestor. This

---

[198] Dmitri Meeks, "Notes de Lexicographie," *RdE* 26 (1974): 56.
[199] Meeks, "Notes de Lexicographie," 59 n. 10.
[200] Meeks, "Notes de Lexicographie," 52–65.
[201] Raymond O. Faulkner, *The Ancient Egyptian Coffin Texts* (London: Aris & Phillips, 2004), 128. Faulkner translates *3bwt* as "family." It seems more likely that the deceased speaker would be said to do battle with other spirits than with the enemy's living family. Note also Spell 147, "As for any soul or any god who shall cause N's *3bwt* to be taken from him, N shall cause his head to be broken ..." (Faulkner, *Coffin Texts*, 124). Cf. Meeks, "Notes de Lexicographie," 56.
[202] Meeks, "Notes de Lexicographie," 58.
[203] Meeks, "Notes de Lexicographie," 62.
[204] Meeks, "Notes de Lexicographie," 64.
[205] Jean Yoyotte, "Hera d'Heliopolis et le Sacrifice Humain," *Écoles Pratiques des Hautes Études, Ve section, Annuaire Résumés des Conférences et Travaux* 89 (1980–81): 48.

dual sense of "ancestor/statue" would accord well with the biblical אבות: they are the dead ancestors who are represented by statues, much like the *teraphim* (see below). Indeed, as Assmann observed, in Egyptian mortuary-cult art, "[o]ne principle reigned supreme: a depiction was not a depiction of a body, it was itself a body. ... [T]here was no distinction between corpse and statue."[206]

The same principle may have obtained in Judah: if the Israelite אבות sometimes appeared to be numinous entities, and sometimes cultic objects, then perhaps the term denoted either or both. This situation finds better-known analogies in West Semitic *npš/nbš*, which came to mean both the soul and the funerary monument;[207] and in Hebrew אשרה (Asherah/asherah) – generally thought to be a goddess who was symbolized by a wooden pole, אשרה appears in the Bible indicating now one, now the other. Perhaps in the cases of both אבות and אשרה, the Bible reflects a diachronic shift in the sense of the term, but as Othmar Keel and Christoph Uehlinger observed, divinities and their symbols were often interchangeable; the אשרה was de-anthropomorphized in certain periods of Israelite and Judean iconography.[208] They called this process "the substitution of the goddess by the entities through which she worked."[209] Perhaps the אבות, too, were both symbols and divine beings, with the singular אוב being a subsequent development internal to Hebrew.

Israelites did have figurines representing ancestors that were used for divination: in other contexts, these are called *teraphim* (תרפים) (Ezek 21:26; Zech 10:2).[210] Even more clearly than the אובות or the ידענים, the *teraphim* were physical objects of some sort (Gen 31:19–35; Judg 17:5, 18:14–20; 2 Kgs 19:11–17).[211] They have frequently been compared to the Nuzi *ilanū*, "household gods," a term that may be used either for divinized ancestors or the statues that represent

---

[206] Assmann, *Death and Salvation*, 106, 109. Zainab Bahrani has argued similarly about Mesopotamian royal images: "In Babylon and Assyria the king's image functioned as his valid representation ... [so as to] blur the division of real and representation" (*The Graven Image: Representation in Babylonia and Assyria* [Archaeology, Culture, and Society; Philadelphia: University of Pennsylvania Press, 2003], 146).
[207] See *DNWSI*, 744–49; *DJA*, 66.
[208] Othmar Keel and Christoph Uehlinger, *Gods, Goddesses and Images of God in Ancient Israel* (trans. T. H. Trapp; Minneapolis: Fortress, 1998), e.g., 314. See also p. 394: "It is quite improbable that names like 'Asherah' ... always referred to the same reality or concept."
[209] Keel and Uehlinger, *Gods, Goddesses and Images of God*, 147.
[210] For an excellent review of the scholarship and critical issues, see Karel van der Toorn and Theodore Lewis in "תרפים," *TDOT* 15:777–89. The size and number of the *teraphim* are apt to cause confusion. In Gen 31, Rachel can hide the *teraphim* underneath her, and they are clearly plural, whereas in 1 Sam 19, it is singular and apparently large enough to function as a dummy for David. Most likely the term was frozen and applied to any representation of any size of an ancestral god.
[211] Also like many terms surrounding the cult of the dead, the תרפים may have suffered some scribal emendation, if the term comes from רפא (like רפאים), but with the loss of the final *aleph*. For a survey of the more than half-dozen suggestions about the etymology, see van der Toorn and Lewis, "תרפים," 778–79.

them.²¹² There is reason to think that the *teraphim* were once an accepted part of Israelite family religion.²¹³ They are never condemned in the legal codes, but only in 1 Sam 15:23 and the report of their removal by Josiah in 2 Kgs 23:24.

Other texts without any of the aforementioned characteristic terminology also subtly reflect some kind of veneration of the dead in Israel and Judah. Besides Exod 20:12 // Deut 5:16 and Deut 26:14 (see § 4.1), one could add Hos 9:4, which warns that certain unwelcome sacrifices "will be like mourners' bread (לחם אונים):²¹⁴ all who eat of it shall be defiled, for their bread shall be for their hunger only; it shall not come to the house of the LORD." This distinction between what may be eaten and what may be offered almost certainly draws on the principle of Deut 26:14 ("I have not offered any of [my sacred portion] to the dead"). Both texts assume that funerary feasts are allowable; but one may not take from them sacrifices to YHWH. It has also been suggested that 1 Sam 20:6, in which David asks to be excused from Saul's service to be present at "a yearly sacrifice for all the family" (זבח הימים שם לכל־המשפחה) reflects a ritual involving the dead ancestors.²¹⁵ Psalm 106:28 connects the Baal of Peor incident from Num 25 to sacrifices for the dead, although this is clearly not portrayed as a Yahwistic practice in any case.²¹⁶

4.4.2.4 Summary

In sum, the body of evidence in favor of long-standing ancestor cults in Israel and Judah is widespread and diverse, if rather thin. Clearly, such practices came to be condemned by representatives of Yahwism, and thus the record of them has been purged fairly effectively from the Hebrew Bible – so that they constitute, in van der Toorn's phrase, "a hidden heritage."²¹⁷ In spite of the difficulty of interpreting many of the biblical references, I would side with R. E. Friedman and S. D. Overton that "the nature and quantity of them is still too much to write off as a mass of uncertain instances."²¹⁸ The limited extent of the attestations in the biblical text is

---

²¹² See recently Rouillard and Tropper, "*Trpym*," 340–61.

²¹³ Brichto suggests that the *teraphim* were not a threat because they were used for *veneration* of ancestors rather than worship ("Kin, Cult, Land and Afterlife," 47), but this is a doubtful distinction. Note Jacob's disposal of "foreign gods" in Gen 35:2–4 (E) and the discussion by Othmar Keel, "Das Vergraben der 'fremden Götter' in Genesis XXXV 4b," *VT* 23 (1973): 305–36.

²¹⁴ With the textual emendation of אונים for אנשים, the term "mourners' bread" may also be reconstructed in Ezek 24:17, 22.

²¹⁵ Van der Toorn, *Family Religion*, 212–13; Bloch-Smith, *Judahite Burial Practices*, 124. The same term is used in 1 Sam 1:21; 2:19; and 20:6.

²¹⁶ Later Persian and Hellenistic texts such as Tob 4:17, Sir 30:17, and Syriac Aḥiqar no. 10 refer to offerings placed or poured on graves. On the last of these, see J. C. Greenfield, "Two Proverbs of Aḥiqar" in *Lingering over Words: Studies in Ancient Near Eastern Literature in Honor of William L. Moran* (Atlanta: Scholars Press, 1990), 194–201.

²¹⁷ Van der Toorn, *Family Religion*, 206.

²¹⁸ R. E. Friedman and S. D. Overton, "Death and Afterlife: The Biblical Silence," in *Judaism*

due more to a theological decision of Yahwistic scribes than it is to an actual absence of ancestor cults in pre-exilic Judah and Israel.

If one searches for the reasons that ancestor cults were banned, several possibilities suggest themselves. I have already alluded to Bloch-Smith's observation that there was a cultic crisis when northern priests had to be assimilated into Jerusalem, which brought condemnations of necromancy because it competed with Yahwism, as the latter was being redefined. Blenkinsopp views Deuteronomy's prohibition of ancestor cults as an outgrowth of a political desire for centralization, since it correlates with a shift from a lineage-based society to a centralized state.[219] I would add that this process was probably under way already in the eighth century, as the Neo-Assyrian threat caused Hezekiah to expand and fortify Jerusalem and other large cities. Sennacherib's destruction of outlying Judean towns in 701 would have severed the crucial link between land and kin for many families by forcing them to abandon their property. Therefore it is likely that the marginalization of ancestor cults was already happening during Isaiah ben Amoz's time, and that the prophet himself was a proponent of that process (§§ 5.2.2.4; 5.2.3.1).

Mary Douglas has advanced a sociological theory about the end of ancestor cults. She argued that the "colonial regime" imposed by the Neo-Assyrians disenfranchised the Judean elders who were most likely to support an ancestor cult, and dishonored the young, who no longer had military outlet for their ambitions, making the time ripe for a religious revolution on the part of the young.[220] She especially emphasizes the role of the boy-king Josiah: "He is like the founder of a nativistic cult, mustering his young followers against the evil empire, going back to the pure origins of the old religion, rejecting accretions and impurities."[221] Of course, as in many reform movements, the quest for "pure origins" in fact led to something quite new – in Judah's case, a religion purged of access to the dead.

To be clear, I see no need to choose among the theories I have just discussed. It is likely that it took a number of forces working in concert to bring about a change as significant as the banning of ancestor cults from an ancient Near Eastern religion.

---

in *Late Antiquity*, part 4, *Death, Life-after-Death, Resurrection and the World to Come in the Judaisms of Antiquity* (ed. Alan J. Avery-Peck and Jacob Neusner; Handbuch der Orientalistik 55; Leiden/New York: Brill, 2000), 46.

[219] Blenkinsopp, "Deuteronomy and the Politics of Post-Mortem Existence," *passim*.

[220] Douglas, "One God, No Ancestors," 192: "Enduring the frustration, bewilderment, and humiliations of a colonial dependency, the old men find their power is broken, but the young men, freed from their yoke, are relatively short of honour. This can make the country ripe for religious change instigated by the young."

[221] Douglas, "One God, No Ancestors," 193.

4.4.3 The underworld and its deities

4.4.3.1 Terms for and images of the underworld

The underworld in Israelite thought is known primarily by the name *Shĕôl* (sixty-five times),[222] which appears to be a uniquely Hebraic term. Its etymology is disputed. Ludwig Koehler and John Day prefer a derivation from the root I שאה ("to lie desolate") with a suffixed ל (as with כֶּרֶם and כַּרְמֶל).[223] Others perceive a derivation from שאל, "to ask," and thus an original reference to necromancy. This would perhaps have been obscured by a perpetual *qere* on the part of the Masoretes – although the Masoretic pointing would be a perfectly acceptable Qal infinitive construct: "[place of] asking"? or "place where one must answer"? Albright and Walter Baumgartner theorized a connection to *šu'aru*, the underworld abode of Tammuz.[224] For a discussion of older theories, see Tromp, *Primitive Conceptions*, 21–23.[225]

In the end, none of the theories about the etymology of Sheol is convincing enough to have generated any consensus. In such a situation, it seems preferable to remain with the apparent root, שאל; but it would go beyond the data to claim that it is a reference to necromancy.[226]

Sheol is characterized as deep (Deut 32:22; Job 11:7), even as a pit deep underwater (Ezek 28:8). It is dark (Job 17:13; 38:17; Ps 23:4; 88:6; 143:3; Lam 3:6) and dusty (Ps 22:16, 30; 30:10; Job 17:16; Dan 12:2). In the grave one finds forgetfulness (Eccl 9:10) and is forgotten (Pss 31:13; 88:5; Job 24:19–20). (If there was care of the dead in ancient Israel outside of the royal palace, it was likely only for a couple of generations, as elsewhere; thus it was probably about the time one's

---

[222] So *HALOT*; see also Ruth Rosenberg, "The Concept of Biblical Sheol within the Context of Ancient Near Eastern Beliefs: A Thesis" (Ph.D. diss., Harvard University, 1981).

[223] Day, "Development of the Belief in Life After Death," 231; *HALOT*, 1368–70; cf. Arabic *šu'/šu'a*, "catastrophe."

[224] I.e., with (unusual) *r / l* interchange. Albright does not explain how the "bright and fruitful home of Tammuz" became the dark, dusty, silent Sheol. W. F. Albright, "Mesopotamian Elements in Canaanite Eschatology" in *Oriental Studies (Paul Haupt Anniversary Volume)* (Baltimore: Johns Hopkins University Press; Leipzig: Hinrichs, 1926), 143–54; W. Baumgartner, "Miszelle zur Etymologie von 'Sche'ol,'" *TZ* 2 (1946): 233–35. See the argument against *šu'alu* in Heidel, *Gilgamesh Epic*, 173–74. Marjo C. A. Korpel points out that at Emar an underworld goddess called Shualu seems to have been attested; however, the relationship of this early figure to Hebrew Sheol is not at all clear. See Korpel, *A Rift in the Clouds: Ugaritic and Hebrew Descriptions of the Divine* (Münster: Ugarit-Verlag, 1990), 348. For the text, see Daniel Arnaud, *Recherches au pays d'Aštata: Emar VI.3* (Paris: Éditions Recherche sur les Civilisations, 1986), no. 385.

[225] For general bibliography and summary of the propsals for the etymology of שאול, see *TDOT* 14:240–41. It has been obligatory in this discussion to mention the article of Eugène Devaud that links the word to an Egyptian word for the afterlife ("Sur l'étymologie de שאול *š^eôl*," *Sphinx* 13 [1909]: 120–21), but its argument is so sketchy and without conviction that it probably needs to be retired from the bibliography.

[226] Tromp, *Primitive Conceptions of Death*, 23.

bones were cleared away that one was indeed forgotten.) Sheol is also a symbol of sadness (Gen 42:38; 44:29–31) and is nevertheless often described as the end of all people (Ps 89:48; cf. Eccl 8:8). There have been some efforts to argue that Sheol is the fate only of the wicked,[227] but it is only in late texts such as Daniel that any distinction among human fates can be seen.[228]

Other terms also are used for the underworld in the Hebrew Bible, such as the term Abaddon (אבדון), which occurs primarily in poetic contexts (Job 26:6; 28:22; 31:12; Ps 88:12; Prov 15:11; 27:20). It is typically taken to be a noun form from the root אבד, thus "[place of] destruction," although it is intriguing to note that the Egyptians' sacred grove containing the "tomb of Osiris" at Biga was called Abaton (ἄβατον) by classical Greek authors and was a site of death-cult activities.[229] One of the most central and striking characteristics of the Abaton was the command for silence in its precincts,[230] similar to the biblical underworld (Ps 94:17: "If YHWH had not been my help, my soul would soon have dwelled in silence"; Ps 115:17: "The dead do not praise YHWH, nor do any that go down into silence"; cf. Isa 47:5; Jer 48:2).

More naturalistically, the underworld was known in Hebrew as בור ("pit"; Ps 28:1; etc.), שחת (also "pit"; Ps 16:10; etc.) and ארץ ("earth"; Jonah 2:7; Pss 22:30; 71:5; Jer 17:13; etc.; cognate with Ugaritic arṣ).[231] Each of these three terms aptly indicates that the Israelite views of the netherworld most commonly reflected the conditions of the tomb – that is, as dug into the earth, as in other ancient Near Eastern cultures. It is pervasively seen as existing down below; texts suggesting that the dead may go upward, such as Eccl 3:21 and Dan 12:3, stand out in stark contrast and are likely a late development.[232] Although we do not know the technical terminology of Israelite tombs, one might wonder whether "the pit" is the receptacle in tombs into which bones were swept to make way for new burials.

The Israelite afterlife was also susceptible to description by a wide variety of

---

[227] Jarick, "Questioning Sheol," 22–32.

[228] Psalm 73:27–28 might obliquely refer to such a distinction.

[229] For Egyptian inscriptions and classical references, see Hermann Junker, *Das Götterdekret über das Abaton* (Vienna: Alfred Hölder, 1913). Cultic activities are known there from at least the Eighteenth Dynasty onward (*Routledge Dictionary of Egyptian Gods and Goddesses* [London: Routledge, 2005], 123). See also Assmann, *Death and Salvation*, 190.

[230] Junker, *Das Götterdekret über das Abaton*, v–vi.

[231] For discussion of further terms and descriptors for the Israelite netherworld especially in the Psalms, see Sidney Jellicoe, "Hebrew-Greek Equivalents for the Nether World, Its Milieu and Inhabitants, in the Old Testament," *Textus* 8 (1973): 1–19.

[232] 2 Kings 2:11 might suggest an ascent to the afterlife, but should be treated as a special case, since Elijah is not even described as dead. Day persuasively argues that the ascents of Enoch and Elijah were modeled on the Mesopotamian accounts of the flood hero being taken to heaven, since Israelite authors clearly knew the flood traditions, and the Mesopotamian accounts use the verb *laqû*, cognate with לקח in Gen 5:24 and 2 Kgs 2:10 ("Development in the Belief in Life after Death," 238–39).

images. Death can be portrayed as a snare or trap (2 Sam 22:6; Pss 18:5; 116:3) or as a prison (Job 17:16; Jonah 2:7). Other texts clearly derive from mythic traditions: Sheol swallows (Num 16:28–34; Ps 69:15; Isa 5:14) and is elsewhere known as a gated city (Job 38:17; Ps 9:13) – an image also found in the other major cultures covered in chapters 1–3. Job 33:18 may reflect the common motif of death as a river crossing (Ḫubur, Styx), if the term שֶׁלַח there is to be interpreted as a cognate of Akkadian *šalḫu/šiliḫtu*, "canal."[233] Ezek 31:15 more clearly describes the "rivers (נהרות) of Sheol."

Tromp surveyed and assessed more than two dozen other terms for the underworld in biblical texts, most of which occur only a few times.[234] In addition to terms that reflect conditions of the tombs, they seem to gather around certain other loci: untamed wilds of nature, such as the uncultivated wasteland and the watery depths.

Finally, there are references in the wisdom literature that might suggest an awareness of longstanding Egyptian ideas about the judgment of the dead.[235] These include the weighing of the heart (see § 2.4.3.) in Prov 21:2: "All a man's ways are right in his own eyes, but YHWH weighs the heart" (also 16:2; 24:12) and Job 31:6 "Let me be weighed in a just balance, and let God know my integrity!" An even more elaborate adaptation of the motif of the judgment of the dead appears in Job 33:22–26:

> His soul draws near the Pit,
>   and his life to those who bring death.
> Then, if there should be for him an angel,
>   a mediator, one of a thousand,
>   one who declares him upright,
> and he is gracious to him, and says,
>   "Deliver him from going down into the Pit;
>   I have found a ransom;
> let his flesh become fresh with youth;
>   let him return to the days of his youthful vigor."

---

[233] Cf. Marvin Pope, *Job: Introduction, Translation, and Notes* (AB 15; 2nd ed.; Garden City, N.Y.: Doubleday, 1965), 218; Eduard Dhorme, *A Commentary on the Book of Job* (trans. H. Knight; London: Nelson & Sons, 1967), 496–97 (French orig. *Le Livre de Job*, 1927). Against this idea, see Dominic Rudman, "The Use of Water Imagery in Descriptions of Sheol," *ZAW* 113 (2001): 240–44.

[234] Tromp, *Primitive Conceptions of Death*, 21–99. These include "the hidden place" (טמון / סתר); "the broad place" (מרחב); "field of death" (שדמות); "miry depths" (המיר); "miry bog" (טיט היון); "depth" (מצולה / מעמק / תהום); "sea" (ים); "great waters" (מים רבים); "ruin" (חרבה / משעה); "fortress / silence" (דומה); "house / tomb" (בית); "dust" (עפר); "descent" (ירדן); and "land of forgetfulness" (ארץ נשייה). His precursors included Paul Dhorme, "Le séjour des morts chez les Babyloniens et les Hébreux," *RB* 4 (1907): 59–78.

[235] Hugo Gressmann, *Israels Spruchweisheit im Zusammenhang der Weltliteratur* (Berlin: K. Curtius, 1925), 43–44; R. B. Y. Scott, *Proverbs. Ecclesiastes: Introduction, Translation, and Notes* (AB 18; Garden City, N.Y.: Doubleday, 1965), 106; J. Gwyn Griffiths, *The Divine Verdict: A Study of Divine Judgement in the Ancient Religions* (Leiden: Brill, 1991), 299–302.

Then he prays to God, and finds favor with him,
he comes into his presence with a shout of joy,
and God repays him for his righteousness.

This is surely not exactly like the native Egyptian scenes; not only does the angelic mediator not have a clear analogue in Egyptian texts, but the text goes on in v. 27 to confess guilt (a far cry from the negative confession of the Book of the Dead) and to attribute the supplicant's survival only to divine grace. However, the rhetoric of restoring the flesh to youthfulness is quintessentially Egyptian – that is precisely the afterlife hope attested in numerous funerary texts. The author of Job has cleverly adapted that rhetoric to the idea of healing from sickness, rather than restoration from death (a distinction that is in any case not sharply drawn in biblical rhetoric; see § 4.6.2). Biblical authors were clearly acquainted with such Egyptian imagery, but as Day points out, they have adapted it "into an image of Yahweh's judgment in this life."[236] In the next chapter, we will see that Isaiah repeatedly demonstrates a knowledge of foreign ideas, but he too adapts them to his own purposes.

4.4.3.2 Underworld gods

Death is personified quite clearly at times in the Bible, just as in the Baal Cycle. One of the most famous references to the swallowing god of Death is found in Isa 5:14 ("Sheol has enlarged its appetite and opened its mouth beyond measure"), which will be discussed in detail in the next chapter (see § 5.2.2.1). There are also others. Habakkuk 2:5 describes an arrogant Babylonian ruler who "makes his gullet wide like Sheol, and is as insatiable as Mot." One might also mention Job 28:22 (where Death speaks), Ps 49:14 (Death as shepherd), and Hos 13:14 ("Death, where are your plagues?").[237]

The lament of Jer 9:20 – "Death has come up into our windows, it has entered our palaces, to cut off the children from the streets and the young men from the squares" – is also highly reminiscent of other cultures' fears of demonic assaults. It has been observed that Baal's refusal to have a window built in his palace in CAT 1.4 v 58–vi 15 may reflect a similar fear of Death coming in the window.[238] In addition, Song 8:6 ("love is as strong as death," כמות אהבה עזה) is sometimes thought to reflect the language used in the Baal Cycle to describe the battle of Baal and Mot ("Mot is strong, Baal is strong," mt ʿz bʿl ʿz, repeated three times in CAT 1.6 vi 17–20).

---

[236] Day, "Development of the Belief in Life after Death," 249.
[237] In Hos 13:14, the term for "plagues" is דבריך, recalling the Ugaritic term for the underworld, arṣ dbr, "Land of Plague" (e.g., CAT 1.5 vi 6).
[238] Mark Smith, "Death in Jeremiah ix, 20," UF 19 (1987): 289–93; John Day, Yahweh and the Gods and Goddesses of Canaan (JSOTSup 265; Sheffield: Sheffield Academic Press, 2000), 190–92. Mot may also be portrayed as a demon threatening humans in CAT 2.10.

This assortment of data shows that biblical authors were aware of Syro-Palestinian traditions akin to those of Ugarit. It is clear that they could choose to make a point or paint a picture by alluding to West Semitic mythological traditions that were outside of typical Yahwistic theology. It is not likely, however, that Mot had a cult in Judah or Israel, or was commonly regarded as an active divine presence (§ 5.2.3.3).

Molek and child sacrifice

The chthonic god Malik/Molek was certainly known to the Israelites (Lev 18:21; 20:2–5; 2 Kgs 23:10; Jer 32:35; Isa 57:9 [emended from מֶלֶךְ]). G. C. Heider and John Day have shown in recent monographs that Molek (however vocalized) is a distinct god,[239] despite some scribal confusion of Molek with the Ammonite Milcom.[240] It does not seem likely that Milcom, as a national god in Ammon comparable to YHWH in Judah, would have had such a different persona from YHWH. (By comparison, the Moabite national deity Chemosh is portrayed in the Mesha inscription as very much like YHWH.)[241] Whatever the original vocalization of the name *Mlk* (which varied widely in different languages), the biblical pointing as Molek seems to reflect a perpetual *qere* using the vowels of *bōšet*, "shame."[242]

---

[239] Heider, "Molech," *DDD*, 581–85; idem, *Cult of Molek*; John Day, *Molech: A God of Human Sacrifice in the Old Testament* (Cambridge: Cambridge University Press, 1989); idem, *Yahweh and the Gods*, 209–16. The theory that these biblical occurrences of the word מלך actually reflect a common noun cognate with the Punic *molk/mulk* (a term for child sacrifice) was once prevalent, but is no longer in favor. For the older theory, see Eissfeldt, *Molk als Opferbegriff*; Wolfram von Soden, review of Eissfeldt, *Molk als Opferbegriff*, *TLZ* 61 (1936): 46. The contexts in which מלך is used strongly suggest the name of a deity rather than that of a sacrifice; e.g., Lev 20:5; Deut 12:31; Jer 19:5; 32:35. See Dennis Pardee, review of Heider, *Cult of Molek*, *JNES* 49 (1990): 372; Heider, "Molech," 582. A final theory is that the name Molek refers to Adad(-milki), which was advanced by Moshe Weinfeld, "The Worship of Molech and the Queen of Heaven and Its Background," *UF* 4 (1972): 133–54. However, the Akkadian texts he adduced in support of this theory (pp. 144–45) are not even cultic texts, but rather curse formulae in legal documents against one who would break a legal agreement. This is a very different situation from what the biblical text portrays.

[240] For example, Milcom appears in 1 Kgs 11:5, 33, while Molek is named in 11:7. The two names are also collocated in 2 Kgs 23:10 and 13. The name is sometimes pointed as if it were מֶלֶךְ with a third masculine plural pronominal suffix (מַלְכָּם, "their king"), e.g., Jer 49:1, 3; Zeph 1:5.

[241] It is of course possible that the *entire* biblical portrait of Molek is a slanderous fabrication, under which lies the Ammonite Milcom – but on that assumption, the whole religio-historical enterprise would be pointless.

[242] This theory is propounded by Moshe Weinfeld in "The Moloch Cult in Israel and Its Background," in *Proceedings of the 5th World Congress of Jewish Studies*, vol. 1, *Hebrew University, Jerusalem, 1969* (Jerusalem: World Union of Jewish Studies, 1973), 37–61. It is adopted by Day (*Yahweh and the Gods*, 56–58) and by Albertz (*History of Israelite Religion*, 1:192). Notably, the *bōšet* theory is questioned by Heider, who thinks Molek is a Qal active participle, by comparison with the LXX translation *archōn*, "ruler" (*Cult of Molek*, 223–28).

Molek is repeatedly portrayed as a god who received child sacrifices (see Ezek 16:21; 23:37–39 in addition to the above). Efforts to show that the Bible does not portray actual child sacrifice in the Molek cult, but rather dedication to the god by fire, have been convincingly disproved.[243] Child sacrifice is well attested in the ancient world, especially in times of crisis. King Mesha of Moab sacrifices his firstborn son (2 Kgs 3:27) and a battle turns in his favor; similar fiery child sacrifices are attested in Phoenician cities such as Carthage, Sicily, Sardinia, and Cyprus.[244] There are other references to cultic immolations of children and adults in Mesopotamian and Egyptian texts of Isaiah's period, but these seem to have had a punitive rather than a propitiatory function (see § 5.2.1.2).

The Bible portrays the cult of Molek is portrayed as having Canaanite roots (Lev 18:21–27; Deut 12:31; 2 Kgs 16:3; 21:2), and there is indeed evidence for child sacrifice in ancient Syria-Palestine.[245] Israelite and Judean kings are accused of participating in such a cult (2 Kgs 16:3 [Ahaz]; 17:17 [the northern kingdom]; 21:6 [Manasseh]), and the same practices are condemned by the prophets.[246] In its biblical portrayal, the child-sacrifice cult is closely associated with the valley of (Ben-)Hinnom, גי (בן־)הנום. The valley is typically identified with the present-day Wadi er-Rababi, to the west of Jerusalem.[247] Within the valley, the specific site of the cult seems to have been Topheth, cognate with the Aramaic *tapya*, "stove, fireplace"[248] and derived from the root *ʾpʾ*, "bake."

Despite the Bible's claims that these kings were influenced by Canaanite practices, it has sometimes been argued that child sacrifice was initially a Yahwistic directive as well, in light of the command to "give" the firstborn sons to YHWH (Exod 22:28b–29); even in its present setting, that commandment sits uncom-

---

[243] Weinfeld has adduced practices from Mesopotamia and elsewhere in which the children in question were merely dedicated to a god (e.g., Adad) in a ritual of passing through fire. There is always the possibility of propagandistic exaggeration, but if so, it was carried out in a remarkably consistent way by numerous biblical authors. Better in this case to presume, with Morton Smith, that "texts mean what they say" ("A Note on Burning Babies," *JAOS* 95 [1975]: 478.

[244] King and Stager, *Life in Biblical Israel*, 359–61. See classical references at Day, *Molech*, 87–91. This interpretation has been contested in recent years, most notably by Hélène Benicho-Safar, *Les tombes puniques de Carthage: Topographie, structures, inscriptions et rites funéraires* (Etudes d'antiquités africaines; Paris: Editions du centre national de la recherche scientifique, 1982), 343. As this book goes to press, a new study of the Carthage remains by physical anthropologists has argued that "while the Carthaginians may have occasionally sacrificed humans … Tophets were cemeteries for those who died shortly before or after birth, regardless of the cause." See Jeffrey H. Schwartz et al., "Skeletal Remains from Punic Carthage Do Not Support Systematic Sacrifice of Infants," *PLoS ONE* 5 (2010): e9177.

[245] Day, *Molech*, 18, esp. n. 11. See also A. R. W. Green, *The Role of Human Sacrifice in the Ancient Near East* (SBLDS 1; Missoula, Mont.: Scholars Press, 1975).

[246] Jeremiah 7:31–32; 19:5–6, 11; cf. 2:23; 3:24 and Ezek 16:20–21; 20:25–26, 30–31; 23:36–39.

[247] See J. A. Dearman, "The Tophet in Jerusalem: Archaeology and Cultural Profile," *JNSL* 22 (1996): 59–71; Duane F. Watson, "Hinnom Valley (Place)," *ABD* 3:202–3.

[248] Day, *Yahweh and the Gods*, 212.

fortably until Exod 34:9 instructs the Israelites to redeem their firstborn sons from sacrifice. Could it be that, in some period, some of the firstborn were not redeemed in "normative" Yahwism but rather sacrificed? The (near-)sacrifice of Isaac at God's command (Gen 22) seems to supply a narrative rationale for such a practice, as does Jephthah's vow to sacrifice his daughter in Judg 11:29–40. Despite the pathos of both accounts, both Abraham (Gen 22:2) and Jephthah (Judg 11:29) are portrayed as acting according to the will of YHWH. As Jon D. Levenson remarked, "If it is, in fact, a mistake for us to read the requirement to sacrifice the first-born son in Exod 22:28–29 independently of the provisions for redemption that appear in other texts, it is a mistake of a sort that numerous Israelites seem to have made."[249]

Ezekiel's explanation of child sacrifice is troubling from a theological standpoint, in that it suggests that God did command it, but only as a punishment. In 20:25–26, God says, "I gave them statutes that were not good and ordinances by which they could not live. I defiled them through their very gifts, in their offering up all their firstborn, in order that I might horrify them." Then again, this text is part of a somewhat revisionist version of Israel's history on Ezekiel's part. Furthermore, there are differences between the Ezekiel and legal texts, on the one hand, and the Molek rites on the other – the primary one being that the sacrifice of the firstborn relates only to males, whereas the Molek cult is repeatedly said to involve sacrificing daughters as well as sons. Even if child sacrifice was at certain times practiced in the name of YHWH, still YHWH was not identical with Molek, nor were they confused.

Jeremiah disputes that child sacrifice was ever YHWH's will, but perhaps protests too much. In 32:35, God objects that the Judeans sacrificed children "though I did not command them,[250] nor did it enter my mind that they should do this abomination." Whether or not it was ever orthodox, language such as this suggests that *someone* claimed it was. Charles A. Kennedy has further reconstructed a reference to child sacrifice in a cult of the dead at tombs in the post-exilic period in Isa 57:5–6: "You who are in heat among the great trees/ and under every green tree, who slay your children in (rock-cut) tombs/ among the clefts in

---

[249] Jon D. Levenson, *The Death and Resurrection of the Beloved Son: The Transformation of Child Sacrifice in Judaism and Christianity* (New Haven: Yale University Press, 1993), 4. Jacob Milgrom argues that YHWH never intended the killing of first human beings, but his subtle exegesis only supports Levenson's point; furthermore, Milgrom does not adequately address Ezek 20:25–26. See Milgrom, "Were the Firstborn Sacrificed to YHWH? To Molek? Popular Practice or Divine Demand?" in A. I. Baumgarten, ed., *Sacrifice in Religious Experience* (Leiden: Brill, 2002), 49–55.

[250] Day's repeated insistence that this phrase should be translated "which I forbade," in light of other occurrences of לא צויתי does not adequately address the next phrase (*Yahweh and the Gods*, 215–16; *Molech*, 68).

the rocks:/ Among the dead of the tomb is your portion,/ they, they are your lot..."²⁵¹

The biblical law does, as we have already noted, contain commandments against child sacrifice; the question is to what period those laws date. Whereas I am inclined to believe in the relative antiquity of the prohibitions, it does not seem impossible that human sacrifice could have survived, beyond the grasp of the emergent Jerusalem orthodoxy of the divided monarchy.²⁵² It is hard to understand why the Hebrew Bible would refer to it repeatedly otherwise.

4.4.3.3 Demons

Mot and Molek were not the only dangerous supernatural powers afoot in the Bible. Although Jewish interest in demonology would peak much later, demons also appear sporadically in the Hebrew Bible. There is of course the divine adversary *haśśāṭān* (1 Chr 21:1; Job 1–2; Zech 3:1–2), but also unspecified demons that stalk in darkness (Ps 91:6), sneak into windows (Jer 9:20), and terrorize suffering people (Pss 55:5; 88:16). Rešeph becomes a henchman in YHWH's wrathful retinue in Hab 3:5 "Before him went Pestilence, and Plague (רֶשֶׁף) followed close behind." The plural רְשָׁפִים are loosed in Ps 78:48–49 as "a troop of destroying angels."²⁵³ Job 18:13–14 also reflects demonic attack in strikingly Mesopotamian terms: "the firstborn of Death (בְּכוֹר מָוֶת) consumes their limbs. They are torn from the tent in which they trusted, and are marched before the king of terrors (לְמֶלֶךְ בַּלָּהוֹת)." The "firstborn of Death" alludes to a demon or deity of sickness, perhaps Rešeph, while the "king of terrors" is reminiscent of the image of Namtar from the Underworld Vision.²⁵⁴

---

²⁵¹ Charles A. Kennedy, "Isaiah 57:5–6: Tombs in the Rocks," *BASOR* 275 (1989): 47–52. Kennedy's translation is based on the use of נחל in Job 21:33 and 28:4, where he takes it to refer to a grave shaft; and also on the use of *ḥ-l-q* in Ugaritic, where it often refers to "perishing" in parallel with *m-t*, "to die" (e.g. 1.5 vi 10; 1.6 i 42).

²⁵² Francesca Stavrakopoulou has argued that "three possible cults of child sacrifice may plausibly have existed within Judah: the firstborn sacrifice, the *mlk* sacrifice, and the sacrifice to the *šadday*-gods" (*King Manasseh and Child Sacrifice*, 299). Even this extremely tentative phrasing may suggest more clarity than actually exists. While her analysis represents a helpful gathering and sorting of the data, I do not think that these three categories reflect "the historical reality of of child sacrifice." The theory of a child-sacrifice to the *šadday*-gods, which is based largely on the fragmentary Deir ʿAlla texts, is particularly speculative.

²⁵³ Both Hab 3:5 and Ps 78:48–49 emphasize the degree to which demons are made subservient to YHWH in the Bible, as does the Job prose tale. See André Caquot, "Anges et démons en Israël," in *Génies, anges, et démons* (Sources orientales 8; Paris: Seuil, 1971), 118.

²⁵⁴ Various other theories have been advanced about this passage, including William Irwin's theory that the ruler is Ereškigal ("Job's Redeemer," *JBL* 81 [1963]: 217–29) and Nahum Sarna's suggestion of a Ugaritic background ("The Mythological Background of Job 18," *JBL* 82 [1963]: 315–18). Day perceived a Molek reference here (*Molech*, 55, 84). Judit M. Blair urges caution in using comparative data to study demons in the Bible: *De-Demonizing the Old Testament: An Investigation of Azazel, Lilith, Deber, Qeteb and Reshef in the Hebrew Bible* (FAT II/37. Tübingen: Mohr Siebeck, 2009).

Demons are also often portrayed semi-naturalistically as wild animals (e.g., Ps 22:13–19),[255] sometimes haunting wastelands as in other ancient Near Eastern cultures. Perhaps the most obvious reference is in Isa 34:14, to Lilith, a well-known Mesopotamian demon (1.4.2.).[256] Apart from a possible association of wastelands with unburied corpses, I find no explicit link between demons and the dead in general, unlike in Mesopotamia.[257]

References to demons in literary texts such as Job are not always reflective of any general belief in their power. However, Mowinckel plausibly perceived a number of the Psalms as prayers for protection from demonic forces, which would reflect a genuine religious concern.[258]

4.4.4 YHWH and the dead

Historians of religion have sometimes proceeded as if YHWH had been thought to have no commerce with death and the underworld in the mainstream preexilic religion. Mowinckel expressed this idea with great force:

Yahweh was kept as far away from death and the realm of the dead as possible. Yahweh has nothing to do with the realm of the dead, where he makes no 'wonders'; the dead 'are torn out of his hand,' a thought which is emphasized so strongly that logically it enters into opposition to the belief in the omnipotence of Yahweh.[259]

Mowinckel was not alone in this view; Tromp compiled a compendium of similar comments by prominent scholars, and this perspective is still widespread, especially among nonspecialists in Hebrew Bible.[260] One prominent recent exponent of this view was Ziony Zevit, who wrote, "Yahwism as presented in extant biblical texts conceived of YHWH as lord of the living. Death was the ultimate contamination of all that was particularly sacred to him."[261]

---

[255] Mowinckel *Psalms in Israel's Worship*, 2:2–8; Brent A. Strawn, "Psalm 22:17b: More Guessing," *JBL* 119 (2000): 439–51, esp. p. 447; Christopher B. Hays, "Chirps from the Dust: The Affliction of Nebuchadnezzar in Daniel 4:30 in Its Ancient Near Eastern Context," *JBL* 126 (2007): 313.

[256] For discussion of Lilith, see Manfred Hutter, "Lilith," *DDD²*, 520–21; G. R. Driver, "Lilith," *PEQ* 91 (1959): 55–57; Lowell K. Handy, "Lilith," *ABD* 4:324–25; Walter Farber, *Schlaf, Kindchen, Schlaf! Mesopotamische Baby-Beschwörungen und -Rituale* (Mesopotamian Civilizations 2; Winona Lake, Ind.: Eisenbrauns, 1989); Vincent Tanghe, "Lilit in Edom," *ETL* 69 (1993): 125–33.

[257] André Caquot finds a possible connection between the dead and demons in Job 30:2–8 ("Anges et démons en Israël"). Given the book of Job's seeming familiarity with Mesopotamian ideas, this is an intriguing possibility, but should not be overemphasized.

[258] Sigmund Mowinckel, *The Psalms in Israel's Worship* (tr. D. R. Ap-Thomas; Oxford: Basil Blackwell, 1962; Reprint, Grand Rapids: Eerdmans, 2004), 2:2–4.

[259] Mowinckel, *Psalms in Israel's Worship*, 1:138.

[260] Tromp, *Primitive Conceptions of Death*, 197–202. For a recent example, see Assmann, *Death and Salvation*, 11: "[I]n the Old Testament world ... the divine and death were kept as far apart as possible."

[261] Zevit, *The Religions of Ancient Israel*, 664.

On a fresh reading, however, it would seem that such claims are much too simple, as are models in which there is a sudden shift in the postexilic period to belief in afterlife and YHWH's authority over the underworld. Instead it is possible to see a growth in these aspects.[262] The extension of God's power into Sheol is expressed already in Amos 9:1–2:[263]

לא־ינוס להם נס ולא־ימלט להם פליט: אם־יחתרו בשאול משם ידי תקחם ואם־יעלו השמים משם אורידם:

Not one of them will flee away, not one of them will escape. If they dig into Sheol, from there my hand will take them; though they climb up to heaven, from there I will bring them down.

This eighth-century text[264] is among the earliest in the Hebrew Bible that shows YHWH's full access to the underworld.[265] This may be part of a larger tradition; Alan Cooper has argued that Ps 24:7–10 is "a fragment or remnant of a descent myth – a myth in which a high god, forsaking his ordinary domain, descends to the netherworld, where he must confront the demonic forces of the infernal realm."[266] The phrase פתחי עולם ("doors of eternity") and the command that they be opened resonate with Egyptian mythology,[267] and even more so with the

---

[262] Gönke Eberhardt refers to "einer Kompetenzausweitung JHWHs auf die Unterwelt" ("an expansion of YHWH's authority over the underworld") (*JHWH und die Unterwelt: Spuren einer Kompetenzausweitung JHWHs im Alten Testament* [FAT II/23; Tübingen: Mohr Siebeck, 2007], 393). Marduk's domination of the Babylonian pantheon may be a significant analogue for Israelite monotheism; both deities seem to have assimilated the epithets and roles of other deities. For example, regarding YHWH's absorption of solar aspects and its relevance for the development of control over the underworld, see Eberhardt, *JHWH und die Unterwelt*, 396–98. Mark Smith seems to reverse the usual understanding of this process when he comments that "the wedge between Yahweh and the dead or the underworld may reflect ... a tendency that was emerging within Israelite religion," but this comment refers to the increasing condemnation of mortuary religion, not to Yahweh's commerce with and control over the underworld ("Recent Study of Israelite Religion in Light of the Ugaritic Texts" in *Ugarit at Seventy-Five* [ed. K. Lawson Younger Jr.; Winona Lake, Ind.: Eisenbrauns, 2007], 18).
[263] See also Ps 139:8.
[264] H. W. Wolff, *Joel and Amos* (Philadelphia: Fortress, 1977), 107: "The five reports of visions [including 9:1–4] ... must certainly, on the basis of their autobiographical style, be traced to Amos himself." See also Jörg Jeremias, *The Book of Amos* (OTL; Louisville, Ky.: Westminster John Knox, 1998), 6. Amos 9:1–4 is not among the passages that F. I. Andersen and D. N. Freedman noted as having attracted doubt regarding their authenticity: *Amos: A New Translation with Introduction and Commentary* (AB 24A; Garden City, N.Y.: Doubleday, 1989), 142.
[265] Eberhardt comments that "die Rede von JHWHs Zugriff auf die Flüchtenden in der Unterwelt noch mit einem gewissen Überraschungsmoment einhergeht" ("The word of YHWH's access to those who are fleeing in the underworld still carries with it a certain element of surprise"), but it is hard to say how he knows this. After all, the parallel statement that YHWH can bring them down from heaven is probably not intended to be surprising. See Eberhardt, *JHWH und die Unterwelt*, 393–94.
[266] Alan Cooper, "Ps 24:7–10: Mythology and Exegesis," *JBL* 102 (1983): 43.
[267] E.g., Pepi's Spell 4 in the Pyramid Texts: "The sky's door has been opened to you; the Cool Waters' door has been made to pull open to you; and you will find the Sun standing waiting for you. He will take hold of your arm, lead you into the sky's dual shrines, and put you on Osiris' throne." Cited in Allen, *The Ancient Egyptian Pyramid Texts*, 100.

descent of Ištar through the seven gates of the underworld (§ 1.4.3), but they are reused in the psalm to assert the Warrior YHWH's power.

Further texts likely to be preexilic that indicate YHWH's power over death include the affirmation that he "kills and brings to life ... brings down to Sheol and raises up" (1 Sam 2:6; Deut 32:39). As John T. Willis has remarked, this claim "is similar to a number of statements in early Hebrew poems."[268] Although proverbs are difficult to date with certainty, one might also mention Prov 15:11: "Sheol and Abaddon lie open before YHWH – how much more human hearts!"[269] In a comparison of this sort (reminiscent of the rabbinic *qal wahomer*), the first term must seem obvious to the hearer in order to elucidate the second.

Already in the preexilic period, therefore, YHWH was seen as a God who saved from death. In light of the parallels between biblical prayer and the prayer of other ancient Near Eastern civilizations (particularly Mesopotamia), this conclusion might have been predicted. In these cultures, prayer was first and foremost a response to suffering – be it on account of sickness, mistreatment, or other causes. In such a condition, the supplicant commonly portrayed him- or herself as approaching death. YHWH, like other gods, was perceived to have the power to save from this near-death condition (see § 1.4.3). Bernd Janowski has framed his study of the Psalter in two parts: "Von Leben zum Tod," ("From Life to Death"), and "Vom Tod zum Leben" ("From Death to Life") – and indeed the Psalter manifests clearly the Israelite affirmation that YHWH has power over *both* life and death.[270] In some cases, it would seem that God's salvation was needed *prior* to death (e.g., Ps 13:3: "Give light to my eyes, *lest* I sleep the sleep of death"; also 28:1; 143:7). At other times the psalmist states quite nakedly that God redeems from death (e.g., Ps 56:14: "You have delivered my soul from death"; also Pss 9:14; 49:15; 68:21; 103:4; Hos 13:14; Lam 3:55–58) and brings people up from Sheol (Pss 30:3; 86:13; Jonah 2:2). Gary Anderson has suggested that this progression from Sheol to salvation in the Psalms was somehow enacted ritually.[271] In more poetic terms, God is frequently said to have the power to turn darkness into light (Amos 5:8; Job 12:22, cf. Job 10:22), probably also evocative of salvation from death, since the tomb was characterized by darkness.[272]

---

[268] John T. Willis, "Song of Hannah and Psalm 113," *CBQ* 35 (1973): 147.

[269] Eberhardt repeatedly appeals to redaction-critical arguments or follows late dating schemes to explain such passages as these as postexilic.

[270] Bernd Janowski, *Konfliktgespräche mit Gott: Eine Anthropologie der Psalmen* (Neukirchen-Vluyn : Neukirchener Verlag, 2003). See also C. Barth, *Die Errettung vom Tode*, esp. part III.

[271] Anderson's foremost piece of evidence is Ps 30:9–13: "'What profit is there in my death, if I go down to the Pit? Will the dust praise you? Will it tell of your faithfulness? Hear, O LORD, and be gracious to me! O LORD, be my helper!' You turned my mourning into dancing,/ you stripped off my sackcloth,/ you girded me with joy./ Thus my heart will sing your praise and not be silent." He believes this reflects a "ritual descent to Sheol" followed by a inverse movement to deliverance (*A Time to Mourn, a Time to Dance: The Expression of Grief and Joy in Israelite Religion* [University Park, Pa.: Pennsylvania State University Press, 1991], 87–97).

YHWH's authority over death is also enacted by Elisha in the (admittedly exceptional) story of the Shunammite woman (2 Kgs 4:32–37; cf. 8:5). The man of God "personifies the deity,"[273] in this case channeling YHWH's power to raise the dead. In the same general context, Jehoram's question, "Am I God, to give death or life?" (2 Kgs 5:7) reflects the same assumption about YHWH's power.

In early strata of the book of Hosea, the assertion that YHWH raises the dead becomes the basis for images of his salvation of the nation:

> Come, let us return to the LORD;
> for it is he who has torn, and he will heal us (ירפאנו);
> he has struck down, and he will bind us up.
> After two days he will revive us (יחינו);
> on the third day he will raise us up (יקמנו),
> that we may live before him. (6:1–2; cf. 13:14)[274]

As with similar Mesopotamian imagery, some scholars have objected that this is not a description of resurrection, but only of healing[275] – but again, this introduces a modern distinction that was much less clear to the ancient authors (§ 1.4.3). Death was not different from sickness; the two phenomena existed on the same continuum, with death lying at one extreme end of the spectrum.[276] In any case, Hosea's use of the verb חיה establishes a lexical connection with much older ancient Near Eastern texts such as the Aqhat Epic (*k b'l . k yhwy . y'šr*, "As Baal, when he revives..."; *CAT* 1.17 vi 30–33; see § 3.3.3.2). Indeed, the idea of rising from the dead on the third day has precedents as ancient as the Sumerian Inanna traditions and Egyptian Osiris traditions.[277] John Day cleverly suggests that the Hosea account is part of the polemic against the cult of Baal. He argues that Hosea's message was that "it is not Baal who dies and rises but Israel that dies

---

[272] So already Heidel, *Gilgamesh Epic*, 219 n. 250: "'light' and 'life' are sometimes used as interchangeable terms."

[273] David L. Petersen, *The Prophetic Literature: An Introduction* (Louisville, Ky.: Westminster John Knox, 2002), 6. See also Levenson, who suggests that the eighth-century prophets' (esp. Hosea's) convictions about resurrection stemmed from folkloristic traditions such as these about Elisha (*Resurrection and the Restoration of Israel*, 206).

[274] It is notoriously difficult to place texts from Hosea in historical context, but 6:1–2 is located in what is usually taken to be one of the most securely "authentic" sections. Day places it in the eighth century ("Development of the Belief in Life after Death," 242). See also F. I. Andersen and D. N. Freedman, *Hosea: A New Translation with Introduction and Commentary* (AB 24; Garden City, N.Y.: Doubleday, 1980), 68–76, esp. 73. Wolff wrote that both these texts (6:1–2; 13:14) are in largely authentic sections of the book, although he thought that 6:1–3 may have been an early redactional insertion based on psalms with "Canaanized" themes.

[275] E.g., James Mays, *Hosea* (OTL; London: SCM, 1969), 95; H. W. Wolff, *Hosea* (Hermeneia; Philadelphia: Fortress, 1974), 117; Wilhelm Rudolph, *Hosea* (KAT 13/1; Gütersloh: G. Mohn, 1966), 135; G. I. Davies, *Hosea* (OTG; Grand Rapids: Eerdmans, 1992), 161.

[276] Levenson, *Resurrection and the Restoration of Israel*, 205; J. Andrew Dearman, *The Book of Hosea* (NICOT; Grand Rapids, Mich.: Eerdmans, 2010), 193–94.

[277] For references, see Wolff, *Hosea*, 117–18.

for worshipping Baal, followed, if repentant, by resurrection."²⁷⁸ Both חיה and קום are picked up again in later biblical references to resurrection (e.g., Isa 26:14, 19; Job 14:12, 14).²⁷⁹

To grasp the broad historical extent of these traditions regarding revivification is to recognize that the biblical texts cannot be fitted into a simple evolutionary model. It is no doubt true that Israelite thought about the restoration from death became more elaborate and central over time, but it is also true that from the early stages of biblical literature, YHWH was always portrayed as a god who had the power to save from death, and who was quite able to access and control the underworld, even if such actions were seen as exceptional. Surely expressions of belief in the raising of the dead have always been extravagant expressions of faith.

It seems unfruitful to ask whether they meant claims about revivificaiton "literally." Francis I. Andersen and David Noel Freedman formulated the matter carefully, and in my view correctly, in their comments on Hos 6:

> The language of resurrection can be used dramatically to describe the recovery of a sick person from illness ... but it does not follow that such language was exclusively metaphorical, and even if so, it must have been grounded in a certain type of expectation about the future life. Its currency testifies to the fact that the idea of resurrection after death was entertained.²⁸⁰

Certainly the Israelites had no systematized "doctrine of resurrection" in the preexilic period – in either the later Christian sense or the sense of any regular expectation – but just as certainly, they did claim that their God *could* raise the dead.²⁸¹

Interpreters who approach biblical texts strictly in terms of the history of religion and ask only what was a normative belief may not be attentive enough to the literary creativity of early Israelite authors, since any creative idea always begins as a minority perspective. As Ellen Davis has argued, Ps 22:30's reference to the dead as being under YHWH's rule is "better explained in terms of the poet's extravagance of expression than in terms of the more sober development of religious dogma."²⁸² How is one to assess what such authors *meant* by what

---

²⁷⁸ Day, "Development of the Belief in Life after Death," 245. For literature on dying and rising gods, see Tryggve N. D. Mettinger, *The Riddle of Resurrection: "Dying and Rising Gods" in the Ancient Near East* (Stockholm: Almqvist & Wiksell International, 2001); or Dearman, *The Book of Hosea*, 194–95.

²⁷⁹ Day, *Yahweh and the Gods*, 119.

²⁸⁰ Andersen and Freedman, *Hosea*, 421.

²⁸¹ It was presumably with an eye to the Christian doctrine that Robert Martin-Achard wrote: "The writers of these hymns [that speak of resurrection] did not envisage the resurrection of the dead, they are simply asserting that the Living God is able to intervene, effectively, everywhere and at all times, even in the darkest hour." Robert Martin-Achard, *From Death to Life: A Study of the Development of the Doctrine of the Resurrection in the Old Testament* (trans. J. P. Smith; Edinburgh: Oliver and Boyd, 1960), 57.

²⁸² Ellen F. Davis, "Exploding the Limits: Form and Function in Psalm 22," *JSOT* 53 (1992): 93–105.

they said? Nick Wyatt's comment about certain aspects of Ugaritic theology applies well to the Israelite rhetoric of resurrection: "The language ... was of course symbolic – when is language *not* symbolic? – but all the more real for so being."[283]

By the postexilic period, the "minority report" becomes more widespread, and it is patent that YHWH's authority extends to the underworld. This can be seen in texts like Ps 139:6–7 ("Where can I go from your spirit? Or where can I flee from your presence? If I ascend to heaven, you are there; if I make my bed in Sheol, you are there") or more bluntly still in Job 26:6 ("Sheol is naked before God, and Abaddon has no covering"). Similarly, in Job 38:17 YHWH asks, "Have the gates of death been shown to you? Have you seen the gates of the shadow of death?" – implying that they are indeed in YHWH's purview. Despite scattered allusions, there is no god of the underworld to challenge YHWH in the Hebrew Bible; he is a God of the living and the dead alike. This might be understood in terms of the development of monotheism: With the staunchly monotheistic pronouncements of Second Isaiah, YHWH *had* to be god of of the underworld, because there *was* "no other" (Isa 45:5–6, etc.).

Some caveats are in order. First, there are certainly conflicting, negative traditions about hope for YHWH's salvation after death. Job 7:9 says, "As a cloud vanishes and is gone, so the one who goes down to the grave does not return." And even a king such as David is portrayed as despairing of the return of his son: "Now he is dead; why should I fast? Can I bring him back again? I shall go to him, but he will not return to me" (1 Sam 12:23). Second, salvation from death is an exceptional and individual matter in the early periods of Israelite religion: one may pray for it, but it is not a general expectation, much less a dogma.[284] As is commonly observed, it is not until Isa 26 or Ezek 37 that biblical writers envisioned a group or national resurrection (see further discussion in § 5.2.4.2). Levenson has recently drawn attention back to this intermediate phase, in which resurrection is promise for the whole nation, but not for the whole world.[285] Scenes of national resurrection more detailed than those of Hosea are envisioned in Ezek 37 and Isa 26; the latter will be taken up in detail in the next chapter. Finally, one could even doubt that Dan 12 has intimations of a "doctrine of a general resurrection" – there it is still "many" (רבים) who will rise, not all. That is to say, Dan 12 is still some distance from Paul's interpretation of Isa 45:23 in Rom 14:10–11: "For we will all (πάντες) stand before the judgment seat of God. For it

---

[283] N. Wyatt, "The Religion of Ugarit: An Overview," in *Handbook of Ugaritic Studies* (ed. W. G. E. Watson and N. Wyatt; Leiden: Brill, 1999), 561.

[284] So also Eberhardt, *JHWH und die Unterwelt*, 394.

[285] Levenson, *Resurrection and the Restoration of Israel*. As Childs pointed out, this is not entirely a new observation ("Death and Dying in Old Testament Theology," 90). Nationalistic resurrection is, at a later point, reinterpreted as individual resurrection, as in the Qumran pseudo-Ezekiel text 4Q385.

is written, 'As I live, says the Lord, every knee shall bow to me, and every tongue (πᾶν γόνυ καὶ πᾶσα γλῶσσα) shall give praise to God.' "

Although Judah did not know of a belief in a group (let alone universal) resurrection in the period of Isaiah's career, the ideas that YHWH saved from death and had power over Sheol predated him. That the gods had the power to revive the dead in some way was known much earlier in Ugarit (Baal) and Mesopotamia (Marduk) and was a central point of Egyptian religion. In chapter 5, I discuss the particular literary and theological use of similar claims in Isaiah (see esp. §§ 5.2.2.3–4; 5.2.4).

4.5 Historical conclusions

The late Iron Age in Judah, the cradle of the book of Isaiah, was a point of convergence, a beach washed by the various currents of the whole Near East. In the matter of beliefs and practices surrounding death, the complex pattern left behind in the sand shows similarities to each of the surrounding cultures, but also differences. This was the situation into which the prophets waded.

A handful of the beliefs and practices reflected in the Bible were common to the entire ancient Near East: the fear of an unhappy afterlife; the conviction that proper burial was a necessity and that the deceased needed some material provision, however simple, for the journey to the afterlife; mourning customs such as sackcloth and wailing; and the idea of sickness as a demonic affliction.

Judeans shared other tenets with at least some of their neighbors: the imagery of the underworld as dusty and dark, but conversely the hope to be with the deity in a better life to come; the belief that its god could save from death; the use of necromancy; a special concern for dead kin as a link to the land; the institution of the *mrzḥ* and the idea of the mighty dead as *rpʾm*; the personification of Death and the cult of a chthonic deity *Mlk*; and perhaps child sacrifice in times of crisis. To be certain, many of these are somewhat submerged, in the Masoretic form of the biblical text, beneath the theological editing of tradents and scribes.

Conclusions about the roots of the aforementioned similarities are necessarily bound up with assumptions about the origins of Israel and its religion. The complexity of those matters means that catchphrases and simple models will not serve well. Just as Israel likely coalesced as a "mixed multitude" from different populations and different backgrounds[286] and lived as one nation among many in ancient Palestine, so its religion reflected these multiple influences.

No doubt some of the similarities are due to the influence and appeal of

---

[286] See Ann E. Killebrew, *Biblical Peoples and Ethnicity: An Archaeological Study of Egyptians, Canaanites, Philistines, and Early Israel (ca. 1300–1100 B.C.E.)* (Archaeology and Biblical Studies 9; Atlanta: Society of Biblical Literature, 2005), 149–96.

4.5 Historical conclusions   191

foreign religions. Yahwists were certainly prone to co-opt elements of other cults; to take a familiar example, Baal the Cloud-Rider becomes YHWH the Cloud-Rider (Ps 68:5; Isa 19:1).[287] J. J. M. Roberts has remarked that Yahwism's "ability to take up elements of its environment, even hostile elements, and transform them into supporting structures" is part of its essence.[288] Isaiah and his early tradents were masters of that process, as the following chapter will show.

Nevertheless, it certainly seems that some form of ancestor cult and belief in afterlife and resurrection was as "indigenous" to Israelite religion as anything else. As Spronk wrote, "when ideas are borrowed from other religions this practically always implies that these ideas fit in with a development within the borrowing religion itself."[289] The "borrowing" culture or religion is somehow fertile, ready to receive the idea that is borrowed; often similar beliefs and practices are already present, albeit in less prominent forms. In other words, Israel would be particularly susceptible to new religious influence from, say, Assyria, in instances where its Syro-Palestinian traditioning already supplied a foothold. Specifically, it might be theorized that the Assyrian fascination with the underworld found a home in Israel because of the preexisting West Semitic tradition of cults of the dead. In any case, the religious situation in Judah must be treated as a distinct entity and evaluated primarily on the basis of the indigenous data, rather than under the assumption that influence from Assyria or other nations was determinative.

In that vein, there are a number of points at which, in the biblical portrait, Israelite religion differed from those of its neighbors: its preference for bench tombs; its prohibition of excessive mourning practices such as gashing the flesh and shaving the head; its distinctive terminology for the underworld; its extensive polemic about the weakened state of the dead (and its lack of connection between demons and the dead); its emphatic concern for defilement by contact with the dead.

It is not surprising that Israel's God – whose jealousy was both famous and ancient (Exod 20:5, etc.)[290] – should have been understood to bristle at sharing worshipers' attention with powers of the underworld. Therefore, such powers eventually moved from being benignly tolerated to being perceived as inherently

---

[287] On Ps 68, see, e.g., W. F. Albright, *Yahweh and the Gods of Canaan*, 26–28; Bill T. Arnold and Brent A. Strawn, "*b'yāh š'mô* in Psalm 68,5: A Hebrew Gloss on an Ugaritic Epithet?," *ZAW* 115 (2003): 428–32.

[288] J. J. M. Roberts, "In Defense of the Monarchy: The Contribution of Israelite Kingship to Biblical Theology," in *Ancient Israelite Religion: Essays in Honor of Frank Moore Cross* (ed. P. D. Miller, Jr. et al.; Philadelphia: Fortress, 1987), 380. Mark S. Smith might call this process "convergence"; see *Early History of God*, 54–59.

[289] Spronk, *Beatific Afterlife*, 85.

[290] Cf. Miller, *Religion of Ancient Israel*, 14; Robert P. Gordon, "Introducing the God of Israel," in *The God of Israel* (ed. Robert P. Gordon; Cambridge: Cambridge University Press, 2007), 6.

demonic and deadly. This issue came to a head over necromancy, which, as chapter 5 demonstrates, was frequently seen as being in competition with the word of YHWH.

Even if such a generalized account is correct, it is not complete. One must take seriously the coexistence of competing and even conflicting beliefs and practices in monarchic Judah. Jerusalem would have been host to an assortment of competing religions, and to competing viewpoints and practices within Yahwism itself.[291] The competition and conflict among viewpoints is what gives so many biblical texts their passionate force. Sometimes the "opposing" views about death and the dead are submerged and scorned (Deuteronomy); at other times they are ridiculed and subverted (Isa 14); and sometimes they are so present and alive in the text that it is hard to know which is the "dominant" view (Job; 1 Sam 28). At other times, "outside" views even breach the canon itself (Ecclesiastes), so that an "inside-outside"/orthodox-vs.-heretical model loses its coherence. Nevertheless, the reconstruction offered here does posit that "mainstream" Yahwistic views existed (and that they changed over time). There is no reason to believe that ancestor worship was ever an integral part of Yahwism, only one that was tolerated; just as the *kispu* was a separate phenomenon from the worship of high gods and national deities in Mesopotamia, so, likely, were comparable practices in Israel.[292]

The question of prohibition of death-cult practices is a separate one. As far as texts can tell us, it would seem to be first in the eighth-century prophets, roughly contemporaneous with the reforms initiated by Hezekiah, that one sees a broad critique of death cults. The argument of Bloch-Smith and Smith that necromancy was forbidden early on is cogent, and I would add that human sacrifice, which was probably never practiced with regularity in Israel, probably came under criticism at about the same time. However, if the "reforming kings" of the Iron Age (primarily Josiah and Hezekiah) succeeded in imposing any sort of "orthodoxy," it probably was very limited in geographical extent and inconsistently enforced over time. It needs only to be pointed out that this time of religious change and conflict coincided with Isaiah's career.

---

[291] Insofar as Jerusalem was the multicultural city that archaeology indicates, there were certainly cultural elements in Judah that preserved beliefs and practices that would be condemned by the Yahwists who composed the Bible. See Elizabeth Bloch-Smith, "Israelite Ethnicity in Iron I: Archaeology Preserves What Is Remembered and What Is Forgotten in Israel's History," *JBL* 122 (2003): 425; also Friedman and Overton, "Death and Afterlife," 56. These elements no doubt were part of what biblical authors characterized as "Canaanite."

[292] That is not to say that there was no royal cult of the dead which would have taken on a nationalistic flavor; Charles A. Kennedy went too far when he asserted that the Israelite cult of the dead was "totally divorced from public and national concerns" ("Dead, Cult of the," *ABD* 2:108).

4.6 The Rhetoric of Death in the Hebrew Bible

4.6.1 Rhetoric and the Bible

Having surveyed the cultural backgrounds of death in the ancient world during the period when much of Isa 1–39 was composed, one can now turn and observe more clearly the ways in which the background was taken up and employed in the book to serve rhetorical ends.

The term "rhetoric" may require some clarification. I am not working with an especially "thick" definition, but rather a simple one: rhetoric, according to the *Oxford English Dictionary*, is "the art of using language so as to persuade or influence others."[293] This sense of rhetoric is more fundamental than either the various schools of "rhetorical criticism" within biblical studies, or even the Greeks' scholastic systematizations. As George Kennedy has observed, rhetoric existed before "rhetoric" –

...that is, before it had the name that came to designate it as a specific area of study. 'Rhetoric' in this broader sense is a universal phenomenon, one found even among animals, for individuals everywhere seek to persuade others to take or refrain from some action, or to hold or discard some belief.[294]

One may, therefore, speak of rhetoric in ancient Near Eastern prophecy in general, and specifically in Isaiah, since inspiring action and belief was surely among the goals of the texts studied here.

"Rhetoric" comes from the Greek ῥητορική – "the art of speaking" – a term that captures an important aspect of Isaian rhetoric. The reigning assumption of this study is that many of the oracles of Isaiah can still best be understood as delivered *to their initial historical context*, although all have been reframed, and many altered, in later stages. As I noted at the outset, I assume that the prophecies of Isaiah ben Amoz were initially compiled in the reign of Hezekiah, and I share the increasingly popular conclusion that a major edition of the book was produced during the reign of Josiah – prior to its augmentation and reframing in the exilic and postexilic periods.[295] Only with respect to the passages in Isa 25 and 26 do I expect this conclusion to be particularly controversial.

Isaiah's oracles would have been compiled in a manner similar to the way that contemporaneous Neo-Assyrian prophecies were compiled and edited in the

---

[293] *OED*, s.v. "rhetoric" (accessed electronically). Ruth Majerick offers a slightly broader definition: "Rhetoric is the art of composition by which language is made descriptive, interpretive, or persuasive" ("Rhetoric and Rhetorical Criticism," *ABD* 5:710).

[294] George Kennedy, *Comparative Rhetoric: An Historical and Cross-Cultural Introduction* (Oxford: Oxford University Press, 1998), 3.

[295] See the recent review of literature by Matthijs J. de Jong, *Isaiah among the Ancient Near Eastern Prophets: A Comparative Study of the Earliest Stages of the Isaiah Tradition and the Neo-Assyrian Prophecies* (VTSup 117; Leiden: Brill, 2007), 7–10.

years shortly after their delivery, in response to major events. The individual texts surveyed in the following chapter all have a literary character, but literary elements were often added to, for example, Neo-Assyrian prophecies very shortly after their delivery.[296] Neo-Assyrian oracles were often incorporated into historical or literary texts within the lifetimes of the kings to whom they were delivered.[297] It would be a mistake to assume that literary reworkings of prophecies are necessarily late. In the case of the thirteen pericopae studied here, a case can be made that all are from the seventh century or earlier (with due allowance for ongoing, light editing and the corruptions that accrue from repeated copying).

What does it mean to read prophetic rhetoric in context? As I have already noted in the general introduction, I share Laurent Pernot's assumption that "rhetoric is tied to historical settings, to social, political, and intellectual conditions."[298] Thus, the reader of Isaiah does well to try to enter imaginatively into the world in which these oracles were first delivered. A significant scholarly tradition has laid the groundwork for reading the prophets, and Isaiah in particular, within their historical and social contexts.[299]

I hope to recapture some of the *immediacy* of these texts. There is a dense, prepared character to Isaiah's speeches; they are rich with allusions and *double entendres*. But preparation is a mark of great rhetoricians. Thus, no strict distinction is made here between "spoken" and "literary," as many scholars have done, because its confuses more than it clarifies.[300] The earlier assumption that the utterances of early Israelite prophets could not have been more than brief exclamations can confidently be judged incorrect in light of the increasing awareness of the sophistication of oral compositions and performances in the ancient world.[301]

---

[296] De Jong, *Isaiah among the Ancient Near Eastern Prophets*, 357–442.

[297] See Martti Nissinen, *Prophets and Prophecy in the Ancient Near East* (WAW 12; Atlanta: Society of Biblical Literature, 2003), 133–77.

[298] Laurent Pernot, *Rhetoric in Antiquity* (trans. W. E. Higgins; Washington, D.C.: Catholic University of America Press, 2005), xii.

[299] Petersen, *Prophetic Literature*, 8–12, 50–60; John H. Hayes and Stuart A. Irvine, *Isaiah: the Eighth-Century Prophet: His Times and His Preaching* (Nashville: Abingdon Press, 1987), 17–66; see further bibliography in chapter 1 n. 62 above.

[300] It is difficult to determine precisely where certain studies place Isaiah on the old continuum that Gunkel stretched out between spoken and written prophecy. Even Gunkel himself is not clear, referring to the beginnings of written prophecy as "a few brief words such as Isaiah wrote or sealed, or ... a few extensive proverbs or poems." See Hermann Gunkel, "The Prophets: Oral and Written" in *Water for a Thirsty Land: Israelite Literature and Religion* (ed. K. C. Hanson; Fortress Classics in Biblical Studies; Minneapolis: Fortress, 2001), 85–133, 134–70, here 89. (If a "poem" as large as Isa 14:4b–21 is what Gunkel had in mind, then we have no disagreement.) G. Kennedy, too, is somewhat equivocal, but could be understood to doubt the likelihood of eloquent spoken prophecy: "Prophets may be assumed to have gone about the county crying 'woe,' but the dramatic synthesis into a dialogic frame, as found in our texts, can only be imagined as a product of written composition, drawing on varied sources, subject to scribal editing" (Kennedy, *Comparative Rhetoric*, 137).

4.6 The Rhetoric of Death in the Hebrew Bible 195

There is reason to think that extended oral performance from memory was common in antiquity. As the famous speech of Thamus in Plato's *Phaedrus* shows, the idea that verbal artistry requires writing is a modern prejudice. Thamus's comment was that writing would only "create forgetfulness in learners' souls" (*Phaedr.* 275). At the risk of comparing apples to oranges, the reader might recall that the lengthy orations of Homeric epic are assigned to roughly the same period as that of the preexilic edition of Isaiah.[302]

If one compares prophetic oracles from elsewhere in the ancient Near East, the enigmatic and terse reports of prophets at Mari may condition the reader to conclude with Hermann Gunkel that originally prophecy was limited to brief statements. And indeed, certain aspects of Isaiah's career (such as the performance of Isa 20) do reflect less verbose prophetic traditions. However, in a body of work much closer to him in history, the Neo-Assyrian prophecies, one frequently finds prophecies of a length equal to roughly five to ten biblical verses.[303] Some of the passages studied in the next chapter are slightly longer than that, but that does not necessarily mean that they are composite. Along with the similarities between Judean and Neo-Assyrian prophecies there are differences, and Matthijs J. de Jong points out that one of these is that prophets seem to have had a larger stature in Judah than in the grander society of Assyria: "Whereas the Assyrian prophets remained in obscurity, Isaiah's star rose quickly."[304] It may be that the preservation of longer oracles is related to Isaiah's greater stature.

Overviews of recent scholarship regarding prophetic rhetoric are readily available, and I will not repeat them here.[305] For readers familiar with that body of literature, suffice it to say what the preceding chapters already indicate: that this study is one of many that seek to reestablish the historical grounding of biblical rhetoric in the wake of literary approaches that have become "more and more

---

[301] See particularly Susan Niditch, *Oral World and Written Word* (Louisville, Ky.: Westminster John Knox, 1996). Also, Donald B. Redford notes the two-way process of textualization and performance: performances could be written down, and texts could be performed: "History and Egyptology," in *Egyptology Today* (ed. R. H. Wilkinson; Cambridge: Cambridge University Press, 2008), 27–30.

[302] On older theories of classicists regarding the formation of the Homeric epics, and the tendency of earlier generations of scholars perceive that long oral compositions were unlikely, see Albert B. Lord, *The Singer of Tales* (Cambridge, Mass.: Harvard University Press, 1964), 10–12.

[303] Simo Parpola, *Assyrian Prophecies* (SAA 9; Helsinki: Helsinki University Press, 1997), *passim*; Nissinen, *Prophets and Prophecy in the Ancient Near East*, 97–132.

[304] De Jong, *Isaiah among the Ancient Near Eastern Prophets*, 459. R. R. Wilson noted some time ago that Isaiah was taken as an important and "central" prophet by both the Deuteronomistic and Chronistic authors. See *Prophecy and Society in Ancient Israel* (Philadelphia: Fortress, 1980), 270–74.

[305] A very readable and up-to-date summary is provided by Brad E. Kelle, *Hosea 2: Metaphor and Rhetoric in Historical Perspective* (Academia Biblica 20; Atlanta: Society of Biblical Literature, 2005), 21–34.

detached from historical criticism."[306] However welcome and beneficial those methods are, they should not cause the reader to lose sight of the fact that, like other ancient Near Eastern prophecies, "[Isaiah's] oracles relate to particular historical circumstances, and [Isaiah] sought to interfere in events of major political significance."[307]

Thus, the guiding assumption here is that the book of Isaiah's rhetorical pieces were "designed to achieve certain results with a given audience in a particular setting," and that one should attempt to describe the "rhetorical-historical situation" of a text.[308] That does not mean merely an historical period but the "discursive universe" of the text:[309] its genre, the cultural (and religious) milieu in which it originated, and its audience and their presumed interpretive competencies.[310] The discussions of mechanisms of influence in chapters 1 and 2 are intended to suggest ways in which certain ideas that were not prominent in the Syro-Palestinian stream of tradition might have entered the "discursive universe" of an eighth-century Judean prophet.

4.6.2 Uses of the rhetoric of death the Hebrew Bible

The passages in Isaiah that I propose to study are only a few examples from a rather large body of texts within biblical literature that employ imagery of life and death for rhetorical ends. A survey of references to death suggests that the rhetorical employment of death in the Hebrew Bible is rather straightforward and most often falls into certain distinct categories, appearing in four contexts: (1)

---

[306] Kelle, *Hosea 2*, 28. Kelle is speaking of what he calls the "Muilenburg school" of rhetorical criticism, but the comment is even more true when viewed more broadly. The drifting of rhetorical concerns from historical context was not Muilenburg's original intention, as is attested by his comment "The prophets do not speak *in abstracto*, but concretely" (James Muilenburg, "Form Criticism and Beyond," *JBL* 88 [1969]: 6). On history and rhetorical criticism, see also Thomas B. Dozeman, "OT Rhetorical Criticism," *ABD* 5:712.

[307] De Jong, *Isaiah among the Ancient Near Eastern Prophets*, 463.

[308] Kelle, *Hosea 2*, 33, 27.

[309] Cf. Stefan Alkier, "Die Bibel im Dialog der Schriften und das Problem der Verstockung in Mk 4: Intertextualität im Rahmen einer kategorialen Semiotik biblischer Texte," in *Die Bibel im Dialog der Schriften: Konzepte Intertextueller Bibellektüre* (ed. S. Alkier and R. B. Hays; Tübingen: Francke, 2005), 1–22, esp. 6–11.

[310] This last item, the audience's interpretive competency, is not to be taken as decisive. Ancient Near Eastern texts are full of plays on words and signs that could not have been understood by a very wide audience. Thorkild Jacobsen has observed that in the Sumero-Akkadian scribal culture, "scribes of the first millennium B.C.E. ... were conversant with a highly artificial and abstruse style in which to compose cryptic pseudo-Sumerian texts.... [O]ne can only guess that such a style was considered a proof of supreme learning" (Thorkild Jacobsen, "Abstruse Sumerian," in *Ah, Assyria...: Studies in Assyrian History and Ancient Near Eastern Historiography Presented to Hayim Tadmor* [ed. Mordechai Cogan and Israel Eph'al; Jerusalem: Magnes Press, 1991], 291). Comparable phenomena may be found to some extent in biblical texts.

psalmic laments; (2) legal punishment clauses; (3) wisdom dichotomies (or alternatives); and (4) prophetic judgment-speeches.[311] All of these traditions would have been well developed by the time of Isaiah ben Amoz's career, and all of them draw on death's negative connotations, holding up death as an unwelcome destination and as a punishment. One could identify a fifth, "pessimistic" tradition in which death is welcomed, which stands in some tension with the aforementioned types of rhetoric.[312] However, examples of that view are so uncommon as to call into question its status as a "tradition"; better to call it a reaction *against* tradition.

The rhetoric of death in psalmic laments has already been alluded to above (§ 4.4.4); in the Psalms, as in much older Mesopotamian prayers, supplicants frequently describe their suffering in terms of encroaching death. For example, Ps 18:5–6: "The cords of death encompassed me; the torrents of perdition assailed me; the cords of Sheol entangled me; the snares of death confronted me." In such passages, the rhetorical purpose is to impel God to act on one's behalf, or to emphasize the depths of suffering from which God has saved the speaker who is giving thanks.

Another very early manifestation would have been in legal material; death is threatened as a punishment in every ancient Near Eastern law collection. For example, the Book of the Covenant includes repeated provisions that various kinds of transgressors "will surely be put to death" (מוֹת יוּמָת; Exod 21:12, 15, 16, 17, 28, 29; 22:2, 19). Although presented as actual punishments, such death-penalty clauses also had an apodictic aspect; from a rhetorical standpoint they were meant to be just as absolute as the commandments of the Decalogue.[313] Death is the ultimate and final legal punishment.

Another strand of rhetoric with a strong claim to antiquity is the "two paths" motif in biblical wisdom literature,[314] for example, Prov 14:12: "There is a way that seems right to a person, but its end is the way to death." By contrast, "In the path of righteousness there is life, in walking its path there is no death" (Prov 12:28). Other examples of this motif include Prov 15:24; 16:25; 21:16; 28:18; and Ps 1 in its entirety (culminating with "the way of the wicked will perish"). If one expands the horizon slightly, to include texts in which wisdom is equated with

---

[311] I use Claus Westermann's term (*Basic Forms of Prophetic Speech* [trans. Hugh Clayton White; Louisville, Ky.: Westminster John Knox, 1991], 129–209), but the form-critical nomenclature is not of primary importance.

[312] This may be seen most obviously in Job (e.g., 3:11: "Why did I not perish at birth, and die as I came from the womb?"). However, it can also be seen in cases of prophets' feeling persecuted, e.g.. Moses (Num 11:15), Elijah (1 Kgs 19:4), and Jeremiah (20:7–18, etc.).

[313] Rifat Sonsino, "Law (Forms of Biblical Law)," *ABD* 4:252.

[314] On the imagery of "path" in general, see William P. Brown, *Seeing the Psalms: A Theology of Metaphor* (Louisville: Westminster John Knox, 2002), 32–53. Also Richard W. Medina, "Life and Death Viewed as Physical and Lived Spaces: Some Preliminary Thoughts from Proverbs," *ZAW* 122 (2010): 199–211.

life and its rejection with death, the instances pile up more quickly still: Prov 13:14; 14:27; 21:6; 23:14; etc.[315] Various Hebrew terms are used for the two paths – e.g., דרך, ארח, נתיבה – and the metaphors of snares[316] and wandering (e.g., Prov 21:16) are related to the same "path" imagery, so the images seem to spring from a common and ancient tradition rather than demonstrating literary associations between texts. Unlike in the legal material, a certain mythological aspect is apparent in many of these texts; the repercussions are not merely physical death, but consignment to the unhappy underworld. This is clear in cases where the Strange Woman (אשה זרה) is the hostess of Sheol and the guide on its path: "Her house is the way to Sheol, going down to the chambers of death" (Prov 7:27); "Her feet go down to death, her steps follow the way to Sheol" (Prov 5:5; cf. also 2:18; 8:35–36; 9:1; Eccl 7:26). Assmann has observed of Egyptian thought that in some contexts "the phrase 'life and death' is tantamount to 'good and evil,'"[317] and so this is another among the affinities between Israelite and Egyptian wisdom.

The motif of the choice between life and death explodes in the classical prophets and in Deuteronomistic literature, which may be related corpora, with both emerging from the Neo-Assyrian and Neo-Babylonian periods. The close of Moses' monologue in Deut 30 may be the most prominent manifestation:

> See, I have set before you today life and prosperity, death and adversity. If you obey the commandments of the LORD your God that I am commanding you today, by loving the LORD your God, walking in his ways, and observing his commandments, decrees, and ordinances, then you shall live and become numerous, and the LORD your God will bless you in the land that you are entering to possess. But if your heart turns away and you do not hear, but are led astray to bow down to other gods and serve them, I declare to you today that you shall perish; you shall not live long in the land that you are crossing the Jordan to enter and possess. I call heaven and earth to witness against you today that I have set before you life and death, blessings and curses. Choose life so that you and your descendants may live. (Deut 30:15–19)

Precisely the same sort of rhetoric manifests itself more concisely in the exhortations of the prophets, particularly by the time of the exile:

> And to this people you shall say: Thus says the LORD: See, I am setting before you the way of life and the way of death. (Jer 21:8)

---

[315] Language of hunters' snares such as that of 14:27 – "The fear of the LORD is a fountain of life, so that one may avoid the snares of death" – perhaps suggests another taproot in psalmic poetic language, e.g., Ps 18:5; 2 Sam 22:6. The image of snares may be another way to express the idea, "be careful where you walk." See Peter Riede, *Im Netz des Jägers: Studien zur Feindmetaphorik der Individualpsalmen* (Neukirchen-Vluyn: Neukirchener Verlag, 2000).

[316] See also the passage concerning the "wicked woman" in 4Q184, which says, "her paths are paths of death ... Her gates are the gates of death, in the entrance to her house Sheol proceeds. All those who go to her will not come back, and all those who inherit her will descend to the pit" (ll. 9–11).

[317] Assmann, *Death and Salvation*, 285.

4.6 The Rhetoric of Death in the Hebrew Bible

Have I any pleasure in the death of the wicked, says the Lord GOD, and not rather that they should turn from their ways and live? (Ezek 18:23; cf. 18:32)

Say to them, As I live, says the Lord GOD, I have no pleasure in the death of the wicked, but that the wicked turn from their ways and live; turn back, turn back from your evil ways; for why will you die, O house of Israel? (Ezek 33:11)

One might conclude, then, that the "wisdom alternative" was taken up by the prophets[318] (and put in the mouth of Moses, the paradigmatic prophet[319]) particularly after the eighth century. Since there is no evidence of this motif in Israelite literature prior to Isaiah, one might conclude that Isaiah was primarily responsible for raising the "life-or-death alternative" to prominence as a major rhetorical device, elaborating the "two paths" theology found in wisdom literature in a complex and influential way.

It would require a more detailed study to determine the most likely cultural taproot of the motif prior to its incorporation in biblical literature. However, it is notable that the motif of the choice between life and death is characteristic of military rhetoric, as besieging powers frequently offered that choice to the besieged city, hoping to avoid the trouble of a siege (see §§ 1.2; 5.2.1.4).

A final major type of rhetoric employing imagery of death is found most often in prophetic judgment speeches (or "prophecies of disaster"[320]) and might be characterized as "aversion therapy" – the association of certain beliefs and actions with death imagery so graphic and horrifying as to make them unappealing.[321] This most commonly takes the form of the exposure of corpses. This was an awful fate because it denied a restful afterlife to the ones exposed (§§ 1.4.1; 2.5.4.1); it was also, of course, repulsive at a purely natural level. The repeated

---

[318] Samuel Terrien saw influence of wisdom traditions about death in Amos, although he did not mention this specific theme in his brief article ("Amos and Wisdom" in B. W. Anderson and W. Harrelson, eds., *Israel's Prophetic Heritage: Essays in Honor of James Muilenburg* [ed. B. W. Anderson and W. Harrelson; New York: Harper & Bros., 1962], 110–11).

[319] David Petersen explores the relationship between Moses and the prophets in "The Ambiguous Role of Moses as Prophet," in *Israel's Prophets and Israel's Past: Essays on the Relationship of Prophetic Texts and Israelite History in Honor of John H. Hayes* (ed. B. E. Kelle and M. B. Moore; New York: T&T Clark, 2006), 311–24. Petersen concludes that the identification of Moses as a prophet is a relatively late phenomenon, and that a text such as Deut 34:10 is actually a move to limit the prestige of prophecy, since no prophet has come along to match Moses. If that is the case, it may be that the retrojection of the theme of life and death into Moses' message served a similar purpose: it asserted that Moses had already "modeled" the themes of the prophets' proclamations.

[320] Eugene March, "Prophecy," in *Old Testament Form Criticism* (TUMSR 2; ed. John H. Hayes; San Antonio: Trinity University Press, 1977), 159–62.

[321] According to G. Kennedy, there are three types of "artistic" rhetoric in the Western tradition: ethos (credibility of the speaker), logos (rational argumentation), and pathos (awakening the audience's emotions) (*Comparative Rhetoric*, 6). Isaiah's use of underworld imagery falls almost entirely under the third heading, intending to inspire a visceral sense of revulsion. On the other hand, a passage such as ch. 6, with its claim to divine mission, seeks to build ethos.

threat of corpse exposure suggests a particularly strong aversion to the dead body in Judean culture. Thus, in addition to the aforementioned factors, cultic-purity issues and legal prohibitions of contact with the dead were probably also at work.[322]

"Aversion therapy" was taken up by Isaiah, as ch. 5 will show, and Jeremiah and Ezekiel seize on it with special enthusiasm, becoming the exemplars of the technique:[323]

Thus says the LORD: "Human corpses shall fall like dung upon the open field, like sheaves behind the reaper, and no one shall gather them." (Jer 9:22; cf. 7:33–8:2)

I will fling you [Pharaoh] into the wilderness, you and all the fish of your channels; you shall fall in the open field, and not be gathered or picked up. To the animals of the earth and to the birds of the air I have given you as food. (Ezek 29:5; cf. 6:5–7)

Grotesque imagery of the dead – particularly the accursed dead – is used for rhetorical purposes in various instances around the ancient Near East,[324] but it is likely that such imagery in the prophets reflects Judeans' direct historical familiarity with the horrors of warfare, suffered at the hands of the Mesopotamians. In some cases, such as Nah 3:1–3, this is particularly clear:

Hôy, city of bloodshed, utterly deceitful, full of booty – no end to the plunder! The crack of whip and rumble of wheel, galloping horse and bounding chariot! Horsemen charging, flashing sword and glittering spear, piles of dead, heaps of corpses, dead bodies without end – they stumble over the bodies!

Such physical dispersal of corpses runs as a literary motif throughout the inscriptions of the Assyrian kings:

Texts as early as Šalmaneser I [described] enemy corpses covering wide plains, ravines, wadis, ditches, city streets and squares, filling entire valleys – like *ašagu*-shrub in the desert, like herds of cattle after a plague. Corpses are carried away by rivers (as early as Tiglath-

---

[322] I am sympathetic to the newer theories that argue that at least parts of the Priestly and Holiness codes already existed in the eighth century BCE. See Moshe Weinfeld, *The Place of the Law in the Religion of Ancient Israel* (Leiden: Brill, 2004), *passim*; Knohl, *Sanctuary of Silence*, 200–213. The idea that the purity laws regarding contact with dead were already in place early on is specifically supported by Friedman and Overton ("Death and Afterlife," 54).

[323] So also Brichto, "Kin, Cult, Land and Afterlife," 37. On Jeremiah's "rhetoric of horror," see Amy Kalmanofsky, *Terror All Around: The Rhetoric of Horror in the Book of Jeremiah* (London: Continuum, 2008).

[324] For example, from the Egyptian Book of Caverns (eighth century B.C.), one finds a description of a cauldron containing "the heads and hearts of the damned, a second simmer[ing] with their bound bodies, upended and headless, and a third ... reserved for their souls, their shades and their 'meat.' Traversing above, the Sun-god admonishes the demons and serpents to do their duty: 'spew flame, kindle the flames beneath that cauldron bearing the enemies of Osiris!' There is 'no escape' here either: 'you are butchered in the Place of Destruction, your souls are destroyed, and your shades too.'" For discussion of this and other Egyptian examples, see Erik Hornung, "Black Holes Viewed From Within: Hell in Ancient Egyptian Thought," *Diogenes* 42 (1994): 133–56.

pileser I), they "cover the surface of the sea" (Šalmaneser III), are even piled up to the edge of the sea (Sargon II). In two cases (Šalmaneser III, Aššurbanipal), the king claims to have dammed major rivers (the Orontes, the Ulai) with corpses. Human blood dyes rivers, fields, mountains, the sea, and even flows through mountain creek beds and city-streets "like a river."[325]

Indeed, Delbert Hillers has argued that these images are a direction reflection of Mesopotamian curses.[326] Thus the Assyrian kings were simply asserting that they had done what they had promised to do to those who opposed their power.

The recurrent focus on corpse exposure and piles of dead bodies in prophetic literature suggests that the theme froze into a fixed literary topos at some point, but there is no sign that this was so prior to Isaiah's prophetic career. The vast destruction and carnage of the Neo-Assyrians' regional campaigns first reached Israel and Judah during that time, which suggests his work as a natural leaping-off point for the literary motif.

---

[325] Seth Richardson, "Death and Dismemberment in Mesopotamia: Discorporation Between the Body and the Body Politic" in *Performing Death: Social Analyses of Funerary Traditions in the Ancient Near East and Mediterranean* (ed. N. Lanieri; Chicago: University of Chicago Press, 2007), 189–208, here 200. See citations of primary texts there.

[326] Delbert R. Hillers, *Treaty-Curses and the Old Testament Prophets* (Rome: Pontifical Biblical Institute, 1964), 68–69. Interestingly, Hillers cites parallels from the *Maqlû* incantation series (IV 42–44; VIII 85–89) rather than historical texts or treaties.

5. The Rhetoric of Death in Isaiah 1–39

5.1 Introduction

Having sketched the cultural backgrounds of death in the ancient world during the time in which much of Isa 1–39 was composed, it is now possible to observe more clearly the ways in which that backdrop was transposed in the book to serve rhetorical ends.[1] This chapter identifies the occurrences of death imagery in the book and analyzes their rhetorical functions. Although the project centers on religious and theological rhetoric, I have argued that such rhetoric is only comprehensible in light of historical, cultural, and political realities (§ 4.6.1).

5.2 Texts

5.2.1 Threats of unhappy afterlife

Death imagery in Isaiah frequently appears in threats of unhappy afterlife. Nowhere in the book is that motif developed more extensively than in the taunt song about the fallen king in ch. 14:

5.2.1.1 Isaiah 14:4–23: The tyrant in Sheol

(1) For the LORD will take pity on Jacob,
   and will again choose Israel
   And he will give them rest upon their land.
And the sojourner will join himself to them

---

[1] I borrow the idea of transposition from Julia Kristeva, for whom it was a preferred alternative to "intertextuality." Transposition refers to "the passage from one signifying system to another." See Kristeva, *La revolution du langage poétique: L'avant-garde à la fin du XIXe siècle: Lautréamont at Mallarmé* (Paris: Seuil, 1974), 60. In this case, the transposition is out of the various other cultures already described, and into Isaiah's text. See Christopher B. Hays, "Echoes of the Ancient Near East?: Intertextuality and the Comparative Study of the Old Testament" in *The Word Leaps the Gap: Essays on Scripture and Theology in Honor of Richard B. Hays* (eds. J. Ross Wagner et al.; Winona Lake, Ind.: Eerdmans, 2009), 20–43.

And attach himself to the house of Jacob.[2]
(2) And nations shall seize them and bring them to their place. But the house of Israel shall possess them upon the LORD's land as male and female slaves.
(3) And they shall be captors to their captors;
And have dominion over those who oppressed them.
On that day the Lord will give rest to you from your suffering and turmoil
And from the hard service that you were made to serve.
(4) Then you shall lift up this *māšāl*[3] against the king of Babylon:

How the oppressor has ceased!
(How) the flood[4] has receded!
(5) The Lord has broken the rod of the wicked,
and the staff of the oppressors.
(6) The one who battered the peoples in rage,
– battery without respite –
who dominated the nations with anger,
relentless persecution.
(7) (Now) all the earth is at rest, at peace,
They burst out in song!
(8) Even the junipers and cedars of Lebanon are joyful:
"Since you were laid low, no logger comes up for us!"
(9) Sheol below stirs to meet your arrival,
the Rephaim rouse themselves,
all the chiefs of the land arise from their thrones,
all the kings of the nations.
(10) All of them sing, and say to you:
"Now even you are wasted away like us –
You have become like us!"
(11) Your pride is brought down to Sheol,[5]
and the noise of your harps.[6]

---

[2] On vv. 1–3 as poetry, see discussion below.

[3] I deem *māšāl* to be a technical literary term with no adequate English analogue, which is thus best left untranslated. See Jeremy Schipper, *Parables and Conflict in the Hebrew Bible* (Cambridge: Cambridge University Press, 2009), 1–22.

[4] Reading מרהבה (following 1QIsaᵃ, LXX, Peshitta, Targums) for MT מדהבה. The reference here is quite likely to the king as the embodiment of the Assyrian military, which in turn is sometimes portrayed as a flood (Akk. *abūbu*) in Neo-Assyrian literature. The adoption of the root רהב could have evoked the destroying sea monster Rahab in a phonological wordplay. The prophet uses Rahab mythology rhetorically in 30:7 as well. An alternate possibility, in light of the reference to the "bee (דבורה) that is in the land of Assyria" in 7:18, is some connection to Old Aramaic *dbhh* (*KAI* 222A:31), which is sometimes thought to be related to *dbrh* II, "bee, wasp" (see references in *DNWSI*, 238).

[5] There is no clear indication where the speech of the Rephaim ought to end – conceivably it could run all the way to v. 18, where the kings are again referred to in the third person – but v. 11's statement "Your pride is brought down to Sheol" seems to me to presume a perspective outside Sheol.

[6] If this image does not seem to add to the portrait or fit with parallelism, it is probably because it is an example of paronomasia. In this context, the consonantal Hebrew text המית נבליך unmistakably evokes the verb "to kill" (Hiphil of מות) and the noun "corpse," נבלה. In fact, it is

Maggots⁷ are spread out beneath you,
and worms are your shroud.

(12) How you are fallen from heaven, Hêlēl of the dawn!
You are cut down to the ground,
helpless on your back.⁸

(13) You said in your heart: "I will ascend the heavens,
I will exalt my throne above the stars of El.
I will be seated atop the mountain of the assembly,
at the heights of Zaphon.

(14) I will ascend to the cloudy heights.
I will be like the Most High."

(15) But instead you are brought down to Sheol,
to the depths of the pit.

(16) Those who see you stare at you,
and they marvel:
"Is this the man who made the earth tremble,
the one who shook kingdoms,

(17) the one who made the world a wasteland,
tore down its cities,
and did not open the prison for his captives?"⁹

(18) The kings of the nations lie in glory,
each in his house.¹⁰

---

possible that 1QIsaᵃ has emphasized this sense; it reads נבלתך, which could represent either "your folly/sin" or "your corpse." Furthermore, in 1QIsaᵃ, Donald W. Parry and Elisha Qimron read המות instead of המית ("sound") (*The Great Isaiah Scroll (1QIsaᵃ): A New Edition* [Leiden: Brill, 1999]). המות could be either an alternate abstract noun (הָמוּת) with the same meaning as המית, or perhaps even a form of מות (thus "the death of your corpse"?). The latter meaning is probably not primary, since it would require emendation to work grammatically, but it might represent a *double entendre*. In any case, an inspection of the photographs of 1QIsaᵃ shows that this letter is difficult to identify, typical of י/ו confusion in Qumran scrolls.

⁷ Bernard Gosse thinks רמה is a late term, a key reason for his proposing a late date for the passage as a whole (*Isaïe 13,1.14,23 dans les traditions littéraires du livre d'Isaïe et dans la tradition des oracles contre les nations* [OBO 78; Göttingen: Vandenhoeck & Ruprecht, 1988], 218). However, *rmh* appears in the Deir 'Alla inscription, which was copied onto a plaster wall ca. 880–770, and possibly was composed even earlier. The relevant line is ii.24°: *rmh.mn.gdš*, "a maggot from a tomb/grave."

⁸ Here I read על־גוים ("weak/helpless on your back") rather than על־גוים. This was proposed by Raymond C. Van Leeuwen, who pointed out that 1QIsaᵃ reads *gwy*, which he took as a short form of *gwyh* ("torso, back") found in Dan 10:6. (He adduces similar nouns with such by-forms.) He finally argues that MT scribes added an enclitic *mem*. He compares this with a comment from the *Gilgamesh Epic* ("Isa 14:12, *ḥôlēs ʿal gwym* and Gilgamesh XI, 6," *JBL* 99 [1980]: 173–84).

⁹ Emending the MT to לאסורים לא פתח בית הכלא, with the superfluous כל from the following phrase כל־מלכי גוים. Cf. Hans Wildberger, *Isaiah 13–27: A Commentary* (Continental Commentaries; Minneapolis: Fortress, 1997), 46.

¹⁰ H. R. Page suggests that "house" refers to temples (*The Myth of Cosmic Rebellion: A Study of Its Reflexes in Ugaritic and Biblical Literature* [VTSup 65; Leiden: Brill, 1996], 136). More likely it refers to tombs (Isa 22:16; Job 17:13; בית עולם in Eccl 12:5; in inscriptions, see *DNWSI*, 159), but in any case the point of v. 17 seems to be safe interment within the family property, which the tyrant does not receive.

(19) But you are cast out from your grave
    like an abhorrent corpse,[11]
clothed with the murdered,
    those pierced with the sword.
    those who go down to the stones of the pit
like a trampled corpse.
(20) You shall not be joined with them in burial
    for you destroyed your land,
    you killed your people.
The seed of evildoers will never again be named.
(21) Prepare for his sons a slaughtering block[12]
    on account of their father's guilt –
lest they rise up and inherit the earth
    and fill the face of the world with fortresses.[13]
(22) I shall rise up against them, says YHWH of hosts,
    and I shall cut off from Babylon name and remnant, scion and seed.

---

[11] I have an hypothesis about the term that I have not been able adequately to research and develop by the time this book went to press; so for the present I adopt the traditional solution that goes back to the Old Greek (ὡς νεκρὸς ἐβδελυγμένος). It is possible to read נֵשֶׁר rather than the MT's נֵצֶר, which is perhaps a later scribal emendation to connect the poem to Nebuchadnezzar (so Wildberger, *Isaiah 13–27*, 46). The vulture is an unclean bird and is associated with the dead throughout the ancient Near East (§ 1.4.2). The unburied or unhappy dead were thought to haunt the living in the form of birds. See Christopher B. Hays, "Chirps from the Dust: The Affliction of Nebuchadnezzar in Daniel 4:30 in Its Ancient Near Eastern Context," *JBL* 126 (2007): 303–23. The frequent move to read נֵפֶל, "miscarriage," does not make a very coherent image with the grave in the first colon. Baruch Halpern connects נצר to postbiblical נֵצֶל, "flesh from a corpse which has become detached," based on a rare *r / l* confusion. See "The Plaster Texts from Deir 'Alla," in *The Balaam Text from Deir 'Alla Re-Evaluated: Proceedings of the International Symposium Held at Leiden, 21–24 August 1989* (ed. J. Hoftijzer and G. van der Kooij; Leiden: Brill, 1991), 68–70. This theory is deemed highly unlikely by Jo Ann Hackett in her response in the same volume and is not adopted here.

[12] מַטְבֵּחַ: In comparing the roots טבח and זבח, one notes that טבח is disproportionately used of human slaughter, while זבח is far more typical in instances of common sacrificial practice.

[13] This line refers to the building of outposts; Assyrians brought their architecture with them into their provinces, essentially building their own cities in occupied areas. More importantly, עִיר refers not only to cities but also to fortified citadels within a city (thus the עִיר דוד). Ramat Rahel, near Jerusalem, is usually understood to have been such a Neo-Assyrian citadel (see Nadav Na'aman, "An Assyrian Residence at Ramat Rahel?" *Tel Aviv* 28 [2001]: 260–80). John H. Hayes and Stuart A. Irvine theorized that a number of passages in Isaiah inveigh against an Assyrian citadel in Jerusalem where Assyrian forces might have been quartered after the Ashdod revolt of 712/711, e.g., Isa 25:2 (*Isaiah the Eighth-Century Prophet: His Times and His Preaching* [Nashville: Abingdon, 1987], 296–97). Cf. the reference to citadels in Aroer in Isa 17:2, and, by comparison, the accounts of the Seleucid citadel in Jerusalem in 1 Macc 1:33–35, 6:18–27; 11:20–23; 13:49–52. In light of all this, Wildberger's comment that this line evokes "modern postulates about protecting the environment" (*Isaiah 13–27*, 73) is wildly off the mark.

(23) I shall make it a preserve for the owl[14]
and a pool of muddy water.[15]
And I will sweep her with a broom of destruction,
says YHWH of hosts.

Isaiah 14 finds its place within the oracles against the nations in Isaiah 13–23. More narrowly, 13:1–14:23 is a collection of oracles nominally addressed to Babylon.[16] The center and largest section of ch. 14 is a mock lament for "the king of Babylon," who sought divine greatness but found an ignominious death. Because the description of the tyrant sounds very much like the Assyrian kings described in, for example, Isa 10:12–15; because there is no reference to Babylon in 14:4b–21; and because the profile of the king does not seem to fit any Babylonian or Persian monarch (see below), the most common conclusion is that the song proper is a Neo-Assyrian-period composition that an exilic or postexilic redactor has paired with the Babylon oracle of ch. 13 by framing it with vv. 1–4a, 22–23.[17] Linguistic arguments about the date of the song are amenable to this interpretation, but inconclusive.[18]

There is a relatively broad consensus that vv. 1–4b are a redactional addition, since it is often taken for prose and employs themes – such as divine pity, restoration, and the reversal of foreigners' oppression – which have many echoes in postexilic texts, not least in Deutero-Isaiah. That consensus has been challenged by Seth Erlandsson,[19] however, and the issue is not completely clear-cut. First, the tendency to typeset all of vv. 1–3 as prose (NRSV, Blenkinsopp, Wildberger) ignores some rather strong parallelism in vv. 1 and 2b, which I have indicated in my translation above. The references to Jacob and (the house of) Israel, while they hardly *necessitate* an early date, at least *might* evoke the situation of the northern refugees in Judah after the fall of Samaria in 722/721, a major event

---

[14] The association of owls with wastelands and the spirits of the dead has already been mentioned in § 1.4.2. קפד is sometimes translated "hedgehog," but the owl seems more comprehensible as a symbol of a haunted wasteland than the rather innocuous hedgehog.

[15] Cf. Ugaritic terms for underworld, § 2.2.2.2: *hmry* ("cesspool/muddy pit,"), *mk* ("sinking down/collapsing") and *ḫḫ* ("mire/hole").

[16] Although 14:24–27 probably dates to the Neo-Assyrian period, like 14:4b–21, those verses are left out of account here because they are a separate form-critical unit and do not contribute to the theme under investigation.

[17] Brevard S. Childs (*Isaiah* [OTL; Louisville, Ky.: Westminster John Knox, 2001], 127) deemed it the majority view that the reference to the "King of Babylon" was redactional.

[18] Erlandsson argued on linguistic grounds that the song may well be from the Neo-Assyrian period, while Wildberger, Gosse, and others argue that it is later. The problem with arguments for its lateness is that, as Wildberger observed (*Isaiah 13–27*, 54), the clearest parallels are with Deutero-Isaiah (e.g., the phrase פצח רנה). In such cases it is difficult to prove whether one is dealing with common authorship or influence of the earlier on the later. As I mentioned in the translation note to v. 11, Gosse's linguistic evidence is not very strong.

[19] Seth Erlandsson, *The Burden of Babylon: A Study of Isaiah 13:2–14:23* (ConBOT 4; Lund: Gleerup, 1970), 162.

during Isaiah's career. Similarly, the settling of aliens in the land of Jacob (vv. 1–2) began immediately after that crisis, under Sargon. Finally, the use of the term רָגַז in v. 3 foreshadows the verbal forms of רגז in vv. 9, 16. While רגז has various senses in relatively wide use in Biblical Hebrew, it seems to have been practically a technical term for disturbing *the dead*, as one can see in 1 Sam 28:15 and in the funerary inscription of Tabnit of Sidon, where it is used no fewer than three times (*KAI* 1.9A:5, 1.13:4, 6, 7). The *māšāl* is to be delivered "when the Lord gives you rest," a phrase which could even be taken to mean "when you rest in the grave," so that it is the deceased who mock the king throughout, and not only in the two speeches (vv. 10, 16b–17). If vv. 1–4b are indeed redactional, then the choice of רגז in v. 3 is at least the work of a sensitive redactor.

Reversal of royal funerary expectations

The *māšāl* can clearly be divided into two major sections, each one introduced by the particle אֵיךְ (vv. 4b, 12). Some commentators further divide the composition into stanzas, but there is not a strict regularity to the form – that can be imposed only through major textual emendations.[20] It has long been observed that the passage is a mock lament[21] written in 3+2 *qînâ* meter, and Gale Yee has shown that it can fruitfully be compared with a typical dirge form as found in 2 Sam 1:19–27.[22] Although not every part of this paradigmatic dirge is mirrored in Isa 14, the latter's parodic nature is apparent when the two compositions are set side-by-side.[23] The *māšāl* is a tour de force, inverting most of the expected elements of lament for a king. Rather than a catalogue of the deceased monarch's strengths and achievements, there is a list of faults and grievances suffered at his hands. After his violence has ceased and there is silence on the earth, the sound that is heard is not mourning or wailing but joyful song. This is truly *not* the funeral service for which the tyrant would have wished.

In Nabonidus's inscription concerning his mother's burial, representatives

---

[20] E.g., W. L. Holladay, "Text, Structure, and Irony in the Poem on the Fall of the Tyrant, Isaiah 14," *CBQ* 61 (1999): 633–45. Joseph Blenkinsopp sees "little evidence of editorial manipulation and expansion" in vv. 4b–21 (*Isaiah 1–39: A New Translation with Introduction and Commentary* [AB 19; New York: Doubleday, 2000], 285).

[21] Karl Budde, "Das hebraische Klagelied," *ZAW* 2 (1882): 1–52.

[22] Gale A. Yee, "The Anatomy of Biblical Parody: The Dirge Form in 2 Samuel 1 and Isaiah 14," *CBQ* 50 (1988): 565–86. On form-critical issues, see also Marvin A. Sweeney, *Isaiah 1–39, With an Introduction to Prophetic Literature* (FOTL 16; Grand Rapids: Eerdmans, 1996), esp. 228.

[23] According to Yee, the parts of a dirge include: (A) Rhetorical introduction announcing the death (2 Sam 1:19::Isa 14:4b); (B) Suppression of the news of death from enemies (2 Sam 1:20:: -); (C) Description of nature at the person's death (2 Sam 1:21:: Isa 14:7–11); (D) Description of the person's life (2 Sam 1:22–23:: Isa 14:5–6); (E) Call to mourners to weep (2 Sam 1:24–25:: Isa 14:16–17); (F) Expression of the singer's personal grief (2 Sam 1:26–27:: Isa 14:18–21). The B element is missing from Isa 14, and the attested elements are arranged A-D-C-E-F.

come from throughout the empire (§ 1.4.1); thus the cypresses of Lebanon might be understood to stand in for delegates from that region, creating a carnival rendition of real mourning practices.[24] Mesopotamian rulers had long boasted of cutting the cedars of Lebanon (a tradition that stretched back to Gilgamesh);[25] by contrast, not only is the king in Isa 14 mocked by the cedars, but he himself is "cut down" (v. 12), making him a failure in relation to his mythic prototypes and his own propaganda. The trees carry a further connotation: A longstanding tradition of Mesopotamian kingship held that the very land was healthier and more fruitful under good rule, but suffered under bad rule.[26] Thus, the singing of the natural world (symbolized metonymically by the cypresses) after the king's death is a pointed critique of his rule. The wasteland imagery of vv. 22–23, while probably a later addition, similarly points to the result of bad rule: the tyrant's land will be haunted by owls (representing spirits of the dead) and reduced to a bog (perhaps evoking imagery of the underworld as a "muddy pit"; see § 3.3.3.3).

The reversal of royal hopes continues as the scene shifts to the underworld: the king does not receive the greeting he would presumably have expected there. In the Ugaritic Royal Funerary Text (*CAT* 1.161), which has deep affinities with the Mesopotamian royal *kispu* ritual (§§ 1.4.1; 3.3.3.2), one may perceive a more typical scene that a ruler would have hoped for upon his arrival in the underworld. There the spirits of the royal ancestors are summoned to welcome the newly deceased to a place of honor among them.[27]

Isaiah 14 toys with such expectations, showing the Rephaim stirring and assembling as if to fulfill their usual role of greeting, but instead they chide the new arrival. It is not often remarked how gentle their taunt is, however; although not exactly kind, it is almost collegial: *You're one of us now*. Misery loves company. It is only when the narrator resumes ("Your pride is brought down to Sheol") that

---

[24] I am using "carnival" as a technical literary category incorporating the subversion of power structures. See further: Mikhail Bakhtin, *Rabelais and His World* (trans. Helene Iswolsky; Cambridge, Mass.: M. I. T. Press, 1968).

[25] *Gilgamesh* Tablet V.291–97, etc. See Assyrian and Babylonian royal inscriptions in *ANET*, 276, 291, 307; this rhetoric is thus accurately reflected in Isa 37:24–25 and 2 Kgs 19:23. Van Leeuwen, "Isa 14:12," 184.

[26] See, paradigmatically, Samuel N. Kramer, trans., "The Curse of Agade," *ANET*, 646–51.

[27] While there is no direct parallel in Mesopotamian literature to this greeting in the underworld, it does not seem unreasonable to think that there was a similar expectation, given that the dead monarchs were invoked for other purposes. In any case, the intended audience of this text would not have been the Mesopotamian king himself, but rather hearers accustomed to the West Semitic mythological traditions that are reflected here. See further: J. Glen Taylor, "A First and Last Thing to Do in Mourning: KTU 1.161 and Some Parallels," in *Ascribe to the Lord: Biblical and Other Studies in Memory of Peter C. Craigie* (ed. Lyle Eslinger and J. Glen Taylor; JSOTSup 67; Sheffield: JSOT Press, 1988), 151–77. This theme of welcoming the dead into the underworld is found in Egyptian literature as well: In Egyptian funerary songs, the congregated dead say, "Welcome safe and sound!" to the new arrival, and, "How good is this which happens to him!" See Kanawati, *The Tomb and Beyond*, 48; and Erich Lüddeckens, *Untersuchungen über religiösen Gehalt, Sprache und Form der ägyptischen Totenklage* (MDAIK 11; Berlin: 1943), 100.

the taunt takes its first truly vicious turn: the dead king is to be grotesquely covered in parasites rather than with a royal cloak. One need only think of the massive stone sarcophagi of the Neo-Assyrian kings (§ 1.4.1) – which were seemingly intended to protect against the filth and disturbance that were typical of common burials – to see what a particularly awful prospect Isaiah's image would have seemed. Verse 11 is where one first learns of the ruler's pride; the indictment at the beginning of the *māšāl* only concerns violence and anger. Along with underworld imagery, then, the theme of pride serves to link the two halves of the composition, since hubris and ambition are the focal point of the second section, which follows directly.

It is remarkable how thoroughly the curse employs the images of the underworld and its terrors as they were perceived in many ancient Near Eastern religions, including that of the Neo-Assyrians; the imagery that accomplishes this is particularly densely packed in this second section. The taunt subverts every hope that a Mesopotamian monarch might have had for the afterlife. He will be powerless (vv. 10, 12, and implicitly in 16–17); his body will be infested (v. 11); not only will he not take his place among the divinized royal dead (v. 18), but his corpse will be defiled and cast out in a heap of bodies; that treatment suggests the disposal of the corpses of a defeated army, akin to the mass grave discovered at Lachish related to its destruction.[28] Thus, he will have no rest at all – in v. 19; בור, "pit," does double duty as an ignominious grave and as a term for the unhappy underworld. All of these outcomes are recognizably nightmarish for a Mesopotamian king.

The text's remarks on the inversion of the tyrant's status invite comparison to a form of ancient Near Eastern rhetoric that remarks on reversals of fortune. Although the most-studied manifestation of this type of rhetoric is the Egyptian "once-now" formula, both Hebrew (e.g., 2 Sam 1:23–25) and Akkadian laments (e.g., *Gilgamesh* XII:96–99) also loosely employ the "once-now" form. Each of these examples indicates that the "once-now" comparisons probably originated in funerary laments,[29] but they came to have a home in other genres.[30] In some Egyptian texts, as in Isaiah 14, this rhetoric of inversion served as social commentary.[31]

---

[28] A. F. Rainey, "The Fate of Lachish during the Campaigns of Sennacherib and Nebuchadrezzar," in *Investigations at Lachish: The Sanctuary and the Residency (Lachish V)* (Institute of Archaeology, Tel Aviv University, 1975), 45–60; David Ussishkin, "Answers at Lachish," *BAR* 5 (1979): 16–39.

[29] For a "once-now" composition in a lament from the Ramesside era, see Jan Assmann, *Death and Salvation in Ancient Egypt* (trans. David Lorton; Ithaca, N.Y.: Cornell University Press, 2005), 114: "The glib one, silence has befallen him, / The wakeful one is asleep, / The one who took no sleep at night is weary every day" (from the tomb of Nefersekheru).

[30] For discussion of the adaptation of the form, see Peter Seibert, *Die Charakteristik: Untersuchungen zu einer altägyptischen Sprechsitte und ihren Ausprägungen in Folklore und Literatur* (Ägyptologische Abhandlungen 17; Wiesbaden: Harrassowitz, 1967), 20–25.

[31] In Egyptian images of a "world upside down," the lowly are exalted and the mighty are

There is one further step in the tyrant's destruction that it is nowhere noted in the literature: the elimination of his mortuary care by the extinguishment of his line. It is commonly argued that vv. 20b–21 are part of the later redaction of the text; insofar as they turn their attention to the sons of the monarch, they are taken to reflect later concerns. Such an approach overlooks important details: In the first place, זרע, "seed," is singular in v. 20. It could be a collective noun (so NRSV, NIV, JPS, and nearly all modern translations), but more likely it is the tyrant himself who is "the seed of evildoers," the descendant of a long line of Assyrian kings who troubled Israel and Judah. Second, a man is not completely destroyed, whether in Mesopotamia or Egypt or elsewhere in the ancient Near East, until he is forgotten; that is the "second death."[32] Conversely, one is happy in the afterlife as long as he has a caretaker to tend his grave and make the proper offerings; if there are sons to invoke his name, the tyrant has some hope of a blessed afterlife. The sons must be killed so that the tyrant will not be invoked. Thus vv. 20b–21 are actually one unified thought: "Prepare for his sons a slaughtering block (so that) the seed of evildoers will never again be named." This is not to deny more worldly motives here – the text may also allude to ending a hostile political dynasty and/or denying eternal fame – but the literary setting points even more strongly to the common Akkadian phrase, *šumu zakāru*, "to call on the name,"[33] a common term for summoning the dead in Mesopotamian funerary rituals. In the Ugaritic royal funerary ritual text (*CAT* 1.161), the same root (*qrʾ*) is used for the invocation of the Rapi'uma (lines 2–12) as Isa 14:20 uses. These verses therefore complete the progression of the taunt song and is likely to be part of the original composition, while vv. 22–23 seem to be a redactor's means of connecting the mock lament to the Babylon oracle in ch. 13.

The myth of Hêlēl

Thus far the tyrant's fall. But what about his attempted assault on the heights of the heavens? What is this mythic material in which the prophet clothes the king?

---

brought low, as in the Admonitions of Ipuwer: "He who could not make a coffin owns a tomb; See, those who owned tombs are cast on high ground; he who could not make a grave owns a treasury."Adapted from Miriam Lichtheim, *Ancient Egyptian Literature: A Book of Readings* (3 vols.; Berkeley: University of California Press, 1973–80), 1:156. Lichtheim argues that the text is a reflection on the theme of "order versus chaos." It is interesting to note that whereas the imperial Egyptians saw the inversion of order as chaotic and dangerous, the author of Isa 14 clearly saw it as desirable.

[32] Brian B. Schmidt correctly shows that the "second death" was a concern for Israelites, although I would contest some of his conclusions: "Memory as Immortality: Countering the Dreaded 'Death After Death' in Ancient Israelite Society," in *Judaism in Late Antiquity*, part 4, *Death, Life-after-Death, Resurrection and the World to Come in the Judaisms of Antiquity* (ed. Alan J. Avery-Peck and Jacob Neusner; Handbuch der Orientalistik 55; Leiden/New York: Brill, 2000), 87–100.

[33] *CAD* Z, 18; also attested in the N-stem, analogous to the Niphal form of קרא in Isa 14:20.

The phrase הֵילֵל בֶּן־שַׁחַר in v. 12 has been an obsession among scholars of the ancient world; numerous theories have been propounded regarding this figure to whom the proud king is likened. With each new current in the field, and each new set of texts, new proposals have been set forward. Even religions without any attested myths have been suggested as the ground for this extended metaphor![34] The broad outlines of this discussion merit a brief survey.

In earlier scholarship, the name Hêlēl was connected to the Arab moon god Hilâlu, primarily because of lexical similarity.[35] (Moon gods, however, are not typically portrayed as hot-headed like the tyrant in Isa 14.) In the nineteenth century, Hermann Gunkel tentatively connected Hêlēl to the Greek myth of Phaeton and ultimately to nature myths,[36] and the Phaeton theory continues to be championed up to the present.[37] However, the story of a hot-headed boy borrowing power from his father and *accidentally* inflicting harm does not seem a natural wellspring for an allusion about a vicious tyrant. Moreover, the possibility is slight that this myth was in the mind of a preexilic prophet: The earliest extant version of the Greek myth (fragments from Euripides) dates to the late fifth century.[38] It is usually theorized either that the influence ran from East to West in the "Heroic Age,"[39] or that both traditions partook of a common eastern Mediterranean tradition.[40]

---

[34] Ulf Oldenburg, "Above the Stars of El: El in Ancient South Arabic Religion," *ZAW* 82 (1970): 187–208. This article argues on the basis of divine epithets alone that a South Arabic myth lies behind the Isaianic text.

[35] H. W. Haussig, *Wörterbuch der Mythologie*, vol. 1 (Stuttgart: E. Klett, 1965), 447. Although still retained as a suggestion in *HALOT*, this connection no longer generates significant scholarly support.

[36] Gunkel was equivocal about the mechanism of the myth's transmission to Israel and inclined instead toward exilic Babylonian influence. Hermann Gunkel, *Creation and Chaos in the Primeval Era and the Eschaton: A Religio-Historical Study of Genesis 1 and Revelation 12* (trans. K. W. Whitney; Grand Rapids: Eerdmans, 2006): 89–91 (German original, 1895).

[37] E.g., J. C. Poirier, "An Illuminating Parallel to Isaiah XIV 12," *VT* 49 (1999): 371–89. In the late version of the myth (in Book 2 of Ovid's *Metamorphoses*), Phaeton begs his father, Helios, to borrow his chariot that pulls the sun across the sky. Helios balks, but Phaeton insists. During the ride, he loses control of the chariot, and the sun goes too high, chilling the earth, and then too low, burning the earth. Finally Zeus is impelled to strike Phaeton down with a thunderbolt. Certain details commend this theory: the "scorched earth" of Phaeton's ride might well resonate with a tyrant's violent campaigning (although then one might have expected fire imagery, which is absent from Isa 14); furthermore, Phaeton is struck down for his flawed ambition, which is an important aspect of the biblical image.

[38] Phaeton was mentioned by Hesiod (ca. 700 BCE), but there is no consensus about whether a myth akin to that of Euripides (or, still later, Ovid) was found in his writings. Even the fragmentary Euripides myth requires significant reconstruction from later texts. See discussion in C. Collard, M. J. Cropp, and K. H. Lee, *Euripides: Selected Fragmentary Plays*, vol. 1 (Warminster: Aris & Phillips, 1995), 195–203; also *Brill's New Pauly: Encyclopedia of the Ancient World: Antiquity* (ed. Hubert Cancik and Helmuth Schneider; Leiden/Boston: Brill, 2002–7), vol. 6, s.v. "Phaeton."

[39] P. C. Craigie, "Helel, Athtar and Phaeton (Jes 14:12–15)," *ZAW* 85 (1973): 223–25: "The

With the discovery of the Ras Shamra texts and the search for eastern Mediterranean cognates, Ugaritic deities came into the discussion. The references in v. 13 to Zaphon and the "mount of assembly" clearly evoke the mythology of Baal's divine throne. Therefore, foremost among the suggested myths has been that of ʿAthtar, a minor astral deity who tries to assume the throne of Baal after the latter is killed by Mot (CAT 1.6 i 43–65).[41] The only thing really in favor of this connection is the epithet ʿṯtr ʿrẓ, "terrible ʿAthtar" – it sounds like the moniker of a tyrant, even if ʿrẓ is only tentatively understood, based on the Heb. ערץ.[42] Here too, however, the issues militating against any close connection to Isa 14 are numerous: ʿAthtar may be called "terrible," but he ascends only when chosen and invited by other deities; he exhibits no apparent hubris. Similarly, when he sees that he is much too small to fill mighty Baal's throne, he willingly steps down. Moreover, he is not ruined or destroyed by his fall; although he abdicates the throne of heaven, he returns to rule the entire earth.[43] Furthermore, why should ʿAthtar be called Hêlēl?[44] Finally, the phrase בן־שחר would then seem to cause

---

principal difficulty in positing Greek antecedents to Jes 14:12–15 lies in the fact that the weight of the evidence indicates Near Eastern influence on early Greek literature, rather than vice versa" (224).

[40] E.g., C. H. Gordon, *Before the Bible: The Common Background of Greek and Hebrew Civilizations* (New York: Harper & Row, 1962), *passim*. The theory that there is direct Greek influence on Isaiah thus necessitates an impossibly late dating of the text at hand. To my knowledge, the only modern study of the text that dates it to the Hellenistic period is Poirier's "Illuminating Parallel."

[41] On ʿAthtar's nature, see Mark S. Smith, "The God Athtar in the Ancient Near East and His Place in KTU 1.6 I" in *Solving Riddles and Untying Knots: Biblical, Epigraphic, and Semitic Studies in Honor of Jonas C. Greenfield*, eds. Ziony Zevit, Seymour Gitin, Michael Sokoloff (Winona Lake, Ind.: Eisenbrauns, 1995), 627–40. Smith argues that ʿAthtar was actually in competition with Baal in a way analogous to the competition between YHWH and Baal ("Yahweh, El, and the Divine Astral Family in Iron Age II Judah," in *Symbiosis, Symbolism and Power of the Past: Canaan, Ancient Israel, and Their Neighbors from the Late Bronze Age through Roman Palaestina* (Winona Lake, Ind.: Eisenbrauns, 2003), 265–77.

[42] See DUL 185–86, s.v. ʿrẓ. For an attempt to argue for ʿAthtar's fearsomeness, see M. S. Heiser, "The Mythological Provenance of Isa. XIV 12–15: A Reconsideration of the Ugaritic Material," *VT* 51 (2001): 354–69. For ערץ in Biblical Hebrew, see Ps 10:18; Isa 2:19, 21; 8:13; 29:23; 47:12; etc.

[43] It is sometimes pointed out that *ymlk.b.arṣ* in CAT 1.6 i 65 might be translated "he rules in the underworld," improving the parallel with Isa 14. This interpretation seems unlikely, since Mot is king of the underworld in the Baal Cycle. In any case, Hêlēl does not "rule" the underworld; he is not even welcome there; he rules *on the earth*.

[44] It seems that in South Arabian inscriptions, ʿAthtar is referred to as Venus, the 'Day Star' (Oldenburg, "Above the Stars of El," 187–208; Heiser, "Mythological Provenance," 356). This does at least supply an astral aspect for ʿAthtar, but why should Venus be further encoded as Hêlēl? Wrote Klaas Spronk: "no convincing answer has been given to the question why Athtar would have been called *hyll* (literally: 'the shining one') in Isa. 14" (Spronk, "Down with Hêlēl!: The Assumed Mythological Background of Isa. 14:12," in *"Und Mose schrieb dieses Lied auf": Studien zum Alten Testament und zum Alten Orient* [FS O. Loretz] [ed. M. Dietrich, I. Kottsieper; AOAT 250; Münster: Ugarit-Verlag, 1998], 719).

problems – there is a Ugaritic deity named šḥr/Šaḥar (CAT 1.23), who is not a parent to ʿAthtar.

Since the theories of Greek and Ugaritic influence do not satisfy, there has been a movement toward Mesopotamian comparisons.[45] These, however, are generally limited in their scope. For example, it may be that certain phrases of the *Gilgamesh Epic* are reflected in Isa 14,[46] but it can hardly explain the whole mythic background of Hêlēl. The same may be said for connections to the Erra and Etana myths. Marvin Sweeney's theory – that Ištar's descent to the netherworld is analogous to the Hêlēl account – needs to be similarly circumscribed.[47] Ištar/Inanna descends to the netherworld and is stripped (and thus humbled) in the process, but there is no hubris or ambition. Furthermore, she returns to her former status.

It is safe to say that none of these theories about the underlying mythic model has commanded consensus, although there is general agreement that the *terminology* has "Canaanite" antecedents in Ugaritic texts. Two things need to be observed about these efforts to locate a parallel myth to that of Hêlēl. First, the fall of the hubristic one is a mytheme of vast geographic and cultural extent; it can be found in various manifestations not only all over the ancient Near East, but all over the world.[48] Because of this, and especially because no really apt literary analogue has ever been proposed, it is important to recognize that Isa 14 is best deemed a particularly Israelite employment of a widespread mythic tradition. As P. C. Craigie remarked, the differences between Isa 14 and the Ugaritic texts "are to be explained by poet's licence in adaptation, rather than in seeking a closer, though very dubious, parallel."[49]

---

[45] An extensive discussion can be found in R. Mark Shipp, *Of Dead Kings and Dirges: Myth and Meaning in Isaiah 14:4b–21* (AcBib 11; Leiden: Brill, 2002), 85–112.

[46] Cf. Van Leeuwen, "Isa 14:12"; R. H. O'Connell, "Isaiah XIV 4B–23: Ironic Reversal Through Concentric Structure and Mythic Allusion," *VT* 38 (1988): 407–18. The most interesting of these resonances is between Isa 14:10's "Now even you are wasted away like us – you have become like us!" and Gilgamesh's reaction to Utnapishtim in XI:3–4: "Your features are not strange; you are like I am! You are not strange at all; you are like I am!"

[47] Sweeney writes: "It would appear that Isaiah's taunt song and use of motifs from the myths that accompany the mourning rites for the dead fertility god in the ancient Near Eastern world is an attempt to satirize the death of Sargon II in relation to one of the most fundamental patterns of ancient Near Eastern religiosity: the death and rebirth of the fertility god or goddess, which governs the dry and rainy seasons of the land, and thus determines the seasons of fertility and lack thereof" (*Isaiah 1–39*, 238). It is difficult to perceive how this amounts to effective satire. Gunkel already noted this idea (*Creation and Chaos*, 320 n. 51).

[48] Donald E. Gowan, *When Man Becomes God: Humanism and Hybris in the Old Testament* (Pittsburgh Theological Monographs 6; Pittsburgh: Pickwick, 1975), 45–67; Hans J. L. Jensen, "The Fall of the King," *SJOT* 1 (1990): 121–47; Joseph Jensen, "Helel ben Shahar (Isaiah 14:12–15) in Bible and Tradition," in *Writing and Reading the Scroll of Isaiah: Studies of an Interpretive Tradition* (ed. C. C. Broyles and C. A. Evans; VTSup 70; Leiden: Brill, 1997), 339–56.

[49] Craigie, "Helel, Athtar and Phaeton," 225. Craigie speaks specifically of Greek parallels; I am construing the statement more broadly. As examples of assuming too much literary influ-

Perhaps there is no direct literary referent for vv. 12–15; perhaps Gunkel was right that one should not think of Isa 14 as the result of "an author who copied another author. We have to deal, in the interpretation of myths and legends, not only with written texts and literary works, but far more often with oral tradition."[50] The biblical authors, like any others, made use of the raw material of their surrounding culture. Whether or not the dirge is authentic to Isaiah, it is certainly an original and creative literary work.

The author's independence and creativity are on display in v. 4, where the author synthesizes Assyrian military propaganda and ancient Near Eastern myth: the term מרהבה, which I have translated "flood" (a common symbol for the Assyrian king and military in inscriptions[51]), may create a phonological allusion to Rahab (רהב), the Hebrew version of the primordial watery chaos monster[52] whom YHWH crushes in Ps 89:11, Isa 51:9, Job 26:12, etc. In the Hêlēl passage, too, he works the stuff of myth into his own creation.

The rhetoric in historical context

If indeed the author of Isa 14 is not bound by the narrative structures of prior myths, but rather has his own message to bring across,[53] then what is that message? It is almost trite to say that the truth the text wishes to communicate is that death and disgrace await the tyrant who terrorizes the earth and vaunts himself to the status of king of the universe – but "king of the universe" (*šar kiššati*) was, in fact, a title claimed by a long line of Assyrian kings.[54] Since the desire to overthrow tyranny would be at home in any number of historical periods, many commentators are satisfied to read the text without reference to specific historical events,[55] but it becomes more interesting and comprehensible when set against a specific cultural and historical backdrop.

---

ence: "In the Bible we have a quotation from Canaanite poetry in which the god [Ashtar] appears as Helel, 'son of dawn' " (W. F. Albright, *Archaeology and the Religion of Israel* [2nd ed.; Baltimore: Johns Hopkins University Press, 1955], 84). Or again: "[The author of Isa 14], familiar as he was with Ugaritic religious texts, also knew that in the Ugaritic language, ʾarṣ could refer to either the earth or the Underworld" (Heiser, "Mythological Provenance," 368).

[50] Gunkel, *Creation and Chaos*, 91.

[51] For example, from the annals of Adad-nirari II (911–891): "The roar of the king is as strong as the destructive flood." See A. K. Grayson, *Assyrian Royal Inscriptions II: From Tiglath-Pileser I to Ashur-nasir-apli II* (Wiesbaden: Harrassowitz, 1976), XCIX 2.

[52] Wildberger, *Isaiah 13–27*, 56; Cf. Lītān (Leviathan) in the Baal Cycle or Tiamat in *Enuma Eliš*.

[53] As W. S. Prinsloo observed: "[T]he intention of Jes 14:12–15 is not to convey a myth. It is rather to use a myth, or certain components of it, in a particular way in order to communicate certain truths." W. S. Prinsloo, "Isaiah 14 12–15: Humiliation, Hubris, Humiliation," *ZAW* 93 (1981): 436.

[54] The title is not, of course, a determinative consideration for an Assyrian reference, since it was claimed by a number of rulers down to the fourth century BCE. Cf. *CAD* K, 458.

[55] E.g. Wildberger, *Isaiah 13–27*, 76; Otto Kaiser, *Isaiah 13–39: A Commentary* (trans. R. A. Wilson; OTL; Philadelphia: Westminster, 1973), 30–31.

To what king did the mock dirge originally refer, then? The superscription referring to "the king of Babylon" does not necessarily indicate the Neo-Babylonian period, as is usually assumed; rulers native to both Babylonia and Assyria claimed that title – even a Persian such as Cyrus the Great is once called "king of Babylon" (Ezra 5:13). Furthermore, Stephanie Dalley has pointed out that the confusion of Assyria and Babylon is of great antiquity and extent.[56] As an example, the "King of Babylon" in the seventh-century Aramaic Adon Papyrus, written from a West Asiastic ruler to the pharaoh, is widely thought to be an Assyrian.[57] Intra-Mesopotamian political distinctions seem to have been murky to outsiders throughout classical history.[58] The most surprising effects of this confusion are seen in errors such as classical authors' attribution of the Hanging Gardens to Babylon, when they really seem to have been in Nineveh. Dalley cogently argues that the confusion of Babylon and Assyria is datable to the Neo-Assyrian Period itself.[59]

The biblical text may supply other clues, however. The shifts in verbal aspect are significant. Most of the song's key verbs are in the perfect aspect, inviting the reader to understand them as telling of past events ("YHWH has shattered," "How you are fallen," "You have been cast out"); their sheer number precludes reading them as prophetic perfects. However, v. 20 switches to the imperative ("prepare an executioner's block for his sons ... so that they will never rise ..."), expressing only a wish, not an historical fact. Thus, one does not have to identify a king whose line was in fact extinguished, but the king in question should have been experienced by Israel as an oppressive, violent tyrant, and he should not have been buried. The imagery of being covered ("clothed") in a pit with corpses that have been pierced by the sword further suggests a death suffered in military conflict.[60] There is only one Mesopotamian monarch known to Israel who fits

---

[56] Stephanie Dalley, "Nineveh, Babylon, and the Hanging Gardens: Cuneiform and Classical Sources Reconciled," *Iraq* 56 (1994): 45–58.

[57] See recently Alberto R. Green, "Esarhaddon, Sanduarri, and the Adon Papyrus" in *Inspired Speech: Prophecy in the Ancient Near East, Essays in Honor of Herbert B. Huffmon*, eds. J. Kaltner and Louis Stulman (Edinburgh: T & T Clark, 2004), 88–97, and also literature cited there.

[58] Dalley, "Nineveh, Babylon, and the Hanging Gardens," 48. As she notes, even the Babylonian ruler Nabonidus' own king-lists ignored shifts from Assyrian to Babylonian rule.

[59] Dalley implies that the confusion began when Sennacherib destroyed Babylon and carried off its gods in 689, so that Nineveh "became Babylon" (Dalley, "Nineveh, Babylon, and the Hanging Gardens," 49). However, as I will argue below, the confusion might be pushed back slightly earlier to Sargon II's assumption of the throne in Babylon.

[60] Saul Olyan makes the provocative and interesting point that the phrase השלכת מקברך in v. 19 suggests that the king was buried in his grave and then disinterred ("Was the 'King of Babylon' Buried Before His Corpse Was Exposed? Some Thoughts on Isa 14,19," *ZAW* 118 [2006]: 423–26). He rightly points out that, if this were so, then it presents "difficulties for the identification of the 'King of Babylon' with Sargon II or other known monarchs who were never buried." However, other aspects of the verse still point to a death in battle, and since Olyan offers no competing theory, there is little to discuss.

this portrait: Sargon II.[61] As Hayim Tadmor has noted, "Sargon was the first and only Assyrian king in the Assyrian Empire to fall on the battlefield and not to receive fitting burial."[62]

There is, in fact, nothing in the taunt that excludes Sargon II. The charge that the tyrant "destroyed his land and killed his people" (v. 20) might be related to Sargon's warring with Babylon in the late eighth century,[63] which certainly involved the killing of fellow Mesopotamians. If Sargon is in view, then even the dirge's superscription may be datable to the Neo-Assyrian period. After 710, when Sargon forced Merodach-Baladan of Babylon to flee, he took his throne and was himself crowned king of Babylonia.[64] The recognition that an Assyrian might be called "king of Babylon" by a biblical author has been a hard-won realization (against the admittedly natural view that Isa 14:4a is redactional), but it is now a widely held opinion.[65] It should not be surprising that a ruler should

---

[61] This is not the place for a survey of the other proposals, such as is already available in a number of sources cited here. The other kings who have received significant support in recent times are Sennacherib, Nebuchadnezzar, and Nabonidus. Suffice it to point out only the primary problems with these suggestions: Sennacherib died peacefully and passed on the empire to his son Esarhaddon without incident. One major consideration against the Babylonian rulers generally suggested is that Babylon was never destroyed between 689 and the late fourth century BCE – thus, the picture of a city destroyed would be an imaginative invention only. Nebuchadnezzar also died at home, in Babylon. Nabonidus was not at all the international terror that the taunt envisions, least of all to Judeans, whose homeland was already destroyed when he ascended the throne in 556. Finally, the case laid out by Hayes and Irvine, that Tiglath-Pileser III is in fact the Hêlel of Isa 14, deserves more serious consideration than it receives. As they showed, Tiglath-Pileser also conquered Babylon (in 729 BCE) and also "took the hand of Bel" at the Babylonian New Year's festival (and even proclaimed his "priesthood" over the city). Furthermore, he was every bit as much a warrior and empire-builder as any other Assyrian king. See Hayes and Irvine, *Isaiah: The Eighth-Century Prophet*, 227–29. The matter hangs, however, on the question of Tiglath-Pileser's death: Hayes and Irvine theorize that he died on campaign to Damascus in 727, but this is an argument from silence. There is nothing else in the Assyrian record to suggest that he did not receive a normal burial, and in fact the tone of the "Sin of Sargon" text suggests that a death on the battlefield was truly an exceptional fate. Furthermore, although Tiglath-Pileser would have been well known to Israel and Judah, one must assume that the Neo-Assyrians would be even more prominent in the public consciousness after the destruction of Samaria in 722. Sargon, the later king, thus fits the profile better.

[62] Hayim Tadmor, Benno Landsberger, and Simo Parpola, "The Sin of Sargon and Sennacherib's Last Will," *SAAB* 3 (1989): 29. (The passage is cited by Tadmor.) See also Herbert Chanan Brichto, "Kin, Cult, Land and Afterlife – A Biblical Complex," *HUCA* 44 (1973): 25.

[63] In the confusion after the death of Shalmaneser V in 722, Babylon had crowned its own king, Merodach-baladan, whom Sargon allowed to stay in power for the sake of expedience. Once uprisings elsewhere in the empire were quelled, Sargon turned on Babylon and took control of it again.

[64] A. K. Grayson, *Assyrian and Babylonian Chronicles* (Texts from Cuneiform Sources; Locust Valley, N.Y.: J. J. Augustin, 1975), I.ii.1–5. Line 5: $\check{S}arru$-$k\hat{i}n$ ina $B\bar{a}bili^{ki}$ $^{d}B\bar{e}l$ ina $k\acute{u}ss\hat{e}$ $itta\check{s}ab$; "Sargon ascended the throne in Babylon"; see idem, "History and Culture of Assyria," *ABD* 4:744.

[65] H. L. Ginsberg wrote: "In view of Sargon's notorious Babylonism, whose manifestations included a three years' residence in Babylon and the stressing of both his Babylonian titles and of

adopt the title of the religious and cultural center of his region, even if he originated somewhere else; it is akin to the way Kushite rulers took the title "pharaoh" in Egypt.

A final argument in favor of Sargon is that his death on the battlefield seems to have been on a campaign to Tabal, a mountainous region in northern Syria.[66] This is also roughly the area of Mt. Zaphon (usually associated with present-day Jebel ʾel-Aqraʿ). The reference to Zaphon in 14:13 would be a fusion of myth and history; certainly the terminology evokes West Semitic myth, but it also represents Sargon's failed and fatal attempt to enthrone himself in the northern mountains.[67] If that is the case, then although much of the imagery of 14:12–15 is of mythic stock, it refers to concrete historical events involving a Mesopotamian king. The mythic material becomes for the prophet "an extended figure of speech."[68]

The identification of the king as an Assyrian indicates that one might look to Neo-Assyrian mythology for the meaning of the title הילל בן־שחר. The theory propounded here addresses the problem common to all of the theories relating the name to Ugaritic and Greek myths: they do not adequately explain the name Hêlēl. If the author meant to evoke, for example, ʿAthtar, why would the name Hêlēl best evoke that association? Even if ʿAthtar had an astral/solar aspect connected to a "shining" heavenly body, Hêlēl is a *hapax legomenon* that has been understood as "Shining one" by reference to an Akkadian root (*ellu*). That root, however, is scarcely *ever* used to describe light or heavenly bodies in Akkadian,

---

his benefactions to the inhabitants and temples of the southern metropolises in an account intended for foreigners (the Cyprus Stela), it would not be remarkable if Isaiah regarded Babylon (a city whose name was presumably far more familiar to him ... than Calah ... let alone Dur-Sharrukin, of which he probably never heard), as the center of the Assyrian empire" ("Reflexes of Sargon in Isaiah after 715 B.C.E.," *JAOS* 88 [1968]: 49). Alasdair Livingstone observes that "Assyrian scholars were interested in Babylonian practices, and at times when Babylonia was under Assyrian rule Assyrian kings performed rites in Babylon" (*Mystical and Mythological Explanatory Works of Assyrian and Babylonian Scholars* [Oxford: Clarendon, 1986], 131); see Grayson, *Assyrian and Babylonian Chronicles*, I.ii.1': (Šarru-kîn qāt ᵈBēl iṣ-ṣa-[bat]; "Sargon took Baal's hand"). See also Erlandsson, *Burden of Babylon*, 164; Miklós Köszeghy, "Hybris und Prophetie: Erwägungen zum Hintergrund von Jesaja XIV 12–15," *VT* 44 (1994): 549; Shipp, *Of Dead Kings and Dirges*, 158–62.

[66] J. D. Hawkins, "The Neo-Hittite States in Syria and Anatolia," in *The Cambridge Ancient History* (2nd ed.; Cambridge: Cambridge University Press, 1982), 3.1:422; Tadmor, Landsberger, and Parpola, "Sin of Sargon," 28.

[67] For a version of this theory, see W. R. Gallagher, "On the Identity of Hêlēl Ben Šaḥar," *UF* 26 (1994): 145–46. Zaphon, if it is correctly identified, is not exactly in Tabal; but then, the precise location of Sargon's death was probably no clearer to eighth-century Judeans than it is to us today – thus the association with Zaphon would not be surprising.

[68] Brevard S. Childs, *Myth and Reality in the Old Testament* (2nd ed.; London: SCM, 1962), 71. We must demur from Childs's judgment that the myth is thereby "demythologized," preferring Page's perspective that "a political event has been mythologized, and a mythological event has been politicized" (*Myth of Cosmic Rebellion*, 131).

but instead normally refers to cleanness and purity.[69] The verb הלל, "to shine," does exist in Hebrew, but is not attested until Job and Sirach.[70] The possibility cannot be excluded that this could be a lone early manifestation of a known verb, but one must conclude that if an Israelite author had wanted to convey "shining one," or "morning star," surely there were more comprehensible ways to do so.

A new interpretive tack is thus in order, and W. R. Gallagher has supplied a promising suggestion, and arguing that Hêlēl should be understood as a West Semitic equivalent of the Mesopotamian Enlil/Illil.[71] He shows that both had strong astral aspects and that the phonetic change from Illil to Hêlēl is plausible.[72] Illil's character meshes with that of the tyrant in Isa 14 in important ways: he was a "devastator" and a god of war;[73] he was also initiator of the flood in Mesopotamian tradition, a provocative connection to Neo-Assyrian imagery, which as we have already noted compared its military assaults to a flood. Illil is also compared to the rising sun in a first-millennium Akkadian text: "When Šamaš rises, he is Enlil."[74]

Hêlēl's fall can also be related to Enlil/Illil. A text from Nineveh recounts a myth in which divine beings break the wings of Enlil and Anu and cast them down into the Abyss (*apsû*).[75] In the same text, it is said that Marduk "cast a [sp]ell against Illil in the Abyss, and consi[gned him] to the Anunnaki," that is, the underworld gods. As Gallagher points out, Marduk's elimination of these older gods "was similar to eliminating a dynasty."[76] In other first-millennium texts, Illil is also consigned to the underworld by other gods;[77] thus, in this time

---

[69] *CAD* E, 104. This fact is never, to my knowledge, noted in the secondary literature by proponents of the ʿAthtar or Phaeton theories.

[70] *hll* is not attested in Northwest Semitic inscriptions, to my knowledge.

[71] W. R. Gallagher, "On the Identity of Hêlēl Ben Šaḥar," *UF* 26 (1994): 145–46. Gallagher points out that there exists an Ugaritic deity *hll* (*CAT* 1.17 ii 26–27; 1.24 6, 15, 41–42), but apart from supplying a possible W. Semitic cognate for the divine name Enlil, there is little in the Ugaritic texts that advances his argument. I am indebted to Mark Smith for his insight on this matter in personal communication.

[72] One may compare the change: Sum. é-gal ("palace") > Ug. *hkl* > Heb. *hykl* :: Sum. ᵈen-lil > (Ebla. ᵈi-li-lu >) Ug. *hll* > Heb. *hyll*.

[73] His first-millennium epithets included "the bull which makes the heavens and the earth quake," "the net which overthrows the enemy land," and "lord of weapons." For texts and references, see Gallagher, "On the Identity of Hêlēl Ben Šaḥar," 140.

[74] (ᵈŠamas ina niphī(kur)-šú ᵈEn-líl) For the text, see E. F. Weidner, "Ein astrologischer Sammeltext aus der Sargonidenzeit," *AfO* 19 (1959/60): 110. For discussion see Livingstone, *Mystical and Mythological Explanatory Works*, 47. Gallagher is troubled that Illil does not seem to be a "son of dawn" in any mythical texts, but this may be an overly literal reading of the Hebrew; a בן־שחר may simply be a heavenly body that is "part of the morning sky." See *HALOT*, 138 (s.v. בֵּן, entries 6, 7).

[75] For text and discussion, see Alasdair Livingstone, *Court Poetry and Literary Miscellanea* (SAA 3; Helsinki: Helsinki University Press, 1989), 115–70.

[76] Gallagher, "On the Identity of Hêlēl Ben Šaḥar," 141.

[77] Gallagher, "On the Identity of Hêlēl Ben Šaḥar," 142.

period one can perceive the outlines of the fall of a star god. The point of these texts is "to give Marduk unchallenged supremacy in the Mesopotamian pantheon"[78] as part of a program of pro-Babylonian propaganda.

Therefore it is specifically pro-Marduk mythological rhetoric that Isaiah most nearly invokes here,[79] although YHWH has taken over Marduk's role by casting down Hêlēl. Insofar as "[d]er Gott Aššur ... scheint in der Sargonidenzeit die Verkörperung der grenzlosen Machtansprüche des Königs zu sein"[80] – and in the same period "Aššur was commonly equated with Enlil"[81] – it is very easy to imagine that this myth of Illil/Enlil's fall could have taken on anti-Assyrian, anti-imperial meanings, both in Babylon, where Marduk was the city god, and in Judah.[82] The use of myths as political rhetoric in ancient Mesopotamia is well known.[83] This possibility becomes more provocative still in light of the apparent diplomatic alliance between Jerusalem and Babylon against Assyria during Isaiah's prophetic career (2 Kgs 20:12–21 // Isa 39).[84]

If it is correct that Isa 14 reflects Isaiah's adaptation of Babylonian anti-Assyrian propaganda, it would lend further support to Erlandsson's assertion that these verses have their historical setting between roughly 722 and 689 (the destruction of Babylon by Sennacherib). This same context explains for Miklós Köszeghy why Isaiah did not name Aššur directly, preferring the closely related

---

[78] Gallagher, "On the Identity of Hêlēl Ben Šaḥar," 142; Livingstone, *Mystical and Mythological Explanatory Works*, 153–54.

[79] In recent years, a number of scholars have emphasized royal ideology in studies of this text; however Spronk ("Down with Hêlēl!" 721) and Wyatt ("The Hollow Crown: Ambivalent Elements in West Semitic Royal Ideology," *UF* 18 [1986]: 421–36) emphasize its Ugaritic forms, while Shipp (*Of Dead Kings and Dirges*, 151) mentions its Sumerian form. Only Köszeghy ("Hybris und Prophetie," *passim*) emphasizes Neo-Assyrian ideology, which is, after all, the most natural place to look for a composition mocking a Neo-Assyrian monarch.

[80] ("The God Aššur ... seems to be, in the Sargonid era, the embodiment of the king's boundless claims to power.") Köszeghy, "Hybris und Prophetie," 550.

[81] Livingstone, *Mystical and Mythological Explanatory Works*, 131.

[82] To explicate the inner workings of Mesopotamian myth enough to prove this point would require more effort and space than it merits in this context. But it is not unreasonable to think that this conflict between Marduk and Enlil/Illil would have taken on special meaning during the first-millennium wars for supremacy between Assyria and Babylon. What a convenient vessel for Babylonian rhetoric: the Assyrian king's "boundless claims to power" meet their end as Marduk overthrows Aššur/Enlil.

[83] For example, one could mention the Assyrian version of *Enuma eliš* in which Aššur(/Anšar) replaces the Babylonian Marduk; for a brief discussion and further references, see K. Lawson Younger, Jr., "Assyrian Involvement in the Southern Levant at the End of the Eighth Century B.C.E.," in *Jerusalem in Bible and Archaeology: The First Temple Period* (ed. Andrew G. Vaughn and Ann E. Killebrew; SBLSymS 18; Atlanta: Society of Biblical Literature, 2003), 255. Peter Machinist also has discussed the role of literary texts in Mesopotamian politics in "Literature as Politics: The Tukulti-Ninurta Epic and the Bible," *CBQ* 38 (1976): 455–82.

[84] The historicity of this account may of course be questioned, but it seems to be a rather typical diplomatic event – albeit one reinterpreted in light of later concerns. It is adopted as historical by Jean-Claude Margueron in "Babylon (Place)," *ABD* 1:563.

Hêlēl as a cipher: Assyria was still very much in power in Palestine, despite Sargon's failure and death, and it was not safe to speak openly against the empire. Assuming a public *Sitz im Leben* for the mock dirge, Köszeghy writes:

Jesaja wollte natürlich die ganz konkreten Hinweise soweit wie möglich vermeiden. Ein Dichter, der gerade ein Lied improvisiert, muss sich nicht unbedingt immer ganz konkret ausdrücken. Zum anderen war es gefährlich, ein solches Lied öffentlich vorzutragen. Es ist allgemein bekannt, wie intensiv die Spionage in den Nachbarländern des neuassyrischen Reiches war.[85]

Therefore one can explain the camouflage inherent in the name Hêlēl as a political necessity. This may even help to explain the term מָשָׁל in v. 4a: the song likens one thing to another; it is a not-so-subtle riddle to be decoded by those with ears to hear.

Isaiah's employment of West Semitic mythological imagery does not refer to any specific literary work that existed in the West, but reflects his fresh adaptation of a Mesopotamian mythological motif. I have already mentioned this above in connection with Zaphon; one might also add that Rephaim and Sheol are uniquely West Semitic, or uniquely Hebraic terms, respectively, but they are used to lampoon the expectations of a Mesopotamian monarch. Here as elsewhere, the reader must recognize the diverse, hybridized nature of Isaiah's discursive universe; the prophet and his tradents had many cultural influences to draw on in their environment.

In sum, we have seen that death and the underworld are the major sources of imagery for the taunt. The following elements all are related to death:

1. the terms שאול and רפאים (vv. 9, 11, 15)
2. the enthronement and glorification of dead kings (vv. 9, 18)
3. the weakness of the dead (vv. 10, 12)
4. the wordplay on מות and נבלה in v. 11
5. the name Hêlēl as a cipher for the god Enlil/Illil who was cast into the netherworld by the high god
6. the mythological connotations of בור (v. 15)
7. the concern for the integrity of the corpse and the horror of corruption and exposure (vv. 19–20)
8. the concern for progeny in order to invoke the deceased's name and to provide mortuary offerings (vv. 21–22)
9. mud imagery evoking the underworld (v. 23)

---

[85] Köszeghy, "Hybris und Prophetie," 553: "Isaiah naturally wanted to avoid completely concrete references as much as possible. A poet who improvises a song does not necessarily have to express himself completely concretely at all times. On the contrary, it was dangerous to speak such a song publicly. It is well-known how intensive the espionage was in the countries neighboring the Neo-Assyrian Empire."

Perceiving these allusions is important at the level of literary comprehension, but they also strongly suggest that those beliefs and practices referenced were familiar to Isaiah's preexilic audience. Yee remarked of the dirge form that "only literary works or forms which are familiar can be parodied successfully,"[86] and the same applies to mythic material. Isaiah inhabited a religious environment that was complex; it was acquainted with diverse beliefs and practices. Not only did Judeans surely take part in certain religious practices that were recognizably "foreign" during Isaiah's period, but also that representatives of YHWH were still negotiating their understanding of and relationship to the divine, so that the boundaries of Yahwism itself would not have seemed as clear to the prophet's contemporaries as they might in historical retrospect. Isaiah himself no doubt had a significant role in defining those boundaries, including in some of the passages that follow.

5.2.1.2 Isaiah 30:27–33: A pyre for the king

The Assyrian king is again the object of condemnation and punishment in Isa 30:

(27) Look there![87] The Lord is coming from far away,
his anger ablaze, (his) smoke-cloud[88] thick,
His lips are full of fury,
and his tongue like a devouring fire.
(28) His breath is like a river,
one that floods up to the neck,
and he will divide[89] and winnow the nations with a sieve of destruction,[90]

---

[86] Yee, "Anatomy of Biblical Parody," 567.

[87] The decision to emend שֵׁם to שֵׁם is not difficult. There is no other place in the Hebrew Bible where שֵׁם יהוה can be understood as the active subject of a verb, and שֵׁם הוה is a common exclamation (Gen 29:2; 2 Sam 15:36; 1 Kgs 14:2; 17:10; Jer 36:12; Ezek 3:23; 8:4, 14; 46:19). Neither is there cause to remove שֵׁם, insofar as Liudger Sabottka shows that the line length (based on syllable-count) is perfectly regular ("Is 30,27–33: Ein Übersetzungsvorschlag," *BZ* 12 [1968]: 244): "Auffallend ist die Ausgewogenheit der einzelnen Zeilen, selbst in der Zahl der Silben."

[88] Read מַשְׂאָה for MT מַשָּׂאָה. Regarding מַשְׂאָה (found in Lachish 4:10), see Victor Sasson, "An Unrecognized 'Smoke-Signal' in Isaiah XXX 27," *VT* 33 (1983): 90–95. This reveals a connection between smoke and fire that makes more sense than the alternative translation, "heavy burden."

[89] This difficult verse is further complicated by 1QIsa^a's reading וחצה לנופה rather than יחצה להנפה. The usual translation – e.g., NRSV: "his breath is like an overflowing stream that reaches up to the neck" – treats the common verb חצה differently from almost all other occurrences. See further comment below.

[90] This image is usually thought to be somewhat incoherent, an example of bad parallelism. The image seems reasonable, however, as a portrait of the Mesopotamian practice of population displacement after wars. The nations are divided and scattered, and תעה picks up the double sense of "wander (geographically)" and "go astray (culturally/religiously)." Although H. L. Ginsberg's suggestion to read נפו as "yoke" would be an excellent play on the common Neo-Assyrian "yoke of Aššur," the Arabic etymology is too speculative, and Isaiah uses the more common על elsewhere (Ginsberg, "An Obscure Hebrew Word," *JQR* 22 [1931–32]: 143–45). On the yoke of Aššur and its familiarity in Palestine, see Christopher B. Hays, "Kirtu and the 'Yoke of the Poor': A New Interpretation of an Old Crux (KTU 1.16 VI:48)," *UF* 37 (2005): 361–70.

and (put) a bit of wandering in the jaws of the peoples.
(29) There will be singing for you
    as on the night that a festival is kept,
    and the heart's joy will be like going with flute
    to come to the mountain of the LORD,
    to the rock of Israel.
(30) The LORD will make heard his majestic voice,
    and unveil the descending blow of his arm,
    in furious anger, and a flame of consuming fire.
    in rain and storm and hail.
(31) And the LORD's voice shall terrify Aššur;
    with a rod he will smite (it).
(32) And every breach[91] beneath[92] the foundation wall,
    which YHWH will bring down upon him,[93]
    will be with timbrels and lyres[94] and battles,
    raising (his arm?), he will fight against it.[95]
(33) For his[96] burning place was arranged long ago,
    it is[97] indeed made ready for a king;
    he has made[98] its wood-pile wide and deep;
    fire and wood in abundance.[99]
    And the breath of the LORD, like a stream of brimstone, ignites it.

This has proved an extraordinarily difficult passage, with interpreters often assuming that some sections of it were muddled in transmission. Thankfully, v. 33, which is most significant for the present purpose, is also the clearest and fullest image. The pericope is the last in a sequence of oracles of different types which, whether or not they were composed at the same time, are arranged around a common theme: Trust in YHWH rather than in an alliance with Egypt.

From a form-critical standpoint, vv. 27–33 comprise a theophany re-

---

[91] מעבר commonly means "ford, crossing," and is used here to describe a breach in the wall of a besieged city. See discussion below.
[92] Read מַשָּׁה for MT מָשָׂה. The MT vocalization has been influenced by שׁבט from the previous verse.
[93] Similar to the problems in v. 28, נוח is understood here in a completely unique sense in most translations; nowhere else does it refer to blows being laid down (as in NRSV, NIV, NJB). I am proposing another unusual sense. If nothing else, it allows one to avoid the common emendation of מוסדה to מוסרה, which is merely an attempt by tradents to make sense of the passage. MT and 1QIsaᵃ agree on מוסדה. Presumably the suffix in עליו refers to the king.
[94] This line has always been problematic; it may be that the image of an assault on city walls gives some inkling about its significance. One might consider also the Israelite siege of Jericho, as it is told in Josh 6. There, the instruments of siege are trumpets rather than lyres or timbrels. See discussion below.
[95] This feminine suffix apparently refers to a city, probably Aššur.
[96] Reading טפתה, i.e., an archaic third person masculine singular suffix.
[97] 1QIsaᵃ: היה for MT K: הוא, Q: היא.
[98] Presumably the agent here is YHWH. 1QIsaᵃ interprets the verse loosely, using imperatives rather than the MT's indicatives.
[99] This phrase would seem to be a later gloss to explain the unusual word מדרה.

port,[100] a vision in which the Divine Warrior comes in the garb of natural forces (fire and water) to smite Assyria, completing the story in which YHWH, not Egypt, saves Judah. However, the expected sequence of YHWH's arrival (vv. 27–28) and punishment of Assyria (vv. 30–31, 33) is interrupted by images of singing and celebrating at a festival (vv. 29, 32). Hans Wildberger argues on the basis of these thematic shifts that vv. 29 and 32 are interpolations. Instead, it appears that the combination of martial and festal imagery represents a rare biblical reflection of the ancient Near Eastern phenomenon of burning enemies in a cultic ceremony (see below).

The description of the Divine Warrior's destruction of Assyria creates a complex episode of *ius talionis* ("retributive justice") in which YHWH abuses the Neo-Assyrians as they abused their enemies.[101] Terms that are used elsewhere in Isa 1–39 to describe Assyrian domination are here part of YHWH's attack, notably the rod (v. 31, cf. 10:5, 15, 24; 14:5, 29) and the flood (v. 28 and 30b; cf. 8:8; 28:2, 15–18; Nah 1:8). Even the phrase "up to the neck" (עד־צואר) is repeated from 8:8, but in 30:28 it is applied to YHWH's breath.

The images of v. 28b have sometimes been deemed troubling – *Why should YHWH wish to punish or mislead the nations?* – but these also likely had as their background the practices and rhetoric of the Mesopotamians. The practice of deporting populations and repopulating cities with foreigners after a war did involve the "dividing" and "sifting" of the peoples (v. 28b). The inscriptions of each of the Neo-Assyrian kings are full of references to deporting thousands of people,[102] redrawing borders, and dividing conquered nations.[103] Jeremiah mournfully reflects these same practices as the will of YHWH in 15:7: "I have winnowed [the inhabitants of Jerusalem] with a winnowing fork in the gates of the land (or 'underworld');[104] I have bereaved them, I have destroyed my people."[105] As John Day wrote of Hosea's polemic against the Baal cult, "polemic can sometimes involve taking up one's enemies' imagery and re-utilizing it for one's own purposes."[106]

---

[100] Sweeney, *Isaiah 1–39*, 394.

[101] The theme of YHWH as a god who repays his enemies according to the nature of their misdeeds is widespread in the Hebrew Bible; e.g., Hos 12:3; Obad 15; Exod 4:22–23; Judg 1:6–7; Isa 59:18; Jer 25:14; Job 34:11. For a full discussion, see Patrick D. Miller, *Sin and Judgment in the Prophets: A Stylistic and Theological Analysis* (SBLMS 27; Chico, Calif.: Scholars Press, 1982).

[102] For references to the Neo-Assyrian practices of deportation and depopulation, see, e.g., CAD N/2, 3–4 (s.v. *nasāḫu*, 1b).

[103] For references to the Neo-Assyrian practice of dividing peoples, see, e.g., CAD Z, 77 (s.v. *zâzu*, 2a).

[104] שערי הארץ; cf. "gates of Sheol" (Isa 38:10); "gates of death" (Job 38:17; Pss 9:14; 107:18). See Mitchell Dahood, "The Value of Ugaritic for Textual Criticism," *Bib* 40 (1959): 164–65; Nicholas J. Tromp, *Primitive Conceptions of Death and the Nether World in the Old Testament* (BibOr 21; Rome: Pontifical Biblical Institute, 1969), 30–31.

[105] Jeremiah 15:7 uses a form of זרה for "winnow," rather than forms of נוף, as Isa 30:28 does.

[106] John Day, *Yahweh and the Gods and Goddesses of Canaan* (Sheffield: Sheffield Academic Press, 2000), 118.

Fig. 5.1 A Neo-Assyrian relief from the palace at Nineveh depicts captives being led away after the fall of Lachish.

As for the "bit of wandering in the jaws of the people," the image of captives led around like cattle is also quite familiar from Neo-Assyrian royal reliefs, such as that which portrays the fall of Lachish (Fig. 5.1). Furthermore, "nations" and "peoples" may refer to the Neo-Assyrians' enlistment of soldiers from disparate regions, as is well-attested in their own inscriptions and art:

[T]he Assyrians ... conscripted subject peoples into their forces on equal terms with native Assyrians. Each ethnic group retained its identity for fighting purposes, constituting, according to the numbers involved, a regiment or smaller unit, retaining both the type of weapon and form of dress associated with the region of origin. Thus we find depicted on the bas reliefs such groups as bowmen, slingsmen, swordsmen, pike-bearers, light infantry, and heavy infantry, often distinguished by their footwear, clothes and headgear as well as by their weapons.[107]

Isa 29:7 also seems to reflect this historical reality, when it refers to "the multitude of all the nations that fight against Ariel."

---

[107] H. W. F. Saggs, *The Might That Was Assyria* (London: Sidgwick & Jackson, 1984), 244.

In addition to the reflections of the Neo-Assyrians' practices, there is an echo of their rhetoric in the "majestic voice of YHWH" that strikes fear in Aššur (v. 31); the phrase מקול חתת is not a common one in the Bible (it occurs only here and in 31:4), but it is analogous to the "fearsome lordly radiance" (*melammu bēlūti*) of the god Aššur and the Assyrian kings, which the latter repeatedly claimed had terrified their foes in battle. To take only one example among many, from one of Sennacherib's inscriptions: *pulḫi melamme bēlūtiya isḫupušu* ("the terror of my lordly radiance overwhelmed him").[108]

Finally, YHWH's besieging of the city in v. 32, although difficult to translate, seems to reflect very similar Assyrian practices, based on royal inscriptions. The most obvious example is from the famous passage in the Rassam Cylinder and its later copies, describing Sennacherib's siege and destruction of Judean cities:

As for Hezekiah of Judah, who did not submit to my yoke, I besieged 46 of his fortified walled cities and surround smaller towns, which were without number. Using packed-down ramps (*aramme*) and applying battering rams, infantry attacks by mines (*pilši*), breeches (*niksi*) and siege machines (*kalbannate*), I conquered them.[109]

Each Akkadian term refers to a relatively well-attested Assyrian technique of siege warfare, and these methods would have been known at the Jerusalem court. (The well-known Nineveh reliefs depicting the siege of Lachish also confirm how familiar these tactics would have been in Judah.) The motif of YHWH making a siege at city walls is not at all uncommon, whether directly or through intermediate human agency; see Isa 25:12 and 29:3 (perhaps also 5:5 and 22:5); Jer 50:15; Ezek 13:14; 26:3–14. The collocation of that image with that of celebratory music, while unusual, does find a fascinating analogue in the account of the siege of Jericho in Joshua 6 (esp. v. 20).[110] Given that the fall of a city would have been cause for celebration on the part of the attackers, the combination of imagery is not so incomprehensible.

S. Z. Aster has recently pointed out that this type of "replacement theology," in which YHWH replaces the Neo-Assyrian king, is a common rhetorical move in Isaiah.[111] His examples have included Isa 2:5–22; 6:1–7; and 10:5–22, 28–34 (in

---

[108] D. D. Luckenbill, *The Annals of Sennacherib* (Oriental Institute Publications 2; Chicago: University of Chicago Press, 1924), 29 ii 38. See further examples at "*melammu*," CAD M/2, 9–12. The image of the god's voice thundering to inspire fear is commonly ascribed to Adad (see references at *rigmu*, "voice," CAD R, 332). Given the early convergence of Baal's storm-god characteristics to YHWH, this would be a natural point of contact for the Assyrian imagery in a West Semitic context.

[109] Trans. M. Cogan, COS 2.119B; for the Akkadian text, see Luckenbill, *Annals of Sennacherib*, 32–33.

[110] In addition to the blowing of the shofars, Joshua commands the people, "Shout (הריעו), for the Lord has given you the city" (6:16); the verb רוע has both the sense "raise the war-cry" and "shout for joy."

[111] Shawn Zelig Aster, "The Image of Assyria in Isaiah 2:5–22: The Campaign Motif Revi-

addition to Micah 4:1–5). One could now add Isa 30:27–33 to the list of instances in which YHWH is garbed in Assyrian imagery and acts like an Assyrian ruler.

It may seem odd that YHWH takes on roles and characteristics of the Mesopotamian king and military, but ch. 10 previously laid groundwork for the idea with the claim that the Assyrian king attacked Judah only by YHWH's will. So already YHWH had been said to work *through* the Assyrians, but in Isa 30:27–33 YHWH becomes the active agent, while the Assyrian king and military become the objects of the assault and suffer the same things they were accustomed to inflicting. To reiterate, the employment of *ius talionis*, retributive justice, is quite typical of Isaiah (e.g., 30:16).

The passage's final image, the burning of the Assyrian king in v. 33, may at first glance seem ill-fitted with what has gone before. This is especially true if one erroneously imports the deity Molek into the text.[112]

Nonetheless, the references to the woodpile and fire clearly evoke images of cultic burning, and the word תפתה (v. 33) has caused many scholars to theorize a connection to the cult of child sacrifice at the Topheth outside Jerusalem.[113] Contrary to those theories, this is no ordinary sacrifice to Molek, if other biblical texts are any indication, for two reasons. First, the Topheth sacrifice is never portrayed in the Bible as a means to expurgate evil – the sacrificial victims of the rites are (presumably innocent) children, not enemies (2 Kgs 23:10; Jer 7:31–32).[114] It is not correct that the Neo-Assyrian king here is "portrayed as a helpless baby"[115] – nothing in the passage supports that idea. Second, the topo-

---

sited," *JAOS* 127 (2007): 249–78; also *idem*, "Isaiah 2:2–4 and Micah 4:1–5: The Vision of the End of Days as a Reaction to Assyrian Power" (paper delivered at the Annual Meeting of the Society of Biblical Literature, San Diego, 2007). Another discussion of the Isaianic reaction to Neo-Assyrian imperial claims is Baruch Levine, "Assyrian Ideology and Israelite Monotheism," *Iraq* 67 (2005): 411–27.

[112] Many interpreters (including Blenkinsopp, Wildberger, Sweeney, and Barth) read מֹלֶךְ (the DN "Molek") instead of the MT's מֶלֶךְ ("king"). The MT is to be retained, however; not least because otherwise, the person to be burned would not be identified. Furthermore, the author clearly approves of the punishment meted out here, whereas neither Isaiah nor an Isaianic tradent is likely to have advocated a Molek ritual as a solution for anything. Third, the parallelism in v. 33 shows that the idea of the fire-pit's great depth and width is directly related to the importance of its *royal* victim (the one thought follows directly from the other: "It is indeed ready for a king – he has made his woodpile wide and deep"). Molek should therefore not be read into the text.

[113] Francesca Stavrakopoulou, *King Manasseh and Child Sacrifice: Biblical Distortions of Historical Realities* (BZAW 338; Berlin: Walter de Gruyter, 2004), 202; Brian P. Irwin, "Molek Imagery and the Slaughter of Gog in Ezekiel 38 and 39," *JSOT* 65 (1995): 93–112.

[114] Blenkinsopp compares this scene to an *auto-da-fé*, a ritualized public punishment of heretics used during the Spanish Inquisition (*Isaiah 1–39*, 424). At a deep level, it may indeed be that rituals of exorcising evil forces lie somewhere in the background of this passage; fire and running water were both among the methods of combating evil ghosts in the ancient Near East (Jean Bottéro, "Les morts et l'au-delà deans les rituels en accadien contre l'action des 'revenants,'" *ZA* 73 [1983]: 177–78).

[115] Stavrakopoulou, *King Manasseh and Child Sacrifice*, 203; cf. Heider, *Cult of Molek*, 322.

nym Topheth never occurs with a suffix, as the word does here; thus, תפתה in 30:33 is to be understood not as a specific location near Jerusalem (which took its name from the common noun used here) but in a prior and more basic sense of a place where humans are burned,[116] and perhaps also a place where they are buried (so Jer 7:32; 19:11).

One must distinguish between burning children to propitiate a deity and burning enemies (and sometimes their children) as punishment for rebellion or other transgressions. There are numerous instances of the latter in Neo-Assyrian sources.

In Mesopotamian thought, burning to death could be considered "the worst fate of all"[117] – and at least in the Sumerian composition "Bilgamesh and the Netherworld," the ghost of the one who burns to death goes up in smoke and has no place in the netherworld.[118] Esarhaddon includes among his treaty curses in his succession treaty the imprecation that, should the vassal transgress, "May Girra ... burn up your name and your offspring."[119] Such curses seem to have been carried out by the Assyrians. Aššurnasirpal II tells in one of his inscriptions of burning a defeated city ruler,[120] and another relates the burning of adolescents.[121] (Such practices do not seem to be out of step with Assyrian norms in general, insofar as the burning of children is also found in Neo-Assyrian documents as a legal punishment for a party who breaks a contract.[122]) Even the cultic aspect of the killing in Isa 30 finds echoes in Assyrian slaughters: as Seth Richardson points out, "enemies were executed not only 'like pigs,' but upon actual

---

[116] Hans Wildberger, *Isaiah 28–39: A Commentary* (Continental Commentaries; Minneapolis: Fortress, 2002), 202. Contra Willem A. M. Beuken, "Isaiah 30: A Prophetic Oracle Transmitted in Two Successive Paradigms," in *Writing and Reading the Scroll of Isaiah: Studies of an Interpretive Tradition* (ed. Craig C. Boyles and Craig A. Evans; VTSup 70; Leiden: Brill, 1997), 387.

[117] George, *The Babylonian Gilgamesh Epic*, 14. George bases this comment primarily on the fact that burning is the final type of death mentioned in "Bilgamesh and the Netherworld," although he notes that the aversion was longstanding.

[118] George, *The Babylonian Gilgamesh Epic*, 776. See discussion above at § 1.4.1.

[119] Simo Parpola, in *Neo-Assyrian Treaties and Loyalty-Oaths* (ed. Simo Parpola and Kazuko Watanabe; SAA 2; Helsinki: Helsinki University Press, 1988), 51 (6.524–25). The word for "offspring" here is NUMUN (Akk. *zēru*), which equally can mean "seed (for planting)." This curse appears in a context that includes agricultural imagery, and thus the "seed" could be understood more literally, but the association with the "name" and the straightforward curse against offspring that follows (6.534–39) affirm this interpretation.

[120] A. K. Grayson, *Assyrian Rulers of the Early First Millennium BC* (Royal Inscriptions of Mesopotamia, Assyrian Periods 2; Toronto: University of Toronto Press, 1991), 101.1 i.111.

[121] Grayson, *Assyrian Royal Inscriptions II*, 176. See also *CAD* Š/2, 52 (s.v. "šarāpu," 1.g.).

[122] For example, "His eldest son will be burnt in the sacred precinct of the god Adad"; "He will burn his son to Adadmilki, his eldest daughter, with two se'ahs of cedar resin, to Belet-seri," etc. These texts were first collected and translated by K. Deller, review of R. de Vaux, *Les sacrifices de l'Ancien Testament*, *Orientalia* NS 34 (1965): 382–386, and have since been discussed by Moshe Weinfeld ("The Worship of Molech and the Queen of Heaven and Its Background," *UF* 4 [1972]: 133–54) and Morton Smith ("A Note on Burning Babies," *JAOS* 95 [1975]: 477–79).

slaughtering tables."[123] Given how many Israelite and Judean cities the Assyrians destroyed in the late eighth century, it is hard to imagine a Judean intellectual *not* being aware of such practices and not being incensed by them. It may well have been precisely this sort of horrific act that convinced a Judean author that the Assyrian monarch himself deserved just such a fate. Indeed, this unforgettable image ended up having a long afterlife of its own, as Gene M. Tucker remarked: "It was not the hell of subsequent tradition, but it certainly provided some of the imagery for later ideas of that place."[124] The recognition of the punitive nature of the burning brings this final verse into a more logical association with the *ius talionis* theme of the rest of the passage.

Although Assyrian practice and rhetoric are the most likely avenues for the image to have reached Isaiah, there is evidence of burning enemies as punishment in Egypt at that time as well,[125] suggesting that the idea had broader cultural currency, and it may even have had an early foothold in West Semitic myth.[126]

---

[123] Seth Richardson, "Death and Dismemberment in Mesopotamia: Discorporation between the Body and the Body Politic," in *Performing Death: Social Analyses of Funerary Traditions in the Ancient Near East and Mediterranean* (ed. N. Lanieri; Chicago: University of Chicago Press, 2007), 197. He cites Riekele Borger, *Beiträge zum Inschriftenwerk Aššurbanipals: Die Prismenklassen A, B, C = K, D, E, F, G, H, J und T sowie andere Inschriften* (Wiesbaden: Harrassowitz, 1996), 108, Prism B VI 87–89. Same text: A. C. Piepkorn, *Historical Prism Inscriptions of Ashurbanipal* (AS 5; Chicago: University of Chicago Press, 1933), 1:74–75, lines 88–89.

[124] Gene M. Tucker, "Isaiah 1–39," in *The New Interpreter's Bible* (ed. L. E. Keck; Nashville: Abingdon, 2001), 6:256. See also N. Wyatt, "The Concept and Purpose of Hell: Its Nature and Development in West Semitic Thought," *Numen* 56 (2009): 178.

[125] There is good evidence for the burning of political rebels on the brazier of the goddess Mut in Egypt during the Third Intermediate Period. The classical Egyptian historian Manetho (third century BCE) reported that the Nubian pharaoh Shabako (721–707 BCE) burned alive Bocchoris, who was Tefnakht's successor at Sais. Bocchoris had broken a covenant "by proclaiming himself king. In succeeding Tefnakht, Bocchoris had compounded the offence, since the vassal treaty which one may assume accompanied the oath was probably binding on descendants, and he was therefore a subject in revolt against his overlord" (Anthony Leahy, "Death by Fire in Ancient Egypt," *Journal of the Economic and Social History of the Orient 27* [1984]: 201). Another native Egyptian text also portrayed Mut as a destroyer of "rebels," a goddess who consumed with fire those who undermined Egyptian authority. The text is the "Ritual to Repulse the Aggressor," which combines an earlier ritual (probably New Kingdom) and a later commentary (probably Third Intermediate Period, i.e., roughly 1100–650 BCE). Two of its sections show that death by fire was likely a real punishment, at least in the later period (Jean Yoyotte, "Hera d'Heliopolis et le sacrifice humain," *Écoles Pratiques des Hautes Études, V^e section, Annuaire Résumés des Conférences et Travaux 89* [1980–81]: 31–102). Formula 2 of the ritual refers to the punishment of "20 enemies [who were] conspirators." In the later commentary, the punishment is spelled out in considerably greater detail: "Let them be cursed so that they are burned in the brazier of Mut" (Yoyotte, "Hera d'Heliopolis," 80). Again in Formula 7 it is primarily the Third Intermediate Period commentary that is of interest: "The wrath of the Great One is against you, that you should be destroyed ... your flesh is incinerated, your *ba*-soul will not escape in the brazier of Mut ... which is in Heliopolis" (Yoyotte, "Hera d'Heliopolis," 81–82). It is generally accepted that this text reflects the practice of human immolation. There are also Hellenistic references to human sacrifice to Mut. Most notable are the many accounts of the Egyptian king Busiris, who supposedly slaughtered foreigners; and the sacrifice of the Typhonian men (Diodorus Siculus 1.88): "Men the color of Typhon [i.e., red] were of old sacrificed by kings by the

All these references indicate that what the author envisions is not as much a sacrifice as a *punishment* against an enemy king who had rebelled against the Cosmic King, YHWH. Both the political and cosmic orders are threatened until YHWH intervenes. Through an imaginative synthesis of cultic and military motifs, the prophet again turns imperial violence and rhetoric back against the *imperator*.

In order to argue that Isa 30:27–33 echoes motifs from the Neo-Assyrian period (or the Third Intermediate Period in Egypt), it would help to show that the passage is at home in that era. And indeed, the prospective nature of the passage, which I conveyed in my translation, strongly suggests that the punishment of the Assyrian king had not yet happened; the verbs point to future events (beginning with the inceptive participle בָּא in v. 27). As with the threat against the proud boasting of the king in Isa 10, this passage looks *ahead* to a time when the Assyrians would be definitively silenced.

The location in which this scene of divine vengeance is to be acted out is an important issue for understanding the passage. It is widely assumed that the defeat of Assyria envisioned here takes place in Jerusalem, so that it is an expression of Zion theology, the idea that YHWH protects Jerusalem.[127] Verse 29, which refers to the הר יהוה and the צור ישראל is surely the reason for this conclusion. However, that verse only *compares* the joy of seeing Assyria humbled to the joy of ascent to Zion; it does not locate the destruction being narrated.[128]

---

grave of Osiris." (For a full discussion of classical evidence, see J. Gwyn Griffiths, "Human Sacrifice in Egypt: The Classical Evidence," *ASAE* 48 [1948]: 409–23. Also Yoyotte, "Hera d'Heliopolis," *passim.*) There are a handful of iconographic portrayals of human slaughter in Egyptian iconography, but their significance is disputed (Yoyotte, "Hera d'Heliopolis," 36–39). As another example, at the temple of Philae, an inscription reads, "May you deliver these scheming men who detest the King to the brazier of Mut ... and thus slaughter His Majesty's adversaries" (Georges Bénédite, *Le temple de Philae*, [Mémoires publiés par les Membres de la Mission Archéologique Française au Caire 13; Paris: Ernest Leroux, 1893], 116, 19; Yoyotte "Hera d'Heliopolis," 77). There is a general scholarly consensus that this was no mere attempt by Western authors to portray Egypt as barbaric, but rather reflected actual historical practice in the Third Intermediate Period. Ramesside rulers sometimes claimed to have "burned the flesh of my enemy with my rays." If YHWH is the one who burns the enemy, and if YHWH is being cast as a king, then the imagery of the pharaohs may lie somewhere in background of the biblical description as well, albeit more indirectly (solar imagery is not present in Isa 30:27–33 as in the Egyptian examples). For examples of such Egyptian rhetoric, see Michael G. Hasel, *Domination and Resistance: Egyptian Military Activity in the Southern Levant, ca. 1300–1185 B.C.* (Leiden: Brill, 1998), 84–86. I do not know of examples of such rhetoric among the sparse corpus of Iron Age Egyptian royal inscriptions.

[126] The imagery of Isa 30:28, 33 also draws on a Syro-Palestinian mythic background, that of Anat's destruction of Mot in the Baal Cycle. Just as YHWH winnows the enemy nations and burns the Assyrian king, so Anat "seizes Mot, son of El. With a knife she splits him; with a sieve she winnows him; with a fire she burns him" (*CAT* 1.6 ii 30–34: tiḥd / bn . ilm . mt. b ḥrb / tbqʿnn . b ḥtr . tdry-/-nn b išt tšrpnn).

[127] J. J. M. Roberts, "The Davidic Origin of the Zion Tradition," *JBL* 92 (1973): 329–44.

[128] Verse 32, if it were comprehensible, might lend support to this theory, but it is not.

Furthermore, YHWH presumably would not have to come there "from far away," as v. 27 states, since Zion theology also holds that YHWH is enthroned in the temple.

A better approach is offered by Hermann Barth and W. A. M. Beuken,[129] who defend the minority position that an Assyrian locale is envisioned. In Isaiah's prophecies, YHWH is mobile, as when he travels to terrify Egypt in 19:1 (the same verb, בוא, is employed). If YHWH also journeys to inflict Assyria's destruction, then where does it take place? Although it may be unwise to build any firm historical theories on v. 32, the text does seem to refer to a siege of a city and the breaching of its foundation wall. If so, the most likely city is Aššur itself, which is referred to in the previous verse and which was destroyed by the Medes and Babylonians in 614, while Josiah was still on the Judean throne.[130]

Wildberger and others connect the passage to Isaiah himself, and in light of the lexical and thematic connections that have been noted with apparently authentic (or at least preexilic) passages, and also with Neo-Assyrian records, it is most unlikely that Assyria is merely a cipher for some other, later world power.[131] Suffice it to say that the fall of Assyria, which stretched over many years, was in sight, but was still not complete when the text was written. Many will find it easiest to imagine the scene as the work of a tradent in a time when Assyria was actually under attack in its own land, in the last quarter of the seventh century; the question is how far the original prophet's foresight extended.

In conclusion, Isa 30:27–33, much like 14:4b–21, subverts the expected order of the Neo-Assyrian king's world. Isaiah 14 upended the tyrant's hopes for the afterlife, while the present passage turns the imagery of his own military fury against him. Thousands of years after they were written, the anger of these passages is still fresh and seething. The very excess of wrath may be seen as a direct inversion of Assyrian practice; as Richardson said of Aššurnasirpal II's abuse of rebel rulers: "there can be no doubt that the royal punishments went beyond the threat of what merely could be visited on the living body, but also on the dead one."[132]

---

[129] Hermann Barth, *Die Jesaja-Worte in der Josiazeit: Israel und Assur als Thema einer produktiven Neuinterpretation der Jesajaüberlieferung* (WMANT 48; Neukirchen-Vluyn: Neukirchener Verlag, 1977), 99–100; Beuken, "Isaiah 30," 387.

[130] This would require the revision of A. K. Grayson's assertion that the city Aššur is "never specifically referred to in the Bible" (*ABD* 1:500). Marvin Sweeney thinks that the reference to a nighttime festival in v. 29 accords well with the Josianic emphasis on Passover (2 Kgs 23:21–23), which was held at night in that period. The celebration over the smiting of the Assyrians would also make sense at a time in which the empire was crumbling, as it was during Josiah's reign.

[131] The destruction it portrays is sometimes analyzed as an apocalyptic battle – for example, by Kaiser, who places it in the Hellenistic period (*Isaiah 13–39*, 310). The text does refer to the punishment not only of Assyria but also of "nations" and "peoples"; however, an explanation of these terms in light of the multinational Assyrian military has already been suggested above.

[132] Richardson, "Death and Dismemberment in Mesopotamia," 197.

The author of Isa 30:27–33 would not be outdone in creative wrath by the Assyrians. He took the image of the Topheth, a place of burning, and in light of Assyrian practice, envisioned it as a place where YHWH's punishment upon the enemy king could be exacted in a ritual of vindication, accompanied by the celebration of YHWH's people. The same sort of precisely calibrated retribution is envisioned in Ps 137:8–9, another passage that is likely to make many modern readers uncomfortable:

> Happy shall they be who pay you back what you have done to us!
> Happy shall they be who take your little ones and dash them against the rock!

Unfortunately, parts of Isa 30:27–33 do not render up their meaning easily, but the Topheth appears to be the lynchpin that holds together the seemingly disparate pictures of warfare and cult in the complex imagery of the passage.

5.2.1.3 Isaiah 22:15–19: Shebna's tomb

It is not only foreigners who suffered Isaiah's wrath or his condemnation to an unhappy afterlife:

> (15) Thus says the Lord, YHWH of hosts: Go now to this stela,[133] to[134] Shebna, who is over the house, and say to him:[135]
> (16) "What are you doing here?[136]
>   And whom do you have here,
>   that you have cut for yourself a tomb here? –
> you who cuts his grave on high
>   and carves for himself a dwelling in the cliff![137]
> (17) The Lord is about to hurl you down, O mighty man!
>   He is indeed going to cover you with darkness;

---

[133] Read *sikkān* or *sikkōn* for *sōkēn* (see below). This term is misunderstood in 1QIsa^a as a Qal participle (סוכן).

[134] Read אל for MT על, following 1QIsa^a. The MT reflects a scribal error due to the interchangeability of these prepositions in later periods.

[135] This phrase ("and say to him") is present in two Hebrew manuscripts, LXX, Vulgate, and Targums.

[136] Verse 16 is rarely typeset as poetry, but the repetition of the phrase לך פה and the parallelism between "grave on high" and "dwelling in the cliff" suggests that this is at least poetic prose, and the versification is an effort to capture that. On the continuum between poetry and prose in Hebrew, see David L. Petersen and Kent Harold Richards, *Interpreting Hebrew Poetry* (Minneapolis: Fortress, 1992), 13–14.

[137] There is no problem in the combination of second person address with the participles חקקי and חצבי; as Ginsberg realized, this construction is very much like that in *hôy*-oracles. He points the reader to Isa 5:8, 11–12; 10:1, etc., and especially Hab 2:6–8, 9–10, 15–17, "as illustrating the continuation of such a clause with the second person" ("Gleanings in First Isaiah," in *Mordecai M. Kaplan Jubilee Volume on the Occasion of His Seventieth Birthday* (ed. Moshe Davis; New York: Jewish Theological Seminary, 1953), 256. See also J. T. Willis, "Textual and Linguistic Issues in Isaiah 22,15–25," *ZAW* 105 (1993): 377–99.

(18) He will indeed unroll (from your head its) wrapping,
 – (rolling it) like a ball into the 'wide land.'
 There you shall die, with your glorious chariots,
 you disgrace to the house of your lord!
(19) I will thrust you from your monument,
 and he[138] will pull you down from your platform."

Isaiah 22:15–19 is part of a larger prophetic announcement of judgment, which continues with the ascension of Eliakim in the place of Shebna in vv. 20–24. A final judgment oracle (seemingly against Eliakim, but perhaps resuming the sentence against Shebna) concludes the passage in v. 25. Although vv. 20–25 obviously are related to vv. 15–19 in the present form of the text, they take up different images and may be a later addition, raising different critical issues. As the present research will show, vv. 15–19 have the integrity of a self-contained unit, and they will be addressed as such.[139]

Some debate surrounds the historicity and role of Shebna. He is referred to as אשר על־הבית. This term refers to a sort of majordomo or administrator of the royal estate, with broadly construed duties,[140] or perhaps specifically oversight over the palace and royal family.[141] In either case, the Shebna addressed in this oracle is a person of stature, but not royal. One encounters a scribe named Shebna also in Isa 36–37; "scribe" is generally taken to be a lower rank, leading to the theory that he was demoted after this oracle was delivered.[142]

The interpretation of this passage has been hampered by scholars' refusal to take its accusation seriously. J. T. Willis calls the tomb "a matter of secondary importance" – an amazing claim, since the tomb is the *only* subject of the indictment. Yet Willis is in good company; Joseph Blenkinsopp wrote: "the punish-

---

[138] One final point regarding v. 19: As Willis has shown, it is not uncommon for the subject to switch from first to third person (or vice versa) within an oracle (see Isa 14:30; 10:12) ("Textual and Linguistic Issues," 390–91). The third person form clearly refers to YHWH, who has already been assaulting Shebna; what would be odd is the suggestion of v. 19a that the prophet himself will get involved.

[139] Wildberger treats vv. 15–19 separately, since he is less confident of the authenticity of the rest.

[140] Tryggve N. D. Mettinger takes it to be a calque for the Egyptian *mr pr wr*, "administrator of the royal domains," and it was a high-ranking position under the Egyptian pharaohs, as seemingly also under the later Judean kings: Mettinger, *Solomonic State Officials: A Study of the Civil Government Officials of the Israelite Monarchy* (ConBOT 5; Lund: Gleerup, 1971), 78–79. However, Robert M. Good has since argued that the title *ʿl bt* was used at Ugarit, and so was likely to be essentially indigenous to the Levant by Isaiah's time: Good, "The Israelite Royal Steward in the Light of Ugaritic *ʿl bt*," *RB* 86 (1979): 580–82 ; idem, "The Ugaritic Steward," *ZAW* 95 (1983): 110–11.

[141] Scott C. Layton, "The Steward in Ancient Israel: A Study of Hebrew (ʾašer) ʿal-habbayit in Its Near Eastern Setting," *JBL* 109 (1990): 633–49.

[142] Any discussion of this question depends on the complicated issue of the relationship between the present text and Isa 36–37. Since the matter is tangential to the issues at hand, I set it aside.

ment threatened seems to be quite disproportionate to the offense, and practically unintelligible except on the assumption that the text is silent about the real reason for the hostility it displays."[143] Wildberger agrees, "The elegant grave must have been just one symptom which showed that this official was arrogant to the core."[144] These comments represent a long tradition of assuming that Shebna's real trespass must be only implicit. Some scholars say he must be a foreigner, with no connection to the people or the land.[145] But there is no manifest sign of this; Shebna is likely a short form of a known Yahwistic moniker, Shebaniah/ Shebanyahu.[146] Others claim that he is a parvenu – the omission of a patronym both here and in Isa 36–37 could indicate that he was of low birth – and that he has overstepped his social status and "is consequently being put in his place as a social climber" by Isaiah.[147] But is this the same Isaiah who consistently rails against the abuses committed by the powerful (5:8, 13–14) and the misdeeds of the Jerusalem leadership (1:10; 3:12; 22:3)? It is not impossible to construct an ideological profile that would contain both viewpoints, but it seems an improbable contrast. There is no denying that Shebna may have been pompous, or that excessive pride is certainly an issue over and over again in Isaiah – but it cannot be the only one.

I will demonstrate that the tomb itself really *is* the main problem – it is the focal point of the oracle (to an even greater extent than is usually recognized), and the threefold repetition of פה in v. 16 (מה־לך פה ומי לך פה כי חצבת לך פה קבר) causes most exegetes to conclude that the prophet must be delivering the oracle *at the tomb itself*. In light of the data already presented about Judean and foreign burial practices in chapters 1–4, Isaiah's problem with the tomb appears to have multiple facets. First, one might point to its excessive individuation, which would have marked a sharp break from Judean burial traditions. The line מה־לך פה ומי לך פה is quite ingenious as Hebrew poetry. The phrase מה־לך פה is a common one in Hebrew prose; it is an idiom for "what are you doing here?" (e.g., 1 Kgs 19:9, 13). However, since the ל can express possession, it allows Isaiah to use a parallel but far less common construction: "Whom do you have here?" This phrase is never, to my knowledge, properly explained in secondary literature on Isa 22. It does not mean "whom do you have here to authorize you to hew out a tomb for yourself?"[148] as if Shebna needed a building permit (cf. NIV). Nor does it mean

---

[143] Blenkinsopp, *Isaiah 1–39*, 338.
[144] Wildberger, *Isaiah 13–27*, 389.
[145] E.g., Kaiser, *Isaiah 13–39*, 153.
[146] See F. W. Dobbs-Allsopp et al., *Hebrew Inscriptions: Texts from the Period of the Monarchy* (New Haven: Yale University Press, 2003), 508. The theory that "Shebna" is related to Egyptian *šbnw* seems to have fallen from favor. *Šbnw* is attested in the Egyptian onomasticon only in the Middle Kingdom. See Hermann Ranke, *Die Ägyptischen Personennamen* (Glückstadt: J. J. Augustin, 1935), 1:325 nn. 11–12.
[147] Blenkinsopp, *Isaiah 1–39*, 338. See also J. T. Willis, "Historical Issues in Isaiah 22,15–25" *Bib* 74 (1993): 62–63.
[148] So Blenkinsopp, *Isaiah 1–39*, 335–36.

"You do not have anyone (no ancestors, no relatives) whose background could make it appropriate for you to erect such an elaborate grave site,"[149] as if Shebna simply doesn't come from a good family (a variety of the parvenu theory). It *does* refer to family – the other two examples of the phrase in the Hebrew Bible suggest that the question מי לך typically did[150] – but the implicit question is, "where is the *rest of your family* buried?" In eighth-century Jerusalem, even most elites would have been buried in a rock-cut bench tomb, one where multiple generations of a family would be successively laid to rest. The period of Hezekiah's reign saw just such a trend: the rise of tombs that were richer and more elaborate and also showed greater individuation (§ 4.3). To say that a shift can be perceived is not to say that such individual burials were common; Shebna's tomb, carved out "for himself" alone (v. 16), would have been exceptional.[151]

This interpretation invites reflection on the Silwan cemetery, a grouping of some fifty Iron Age tombs discovered over the course of the past century or so in the town of Silwan, on the hillside facing the Ophel and City of David. They are large and characterized by fine stonework and features reflecting their builders' intention that they be used only for themselves and not for their descendants: for example, individual bathtub coffins, personal names inscribed in stone, and a lack of bone pits. Concluded archaeologist David Ussishkin: "Our tombs were prepared for the burial of relatively few people and they cannot be considered as 'family tombs.'"[152] Despite their individual purpose, these tombs are also the size of a small Iron Age house, which suggests that even the phrase "a dwelling (משכן) in the cliff" contains a certain condemnation of selfish ostentation: why should one corpse need an entire house? (Insofar as the most common referent of משכן in the Bible is the abode of God, it could be supposed that the term conveys a sense of hubris, or even refers to hopes for divinization after death.)

One of the tombs bore the following inscription, which was chiseled off from the lintel and later transcribed by N. Avigad:[153]

זאת [קברת ...]יהו אשר על הבית אין פה כסף וזהב כי אם [עצמתו]
ועצמת אמתה אתה ארור האדם אשר יפתח את זאת

---

[149] Wildberger, *Isaiah 13–27*, 387.
[150] The two instances are Gen 19:2, where the angels are asking Lot what other family he has in Sodom; and Gen 33:8, where Esau asks Jacob who all these members of his household are whom he has been sending ahead of him.
[151] David Ussishkin, "The Necropolis from the Time of the Kingdom of Judah at Silwan, Jerusalem," *BA* 33 (1970): 45: The "exclusiveness [of the individual Silwan tombs] becomes more apparent if we consider the fact that tens of thousands of people were buried in Jerusalem in the period of the First Temple, almost certainly in tombs of types characteristic of the period." On the antifamilial nature of the individual tombs as a social and theological problem, see also Stephen L. Cook, "Funerary Practices and Afterlife Expectations in Ancient Israel," *Religion Compass* 1 (2007): 22.
[152] Ussishkin, "Necropolis," 45.
[153] N. Avigad, "The Epitaph of a Royal Steward from Siloam Village," *IEJ* 8 (1953): 137–52.

The translation: "This is [the grave of ...]yahu who was over the house. There is no silver or gold here, but rather [his bones] and the bones of his slave-wife with him. Cursed be the man who will open this."[154] This has come to be known as the "Tomb of the Royal Steward," and from Avigad's first publication of the inscription, he promulgated the idea that it was the tomb of Shebna (although Avigad coyly attributed the idea to Yigael Yadin). From paleographical and orthographical standpoints, a late-eighth-century date is plausible.[155] However, although the phrase "who is over the house" suggests that the tomb's inhabitant indeed had the same position as Shebna, the Yahwistic theophoric element is hardly helpful in determining anything, given the predominance of such names,[156] and given the fact that Shebna's name has no theophoric element in the biblical text. Still, the identification has always been tempting to make, since it is easy to imagine one of these Silwan "graves on high" having been the object of Isaiah's condemnation. John D. W. Watts suggests that Shebna was "preoccupied by dignity in death while most people in Jerusalem were still hoping to live."[157] This would be consonant with the condemnation of those who feast while Jerusalem is under threat in 22:12–14. Isaiah repeatedly criticizes those who are focused on personal enjoyment and gain during times in which the prophet perceived Judah to be in crisis.

A second possible objection to the tomb is its display of foreign influence: non-native features of the preexilic tombs in the Silwan cemetery have long been noted. Perhaps the most striking foreign architectural element was pyramid-shaped monumental caps very much like those of Egyptian tombs of a similar period (Fig. 5.2). The stones that formed the pyramid were found toppled in the Tomb of Pharaoh's Daughter[158] (a romantic title with no proof to support it, but evocative of the architectural features). Similar bases show that at least two other tombs nearby also had pyramid tops as well, and Avigad argued that the Tomb of the Royal Steward had one as well.[159] Other elements seen nowhere else in Iron Age Judah included "entrances located high above the surface, gabled ceilings, straight ceilings with a cornice, trough-shaped resting-places with pillows, above-ground tombs, and inscriptions engraved on the façade."[160] Even the in-

---

[154] The similarity of the inscription to that of Tabnit of Sidon (*KAI* 1.13, *COS* 2.56) is remarkable, extending even to the assertion that there are no precious metals within (see § 2.3 above).

[155] Avigad, "Epitaph of a Royal Steward," 149–50. Orthographically, the *plene* spelling of ארור was perceived by Avigad as a hindrance to an eighth-century date, but now other inscriptions with *plene* spellings dating from the same period have been found (Mettinger, *Solomonic State Officials*, 72).

[156] Jeffrey H. Tigay, *You Shall Have No Other Gods: Israelite Religion in the Light of Hebrew Inscriptions* (HSS 31; Atlanta: Scholars Press, 1986).

[157] John D. W. Watts, *Isaiah 1–33* (rev. ed.; WBC 24; Nashville: Thomas Nelson, 2005), 348.

[158] Ussishkin, "Necropolis," 40.

[159] Avigad, "Epitaph of a Royal Steward," 151.

[160] Ussishkin, "Necropolis," 45.

Fig. 5.2 Reconstruction of an Egyptian tomb chapel from Deir el-Medina. Source: D'Auria et al, eds., *Mummies and Magic*, 24.

clusion of the names in the inscription might be considered an Egyptianizing practice, since the deceased was consistently named in ancient Egyptian tomb inscriptions as well.[161] In sum, "The architecture of the tombs and the burial traditions sharply differ from anything known from contemporary Palestine."[162] Moreover, much of the tombs' external architecture is damaged by many layers of later civilization and quarrying over the centuries; their unusual character would be much more apparent had not a monastery and then a city been successively built on top of them.

These Silwan tombs were thus constructed under Egyptian influence. Despite their uncommon architecture, they are exceptional only in the manner and degree to which they manifest Egyptian influence; that influence was widespread in Iron Age Judah, including in grave goods such as Egyptian (or Egyptianizing) scarabs that symbolized renewed life.[163] The increased interest in Egyptian tomb

---

[161] "Unveränderlicher Bestandteil des Denkmals blieben seit frühester Zeit jedoch der Name des Toten und fast immer eine ihn darstellende Bildnisfigur" (Peter Munro, *Die spätägyptischen Totenstelen* [Glückstadt: J. J. Augustin, 1973], 5).

[162] Ussishkin, "Necropolis," 45.

[163] For example, in the Tel Halif tombs: Biran, Avraham and Ram Gophna. "An Iron Age

forms in eighth-century Judah corresponds to a similar interest in Egypt itself; it has already been demonstrated that there was a classicizing movement in Egyptian culture under the Twenty-fifth and especially the Twenty-sixth Dynasties (ca. 747–656; cf. § 2.4.1) – that is to say, just before and throughout the career of Isaiah. This movement was reflected above all in funerary architecture, as the new, Nubian pharaohs and their high officials sought to be buried in Thebes like their Delta predecessors. They built lavish cliff tombs with mortuary chapels, often topped by small pyramids (see illustration).[164] Unquestionably, the Silwan tombs did not approach the size and grandeur of their Egyptian models, but there is no reason they should not have originally had cultic installations at the entryway for mortuary care, as did Egyptian tombs. Of course, in the Silwan cemetery one does not find pure manifestations of a style, but designs with hybridized provincial imitations; Ussishkin suggested that analogues are to be sought in Phoenicia.

Indeed, the Iron Age Phoenician cemetery at Tyre (§ 3.4) sheds light on both of the foregoing points: (1) It displayed a "egalitarian ideology" in the relative uniformity of its burials across social classes, and one suspects that the same ideology was dominant in Judah; (2) It showed Egyptian influence in the presence of scarabs interred with the bodies. Whereas Phoenician society was presumably tolerant of this influence, Isaiah was not.

Verses 15 and 19 offer evidence that Shebna's tomb included some obvious cultic installation, in contrast to most Judean tombs of the Iron Age. In v. 15, Isaiah is instructed to go to "this סכן," and it is typically asserted that סכן is a second title for Shebna. The term would be a biblical *hapax legomenon*, widely taken to refer to a governor or high administrator.[165] But is it a title at all? The

---

Burial Cave at Tel Halif." *IEJ* 20 (1970): 168–69. On the meaning of the scarabs, see S. J. Watson, "Death and Cosmology in Ancient Egypt," *JNSL* 17 (1991): 158–59. Says Erik Hornung: "The solar corpse takes the form of a scarab beetle, thus bearing within himself the germ of regeneration, as the scarab dung beetle is the rejuvenated morning form of the sun" ("Black Holes Viewed from Within: Hell in Ancient Egyptian Thought," *Diogenes* 42 [1994]: 148).

[164] See § 2.4.1. Note also Mettinger, *Solomonic State Officials*, 78: "Tombs of excellent quality are known for several of the [Egyptian] high stewards."

[165] If it is a title, then the sheer volume and diversity of the comparative evidence from both Ugarit and Mesopotamia will make it impossible to go beyond generalities. Willis treats the title as if it derived from Akkadian *šakānu*, "to place, set up, establish, etc." Derived from this root, the nouns *šakkanakku* and *šaknu* (II) are widely used in Mesopotamian texts of governors of provinces, military officers, and other authorities of unknown status (*CAD* Š.1 116–57, 170–76, 180–92). Ugaritic *skn* is also a term for a "prefect, governor, mayor, manager, administrator" (DUL 757–59) from a root meaning "care for." This same root is attested in the Amarna letters from Jerusalem as a West Semitic loanword. It is surely also this West Semitic root that is reflected in the feminine form סכנת, "caretaker," used only of Abishag's relationship to David (1 Kgs 1:2, 4) – but that relationship hardly sheds light on the term used here! Given the combination of biblical silence and comparative morass, the present author despairs of learning much else about this position, if it is a role in Israelite/Judahite government. There is a large literature about the relationship between these roots; see *DNWSI*, 786, s.v. "skn." For further discussion of

biblical record of the administration at Jerusalem is not skimpy, nor would there be any reason for editors to purge from the text a prominent administrative title. Yet no other official in the Hebrew Bible, nor in extrabiblical Hebrew inscriptions,[166] bears this title. For a fresh reading, I return to the Isaianic text: לך־בא אל־ הסכן הזה אל־שבנא אשר על־הבית. Although many remark that the prophet must be at the tomb, none seems to make the connection that *skn* has another meaning in West Semitic: "mortuary stela" (see *DUL* 759).[167] The reader has already encountered this word in Ugaritic in the Dagan stelae (*CAT* 6.13–14; § 3.3.3.3) and the Duties of an Ideal Son (*CAT* 1.17 I:26–34 et pars.). Mettinger has pointed out evidence for the use of *sikkanû* (stelae) in mortuary cults in Sumer, Ebla, Mari, and Phoenicia.[168]

Furthermore, stelae were an integral part of Egyptian tombs throughout ancient history;[169] they were markers of stone or wood identifying the owner of a tomb and including offering prayers for the care and feeding of his or her spirit, thus serving much the same function as W. F. Albright theorized for מצבות in ancient Palestine (§ 4.1).[170] They were also typically, in ancient Egypt, part of the *external* architecture of tombs, so if Egyptianizing tombs such as those at Silwan ever had them, they would be long gone, as the area was built over. In addition, Egyptian funerary stelae from the Third Intermediate Period were made of wood (Fig. 5.3), which would be far less likely than stone to survive. Indeed, again at the Iron Age Phoenician cemetery in Tyre, "'notables' of the community had the right to a stone funeral stela containing engraved symbols and funerary formulae

---

the titles, see Mettinger, *Solomonic State Officials*; J. T. Willis, "'*ab* as an Official Term," *SJOT* 10 (1996): 115–36; Avigad, "Epitaph of a Royal Steward," 137–52.

[166] The title *skn* appears in Phoenician inscriptions. It is also found in a Hebrew inscription on a broken ivory from Nimrud. However, the entire text reads "]*lskn skn xx*[... " Nothing indicates that this is a title. In fact, Wolfgang Röllig's introduction offers, among other suggestions for the enigmatic texts on the back of ivories: "Bezeichnen vielleicht die Buchstaben einen bestimmten Teil des Möbelstückes, für den diese Elfenbeinplatte bestimmt war?" ("Perhaps the letters designate a certain part of the piece of furniture, for which this ivory plate was intended?") (*Neue Ephemeris für semitische Epigraphik*, vol. 2 [ed. Rainer Degen et al.; Wiesbaden: Harrassowitz in Komm., 1974], 49). In other words, for all one knows the ivories might have been part of a piece of cultic hardware called a *skn*. And in any case one unusual item from Nimrud could hardly be taken as definitive evidence about Judean government.

[167] In Hebrew, the word should probably be pointed סֻכָּן or סִכָּן; cf. Emar Akkadian *sikkānu*. For further lexicographical discussion of the occurrences of the root *skn* in Hebrew, see M. Dietrich, O. Loretz and J. Sanmartin, "Zur ugaritischen Lexicographie (XII)," *UF* 6 (1974): 41–44.

[168] Tryggve N. D. Mettinger, *No Graven Image? Israelite Aniconism in Its Ancient Near Eastern Context* (ConBOT 42; Stockholm: Almqvist & Wiksell International, 1995), 115–16, 131–32.

[169] Regina Hölzl, "Stela," in *Oxford Encyclopedia of Ancient Egypt* (Oxford: Oxford University Press, 2001), 3:319–24; Karl Martin, "Stele," in *Lexikon der Ägyptologie* (Wiesbaden: Harrassowitz, 1986), 6:1–6.

[170] See also Elizabeth Bloch-Smith, *Judahite Burial Practices and Beliefs about the Dead* (JSOTSup 123; Sheffield: JSOT Press, 1992), 113; Karel van der Toorn, *Family Religion in Babylonia, Syria and Israel: Continuity and Change in the Forms of Religious Life* (Leiden: Brill, 1996), 220–22.

Fig. 5.3 Wooden funerary stele, Egyptian, Third Intermediate Period. From the collection of the Michael C. Carlos Museum, Emory University.

inscribed as epitaphs for the deceased," and "[t]he stelae were set up directly on top of the graves" so that "the upper part of the stela ... was visible on the surface."[171] Furthermore, "[t]races of wooden imprints at the edge of some graves suggest the presence of markers made of organic material."[172] I suggest that the same was true of elites in Jerusalem.

---

[171] Aubet, "The Phoenician Cemetery of Tyre," 154.
[172] Aubet, "The Phoenician Cemetery of Tyre," 148.

Adopting this translation quite plausibly reveals the true import of v. 15b: "Go to this mortuary stela, to Shebna who is master of the house (and say): 'What are you doing here?'" In the same way, Isaiah is sent in 7:3 to meet a person, Ahaz, at a specific place, Fuller's Field.[173] It would not be odd to use the term סכן to indicate the entire tomb, since a funerary stela, "*pars pro toto*, embodied the most important and essential purpose of the tomb and was a surrogate for it."[174]

This reading not only eliminates the unparalleled and possibly contradictory title for Shebna, but it also sets the location, which is a point of great emphasis. Furthermore, it makes the passage more coherent by placing the focus on the tomb from the beginning.

I would argue further that related cultic installations are referred to again in v. 19. Verse 19 has not attracted special notice from interpreters; it is typically seen as a mere "link" (whether redactional or original) between the Shebna oracle and the announcement of Eliakim as a replacement.[175] Commentators also sense other irregularities: Blenkinsopp remarks that v. 19 is a "rather bland statement about Shebna's dismissal from office ... following the intemperate language preceding it,"[176] while Wildberger says that it is "hardly the job of a prophet to threaten someone with removal from their position in the government."[177]

Since this verse seems so ill-fitted to its context under the usual understanding, it is curious that no one remarks on its unusual vocabulary: מצב never means "office" in the sense of "job" in the Hebrew Bible, nor in Northwest Semitic inscriptions.[178] In inscriptions, however, it *does* regularly mean "stela, image, idol, sacred stone."[179] It is etymologically related to the common term מצבה, the cultic "standing stones" that mark various holy places in the Old Testament and were condemned by the Deuteronomists.[180] Such stones had various cultic functions, but memorial markers were one of the common ones.[181] Of special interest in this connection are the מצבות erected as a grave-marker for Rachel (Gen 35:20), and

---

[173] In 7:3 one also finds combined indications of where to go and whom to go to: צא נא לקראת אחז ... אל־קצה תעלת הברכה העליונה אל־מסלת שדה כובס, "Go to meet Ahaz, to the end of the aqueduct of the upper pool, to the highway to the Fuller's Field."

[174] Alan R. Schulman, "Some Observations About the ₃ḥ iḵr n Rʿ Stelae," *BO* 43 (1986): 304.

[175] Wildberger states: "Without any doubt, v. 19 is a later addition ..." (*Isaiah 13–27*, 382). Blenkinsopp says: "most commentators ... read this verse as marking the transition from Shebna to Eliakim and therefore as an addition" (*Isaiah 1–39*, 337). See also Tucker, "Isaiah 1–39," 196.

[176] Blenkinsopp, *Isaiah 1–39*, 337.

[177] Wildberger, *Isaiah 13–27*, 382.

[178] It means "place (of standing)" in Josh 4:3, 9; and it means "garrison" in 2 Sam 23:14 and a number of times in 1 Sam 13–14.

[179] See references in *DNWSI*, 675–76.

[180] Genesis 28:18; 28:22; 31:13; 35:14; 31:45, 51, 52 (bis); Exod 24:4; Hos 3:4; 10:1, 2. As a foreign practice: Exod 23:24; 34:13; Deut 7:5; 12:3; 2 Kgs 3:2; 10:26, 27. Deuteronomic condemnations: Deut 16:22; 1 Kgs 14:23; 17:10; 18:4; 23:14; 2 Chr 14:2; 31:1; cf. Mic 5:12; Lev 26:1.

[181] Izaak J. De Hulster, *Iconographic Exegesis and Third Isaiah* (FAT/II 36; Tübingen, Germany: Mohr Siebeck, 2009), 151–68.

as a personal memorial by Absalom (2 Sam 18:18). It is also worthy of mention that Israelites were capable of using the term מצבות to describe features of Egyptian architecture (Ezek 26:11; Isa 19:19) and also probably to describe a "compound monument," that is, the whole of the tomb.[182] In the context of this oracle, it seems most logical to interpret והדפתיך ממצבך to mean "I will thrust you from your monument (= tomb chapel)."

The term מעמד presents slightly different issues: It does indeed mean "job, duty" twice in the writings of the Chronicler (1 Chr 23:28; 2 Chr 35:15), but there is reason to think that this is a late usage that would not have been intended by a preexilic prophet. In Ps 69:3, it is used as the Psalmist feels himself drowning, and "there is no place to stand" (אין מעמד). The image of a foothold seems quite appropriate to the setting of a tomb cut into a cliff. "He will tear you down from your foothold" makes rather good sense with the image of YHWH hurling Shebna away. There is also, once again, a possible architectural aspect to the term; it is restored in a Palmyrene inscription with the meaning "raised, erected object⟩ altar," and may thus be related to the more common עמוד, "pillar, platform."[183] It is not clear what precise significance is envisioned for this platform; it could be an altar or other cultic installation, but the syntax suggests that it is a platform or pedestal on which Isaiah portrays Shebna exalting himself.[184]

In further support of the foregoing interpretation, the verbs הדף (usually "push") and especially הרס (usually "tear down") by their nature express physical force. Although הדף is sometimes used in a metaphorical sense (Deut 6:16; Job 18:18), neither verb has anything to do with removal from office in the Hebrew Bible.

In sum, the idea in this passage that Shebna is being fired from a job has been forced on the text and is impossible to sustain. Instead, the image is of the tomb as a lofty place in which Shebna seeks to enshrine himself but from which YHWH rips him out and hurls him onto a wide, unsheltered land. The ensuing passage, in which Eliakim is called to take Shebna's place, may create a *double entendre* by emphasizing administrative duties. (Wordplay in general, and paronomasia/*double entendre* in particular, are pervasive in Isaiah.[185]). But in v. 19 the references to

---

[182] The same can be said of Hebrew (מצב(ה as of Egyptian *wḏ*: "Stele," in *Lexikon der Ägyptologie*, 6:1. Thus the phrase "thrusting you from your מצב" does not create an awkward image.

[183] Two kings of Judah are said to stand על־עמודו in public ceremonies. This is generally translated awkwardly as "the king stood by the pillar." More likely, it should be "the king stood on the platform." Is it an accident that the two kings in question are seven-year-old Jehoash (2 Kgs 11:14) and eight-year-old Josiah (2 Kgs 23:3)? These are kings who would need to stand on a platform! This point is also argued by Arnulf Kuschke and Martin Metzger, "Kumudi und die Ausgrabungen auf Tell Kāmid el-Loz," in *Congress Volume: Uppsala, 1971* (Leiden: Brill, 1972), 163–66.

[184] Altars are found in Egyptian tombs, so perhaps Isaiah is either misunderstanding or purposely co-opting the feature in a way somewhat different from its actual cultic role.

[185] See J. J. M. Roberts, "Double Entendre in First Isaiah," *CBQ* 54 (1992): 39–48; also Im-

the tomb are quite clear. Verses 15 and 19 therefore suggest that Shebna's pride is not the only issue at stake for Isaiah; cultic/theological concerns are also interwoven in the oracle. The repeated references to cultic structures are likely associated with cult-of-the-dead practices that the prophet elsewhere condemns (e.g., 8:19–20).[186]

The most difficult portion of the text has always been vv. 17b–18. The start of v. 17 clearly threatens that YHWH will "hurl Shebna down," and in some way the rest of vv. 17–18 elaborate that threat. In light of the picture of a "tomb on high," the significance of this threat should be rather obvious: Shebna is going to be cast from his grave and thus be deprived of a peaceful afterlife, much like the tyrant in Isa 14. The passage has generally been explained by analogy with Jer 22:26 – "I will hurl you (הטלתיך) and the mother who bore you into another country, where you were not born, and there you shall die" – in which case it is quite obviously a reference to the Babylonian exile. Of course, exile was already a familiar punishment to Israel and Judah prior to the sixth century (e.g., Amos 7:11); thus, it might be in view here even if the passage is "authentic." I would like to suggest, however, that the very difficult verb forms are best explained by the assumption that the prophet picks up the image of v. 17a by at least punning on corpse violation.

The options typically presented for עטה in v. 17b are truly unpalatable. Most translations understand it by analogy with an Arabic verb 'tw, "to seize, grasp" (so BDB, NRSV, NIV, NJB). The solution of HALOT ("to delouse") is worse still; as Blenkinsopp astutely remarks, "why delouse a garment and then throw it away?"[187] Furthermore, the only other supposed occurrence of עטה II ("to delouse") that HALOT cites (Jer 43:12) is also unclear and therefore not relevant. The LXX has its own free translation,[188] and 1QIsa[a] seems confused as well.[189]

Under these circumstances, it seems better to return to firm ground: עטה (I), "to cover over, wrap." When Samuel rises from the dead to speak to Saul, he is wrapped in a robe (הוא עטה מעיל; 1 Sam 28:14). As one can see from the contrast

---

manuel M. Casanowicz, "Paronomasia in the Old Testament," *JBL* 12 (1893): 105–67, esp. chart p. 167; Edwin M. Good, *Irony in the Old Testament* (2nd ed.; Sheffield: Almond, 1981), 121–25; and note the large number of examples from Isaiah in Stefan Schorch, "Between Science and Magic: The Function and Roots of Paronomasia in the Prophetic Books of the Hebrew Bible," in *Puns and Pundits: Word Play in the Hebrew Bible and Ancient Near Eastern Literature* (ed. Scott B. Noegel; Bethesda, Md.: CDL, 2000), 205–22.

[186] See also W. Boyd Barrick, *The King and the Cemeteries: Toward a New Understanding of Josiah's Reform* (VTSup 88; Boston: Brill, 2001), 168.

[187] Blenkinsopp, *Isaiah 1–39*, 336.

[188] ἀφελεῖ τὴν στολήν σου καὶ τὸν στέφανόν σου τὸν ἔνδοξον – "he will remove your robe and your crown of glory"

[189] 1QIsa[a] complicates the matter by reading יעוטך, as if it had understood an irregular form from the root עיט, "to attack with screams (like a bird of prey)." But the next word is still עטה, so the intention is unclear. The י at the start of יעוטך is also the result of a correction (Parry and Qimron, *Great Isaiah Scroll*, 35), so the scribe seems to have had a problem here.

between Isa 61:10 ("[YHWH] has covered me with the robe of righteousness") and Ps 89:46 ("You [YHWH] have covered him with shame"), עטה is a neutral word in Hebrew, well-suited to wordplay. One can well imagine that being "covered" or "cloaked" was a hope for deceased Israelites; the image of cloaking/ covering evokes the desire not to be disturbed. The image may be more straightforward still, since both textual and archaeological data indicate that Judeans of high rank were commonly buried in cloaks (§ 4.3). Alternately, it might evoke bathtub coffins like those of the elite Silwan tombs, which were fitted with stone covers. But cloaking also could be used in a negative sense. In Ps 109:19, the Psalmist asks that the enemy's curses "be like a garment that he wraps around himself (יעטה) ... and, in v. 29 of the same Psalm, he prays that his accusers "be wrapped (יעטו) in their own shame as in a mantle." Furthermore, עטה has a cognate in Akkadian, *eṭû*, "be dark," which is used in negative contexts such as this curse against military opponents from the Tukulti-Ninurta Epic: "O Šamaš, lord of judgment, darken (*uṭṭi*) the eyes of the troops of Sumer and Akkad!"[190] Perhaps, therefore, Isaiah is turning a hope of protection into a threat of vengeance: Shebna will be covered over in the sense of extinguishment or blotting out.

The situation with צנף is similar. Here too one encounters a verb with a relatively common sense (in this case "wrap, wind") that is supposed to mean something different, especially for this context. A number of modern translations assert that the basic sense of צנף is "to go in circles," and they thus seem to picture Shebna being flung from something like a sling (NRSV), or rolled into a ball (Wildberger, Blenkinsopp, NIV, NJB). Against these suggestions, צנף never bears this meaning elsewhere; in nominal forms it refers to some sort of wrap upon the head, and in the only other verbal occurrence (Lev 16:4) it refers to the wrapping of the same.[191]

There is no neat solution to this problem, but I think that the few exegetes who have suggested over the years that there is a reference to Egyptian burial wrappings are on the right track, given the context.[192] I would suggest that צנף can mean both "wrap" and "unwrap," and that the underlying image here is of YHWH unwrapping the mummified corpse of Shebna after he has uncovered it.

The parallel between כדור in this verse and a cognate noun in Anat's slaughter in the Baal Cycle deserves closer attention:

---

[190] Tukulti-Ninurta Epic, ii 30. Demons are said to be "like vultures with spread wings that darken the daylight" (*CT* 16 42:8; cf. *CAD* E, 412).

[191] The Tanakh translation faithfully tries to follow the garment metaphor – "The LORD is about to shake you severely, fellow, and then wrap you around Himself./ Indeed, He will wind you about Him as a headdress, a turban. Off to a broad land!" Not only is this final phrase disjointed and abrupt; one might also ask why the Lord would wrap around himself one whom he is punishing. And if he is wearing Shebna, then is the Lord also "off to a broad land"?

[192] Kurt Galling, *Biblisches Reallexikon* (HAT 1; Tübingen: Mohr Siebeck, 1937), 239: "Auf ägyptischen Brauch der Leichenumwicklung scheint Jes 22:18 anzuspielen." Also R. E. Clements, *Isaiah 1–39* (NCB; Grand Rapids: Eerdmans, 1980), 189.

Thereupon 'Anatu begins to smite her adversaries in the valley ...
Under her, heads are like balls (*k kdrt*),
above her, hands are like locusts,
heaps of fighters' hands are like (heaps of) grasshoppers. (*CAT* 1.3 ii 5–6, 9–11)

Since this seems to be the only other instance of *kd(w)r*, "ball," in extrabiblical Semitic texts, one wonders whether the term was traditionally related to an ancient idiom akin to the modern phrase, "making heads roll." That would appear to be what this passage envisions as well: As YHWH unwraps the head of Shebna, it rolls like a ball down into the valley (indeed, it is tempting to see כדור as a play on קדרון, "Kidron"). Since the root דור has the sense of "make a round" in rabbinic Hebrew, it seems likely that a later scribe removed a *kaph*, mistakenly taking it for a dittography, and that the text originally read ככדור.[193]

Even if כדור does mean "ball," the syntax of צנוף יצנפך צנפה is still unclear. I would suggest that it is allowable to supply the word "head," since that is the sort of wrapping to which צנף typically refers. Thus: "He will indeed unwrap your head-wrapping, (rolling your head) like a ball into a wide land." Perhaps there is another *double entendre* here: the headgear is a mark of Shebna's office or stature, but is compared by the prophet to the wrappings of a corpse.

It is not at all clear that ארץ רחבת ידים refers to a foreign country; "the wide land" (*erṣetu rapaštu*) was a term for the underworld in Akkadian (§ 1.4.3), and there are similar phrases in the Bible,[194] so the text may refer to Shebna's expulsion there. Alternately, it may simply indicate a wide-open area without shelter for the dead, perhaps the Kidron Valley below.[195] Blenkinsopp remarked that "[t]he prospect of death in a foreign land, no doubt Mesopotamia, constitutes a brutally direct negation of this official's tomb-building in or near Jerusalem."[196] But expulsion from the tomb and banishment to the underworld is even more brutally direct. Another problem with the theory that exile is in view is noted by Willis: "it is not logical to announce that one will be removed from office after announcing that he will go into exile. Removal from office must precede being taken into exile."[197] On my revised reading, however, corpse exposure quite naturally follows removal from the tomb.

---

[193] Brichto, "Kin, Cult, Land and Afterlife," 35.
[194] Especially Job 38:17–18: "Have the gates of death been revealed to you, or have you seen the gates of deep darkness? Have you comprehended the wide places of the earth (רחבי־ארץ)?" But see also Pss 18:20; 31:9; 118:5. For commentary, see Mitchell J. Dahood, *Psalms: Introduction, Translation, and Notes* (3 vols.; AB 16, 17, 17A, Garden City, N.Y.: Doubleday, 1966–70), 1:185; Tromp, *Primitive Conceptions of Death*, 47–48. Finally, one might note also the description of the underworld as "utterly endless" in Book of the Dead, Spell 175.
[195] I agree with Watts that "[t]he term is not specific enough for the interpretations laid on it" (*Isaiah 1–33*, 348).
[196] Blenkinsopp, *Isaiah 1–39*, 337.
[197] Willis, "Historical Issues," 64.

If it is correct to see in צִיּוֹן another reference to Egyptianizing burial practices, it may to some extent reflect aspects of Shebna's actual burial plans, given the unusual Silwan tombs, but it may also be that Isaiah is vilifying Shebna as a traitor to Judah. It is frequently supposed that Shebna was a part of the pro-Egyptian party that Isaiah so despised (Isa 11:15; 19:1–15; 20; 30:1–7), perhaps even its leader.[198] After all, Egyptian political and artistic influence seem to have been correlated.[199] In portraying Shebna as embracing foreign burial customs, Isaiah might have hoped to stir passions against him and his political views, much as the Roman emperor Octavian portrayed Mark Antony as an immoral traitor for leaving his wife and family for the Egyptian Cleopatra. The rhetoric runs: How can we trust a man who prefers an Egyptian (after)life? One advantage of the reading presented here is that it makes it possible to maintain the long-standing assumption that a political dispute underlies the condemnation, even if the actual language of the condemnation is primarily religious.

In light of Isaiah's anti-Egyptianizing rhetoric, the reference to "glorious chariots" (v. 18) may also take on a different significance. Their presence in the text does not seem to have been adequately explained, despite the efforts of scholars to show that they symbolize excessive pomp. That motif is apparent only in 1 Sam 8:11; it simply does not seem to have been a prominent enough idea for Isaiah to refer to it without any sort of context or development. If the usual understandings of the passage are correct, then Shebna is being sent into exile with these chariots – but who was ever taken into exile on a glorious chariot? Or what administrator who died in exile was ever honored by having his body carried on such a chariot (cf. Tanakh)?[200] Instead, since the text portrays things being thrown out from a tomb, perhaps the image is of chariots as grave goods. Chariots, including miniaturized ones, are well known from elite graves in Egypt[201] and throughout the ancient Near East.[202] Tutankhamun's tomb, one of the few royal

---

[198] E.g., Wildberger, *Isaiah 13–27*, 381; Kaiser, Isaiah *13–39*, 151. A. Auret hypothesized that Shebna might have been an Assyrian official foisted on Hezekiah by his suzerain. But this theory does not square with the comparative data: (1) it does not seem to have been Neo-Assyrian practice to install merely a high official; and (2) the name Shebna has never been explained as a Mesopotamian one. See Auret, "A Different Background for Isaiah 22:15–25 Presents an Alternative Paradigm: Disposing of Political and Religious Opposition?" *OTE* 6 (1993): 46–56.

[199] Glenn Markoe, "The Emergence of Phoenician Art," *BASOR* 279 (1990): 23: "Egyptian artistic influence in the Levant did not remain constant throughout the Late Bronze and Iron Ages, but fluctuated according to the extent of Egyptian political and commercial involvement in the region."

[200] One possible explanation would be an Assyrian parade in which dead enemies were displayed (see Richardson, "Death and Dismemberment in Mesopotamia," 199 n. 45). However, a mere steward seems unlikely to have been accorded such treatment, which was usually reserved for kings.

[201] For a list of chariots in Egyptian tombs, see M. A. Littauer and J. H. Crouwel, *Chariots and Related Equipment from the Tomb of Tutʿankhamūn* (Tutʿankhamūn's Tomb Series 8; Oxford: Griffith Institute, 1985), 67–69.

[202] E.g., at Ebla; cf. Paolo Matthiae, "New Discoveries at Ebla: The Excavations of the Western Palace and the Royal Necropolis of the Amorite Period," *BA* 47 (1984): 25.

Egyptian burials not thoroughly robbed in antiquity, included no fewer than six, of which three were extensively covered in precious metals. In the eighth and seventh centuries, a whole sequence of Kushite pharaohs were buried with their chariot horses and some associated items.[203] Chariots as grave provisions are known also from ancient Mesopotamia, where they were "a conspicuous component of the burial goods of kings and other wealthy citizens."[204] Chariots were "status-conferring vehicles,"[205] in death as in life. Strangely, archaeologists have not recovered Neo-Assyrian chariots or models, but this appears to be merely an accident of preservation, since numerous Neo-Assyrian reliefs show the Neo-Assyrian kings on chariots, and scholars conclude that they were certainly well known in first-millennium Mesopotamia.[206] The comparatively small scale of the Silwan tombs is not a hindrance to this theory, since chariots often filled most of a burial chamber, or had to be disassembled to fit into tombs.[207] The chariots popular in the ancient Near East were not of great size or heft; they were small, light, and intended only for one or two riders. Chariots are also found miniaturized as votive models, and similar ones could have been included as grave goods.

The understanding of this verse must remain conjectural, since the provisions from the Silwan tombs have long since disappeared, and they may have been as unusual (for Judah) as were the tombs themselves. In any case, the theory is not that there was actually a chariot present when the oracle was delivered, but that Isaiah was referring to a foreign burial practice that would have been deemed

---

[203] The pharaohs are Piankhy, Shabako, Shebitku, and Tanwetamani; their tombs at El Kurru have twenty-four horse burials associated with them. See Dows Dunham, *The Royal Cemeteries of Kush*, vol. 1 (Cambridge, Mass.: Harvard University Press, 1950), 110–17 and plate IV; also Lisa A. Heidorn, "The Horses of Kush," *JNES* 56 (1997): 105–14; and W. Stevenson Smith, *The Art and Architecture of Ancient Egypt* (rev. ed. with additions by W. K. Simpson; New Haven: Yale University Press, 1998), 232.

[204] J. N. Postgate, *Early Mesopotamia: Society and Economy at the Dawn of History* (London: Routledge, 1994), 246. Since chariots continued to be used ceremonially by the Mesopotamians through the Neo-Babylonian period (A. Leo Oppenheim, *Ancient Mesopotamia: Portrait of a Dead Civilization* [Chicago: University of Chicago Press, 1964; rev. ed. by Erica Reiner, Chicago: University of Chicago Press, 1977], 193), it is likely they also continued to be used in elite burials. The phenomenon appears to have been rather widespread, since "chariot burials" have been found from Iron Age Great Britain, fourteenth- to ninth-century BCE China, and Roman-period Athens. Other wheeled vehicles were buried with the dead in the Urals and in Kültepe in the early second millennium, although these may not have been "true chariots." See M. A. Littauer and J. H. Crouwel, "The Origin of the True Chariot," in *Selected Writings on Chariots and Other Early Vehicles, Riding and Harness* (Culture and History of the Ancient Near East 6; Leiden: Brill, 2002), 45.

[205] Littauer and Crouwel, "Origin of the True Chariot," 50.

[206] Archaeologists' failure to locate most of the Neo-Assyrian royal graves is well known. See M. A. Littauer, "New Light on the Assyrian Chariot," in *Selected Writings on Chariots and Other Early Vehicles, Riding and Harness* (Culture and History of the Ancient Near East 6; Leiden: Brill, 2002), 246–57.

[207] Littauer and Crouwel, "Origin of the True Chariot," 51; Littauer and Crouwel, *Chariots and Related Equipment*, 98.

strange and excessive by Judean standards but was within the realm of possibility in the context of the surge in burial preparations under Hezekiah. As a critic might express the point in English vernacular: *He's already got a pyramid, a coffin, a stele, and an inscription.... Next thing you know, he'll be putting a gilded chariot in that tomb.*

Having laid out this new reading at some length, it is necessary to retrench: the phrase שמה תמות (v. 18) is problematic for the interpretation offered here. If the image is of a tomb being violated, then is the inhabitant not already dead? How can he die after being cast out? There are ways to rationalize the image: Perhaps it could be taken as a stative ("there you will lie dead"); or perhaps it refers to the "second death," in which case it would continue the string of references to Egyptian beliefs.[208] To an Egyptian, only death without proper burial was truly death.[209] It is also possible that one is dealing here with a typically Isaian *double entendre* that does not work as well as some others, or that the delicate imagistic work has been corrupted by a redactor or copyist.[210] In any case, the simple juxtaposition of the tomb ("here") in v. 16 and YHWH's "hurling" in v. 17 already creates the image of disinterment; I have merely tried to show that that image is carried through the passage much more thoroughly and coherently than is usually thought to be the case.

At a minimum, one can say that Isa 22:15–19 demonstrates the same tendency on Isaiah's part to threaten unsuccessful burial and unhappy afterlife; it is not only foreign enemies who are the target of such condemnation, but Judean opponents as well. If the analysis presented here is correct, then it also shows that Isaiah was concerned here as much with theological and cultic transgressions as with political ones. It eliminates the need for special pleading regarding the translation of seven different words (מצב, צנפה, יצנפך, צנוף, עטה, יעטה and מעמד) and also removes a reference to a governmental title known from no other biblical or inscriptional Hebrew text. Furthermore, it reveals in the text the plausible coherence of a unified prophetic utterance: the matter at hand is the

---

[208] For examples of tomb desecration as a way of inflicting the second death, see Aidan Dodson, "Death After Death in the Valley of the Kings," in *Death and Taxes in the Ancient Near East*, 53–59.

[209] The story of Sinuhe provides a possible example of this sort of reasoning. Sinuhe is an Egyptian official who leaves Egypt and finds success living in Palestine. However, in his old age he prays to return to Egypt to be buried, and the pharaoh invites him back. When he receives the pharaoh's letter, he exclaims, "Truly good is the kindness that saves me from death!," and he calls the pharaoh "lord who saves from the West" (Lichtheim, *Ancient Egyptian Literature*, 1:230). As Assmann observes, "dying abroad would be death, while dying in the homeland, in the favor of the king, and being buried in a tomb presented by the king, would be life" (Assmann, *Death and Salvation*, 179).

[210] For example, it might be possible to take שמה תמות as a late addition, perhaps under the influence of Jer 22:26 (which ends with שם תמותו), but the stability of the text of Isaiah in its various forms makes this an unappealing theory.

tomb, which is the symbol for all the underlying problems. The oracle is delivered there and refers to its builder, its architecture, its provisions, and (by association) its cultic practices. It also, however, *connects* hints of Egyptianizing elements in the Silwan tombs and in the text to the (anti-Egyptian) political background that is apparent elsewhere in Isa 1–39.

5.2.1.4 Isaiah 36:11–12: A hellish meal

A high Neo-Assyrian official trying to convince Jerusalem to capitulate to Sennacherib issues another kind of death threat against the city's people:

(11) And Eliakim, Shebna, and Joah said to the *rab šaqeh*, "Please, speak to your servants in Aramaic, for we understand it; do not speak to us in Judean in earshot of the people who are on the wall.

(12) But the *rab šaqeh* said, "Was it only to you and your master that my master sent me to speak these words? Was it not to the men sitting on the wall, (who are) to eat their excrement and drink their urine?"

This brief exchange and its parallel in 2 Kgs 18:26–27[211] are part of the larger biblical account of Sennacherib's attack on Judah in 701. The extensive body of research surrounding this passage and the historical event it recounts has already been summarized in § 1.2, so I will recapitulate only briefly: the exchange cited here is part of the so-called B1 narrative (Isa 36:1–37:9a, 36–37 // 2 Kgs 18:17–19:9a, 36–37), the longest of the four in the Hebrew Bible. The others are 2 Kgs 18:13–16 (A); Isa 37:9b–35 // 2 Kgs 19:9b–35 (B2), and 2 Chr 32:1–22 (C). To speak of four accounts in the Bible usually presumes that they were successively edited and augmented, building on the first, annalistic version in A.[212]

To say that B1 is not the earliest version of the event, however, is not to say that it is purely fictional. Assessments of B1's historical value have pointed in two directions. On the one hand, it shows genuine acquaintance with Neo-Assyrian rhetoric. Wrote Peter Machinist:

> The address was doubtless not the invention – or at least not the full invention – of the Deuteronomist writers, but something that gives every indication of being rooted in actual historical practice. Other examples of such "psychological warfare" can be illustrated in Neo-Assyrian texts – letters and annals – as well as reliefs, and the address, parallel to its sensitivity to Judaean matters, is permeated by Assyrian phraseology and imagery.[213]

---

[211] The text of the Kings passage is identical apart from the addition of להם in the phrase "the *rab šaqeh* said *to them* ..."

[212] The theory of multiple biblical sources goes at least as far back as Bernhard Stade, "Miscellen 16. Anmerkungen zu 2 Kö 15–21," *ZAW* 6 (1886): 172–86. For more recent studies of the theological redaction of the biblical account, see Brevard S. Childs, *Isaiah and the Assyrian Crisis* (SBT 2nd series, 3; London: SCM, 1967); and R. E. Clements, *Isaiah and the Deliverance of Jerusalem: A Study of the Interpretation of Prophecy in the Old Testament* (JSOTSup 13; Sheffield, Eng.: Dept. of Biblical Studies, University of Sheffield, 1980); William R. Gallagher, *Sennacherib's Campaign to Judah: New Studies* (Studies in the History and Culture of the Ancient Near East 18; Leiden: Brill, 1999).

Machinist concludes that all three versions show "at their core a clear knowledge of Assyrian officialdom and techniques of war, and the definite impress of Assyrian power."[214] These observations are prefigured by the research of Chaim Cohen showing numerous specific details of lexicon, phraseology, and imagery in which the biblical speech matches historical Assyrian rhetoric as reflected in royal inscriptions.[215] Even the claim that the land's own deity has given it over to the Assyrians finds clear inscriptional analogues, such as Sargon's claim that Marduk had given Babylon over to him.[216] Furthermore, W. G. Lambert has recently adduced a record of similar Assyrian employment of intimidating rhetoric in a letter from two officers to Tiglath-Pileser III; in that case, the threats were against a city in Babylonia.[217] Finally, Bradley J. Parker finds that the promise of re-settling a family together and giving them farmland, housing, and even cattle is consistent with Assyrian practice elsewhere.[218]

On the other hand, certain parts of the speech contain Deuteronomistic terminology and idioms. This fact, along with the passage's location within the Deuteronomistic History, leads many to conclude that it has undergone significant editing. While the historians' ideology certainly shapes the retelling, that does not abolish the question of the extent to which the reportage is based on accurate memory or records.[219] The B1 account in which 36:12 is found is usually taken to be earlier than B2, and the verse's imagery is certainly not Deuteronomistic. Therefore it has a claim to be part of the underlying "Neo-Assyrian" layer of the speech, be it from shortly after 701 or from a Josianic redaction.

Ehud Ben Zvi has rightly drawn a connection between this passage and texts

---

[213] Peter Machinist, "The Rab Šaqeh at the Wall of Jerusalem: Israelite Identity in the Face of the Assyrian 'Other,'" *HS* 41 (2000): 159.

[214] Machinist, "Rab Šaqeh at the Wall of Jerusalem," 166; cf. Childs, *Isaiah*, 273.

[215] Chaim Cohen, "Neo-Assyrian Elements in the Speech of the Rab-Šāqê," in *Israel Oriental Studies 9* (Tel Aviv: Tel Aviv University, 1979), 32–48.

[216] Cf. Tadmor, Landsberger, and Parpola, "Sin of Sargon," 28.

[217] W. G. Lambert, "Mesopotamian Sources and Pre-Exilic Israel," in John Day, ed., *In Search of Pre-Exilic Israel: Proceedings of the Oxford Old Testament Seminar* (London: T & T Clark International, 2004), 361. Lambert cites H. W. F. Saggs, *The Nimrud Letters* (CTN 5; British Institute for the Study of Iraq, 2001): 20–21.

[218] Parker, *The Mechanics of Empire*, 263.

[219] Thucydides' method, which is probably not unlike that of the historians who recorded this passage, is often cited to disparage the historicity of speeches: "it was in all cases difficult to carry them [the speeches] word for word in one's memory, so my habit has been to make the speakers say what was in my opinion demanded of them by the various occasions, of course adhering as closely as possible to the general sense of what they really said" (*History of the Peloponnesian War* 1.22). For a discussion of the similar method of presenting speeches in Herodotus, see Donald Lateiner, *The Historical Method of Herodotus* (Journal of the Classical Association of Canada Supplementary Volume 23; Toronto: University of Toronto Press, 1989), 19–26. Regarding the Deuteronomistic Historian's intention to write accurate history, see Baruch Halpern, *The First Historians: The Hebrew Bible and History* (San Francisco: Harper & Row, 1988), 1–35.

such as Jer 21:8–10 and Deut 30:15, where "the main topic is the choice between a way of life and a way of death."[220] These texts undoubtedly have that theme in common, although Ben Zvi does not make it precisely clear on what basis he has deduced that the *rab šaqeh*'s speech offers that choice, since neither life nor death is actually mentioned in Isa 36–37. Of course, even a passing acquaintance with the Neo-Assyrians' military practices makes it clear that death awaited many who resisted their attacks or sieges (§ 1.2), so presumably Ben Zvi meant that the *rab šaqeh*'s reference to eating excrement and drinking urine evokes the conditions of a besieged city in its final throes, when its food and drinking water have been exhausted.

It seems to have been a relatively common tactic of ancient military rhetoric to present to a besieged city the choice between life and death, in explicit and sometimes graphic terms. I have already noted the Assyrian preference for frightening talk over military action (§ 1.2–3), and the same kind of terrorizing rhetoric seemed to have been employed by the Kushite rulers of Isaiah's time as well.[221] In other words, this tactic was widely diffused among Judah's neighbors and would have been known to court elites there, and the specific linguistic characteristics indicate Assyrian tendencies.

That argument would be accurate, but there is a mythological level to the *rab šaqeh*'s threat as well. The fear of eating excrement and drinking urine is well attested in Egyptian books of the dead (§ 2.4.3); chap. 53 of the "Book of Going Forth by Day" includes this aspiration for the afterlife: "I will not eat excrement, I will not drink urine"; and the same ideas can be found in magical papyri.[222] In connecting these ideas to the *rab šaqeh*'s speech, Paolo Xella was forced to hypothesize that since Mesopotamian texts commonly refer to the dead as eating dust and drinking muddy water (see § 1.4.3), it was a small step to the idea of consuming excrement.[223] But one can add to Xella's data a curse found in treaties of the Assyrian kings such as Aššur-Nirari V (755–745): "Let dust be their food, pitch their ointment; ass's urine their drink."[224] As Meir Malul has pointed out,[225]

---

[220] Ehud Ben Zvi, "Who Wrote the Speech of Rabshakeh and When?" *JBL* 109 (1990): 88.
[221] In Piye's victory stele, he recounts quelling a Saite-led uprising at the city Per-Sekhemkhepperre. When he reaches the stronghold and finds it prepared to fight, he issues this proclamation: "O you who live in death, you who live in death; you poor wretches, you who live in death! If the moment passes without your opening to me, you will be counted slain according to the King's judgment. Do not bar the gates of your life, so as to be brought to the block this day! Do not desire death and reject life!" And again later: "His majesty sent to [Mer-Atum], saying: "Look, two ways are before you; choose as you wish. Open, you live; close, you die. My majesty will not pass by a closed town!" Cf. Victory Stele of King Piye, lines 77–78, 82. Lichtheim, *Ancient Egyptian Literature*, 3:74. According to the stele, both cities capitulated immediately.
[222] J. F. Borghouts, *Ancient Egyptian Magical Texts* (Nisaba 9; Leiden: Brill, 1978), Spell 22.
[223] Paolo Xella, "Sur la Nourriture des Morts," in *Death in Mesopotamia: Papers Read at the XXVIe Rencontre Assyriologique Internationale* (ed. Bendt Alster; Mesopotamia 8; Copenhagen: Akademisk Forlag, 1980), 151–60.
[224] For the Aššur-Nirari V treaty, see *AfO* 8 25 iv.15. (Also *ANET* 539.) The curse is partly re-

reference to eating dust as food is the same as the lot of the dead as described in the Descent of Ištar and Nergal and Ereškigal (and elsewhere; see § 1.4.3), and in the *rab šaqeh*'s speech the threat seems to have had similar mythological force. Insofar as the *rab šaqeh* was charging Hezekiah with breaking a Neo-Assyrian covenant, it seems natural that he should have used similar language derived from treaty stipulations.

From there, it seems quite safe to assume that Judean elites who were part of the same *koine* culture as the Assyrians and the Egyptians would have heard in the *rab šaqeh*'s words not only the treat of a horrible, suffering death but also an allusion to an unhappy afterlife. Whether this allusion was intended by the authors of the actual Neo-Assyrian treaties cited above,[226] or whether it was the creative invention of the *rab šaqeh*,[227] or whether, finally, it would have depended upon the biblical author to imagine this threat,[228] it was surely part of the discursive universe of the Iron Age Levant, and thus potentially within the cultural compentency of any and all of the above.

In the final accounting, the data are insufficient to determine whether this synthesis of Assyrian and Egyptian motifs is more likely a result of the rhetorical ingenuity of an imperial intellectual or the literary creativity of a historian. One *can* say that in its present location, the threat seems to look in both directions in history: backward, to the historical reality of an empire that actually did threaten death to those who opposed it; and forward, in that it seems to have been elaborated by the Deuteronomistic Historian into a much clearer choice between death and life. In Isa 36:16–17, the *rab šaqeh* offers a positive alternative in Deuteronomistic language: "Make your peace with me and come out to me; then everyone of you will eat from your own vine and your own fig tree and drink water from your own cistern, until I come and take you away to a land like your

---

used in a treaty of Esarhaddon (680–669). See D. J. Wiseman, *The Vassal Treaties of Esarhaddon* (Iraq 20, pt. 1; London: British School of Archaeology in Iraq, 1958), 491.

[225] Meir Malul, "Eating and Drinking (One's) Refuse," *Nouvelles Assyriologiques Brèves et Utilitaires* (1993): 82–83.

[226] The Neo-Assyrians were great collectors of foreign wealth and curiosities and surely also absorbed many foreign ideas in the process. See Allison Karmel Thomason, *Luxury and Legitimation: Royal Collecting in Ancient Mesopotamia* (London: Ashgate, 2005): 119–214; Amélie Kuhrt, *The Ancient Near East, c. 3000–330 BC*, vol. 2 (Routledge History of the Ancient World; London: Routledge, 1995), 2:518–19.

[227] Any Assyrian diplomat would have been relatively learned. It has been argued that the *rab šaqeh* was a diplomat with special training and diplomatic knowledge of Judah (Brevard S. Childs, *Isaiah and the Assyrian Crisis* [SBT, 2nd series, 3; Naperville, Ill.: Alec R. Allenson, 1967], 82); or even a native speaker of Hebrew, perhaps an exile from the northern kingdom who had risen in the Neo-Assyrian administration (Mordechai Cogan and Hayim Tadmor, *II Kings: A New Translation with Introduction and Commentary* [AB 11; Garden City, N.Y.: Doubleday, 1988], 230; cf. *b. Sanhedrin* 60a).

[228] It could be that although the inclusion of this threat in the text of the speech was triggered by a memory of actual Neo-Assyrian rhetoric, it reflects instead a specific fear that is closer to home in Egypt, to the south.

own land, a land of grain and wine, a land of bread and vineyards." As is well known, Deuteronomy may have been the result of a reaction against Neo-Assyrian hegemony and in some ways the mirror image of the Sargonids' loyalty oaths.[229] If so, then perhaps the sort of life-and-death choices that are found both in Isa 36:11–17 and in Deut 30:15 also reflect Neo-Assyrian rhetoric. If so, then Isaiah's use of threats of an unhappy afterlife also ultimately owe something to the terrorizing rhetoric of Judah's imperial hegemon.

At the end of the account of the siege, of course, the Judeans escape unscathed, and it is the Assyrians who perish in great numbers (Isa 37:33–36) – and the hearer of the story would implicitly understand that as soldiers who died on campaign, the Assyrians would have been among the unburied, uncared-for, unhappy dead. Thus the *rab šaqeh*'s threat is turned back against his own side. Although the prose account of the siege in Isa 36–37 does not bear much literary resemblance to the prophecies of Isaiah, it is very much at home in the book, since the reversal of Assyrian rhetoric loomed large among the prophet's techniques.

5.2.2 Comparisons of the living to the dead

5.2.2.1 Isaiah 5:11–17: The nobility's parade to hell

(11) *Hôy*, those who get up early in the morning and chase after beer;
    and stay up late at night so that wine pursues them![230]
(12) whose feasts consist of lyre and harp, tambourine and flute and wine,
    but who have no regard for the deeds of the LORD, nor see the work of his hands!
(13) Therefore my people go into exile without knowledge,
    its nobility dying[231] of hunger, and its crowd parched with thirst.
(14) Therefore Sheol widens her throat
    and opens her maw in a measureless gape –
    down go her splendor and her crowd and her uproar,
    and the one who exults in her.
(15) Humanity will be humbled,[232] and each one will be brought low;[233]
    The eyes of the proud will be humbled.

---

[229] E.g., Eckart Otto, *Das Deuteronomium: Politische Theologie und Rechtsreform in Juda und Assyrien* (BZAW 284; Berlin: De Gruyter, 1999).

[230] This turn of phrase, though odd to the modern ear, is in keeping with Isaiah's penchant for *ius talionis*. See Roberts, "Double Entendre in First Isaiah," 39–48.

[231] Reading מָתֵי ("dying of") for מְתֵי ("men of") as the parallelism strongly suggests – although there would be a certain logic to describing the drinking, feasting, ravenously acquisitive nobles as "men of hunger."

[232] Read יִשַּׁח (1QIsaᵃ) for MT וַיִּשַּׁח.

[233] Read וְיִשְׁפַּל for MT וַיִּשְׁפַּל.

(16) But the Lord of hosts will be exalted in judgment,
    and the Holy God will show himself holy in righteousness.
(17) And lambs shall graze as in a pasture,
    and among ruins fatling kids shall feed.[234]

This passage is part of a sequence of oracles in 5:8–24 that are introduced by the particle *hôy*. The sense of the oracle is, at one level, straightforward: revelers will parade straight to the underworld, taking with them their wealth and clamor. The immediate indictment may be drinking and partying, but in context it is clear that these things do not constitute the primary issue. In Isaiah's view, the elites' drunken carousing exemplifies their lack of concern for others. The entire sequence of woes in 5:8–22 is bracketed by references to failures of "social justice," including violence (5:7), land-grabbing (5:8), and legal malfeasance (5:23), in contrast to the calls to משפט ("justice," v. 7) and צדקה ("righteousness," v. 16).

Isaiah was not the first to associate social disorder and death; older Egyptian portraits of the "topsy-turvy world" employ analogous imagery. The most famous example is in the "Prophecy of Neferti":

> I show you the land in deep sickness;
> the weak is now strong,
> one greets the one who once greeted.
> I show you the undermost uppermost,
> what lay on its back now has its belly below.
> *One will live in the realm of the dead.*
> The beggar will heap up riches, etc.[235]

Similarly, in Isaiah's own time the Kushite ruler Piye addressed rebels against his power in this way "O you who live in death, you who live in death; you poor wretches, you who live in death!"[236] (see further § 5.2.1.4). As Assmann says, "When the social order is overturned, men live in a topsy-turvy world, a realm of death."[237] Naturally, the social order envisioned by Isaiah is quite different from that of the Middle Kingdom Egyptian society out of which this text came – he envisions greater equity, whereas the Egyptian elites seem to have envisioned the maintenance of social boundaries – but the outcome is similar: those who rebel against YHWH's righteous rule are portrayed as the dead.

---

[234] Reading וְהָרְבוֹת מֵחִים גֵּדִים. For discussion, see Hans Wildberger, *Isaiah 1–12: A Commentary* (Continental Commentaries; Minneapolis: Fortress, 1991), 191–92.

[235] Neferti, 54–56; Wolfgang Helck, *Die Prophezeihung des Nfr.tj* (Wiesbaden: Harrasowitz, 1970), 46–47. Cited in Assmann, *Death and Salvation*, 139. Lichtheim translates the penultimate cited line: "Men will live in the graveyard" (*Ancient Egyptian Literature*, 1:143). Similar ideas seem to be expressed in the "Babylonian Theodicy," ll. 181–87; see W. G. Lambert, *Babylonian Wisdom Literature* (Oxford: Clarendon, 1960), 81. In that case, however, the disorder seems to be more personal than social.

[236] Lichtheim, *Ancient Egyptian Literature*, 3:74.

[237] Assmann, *Death and Salvation*, 139.

The description of the feast in 5:11 employs imagery similar to that of the *marzēaḥ* (see §§ 4.4.1.3; 3.3.3.2.3); other passages in Isaiah also associate drunkenness with cults of the dead – as he does in chs. 19 and 28 (§ 5.2.3.2–3), and as the Ugaritic texts perhaps do.[238] Indeed, Reinhard Fey argued that Isa 5:11–13 is dependent on Amos 6:1–7, which refers to the *marzēaḥ*.[239] John McLaughlin concludes that it is not a *marzēaḥ*, because Isaiah substitutes the word מִשְׁתֶּה for מַרְזֵחַ,[240] but he does note that it adapts the Amos text to "a different situation."[241] To be sure, Isaiah *compares* the feasting of the wealthy to a celebration of death; but it is not clear that he equates them. It is possible that both the people's disregard for YHWH and his work (v. 12) and the charge of a lack of knowledge (v. 13) refer to the abandonment of YHWH's divinatory cult in favor of consulting the dead. If so, his claim would be that true knowledge is found not through necromancy but through YHWH's prophets.

Verse 14 refers to the tradition of the voracious swallowing of the underworld. This is usually considered a West Semitic tradition, on the basis of the characterization of Mot in the Baal Cycle (*CAT* 1.5).[242] However, in my view the imagery is more likely to have Egyptian roots, since the Egyptian underworld was full of swallowers, at least as far back as the New Kingdom – a period when Egyptian culture was certainly influential in the Ugarit. The most famous swallowers in Egyptian myth were the serpent Apophis and the hybrid monster Ammut who devoured souls who were judged impure (§ 2.4.3), but there were also underworld demons named "[those] who devour millions," and the entry gate to the underworld in the *Amduat* (from the Egyptian New Kingdom) was named "All-Devourer," and door-keepers in the Book of Gates are also called "Devourers."[243] Much less famous are some intriguing episodes in first-millennium Mesopotamian texts of the dead swallowing the living[244] and of corpses being swallowed up by the earth.[245]

---

[238] See also Bernhard Lang, "Life after Death in the Prophetic Promise," in *Congress Volume: Jerusalem 1986* (ed. J. Emerton; VTSup 40; Leiden: Brill, 1988), 146.

[239] Both texts are *hôy*-oracles and share some common vocabulary; another key sign of this dependence is Isaiah's use of גלה in the Qal here (cf. Amos 6:7), the only such occurrence in the book apart from 24:11. Reinhard Fey, *Amos und Jesaja: Abhängigkeit und Eigenständigkeit des Jesaja* (Neukirchen-Vluyn: Neukirchener Verlag, 1963), 10–22.

[240] John L. McLaughlin, *The Marzēaḥ in the Prophetic Literature: References and Allusions in Light of the Extra-Biblical Evidence* (Leiden: Brill, 2001), 155–62.

[241] McLaughlin, *Marzēaḥ in the Prophetic Literature*, 183.

[242] Cf. Marvin Pope, "The Cult of the Dead at Ugarit," in *Probative Pontificating in Ugaritic and Biblical Literature: Collected Essays* (ed. Mark S. Smith; Münster: Ugarit-Verlag, 1994), 234.

[243] Hornung, "Black Holes Viewed From Within," 134–35.

[244] Descent of Ištar, 19: "I shall raise up the dead and they shall devour the living" (*u-še-el-la-a mi-tu-ti* KÚ.MEŠ *bal-ṭu-ti*); cf. *COS* 1.108, p. 381.

[245] See *CAD* A.1, 254 ("*akālu*," 5d). The original texts are published in E. A. W. Budge and L. W. King, *The Annals of the Kings of Assyria* (London: British Museum, 1902), 301 (ii.18) and 358 (iii.41) but the translations there do not reflect *CAD*'s reinterpretations.

All this indicates that the mytheme of Death the Swallower was rather widespread by the eighth century, but it is a quintessentially Isaianic move to threaten that those who seek the god of the underworld in cultic or necromantic rituals will end up being swallowed by the underworld.

Verse 13's references to hunger and thirst represent another instance of *ius talionis*: those who filled themselves with food and drink are to be empty. This punishment resonates with the rhetoric of the *rab šaqeh* in 36:12, and a similar threat of death by siege may lie behind the imagery of 5:13. It would be in keeping with Isaiah's general message to refer to Assyria again here as the agent of punishment (cf. 5:26–30, etc.). Continuing the *ius talionis* theme, a multiple reversal is found in v. 14 – the high and mighty go downward to the underworld, and their hunger and thirst mean that Sheol's gullet can be filled to bursting.[246] These reversals are reprised and echoed in vv. 15–16: humans descend, while God is exalted.[247]

Those who go down to Sheol belong to her (v. 14). A number of translations and commentators supply a predicate different from Sheol for the feminine suffixes, however – typically Jerusalem.[248] This assumption risks artificially determining the date of the oracle, which may initially have been directed against the northern kingdom.[249] Furthermore, the idea that Sheol has her own "crowd" who party raucously with her would not be an novel idea; it is implicit in the wisdom literature as well.[250] In Proverbs, the wicked woman functions as a hostess and

---

[246] If the reading "dying of hunger" in v. 13 is correct, then these two לכן-clauses have the same thrust ("nobility are dying" :: "Sheol swallows them"). Therefore there are literary connections uniting vv. 11–14, and the occasional form-critical objections that an oracle should not have two announcements of judgment overlook the fact that repetition is characteristic of oral style and poetic rhetoric.

[247] Verse 17 introduces wasteland imagery of a ruined city that has become a pasture for animals, a widespread motif in the Bible and beyond. Whether original or redactional, they are peripheral to our topic.

[248] Notably NRSV: "the nobility of Jerusalem and her multitude go down, her throng and all who exult in her." See also James G. Williams, "The Alas-Oracles of the Eighth Century Prophets," *HUCA* 38 (1967): 75–91. By contrast, NJB supports my understanding: "Sheol opens wide its throat and gapes with measureless jaw and down go her noblemen and populace and her loud revellers merry to the last!"

[249] Both Sweeney and Christopher R. Seitz take this view. As Seitz points out, not only did the northern kingdom experience a major exile in 722/721, but the conclusion of the chapter in vv. 25–30 strongly suggests a perspective prior to the Babylonian Exile for the chapter as a whole: "his anger has not turned away, and his hand is stretched out still." Seitz argues that Isaiah here uses the experience of Israel as a warning to Judah (Christopher R. Seitz, *Isaiah 1–39* [Int; Louisville, Ky.: Westminster John Knox, 1993], 50). Cf. also Sweeney, *Isaiah 1–39*, 130–31. For an opposing opinion, see Clements, who views all of vv. 14–17 as a postexilic addition (*Isaiah 1–39*, 34).

[250] I do not intend to argue any broad thesis about Isaiah's relationship to wisdom traditions; for discussion, see J. William Whedbee, *Isaiah and Wisdom* (Nashville: Abingdon, 1971); J. Fichtner, "Jesaja unter den Weisen," *TL* 74 (1949), cols. 75–80; Wildberger, *Isaiah 28–39*, 596–615. See also Samuel Terrien, "Amos and Wisdom," in *Israel's Prophetic Heritage: Essays in*

lover for fools. She sits at the door of her house, calling to passers-by, "but they do not know that the Rephaim are there, that her guests are in the depths of Sheol" (Prov 9:18). Furthermore, in Prov 9:13 she is described in terminology found also in the description of the partying horde in Isa 5: "The foolish woman is loud (המיה; cf. המון, vv. 13–14); she is ignorant and knows nothing (בל־ידעה; cf. בלי־ דעת, v. 13)." Like those whom the wicked woman leads to Sheol, the revelers of Isa 5:13–14 are noisy and lack knowledge.

Isaiah 5:11–17 makes use of wisdom traditions in other ways. Notably, Prov 23 helps to explain the phrase עלז בה (5:14), which usually causes consternation for commentators.[251] Proverbs 23:16 reads, "My heart will rejoice (תעלזנה) when your lips speak what is right." "What is right" is defined, as so often in wisdom literature, in opposition to what is wrong. Proverbs 23 as a whole is built around the theme of eating and drinking, and it warns against the sort of gluttony and excess that are also referenced in Isa 5:

> Do not be among those who guzzle wine, gorge themselves on meat;
> for the drunkard and the glutton will come to poverty,
> and drowsiness will clothe them with rags. (Prov 23:20–21)

This connection to Isa 5 is cemented by the phrase מאחרים על־היין ("those who linger over the wine") in Prov 23:30 (cf. מאחרי בנשף יין ידליקם in Isa 5:11). Proverbs 23 also contains a link to underworld themes when it advises, "beat them with the rod, you will save their lives from Sheol" (23:14). The *fear* of the parents in Prov 23 is identical to the *fate* of the revelers in Isa 5: they have rejoiced in the wrong things and gone to Sheol. Thus, the passages in Isaiah and Proverbs alike warn the hearer not to eat and drink to excess; one must discipline oneself to rejoice in what is right or end up in Sheol.[252]

It would appear that Isaiah appropriated this set of motifs from wisdom traditions as a subset of the "life-and-death alternative" theme (§ 4.6.2). Isaiah's reliance on wisdom traditions helps confirm the theory presented in § 4.6.2 that the life-and-death choice is originally a wisdom motif.

Honor of James Muilenburg (ed. B. W. Anderson and W. Harrelson; New York: Harper & Bros., 1962), *passim*.

[251] Wrote Blenkinsopp: "'the one exulting in her,' has defied explanation" (*Isaiah 1–39*, 210). J. A. Emerton viewed it as enough of a problem to emend the text to read עז לבה, "the strength of her heart," so that Zion's courage/stubbornness disappears along with the throng; see J. A. Emerton, "The Textual Problems of Isaiah v 14," *VT* 17 (1967): 135–42. However, only the Syriac offers any support for Emerton's reading.

[252] One might also mention, in this connection, Prov 1:11–12, where sinners say to the child, "let us wantonly ambush the innocent; like Sheol let us swallow them alive and whole, like those who go down to the Pit." In Isa 5, the situation is reversed and sinners are swallowed up.

5.2.2.2 The hôy-oracles

Given the preponderance of *hôy*-oracles both in Isa 5 and in chs. 28–29 (the discussion of which is to follow), and given that the form is originally related to a cry of mourning, a brief discussion is warranted.

The literary form of the *hôy*-oracle is relatively simple: they are (1) introduced by the interjection *hôy* and followed by (2) a substantive participle or noun identifying the object. Sometimes (3) the indictment is elaborated, and eventually (4) a judgment is announced. Claus Westermann rightly observes that "the first part – the actual cry of woe – has a very stable structure, whereas in the second part a greater freedom prevails."[253] In other words, there may be no immediate sentence of judgment, or there may be multiple judgment clauses. I would go so far as to say that parts (3) and (4) are not integral to the *hôy*-oracle, as one can see in the repetition of (1) and (2) in vv. 18, 20, 21 and 22 without any announcement of judgment. In fact, the cry *hôy* already contains its own death sentence, at least in its early occurrences in prophetic literature, because the cry *hôy* was an announcement of death.

Various theories have been propounded over time for the *Sitz im Leben* of the *hôy*-oracles, including covenant curses (Claus Westermann)[254] and wisdom literature (Erhard Gerstenberger).[255] The overwhelming weight of scholarship, however, indicates that the cry *hôy* derived historically from cries of mourning for the dead.[256] As Waldemar Janzen concluded in his monograph on the topic: "in the prophetic use of *hôy* in the eighth century, there is strong evidence for a living awareness of the background of *hôy* in funerary lamentation."[257] A number of narratives demonstrate this use of *hôy*, such as the death of the man of God in 1 Kgs 13. At his graveside, "they mourned over him, saying, '*Hôy*, my brother!' " (1 Kgs 13:30). Or again, Jeremiah's account of the mourning for Jehoiakim: "They shall not lament for him, saying, *hôy*, my brother! ..." (Jer 22:18). The eighth-

---

[253] Claus Westermann, *Basic Forms of Prophetic Speech* (trans. H. C. White. 1967; Louisville, Ky.: Westminster John Knox, 1991), 193.

[254] Westermann, *Basic Forms of Prophetic Speech*, 190–94.

[255] Erhard Gerstenberger, "The Woe-Oracles of the Prophets," *JBL* 81 (1961): 249–63.

[256] Waldemar Janzen, *Mourning Cry and Woe-Oracle* (BZAW 125; Berlin: De Gruyter, 1972); and previously R. J. Clifford, "The Use of *hôy* in the Prophets," *CBQ* 28 (1966): 458–64; Gunther Wanke, "אוֹי und הוֹי," *ZAW* 78 (1966): 215–18; H. J. Krause, "Hôj als prophetische Leichenklage über das eigene Volk im 8. Jahrhundert," *ZAW* 85 (1973): 15–46; and Williams, "Alas-Oracles," 86. See also Jacques Vermeylen, *Du prophète Isaïe à l'apocalyptique: Isaïe, I–XXXV, miroir d'un demi-millénaire d'expérience religieuse en Israël* (2 vols.; EBib; Paris: J. Gabalda, 1977–1978), 2:603–52.

[257] Janzen, *Mourning Cry and Woe-Oracle*, 84. Although Janzen concluded that comparative linguistic data on types of cries is not determinative of the meaning of biblical הוֹי, the comparison to the Akkadian cry *ūa* valid, and it is often used in contexts related to mourning and death. We can also add a further relevant example beyond Janzen's: It is uttered by the Neo-Assyrian prince Kummâ when he awakes from his "Underworld Vision" after Nergal nearly kills him. See Livingstone, "Court Poetry," 76 (r. 31).

century prophets also show clear awareness of the *hôy*-particle's origin in death or funerary lament.[258] This is certainly the case in Micah ("*Hôy*, you who devise wickedness! ... On that day they shall take up a taunt song against you, and wail with bitter lamentation (נְהִי)" (Mic 2:1, 4),[259] and especially in Amos 5:

> Therefore thus says YHWH, the God of hosts, the Lord:
> In all the squares there shall be wailing;
>   and in all the streets they shall say, "*Hô! Hô!*"
> They shall call the farmers to mourning,
>   and those skilled in lamentation, to wailing;
> in all the vineyards there shall be wailing,
>   for I will pass through the midst of you, says the LORD.
> *Hôy*, you who desire the day of the LORD!
>   Why do you want the day of the LORD?
> It is darkness, not light;
>   as if someone fled from a lion,
>   and was met by a bear;
> or went into the house and rested a hand against the wall,
>   and was bitten by a snake.
> Is not the day of the LORD darkness, not light,
>   and gloom with no brightness in it? (Amos 5:16–20)

In Isaiah as well, *hôy*-oracles are repeatedly found in close proximity to language either proclaiming or predicting death (see chart 5.1), suggesting that Isaiah too was familiar with the particle's original funerary lament context.

Chart 5.1: The Hôy-Oracles of Isaiah 1–33

Hôy-oracle(s)	Death imagery
1:4	1:5–6 ("The whole head is sick, the whole heart faint ... there is no soundness in it, but bruises and sores and bleeding wounds ... your land is desolate ...")
1:24	1:21–26 ("I will pour out my wrath on my enemies ... rebels and sinners shall be destroyed together")
5:8	5:9 ("Surely many houses shall be desolate, large and beautiful houses, without inhabitant.")

---

[258] As Janzen shows, this background seems to have been forgotten and obscured in later *hôy*-oracles.

[259] Compare the use of נְהִי in Jer 31:15; Amos 5:16.

Hôy-oracle(s)	Death imagery
5:11	5:14 ("Therefore Sheol has enlarged its appetite," etc.)
5:18, 20, 21, 22	5:24–25 ("the anger of the LORD was kindled against his people, and he stretched out his hand against them and struck them; the mountains quaked, and their corpses were like refuse in the streets")
10:1	10:3–4 ("What will you do ... so as not to ... fall among the slain?")
10:5	10:16–18 ("The LORD of hosts will send wasting sickness among his stout warriors, and under his glory a burning will be kindled, like the burning of fire. The light of Israel will become a fire, and his Holy One a flame; and it will burn and devour his thorns and briers in one day.")[260]
17:12	17:14 ("Before morning time, they are no more")
18:1	18:5–6 ("[The LORD] will cut off the shoots with pruning knives, and cut down and take away the spreading branches. They will all be left to the mountain birds of prey and to the wild animals; the birds will feed on them all summer, the wild animals all winter.")[261]
28:1	28:14–21 ("'We have made a covenant with death'")
29:1	29:1–4 ("Your voice will come from the ground like the voice of a ghost")

---

[260] This is, obviously enough, a reflection of the death and burning of Assyrian soldiers and king recounted elsewhere in Isaiah: see 14:3b–21; 30:27–33; 37:36.
[261] The image of cutting branches as judgment is clear enough; the reference to birds reflects imagery of corpse exposure, as after a battle or other slaughter. See discussion and citations in § 4.6.2.

Hôy-oracle(s)	Death imagery
29:15	29:15 ("You who go deep to hide counsel from the Lord, whose deeds are done in a dark place."[262])
30:1	--
31:1	31:3 ("They will all perish together")
33:1	33:1 ("When you have ceased to destroy, you will be destroyed.")

Janzen showed that, over time, the cry *hôy* lost its funerary association, so that in, for example, Zech 2:10–11, it has no apparent funerary (nor even negative) connotations.[263] In the eighth century, however, that connotation was still very much alive. As J. G. Williams wrote, "when those to whom the prophets preached heard the initial exclamation, '*hôy!*', they would have immediately associated it mentally and emotionally with mourning for the dead."[264] The examples in Isaiah emphatically confirm this; it is remarkable how often in Isaiah the particle *hôy* calls the reader or hearer's attention to impending death.

Having established that the cry *hôy* had funerary associations in the period of Isaiah's ministry clarifies its rhetorical impact: it *proleptically* announces the death of its object. As Gunkel remarked, "How powerful and glorious it must have been when they lamented those as already fallen who now were enjoying the best of fortunes."[265] It is rather analogous to the Hebrew grammatical phenomenon of the "prophetic perfect," proclaiming the future as a completed fact.[266] In its prophetic employment, the cry loses its genuine sense of mourning and takes on polemical or satirical overtones.[267] Ronald E. Clements and others miss the point in objecting that there is a shift in meaning from "cry of grief" to "cry of

---

[262] Almost certainly a reference to necromantic divination.

[263] This observation also answers Roberts's argument that Isa 55:1 disproves the *hôy*-oracle's funerary association (J. J. M. Roberts, *Nahum, Habakkuk, and Zephaniah: A Commentary* [OTL; Louisville, Ky.: Westminster John Knox, 1991], 118–19). The text is late and so is accounted for by Janzen's theory.

[264] Williams, "Alas-Oracles," 86.

[265] Hermann Gunkel, "The Prophets: Oral and Written" in *Water for a Thirsty Land: Israelite Literature and Religion* (ed. K. C. Hanson; Fortress Classics in Biblical Studies; Minneapolis: Fortress, 2001), 113; see also Clifford, "Use of *hôy* in the Prophets," 464.

[266] George L. Klein, "The 'Prophetic Perfect,'" *JNSL* 16 (1990): 45–60. Bruce Waltke and Michael O'Connor also call this the *accidental perfect*, in which "a speaker vividly and dramatically represents a future situation both as complete and as independent" (*Introduction to Biblical Hebrew Syntax* [Winona Lake, Ind.: Eisenbrauns, 1990], 490).

[267] Ze'ev Weisman, *Political Satire in the Bible* (Atlanta: Scholars Press, 1998), 84.

anger"[268] – *hôy* is no ordinary cry of anger, but a cry of *mock grief* for those who will not actually be lamented, much as Isa 14's mock dirge scorns the dead tyrant. Isaiah uses the cry *hôy* over and over again – no fewer than eighteen times in chs. 1–33[269] – another indication of the centrality of death imagery in the book's rhetoric, and another artful employment of it.

In conclusion, Isa 5:14 is not only one of the most powerful images associating Isaiah's enemies with the underworld; it is also the key to the entire chapter, especially the sequence of *hôy*-oracles. The *hôy*-oracles in fact make a claim about their objects analogous that of 5:14: they are judged by YHWH and are as good as dead already.

5.2.2.3 Isaiah 29:1–8: A "near-death experience" for Jerusalem

Isaiah 29:1–8 is among the *hôy*-oracles in which the object of the mock lament is clearly portrayed as dead:

(1) *Hôy*, ʾUruʾel,[270] ʾUruʾel, city where David camped[271]
     Add year to year, let the festivals circle round,
(2) But I will corner ʾUruʾel,
     and she shall be an object of mourning and lament,
     and she will be like an *ʾarīʾel*[272] to me,
(3) For I will encamp around you like a wall,[273]

---

[268] R. E. Clements, "The Form and Character of Prophetic Woe Oracles," *Semitics* 8 (1982): 27–28.

[269] Although the majority of these instances are considered "authentic," the case presented here hardly depends on the authenticity of every one. It would be interesting, however, to analyze whether the oracles can be dated to some extent based on their awareness of the funerary *Sitz im Leben* – for example, do the *hôy* oracles in Isa 1 and 30 represent a later stratum, since death imagery is less clear or absent?

[270] ʾUruʾel refers to Jerusalem; see discussion below.

[271] There is debate about the sense of חנה here. It is not likely to refer to a siege of the Jebusite city by David, since no such event is related anywhere (it would have to be inferred in 2 Sam 5). It seems more probable that it reflects the rhetoric of the envisioned Neo-Assyrian attackers, who refer to the rule of the Davidic dynasty in Jerusalem as merely temporary, like an encampment.

[272] The primary meaning here is likely "altar hearth," but the word is potentially polysemic (see below), thus my decision not to translate it.

[273] דור here is cognate with Akk. *dūru*, "wall," and Ug. *dr*, "circle." The simile *kima dūri* is used by Aššurbanipal to describe the siege of a city in Elam; see Annals iv.125 in Maximilian Streck, *Assurbanipal und die letzten assyrischen Könige bis zum Untergange Ninevehs* (Leipzig: Zentralantiquariat, 1975), 42. This image of a wall cutting off supplies and communication in fact may be an accurate reflection of Sennacherib's siege of Jerusalem in 701. As Stephanie Dalley has remarked, the term URU *ḫalsu* in Sennacherib's account does not mean full-scale "earth-works," but rather "fort." Indeed, the translation makes better sense when emended in this way: "As for Hezekiah, ... I locked (him) up within Jerusalem ... like a bird in a cage. I surrounded him with forts, and made it unthinkable for him to exit by the city gate" (after M. Cogan, *COS* 2.119B). In Dalley's view, this means that a smaller group of Assyrians (without the king, as portrayed) blockaded the city "in a passive way without attempting to besiege it in an active way"

I will encircle you with installations, and raise up siege works against you.
(4) You shall be brought low; from the ground you shall speak;
from low in the dust your speech shall come,
and your voice shall be like a ghost from the earth,
and your speech shall whisper from the dust.
(5) But the multitude of your enemies will be like fine dust,
and the terrible horde like passing chaff –
(6) Suddenly, in an instant, the Lord of Hosts will visit you
with thunder and earthquake and a mighty voice,
with whirlwind and tempest, and flames of devouring fire.
(7) And the horde of nations fighting against ʾUruʾel,
and all who make war on her and her fortress,[274] and besiege her,
will be like a dream, a vision of the night.
(8) And it will be just as when a hungry man dreams that he is eating,
but he awakes and his mouth is empty;
Or when a thirsty man dreams that he is drinking,
but he awakes and his throat is dry.
Thus it will be for all the horde of nations
who fight against Mount Zion.

A number of aspects of this passage resonate with other parts of Isaiah; not only the cry *hôy*, but the siege imagery in v. 3 also evokes similar scenes in Isa 30 and 36–37. And like the latter passage, those who are besieged are likened here to the dead: they will be low and will speak "from the ground," with all the underworld connotations that ארץ carries (§ 4.4.3.1). Furthermore, the root צפף, in the same Pilpael stem found here, is used to describe the twittering of ghosts in Isa 8:19. In other words, the threat issued against the city here is akin to that of the *rab šaqeh* – i.e., that its inhabitants will die and be like miserable ghosts – albeit couched in different underworld imagery.

Just what is this city, with its obscure name? The reference to Zion in v. 8 identifies אריאל as Jerusalem, and although v. 8 is often taken to be redactional (see below), there is no reason to think that the original oracle concerned any other city. The understanding of אריאל, repeated five times in the Masoretic form of this passage (though not in 1QIsaᵃ, on which see below), is of great significance in the present research. Four times (in vv. 1–2a, 7) it must be a name for a city, as v. 1's apposition makes clear. By contrast, the *kaph* preposition in v. 2b indicates that the occurrence there is different, a simile that somehow plays on the city's name.

Theories attempting to explain this literary device abound, but no etymological argument regarding אריאל has proved overwhelmingly convincing:

(Dalley, "Recent Evidence from Assyrian Sources for Judaean History from Uzziah to Manasseh," *JSOT* 28 [2004]: 392).

[274] For מצדתה, read מְצָרֶתָהּ with 1QIsaᵃ.

1. The most obvious Hebrew etymology, "lion of god," is sometimes supported by comparison with Gen 49:9 ("Judah is a lion's whelp [גור אריה]"), but this is a fragile logic. There is no other support forthcoming for such an equation, and Judah is not equivalent with Jerusalem.
2. The old proposal to connect the element ארי to a supposed Arabic term *iryat* meaning "hearth" was dismissed by Albright, since there are no cognates, nor is there is a verb *ʾrh*, "to burn," as is sometimes posited.[275]
3. Albright's theory that Akkadian *arallû* could mean "mountain of god" (which would have made it a neat wordplay on Zion) has also been proven false.[276]
4. On the other hand, the connection to Akkadian *arallû*, "underworld," remains fascinating even if the requisite phonological shifts do not fall neatly into place.[277] In light of the imagery of mourning and lament (v. 2) and the reduction to dust (v. 4), it may be that the Hebrew אריאל at least plays on *arallû*.

Ronald Youngblood argues that the name of the city in vv. 1–2a, 7 should be read ʾŪrûēl, in keeping with the reading of 1QIsaᵃ: ארואל.[278] While it is true that *waw* and *yod* are often very difficult to distinguish in the Dead Sea Scrolls, consultation of the photographs confirms the reading.[279] Youngblood rightly points out that the first element in the name Jerusalem was consistently vocalized with *u*-sounds, both in Akkadian (Amarna: *Ú-ru-sa-lim*; Sennacherib: *Ur-sa-lim-mu*) and in Syriac (ʾŪrišlem) and Nabatean (ʾŪršālîm). In the case of the Akkadian forms, scribes may well have conflated the element "Uru" with the Sumero-Akkadian determinative URU, marking cities – whether or not that etymology of Jerusalem's name is accurate.[280]

---

[275] W. F. Albright, "The Babylonian Temple-Tower and the Altar of Burnt-Offering," *JBL* 39 (1920): 139.

[276] This etymology has a long history; see William Henry Cobb, "The Ode in Isaiah XIV," *JBL* 15 (1896): 18–35. More recently, it is sustained by Blenkinsopp, *Isaiah 1–39*, 401.

[277] See Herbert G. May, "Ephod and Ariel," *AJSL* 56 (1939): 53–54.

[278] Ronald Youngblood, "Ariel, 'City of God,'" in *Essays on the Occasion of the Seventieth Anniversary of the Dropsie University* (Philadelphia: Dropsie University, 1979), 458–59. Cf. Parry and Qimron, *Great Isaiah Scroll*, 47. Dewey Beegle suggested that ארואל is merely a biform, like Peniel/Penuel; he does not offer any explanation of the form or its appearance here, however (Beegle, "Proper Names in the New Isaiah Scroll," *BASOR* 123 [1951]: 29). E. Y. Kutscher points out that the LXX seems to have had ארואל in its *Vorlage* and understood it as a city in Moab. This does not shed much light on the sense of the Hebrew text, however, since the LXX is loose and exegetical at this juncture. See Kutscher, *The Language and Linguistic Background of the Isaiah Scroll (1 Q Isaᵃ)* (Leiden: Brill, 1974), 97–98.

[279] *Scrolls from Qumrân Cave I: The Great Isaiah Scroll, the Order of the Community, the Pesher to Habakkuk, From Photographs by John C. Trever* (Intro. by Frank Moore Cross; Jerusalem: Albright Institute and The Shrine of the Book, 1972), 60–61.

[280] Brent A. Strawn has recently renewed the objection of Samuel Feigin that the Akkadian orthography merely reflects the pronunciation *Ierušalem. See Strawn, *What Is Stronger Than a Lion?: Leonine Image and Metaphor in the Hebrew Bible and the Ancient Near East* (OBO 212; Fribourg: Academic Press; Göttingen: Vandenhoeck & Ruprecht, 2005), 70 n. 6. If, however,

Youngblood argues that an Ur-text had אַרוּאֵל four times and אֲרִיאֵל once, but that 1QIsaᵃ and MT each subsequently flattened out the spellings in different ways, both thereby losing the original Isaianic paronomasia on the similar-sounding words "ʾUruʾel" (indicating Jerusalem) and "ʾar(i)ʾel" (indicating an altar-hearth). Thus perhaps Isaiah, in this threat against Jerusalem, apes the Akkadian pronunciation of the Neo-Assyrians, the greatest enemies of Judah during that historical period, and substitutes the more generic ʾēl for šlm, since the latter was probably understood as a theophoric element.[281] ʾUruʾel seems a heavily camouflaged term for Jerusalem, but perhaps a prophecy that YHWH would attack Jerusalem was sufficiently scandalous in this period (at least in some circles) that camouflage seemed advisable.

If one assumes that there is a play on words here, it is difficult to determine with certainty the other senses of ʾryʾl that are in play, since the other occurrences of similar terms are rather limited. Both the Mesha inscription's ʾrʾl and Ezek 43:15–16's אֲרִיאֵל/הַראֵל strongly suggest that a cultic item is in view. The Moabite king Mesha claims to have taken an ʾrʾl at least from the city ʿAṭarot and dragged it before Chemosh, and likely did the same with two ʾrʾlm from Nebo.[282] That the Ezekiel text refers to a part of the altar is clear.[283] The word אֲרִאֵל in 2 Samuel 23:20 ("Benaiah ... smote two אֲרִאֵל of Moab.") may also fit the altar theory, since it is quite possible to smite (נכה) inanimate objects.[284] Most difficult of all is the reference to אֶרְאֶלָּם in Isa 33:7, which seems to require a personal meaning (based on the parallelism with "messengers"). However, there is not enough context to determine what sort of people these are.[285]

Youngblood has correctly presented his data, then the syllabic spellings from the Amarna letters and Sennacherib's annals seem to answer this objection. Strawn thinks it unlikely that the Qumran text should have preserved an older spelling – but if not at Qumran, where else would an older spelling be preserved?

[281] Cf. H. B. Huffmon, "Shalem," *DDD²*, 755–57.

[282] The reconstruction of the broken section of lines 17–18 is matter of debate. The question is what Mesha dragged from Nebo. It could read ʾ[rʾ]ly yhwh, "the ʾrʾls of YHWH," or ʾ[t k]ly yhwh, "the vessel of YHWH." In favor of ʾrʾl is that fact that the verb shb, "drag" is used of ʾrʾl in lines 12–13. The object marker ʾt is used with ʾrʾl in line 12 and would not fit here, but this is hardly determinative. Furthermore, the "vessels of YHWH," as they are portrayed in the Bible, do not seem to be so large as to need to be "dragged," unless they were assumed to be somehow bundled together. Thus, I favor the reading ʾrʾly. See Samuel Feigin, "The Meaning of Ariel," *JBL* 39 (1920): 134.

[283] The odd spelling אֲרִאֵיל may be a scribal error under the influence of the reference to "horns" in the same verse (i.e., because אִיל = "ram"). Feigin believed that "[t]he different spellings ... indicate that the word is a loan from a foreign language and variously adapted by popular etymology to Hebrew speech-consciousness" ("Meaning of Ariel," 135).

[284] Cf. Amos 3:15; 6:11; 2 Kgs 15:16. The variety of solutions offered by the versions only indicates their own efforts to clarify: e.g., LXX: "two sons of Ariel"; Vulgate: "two lions"; Targums: "two great men." The parallel text in 1 Chr 11:22 reads אֲרִיאֵל.

[285] May suggests that they are those who bear the *ariel* when it is moved around, as for a battle ("Ephod and Ariel," 57–58.)

A further level of perplexity is what sort of cultic item an אראל is in the Mesha Inscription: is it identical to the part of the altar in Ezek 43, or is it a divine image or palladium, as is sometimes suggested?[286] The image of theft of a statue would coincide with the common ancient practice of "godnapping," but, at most, ancient Israel seems to have had relatively formless stelae representing the divine presence (as, for example, at Arad). That some other cultic item besides an image could be in view is supported by the account of the Philistines' theft of the ark in 1 Sam 4–6, in which the ark is placed beside Dagon much as Mesha dragged the *ʾrʾly* before Chemosh. In the final accounting, the image of a part of the altar makes much better sense in Isaiah's imagery than does a divine image.

Thus it seems that some object of cultic hardware is in view in 29:2b. Although the data are refractory, the primary referent of אריאל in v. 2b is likely an altar hearth, so that the common conclusion is basically correct in that the simile כאריאל evokes a city burning and flowing with blood like a sacrificial altar.[287] Nevertheless, the text is best served by an approach willing to countenance literary ambiguity, since the term אריאל is also likely to pick up echoes of a Mesopotamian term for the underworld (*arallû*).[288] Thus, the message is a graphic one: Jerusalem is threatened with a bloody death and will be filled with the dead, like the underworld.

This threat of death is averted when YHWH intervenes in vv. 5–8, but was this the original thrust of the oracle? The compositional integrity of vv. 1–8 has long been questioned – many interpreters see the salvation of Jerusalem as a redactional addition, dating sometime after the withdrawal of Sennacherib in 701.[289] Some interpreters exclude vv. 5bβ–6 from the imagery of salvation, setting it aside as part of an original judgment oracle (thus limiting it to vv. 5a–bα, 7–8). This makes too much of the essentially neutral verb פקד in v. 6, assuming that it always indicates judgment; YHWH's theophany with all the natural forces named in v. 6 does not have to be a negative thing for Jerusalem; these forces are salvific in, e.g., Pss 18:7–15; 77:19; 83:13–15; etc.[290] Isaiah 17:12–14 offers another particularly clear example, in which the roaring nations are blown away like chaff by the same theophanic wind described in 29:5–6. The passages share vocabulary such as המון, מץ, and סופה, and in both passages the threat is gone by morning.

---

[286] See Feigin, "Meaning of Ariel"; May, "Ephod and Ariel."

[287] Herodotus reported that the city of Ecbatana was built with painted walls rising in seven concentric circles, and Pirjo Lapinkivi has hypothesized that this was meant to echo the shape and colors of a ziggurat (*Ištar's Descent*, 80). Perhaps a city could be imagined as an altar, just as it could be imagined as a ziggurat.

[288] As Blenkinsopp has written, it seems that "the designation is deliberately cryptic and polyvalent" (*Isaiah 1–39*, 401).

[289] With various nuances, see Clements, *Isaiah 1–39*, 235; Vermeylen, *Du Prophète Isaïe à l'Apocalyptique*, 1.401–4; Kaiser, *Isaiah 13–39*, 264–68.

[290] Indeed the simultaneous terrifying and beneficent aspects seem to be inherent in theophanies (cf. Theodore Hiebert, "Theophany in the OT," *ABD* 6:508).

There is a larger question at stake in these redactional arguments, one that involves the essential character of Isaiah's prophecies, and his use of images of death and life: Did he prophesy only judgment and destruction, or also salvation?[291] Matthijs J. de Jong, in his study of the redaction of First Isaiah in light of the recording and compilation of Assyrian prophecies, concluded as follows:

> The eighth-century prophetic material within First Isaiah and its earliest elaboration in the Assyrian period ... are distinctly different from what is supposedly the main characteristic of biblical prophecy: the proclamation of unconditional judgement. The eighth-century prophetic material is partly marked by positive aspects ..., and the critical sayings address a quite specific group of people; furthermore, the seventh-century revision is of an unambiguously positive tone.[292]

Hans Barstad reached similar conclusions in his study of Isaiah and Mari prophecies.[293] Indeed, there is a growing consensus that the "judgment-only" criterion is inadequate.[294] As Childs wrote, "The complexity of the oracle derives from its basic theological content. God both kills and brings to life."[295] There has been in recent times a surprisingly broad willingness to accept the unity of vv. 1–7, with only v. 8 as perhaps a gloss,[296] and that position is also adopted here.

G. C. I. Wong helpfully focuses the discussion about the passage's redaction on the issue of the dream, which is the dominant metaphor in vv. 7–8.[297] Wong's theory is that (contrary to most redaction theories) v. 7 was initially part of the oracle of judgment: the hordes would overrun Zion "like a bad dream." According to Wong, v. 7 was later reinterpreted by the addition of v. 8, which shifted the dreaming subject from Jerusalem to its attackers, who were to awake with their dreams of conquest unfulfilled. The weakness in Wong's theory is that no historical experience is ever likened to a nightmare in classical Hebrew rhetoric, as it might be in various modern languages.

The dream in 29:7 can only function as a salvation oracle, because dreams are

---

[291] For the background of this discussion, see Wildberger, *Isaiah 28–39*, 630–32, and literature cited there.

[292] Matthijs J. de Jong, *Isaiah among the Ancient Near Eastern Prophets: A Comparative Study of the Earliest Stages of the Isaiah Tradition and the Neo-Assyrian Prophecies* (Leiden: Brill, 2007), 448–49. It should be noted that de Jong's assessment of 29:1–8 differs from my own.

[293] Hans Barstad, "*Sic Dicit Dominus*: Mari Prophetic Texts and the Hebrew Bible," in *Essays on Ancient Israel in Its Near Eastern Context: A Tribute to Nadav Naaman* (ed. Y. Amit, E. Ben Zvi, I. Finkelstein, and O. Lipschits; Winona Lake, Ind.: Eisenbrauns, 2006), 21–52.

[294] See, e.g., Marvin A. Sweeney, "Dating Prophetic Texts," *HS* 48 (2007): 55; Childs, *Isaiah*, 215–16.

[295] Childs, *Isaiah*, 218.

[296] Barth, *Die Jesaja-Worte in der Josiazeit*, 184–90; Robin L. Routledge, "The Siege and Deliverance of the City of David in Isaiah 29:1–8," *TynBul* 43 (1992): 181–90. So also Blenkinsopp, Wildberger; see below. One must also reckon again here with the possibility of a "self-extended oracle," that is, one that the prophet himself adapted to a new situation. See William Holladay, *Isaiah: Scroll of a Prophetic Heritage* (Grand Rapids: Eerdmans, 1978), 59, 84.

[297] G. C. I. Wong, "On 'Visits' and 'Visions' in Isaiah XXIX 6–7," *VT* 45 (1995): 370–76.

overwhelmingly a divinatory (or revelatory) device in the Bible. The "dreamer of dreams" in Deut 13 is a parallel figure to the prophet, and dreams were commonly mantic devices throughout the ancient world.[298] Thus, it is true that there are references to bad dreams, but they are, so far as I can see, always *warnings of an evil to come*, rather than a reflection of an evil already suffered. Job 33:15–18 is a clear statement of dreams' future aspect in ancient Israelite culture:

> For God speaks in one way, and in two,
>   though people do not perceive it.
> In a dream (חלום),
>   in a vision of the night (חזיון לילה),
> when deep sleep falls on mortals,
>   while they slumber on their beds,
> then he opens their ears,
>   *and terrifies them with warnings,*
> *that he may turn them aside from their deeds,*
>   and keep them from pride,
> to spare their souls from the Pit,
>   their lives from traversing the River.

A perusal of other occurrences of חלום in the Bible demonstrates that this theme of dreams as foretelling is commonplace (see Gen 20:3; 41:25; Dan 2; etc.). In a related manner, dreams in the Bible also reveal the divine will (Num 12:6; 1 Sam 28:6, 15; 1 Kgs 3). Dreams may foretell negative events, but they are not used to describe negative events.

In light of all this, the dream in vv. 7–8 must almost certainly be viewed as pointing to a future event. Its surprising shift is not introduced by redactional work; rather, the reversal of the attackers' expectation is part of Isaiah's own message, as in Isa 10:12–19.

In most of the aforementioned dream passages, the dream is a frightening warning, by contrast with the salvation oracle issued in 29:7–8, but our text finds an ideal analogue in Ps 73:17–20; there, the Psalmist reflects that in his bitterness against his enemies he had almost given up hope,

> ... until I went into the sanctuary of God;
>   then I perceived their end.
> Truly you set them in slippery places;
>   you make them fall to ruin.

---

[298] See A. Leo Oppenheim's discussion of dream-omina in "The Interpretation of Dreams in the Ancient Near East: With a Translation of an Assyrian Dream-Book," *Transactions of the American Philosophical Society*, n.s. 46/3 (1956): 179–373. Note also the Netherworld Vision of an Assyrian Prince, in which the dreaming ruler sees horrific beings in the underworld as a warning – in that case, as I have already observed, probably a warning not to neglect the cult of the underworld gods (§ 1.2.3.3). On oneiromancy at Mari, see Moshe Weinfeld, "Ancient Near Eastern Patterns in Prophetic Literature," in *Prophecy in the Hebrew Bible: Selected Studies from Vetus Testamentum* (compiled by David E. Orton; Leiden: Brill, 2000), 91–95.

How they are destroyed in a moment,
swept away utterly by terrors!
They are like a dream (כהלום) when one awakes (הקיץ);
on awaking you despise their phantoms.

The practice of dream-incubation in a sanctuary was widespread in the ancient world. In this case, the Psalmist receives a vision of the destruction of his enemies that is quite similar to that of Isa 29:7–8. Although different terminology is used for the suddenness of the dispersal (כרגע in Ps 73:19; פתאם לפתע in Isa 29:5), the same vocabulary is used for the dream and the waking. Such *Heilsorakeln* would no doubt have been staples in the repertoires of diviners at royal courts throughout the ancient Near East.[299]

The shift from warning (vv. 1–4) to salvation oracle (vv. 5–8) marks this text as more complex, rhetorically, than an ordinary divinatory response. It is still conceivable however, that Isaiah has employed that *Gattung* in a new creation, as he has other *Gattungen* in other instances. West Semitic inscriptions of Isaiah's period, such as the Zakkur Inscription, show similar literary creativity.[300] A fruitful comparison could also be made to the "Underworld Vision of an Assyrian Prince" (§ 1.4.3), which Seth Sanders called "fascinating for its generic promiscuity, reworking previously separate features" found in other genres.[301] Like that terrifying vision, Jerusalem's nightmare seems to have been reported from a retrospective standpoint, after stability had been achieved.

Compositional unity is significant because it affects the way one sees Isaiah using the rhetoric of death. Commentators arguing for the unity of the whole pericope point out that the expected deliverance of the city reflects a Zion theology that is consistent with Isaiah's own perspective.[302] Blenkinsopp calls this a

---

[299] See *Queries to the Sungod: Divination and Politics in Sargonid Assyria* (ed. Ivan Starr; SAA 4; Helsinki: Helsinki University Press, 1990). See also, e.g., 1 Kgs 22:6.

[300] Jonas C. Greenfield has remarked of the Zakkur Stele that its use of the *Heilsorakel* and *Danklied* forms in shaping a royal inscription suggests that "literary Aramaic of the eighth century B.C... was richer and more diverse than we usually think." See J. C. Greenfield, "The Zakir Inscription and the *Danklied*," in *Proceedings of the Fifth World Congress of Jewish Studies, 1969* (Jerusalem: Magnes, 1971), 191.

[301] Seth Sanders, "The First Tour of Hell: From Neo-Assyrian Propaganda to Early Jewish Revelation," *JANER* 9 (2009): 156. Sanders sees the Underworld Vision as comparable to Isaiah: "[A]s a late pre-exilic text the Underworld Vision also helps us understand the shifts that made such authoritative prophetic narratives as Exodus, as well as Deuteronomy, Isaiah, Jeremiah, and Ezekiel possible. The Underworld Vision, along with the contemporary Erra epic, is the first Mesopotamian mythic narrative that claims to have been revealed to a living, historical human being. During a renaissance that was also a crisis of tradition, new mythic narratives were introduced under the rubric of personal experience: people now claimed, as individuals, to have experienced mythic events" ("The First Tour of Hell," 168–69).

[302] Hugo Gressmann wrote that Isaiah believed, "As the sun shines in the underworld and causes tremendous joy among the dead, so a period of weal must follow a period of woe.... Isaiah confidently awaited the hour when God would be pleased to intervene and scatter the hosts of the enemy like the ghosts of the night" (*The Tower of Babel* [New York: Jewish Institute of Religion Press, 1928], 86).

"near-death experience" for Jerusalem:³⁰³ the city is pressed to the point of death, as an Assyrian siege might have done, but is ultimately promised salvation.

Wildberger calls attention to the rhetorical suspense of the first four verses: assuming that the threat is delivered by the prophet, in whose assumed voice is he speaking? It seems clear that a siege is envisioned – the language once again evokes the Neo-Assyrian inscriptions³⁰⁴ – but of course YHWH is portrayed elsewhere as the ultimate cause of the Assyrian assault (Isa 10), and here he is "identified with the besieging peoples," as Watts rightly observed.³⁰⁵ Is it too much to envision that the prophet is telling a story in which neither the implied audience (Jerusalem) nor the implied speaker (Assyria) knows what is coming during the first four verses – in which both proceed without understanding the deeper plans of God, which are revealed only at the last moment, in the salvation of God's city? The words of vv. 1–4, which appear to reflect the divine will, are revealed in a twinkling as merely a passing stage, a beating intending to teach (cf. Isa 19:22; Judg 2:11–19; Prov 23:14). Whether this passage is part of a later preexilic redaction or (as seems more likely) authentic, in its present form it captures just that tension: YHWH oppresses unto (the verge of) death through the agency of human foes, but holds out deliverance and life to the faithful.³⁰⁶

5.2.2.4 Isaiah 8:16–9:6: Those who consult the dead are like them

As early as the translation of the Old Greek and the other ancient versions, the end of Isa 8 was already a source of consternation. The variations among ancient witnesses show that translators had widely divergent views about what the text was trying to say. Recent exegetes call it "perhaps the most enigmatic ... in the entire book of Isaiah,"³⁰⁷ "one of the most difficult ... in the book,"³⁰⁸ and "a near paradigm of ambiguity."³⁰⁹ This is likely due not *only* to problems with the text's transmission, but also to ambiguities that the author intended to create. Nevertheless, what emerges is a stark contrast between a life of misery, darkness, and uncertainty under the influence of necromantic divination and a life of riches, freedom, and triumph under the rule of a righteous king:

---

³⁰³ Blenkinsopp, *Isaiah 1–39*, 401.

³⁰⁴ See translation note on 29:3 above. Also Brian B. Schmidt, *Israel's Beneficent Dead: Ancestor Cult and Necromancy in Ancient Israelite Religion and Tradition* (FAT 11; Tübingen: Mohr Siebeck, 1994), 163–64.

³⁰⁵ Watts, *Isaiah 1–33*, 449.

³⁰⁶ On YHWH's use of foreign nations to punish and correct his people, see recently Terence E. Fretheim, "God and Violence in the Old Testament," *WW* 24 (2004): 18–28.

³⁰⁷ Marvin Sweeney, "A Philological and Form-Critical Reevaluation of Isaiah 8:16–9:6," *HAR* 14 (1994): 215.

³⁰⁸ C. F. Whitley, "The Language and Exegesis of Isaiah 8:16–23," *ZAW* 90 (1978): 28.

³⁰⁹ R. P. Carroll, "Translation and Attribution in Isaiah 8.19f," *BT* 31 (1980): 127.

(16) Bind up the testimony,
    seal the instruction among my disciples.
(17) I will wait for the Lord, who is hiding his face from the house of Jacob,
    and put my hope in him.
(18) Here I am, and the children whom the Lord has given to me as signs and portents
    in Israel, from the Lord of hosts, who dwells on Mount Zion.

(19) And if they say to you, "Consult the ghosts and familiar spirits that twitter[310] and murmur! Should a people not consult its ancestors[311] – (should it not consult) the dead on behalf of the living – (20) for[312] instruction and testimony?"

Surely they will say such a thing – but it has no dawn. (21) (The one who says it) will cross over, oppressed and starving, and since when it is hungry it grows wrathful, then it will curse by its dead kings[313] and by its ancestors, and turn to rebellion.[314]

(22) And to the underworld it shall look, and behold, distress and darkness – exhaustion,[315] siege, and exile[316] into deep darkness.[317]

(23) But there was no exhaustion for the one[318] who was besieged –

As in the former time he brought into contempt
    the land of Zebulun and the land of Naphtali,
So in the latter time he oppressed
    the Way of the Sea, the land beyond the Jordan, Galilee of the nations.

---

[310] One also notes that ghosts are said to "twitter from below" in the Sumero-Akkadian incatation series *Utukkū lemnūtu* 5:6. See Geller, *Evil Demons*, 208.

[311] Or "its dead"; for אלהים in this sense, see 1 Sam 28:13; cf. Theodore J. Lewis, *Cults of the Dead in Ancient Israel and Ugarit* (HSM 39; Atlanta: Scholars Press, 1989), 131; and already G. R. Driver, "Isaianic Problems," in *Festschrift for Wilhelm Eilers* (Wiesbaden: Harrassowitz, 1967), 44: "The 'gods' in the present passage are the *manes* of each frightened man's family."

[312] A few translators treat this phrase as an interjection by the prophet ("To the teaching and to the testimony!"), e.g., Kaiser, Sweeney, RSV, NIV.

[313] Read מלכו as a suffixed plural (usu. מלכי), spelled defectively. See discussion below.

[314] For מעל, "rebellion" with verbs of turning, see Josh 22:16; 2 Chr 29:6. As Sweeney points out, מעל "is commonly used for treachery against God (Josh 22:22; 1 Chr 9:1; 2 Chr 29:19; 33:19; Ezra 9:2, 4; 10:6)" (Sweeney, "Philological and Form-Critical Re-Evaluation of Isa 8:16–9:6," 221.)

[315] Hophal participle from עיף/עוף, used as a substantive. Cf. Isa 40:30–31.

[316] Literally: "scattering," "expulsion." However, this term is often used of exiled peoples (esp. in Jer 8:3; 16:15; 23:8; 24:9; 27:10, 15; 29:14, 18; 32:37; 46:28; also Mic 4:6; Deut 30:4; etc.), and that is likely the force of the image here. If the consonantal text is correct, it is most likely a Hophal participle with an unassimilated nun (מֻנְדָּח), rather than the Pual suggested by the MT pointing, since neither a Pual nor a Piel is otherwise attested.

[317] The ה in אפלה is directive. For the short form of אפלה, see Amos 5:20.

[318] לה either marks a shift of person from the previous masculine subject, perhaps due to a redactional join; or it could be repointed as an archaic masculine suffix: לֹה.

(9:1) The people who were walking in the darkness
have seen a great light;
those who were dwelling in the land of the shadow of death,
on them light has shined
(2) You have magnified the nation; you have increased its joy.
they rejoiced before you like the rejoicing at the harvest
as men rejoice when they divide spoil.
(3) For the yoke of its burden and the rod on its shoulders,
the scepter of their oppressor you shattered as on the day of Midian.
(4) Every sandal marching like thunder, and every garment rolled in blood
shall be for burning, fuel for a fire.
(5) For a child is born to us, a son is given to us,
and governance shall be on his shoulders
and one shall call his name Wonderful Counselor, Mighty God,
Eternal Father, Prince of Peace.
(6) There shall be no end to the increase of authority and peace;
As for the throne of David and his kingdom, he shall establish it firmly,
and ground it in justice and righteousness, now and forever.
May the zeal of the Lord of hosts do this.

At least two major sections of this pericope can and should be read as unified compositions – 8:16–23aα and 9:1–6 – with the crux that is the remainder of 8:23 standing as a join between them.

It may well be that 8:16–23aα was not composed as a unity, but in the first place, there appears to be no other way to read it as the text of Isaiah now stands; and in the second place, it has a thematic coherence, despite its grammatical and syntactical fissures.[319] Isaiah's instruction and testimony are contrasted with that

---

[319] So also Lewis, *Cults of the Dead*, 128. Others who have argued for the unity of at least vv. 19–22 include, e.g., Driver, "Isaianic Problems," 43–49; Vermeylen, *Du Prophète Isaïe à l'Apocalyptique*, 228–32; Sweeney, *Isaiah 1–39*, 175–87; and Adam S. van der Woude, "Jesaja 8,19–23a als literarische Einheit," in *Studies in the Book of Isaiah: Festschrift Willem A. M. Beuken* (ed. J. van Ruiten and M. Vervenne; Leuven: Leuven University Press, 1997), 129–36. Karel van der Toorn wrote: "Although many authors regard vv. 19–20 as an addition, exilic or post-exilic, I see no conclusive argument against the Isaianic authorship of these verses" ("Echoes of Judean Necromancy in Isaiah 28, 7–22," *ZAW* 100 [1988]: 210). Similarly, Knud Jeppesen writes that "there is nothing in the text to suggest that it is non-Isaianic ("Call and Frustration: A New Understanding of Isaiah viii 21–22," *VT* 32 [1982]: 150); and Blenkinsopp judges that nothing "obliges us to assign a Second Temple date to this appendix" (*Isaiah 1–39*, 245). Against this idea, H. G. M. Williamson writes that "it looks as though we are dealing with the fragment of what was once a more extended discourse. ... [I]t is difficult to believe that these words were written specifically for their present context, or that they have been added by a later scribe or redactor with a view to amplifying what precedes" ("Isaiah 8:21 and a New Inscription from Ekron," *Bulletin of the Anglo-Israel Archaeological Society* 18 [2000]: 51). In this he concurs with G. B. Gray, who deems vv. 19–23 a composite of "three fragments" (*A Critical and Exegetical Commentary on the Book of Isaiah, I–XXXIX* [ICC; New York, Charles Scribner's Sons, 1912], 157–59). R. E. Clements regards 8:19–22 as three separate post-587 additions ("The Prophecies of Isaiah and the Fall of Jerusalem," in *Prophecy in the Hebrew Bible*, 148–63; orig. *VT* 30 [1980]: 421–36). Schmidt also thinks that this passage is a Deuteronomistic addition, since the terms אוב

which is derived from necromancy, and those who advocate consulting the dead are likened to them. Bracketing for the moment the precise historical context, it is clear that vv. 16–20 envision a situation of turmoil and crisis: the Lord has turned his face from "the house of Jacob," and some are advocating forms of divination other than Isaiah's prophecies.[320] The idea that necromancy was a last resort for those whom God ignored is attested also in the account of Saul at Endor (1 Sam 28:6–7: "When Saul inquired of the LORD, the LORD did not answer him, not by dreams, or by Urim, or by prophets. Then Saul said to his servants, 'Seek out for me a woman who is a medium ...'"). In this situation, Isaiah orders that his teachings be stored away until, in the course of events, their accuracy can be assessed. This method for distinguishing between true and false prophecy was probably traditional (assuming that Deut 18:21–22 reflects older received wisdom). Indeed, given the condemnation of necromancy in Deut 18:10–13, all of Deut 18:9–22 may reflect a common concern about the allure of necromancy in times of crisis like those of 1 Sam 28 and Isa 8:16–23aα.

The idea of "YHWH hiding his face," found in 8:17, is frequently associated with impending death, which sets the stage for the images of death and the underworld that follow. The experience of YHWH's neglect is akin to death:

Why do you hide your face? Why do you forget our affliction and oppression?
For we sink down to the dust; our bodies cling to the ground. (Ps 44:24–25)[321]

When you hide your face, they are dismayed;
when you take away their breath, they die and return to their dust. (Ps 104:29)

Answer me quickly, O YHWH;
my spirit fails.
Do not hide your face from me,
or I shall be like those who go down to the Pit. (Ps 143:7)

---

and ידענים appear more often in Deuteronomistic contexts (*Israel's Beneficent Dead*, 147–54). But did the Deuteronomists invent their own terminology for necromantic practices? More likely they adopted terms that already existed. And in Josef Tropper's view, "Die drei [Texte] dem Buch Protojesaja [i.e., 8:19; 19:3; and 29:4] entstammenden Belege sind allesamt im jeweiligen Kontext sekundär; keiner ist Jesajanischer Herkunft, vielmehr scheinen alle drei Verse auf einen einzigen Kommentator der späteren nachexilischen Zeit zurückzugehen" (*Nekromantie: Totenbefragung im Alten Orient und im Alten Testament* [AOAT 223; Kevelaer: Butzon & Bercker, 1989; Neukirchen-Vluyn: Neukirchener Verlag, 1989], 341). As with Schmidt, these data are forced to conform to a larger thesis about the development and banning of necromancy and cults of the dead, a thesis against which I have already argued (§ 2.4.2). In sum (and in part *because of* the manifest difficulty of the text), I conclude that vv. 19–23 existed prior to the compilation of these verses, which was probably Josianic, corresponding to the composition of 9:1–6.

[320] See, among others: Mark Smith and Elizabeth Bloch-Smith, "Death and Afterlife in Ugarit and Israel," *JAOS* 108 (1988): 281–83.

[321] The imagery of vv. 19, 22 also invokes death imagery: "you have broken us in the haunt of jackals, and covered us with deep darkness.... Because of you we are being killed all day long, and accounted as sheep for the slaughter."

As this last example indicates, "YHWH is hiding his face" also commonly means that YHWH is refusing to offer counsel ("Answer me ..."). Isaiah laments that although he has just delivered an oracle, his opponents seek necromantic knowledge, thus bringing YHWH's neglect (and death) upon themselves.

The pressure to consult the dead is more comprehensible in light of the passage's historical and political background, which is different from most others discussed thus far. The text reflects a Judean view of the Syro-Ephraimitic Crisis of 734–731, in which the northern kingdom formed a league with the Arameans against the Assyrians and attacked Jerusalem in an effort to force the Judeans to join in.[322] (In stark contrast to the image of Assyria in later oracles already surveyed above, in Isa 8 the Assyrians are portrayed as a *salvific* flood – indeed, as the very presence of God with Judah [8:7–8]). In a time of political turmoil among the tribes named for the sons of Jacob, it would have seemed that the land had ceased to be in divine favor. Thus, the "house of Jacob" in v. 17 likely does not refer primarily to Judah.[323] Here it indicates first and foremost that the Lord had neglected the northern kingdom, which comprised the majority of the tribes that made up "the house of Jacob," and had deprived its leaders of good counsel – for why else would they attack their brother nation? Judah's long wait for support from Mesopotamia must have been nerve-wracking. It would have been difficult for Assyria to get a message through to Judah past its northern adversaries, and it seems some inhabitants of Jerusalem argued that they should consult the dead for some kind of insight into their situation.

While there is no doubt that the primary sense of the speech is to advocate necromancy, some of its most significant terms playfully admit of more than one understanding, creating a kind of extended *double entendre*:

(19) "Consult the ghosts (אבות) and familiar spirits (ידענים) that twitter and murmur! Should a people not consult its ancestors (דרש אלהיו) – (should it not consult) the dead on behalf of the living – (20) for instruction (תורה) and testimony?" (Isa 8:19–20)

A number of these ideas, taken out of context, sound remarkably like something that even the staunchest and most "intolerant" Yahwist might have said: The term ידענים is certainly from the root ידע, "to know," and similar-sounding substantives from the same root have the sense of "expert, knowledgeable person," e.g., יְדֻעִים (1 Chr 12:33; Job 34:2; Eccl 9:11). Even אבות could be understood

---

[322] See Childs, *Isaiah*, 79; J. Maxwell Miller and John H. Hayes, *A History of Ancient Israel and Judah* (2nd ed.; Louisville, Ky.: Westminster John Knox, 2006), 378–91, 395–98.

[323] On Isaiah's use of the term "Jacob," see J. J. M. Roberts, "Isaiah 2 and the Prophet's Message to the North," *JQR* n.s. 75 (1985): 290–308, here 293–94. Like Roberts, I cannot agree with the view that "house of Jacob" is a clear marker of a postexilic text (contra Blenkinsopp, *Isaiah 1–39*, 282; H. G. M. Willamson, *The Book Called Isaiah: Deutero-Isaiah's Role in Composition and Redaction* [Oxford: Oxford University Press, 1994], 165–67), even if it became a common term of identity in that period. A number of texts with good claims to being preexilic employ it (e.g., Exod 19:3 [E], Mic 3:9).

as "fathers," and indeed that has sometimes been taken to be the etymology of the word (§ 4.4.3.2). Furthermore, it would have sounded natural enough that a people should "consult its God" (a possible understanding of דרש אלהיו; cf. Deut 4:29; 1 Sam 9:9; Pss 53:3; 14:2; 69:33; 77:3; Job 5:8; etc.). Clearly, too, instruction was thought to come from God (Isa 1:10; 2:3; 5:24; 8:16; etc.), and testimony through God's prophets (8:16).[324] Thus, in an impressive barrage of double-talk that translations cannot capture, the words of Isaiah's opponents repeatedly echo theologically acceptable language, while actually advocating for necromancy. (Only the twittering and murmuring and the explicit reference to the dead in v. 19 undermine this alternate reading.)

This sort of speech is referred to throughout the book – speech that obfuscates and buries the truth. For example, in 5:20–21, the prophet condemns those who are "wise in their own eyes, and shrewd in their own sight," who "put darkness for light and light for darkness," etc. (cf. also 30:10–11). In 8:19–20, the prophet parodies his opponents' sly rhetoric directly. They are not clods who bluntly reject Isaiah's teaching – instead, they are portrayed as intelligent and cultivated rhetoricians who adopt the jargon of the Yahwistic cult even in subverting it. Therefore, in order to appreciate the force of vv. 19–20, it is crucial to let the words speak with two voices, that of Isaiah and that of his opponents.

Isaiah counters this speech with similarly complex rhetoric. In v. 20, the phrase אין לו שחר marks the transition between the language of divinatory consultation and that of the grave, and it looks in both directions. The word שחר is usually translated "dawn," which indeed anticipates the imagery of darkness that follows. But the phrase is typically translated as if it referred to the speakers (e.g., NRSV: "Surely, those who speak like this will have no dawn!"; cf. NJPS, NIV, etc.). This is possible only through textual emendation, however, since the speakers are plural (יאמרו), while both the suffix in לו and the syntax indicate that the phrase modifies not the speakers but *the word that is spoken*. It is not often remarked in discussions of this text that the root שחר is commonly used of seeking God (Isa 26:9; Hos 5:15; Pss 63:2; 78:34).[325] If the word is pointed as a Piel infinitive (שַׁחֵר),

---

[324] Good, *Irony in the Old Testament*, 138: "Allegiance is finally at issue. That is what [Isaiah's] theology is all about."

[325] A number of scholars have explained the word here and the possibly related terms in Isa 47:11, 15 (שחרה, סחריך) as connected to the idea of magic or sorcery, by comparison with the Akkadian *saḫīru*, "sorcerer." This might, in fact, be understood as simply a different form of the argument presented here. They argue that the Hebrew שחר in these cases relates to the Akkadian verb *saḫāru* in the D: "turn aside (evil)" (*CAD* S, 47–48, s.v. *saḫāru*, no. 8), whereas I am suggesting that the sense relates to the G stem (under subheading #2), "to turn to/beseech a deity" (*CAD* S, 41–43). Even though the Hebrew root occurs mostly in the D stem (except for Prov 11:27), its other occurrences strongly suggest that it was used in ways akin to דרש, that is, as a term for seeking a god. For the earlier understanding, "magic, power (to bewitch maliciously)," see G. R. Driver, "Hebrew Notes on the Prophets and Proverbs," *JTS* 41 (1940): 162; idem, "Isaianic Problems," 45; Sweeney, "Philological and Form-Critical Re-Evaluation of Isaiah 8:16–9:6," 219–20; Wildberger, *Isaiah 1–12*, 364; and Otto Kaiser, *Isaiah 1–12: A Commentary*

the phrase could mean, "this word, which has no (earnest) seeking" – that is, which is disingenuous and false, rather than earnestly sought from the Lord, as Isaiah's own counsel is.

Verses 21–22 extend the message, adding that no light will be shed by necromantic consultation, and that such pursuits lead only to darkness, suffering, and distress[326] – that is, the condition of the uncared-for dead. These verses also bring more problems with pronouns. The subject is now singular (ועבר), which might be accounted for by the assumption that "the people" are being referred to throughout the passage, sometimes as a collective singular and other times as a plural entity. More troublesome is the lack of an antecedent for the feminine pronoun in the term בה, which describes that into which the subject crosses over. The suffix can refer only to a geographical entity, and short of positing that these verses were imported from some other context,[327] it must be Sheol (or its euphemism ארץ, as in v. 22; both are feminine). The language employed in these verses is clearly similar to the underworld as envisioned throughout the ancient Near East. It is dark (v. 22); its inhabitants are hungry; and because of their hunger they are wrathful.[328] Of course, those images of distress, exhaustion, siege, and exile also might describe the plight of the inhabitants of a city under attack, as Jerusalem would have been in the face of the Syro-Ephraimitic alliance. But when they look to the underworld (אל־ארץ יביט) by means of necromancy – the theme of vv. 19–20 reappears – they see only more darkness.

The phrase וקלל במלכו ובאלהיו may also contain a reference to the cult of the dead, but not in the way that is most often thought. George C. Heider and others have argued that מלכו is a reference to the god Molek,[329] but the word pair "god and king" is known from both extrabiblical and biblical texts,[330] and there is no apparent reference to the Molek cult in the rest of the passage. The translation "it will curse its king and its God" is widely adopted, especially by readers who advocate a strictly historical (as opposed to mythological) understanding of the entire passage, since cursing God and king is precisely what a suffering people

---

(trans. John Bowden; 2nd ed.; OTL; Philadelphia: Westminster, 1983), 199. Even the medieval rabbi David Kimhi proposed a similar play on words in Isaiah. See the comments A. J. Rosenberg in *Isaiah: Translation of Text, Rashi and Commentary*, vol. 1 (Miqra'ot Gedolot) (New York: Judaica Press, 1982), 205.

[326] Similar is the conclusion of Driver, "Isaianic Problems," 49.

[327] For example, Patrick W. Skehan argued that the subject is the Assyrian king, and that vv. 21–22 have been moved from their proper place within 14:24–27 ("Some Textual Problems in Isaia [sic]," *CBQ* 22 [1960]: 47–55), but his case is highly speculative.

[328] In addition to chapters. 1–2 above, see George C. Heider, *The Cult of Molek: A Reassessment* (JSOTSup 43; Sheffield: JSOT Press, 1985), 329.

[329] Heider, *Cult of Molek*, 331. Tellingly, however, John Day leaves it out of his accounting of OT references to Molek (*Molech: A God of Human Sacrifice in the Old Testament* [Cambridge: Cambridge University Press, 1989], *passim*).

[330] Exodus 22:27; 1 Kgs 21:13; Prov. 24:21; Williamson, "Isaiah 8:21 and a New Inscription," 51–55.

might be expected to do.³³¹ In this view, the ב-prepositions, which must otherwise indicate in whose name the subject curses, are taken to be pious scribal emendations (like the substitution elsewhere of ברך, "bless," for קלל, "curse").

However, two factors suggest that supernatural powers are in view, albeit not Molek: First, I am not aware that pious emendation by the insertion of prepositions is attested elsewhere in the Bible; and, second, the phrase אלהיו repeats v. 19 so neatly that the reader ought to be biased toward interpreting the word in the same way here, as "spirits of the dead." Following that tack, one could also interpret מלכו as a plural form ("its kings") – *mlkw* would have been a normal plural suffixed form in preexilic Hebrew.³³² Perhaps these "kings" are in fact the dead (cf. Isa 14:9, 18) just as *mlkm* was a term for the divinized dead in Ugarit (§ 3.3.3.2); it would have been quite understandable for a later scribe to misunderstand this word and point it as a singular. One may conclude that the advocates of necromancy are portrayed as invoking the powerful spirits of the dead to curse their fellow Judeans. The ability to invoke the powers of the dead is of course a widespread belief in ancient Near Eastern religion from the Mesopotamian *kispu* and other funerary inscriptions³³³ to the Egyptian Letters to the Dead, the Ugaritic royal funerary cult, etc.

Much as the wider biblical polemic against the Rephaim portrays them as powerless, here Isaiah implicitly asks why their advocates would expect those who live in darkness and suffering to be able to offer any help to the living who are in the same situation. One arrives at a portrait of the advocates of necromancy as the unhappy dead, their relationship to the underworld disturbed by the prophet's intervention. They curse the prophet, rebel against YHWH, and see no hope (v. 22), whereas the prophet who trusts in the Lord sees the light of the coming salvation.

Verse 23 has attained the status of a major crux, but its grammar and historical referents are of only limited relevance to the present research. A few observations (which are also reflected in the translation above) must suffice: The verse speaks

---

³³¹ Williamson, "Isaiah 8:21 and a New Inscription," 53.

³³² Sandra Landis Gogel, *A Grammar of Epigraphic Hebrew* (SBLRBS 23; Atlanta: Scholars Press, 1998), 155–57. In early Hebrew there was no *yod*-marker of a suffixed plural (מלכו). One might conclude that the nuance was lost on a later scribe who updated the orthography.

³³³ The idea of the dead summoning underworld gods to curse the living is, in fact, attested in Neo-Assyrian funerary inscriptions. In one, a Mesopotamian nobleman curses anyone who would disturb or neglect his burial – and does so in the name of the king of the underworld: "May Nergal, by fever, calamity, and massacre, not spare your life!" (ᵈ*N[e]rgal ina di-ʾi šib-ṭu u šag-ga-áš-ti la i-gam-mi-il nap-šat-su*; Jean Bottéro, "Les inscriptions cunéiformes funéraires," in *La Mort, les morts dans les sociétés anciennes* (ed. G. Gnoli and J. P. Vernant; Cambridge/New York: Cambridge University Press, 1982), 385. The text in question dates to the reign of Aššur-etel-ilî (626–624).) A similar Babylonian inscription from the end of the second millennium curses the one who would open the tomb: "May the (infernal) Anunnaki from below destroy your offspring!" (ᵈ*A-nun-na i-na ša-ap-la-ti [p]iⁱˡ-ri-ʾi-šu [l]iʾ-h[aʾ]-a[lʾ]-li-qu*; Bottéro, "Les inscriptions cunéiformes funéraires," 387).

of two *past* historical events; it is not advisable to translate one perfect-aspect verb as past and a neighboring one as future, as many translations do.[334] Nor is הכביד likely to mean "he glorified," but rather, "he made heavy/oppressed," as is more common. Although G. R. Driver and J. A. Emerton argued that the masculine adjectives "former" and "latter" cannot modify "time," which is usually feminine,[335] later studies have convincingly shown that classical Hebrew is not necessarily so rigid.[336]

Contrary to the older and still popular theory that 8:23 refers to a pair of Neo-Assyrian invasions during the 730s,[337] I concur with Hanan Eshel and Blenkinsopp that the most likely pair of historical events are the deliverance of Judah from two quite distinct northern threats: the first, the intervention of Bar-Hadad of Syria on behalf of Asa of Judah against Ba'asha of Israel (ca. 885 BCE; cf. 1 Kgs 15:18-21 // 2 Chr 16); the second, Tiglath-Pileser III's aforementioned attack on Syria and Israel in 734-731.[338] The implied subject of the verbs קלל and הכביד is YHWH, who is for Isaiah the motive force behind geopolitical events:

As in the former time YHWH brought into contempt
 the land of Zebulun and the land of Naphtali,
So in the latter time he oppressed
 the Way of the Sea, the land beyond the Jordan, Galilee of the nations.

The implicit logic of the transition from v. 22 to v. 23 is that since YHWH has brought this oppression upon the nation, salvation will come only through seeking him (and not other powers such as the dead ancestors).

Both military events in v. 23 are reported in the past tense, and they also seem disjointed from any context – not only from the previous imagery but also from the hymn of 9:1–6, which is entirely different in literary form. It would seem that this text found its way into this position at a later time, perhaps when the hymn was composed. Despite some efforts to argue a postexilic date for the hymn,[339] it

---

[334] Note the same "former/latter" pair in Jer 50:17, there referring clearly to past events.

[335] Driver, "Isaianic Problems," 46–48; J. A. Emerton, "Some Linguistic and Historical Problems in Isa VIII.23," *JSS* 14 (1969): 151–75.

[336] On grammatical grounds: Paul D. Wegner, "Another Look at Isa VIII 23B," *VT* 41 (1991): 481–84. Arguing the same point on literary grounds is Jesper Høgenhaven, "On the Structure and Meaning of Isa VIII.23b," *VT* 37 (1987): 218–21.

[337] E.g., Whitley, "Language and Exegesis of Isaiah 8:16–23," 28–43. There is a minority position that the allusion is to kings of the northern kingdom; see, e.g., H. L. Ginsberg, "An Unrecognized Allusion to Kings Pekah and Hoshea of Israel," *ErIsr* 5 (1958): 61*–65*.

[338] Hanan Eshel, "Isaiah VIII.23: An Historical-Geographical Analogy," *VT* 40 (1990): 104–8; Blenkinsopp, *Isaiah 1–39*, 247.

[339] E.g., Wolfgang Werner, *Eschatologische Texte in Jesaja 1–39: Messias, Heiliger Rest, Völker* (Würzburg: Echter Verlag, 1982), 46. Seitz wonders whether the descriptions of victory in the hymn are to be taken as historical at all: "When one treats the oracle as a traditional accession piece ... the language of military defeat need not conform so closely to historical facts. The cause for joy is not so much pending military victory but the 'birth' of a new ruler, in whose wake such victory will come in due course" (*Isaiah 1–39*, 86).

is entirely in keeping with ancient Near Eastern rhetoric about real kings, and does not reflect any of the later disasters that befell Judah. Indeed, the yoke,[340] rod, and scepter of v. 3 (Isa 10:5, 15; 14:5, 25, 29) and the trampling sandal of v. 4[341] all relate this passage to the Neo-Assyrian oracles in chs. 1–33. Insofar as it tells of the growth of the nation and portrays the breaking of the staff of an oppressor, the common conclusion that it originally was composed for Hezekiah (after the departure of Sennacherib) or Josiah (in anticipation of the Neo-Assyrian empire's crumbling) seems likely.[342]

The assignation of the hymn to the preexilic period is significant, in that 9:1–6 reverses the underworld language of 8:19 in specific ways: the darkness and gloom that characterized those who rejected the Lord's counsel give way to light (9:1), and distress gives way to joy (v. 2). While in no way as startling an image as what one finds in chs. 24–27, this does suggest that the overturning of death – the reversal of the sepulchral order of things that Isaiah saw as resulting from cults of the dead – is entirely plausible as the work of a pre-exilic author, whether it was Isaiah himself or a tradent.

In conclusion, 8:16–8:23aα reflects the challenging situation in which Isaiah prophesied. His word was not heeded, perhaps not even countenanced. The bitter invective against necromancy reflects frustration with the silver-tongued advocates who, in Isaiah's view, turned their backs on YHWH in a crisis. The hymn in 9:1–6 promises light, peace, and prosperity under the rule of YHWH's anointed. Whether or not it is authentically Isaianic, its thrust is already contained *in nuce* in the end of ch. 8: Although there is "no dawn" for necromancy, there is in the word of YHWH.

5.2.3 Other condemnations of cults of the dead

5.2.3.1 Isaiah 7:10–13: YHWH's sign from Sheol?

The reference to Sheol in Isa 7:11 is overshadowed in its context within the Immanuel oracle (7:10–17), the latter half of which has generated a breathtaking

---

[340] The "yoke of Aššur" was an exceedingly common literary motif used in Neo-Assyrian texts to describe their rule over other nations. For discussion, see Hays, "Kirtu and the 'Yoke of the Poor,'" 361–70.

[341] סְאוֹן is a loanword from Akkadian *šēnu* (*CAD* Š.II, 289–92).

[342] H. G. M. Williamson, "First and Last in Isaiah," in *Of Prophets' Visions and the Wisdom of Sages: Essays in Honour of R. Norman Whybray on his Seventieth Birthday* (ed. Heather A. McKay and David J. A. Clines; Sheffield: JSOT Press, 1993). Høgenhaven dates the hymn between 732 and 722 ("On the Structure," 220). Writes Blenkinsopp: "If we compare [9:1–6] with texts known to be postexilic that focus on the Davidic dynasty we certainly note some duplication of themes, ... but nonetheless the differences are more in evidence than the similarities" (*Isaiah 1–39*, 248). Van der Woude also deems the hymn Josianic ("Jesaja 8,19–23a als literarische Einheit").

amount of literature on account of its significance in Christian theology. However, this passage too contains a subtle polemic against necromancy:

(10) And YHWH spoke to Ahaz again, saying: (11) "Ask for a sign from the Lord your God – make it deep as Sheol (שְׁאָלָה) or high above!"
(12) But Ahaz said, "No, I will not ask; I will not test the Lord."
(13) Then Isaiah said, "Hear, O House of David! Is it not enough for you to weary mortals, that you also weary my God?"

Isaiah's offer creates a potential problem of theological consistency, since "a sign from Sheol" might well be understood to refer to necromancy. Unease about this very problem may have led to a pious scribal emendation of the word Sheol.[343] Is the reader supposed to understand that YHWH now condones and even promotes necromancy, which is elsewhere mocked and condemned in Isa 1–39?

YHWH's offer of a sign from Sheol should be read in light of the historical and religious controversy reflected also in 8:16–20 – that is, the competition between prophets of YHWH and advocates of necromancy for divinatory authority and thus for influence in matters of state.[344] (The fact that Isaiah and his advice may be out of favor with Ahaz and the court at about this time could be reflected in the location in which he delivered the previous oracle in 7:3–9: Why else should the prophet have had to meet with the king at some reservoir by a highway?) In Isa 8:19–20, Isaiah tried to undermine the appeal of necromancy. Implicit in that effort is Isaiah's view that Yahwism and necromancy were mutually exclusive; if the king pursued one, it was at the expense of the other. The invitation in 7:11, "ask a sign!", is a plea to seek and heed the word of YHWH at a time when presumably Ahaz was not doing so. Just as the advocates of necromancy did in Isa 8:19–20, Ahaz enunciates a good simulacrum of Yahwism:[345] "I will not test the Lord," echoing a common and seemingly ancient taboo. It is not for mortals to test God (cf. Exod 17:2 [E]; Deut 6:16; Ps 78:56), but rather God who tests (Gen 22:1; Exod 15:25: 20:20 [all E]; Deut 4:34: 8:2: 13:4; Judg 2:22; Ps 26:2: etc.). But in this case, נסה might as well be a synonym for דרש, since Ahaz's reply clearly means, "I will not *consult* YHWH." Blenkinsopp pleads ignorance about the

---

[343] The form שְׁאָלָה has sometimes been taken as an emendation in which the expected form שְׁאֵלָה has been repointed as an infinitive of the root שאל, "to ask." The assumption is that it would be unseemly for YHWH to offer Ahaz a sign from Sheol, since (in a later copyist's view), YHWH had no involvement with the underworld. However, Paul Joüon and Takamitsu Muraoka deem the MT pointing merely an alternative pausal form, chosen to create assonance with מַעְלָה (*A Grammar of Biblical Hebrew* [SubBi 14; Rome: Pontificio Istituto Biblico, 2000], 107 [§ 32c]). If so, then the ה- is directive, expressing extent. In any case, the context has long made it clear to translators that שאלה must refer to something deep, such as the underworld: thus one finds εἰς ᾅδην ("to Hades") in a number of Greek manuscripts (e.g., Aquila, Symmachus, Theodotion; cf. also LXX: εἰς βάθος) and *in profundum inferni* ("in the depth(s) of Hell") in the Vulgate.

[344] So also van der Toorn, "Echoes of Judean Necromancy," 215: "In his prophetic ministry, Isaiah had to combat, among other things, the tendency of this people to resort to necromancy."

[345] Similarly, Childs, *Isaiah*, 65.

reasons for Isaiah's ire: "The terseness of the narrative does not permit a clear sense as to why the refusal of Ahaz to put Yahveh to the test elicited such a testy reply."[346] An answer can now be supplied: it appears that Isaiah's anger derives from Ahaz's decision to turn his back on the prophet's offer of counsel.

The common observation that the word pair שאלה / מעלה creates a merismus here is correct. It does suggest that Isaiah is giving Ahaz "the greatest latitude in making his request."[347] G. Boccaccini accurately expanded Isaiah's words as follows: "Chiedi qualunque cosa; hai dinanzi a te l'universo intero (non cielo e terra solo, ma cielo e Šeol!); sappi che la potenza di Dio è altrettanto immensa."[348] However, the expression of totality is not the extent of the phrase's significance. The reference to Sheol also makes a rhetorical (and theological) claim about YHWH's power over the specific competing source of knowledge, that is: *Why seek mantic knowledge from the dead when YHWH has power over Sheol as well?* The claim is thus analogous to Amos 9:2 – "If they dig into Sheol, from there shall my hand take them; though they climb up to heaven, from there I will bring them down" – although instead of merely asserting the extension of YHWH's power into the underworld (§ 4.4.4), it implicitly *abolishes* the underworld powers by replacing them with YHWH. Mantic recourse to Sheol is portrayed as futile in light of YHWH's power over Sheol.

5.2.3.2 Isaiah 19:1–15: Egypt will consult its ghosts in vain

It is not only Judean necromancy that is mocked and/or condemned in Isaiah, but also that of the Egyptians:

(1) An oracle concerning Egypt:
   Look, the Lord is riding upon a swift cloud;
      he will come to Egypt,
   and the idols of Egypt will shake before him
      and the heart of Egypt will melt within it.
(2) And I will stir up Egypt against Egypt
      and each will fight his brother, and each (will fight) his neighbor –
   city against city, kingdom against kingdom.
(3) And the spirit of the Egyptians shall be crushed within it,
      and I will confound its plan.
   They will consult their gods[349] and their shades,

---

[346] Blenkinsopp, *Isaiah 1–39*, 232.
[347] Blenkinsopp, *Isaiah 1–39*, 232.
[348] "Ask anything; you have before you the entire universe (not merely sky and earth, but sky and Sheol!), know that the power of God is equally immense." G. Boccaccini, "I termini contrari come espressioni della totalita in Ebraico," *Bib* 33 (1952): 178.
[349] Tentatively, read אלהים or אלים for MT אלילים. Lewis points out that the LXX translated τοὺς θεούς here, which it does nowhere else for אלילים, suggesting to him that its *Vorlage* read אלהים (*Cults of the Dead*, 133). The term אלילים is one of Schmidt's arguments for a late date for the passage, since it occurs in putatively late contexts in Isa 2:8, 18; 31:7 (*Israel's Beneficent Dead,*

their ghosts and their familiar spirits.
(4) But I will dam up[350] Egypt by the hand of a hard master
    and a mighty king shall rule over them,
    Says the Lord, YHWH of hosts.
....
(11) Surely the officials of Tanis are fools,
     The wisest of Pharaoh's counselors give stupid counsel.
     How can you say to Pharaoh, "I am a wise man,
     an acolyte of ancient kings"?
(12) Where then are your wise men, that they may tell you
     and make known to you what YHWH of hosts has planned against Egypt?
(13) The officials of Tanis have become foolish,
     the officials of Memphis deceive themselves,
     the cornerstones[351] of her factions lead Egypt astray.
(14) YHWH has poured into her a twisted spirit,
     and they shall make Egypt stumble in all its works,
     like the stumbling of a drunkard in his vomit.
(15) And neither head nor tail, palm branch nor reed,
     will do anything for Egypt.[352]

Contrary to the opinion of many scholars, the oracle concerning Egypt in Isa 19:1–15 is a unified composition.[353] It is generally subdivided into three primary sections – vv. 1b–4, 5–10, and 11–14(15), with the superscription in v. 1a and the possibility of a prose addition in v. 15. Verses 1–4 concern the reaction of Egypt to a crisis that is exacerbated by internal divisions and results in suffering at the hands of a "harsh overlord." Since the primary sense of the verb סכר in v. 4 is "dam up" (cf. Gen 8:2),[354] the Nile Curse passage in vv. 5–10 is not likely to be an

---

157); but this is not a conclusive argument, given the appearance of the word in 10:10–11. Given its occurrence in the Assyrian king's speech in 10:10–11, it may well be a loanword from Neo-Assyrian *ēlilu*, "mighty one," which is frequently used as a divine epithet.

[350] See discussion below.

[351] Read פנות for MT פנת; cf. התעו.

[352] Verse 15 is sometimes taken to be a wisdom saying added secondarily. As is observed by Sweeney, Blenkinsopp, and others, its mere repetition from 9:13 does not indicate that it is secondary here. If the explanation offered at 9:14 is correct, that "palm branch and reed" signify elders and prophets, then the use of v. 15 here makes good sense, whether it is original or not. In light of the context – the conflict within Egypt – it is tempting to see "head and tail" as a reference to Lower and Upper Egypt (represented as parts of a Leviathan-like river-serpent).

[353] The full argument can be found in Christopher B. Hays, "Damming Egypt/Damning Egypt: The Paronomasia of *skr* and the Unity of Isa 19:1–15," *ZAW* 120 (2008): 612–16. The same conclusion was reached independently, and on different grounds, by Hilary Marlow, "The Lament Over the River Nile – Isaiah XIX 5–10 in its Wider Context," *VT* 57 (2007): 229–242. See also Alviero Niccacci, "Isaiah XVIII–XX from an Egyptological Perspective," *VT* 48 (1998): 214–238. Older, opposing views may be found in, e.g., Kaiser, *Isaiah 13–39*, 99–100; Wildberger, *Isaiah 13–27*, 233–39; Vermeylen, *Du Prophète Isaïe à l'Apocalyptique*, 322.

[354] As I have shown elsewhere ("Damming Egypt/Damning Egypt"), damming was both a military tactic carried out by Neo-Assyrian monarchs (*ABL* 273; cf. also *ABL* 543 r. 11; 1108 r. 12; 1244 r. 4) and also, in the Erra Epic (IV.13), a response of a city to the theophanic assault of a

unrelated addition, as Wildberger thought,[355] let alone a late apocalyptic flourish, as Kaiser opined.[356] Sweeney and Childs have further noted the form-critical integrity of vv. 1b–10, which announce YHWH's punishment of Egypt and its consequences.[357] Moreover, there are also thematic connections between v. 3 and vv. 11–14. The references to necromancy in v. 3 connect this section thematically with the condemnation of Pharaoh's counselors as foolish in vv. 11–14; thus they are often treated as an original unity.[358] In light of the phrase בן־מלכי קדם (which may refer to acolytes of a necromantic cult of a dead pharaoh, see below) and the imagery of drunkenness (which is commonly related to cults of the dead [see §§ 3.3.3.2.3; 4.4.1.3]), the connections are even more direct than is usually thought.

Even if these verses are a compositional unity, one might still doubt their authenticity and historical accuracy.[359] Do they reflect genuine knowledge of Egyptian necromantic practices in Iron Age II, or are they a late, fictional amal-

---

deity. In the phrase וסכרתי את־מצרים ביד אדנים קשה, the ב functions as an instrumental marker. (The river in Erra IV.13 is also dammed "by hands.") Thus "damming" is an apt image for this context; there is no need to invent a סכר II that means the same thing as סגר ("hand over"), as *HALOT* does.

[355] Wildberger wrote that "vv. 5–10 describe an economic breakdown, caused when the waters in the 'river' dry up, with no apparent relationship between this and the political crisis in vv. 1–4" (Wildberger, *Isaiah 13–27*, 234, 237).

[356] So Kaiser, *Isaiah 13–39*, 102.

[357] Sweeney also notes the conjunctive *waw*s throughout the passage (Sweeney, *Isaiah 1–39*, 263, 265; Childs, *Isaiah*, 142–43).

[358] Wildberger, *Isaiah 13–27*, 235–37, 249. (The thematic connection is noted by Kaiser (*Isaiah 13–39*, 99), although he does not perceive even vv. 1b–4 and 11–14 as an original unity.) The reference to drunkenness in v. 14 connects it to other Isaianic passages that probably refer to necromantic cults of the dead (certainly 28:7; possibly also 5:11; 22:13; 29:9). See G. R. Driver, "Another Little Drink – Isa 28:1–22," in *Words and Meanings: Essays Presented to David Winton Thomas on His Retirement from the Regius Professorship of Hebrew in the University of Cambridge, 1968* (ed. P. R. Ackroyd and B. Lindars; London: Cambridge University Press, 1968), 47–67; M. H. Pope, review of Schmidt, *Israel's Beneficent Dead* in *JQR* 88 (1997): 91–93; Bernhard Asen, "The Garlands of Ephraim: Isaiah 28, 1–6 and the Marzeaḥ," *JSOT* 71 (1996): 71–87; van der Toorn, "Echoes of Judean Necromancy," 199–217, esp. 212–13.

[359] A number of the themes that Vermeylen noted that are shared with other texts are shared with authentic passages, notably the incompetence of leaders, the recourse to necromancers, drunkenness and stumbling, vomit, etc. His argument that sharing various themes in common with other passages in Isa 1–39 indicates that a later author borrowed them in composing this text; but he does not prove it (Vermeylen, *Du Prophète Isaïe à l'Apocalyptique*, 320–21). Kaiser's hasty dismissal of the possible authenticity of 19:1–15 is based entirely on poetic style, which in turn is supported only by a footnote to T. K. Cheyne, *The Prophecies of Isaiah: A New Translation with Commentary and Appendices*, 3rd ed. (New York: Thomas Whitaker, 1884), 114. Cheyne's comments there hardly warrant Kaiser's journey into the Hellenstic period. Cheyne's only question is whether the passage is authentic or drafted by a disciple, "working of course on the basis of Isaiah's notes"! Only slightly better than Kaiser are commentators who reject the authenticity based on stylistic criteria such as the repetition of מצרים in vv. 1–4. This may or may not be good style, but it needs to be shown, rather than assumed, that this feature is relevant to the question of Isaianic authorship.

gamation constructed by, for example, a Deuteronomistic or later author?[360] It might be argued that the passage is a multicultural mishmash and therefore "only" a literary creation. Schmidt viewed the use of אבות and ידעונים as "symptomatic of the author's ignorance of Egyptian beliefs," but I have already pointed out that it has since been established that necromancy was practiced by the Egyptians (§ 2.4.2)[361] and have argued that אבות (v. 3) may even be a loanword from Egyptian 3bwt, meaning "(symbol of) ancestors" (§ 4.4.2.3). Thus it is far more likely that the Deuteronomistic terminology *derives from* this more or less accurate (if ideologically slanted) portrayal of Egyptian necromancy.

There is certainly evidence of non-Egyptian cultural traditions in these verses: the cloud-rider theophany of v. 1 can be attributed to "Canaanite"/Ugaritic Baal imagery.[362] And not only does the use of the verb סכר in v. 4 show signs of Mesopotamian influence,[363] but also the term used for "shades" in v. 3, אטים. It is a *hapax legomenon* in Biblical Hebrew, and almost certainly a loanword from Akkadian *eṭimmu*.[364] However, those disparate traditions seem to sit side by side with genuine knowledge of Egypt and its culture. As noted in § 2.3, Alviero Niccacci has cogently demonstrated that Isaiah 18–20 as a whole is firmly rooted in both eighth-century political history and in a knowledge of Egyptian culture and even language.[365]

Certainly 19:1–10 reflect accurate insight about Egypt in Isaiah's time. Even Donald Redford, usually a skeptic about Israel's knowledge of Egypt, assumed an eighth-century date for vv. 1–4 and granted the accuracy of its portrait.[366] The references to Tanis (Zoan) in vv. 11, 13 make much more sense prior to ca. 715, when the Twenty-second Dynasty, which had its capital in Tanis, fell to the Twenty-fifth (Nubian) Dynasty.[367]

---

[360] Schmidt believes that these verses are Deuteronomistic (*Israel's Beneficent Dead*, 157–58). Tropper's view (*Nekromantie*, 341) that these verses are postexilic has already been discussed above. Even Lewis seems to take the redactional consensus for granted, although his study demonstrates that the supposed redactor who added 19:3 held the same views of necromancy as did Isaiah ben Amoz (*Cults of the Dead*, 132–34, 137, 174).

[361] For Schmidt's argument against the existence of Egyptian necromancy, see *Israel's Beneficent Dead*, 156 n. 100.

[362] Oswald Loretz, "Der ugaritische Topos *b'l rkb* und die 'Sprache Kanaans' in Jes 19,1–25," *UF* 19 (1987): 101–12.

[363] Two of the three biblical instances in which סכר means "dam up" show signs of specific Mesopotamian influence (the other is Gen 8:2, part of the P flood narrative). See further in Hays, "Damming Egypt/Damning Egypt."

[364] See Lewis, *Cults of the Dead*, 133–34 and further references in n. 16; *CAD* E, 397–401.

[365] Alviero Niccacci, "Isaiah XVIII–XX from an Egyptological Perspective," *VT* 48 (1998): 214–238. Also Marlow, "The Lament Over the River Nile."

[366] Donald B. Redford, "The Relations between Egypt and Israel from El-Amarna to the Babylonian Conquest," in *Biblical Archaeology Today: Proceedings of the International Congress on Biblical Archaeology, Jerusalem, April 1984* (Jerusalem: Israel Exploration Society, 1985), 195.

[367] It is true that the pharaoh Taharqa (Twenty-fifth Dynasty; ruled ca. 690–664) made Tanis the seat of his rule for a time, and that the image of the "harsh overlord" fits well with the

The ensuing verses (vv. 5–10) cannot be specifically related to one period, but do show impressive knowledge of Egyptian culture and economy. Wildberger wrote,

> The author demonstrates a detailed knowledge of the geography of the Nile delta region and has observed economic conditions carefully enough to be able to describe specific problems. ... This type of detailed knowledge cannot be observed anywhere else in the OT.[368]

Wildberger was referring not only to the author's understanding of the Nile's economic impact on Egypt[369] but also to the numerous terms in Isa 19:1–15 that have been perceived as Egyptian loanwords – for example, שׁתת[370] (v. 5), סוּף[371] (v. 6), זנח[372] (v. 6), ערות[373] (v. 7). Even terms like מצור[374] (v. 6) and יאור (פִּי)[375] (vv. 6–8) may reflect specific knowledge of Egypt. This density of potential loanwords in vv. 5–10 is quite exceptional in the Hebrew Bible; whatever Israelite authors knew about Egypt, they did not employ Egyptian cognates with anything like the frequency with which they employed cognates from other Semitic languages. Wildberger seemed to lean toward the conclusion that this was the work of

---

invading Sargonids; however, this period does not square with the image of internal turmoil in vv. 1–4. Vermeylen advanced the theory that 19:1–4, 11–15 refers to Nebuchadnezzar's conquest of Egypt ca. 568–567 (*Du Prophète Isaïe à l'Apocalyptique*, 321), but Tanis was no longer a very significant city politically during that period. It is no great stretch to see Isaiah's image of the subjugation of Egypt by Assyria as a prediction from the late eighth century, issued prior to its accomplishment. It would not have been a hard thing to predict. Roberts associates the oracle with the Kushite Shabako's invasion of the Delta in 720 (J. J. M. Roberts, "Isaiah's Egyptian and Nubian Oracles," in *Israel's Prophets and Israel's Past: Essays on the Relationship of Prophetic Texts and Israelite History in Honor of John H. Hayes* [ed. B. E. Kelle and M. B. Moore; Library of Hebrew Bible/Old Testament Studies 446; New York: T&T Clark, 2006], 206).

[368] Wildberger, *Isaiah 13–27*, 234–35.

[369] Egypt "was conceived of as a body, and the water of the Nile as an elixir of life that gushed forth from it" (Assmann, *Death and Salvation*, 361).

[370] I. Eitan, "An Egyptian Loan Word in Isa 19," *Jewish Quarterly Review* 15 (1924–25): 419–22; Wildberger, *Isaiah 13–27*, 235.

[371] Egyptian *twf(y)*; W. F. Albright, *The Vocalization of the Egyptian Syllabic Orthography* (New Haven: American Oriental Society, 1934), 65; Thomas Lambdin, "Egyptian Loan Words in the Old Testament," *JAOS* 73 (1953): 153; W. A. Ward, "The Semitic Biconsonantal Root SP and the Common Origin of Egyptian CWP and Hebrew SÛP: Marsh(-Plant)," *VT* 24 (1974): 339, 349.

[372] F. Caplice, *Grundlagen der Ägyptische-Semitischen Wortvergleichung* (1936), no. 754; R. Yaron, "The Meaning of ZANAH," *VT* 13 (1963): 237–39.

[373] Egyptian ʿr, WAS 1.213; John D. Currid, *Ancient Egypt and the Old Testament* (Grand Rapids: Baker, 1997), 230; Wildberger, *Isaiah 13–27*, 235; *HALOT*, s.v. "עָרָה."

[374] מצור is often taken to refer to Lower Egypt, while מצרים refers to Upper and Lower Egypt together (Hugo Winckler, *Alttestamentliche Untersuchungen* [Leipzig: E. Pfeiffer, 1892], 172). The argument of P. J. Calderone ("The Rivers of 'Maṣor,' " *Bib* 42 [1961]: 423–32), that מצור derives from the root צור, such that the phrase means something like "mountain streams," has not been adopted.

[375] Egyptian *yrw*; H. Eisling, "יְאֹר" in *TDOT* 5:539–63.

a late author, presumably living in exile in Egypt ("this author is someone who does not know Egypt from secondhand reports only"[376]). However, if vv. 5–10 can no longer be severed from vv. 1–4, then they must be from the eighth century. Thus it is hard to disagree with Sarah Israelit-Groll that Isaiah himself "was acquainted with the Egyptian language and culture," as a part of his "deep sensitivity to and subtle conception of the international affairs of his time."[377] This fits with Isaiah's general message about Egypt that is reflected in chs. 1–33 – Redford implicitly states that Isaiah must have been a "most astute" observer of Egypt to recognize the weak state of its military in his time.[378]

This conclusion should send the reader back to Isa 19's references to necromancy to reconsider whether they are authentic and reflective of actual Egyptian practice. Chapter 2 demonstrated that necromancy was quite common in Egypt by the Third Intermediate Period, as reflected in Letters to the Dead, pseudonymous letters from dead pharaohs, and various localized necromantic cults (§ 2.4.2). Redford has shown that Jerusalem was in contact primarily with the Delta kingdoms during the monarchic period, and Isa 19's references to Tanis and rulers enthroned there fits with this conclusion. If indeed the court of Ahaz or Hezekiah communicated with the Tanites in this period, it is plausible that they would have gathered the picture reported in vv. 11–14: a crumbling kingdom in intellectual disarray, with no counselor able to offer it any helpful advice. As the foregoing discussion of Isa 8 suggested, necromancy and cults of the dead seem to have been a familiar resort in the ancient world in times of crisis, and Isa 19 seems to portray an Egyptian kingdom in a situation analogous to that of Judah in Isa 8.

At a second look, there are, in fact, indications that vv. 11–14 extend v. 3's concern with necromancy. The phrase בן־מלכי־קדם is never convincingly explained in commentaries – how were the Egyptian wise men in any sense "descendants of ancient kings"?[379] This does not seem to have been any common title for a sage in Egyptian literature.[380] Although some priestly positions in Egypt were held by the royal family, in later periods the priesthood was increasingly

---

[376] Wildberger, *Isaiah 13–27*, 234–35.

[377] Sarah Israelit-Groll, "The Egyptian Background to Isaiah 19:18," in *Boundaries of the Ancient Near Eastern World: A Tribute to Cyrus H. Gordon* (ed. Meir Lubetski et al.; JSOTSup 273; Sheffield: JSOT Press, 1998) 300, 303.

[378] Redford, "Studies in Relations between Palestine and Egypt during the First Millennium B.C.: II. The Twenty-Second Dynasty," *JAOS* 93 (1973): 14: "no one save the most astute realized that ... [Egypt] was considerably weaker than she had been in the New Kingdom. The deep impression the Ramesside empire had made throughout the ancient world faded only gradually, and even as late as the Seventh Century Egypt was regarded by the rulers of Judah as a power to be relied upon."

[379] This understanding is reflected in, e.g., NRSV, NJB, Blenkinsopp.

[380] Wildberger suggests a connection to the phrase בני קדם as type of the wise man (1 Kgs 5:10; cf. Isa 2:6), but the intervening מלכי creates a different sense here.

professionalized and even subject to its own hereditary succession.³⁸¹ Instead, the phrase seems likely to refer to a member of a royal necromantic cult such as were popular in Egypt in that period, analogous to the familiar Hebrew phrase בן־ נביאים, "member of a prophetic guild," or the Akkadian *mār bārî*, "member of a group of diviners."³⁸² Thus, a translation such as "acolyte of ancient kings" is more accurate (perhaps this is what NIV translators envisioned with the phrase "disciple of ancient kings").³⁸³ Tanis was the site of the royal necropolis for the Twenty-first and Twenty-second Dynasties; this would have made it a likely location for a royal necromantic cult. "Son of ancient kings" would not, in this view, be a direct calque of an Egyptian title, but rather a Hebrew-speaking prophet's invention to describe the position.

The image of "stumbling/staggering/erring" (תעה; vv. 13–14) functions on two levels. On a geopolitical level, it evokes the clumsy helplessness of Egypt in the face of Assyrian imperialism. Despite their historic influence in Palestine, the Delta kingdoms were repeatedly unable (or perhaps unwilling) to mount any significant resistance to the Nubians' onslaught or the Assyrians' expansion (see § 1.2). However, the language of drunkenness also echoes that which is used elsewhere in the book to describe the practitioners of necromancy.³⁸⁴ This motif is likely in evidence in 5:11; 22:13; and 29:9, but the clearest reference is in 28:7–8, which uses some of the same keywords as 19:14:

> These also reel with wine and stumble (תעו) with beer;
> the priest and the prophet reel with strong drink,
> they are confused with wine, they stagger with strong drink;
> they err in vision, they stumble in giving judgment.
> All tables are full of vomit (קיא);
> excrement is everywhere.

These drunken authorities are some of the same ones who are charged with making a covenant with death in Isa 28. As the next section (§ 5.2.3.3) shows, the religious reality behind the "covenant with death" is complex; the imagery of drunkenness there probably reflects a creative literary fusing of non-mortuary aspects of Egyptian religious practices and mortuary cult practices that were more widespread. Isa 19 focuses more specifically on necromantic aspects of Egyptian religion, but portrays them negatively in a strikingly similar way.

---

[381] See Denise M. Doxey, "Priesthood," in *OEAE*, 3:68–73; Ronald J. Williams, "The Sage in Egyptian Literature," in *The Sage in Israel and the Ancient Near East* (ed. J. G. Gammie and L. G. Perdue; Winona Lake, Ind.: Eisenbrauns, 1990), 27.
[382] *CAD* B, 125.
[383] Assmann points out that "the mortuary cult and wisdom had the same root: the father-son constellation" (*Death and Salvation*, 53), and cites an Old Kingdom text in which the father seeks to teach his son "the words of the 'hearers,' the thoughts of the predecessors, who once served the ancestor-kings."
[384] See Driver, "Another Little Drink," 47–67; Pope, review of Schmidt, *Israel's Beneficent Dead*, 91–93; Asen, "Garlands of Ephraim," 71–87; van der Toorn, "Echoes of Judean Necromancy," 199–217, esp. 212–13.

In conclusion, Isa 19:1–15 is a passage that gives many indications of authenticity and suggests that Isaiah was knowledgeable about Egyptian culture. The text is a unified composition, most likely of the eighth century prior to 715. It is striking that Isaiah's oracle against Egypt focuses not on any perceived lack of military might but on its lack of wisdom and knowledge; in his condemnations of Israel and Judah as well, it is often a lack of understanding that he identifies as the problem (5:13; 6:9; 28:9; 29:24).[385] As elsewhere in the book, Isaiah seizes on necromantic consultations as the exemplar of foolish and misleading divinatory practices.

5.2.3.3 Isaiah 28:1–22: The Covenant with Mut

Isaiah 28:1–22 gathers together a number of the themes already discussed, such as the association of opponents with the dead, the condemnation of drunken cultic activity, and the assertion of the futility of death cults. Its interpretation hinges on the meaning of the prophet's accusation that the Jerusalem leaders have made a "covenant with מות."

Most scholars would agree that at least Isa 28:7–22 is a response to Judah's seeking Egyptian support under the Neo-Assyrian threat. The image of floodwaters strongly evokes the Assyrians, as we have had numerous occasions to observe already (Isa 8:7–8; 14:4; also Nah 1:8, etc.).[386] Toward the end of the eighth century, with the seacoast and the former northern kingdom already firmly under Assyrian control, Judah would have had no nation to turn to for support but Egypt, specifically the Nubian Twenty-fifth Dynasty (732–653 BCE) and perhaps the Saite Twenty-sixth Dynasty (672–525 BCE). Indeed, it has long been observed that a treaty with Egypt underlies the image of the covenant with Death.[387] However, as John Day remarked, "scholars are at a loss to explain satisfactorily why Egypt should be called Death or Sheol."[388] The fact that Isaiah was playing on the name of the Egyptian goddess Mut resolves this long-standing scholarly dilemma.

---

[385] Cf. also 1:3, which, even if redactional, is an accurate summary of Isaiah's concern.

[386] Joseph Blenkinsopp, "Judah's Covenant with Death (Isaiah XXVIII 14–22)," VT 50 (2000): 474.

[387] Paul Auvray, Isaïe 1–39 (Paris: J. Gabalda, 1972), 250–51; Edward J. Kissane, The Book of Isaiah, vol. 1 (Dublin: Browne & Nolan, 1941), 318 ("the meaning is not that they had entered into a compact with the gods of the underworld, but that they had taken adequate measures to ensure the safety of the state"); D. Karl Marti, Das Buch Jesaja (KHC 10; Tübingen: Mohr Siebeck, 1900), 207; Clements, Isaiah 1–39, 230; Sweeney, Isaiah 1–39, 369 (tentatively, and with allowance for an allusion also to the marzeah); Gary Stansell, "Blest Be the Tie That Binds (Isaiah Together)," in New Visions of Isaiah (ed. R. Melugin; JSOTSup 214; Sheffield: Sheffield Academic Press, 1996), 78.

[388] Day, Molech, 85. See also Clements, Isaiah 1–39, 229: "Exactly why Egypt could meaningfully be described metaphorically as 'Death' (Mot) is not clear unless it was the apparent religious preoccupation of that country with death and the care of the dead."

5.2 Texts

(1) *Hôy*, proud garland of the drunkards of Ephraim,
    fading lotus-blossom of its glorious beauty,
    which is upon the head flowing[389] with perfumes[390]
    of those hammered[391] with wine.
(2) See, the Lord had one who was strong and mighty;
    Like a storm of hail, a destroying tempest
    like a downpour of mighty, overflowing waters,
    he brought them to the ground with his hand.
(3) They will be trampled underfoot,
    the proud garlands[392] of the drunkards of Ephraim,
(4) and the fading lotus-blossom of its glorious beauty
    which is upon the head flowing with perfumes
    will be like an early fig, before summer –
    whoever sees it swallows it as soon as it is in his hand.
(5) In that day, YHWH of hosts will be a beautiful garland
    and a wreath of glory to the remnant of his people,
(6) and a spirit of justice to the one who sits in judgment,
    and strength to those who repel the assault at the gate.
(7) These, too, stagger from wine and stumble from beer;
    priest and prophet stagger with beer;
    they are swallowed up[393] on account of wine;
    they stumble on account of beer,
    they err in vision,
    they are unstable in judgment.
(8) For all the tables are full of vomit,
    filth overruns the place.
(9) Whom will he teach knowledge?
    And to whom will he explain the report?
    To children just weaned from milk?
    To those who have hardly outgrown[394] the breast?

---

[389] Read גאי for גיא. Cf. 1QIsaᵃ; also Driver, "Another Little Drink," 48–49. Driver suggests that this unusual term was chosen to create a play on words with גאות in vv. 1, 3.

[390] The plural שמנים perhaps reflects blended aromatic oils used for anointing the head; cf. Song 1:3; 4:10; Amos 6:6.

[391] Cf. הלמות, "hammer," Judg 5:26. There is also an untranslatable play on words here that evokes חלם, "to dream." That is to say, the prophet implies that the dreams and visions of this group (cf. v. 15, 18) are merely alcohol-induced.

[392] Read עֲטֶרֶת to agree with תרמסנה.

[393] HALOT's suggestion to relate this form to בלל abolishes Isaiah's play on words and is not to be adopted. Cf. Roberts, "Double Entendre in First Isaiah," 41–43.

[394] Taking עתיק in the sense of "old"; cf. Marcus Jastrow, *A Dictionary of the Targumim, the Talmud Babli and Yerushalmi, and the Midrashic Literature* (2 vols.; New York: Pardes, 1903), 1129–1130.

(10) For it is "poo-poo,[395] poo-poo; bleh-bleh,[396] bleh-bleh,"
a little here, a little there.
(11) For with derisive speech and a foreign tongue,
he will speak to this people.
(12) He has said to them,
"This is the place of rest; give rest to the weary,
and this is the place of repose – " but they refused to listen.
(13) So the word of the Lord will be for them:
"poo-poo, poo-poo; bleh-bleh, bleh-bleh,"
a little here, a little there.
So that they will go and stagger backward;
They will be broken and snared and captured.

(14) Therefore hear the word of YHWH, you scoffers who rule[397] this people in Jerusalem:[398]
(15) Because you said,
"We have made a covenant with Mut(/Death),
and with Sheol we have made a pact.[399]
When the overwhelming torrent passes over,
It will not reach us,
for we have set a lie as our shelter,
and hidden ourselves in falsehood.
(16) Therefore thus says the Lord, YHWH:
"Look, I am laying[400] in Zion a stone,
a stone of testing,[401] a costly cornerstone,
a foundation of a foundation[402] –

---

[395] See discussion below. 1QIsaᵃ's alternate reading צי for צו unfortunately sheds no light.
[396] See discussion below. This translation is an admittedly insufficient attempt to get at the double sense of nonsensical baby talk and regurgitation.
[397] Another *double entendre* on the dual sense of משל ("to rule"/"to make a proverb") emphasizing the rulers' "ability to coin a clever turn of phrase" (Roberts, "Double Entendre in First Isaiah," 43). Cf. also § 3.3.2.4.
[398] In my view, the best interpretation is that it is the rulers who are "in Jerusalem," rather than the people, but I have allowed the indeterminacy of the Hebrew to remain.
[399] The terms חזה here and חזות in v. 18 have been widely discussed in the secondary literature. Two theories are often cited: that of G. R. Driver, who connected the term to OSA ḥdyt, "things that correspond, agreement" ("Another Little Drink," 58); and that of E. Kutsch, that these terms derive from the common root חזה, "to see," and that ברית is similarly related to the Akkadian barû, "to look upon, inspect" ("Sehen und Bestimmen: Die Etymologie von בְּרִית," in *Archäologie und Altes Testament: Festschrift für Kurt Galling* [ed. Arnulf Kuschke and Ernst Kutsch; Tübingen: Mohr Siebeck, 1970], 165–78). I take the latter view; see further below.
[400] Read יִסַּד; cf. J. J. M. Roberts, "Yahweh's Foundation in Zion (Isa 28:16)," *JBL* 106 (1987): 27–45.
[401] Although בחן may be related to an Egyptian word for a specific type of rock (see discussion below), here I have allowed the obvious play on the Hebrew root בחן ("to test") to take precedence.
[402] Hebrew frequently repeats words for emphasis, such as מעלה מעלה...מטה מטה (Deut 28:43) or the common phrase עדי־עד. Thus this phrase might also be translated "the deepest foundation." More literally, the sort of huge stones envisioned here and in the references to "costly

the one who trusts will not tremble.⁴⁰³
(17) And I will set justice as a measuring line
and righteousness as a plummet.
But hail will sweep away the shelter of falsehood
and waters will overwhelm the hiding place,
(18) and your covenant with death will be covered over,
and your pact with Sheol will not stand.⁴⁰⁴
For when the overwhelming torrent passes through,
you will be its stomping-ground.
(19) As often as it passes through, it will take you –
for morning by morning it passes through, by day and by night,
and it is sheer terror to understand the report.
(20) For the bench is too short to stretch yourself out,
and the shroud too narrow when it is gathered up.⁴⁰⁵
(21) For as on Mount Perazim YHWH will rise up,
as in the Valley of Gibeon he will rage.
to do his deed – strange is his deed,
and to perform his service – foreign is his service!
(22) And now, do not scoff lest your chains become stronger,
for destruction has been determined –
I have heard from the Lord, YHWH of hosts –
against the whole land.⁴⁰⁶

Although much of the work that has been done on this passage is helpful and basically accurate, the passage still seems at best a bit disjointed, due to its mixed imagery of torrential storms, drunkenness, flowers, and small children. This is commonly attributed to rather heavy redactional work in the text; instead, the key to the disparate images is the identity of *mwt*, a figure that, in addition to making sense of the mixed imagery, should meet certain criteria:

---

stones" used in Solomon's house (1 Kgs 5:31; 7:9–11) might indeed be viewed by a builder as "a foundation for a foundation."

⁴⁰³ Cf. Ugaritic √ḥ-š, "to tremble, be alarmed" (DUL 412); Akkadian ḫâšu B, "to worry," *CAD* H 146–47. See already Driver, "Another Little Drink," 60; Roberts, "Yahweh's Foundation," 36.

⁴⁰⁴ There is an untranslatable *double entendre* here: the חזות picks up the double senses of "pact" and "vision," and the verb קום works with either sense: "your pact will not endure" (cf. Amos 7:2; Nah 1:6; Isa 40:8; etc.) or "your vision will not come to pass" (cf. Isa 7:17; 8:10; 14:24; 46:10; etc.).

⁴⁰⁵ 1QIsaᵃ differs remarkably from the MT for much of this verse – it reads משתרריים והממסככה vs. MT's מהשתרע והמסכה צרה. E. Y. Kutscher suggests that "the large number of strange substitutions in this verse makes it seem likely that the text which the copyist transcribed was illegible at this point" (*Language and Linguistic Background of the Isaiah Scroll*, 379; cf. also 289). Although the LXX and Theodotion might have understood something like the Qumran text, it would be very difficult to make sense of.

⁴⁰⁶ It is no use translating this final, dangling phrase as it were part of the flow of the verse, when it is not.

1. *mwt* should plausibly have been known to a Judean author in the period in which the text was composed;
2. *mwt* should be capable of making a covenant, at least figuratively;
3. *mwt* should be a figure known to offer protection; and
4. *mwt* should have some connection to death or the underworld so that the play on Hebrew מות, "death," makes sense.

There is in fact a figure who fits the entire profile: the Egyptian goddess Mut, whose name in Egyptian (*Mwt*) apparently provided the prophet with an irresistible opportunity for *double entendre*.[407] Indeed, this would be only one of a number of bilingual wordplays in the Bible, including one in Isa 10:8.[408]

The phonology of Egyptian *Mwt* and Hebrew *mwt* seems to allow for a wordplay on "Mut" and "death." First, the bisyllabic Masoretic pointing מָוֶת is not historically accurate to eighth-century Judah. Instead, the term would have been pronounced /mawt/; the diphthong did not contract to /ô/ as in northern Hebrew.[409] Second, this is of interest since both the name of Mut and the name of Mot (the god of death) could be spelled the same way in Greek: Μουθ.[410] The Greek spelling attests the preservation of the diphthong in Mut's name as well. An analogous play on words is found in Amos 8:1–2, with קַיִץ ("summer fruit") and קֵץ ("end"). Given the uncertainty about Amos's regional dialect, it is impossible to know just how he might have pronounced the words, but they may have sounded identical.[411] More significantly, the cultural currency of such phonological wordplay suggests that hearers were not too distracted by variations in diphthong pronunciation to appreciate the play.

Mut was also known and worshiped in Isaiah's Judah. As I have shown elsewhere in greater detail,[412] Mut is well-represented in amuletic iconography in the Iron-Age Levant, with dozens of amulets portraying her having been discovered

---

[407] Isaiah's tendency toward wordplay, especially paronomasia, has already been noted above in the discussion of Isaiah 22, (p. 242 n. 186).

[408] Machinist, "Assyria and Its Image," 734–5; Gary A. Rendsburg, "Bilingual Worplay in the Bible," *VT* 38 (1988): 354–56.

[409] W. Randall Garr, *Dialect Geography of Syria-Palestine, 1000–586 B.C.E.* (Philadelphia: University of Pennsylvania Press, 1985), 38–39.

[410] For Mut, see Plutarch, *De Iside et Osiride* 374 B; see also Christian Froidefond, ed., *Isis et Osiris (Plutarque: Oeuvres Morales, Tome V, 2e partie)* (Paris: Belles Lettres, 1988), 305. For Mot, see Eusebius of Caesarea, *Praeparatio Evangelica* 1.10.34. On the etymology of Mut's name, see W. Brunsch, "Untersuchungen zu den griechischen Wiedergaben ägyptischer Personennamen," *Enchoria* 8 (1978): 123–28. The Egyptian *mt* means "death/dead (person)/to die"; there is no native Egyptian etymological connection in Egyptian between *mt* (death) and *mwt* (Mut), although similar wordplay occurs in Egyptian texts as well.

[411] Francis I. Andersen and David Noel Freedman deem it possible "that the pronunciation of both words was originally *qēṣ* in Amos's presentation" (*Amos: A New Translation with Introduction and Commentary* [AB 24A; Garden City, N.Y.: Doubleday, 1989], 796).

[412] "The Egyptian Goddess Mut in Iron-Age Palestine: Further Data From Amulets and Onomastics," *JNES*, forthcoming.

Fig. 5.4 Mut amulet from Iron II Lachish. From Christian Herrmann, *Ägyptische Amulette*, 216.

in Israel and Judah (Fig. 5.4).[413] These are tiny statuettes, just a few centimeters in their largest dimensions, which were either worn on the body or laid atop the corpse at burial[414] (a significant percentage of the Levantine examples were discovered in burial contexts). This indicates that she was sought out by Israelites, Judeans, and others for blessings and protection, much as she was during the same period in Egypt, and that her cult almost certainly had a mortuary aspect as it did in Egypt (see below). She also appears in personal and geographical names such as אחימות ("Brother of Mut"; 1 Chr 6:10), עינמות ("Eye of Mut"; CAI 44, an Ammonite seal), עזמות ("Mut is refuge"; 2 Sam 23:31; 1 Chr 11:33; 12:3; 27:35), and הצרמות ("Settlement of Mut"; Gen 10:26).[415] The limited number of names that has survived in biblical texts and inscriptions is in keeping with the religiously conservative naming practices that obtained in that world,[416] but there is

---

[413] See Christian Herrmann, *Ägyptische Amulette aus Palästina/Israel: Mit einem Ausblick auf ihre Rezeption durch das Alte Testament* (OBO 138; Freiburg, Schweiz: Universitätsverlag; Göttingen: Vandenhoeck & Ruprecht, 1994), esp. 208–25, although my analysis suggests that some of the amulets he identifies with Isis or Sekhmet also could have represented Mut.

[414] See Andrews, "Amulets," *OEAE*, 77.

[415] On these names, in addition to my forthcoming article, see the more cursory analyses in Yoshiyuki Muchiki, *Egyptian Proper Names and Loanwords in North-West Semitic* (SBLDS 173; Atlanta, Ga.: Society of Biblical Literature, 1999).

[416] See Tigay, *You Shall Have No Other Gods*.

enough data to indicate that there existed an active cult of Mut in Isaiah's time that would have been just as tempting as it was to rely on the Egyptians for horses and military support (cf. Isa 20:1–6; 30:1–7; etc.). There is no doubt that a religious "expert" in the region, such as Isaiah, would have been familiar with Mut.

Despite all this, I know of only one other attempt to relate Mut to the Hebrew Bible, that of Manfred Görg, who theorized a quarter-century ago that the references to the "mirrors of the women who served at the entrance to the tent of meeting" (Exod 38:8) were an Israelite reflection of the Kushite-Saite cult of Mut, and suggested that Mut or another Egyptian goddess could even have been the "Queen of Heaven" alluded to in Jeremiah 7 and 44.[417] The relationship of Mut to the "Queen of Heaven" cannot be pursued in a thorough way here, but deserves further investigation.

The Egyptian goddess Mut

The relative lack of attention to Mut, even among Egyptologists, appears to be due not to any defect in the theory but to gaps in scholarly knowledge of Mut, which persisted until relatively recently.[418] Thanks to the work of Herman te Velde, Betsy Bryan, Richard Fazzini, and others over the past three decades, we now know more.

Mut was a goddess who rose to prominence in Egypt late, in the middle of the second millennium BCE.[419] Championed during the 15th century by Hatshepsut, who built a temple to her at Luxor,[420] Mut took her place as the wife of Amun (-Re), a god who rose to primacy at Thebes and who became the chief deity of the Nubian kingdom of Napata. Alongside Amun-Re, Mut achieved great popularity in the New Kingdom, with cults and temples around the Delta. The chief among these was at Thebes, site of the famous Karnak temple complex. Mut is prominent in Ramesside-period inscriptions there and at temples in other places.

The Third Intermediate Period is relatively poor in inscriptions compared to earlier periods (see § 2.2), but it is clear that Mut was a very prominent deity for

---

[417] Manfred Görg, "Der Spiegeldienst der Frauen (Ex 38,8)," *BN* 23 (1984): 9–13. I regret that I was unaware of that piece when my *Vetus Testamentum* article on this topic went to press.

[418] Herman te Velde observed that "little particular attention has been paid to Mut" ("Toward a Minimal Definition," 3), and he noted that Egyptologists as recently as the 1970s could call Mut "a colourless local goddess" and "a rather pallid figure who only achieved eminence as the wife of the powerful Amun" (see citations in "Mut and Other Goddesses," 457). The former scholarly neglect also extended more generally to the later periods of Egyptian history (John D. Ray, "The Late Period: An Overview," in *OEAE*, 2:267).

[419] A fresh discussion of some of the earliest attestations of Mut's name is undertaken by Audrey O. Bolsharov, "Mut or Not? On the Meaning of a Vulture Sign on the Hermitage Statue of Amenemhat III," in *Servant of Mut: Studies in Honor of Richard A. Fazzini* (ed. Sue H. D'Auria; Leiden: Brill, 2008), 23–31.

[420] Betsy M. Bryan, "The Temple of Mut: New Evidence on Hatshepsut's Building Activity" in *Hatshepsut: From Queen to Pharaoh* (New York: Metropolitan Museum of Art, 2005), 181–83.

the Nubians and Saites. The excavators of the Precinct of Mut in Thebes noted: "it seems clear that considerable – one might even say special – attention was given to the Mut Temple during Dynasty XXV and very early Dynasty XXVI."[421] Taharqa added a major gate to the Mut precinct during Dynasty XXV, and Mentuemet, the fourth prophet of Amun at Karnak during the Twenty-sixth Dynasty, wrote:

> I have renewed the temple of Mut-the-Great, Isheru's mistress,[422]
> so that it is more beautiful than before
> I adorned her bark with electrum
> all its images with genuine stone.[423]

Egyptologists frequently remark on Mut's meteoric rise during the New Kingdom and Third Intermediate Period. A hymn to Mut from the reign of Ramesses VI (1142–1134) gives her the epithet "mistress of every city," and its translator concludes that the title may "have been more than purely honorary," since most major Egyptian towns seemingly did have at least guest cults of Amun and Mut at that time.[424]

Mut's mythology was multifaceted, as is typical of Egyptian deities. Her name was written with the vulture hieroglyphic sign, and so she could be portrayed as a vulture in iconography. However, "Mut" means mother (the common noun is identically transliterated as *mwt*),[425] and indeed she was the queen of the gods, and part of the "Theban Triad," with husband Amun and son Khonsu.[426] For this reason she was interpreted as Hera by the Greeks. She was frequently portrayed

---

[421] Richard A. Fazzini and William Peck, "The Precinct of Mut during Dynasty XXV and Early Dynasty XXVI: A Growing Picture," *Society for the Study of Egyptian Antiquities Journal* 11 (1981): 125.

[422] Isheru is the name of a sacred lake that surrounded Mut's temple.

[423] Lichtheim, *Ancient Egyptian Literature*, 3:32. For another example of Dynasty XXV work on the Mut Precinct at Karnak, see Richard A. Fazzini, "A Sculpture of King Taharqa (?) in the Precinct of the Goddess Mut at South Karnak" in *Mélanges Gamal Eddin Mokhtar* (ed. Paule Posener-Kriéger; Cairo: Le Caire Institut Français d'Archéologie Orientale, 1985), 293–306.

[424] H. M. Stewart, "A Crossword Hymn to Mut," *JEA* 57 (1971): 90. The reference is to the Crossword Hymn, horizontal line 22. Cf. László Török, *The Kingdom of Kush: Handbook of the Napatan-Meroitic Civilization* (Leiden: Brill, 1997), 311. For an example from Memphis, see Jocelyne Berlandini, "La Mout Ḥnt-pr-Ptḥ sur un fragment memphite de Chabaka," *Bulletin de la Société d'Égyptologie de Genève* 9–10 (1984–85): 31–40.

[425] Herman te Velde writes: "[I]t is tempting to assume that the name of the goddess actually meant 'mother'" ("The Goddess Mut and the Vulture," in *Servant of Mut: Studies in Honor of Richard A. Fazzini* [ed. Sue H. D'Auria; Boston: Brill, 2008], 243). See also *idem*, "Toward a Minimal Definition of the Goddess Mut," *JEOL* 26 (1979–80): 4.

[426] Török, *Kingdom of Kush*, 308. A first-century BCE relief of Ptolemy XII worshiping Mut has recently been published. In the scene, Mut is enthroned, while Hathor and other goddesses stand behind her in her entourage (W. Raymond Johnson and J. Brett McClain, "A Fragmentary Scene of Ptolemy XII Worshiping the Goddess Mut and Her Divine Entourage," in *Servant of Mut*, 134–40). This process in which other goddesses were subordinated to Mut was clearly under way in the eighth century BCE.

holding a child in her lap. However, she was a figure not only of gentleness but also of maternal ferocity. In this role, she was portrayed "standing behind Amon and raising a protective hand by his shoulder,"[427] and she was also a guarantor of the pharaoh's power – indeed, she was its divine embodiment. One hymn describes her quite literally supporting the pharaoh, sitting "under the king as the throne."[428] A Ramesside hymn called her "King of Upper and Lower Egypt," a title that no other deity in the pantheon claimed:[429]

> She has no equal, the unique one who has no peer.
> There has come into existence none like her within the Ennead.[430]
> There are no goddesses among tens of thousands of her form.
> Her manifestation on earth is kingship.[431]

As the symbol of kingship, she became a national god, not unlike Aššur in Assyria. In this light, it seems entirely natural that she should have been in the position of overseeing treaties between Egypt and its vassals, such as the loyalty-oath that the Saite ruler Tefnakht swore to Piye when the latter conquered Lower Egypt in 725.[432] The relief in the lunette of the stele (Fig. 5.4) portrays Amun seated behind Piye; but standing behind Amun is Mut, as if she were also a guarantor of the whole arrangement:[433]

Mut was in fact thought to enforce covenant curses in the most horrific ways. I have already noted above the ritual texts in which rebels were burned on her brazier, and Manetho's report that Shabako (721–707) burned Bocchoris alive because of his breach of covenant (§ 5.2.1.2). Thus, Mut "not only protected the person of the king but also the state itself with a power which was as fierce as it was final"[434] ... "her arms are a protection around the king and her fiery breath is against his enemies."[435] Such a ritual of burning humans alive both evokes the supposedly protective human sacrifices practiced elsewhere in the ancient world (§ 4.4.3.2), and also would have *enacted* protection for the state (at least in the minds of those who ordered it), by destroying enemies who might have under-

---

[427] Te Velde, "Toward a Minimal Definition," 8.

[428] Lana Troy, "Mut Enthroned," *Essays on Ancient Egypt in Honour of Herman te Velde*, ed. Jacobus van Dijk (Egyptological Memoirs 1; Groningen: Styx, 1997), 302. This is horizontal line 16 from the "Crossword Hymn."

[429] Barbara S. Lesko, *The Great Goddesses of Egypt* (Norman: University of Oklahoma, 1999), 143.

[430] A grouping of nine great Egyptian deities.

[431] Herman te Velde, "Mut and Other Ancient Egyptian Goddesses," in *Ancient Egypt, the Aegean, and the Near East: Studies in Honor of Martha Rhoads Bell* (San Antonio, Tex.: Van Siclen Books, 1997), 2:459–60.

[432] Piye Victory Stela, lines 126–44; Lichtheim, *Ancient Egyptian Literature* 3:79–80.

[433] Lichtheim, *Ancient Egyptian Literature*, 3:66.

[434] Richard H. Wilkinson, *The Complete Gods and Goddesses of Ancient Egypt* (London: Thames & Hudson, 2003), 154.

[435] Te Velde, "Mut and Other Ancient Egyptian Goddesses," 459.

Fig. 5.5 The lunette from the Victory Stele of Piye. Mut is the farthest-left standing figure.

mined Egypt's power.[436] However, Mut's protective aspect also had a comforting side; she was portrayed iconographically as a vulture with protecting wings, as in a statue of Mutemwia, the mother of Amunhotep III, that resides in the British Museum (fig. 5.6).[437] The two sides of Mut, the violent and the protective, are held together in the title "The Eye of Re," by which she is identified with the primordial destructive vengeance of the high god Re, embodied as his daughter, which continued to protect the pharaoh through the uraei that he wore.[438]

Given the "democratization of death" (§ 2.4.2) in later periods in Egypt, it is no surprise that the protective aspect that Mut played vis-à-vis the state and monarchy spread to other elites. An excellent example of the more popular adoration of Mut can be seen in the tomb inscription of a Heliopolitan scribe from the period of Ramesses II (1303–1213), who changed his name from Kiki to Samut ("son of Mut"). The hymn expresses devotion and the expectation of protection:

> As for him whom Mut makes a protégé, no god knows how to assail him,
> the favorite of the king of his time, being one who passes away into honor.
> As for him whom Mut makes a protégé, no evil will attack him,
> and he will be sheltered every day until he joins the necropolis.
> As for him whom Mut makes a protégé, how happy is his life!
> The favors of the king which endue his body belong to the one who sets her in his heart.

---

[436] Such punitive human sacrifice may go back at least as far as the first dynasty. See Bernadette Menu, "Mise à mort cérémonielle et prélèvements royaux sous la Ire dynastie" in *Le Sacrifice humain en Égypte ancienne et ailleurs*. Edited by Jean-Pierre Albert and Béatrix Midant-Reynes (Paris: Soleb, 2005), 122–135.

[437] For a photograph, see Stephen Quirke and Jeffrey Spencer, eds., *The British Museum Book of Ancient Egypt* (London: Trustees of the British Museum by British Museum Press, 1992), 78. For discussion, see Lesko, *Great Goddesses of Egypt*, 141. Mut's protective aspect could also be assumed by human Egyptian queens; see Betsy M. Bryan, "A Newly Discovered Statue of a Queen from the Reign of Amenhotep III," in *Servant of Mut*, 37–39; also Gerry D. Scott III, *Temple, Tomb, and Dwelling: Egyptian Antiquities from the Harer Family Trust Collection* (San Bernardino, Ca.: University Art Gallery, California State University, San Bernardino, 1992), 132–34.

[438] Herman te Vedle, "Mut, the Eye of Re," *Studien zur Altägyptischen Kultur Beihefte* 3 (1988): 395–403.

Fig. 5.6 The statue of Mutemwia in the British Museum.

> As for him whom Mut makes a protégé,
> when he issues from the womb, favor and fate are his,
> and beauty upon the brick. He is destined for honor.
> As for him whom Mut makes a protégé how happy is he whom she loves.
> No god will cast him down, being one who does not know death.[439]

The text is functionally a donation inscription: Samut "found the goddess Mut so powerful a protector that he left all of his property in her temple."[440] It demonstrates the expectation of the goddess' sheltering might.

As the presence of these elements in tombs indicates, Mut's protection extended over this life and the next. Indeed, the inscription of Samut makes no distinction between the two; having experienced the goddess's favor in his life, he expects it in his afterlife as well. Spell 164 from the Book of the Dead reflects a specific expectation of protection in the afterlife, invoking "Mut the divine-souled ..."

---

[439] Te Velde, "Toward a Minimal Definition," 9; see also J. A. Wilson, "The Theban Tomb (No. 409) of Si-Mut, Called Kiki," *JNES* 29 (1970): 187–92; Pascal Vernus, "Les inscriptions de S3-Mut Surnommé KYKY," *Révue d'Égyptologie* 30 (1978): 115–46.

[440] Wilson, "Theban Tomb (No. 409) of Si-Mut," 192.

"... who keeps sound their corpses, ⟨who⟩ preserves them from the execution place of the rebels who are in the (judgment) hall of the evil one, without lassoing them.

The goddess says with her own mouth: "I will do as ye say, (ye goddesses,) ye progeny, for the Son," when they prepare the burial for him.

To be said over ⟨an image of⟩ Mut having three faces – one like the face of *Pḥ3t*, wearing twin plumes, another like a human face wearing the white crown and the red crown, another like a vulture's face wearing twin plumes – and a phallus and wings, with a lion's claw(s).

...

Then he shall be divine among the gods in the god's domain and shall not be kept away forever and ever. His flesh and his bones shall stay sound like (those of) one who is alive; indeed, he shall not die... ."[441]

It would appear that this spell, with its reference to "the execution place of the rebels," conflates the slaughter of traitors on the brazier of Mut with the judgment of the dead in the afterlife. Mut is called upon to keep the deceased from the execution place, so that he or she may reach the happy afterlife. This is a natural development, since the "Ritual to Repulse the Aggressor" already expresses the desire to destroy not only the body but the *ba* of the rebels (on the *ba*, see § 2.4.2). Thus, Mut seems to have increased her power rather as YHWH did: once a guarantor of earthly power, her authority soon reached the underworld, even though she was not originally a chthonic deity.[442] As Barbara Lesko observed, "Mut then was able to rescue and protect the deceased Egyptians who called on her. Thus, at least by the post-Empire or Third Intermediate Period, her power could extend beyond the world of the living and save souls fettered in the Netherworld."[443] There are other indications of Mut's association with the underworld as well. A passage from the Crossword Hymn seems to refer to her as having been present at the creation of the netherworld, and having millions of spirits under her protection.[444] Vulture elements in Egyptian tombs of the Ramesside and later periods might also reflect a belief in Mut's protective power

---

[441] Thomas George Allen, ed. *The Egyptian Book of the Dead: Documents in the Oriental Institute Museum at the University of Chicago* (Chicago: University of Chicago Press, 1960), 160–61. Also relevant is Spell 137A, which portrays the Eye of Re as protector of the dead.

[442] Mut is not the only deity with similar duties; Nut was also known as a protectress and "mother" to the dead. In one very late text, Nut says to the deceased, "My beloved son, Osiris N., come and rest in me! I am your mother who protects you daily, I protect your body from all evil, I guard your body from all evil. I make your flesh perfectly hale" (cited in Assmann, *Death and Salvation*, 170). It is not clear whether some assimilation between Mut and Nut might have taken place, as was common among Egyptian deities.

[443] Lesko, *Great Goddesses of Egypt*, 147.

[444] Vertical line 65: "She is ... as the goddess of Thebes, the mistress who was in the heart, when the netherworld came into existence... . She makes Thebes content. Millions of spirits, which Rēʿ has made for her through his sight, they are known. That is, they are promoted like what she has made." Stewart, "Crossword Hymn to Mut," 103–4. On the Crossword Hymn, see also Troy, "Mut Enthroned," *passim*.

over the dead.[445] All of this helps explain the common presence of Mut amulets in burials, both in Egypt and Palestine.

Details such as the flower garlands and heavy drinking related in Isa 28 were also part of the worship of Mut. Hatshepsut inscribed on a column of the Luxor temple: "[She made it as a monument for her mother Mut] mistress of Isheru, making for her a columned porch of drunkenness anew, so that she might do [as] one who is given life [forever]." Betsy Bryan explains that the reference is to "the location of the Festival of Drunkenness," which took place in the Mut temple,[446] and which continued to be attested down through the Roman period.[447] This festival was connected with the aforementioned Eye of Re myth, in which Re's avenging eye (embodied as a daughter-goddess) is finally subdued when Re gives her red-tinted beer in place of blood, which makes her drunk and pacified. This was re-enacted in Mut's cult; as one text says, "(Tinted beer) is abundantly poured for her at these occasions of the Feast of the Valley, it being more precious/sublime (?) than blood, being the work of the beer goddess in order to appease her heart in her anger."[448] The reference to the "Feast of the Valley" furnishes a connection between Mut's worship and the invocation of the dead; as § 2.4.2 showed, the Feast of the Valley was a mortuary banquet, meant to join the living and the dead in shared festivities.

Importantly, group drunkenness played a role in the communal supplication of the goddess. Bryan states that this was "drinking to become drunk." It was not a social occasion, but rather a case of "pouring it down." This was intended to "create an epiphany, an encounter with the deity," and in the encounter it offered "a communal opportunity to make a request of the deity."[449] The need of the Judeans to request protection from Assyria would have been just such an occasion.

The aspect of Mut's cult involving drunkenness was not forgotten by those in the Third Intermediate who promoted her worship anew. A Twenty-fifth-Dynasty stele from Tell Edfu reflects inebriation as a form of religious practice; the main part of the inscription reads (with emphasis added):

---

[445] The New Kingdom tombs of Pharaohs Merneptah, Siptah, and Ramses IV all had patterns of vultures with spread wings across their ceilings, surely expressing the hope of protection in the afterlife. Furthermore, various Ramesside queens were associated with Mut (Richard A. Fazzini, "Standard Bearing Statue of Queen," in *Mistress of the House, Mistress of Heaven: Women in Ancient Egypt* [ed. A. K. Capel and G. E. Markoe; Cincinnati: Cincinnati Art Museum, 1996], 114–15). Still, on a traditional reading, the Ramesside vulture ceilings are likely better understood as representations of Nekhbet.

[446] Bryan, "The Temple of Mut," 182.

[447] Along the way, such a festival is also reported in Herodotus, *Histories*, 2.60.

[448] Anthony Spalinger, "A Religious Calendar Year in the Mut Temple at Karnak," *RdE* 44 (1993): 176. This text is Greco-Roman, but likely indicative of earlier practices as well.

[449] Betsy Bryan, "Making for Mut a Porch of Drunkenness: A Field Report on a Decade of Excavation at the Mut Temple," lecture delivered at the Bowers Museum, Santa Ana, California, Dec. 11, 2010.

O Mut, celestial and solar goddess, who is the first-ranked in Isheru,

He inebriates himself for you, the priest of Amun who resides at Karnak, the one who is known to the king, son of the priest, second class, of Amun, king of the gods, the eyes and ears of the king, Patenf.

He rejoices for you. Count him among your servants, those whom [you] love ... his patron.

Protect this man *who inebriates himself* for the golden goddess.[450]

The text of the stele also shows a man and his wife presenting gifts before Mut, among them an offering of flowers; the text in front of the man reads, "The giving of floral-offerings of the forest... ."[451] Even closer to Isaiah's imagery of a flower garland is a later text describing the regular rituals for Mut, which says that "a crown of fresh flowers is tied for her ... every day."[452] Another hymn to the lion goddess goes: "When the organizer praises you with his lotus blooms / ... / The virgins rejoice for you with garlands,/ The women with the wreath-crown."[453] Despite a broader ancient Near Eastern tradition of floral motifs on royal crowns which may lie in the background,[454] this is probably the primary referent of Isaiah's text.

---

[450] M. Fernand Bisson de la Roque, "Complement de la stele d'Amenemhêt, fils de PN, Époux de Kyky" *BIFAO* 25 (1925): 48. The reference to the "golden goddess" reflects some form of assimilation between Mut and Hathor, who usually bears that title. The Third Intermediate Period was well along the process of assimilation of goddesses; by the Greco-Roman period, Spalinger can say, "Mut is Hathor and vice-versa" (Spalinger, "A Religious Calendar Year," 181).

[451] R. Engelbach, "Notes of Inspection, April 1921," *ASAE* 21 (1921): 188–96.

[452] Spalinger, "A Religious Calendar Year," 177. Flowers are repeatedly associated with Mut in various other ways as well. The Crossword Hymn refers to Mut as "The lady of the lotuses ... She who is beautiful of face, the lotus being associated with her beautiful face" (Vertical lines 62, 66; Stewart, "Crossword Hymn to Mut," 103, 104). The associations of the so-called blue lotus (*Nymphaea coerulea*, actually a water-lily) with hopes for the afterlife may be significant here: because they open in the morning and close at night, "the Egyptians saw in them an image of rebirth or regeneration. The flowers were used to symbolize the deceased's entering into the underworld and the rebirth in the hereafter to a new life" (Renate Germer, "Flowers," in *OEAE*, 1:541).

[453] This is from the temple of Medamud, for lion goddess Ra-et Tawy. Mut's leonine aspect, usually expressed by assimilation with Sekhmet, makes this relevant to her as well. Bryan, "Making for Mut a Porch of Drunkenness."

[454] As Wildberger has noted (*Isaiah 28–39*, 8), the connection to the carnivalesque, drunken crowning of Oholah and Oholibah in Ezek 23:42–43 is impossible to miss: "The sound of a raucous multitude was around her, with many of the rabble brought in drunken from the wilderness; and they put bracelets on the arms of the women, and beautiful crowns (עטרת תפארת) upon their heads. Then I said, 'Ah, she is worn out with adulteries, but they carry on their sexual acts with her...'" There may be some dependence on Isaiah here, but apparently both texts refer to some form of drunken ritual. Oholah and Oholibah represent Samaria and Jerusalem, and Rolf Jacobson has argued that the crowns in both passages are symbols of kingship, and has adduced iconographic data of floral imagery on ancient Near Eastern crowns (Rolf A. Jacobson, "A Rose by Any Other Name: Iconography and the Interpretation of Isaiah 28:1–6," *Images and Prophecy in the Ancient Eastern Mediterranean* [eds. Martti Nissinen and Charles E. Carter; Göttingen: Vandenhoeck & Ruprecht, 2009], 125–46). I think that he is correct about that point, but when he denies an sociohistorical cultic connection, he misses the prophets'

Flowers in general were common in Egyptian funerary rituals: they were used as funerary offerings to the gods; garlands were used to decorate mummies and burial equipment and were also worn by guests at funerary banquets.[455] Faience collars decorated with floral patterns were placed around mummies' necks. In late versions of the Book of the Dead, "a round floral wreath [is] the symbol of successfully withstanding the Tribunal of the Dead before Osiris."[456] Based on iconographic evidence, it is clear that some similar Egyptian motifs made their way into Judean culture.[457] The term ציץ(/ציצה) found in Isa 28:1, 4 also appears in the description of Solomon's temple in 1 Kgs 6:18, 29, 32, 34, where it seems to refer to lotus blossoms (cf. 1 Kgs 7:19).[458] John Strange has argued that the lotuses used in the decoration of the First Temple were a reflection of Egyptian beliefs about afterlife and resurrection, as they were in Egyptian temples.[459] If these ideas did have currency in Judah, then the choice of נבל to modify ציץ in both instances in Isa 28 seems particularly forceful from a rhetorical standpoint: the lotus symbolizes rebirth, but the prophet announces that it will wither and perish.[460]

Finally, there was a connection between drunkenness and flowers, since the Egyptians may have known how to enhance wine with the narcotic alkaloids in the lotus flower.[461] This narcotic fortification of beer that was already stronger than average regularly led to vomiting in feasts dedicated to Mut, as is portrayed in paintings from the New Kingdom),[462] much like the vomiting that Isaiah condemned in vv. 8, 10, 13.

---

rhetorical employment of this crown imagery *in conjunction with* imagery of actual drunken, cultic feasts to portray the rulers of both cities as faithless (and, in Isaiah's case, drunks as well). That is to say, elite Judeans probably actually *did* know drunken feasts such as this.

[455] Bernhard Asen, in a study of the use of flowers in death-cult rituals, mentions the relevance of Egyptian data but does not note any specific connections ("Garlands of Ephraim," 71–87).

[456] Germer, "Flowers," 543.

[457] Othmar Keel and Christoph Uehlinger, *Gods, Goddesses, and Images of God in Ancient Israel* (trans. Thomas H. Trapp; Minneapolis: Fortress, 1998), 249; see also index for other references.

[458] Cf. *HALOT*, 1023 (ציץ), 1454–55 (שושן); John Strange, "The Idea of Afterlife in Ancient Israel: Some Remarks on the Iconography in Solomon's Temple," *PEQ* 117 (1985): 35–40.

[459] On the Egyptian use of the flower/lotus motif in this way, see De Buck, "La Fleur au Front du Grand-Prêtre," *passim*. On their use in Egyptian temples, see Watson, "Death and Cosmology in Ancient Egypt," 156–58. Strange argues that the lotuses were a deliberate syncretistic flourish by Solomon to "merge the Israelite Religion with the religion of his indigenous subjects" ("Idea of Afterlife," 38). Whether or not the religious and historical presuppositions of that statement can be sustained, his essential point that Solomon may have employed motifs similar to those of Egyptians, and with similar mythological referents, seems sound.

[460] Isaiah 40:6–8 reuses the image but appears to have forgotten the mythological significance of the ציץ, since the lotus is not a flower of the field.

[461] W. Benson Harer, Jr., "Lotus," in *Oxford Encyclopedia of Ancient Egypt* (Oxford: Oxford University Press, 2001), 2:305.

[462] Bryan, "Making for Mut a Porch of Drunkenness."

A final excerpt from an Egyptian harper's song (i.e. a funerary song) ties together flowers, perfumes and wine in a way very much like that of Isa 28:1:

> I have wept! I have mourned!
> O all people, remember getting drunk on wine,
> with wreaths and perfume on your heads![463]

The dual association of these cultic elements with Mut and funerals invites the sort of idea-play in which Isa 28 engages, portraying the goddess' cult as death-seeking behavior. Thus, not only does Mut's mythology illuminate Isa 28, so does her cult: Isaiah takes the cultic practices involved with Mut's worship and portrays them as a funeral for those who are involved, which seems to have required only a small creative leap.

The foregoing sketch should suffice to indicate that Mut is a most apt referent for *mwt* in v. 15: She was a goddess of terrifying power who was held in great esteem by the Nubian and Saite dynasties upon whom Judah leaned in the face of an Assyrian threat. She was understood as a protector of Egypt and its king, to the point that she became known as a destroyer of the nation's enemies, who were burned on her brazier. Her protective role was eventually extended to others in this life and the next; she was worshiped in rites that included inebriation and offerings of flowers; and her name is sounded similar to Hebrew מות.

A point that will become clearer in the ensuing analysis may bear emphasizing here as well: I am not arguing that this text is a completely accurate reflection of Mut's cult, any more than the anti-idol polemics throughout the Hebrew Bible are accurate reflections of iconic cults. Instead, I am arguing that Isaiah has refracted Mut's cult through his own theological lenses.

Competing proposals

No other proposal about the mythical referents of the "covenant with Death" answers remotely as many questions. All have their problems, and generally the same ones: Why should the deity be called *Mwt*, even if he or she was associated with the underworld? Did the deity have a notable protective aspect? And can the theory account for imagery such as that of drunkenness, flowers, and infants?

One popular theory is that *Mwt* refers to Osiris, since he is the king of the Egyptian underworld,[464] but few of the other details of the Isaiah passage fit, and it is more often the goddesses who were invoked for protection in the underworld. In short, the Egyptians aspired primarily to *become* Osiris, not simply to be protected by him.

---

[463] Lüddeckens, *Totenklage*, 149–50.

[464] Bernhard Duhm, *Das Buch Jesaja* (4th ed.; Göttingen: Vandenhoeck & Ruprecht, 1922), 199–200; Johann Fischer, *Das Buch Jesaja*, Teil I (Bonn: Peter Hanstein, 1937), 188; Auvray, *Isaïe 1–39*, 250–51; John Skinner perceived that "Death and Sheol" were Osiris and Isis (*The Book of the Prophet Isaiah, Chapters I–XXXIX* [2nd ed.; Cambridge: Cambridge University Press, 1915], 225).

Day argued that *Mwt* referred to Molek,⁴⁶⁵ but there is no hint of the characteristics of the Molek cult, such as child sacrifice, and no good reason why the god's name should have been obscured here.

The least speculative of older theories is that *Mwt* refers to the familiar, Syro-Palestinian Mot.⁴⁶⁶ It is sometimes elaborated with the idea that Sheol refers to an Egyptian deity, and that the pair reflects joint negotiations with the seacoast and Egypt to find allies against Assyria.⁴⁶⁷ (Going farther still, van der Toorn took the terms כזב, "lie," and שקר, "falsehood," as encoded terms for Chemosh and Milcom.)⁴⁶⁸ The problem with theorizing a covenant with the god Mot known from Ugarit, is that there is no indication that Mot made covenants.⁴⁶⁹ In fact, as Day pointed out, "a Mot cult in Judah is otherwise unknown at this time"⁴⁷⁰ – unlike Mut, one can now add.

The most developed version of the Mot theory is that of Blenkinsopp, who argued that Mot would have seemed an apt treaty partner, because he was the enemy of Baal, whose role was filled in Mesopotamia by Hadad, who in turn "was venerated by the Assyrians as a war deity and [who] ... is also named as a guarantor of treaties, and played an important role in divination and mortuary rites."⁴⁷¹ This argument is not only tortuous, it confuses the issue: If the Judeans' covenant is with Mot, then Hadad's covenant-making and underworld aspects are irrelevant.

Finally, other exegetes decline to address the mythological issues. Wildberger perceived unspecified secret protective rites,⁴⁷² and Kaiser, simply that the proph-

---

⁴⁶⁵ Day, *Molech*, 58–64.
⁴⁶⁶ E.g., McLaughlin, Marzēaḥ in the Prophetic Literature, 184; Theodore J. Lewis, "Mot (deity)," *ABD* 4:923; John F. Healey, "Mot," *DDD²*, 601; H.-J. Fabry, "מות," *TDOT* 8:205–9.
⁴⁶⁷ E.g., Vermeylen, Du Prophète Isaïe à l'Apocalyptique, p. 393 n. 1.
⁴⁶⁸ Van der Toorn, "Echoes of Judean Necromancy," 203.
⁴⁶⁹ Healey, "Mot," 601. J. C. de Moor and Klaas Spronk thought that *CAT* 1.82 included a reference to a covenant with Mot in line 5 ("More on Demons in Ugarit (KTU 1.82)," *UF* 16 [1984]: 239–40), but the correct reading appears to be *tǵrm lmt brqk*, "unite your rays against Mot," rather than *tǵrm lmt brtk*, "You are pledging your covenant to Mot"; see *DUL* 239, 326; also André Caquot, *Textes Ougaritiques*, vol. 2 (Paris: Cerf, 1989), 65 n. 174. *CAT* 1.82 appears to be a collection of apotropaic incantations; see G. del Olmo Lete, *Canaanite Religion According to the Liturgical Texts of Ugarit* (trans. W. G. E. Watson; Winona Lake, Ind.: Eisenbrauns, 2004), 373–76, esp. 374 n. 140. The idea of sickness as a battle *against* Mot is attested in the Kirta epic (1.16 vi 13).
⁴⁷⁰ Day, *Molech*, 85. Ziony Zevit has hypothesized a cult of Mot in ancient Israel on the basis of: Isa 28:15, 18; and a handful of seals with the theophoric element *mwt* (Ziony Zevit, *The Religions of Ancient Israel: A Synthesis of Parallactic Approaches* [London: Continuum, 2001], 604–9. Cf. Tigay, *You Shall Have No Other Gods*, 65–73). I argue against this interpretation in "The Egyptian Goddess Mut in Iron-Age Palestine: Further Data From Amulets and Onomastics," forthcoming. There is no sign of a cult of Mot in Israel or Judah, or even in Ugarit. Furthermore, Egyptian gods are named in similar seals. Therefore, I argue that some of the seals and biblical names are Mut-theophoric, while other names, such as מרימות and ירימות, are non-theophoric.
⁴⁷¹ Blenkinsopp, "Judah's Covenant with Death," 477–78.
⁴⁷² Wildberger, *Isaiah 28–39*, 39–40.

ets' opponents are "*behaving as though* they have made a pact with death and the underworld ... as though they were immortal, though of course only for a time."[473]

Exegesis

Isa 28:1–22 may be roughly divided into four sections: vv. 1–4 (indictment of the northern kingdom); vv. 5–6 (announcement of YHWH's rule);[474] vv. 7–13 (indictment of the southern kingdom);[475] and vv. 14–22 (announcement of judgment). Verses 7–13 expand the indictment of vv. 1–4 and most likely function as the substance of the prophet's case against the Jerusalemite leaders named in v. 14. Older interpretations tended to view the oracle, even vv. 7–22, as highly fragmentary, the result of a complex redactional process.[476] As the ensuing discussion will show, the recognition of the reference to Mut does much to restore coherence to the passage. I will argue that most of vv. 7–22 dates from the end of the eighth century, or perhaps the early seventh, and refers to a crisis brought on by the Assyrian threat to Judah at that time.[477]

It may not even be necessary to theorize two separate redactional layers for the northern and southern sections, although such extensions of old oracles are assumed to have been common.[478] Instead, it may be that Isaiah is using the example of the northern kingdom's collapse as a warning to Jerusalem leadership. The verb of 28:2 (הניח) is perfect in aspect. Although translators almost uniformly take it to be a "prophetic perfect," it is more likely to be a simple reflection on past events: "He brought them to the ground." The former destruction of the northern kingdom in 722 is now connected with a coming destruction: the Samarians, having fled to Judah, have now "infected" Jerusalem and as a result both they and the native Jerusalemites will be trampled again.

---

[473] Kaiser, *Isaiah 13–39*, 251.

[474] The common view that vv. 5–6 are late (see, e.g., Stansell, "Blest Be the Tie That Binds," 68–69) depends on a larger conclusion about the use of the phrase "on that day," which may or may not be an indicator of redactional activity. As Sweeney notes, in the present form of the text, the announcement of vv. 5–6 "sets the tone for the entire passage by stating that YHWH's leadership will be the result of the punishments announced throughout the subsequent verses" (*Isaiah 1–39*, 362).

[475] Sweeney perceives a continued message against Ephraim in vv. 7–13, but I share the common view that וגם אלה marks a shift from the North to the South as the object of the oracle, even though the Judahites are not named until v. 14.

[476] For a summary of redactional theories, see David L. Petersen, "Isaiah 28: A Redaction-Critical Study," in *SBL Seminar Papers, 1979* (ed. P. J. Achtemeier; Atlanta: Scholars Press, 1979), 2:102–4.

[477] On the basic authenticity of the passage, see Wildberger, *Isaiah 28–39*, 37; Sweeney, *Isaiah 1–39*, 355–58. I would take vv. 19b and 22d as expansions. Although I do not agree that there is anything inherently late about the perspective implied in the phrase על כל־הארץ (cf. Wildberger, *Isaiah 28–39*, 45), it does seem to dangle awkwardly at the end of v. 22.

[478] De Jong, *Isaiah among the Ancient Near Eastern Prophets*, 448.

Roberts thinks that the passage is a self-extended oracle based on an original *hôy*-oracle in 28:1–4.[479] Indeed, Isaiah may have associated the Mut cult with the northern kingdom.[480]

The imperfect תרמסנה (v. 3) might seem to contradict the theory that vv. 1–4 postdate the fall of the northern kingdom, but it is not the "Ephraimites" themselves who are threatened but rather the floral garlands that the prophets associate with their anti-Yahwistic practices. It does not seem far-fetched that a Judean prophet should have continued to condemn aspects of the northern kingdom's cultic behavior even after its fall. Long after Samaria's destruction, Israel continued to be viewed in Judah (at least by the Deuteronomists) as a source of wrongdoing and heresy. Alternately, it might be assumed that תרמסנה does not express the future tense but is an archaic preterite form; or that this is simply a nonperfective use of the prefix conjugation – which would be all the more plausible in a poetic context.[481]

The imagery of the raging flood (vv. 2, 15, 17–18) again alludes to YHWH's employment of the Assyrians in judgment, which had already befallen the North and was now threatening the South.[482] There is no reason to look beyond a Neo-Assyrian offensive for the historical setting. Isaiah also associates trampling with Assyria (see 10:6). The year 701 naturally suggests itself, although as chapter 1 showed, less is known about Assyria's campaigns in the West after 689 than one would like; presumably Judah lived for quite some time under the threat of annihilation.[483]

At the time when the oracle was delivered, the Jerusalem leadership lacked faith in its ability to survive and sought out a pact with Egypt. Such a treaty would have been guaranteed by the threat of Mut's wrath, and most likely the Jerusalem

---

[479] On self-extended oracles, see Holladay, *Isaiah: Scroll of a Prophetic Heritage*, 59, 84. Roberts writes that vv. 1–4 may have originated as an oracle against the northern kingdom during the Syro-Ephraimitic War – one that "Isaiah reused in the Assyrian period to introduce his oracle against the Judean leaders, who were just as irresponsible as the northerners had been" ("Yahweh's Foundation," 37; cf. Roberts, "Isaiah's Egyptian and Nubian Oracles," 207). J. Cheryl Exum hints at the same conclusion on literary grounds: "a strong similarity between v. 14ff and vv. 1–4 in terms of both form and content serves to show the Jerusalemites that their situation is not so different from that of their northern neighbors" ("'Whom Will He Teach Knowledge?' A Literary Approach to Isaiah 28," in *Art and Meaning: Rhetoric in Biblical Literature* [ed. David J. A. Clines, David M. Gunn, and Alan J. Hauser; JSOTSup 19; Sheffield: JSOT Press, 1982]: 109–10).

[480] From the eleventh through the seventh centuries, vultures on stamp seals are documented mainly in the North, which could reflect a greater familiarity with Mut there (Silvia Schroer, "Vulture," in *Iconography of Deities and Demons*, accessed electronically in pre-publication on Nov. 12, 2007).

[481] Cf. Waltke and O'Connor, *Introduction to Biblical Hebrew Syntax*, 502–4.

[482] *Pace* Stefanie Ulrike Gulde, who perceived an image of a Canaanite weather-god (*Der Tod als Herrscher in Ugarit und Israel* [FAT/II 22; Tübingen: Mohr Siebeck, 2007], 236–38).

[483] Jeffrey A. Blakely and James W. Hardin, "Southwestern Judah in the Late Eighth Century B.C.E.," *BASOR* 326 (2002): 11–64.

court, at least, would have been warned by the Egyptian representatives of the fate that awaits rebels and traitors.[484] It can be inferred that the covenant ceremony involved the cultic invocation of Mut's protection as a symbol of Egypt's military support for Judah. Priests, prophets, and other leaders in Jerusalem, having lost faith in YHWH's ability to protect the city, participated in the rituals, donning flowers and drinking heavily.[485] The same Egyptian influences in Palestine that Görg identified are relevant here as well. He argued for not only a "pro-Egyptian orientation in parts of the population,"[486] but also a "a pro-Egyptian movement in priestly circles of the late pre-exilic population of Jerusalem,"[487] specifically during the 25th and 26th Egyptian dynasties.

As was demonstrated above, a covenant-making feast for Mut could well have been viewed as necromancy, given Mut's association with the "Feast of the Valley." Indeed, divination and, particularly, necromancy were commonly linked with drunkenness in the ancient world, as with the *marzēaḥ* (§ 4.4.1.3).[488]

Isaiah professed to see no glory in these rites. In place of the garlands for Mut, he objects that YHWH will be the crown of his people (vv. 5–6), but only after the Assyrians have trampled many of them and devoured whatever they can grab (vv. 3–4). The threefold image of the crown, the spirit of wisdom, and strength seems to express the completeness of YHWH's provision for his people, empowering key segments of society: rulers, sages, and warriors. The passage asserts that there is no need to turn to Mut when YHWH can give the people all they need. It is often assumed that the formula ביום ההוא with a positive vision of the future must be a late, proto-apocalyptic form, but there is no clear indication that vv. 5–6 should be taken as a late insertion.[489]

Seeing (or imagining) the scene of debauchery surrounding the bacchanalian rites for Mut, Isaiah condemns those who participate. The wrongdoing has a sociopolitical aspect as well,[490] but these memorable cultic excesses become the peg on which the prophet hangs the oracle. He portrays them as suffering from

---

[484] Here again, one can point to the lunette of Piye's Victory Stele, which represents submission to Piye as also submission to Piye's gods.

[485] So also Blenkinsopp, "Judah's Covenant with Death," 479.

[486] "[P]roägyptischen Orientierung in Teilen der Bevölkerung" (Görg, "Der Spiegeldienst der Frauen," 12).

[487] "[E]iner pro-ägyptischen Bewegung in priesterlichen Kreisen der spätvorexilischen Bevölkerung Jerusalems" (Görg, "Der Spiegeldienst der Frauen," 12).

[488] Van der Toorn, "Echoes of Judean Necromancy," 212–13; Pope, "Cult of the Dead at Ugarit," 245.

[489] ביום ההוא was used in Day of the Lord threats in an early period (e.g., Amos 8:9, etc.) and may just as well have been used for positive oracles. Indeed, Amos 5:18–20 testifies indirectly to a prior belief in the Day of the Lord as a day of salvation, as is attested here.

[490] A comparison of v. 12 with Mic 2:1–11 suggests that the indictment in both cases is the same as that of the series of *hôy*-oracles in Isa 5: the consolidation of property and exclusion of the poor by wealthy landowners. Note the grabbing of land in Mic 2:2, the denial of rest (מנוחה) in Mic 2:10, and the imagery of drunkenness in all three passages.

uncontrolled vomiting and defecation, disgusting habits worthy of babies, not grown adults. He characterizes his opponents as infants *because they seek the care of a mother* (Mut as mother goddess). Worshipers of Mut could indeed refer to themselves as her children, as in a building inscription of Taharqa (r. 690–664) at the Mut temple at Napata: "What he made as his monument for his mother Mut of Napata... ."[491]

Worshippers of Mut even chose to portray *themselves* as suckling children: A silver amulet from El-Kurru shows the Kushite queen Nefrukakashta nursing at the breast of Mut (Fig. 5.8); the vulture hovering over the scene cements the identification. As Sekhmet-Mut, she is also portrayed suckling a king in a blue-glazed amulet from Dynasty 22 (Fig. 5.9). (Again, this reflects Mut's adoption of roles previously fulfilled by other goddesses; a comparable image from the 19th dynasty shows Ramesses II suckling from Anuket [Fig. 5.7]). An actual drinking vessel with two spouts reminiscent of breasts was excavated from the tomb of Nefrukakashta's sister, Queen Khensa, which supports the idea that there was cultic drinking associated with the worship of Mut. Writes Ann K. Capel, "The plaque of Nefrukakashta and the vessel of Khensa were undoubtedly placed in their tombs to ease them through the next rite of passage, when they would be reborn in the afterlife, nourished by the divine milk of the mother goddess."[492]

This, then, is the explanation of Isaiah's depiction of his adversaries in v. 9 as "children just weaned from milk" and "those who have hardly outgrown the breast."

Surely, Isaiah concludes, YHWH will not instruct or enlighten such pitiful, infantile people as these. Much as in Isa 6:9–10, YHWH curses the people not to understand. The odd speech of vv. 10 and 13 (צו לצו... קו לקו) is designed to mock and mislead the Jerusalem leadership (v. 11), because they have already rejected YHWH's word (v. 12).[493] The words קו and צו still resist definitive explanation, but the interpretation that they are an impression of baby talk fits best with the context.[494] By comparison with צאה and קיא in v. 8, these words appear to be

---

[491] Török, *Image of the Ordered World*, 75.

[492] Ann K. Capel, "Goddess suckling a queen," in *Mistress of the House, Mistress of Heaven: Women in Ancient Egypt* (eds. A. K. Capel and G. E. Markoe; Cincinnati: Cincinnati Art Museum, 1996), 118. Mut's role in "divine wetnurse" imagery in Bronze-Age Egypt has now been noted by Stephanie Lynn Budin in *Images of Woman and Child from the Bronze Age: Reconsidering Fertility, Maternity, and Gender in the Ancient World* (New York: Cambridge University Press, 2011), 38–89.

[493] So also Exum, "'Whom Will He Teach Knowledge?'," 122.

[494] Driver, "Another Little Drink," 55; Baruch Halpern, "'The Excremental Vision': The Doomed Priests of Doom in Isaiah 28," *HAR* 10 (1986): 115; Exum, "'Whom Will He Teach Knowledge?',' 121. The other primary theories regarding vv. 10 and 13 are unconvincing. It has been argued that these are a reflection of Akkadian, for example, the commands of an Assyrian taskmaster leading the people into exile (A. van Selms, "Isaiah 28:9–13: An Attempt to Give a New Interpretation," *ZAW* 85 [1973]: 332–39). However, the translations produced on the basis of this assumption do not suit the context well, and it is highly unlikely that the Assyrians gave orders to the inhabitants of Palestine in Akkadian, since the latter would not have understood

Fig. 5.7 Ostracon: Ramesses II suckled by the goddess Anuket (Dynasty 19; limestone with pigment). From *Mistress of the House, Mistress of Heaven: Women in Ancient Egypt* (eds. A. K. Capel and G. E. Markoe; Cincinnati: Cincinnati Art Museum, 1996), 118.

"babyisms" for excrement and vomit, respectively. Indeed, speech acquisition accelerates at about the same time as weaning, after one year of age, with toddlers frequently babbling half-intelligible syllables. As Baruch Halpern notes, "Com-

---

that language, outside of perhaps a few specially trained scribes at the court. Van der Toorn has recently lent support to an older theory that 28:10 and 13 reflect "phrases spoken during séances" (Van der Toorn, "Echoes of Judean Necromancy," 208; quoting Daiches, "Isaiah and Spiritualism," *The Jewish Chronicle Supplement,* July 1921, vi.) Specifically, van der Toorn detects "bird-like twittering and groans" ("Echoes," 209). However, there is no good evidence of cognate sounds or phrases used in this way. A third theory holds that it is Isaiah's opponents who speak these words, mocking the prophet with nonsense talk. However, the phrase is clearly attributed to YHWH in vv. 11 and 13, and implicitly in v. 21.

Fig. 5.8 The goddess Mut suckling a queen of the 25th dynasty (Silver, from El-Kurru). From *Mistress of the House, Mistress of Heaven: Women in Ancient Egypt* (eds. A. K. Capel and G. E. Markoe; Cincinnati: Cincinnati Art Museum, 1996), 118.

Fig. 5.9 Blue-glazed amulet of Sekhmet-Mut suckling a king from Dynasty 22. British Museum. See Carol R. Andrews, *Amulets of Ancient Egypt* (Austin, Tex.: University of Texas, 1994), 23.

parison with English euphemisms (such as 'wee-wee') suggests that herein lies some of the reason for the repetition in the refrain."[495]

On another level, the repeated phrase in vv. 10 and 13 appears to be an allusion to the speech of the Nubians. Much as the Greeks' term for foreigners (βάρβαροι) mocked the "strange" sounds of their speech, so Isaiah refers to the Nubians as the "קו־קו people" in 18:2, 7.[496] YHWH is speaking through the Nubians. Taken as a whole, this complex of imagery conveys that the speech of the Nubians in the Mut cult, which sounds like nonsense and baby-talk to Judeans, is YHWH's way of confusing the Jerusalem leadership and keeping them in the dark. Similar themes of YHWH confusing the people are found in 6:9–10 and 8:22, in which YHWH seems to punish the practitioners of necromancy by causing them to see only darkness. Isaiah repeatedly asserts that YHWH can frustrate forms of divination that are ostensibly outside his purview.

Isaiah condemns the Egyptian pact from another angle as a "covenant with Death." Verse 14's reference to rulers (מֹשְׁלֵי) is nonspecific and intended as a catchall for Jerusalem elites named in v. 7 and those left unnamed.[497] As with instances of paronomasia in earlier passages, the *double entendre* of the ברית את־ מות unfolds in stages. I have already argued that "Mut" and "death" sounded similar. Thus, it is *after* the first colon of v. 15 that it begins to become clear that this is no ordinary comment by the proponents of Mut but rather a self-condemnation placed on their lips. In the first place, the use of ברית to describe apostasy from YHWH is highly unusual – there is no case in which the Israelites are said to make a covenant with any other god.[498] The statement "we have made a covenant with Mut" is thus unique in biblical literature and perhaps already contains an implicit charge of apostasy; some biblical covenants seem to be modeled on suzerainty treaties, and so to make a covenant with Mut was almost certainly, in Isaiah's eyes, to abrogate the covenant with YHWH.[499] The prophet's voice emerges even more strongly in the parallel stich: "with Sheol we have made a pact." At this point the hearer would have grasped fully the paronomasia of *Mwt*: the agreement is not merely heretical, but fatal.

---

[495] Halpern, "Excremental Vision," 115.
[496] The sense of קו־קו in 18:2, 7 is disputed (for a summary of theories, see Wildberger, *Isaiah 13–27*, 208), but its association with the Nubians (Cushites) is not.
[497] So also Wildberger, *Isaiah 28–39*, 37: "To this group belong, first of all, without a doubt, the politicians, but the priests, prophets, wise, and other good 'patriots' in Jerusalem would fit as well."
[498] One might raise in objection the divine name בעל־ברית ("Baal-Berith"/"master of the covenant"; Judg 8:33; 9:4), whom the Israelites are said to worship – but a covenant with this god remains an inference and is never elaborated in the biblical text.
[499] So also Blenkinsopp, *Isaiah 1–39*, 393. Blenkinsopp connects this to the Sinai covenant on the basis of Isaiah's use of חזה by comparison with the account of the seventy elders who "saw God" (ויחזו את־האלהים) on Sinai. Given Isaiah's emphasis on Royal Zion theology, I am more inclined to think he would have referred to the covenant with David; see J. J. M. Roberts, *The Bible and the Ancient Near East* (Winona Lake, Ind.: Eisenbrauns, 2002), 313–57.

When the judgment clause finally arrives, it is rather odd: What does it mean that YHWH will place a stone in Zion? Two features potentially connect v. 16 with Egypt: First, the phrase פנת יקרת מוסד, "a cornerstone precious to the foundation." Perhaps this is YHWH's answer to the "cornerstones of their [Egyptian] tribes," which in 19:13 refers to the sages (and perhaps necromancers) of pharaoh. The rhetorical thrust is that YHWH has a cornerstone of his own, and the one who wishes to stand firm on it will practice faith, justice, and righteousness rather than drunken foreign rites.

The second feature of v. 16 that may evoke Egypt is the term בֹּחַן. The word is a *hapax legomenon* in classical Hebrew, and the best available etymology relates it to the Egyptian *bḥn*, referring to a black or green metamorphic rock.[500] Although this type of stone is apparently not known to have been used for building in Palestine in Isaiah's time, as the context would suggest, there are numerous stelae made of black stone from all over the ancient Near East. Such objects were routinely placed or installed by monarchs as symbols of power and markers of authority or possession, and have been excavated from Iron Age Palestine.[501]

The word בֹּחַן is also likely to have evoked for its hearers the more common Hebrew root בחן ("testing"). In context, the implied test is whether the hearers will trust in YHWH and not fear, or will not trust in YHWH and thus be destroyed (vv. 17–19, cf. also v. 13).[502] There is a clear intertextual relationship between Isa 28:13, 16 and 8:14–15, since both entail the motif of stumbling over a stone placed by YHWH.[503] In 8:14, the stone is YHWH himself, and in 28:16 it seems to at least represent the deity or his word.

Putting together the two halves of this *double entendre*, one wonders whether the building images of vv. 16–17 are merely metaphors and the אבן בחן some ceremonial object such as a stele or palladium, to which Isaiah could point, and

---

[500] Lambdin, "Egyptian Loan Words in the Old Testament," 148. Writes Roberts ("Yahweh's Foundation," 30): "[I]t is not surprising that scholars have searched the languages which were either cognate with Hebrew or which heavily influenced the Hebrew vocabulary for stone names that could explain Hebrew *bōḥan*. The best candidate that has emerged from that search is the Egyptian word *bḥn*, a word that designates schist gneiss, a black or green siliceous schist that was used in Egypt for making statues and a number of scholars have explained the Hebrew *bōḥan* as a loanword from this Egyptian term. H. Wildberger and M. Tsevat reject this identification, because this stone is not found in Palestine, and there is no evidence that the Israelites imported it into Israel for building purposes. This is not a fatal objection, however, because as a loanword *bḥn* could easily have come to designate fine building stones quite distinct from the original Egyptian stone designated by the term."

[501] In addition to the late–10th century stela of Sheshonq I found at Megiddo, there are inscriptions of Sargon II and Esarhaddon. See Wayne Horowitz, Takayoshi Oshima, and Seth Sanders, *Cuneiform in Canaan: Cuneiform Sources from the Land of Israel in Ancient Times* (Jerusalem: Israel Exploration Society and The Hebrew University of Jerusalem, 2006), 19.

[502] Wildberger describes בחן as "almost ... a *terminus technicus*" for divine testing (*Isaiah 1–39*, 42).

[503] Petersen attributed the relationship to a redactional addition in Isa 28:13 ("Isaiah 28: A Redaction-Critical Study," 110).

which might symbolize YHWH's demand for allegiance (as we have seen, YHWH is prone to act like a human sovereign in Isaiah).[504] Could YHWH's "stone of testing" be an answer to an Egyptian monument placed in the Judean court, something akin to the "weapon of Aššur" that Assyrian kings placed in foreign vassal kingdoms to mark their lordship (§ 1.3)? Of course, the comparisons of the line and plummet in v. 17 to justice and righteousness clearly mark those items as metaphorical, so the same might be true of the "stone." If the "foundation stone" has a physical referent at all, it could be almost anything in which Isaiah is calling the people to trust – including the prophet himself. In the end, the meaning of this stone is a matter for conjecture.

The images of hail and rushing water (vv. 17–18) portray YHWH's abolishment of the false shelter of the Mut covenanters through the agency, yet again, of the Neo-Assyrian flood. The covenant will be abolished, and the pact will not stand. I have already noted the paronomasia of חזות; here the meaning "vision" suggests itself even more strongly, given v. 18's phrase חזותכם את־שאול לא תקום – the alternate meaning "your vision of Sheol will not arise" springs easily to mind, recalling the spirit of Samuel rising from the ground (even if there the verb is עלה).[505] The prospect of a Judean covenant with Mut certainly could have looked like "a vision of hell" to a prophet of YHWH.

The inadequacy of Mut's (i.e., Egypt's) shelter is the topic of v. 20 as well. The image of the "bed" evokes the bench tomb,[506] but it is extremely terse and thus requires explanation. Because the prophet is mocking those who seek protection from a goddess known for protecting the dead, he likens them to those who would hide in a tomb and wrap a shroud around themselves. This image may have been a reflection of Egyptian hopes; in ancient Egypt, death could be seen as a re-entry into the protecting womb, with the sarcophagus symbolizing the womb.[507] Texts reflecting this hope were inscribed on coffins. One such text reads:

> My beloved son, Osiris PN,
> come and rest in me!
> I am your mother who protects you daily.

---

[504] Slightly different is the view of Knud Jeppesen, "The Cornerstone (Isa 28:16) in Deutero-Isaianic Re-Reading of the Message of Isaiah," *ST* 38 (1984): 95: "I find it more appropriate to assume that the cornerstone was a real, material stone to which the original prophet was able to point." Jeppesen, however, sees the stone as likely the actual cornerstone of the temple.

[505] The intervening particle את of course makes this a strained reading, but not an impossible one: את could be read as a direct-object marker or emphatic particle rather than a preposition.

[506] Cf. Johnston, *Shades of Sheol*, 177.

[507] Mahmoud I. Hussein, "Anatomy of the Egyptian Tomb,'The Egyptian Tomb as a Womb.'" *Discussions in Egyptology* 49 (2001): 25–33; Jan Assmann, "Death and Initiation in the Funerary Religion of Ancient Egypt" in *Religion and Philosophy in Ancient Egypt* (ed. James P. Allen et al.; Yale Egyptological Studies 3; New Haven, Conn.: Yale University, 1989), 139–40.

I protect your body from all evil,
I guard your body from all evil.[508]

So one can see again here the connection of motherhood, death, the tomb, and protection. Writes Lana Troy: "[Mut] protects the son, her child, from the dangers of the Netherworld, in preparation for rebirth."[509]

Isaiah subverts the hope of protection – "playing dead" may work for certain animals which use it as a tactic for self-defense, but it will not work for the Jerusalemite leaders, he says; the tomb will not have space for them to lie down in comfort and peace, and the protective shroud will be too small to gather around them. The term מסכה is used also in Isa 25:7, where the context makes clear that it specifies a burial shroud similar to the ones used in Judean burials (§ 4.3.)[510] The term מצע, "bed," is from the same root (יצע) that is used in Isa 14:11 of the "bed of maggots" (cf. NRSV), in Ps 139:8 of "making [one's] bed in Sheol," and in Isa 58:5 of "laying down in dust and ashes," so some explicit mourning or funerary connection is possible. Susan Ackerman has argued cogently that Isa 65:4, with its condemnation of those who sit down in graves and spend the night in sheltered places" refers to the practice of incubating dreams with messages from the dead by sleeping in tombs, and so another layer of meaning in this text may be an allusion to the same practice.[511]

The tomb is not just any symbol of futility or false hope; it also should have evoked certain strong aversions in its Judean hearers. The idea of lying down in a tomb (probably unappealing to anyone) would be particularly horrific to one concerned with cultic purity and corpse contamination, as some of Isaiah's audience certainly would have been.

The coming destruction is related by means of a startling twist on what must have been traditional holy-war imagery at the time of the text's composition. The references in 28:21 to YHWH's warring on Israel's behalf at Gibeon (Josh 10:11–12) and Perazim (1 Sam 5:20) refer to precisely the same two natural forces

---

[508] Cited in Assmann, *Death and Salvation*, 170.
[509] Troy, "Mut Enthroned," 310. More typically Nut was the mother goddess in these cases, but given the fluidity of Egyptian theological thought, it is not surprising that this role be applied to another mother goddess such as Mut. In Merneptah's tomb Neith played the role because she was the "protective deity of his corpse."
[510] Pointed differently, מסכה is also a covering or garment in Ezek 28:13. One might perceive a connection between מסכה and מכסה, which is used for the covering of a corpse in Isa 14:11. Neither word is common in classical Hebrew. It is possible that one is dealing with two similarly-spelled words for similar items, but it may also be that מסכה I, "(cast) idol" has exerted some influence in the mind of either the author or a copyist, that is, creating a *double entendre*: "the shroud/false god will not protect you... ."
[511] Susan Ackerman, *Under Every Green Tree: Popular Religion in Sixth-Century Judah* (HSM 46; Atlanta, Ga.: Scholars Press, 1992), 195–202. This would require the revision of her comment that "Other than Isa 65:4aβ, there are, in the Bible, no other explicit condemnations of incubation" (199).

that are named in vv. 2 and 17: hail and flood – but this time YHWH will harness these forces *against* his people, rather than on their behalf. It would have been a "strange" and "foreign" picture, indeed, for the inhabitants of Jerusalem to face the wrath of YHWH (not coincidentally, it is the same picture that is painted by the Neo-Assyrians in 36:10; and by Isaiah in 10:5, etc.). This twist may be seen as an instance of *ius talionis*: those who embraced a foreign god and her strange rites were to be threatened with the strange and foreign wrath of YHWH.

In sum, Isaiah has taken an image of the Jerusalem leadership's drunken festivities supplicating of the Egyptian goddess Mut – and a reasonably accurate one, at that – and has turned it into an picture of faithlessness and failure. That which they hoped would spare life will bring death; and that which they hoped would protect will destroy.

5.2.4 Life's triumph over death

A small assortment of texts that are usually thought to be later than Isaiah of Jerusalem further develop the themes of death and life that were introduced in the passages already surveyed. These passages are more confessional in tone, and they turn more clearly and deliberately toward life. They present YHWH as a God who offers salvation from death, who brings life out of death – a theme that is already intimated (albeit in less overt ways) in Isa 9:1–6 and 29:5–8.

Two of these texts appear in Isa 24–27, a pericope for which the *status quaestionis* has changed markedly over the past thirty years. Detailed *Forschungsgeschichten* are now widely available,[512] so that a brief survey will suffice here. In the wake of Bernhard Duhm and other nineteenth-century critics, generations of students were taught that these chapters were "apocalyptic" in nature and reflected religious ideas that could only have been possible in a late period – as late as the first century CE. However, beginning in the 1970s the pendulum began to swing back toward an earlier date, as the distance between these chapters and Hellenistic apocalyptic became clear.[513] The Isaiah scrolls from the second century BCE at Qumran not only rule out the latest dates that have been advanced; they also suggest the long-term stability of the Isaianic text, in contrast to a book such as Jeremiah.[514] As Dan G. Johnson observed, "the trend in recent years has

---

[512] In addition to the relevant sections of the commentaries of Sweeney and Blenkinsopp, more detail can be found in Dan G. Johnson, *From Chaos to Restoration: An Integrative Reading of Isaiah 24–27* (JSOTSup 61; Sheffield: Sheffield Academic Press, 1988), 11–17; Brian Doyle, *The Apocalypse of Isaiah Metaphorically Speaking: A Study of the Use, Function, and Significance of Metaphors in Isaiah 24–27* (BETL 161; Leuven: Peeters, 2000), 11–45; J. Todd Hibbard, *Intertextuality in Isaiah 24–27: The Reuse and Evocation of Earlier Texts and Traditions* (FAT 16; Tübingen: Mohr Siebeck, 2006), 20–36.

[513] For references, see Hasel, "Resurrection in the Theology of Old Testament Apocalyptic," 269.

[514] Furthermore, the popularizing and explanatory nature of the 1QIsa^a text suggests that

been to place the date of Isa 24–27 much earlier than the previous generation of scholars had done."[515] Since William R. Millar's literary and thematic study, most recent commentators place the text in the sixth century.[516] Furthermore, for reasons that Millar's book makes clear, it has even become possible again to argue for a seventh-[517] or eighth-century date.[518] In short, the text is lacking in linguistic and formal indications of lateness. It is remarkable that Wildberger, in a three-volume commentary, does not argue the case himself but rather cites the slim 1933 study by Wilhelm Rudolph as the definitive word about the date of chs. 24–27.[519] Upon review, it will not bear that weight; Rudolph's conclusions were based largely on the now-discredited claim that the chapters are "apocalyptic" in nature. (Below, I also contest Rudolph's perception that certain passages, especially the ones discussed here, are "eschatological," an idea that still enjoys some acceptance.)

The primary reason for scholars to maintain a postexilic date now is the assumption that the literary relationship of Isa 24–27 to other biblical texts is due to a later author's borrowing of earlier texts.[520] While these chapters are often analyzed independently, "comme un unité littéraire autonome,"[521] scholars also frequently make use of "intertextual" analysis in order to establish both the text's theological/ideological affinities with other biblical texts (or lack thereof) and its place in the relative chronological order of the book's composition.[522] Such research most often draws comparisons with other parts of Isaiah, but other texts such as Amos, Micah, Hosea, and Jeremiah have also been adduced in this regard. The trouble with this species of intertextual analysis is the difficulty of establishing the priority of one text over another. Without recourse to criteria

---

already in the second century BCE, "First Isaiah" was seen as needing interpretation. Kutscher, *Language and Linguistic Background of the Isaiah Scroll*, passim.

[515] Johnson, *From Chaos to Restoration*, 14.
[516] William R. Millar places the text in "the last half of the sixth century B.C." (*Isaiah 24–27 and the Origin of Apocalyptic* [HSM 11; Missoula, Mont.: Scholars Press, 1976], 120). D. Johnson proposes a preexilic section in 587 and a larger exilic section (*From Chaos to Restoration*, 16–17); Sweeney tentatively suggests the late sixth century (*Isaiah 1–39*, 320); Blenkinsopp suggests a date shortly after 539 (*Isaiah 1–39*, 348).
[517] See H. L. Ginsberg, "Isaiah (First Isaiah)" in *EncJud*, 9:58–59; J. H. Eaton, "The Origin of the Book of Isaiah," *VT* 9 (1959): 150–51.
[518] See Hayes and Irvine, *Isaiah the Eighth Century Prophet*, 294–320. John Mauchline also asserted the substantial authenticity of chs. 24–27, while making allowances for later additions. Cf. *Isaiah 1–39: Introduction and Commentary* (London: SCM, 1962), 196–97. For a fuller account of scholars of previous generations who held to both very early and very late dates, see Gerhard F. Hasel, "Resurrection in the Theology of Old Testament Apocalyptic." *ZAW* 92 (1980): 268–69.
[519] Wilhelm Rudolph, *Jesaja 24–27* (BWANT 62; Stuttgart: W. Kohlhammer, 1933).
[520] See, e.g., Blenkinsopp, *Isaiah 1–39*, 346–48; Hibbard, *Intertextuality in Isaiah 24–27*, 32–36.
[521] Vermeylen, *Du Prophète Isaïe à l'Apocalyptique*, 352.
[522] Hibbard, *Intertextuality in Isaiah 24–27*, 2.

such as historical references (which are scanty in chs. 24–27) or linguistic typology, one can just as well assume that the texts in chs. 24–27 have priority, especially in cases where one is dealing with texts in Isa 40–66. For example, J. Todd Hibbard argues that Isa 25:9–10a alludes to such texts as Isa 49:22–23 and 51:5 on the basis of the terms קוה ("to wait on") and ישועה ("salvation") – but "waiting for YHWH's salvation" is a *pervasive* theme, not only in probably early strata of Isaiah (8:17; 33:2) but in the Hebrew Bible as a whole (Ps 25:5; Prov 20:2; etc.)! It is one thing to indicate that there is a common "conversation" among these texts, but Hibbard and others speak of Isa 24–27 as "alluding to" and "building on" these exilic and postexilic texts, when they have established no such historical priority.[523]

In other cases, it is quite likely that both texts drew on a common tradition. For example, Sweeney lays great weight on parallel phrasings in Isa 24:17–18a ("Terror and pit and snare are before you, O dweller of the earth. It shall be that the one who flees at the sound of terror will fall into a pit; whoever climbs from the midst of the pit will be caught in the snare") and Jer 48:43–44a ("Terror, pit, and trap are before you, O dweller of Moab! The one who flees from the terror shall fall into the pit, and everyone who climbs out of the pit shall be caught in the trap").[524] Apparently it is only the broader perspective of the Isaianic passage that makes this parallel relevant for dating, a feature that (as I discuss below) hardly establishes a late date. There is certainly an intertextual relationship between these two texts, as marked by the distinctive alliterative play on the words פחד, פח and פחת,[525] but what is that relationship? To play devil's advocate, Jer 48:43–44 is the text that was demonstrably fluid in a late period[526] (appearing at 31:43–44 in the LXX form of the book), not Isa 24:17–18; is it not empirically easier to conclude that Jeremiah's oracles against the nations were edited at a later date in such a way as to incorporate fragments of other oracles? My point is not to argue that thesis, but only to introduce a measure of "reasonable doubt." Although it would require another study to demonstrate the point, it appears to me that the common dating of Isa 24–27 is the result of intertextual fishing expeditions without adequate methodological controls.

If I have sufficiently problematized the usual late dating of Isa 24–27, I would like to approach two particular passages, 25:6–8 and 26:11–19, with an open mind about their authorship, and would like to suggest that they show distinct

---

[523] For example, Hibbard describes 25:9–10a as "alluding" to and "building on" the texts in Isa 49 and 51 (*Intertextuality in Isaiah 24–27*, 118).
[524] Sweeney, *Isaiah 1–39*, 318–19.
[525] Although the language of snares and traps is widespread in the Bible (e.g., Isa 8:14; Josh 23:13; Pss 69:23; 140:6; 141:9; Lam 3:47), more often מוקש is used for "snare."
[526] See Emanuel Tov, "The Literary History of the Book of Jeremiah in Light of Its Textual History," in *Empirical Models for Biblical Criticism* (ed. Jeffrey H. Tigay; Philadelphia: University of Pennsylvania Press, 1985), 211–37.

relationships with the "covenant with *Mwt*" passage just surveyed (28:1–22). The larger question of the date of chaps. 24–27 would require its own thorough study (indeed, such a study is overdue); I limit myself here to observing that the rhetoric and religious ideas of 25:6–8 and 26:11–19 make more sense in an earlier historical period than in the one in which they are usually placed.

5.2.4.1 Isaiah 25:6–8: "He will swallow up Death forever"

(6) The Lord of hosts will make for all the peoples on this mountain
a feast of rich food, a feast of aged wines –
rich food flavored with marrow[527] and aged, strained wines.
(7) He will swallow up on this mountain
the shroud that is wrapped around all the peoples,
the covering that is spread over all the nations.
(8) He will swallow up Death forever.
The Lord YHWH will wipe a tear from every face,
and he will remove the shame from over the whole land.
For YHWH has spoken.

These verses constitute a distinct literary unit within a larger composition – Sweeney regards them as the "announcement of blessing of the peoples" which is followed by a response in vv. 9–12.[528] (The formula ביום ההוא marks v. 9 as the beginning of the next section, the "announcement of Israel's response.") Verses 6–8 are distinguished not only by form but also by grammar. In vv. 1–5, YHWH is addressed in the second person, whereas in vv. 6–8 he is described in the third person. In general, vv. 1–5 describe past events, whereas vv. 6–8 look to the future. Nevertheless, any number of psalms demonstrate that such shifts are rather normal in classical Hebrew poetry, so although vv. 6–8 are a distinct unit, they may be part of the same composition. There are grammatical and syntactical links: v. 6 begins with a conjunctive *waw*, linking it to what precedes; and v. 3 is characterized by imperfect verbs such as occur in vv. 6–8. Thus, it is not at all clear that vv. 6–8 ought to be treated as a separate and later addition, as Blenkinsopp, for example, does, calling it an "eschatological banquet."[529] As I will argue further along, this passage is not eschatological, although it is idealized.

The welcoming view of the nations in 25:6 is similar to that of 2:3–4; 51:3–4; 56:7 – a list that neither speaks for authorship by the prophet himself nor indicates a later period than that of the rest of the book. Even (presumably authentic) passages such as 3:13[530] reflect the same underlying idea that YHWH possesses

---

[527] The phrase שמנים מחהים is somewhat redundant (perhaps overstated for effect), since the marrow is also fatty. A delicacy in many countries, it is often served spread on toast.
[528] Sweeney, *Isaiah 1–39*, 333.
[529] Blenkinsopp, *Isaiah 1–39*, 357. Cf. also Vermeylen, *Du Prophète Isaïe à l'Apocalytique*, 361.
[530] Blenkinsopp, *Isaiah 1–39*, 199; Wildberger, *Isaiah 1–12*, 141.

and judges the peoples of the earth (a similar early instance of the theme of YHWH's judgment over the earth and nations is found in Ps 82:8).⁵³¹ As is well known, "judging" was not a uniformly negative concept, and the provision of a banquet in 25:6 might be seen as merely the positive face of the Divine Judge (i.e., Ruler).⁵³² This observation throws one back again on the historical question of what event might have occasioned such generosity on YHWH's part.

Another reason sometimes offered for a late date for the passage is its "universalism," but the universalism of the salvation offered in this passage can be seriously doubted.⁵³³ Instead, the breadth of the images here is more likely a response to the breadth of the power of one of the empires that ruled Palestine (whether that of the Assyrians or Babylonians). The Assyrian ruler was said to be "lord of all countries" (šarru EN KUR.KUR) and "king of the universe" (šar kiššati). The word pair "peoples-nations" (גוים-עמים) in v. 7b–c is a common one in biblical parallelism in various periods (e.g., Deut 32:8; Ps 33:10; Zech 8:22),⁵³⁴ but in Isaiah's case, it may also reflect the rhetoric of Neo-Assyrian kings (cf. Isa 14:6) – especially in the inscriptions of Esarhaddon and Aššurbanipal – the king is said to possess "lordship over land(s) and people(s)" (belūt KUR u nišī).⁵³⁵ The assertion of YHWH's rule and beneficence for the peoples might well be a reaction against that universalizing Assyrian rhetoric.⁵³⁶ (The word pair גוים-עמים is also found in Isa 14:6, where it describes those whom the tyrant, probably Sargon II, smote.) Baruch Levine has remarked on the way in which "the threat to the survival of Judah and Jerusalem, emanating from Assyria ... called forth an enhanced God-idea," especially in the prophecies of Isaiah of Jerusalem. He concludes that "universal monotheism is to be seen as a religious response to em-

---

⁵³¹ Vermeylen's idea that this refers to the "peuple juif dispersé sur toute la terre" is quite unlikely (Du Prophète Isaïe à l'Apocalyptique, 362–63). The עמים and גוים of vv. 6–7 are almost certainly inclusive of foreign nations, as in nearly every plural occurrence of these term in the Bible, and "his people" in v. 8 are not portrayed as scattered.

⁵³² Contrary to Kaiser, there is no sign that Israel takes on a "priestly" role here in relation to the nations; the feast here seems to be noncultic and is an unmediated gift of divine grace. The people are in no way a vehicle of YHWH's blessing, as in, e.g., Gen 12:2–3.

⁵³³ For a representative claim about the passage's universalism, see Vermeylen, Du Prophète Isaïe à l'Apocalyptique, 362–63.

⁵³⁴ See E. A. Speiser, "'People' and 'Nation' of Israel," JBL 79 (1960): 157–63.

⁵³⁵ Cf. CAD M/1, 418.

⁵³⁶ So already Gressmann: "Assyria at that time meant the whole world. ... [Isaiah's God has] become the lord of Assyria, indeed the Lord of the world who everywhere wills and creates the good. ... The good God becomes the God of the world, and the national religion the universal religion. Therefore we may say that Israel is indebted for this advance to tacit intercourse with Assyrian religion" (Tower of Babel, 86–87). One might compare the argument of Christoph Uehlinger in Weltreich und "Eine Rede": Eine neue Deutung der sogenannten Turmbauerzählung (Gen 11, 1–9) (OBO 101; Freiburg, Schweiz: Universitätsverlag, 1990). Certainly the word pair "peoples-nations" can also be found in late texts, but I see no pattern of lateness in the list of its occurrences.

pire."⁵³⁷ As noted above (§ 5.2.1.2), Aster gives the name "replacement theology" to this method of subverting the Assyrians' claims – in this case, the claim to be a "universal sovereign, whose power knows no geographic bounds."⁵³⁸ All this subverts the older notion that the passage's breadth of vision is a late feature, and makes the Neo-Assyrian period more plausible.

The passage also, however, employs mythological traditions – most obviously the mytheme of Swallowing Death (see §§ 3.3.3.3; 4.4.3.2, 5.2.2.1). This widespread motif is appropriated for YHWH in much the same way as the Assyrians' claims were. Less often noted, strangely, is its reliance on the image of the blessed dead feasting with a god. This image was present already in the Ugaritic Aqhat epic, where Baal "invites the [revived] one to a feast and offers him drink" (*CAT* 1.17 vi 30–31; § 3.3.3.2.2); and also in the eighth-century BCE Hadad inscription: "May the soul of Panammuwa eat with you [i.e., Hadad], and may the soul of Panammuwa drink [ותשתי] with you"⁵³⁹ (§ 3.4). A similar idea is attested from the Middle Kingdom onward in Egypt; as one stela reads: "May he have a superfluity of offerings and food ... on all the festivals. ... May he sit at the right of Osiris, at the head of the illustrious nobles."⁵⁴⁰ In other words, the author of Isa 25:6–8, having envisioned YHWH's salvation as deliverance from death, connected it to a tradition in which those who are raised to drink and feast with the god who raised them.⁵⁴¹ That tradition seems to have been already well developed in the ancient Near East by the eighth century.⁵⁴²

Millar, too, concluded that "the thematic pattern encountered in Isa 24–27 is ancient, perhaps even having its origin in Canaanite religion."⁵⁴³ In short, he perceived a "thematic pattern of threat, war, victory and feast" that had its roots in a cultic "processional way" that helped to celebrate YHWH's kingship.⁵⁴⁴ However, I think he was mistaken to argue that "the entire created order was being threatened by YHWH, not specific historical enemies."⁵⁴⁵

---

⁵³⁷ Levine, "Assyrian Ideology and Israelite Monotheism," 411.
⁵³⁸ Shawn Zelig Aster, "The Image of Assyria in Isaiah 2:5–22: The Campaign Motif Revisited," *JAOS* 127 (2007): 249–78. I thank Prof. Aster for supplying this article to me in manuscript form.
⁵³⁹ תאכל נבש פנמו עמך ותשתי נבש פנמו עמך (*KAI* 1.214:17, p. 39; *COS* 2.36).
⁵⁴⁰ Stela of the Sealbearer Meri (Louvre C3), from the ninth year Senworset I. Cited in Assmann, *Death and Salvation*, 225.
⁵⁴¹ Despite the notes of judgment in 25:2 and 5, the feast of v. 6 must be sharply distinguished from the "sacrificial feast" tradition expressed in, e.g., Ezek 39:17 and Zeph 1:7. Not only is the bloody imagery of those passages missing from Isa 25, but v. 6 also uses משתה, specifying a banquet without sacrificial overtones, whereas the other passages use זבח.
⁵⁴² This observation would further support the view of Mark Smith and Elizabeth Bloch-Smith: "[T]he possibility should be considered that in Israel the idea of the dead eating evolved into being 'with God,' in a way comparable to KAI 214," that is, the Hadad inscription ("Death and Afterlife in Ugarit and Israel," *JAOS* 108 [1988]: 283).
⁵⁴³ Millar, *Isaiah 24–27*, 81.
⁵⁴⁴ Millar, *Isaiah 24–27*, 101.
⁵⁴⁵ Millar, *Isaiah 24–27*, 106.

As with other sections of Isaiah, the historical context of chs. 24–27 may be important even though the historical references are unclear. Indeed, the innovative twist of these verses is not the hope of revivification, as is often thought, or feasting with a god; if anything, it is the portrayal of political deliverance as national resurrection from the dead, a motif I have already noted in 29:5–8 and 9:1–6.

The historical context of this political deliverance in Isa 25 is more difficult to ascertain than those of the aforementioned passages in Isa 9 and 29. What historical event is it that is related in Isa 25:2–3's portrait of the fall of a citadel and the fear instilled in "a strong people" (עַם־עָז) and "ruthless nations" (גּוֹיִם עָרִיצִים)? "The ruthless" (עָרִיצִים) are also found in 29:5 besieging Jerusalem in a passage we have connected with the events of 701 (§ 5.2.2.3), and the "strong people" could be connected with the "mighty (Assyrian) king" (מֶלֶךְ עַז) of Isa 19:4. But neither of these lexical relationships with eighth-century texts is in any way decisive for the date, since both phrases also have late attestations. The mountain in 25:6 can only be Mt. Zion, not only because of the reference to the הַר צִיּוֹן in 24:23;[546] Zion also seems prohibitively likely because there is no other mountain where YHWH would be said to host a feast (Exod 24:9–11 notwithstanding[547]).

If the feast takes place on Zion, then the "fortified palace of foreigners" (אַרְמוֹן זָרִים) that is destroyed in Isa 25:2 is likely also to be in the proximity of Zion. This term is parallel to קִרְיָה and עִיר; but one may recall from the discussion of 14:21 that עִיר refers not only to whole cities but to fortified precincts within a city (§ 5.2.1.1). The Judean concern for the Assyrians' filling their land with citadels was expressed also in 14:21, so Hayes and Irvine may well be correct that it is the overthrow of an Assyrian citadel that is referred to in 25:2–3. Palaces for Assyrian governors are well known in locations such as Ramat Rahel.

As Hayes and Irvine also point out, when the Maccabees besieged the Seleucid citadel in Jerusalem and expelled the rulers who were quartered there, the event was commemorated in a manner no less joyful than the feast described in 25:6:

The Jews entered it with praise and palm branches, and with harps and cymbals and stringed instruments, and with hymns and songs, because a great enemy had been crushed and removed from Israel. Simon decreed that every year they should celebrate this day with rejoicing. (1 Macc 13:51b–52a)

---

[546] Although 25:6–8 is of course a separate literary unit from 24:23, Clements (*Isaiah 1–39*, 208) and Wildberger (*Isaiah 13–27*, 534) both view the former as the continuation of the latter. Cf. Childs, *Isaiah*, 184.

[547] Exodus 24:9–11 is often cited as an intertext for 25:6, but the two passages share no significant vocabulary whatsoever; the Exodus passage even uses אֱלֹהִים, whereas Isa 25:6 uses יהוה. There is no likely connection between the texts except that made by later interpreters, and perhaps the common ancient tradition of feasting with a god. For the opposing view, see, e.g., Vermeylen, *Du Prophète Isaïe à l'Apocalytique*, 362.

Of course, a mid-second-century date is impossible for the Isa 25 passage – so it cannot be a response to the same event as the Maccabees passage – and there was no other known uprising in Jerusalem prior to that event and after the end of the Neo-Babylonian period that would fit this account.[548] Nor can Cyrus's easy entry into Babylon be made to fit the description of a city reduced to rubble. Despite all that, one cannot follow Hayes and Irvine in attributing this event to an anti-Assyrian uprising in 705–704, for a number of reasons:

1. There is no mention of such an event in either biblical or extrabiblical texts. Hezekiah's offense against Sennacherib upon the death of Sargon seems to have been only withholding tribute (2 Kgs 18:14);
2. the destruction of a citadel would surely have led to a much more serious reprisal from Sennacherib than what Jerusalem actually suffered (§ 1.2–3);
3. other references in the passage likely refer to a later geopolitical situation.

Could it be that "Death" and the "covering" (מסכה) here refer to Egypt, as they did in ch. 28? The use of מסכה connects the present passage to 28:20, where the same word is used to describe a shroud, and where it was also a symbol of Mut and mocked the hope of protection by an underworld deity. (Note also מסכה in 30:1, which is generally taken to indicate an "alliance" with Egypt.) The reference in 25:8 to the removal of the "shame" (הרפה) from the land could be taken the same way, since הרפה is applied to Egypt in Isa 30:5.[549] However, it seems unlikely that the defeat of Egypt by Assyria would have been met with such enthusiasm by Isaiah or anyone in Jerusalem. Despite Isaiah's warnings about reliance on Egypt, its downfall is not a particular occasion for glee, but rather a hard lesson for those Judeans who trusted in it. Moreover, Isaiah and the rest of the biblical history of the period reflect the fact that Egypt was not an imperial power "over the nations" at that time.

The most plausible conclusion is that these terms have different referents, because 25:1–8 was composed during the reign of Josiah.[550] Egypt had been conquered by Assyria, and then the conquerors were conquered as well (Isa 27:7 may reflect this complex sequence of historical events: "Has he struck them down as he struck down those who struck them? Or have they been killed as their killers were killed?"). With the crumbling of the Neo-Assyrian Empire, there was a power vacuum in Palestine, and a later tradent has taken up much of the lan-

---

[548] The reference to the Moabites in v. 10 is not helpful in dating, since Israel and Judah were intermittently in conflict with Moab throughout their history. See J. Maxwell Miller, "Moab" in *ABD* 4:882–93.

[549] Levenson remarks that the reference to this shame "demonstrates the historically particular circumstance to which the oracle speaks." Jon D. Levenson, *Resurrection and the Restoration of Israel* (New Haven: Yale University Press, 2006), 199.

[550] So also Eaton, "The Origin of the Book Of Isaiah," 150–51 and Ginsberg, "Isaiah (First Isaiah)," 58: "[T]he key passage 25:6–12 sounds like nothing so much as an assurance by an early seventh-century writer that Isaiah's prediction 14:24–27 ... of the liberation of the nations as a result of the Lord's destroying Assyria ... will yet come true."

guage of earlier passages to celebrate what seemed to be a major new era of peace and prosperity in Judah's history. In the elation over the restoration of political freedom, an Isaianic tradent envisions the concomitant restoration of YHWH's rule over Palestine, to be celebrated by a great feast on Mount Zion. In this context, the terms "Death" and the "covering/shroud" lose their older, more specific referents and refer to the state of intermittent war and constant insecurity that had characterized the Neo-Assyrian period. The tradent could not have known how short-lived this new golden era would be.

To reiterate for the sake of clarity, the image of swallowing up Death was *not eschatological* in its original composition, however much it may have invited such a reading in later periods. It is very much in line with the images of YHWH overcoming the covenant with Death in Isa 28:15, 18 (and the swallowing of the elites in Isa 5:14); as such, its primary reference is to historical/geopolitical events. It appears to be a sharp theological break only when it is read from the perspective of later Judaism and Christianity.[551] To assign a date to this passage based on the idea that it is apocalyptic and eschatological would be akin to dating the Servant Songs in the first millennium CE because early Christian interpreters read them as a prefiguration of Jesus Christ. As Childs remarks, 25:6–8 is difficult to date precisely because the theme of life's triumph over death is found "throughout the entire Isaianic corpus."[552]

In light of the extensive rhetorical employment of the imagery of death and life by Isaiah of Jerusalem, when the seventh-century author of this text spoke of YHWH swallowing up Death, he would have meant primarily that YHWH would triumph over the power of death, destruction, and chaos that the Neo-Assyrian empire had embodied for Israel and Judah. The text would derive from a period in which the fall of Assyria was not complete but was clearly within view of a perceptive observer.

5.2.4.2 Isaiah 26:11–21: "Your dead shall rise"

The language of these verses is problematic in places, requiring a few emendations as indicated. However, the text is basically stable in the MT and 1QIsaᵃ; the divergences of the Versions usually reflect the same troubles with comprehension that translators still face today, rather than underlying textual variants.

(11) O LORD, high is your hand; they do not see;
    Let them see and be ashamed by the zeal of the people;[553]

---

[551] This is particularly clear when Kaiser conflates 25:8 with 1 Cor 15:54 and Rev 21:4 (*Isaiah 13–39*, 201). A list of those who have claimed that Isa 25:8 is eschatological would be either arbitrarily limited or else impossibly large and unwieldy.
[552] Childs, *Isaiah*, 185.
[553] Despite the near-universal insistence of translations and commentators, there is no reason that the construct chain קִנְאַת־עָם should mean "the zeal *for* the people" (Wildberger, *Isaiah*

let the fiery wrath[554] of your enemies consume them.[555]

(12) O LORD, you will ordain peace[556] for us,
for indeed *you* have accomplished all our works for us.
(13) O LORD our God, other lords besides you have ruled over us
but we will profess your name alone.
(14) The dead do not live; ghosts do not rise
You have dealt with them and destroyed them;
You have eliminated all memory of them.
(15) You have enlarged the nation, O LORD,
you have enlarged the nation, you have glorified yourself.
You have expanded all the boundaries of the underworld.
(16) O LORD, in distress they sought you out;
they poured out an incantation when your discipline was upon them.

(17) As a pregnant woman who draws near to childbirth writhes,
and cries out in her birth-pangs,
so were we because of you, O LORD.
(18) We were pregnant, we writhed,
but we gave birth to wind.
The underworld does not accomplish[557] victories;
they do not cause the rulers of the world to fall.[558]

(19) Your dead will live, your[559] corpses will rise.
Those who dwell in the dust, awake and shout for joy!
Your shadow is a shadow of light,
but you will bring down the Rephaim into the underworld.
(20) Go, my people, enter your rooms and shut your doors behind you
It is only a little while the until the wrath has passed by.

13–27, 551, 562–63), let alone "your zeal for your people" (Blenkinsopp, *Isaiah 1–39*, 366; NRSV, Tanakh, NIV). Wildberger rightly cites Isa 9:6; 37:32; and Zech 1:14 as important texts for comparison; but they show that his translation is unlikely. The first two show that קנאה in the construct form plus a noun means "zeal of X"; whereas the Zechariah text marks the objects of YHWH's zeal with ל prepositions. There is no theological problem with understanding the work of popular zeal as ultimately a manifestation of the divine will; cf. Num 25:11.

[554] Cf. NJB: "with your fiery wrath you will devour your enemies."
[555] See discussion below.
[556] The suggestion to emend to שָׁלוֹם (e.g., Clements, *Isaiah 1–39*, 215) is reasonable, but the context does not demand it.
[557] Read יעשה for נעשה. One could derive almost the same effect by emending to נעשו for a passive sense ("victories are not achieved"), or ישע נעשה ("victory is not achieved").
[558] Read יַפְּלוּ for יִפְּלוּ.
[559] Read נבלתיך; final *kaph* perhaps removed as a pious emendation to remove the possibility of concluding that YHWH had a corpse. Philip C. Schmitz cleverly suggests that נבלתי is a gentilic or an "accusative of state," describing the state in which the dead are first raised: "(As) a corpse they shall rise" ("The Grammar of Resurrection in Isaiah 26:19a–c," *JBL* 122 [2003]: 145–55). Such a form would be unusual, but this suggestion could be adopted without greatly changing the sense of the passage.

(21) For look, the LORD is going out from his place
to visit the iniquity of the ruler of the earth upon him.
The underworld will uncover her blood,[560]
and will conceal her slain no longer.

The pericope identified here for analysis is somewhat artificial, based more on thematic than formal grounds. These verses have been analyzed as belonging to a bewildering number of genres,[561] but I am content to follow Sweeney in viewing ch. 26 as a whole as a single communal song. In his analysis, the verses treated here comprise a "petition to YHWH to act" (vv. 11–19) and an exhortation to wait for YHWH's intervention (vv. 20–21). In my understanding, v. 11 is indeed a petition to YHWH. However, I would call the remainder of vv. 12–19 a confession, in both senses of the word:[562] It is a confession of faith in YHWH and a confession of weakness and error on the part of the speaker, who speaks on behalf of the whole people. (In that sense, it is in the tradition of Isa 6:5: "Woe is me! I am lost, for I am a man of unclean lips, and I live among a people of unclean lips.")

The text begins with the affirmation that it was YHWH who accomplished the victories of his people, a theological idea that was widespread and surely as ancient as Yahwism itself (Exod 14:13–14; Josh 24:31; Judg 2:7, 10; Ps 118:15; etc.). The peace toward which the prophet looks is one enforced by YHWH, not by neighboring empires. But YHWH is like a martial artist, using the wrath of the enemies against them. The oppressive empires will be consumed, the text assures, when *their own wrath* consumes them (אף־אש צריך תאכלם). Most translations (NRSV, NJPS, NIV, etc.) assume that the fire is *YHWH's* wrath burning *against* his adversaries, but without a preposition in the phrase, that is unlikely. The better conclusion seems to be that it is a reflection of the same *ius talionis* theology that Isaiah expressed elsewhere in the book (see discussions of Isa 5; 14; 30, etc.). Arguably this picture has some historical grounding: the Neo-Assyrians' and Neo-Babylonians' destructive tactics surely engendered great unhappiness and unrest, and thereby made their empires harder to manage over the long run.

The expression of trust in YHWH is simultaneously a renunciation of trust in "other lords" (vv. 12–13). One hears in this statement echoes of Isaiah's polemic against Egypt as a source of protection. The confession that "other lords have ruled over us" is often taken as a political statement, but the choice of the verb בעל strongly suggests that the reference is primarily to other gods. The root

---

[560] One might well perceive here a dual image. The second half of the verse suggests the common sense of דמים as "bloodguilt (due to violence)." On the other hand, the earth is personified here in feminine form, and the image of "uncovering her blood(s)" evokes the concern for cultic purity in Lev 20:18, etc.

[561] Hasel, "Resurrection in the Theology of Old Testament Apocalyptic," 270–71.

[562] Kaiser, *Isaiah 13–39*, 210: "[T]he prayer opens in v. 7 with a confession which comes to be the theme of all the rest of the poem."

בעל is rarely if ever used of a human ruler over Israel or Judah. The main use of בעל is in marriage contexts, and the metaphor of God as spouse of Israel had currency in the time of Hosea as well as later in the prophecies of Jeremiah (31:32; cf. 3:14). Thus, the confession is of unfaithfulness to the divine spouse in seeking protection and peace elsewhere, a theme reflected especially in Isa 28.

Why should the dead suddenly appear in this context, unless it is because they were seen as a competing source of divine power and knowledge? Indeed, the opposition between Yahwistic prophecy and necromancy is the key to vv. 13–14. On behalf of the people, the prophet promises to call on YHWH alone (v. 13) – not the dead, nor the Rephaim, who might have been important in guaranteeing the success of kings, as were the *rpum* at Ugarit (§ 3.3.3.2.2). Conquered by YHWH, these latter powers sink down once and for all into eternal forgetfulness (v. 14c). The idea that YHWH glorifies himself by destroying his adversaries is a familiar theological theme (Exod 14:4; Ezek 39:13; cf. Lev 10:3). It should be clear from the foregoing discussion that, at least in the book of Isaiah, the dead were YHWH's competition.

Verse 15 is an unrecognized crux in the interpretation of this section. It is usually taken as a salvific act of God but is in fact a *destructive* one. It is important to note that despite its hymnic ring, the language of v. 15 is not traditional for biblical praise. In fact, the phrases יסף לגוי and רחק (קצוי־)ארץ are used nowhere else in the Bible. I would suggest that these phrases elaborate on YHWH's destruction of the dead spirits just mentioned in v. 14. YHWH has killed his enemies and erased the memory of them ... he has enlarged the boundaries of the *underworld* (by now a familiar sense of ארץ) by adding to the "nation" of the dead. The idea that there are "nations" in the underworld is reflected in Ezek 32, in which Egypt, Assyria, Edom, and other nations are all portrayed as inhabitants of Sheol. The idea that there were nations in the underworld is attested also in Mesopotamian and classical Greek literature.[563] The picture of the immense and ever-expanding size of the underworld is a familiar one in Mesopotamian and Egyptian myth – after all people kept dying, and they had to go somewhere.[564]

This reading resolves a thorny theological question that ought to attract more attention from those who see the salvation of YHWH's people reflected in vv. 15–16: לחש is likely a *non-Yahwistic* incantation of some sort. The term לחש is

---

[563] Exceptionally, the phrase "peoples of the underworld" (UN.MEŠ KI.TA.MEŠ) is also attested in a text from Aššur related to the Tammuz cult. See Erich Ebeling, *Literarische Keilschrifttexte aus Assur* (Berlin: Akademie-Verlag, 1953), 70 r.iii 2; Erich Ebeling, *Tod und Leben nach den Vorstellungen der Baylonier*, I. Teil (Berlin: Walter de Gruyter, 1931), 54, line 29. Furthermore, in the *Odyssey* XI.34, "nations of the dead" (ἐθνέα νεκρῶν) throng to Odysseus when he visits Hades.

[564] Véronique van der Stede, *Mourir au pays de deux fleuves: L'au delà Mésopotamien d'après les sources sumériennes et akkadiennes* (Lettres Orientales 12; Leuven: Peeters, 2007), 91. On the Egyptian underworld as "utterly endless," see § 2.4.3.

never used of prayer to YHWH; it may well be a technical term for incantations that were viewed as heterodox.⁵⁶⁵ Thus, it is difficult to believe that an author would choose this term to reflect acceptable supplication.⁵⁶⁶ It is better not to rest too much on a philologically difficult phrase, but I suggest that the לחש is simply the last gasp of the *enemies*: YHWH disciplined them in an effort to get them to turn from their apostasy, and what did they squeeze out with their last breath? A "foreign" magic spell. They meet their end not with a bang but with a whimper.

The ensuing image of suffering in childbirth begins in v. 17 and turns the focus from those who were destroyed to those who were saved, as marked by the return to first-person pronouns. These, too, suffered under YHWH's oppression and felt the futility of their own efforts; their writhing before their salvation is reminiscent of the "near-death experience" in ch. 29.

Verse 18b requires some interpretive license, and every translation supplies something not in the text. The most common decision is to supply a ב preposition (which could conceivably be omitted in poetry) before ארץ. The most promising example of this emendation, although I do not adopt it, is Levenson's "You make it (i.e., dew) fall on the land of the shades."⁵⁶⁷ Less convincing are translations that treat נפל as "give birth." The resulting translation – "We have won no victories on earth, and no one is born to inhabit the world"⁵⁶⁸ – is profoundly unlikely. The theory that נפל means give birth, based on postbiblical terms for "miscarry/abort," is overly influenced by the imagery of childbearing (v. 17). Nowhere else in classical Hebrew outside this passage does the verb have such a meaning;⁵⁶⁹ and based on the later usage, the translation ought to be, "inhabitants of the world are not *miscarried*," which strains comprehension.

---

⁵⁶⁵ Hebrew לחש may be a reflex of the Akkadian verb *laḫāšu*, which is commonly used in Mesopotamian incantation texts: *CAD* L, 40–41. See Hayim ben Yosef Tawil, *An Akkadian Lexical Companion for Biblical Hebrew: Etymological-Semantic and Idiomatic Equivalents with Supplement on Biblical Aramaic* (Jersey City: Ktav, 2009), 188–89. However, the possibility that לחש might be a loanword is not discussed by Paul Mankowski in *Akkadian Loanwords in Biblical Hebrew* (Winona Lake, IN: Eisenbrauns, 2000). Perhaps this is because in Ugaritic, the root *lḫš* occurs twice, in the nouns *mlḫš* ("exorcist"; *CAT* 1.100:5) and *lḫšt* ("whisper, murmur"; 1.3 iii 23). Then again, there is significant Akkadian influence on Ugaritic as well, and it is not clear whether these terms continued in use in W. Semitic or were re-introduced in Iron Age Judah.

⁵⁶⁶ This would be all the more true if one assumed this text is relatively late, when the idea of "orthodoxy" would have been more developed. It is possible that לחש is instead some amulet or other ornament as in Isa 3:20, particularly if the word צקן were originally related to the root יצק, which would give something like "they cast an amulet." The reference to YHWH's removal from Judah of the נבון לחש ("expert enchanter" [3:3]) is commonly but wrongly taken as a sign that the enchanters were consistent with Yahwism in an early period. It does indicate that such cultic functionaries were part of the court, but the list of officials simply reflects the removal of all advice and leadership, whether consistent with Yahwism or not.

⁵⁶⁷ Levenson, *Resurrection and the Restoration of Israel*, 197.

⁵⁶⁸ NRSV, cf. Tanakh, NJB, etc. NIV implicitly emends to the first person common plural Qal perfect form, נפלנו.

⁵⁶⁹ It is true that the noun נפל, "miscarriage," appears in Ps 58:9; Job 3:16; Eccl 6:3.

The occurrences of נפל in vv. 18–19 do need to be considered together. My translation, however, reflects a theme that is widespread in Isaiah: the fall of earthly powers.[570] The sense of vv. 17–18 is that humans are powerless to achieve victory, and that appeal to the powers of the underworld is similarly useless, because it is only YHWH who overthrows unjust rulers. (Reliance on YHWH is of course a major theme in the original oracles of Isaiah.) Substantive participles from ישב commonly refer to rulers who sit on thrones (Isa 10:13; Amos 1:5, 8; Exod 15:14–15; Lam 4:12).[571] The term תבל, "world," seems to have been specifically chosen to differentiate the world above from the underworld (ארץ). By rereading נעשה as יעשה, we restore the idea that "the underworld does not accomplish victories." This statement of the inefficacy of the dead reprises the theme of v. 14, and the implicit assertion that it is YHWH who causes unjust rulers to fall is akin to the theme of Isa 14.

The claim of v. 19, that YHWH raises the dead, has been taken as a marker of a revolution in theological thought, but this idea needs to be reconsidered.[572] The idea that YHWH raises some up and casts others down is found also in 26:5 and is broadly attested elsewhere in the Bible.[573] Here the promise is extended to those who dwell in the dust – but that is precisely the message of 29:1–8 as well (§ 5.2.2.3); the only difference is that 26:19 explicitly spells out the equation between the "dwellers in the dust" and the dead. Verse 19's reference to "those who dwell in the dust" neatly evokes those who whisper from the dust in 29:4. Even the verb רנן, "shout for joy," might be understood as an intentional contrast to the low chirping of 29:4 (and 26:16): perhaps the message is that those who murmured and whispered like the dead in an empty effort at deliverance now exult aloud in YHWH's salvation. (Silence is one of the characteristics of the world of the dead; cf. Pss 94:17; 115:17.[574])

When compared with Isa 29, or YHWH's abolition of the "covenant with Death" in Isa 28, the salvific revivification of 26:19 does not look so out of place in an early stratum of the book. As we have seen throughout, Isaiah repeatedly compared those who rejected YHWH to the dead; and just as in Isa 29 even some of those who angered YHWH were still saved, so here too. Threatened with death, the people live, by YHWH's grace. The imagery is spelled out more explicitly here than elsewhere, in that the roots for "life" and "death" are used, but it

---

[570] Isaiah 3:8; 8:15; 10:4, 34; 13:15; 14:12; 21:9; 22:25; 24:18, 20; 30:25; 31:3, 8; 37:7.
[571] F. M. Cross, Jr., and D. N. Freedman, "The Song of Miriam," *JNES* 14 (1955): 248–49. In ancient Near Eastern iconography, a seated posture also commonly reflects a position of power.
[572] A good brief summary of older scholarship may be found in Hasel, "Resurrection in the Theology of Old Testament Apocalyptic."
[573] E.g., Ps 75:8; Isa 2:1–12, 17; 2 Sam 22:28; Job 5:11.
[574] See Sidney Jellicoe, "Hebrew-Greek Equivalents for the Nether World, Its Milieu and Inhabitants, in the Old Testament," *Textus* 8 (1973): 6–7. This is also true especially in the Egyptian cult of Osiris: "Osiris was lord of silence, and no one was to raise his voice in his vicinity" (Assmann, *Death and Salvation*, 190).

is the same idea; whether this directness should be taken as stylistically inferior, a later development, etc., is a claim that would be difficult to assess.

A rather explicit parallel to Isa 26:19 is found in 1 Sam 2:6–8: "YHWH kills and brings to life; he brings down to Sheol and raises up." It is possible in either case to read the language of life and death as figurative for worldly flourishing or suffering, as in lament language (§ 4.6.2). There was always room in these texts to interpret them as literal truth, hyperbolic rhetoric, or some combination thereof. It does not seem advisable to insist on dating such texts by means of a typology of religious thought, but rather to take them as expressions of a certain kind of hymnic praise that was the mirror image of the lament language that expressed suffering as encroaching death.

Thus, although the claims of v. 19 look like a major theological innovation at first glance and were taken as typologically late by many older interpreters, they represent at most a small "development" in religious thought. Their message is also integrated into the rhetoric of the passage. The statements that "Your dead shall live, your corpses shall rise" form a counterpoint to the earlier statement that the dead who are summoned to challenge YHWH's authority will not rise (v. 14). In the context of YHWH's abolishment of foreign kings, the opposition between the common dead and "your" (YHWH's) dead seems to imply a nationalistic outlook, not a universalistic one, as is sometimes thought.[575] There is a particularly strong us-versus-them dichotomy in vv. 11–12.

The ensuing phrase in v. 19, כי טל אורת טלך, elaborates on the foregoing in some way, although it is another difficult phrase. I disagree (again) with the most common understanding, which results in a translation such as "your dew is a radiant dew" (lit., "a dew of lights"; see NRSV, NJB, RSV).[576] Various interpretations have been proferred for אורת, but I believe the difficulty lies instead in a misunderstanding of טל. It is true that dew is portrayed as a blessing elsewhere in the Bible (Gen 27:28, 39; Mic 5:6; Zech 8:12; etc.), which would supply the necessary positive sense here. Nevertheless, in every other case, some larger agricultural metaphor supplies the context for the imagery of dew as blessing,[577] and the dew is nowhere else described with the characteristics of light. There is no agricultural imagery at all in Isa 26; the overwhelming theme is of death and life.

To begin instead with what is more certain, אוֹרֹת is a plural of אוֹרָה, "light, brightness, dawn."[578] In Aramaic, טל(ל) (cognate with Heb. צֵל) means "shadow,

---

[575] Note Blenkinsopp's equivocal comments (*Isaiah 1–39*, 369).
[576] NJPS's "dew on fresh growth" relates אורת to the plant named in 2 Kgs 4:39. Whether this idea would be expressed with a construct chain rather than prepositional phrase is doubtful.
[577] With the possible exception of the difficult text of Ps 110:3.
[578] See Jastrow, *Dictionary of the Targumim*, 33.

shade," and, by metaphorical extension, "protection."⁵⁷⁹ The name of the Judean queen Hamital (חמיטל / המוטל = "my father-in-law is protection"; 2 Kgs 23:31; 24:48; Jer 52:1) also contains the Aramaized form of the word. This suggests that there were by-forms in use in Judah during the preexilic period. I would suggest, then, that טל in 26:19 is an Aramaizing form of the word that plays on that dual sense of "shadow"/"protection."⁵⁸⁰ Isaiah 18:4 may be another instance of the biform טל: כהם צח עלי־אור כעב טל בחם קציר: "like the shimmering heat of (sun)light, like a (shade-/dew-)cloud in the harvest heat" – עב and טל are used together nowhere else in BH, and the context here suggests imagery of heat and light, more than moisture. One might also recall Isaiah's condemnation of the advocates of necromancy in 8:20, that they and their advice "have no dawn." The idea here is that those who rely on YHWH's protection, who take shelter under his shade, may look forward to a dawn, a bright hope even in darkness, whereas those who reject him go down to gloom with the Rephaim.⁵⁸¹ YHWH shines light in darkness, as in one of the only other biblical occurrences of אורה, Ps 139:11–12:

> If I say, "Surely the darkness shall cover me,
>   and the light around me become night,"
> even the darkness is not dark to you;
>   the night is as bright as the day,
>   for darkness is as light (כאורה) to you.

The idea that one can hide from God is an idea that is also attributed to some of Isaiah's enemies (e.g., Isa 29:15); it is construed a bit less negatively in the psalm but is still portrayed as futile. In sum, the portrait of YHWH as a god who turns darkness into light is prominent in Isaiah (see 9:2).

"Shade" occurs frequently in Isaiah and always with the more regular צל; one even notes the image of צל עב as divine protection in 25:4–5. Thus the combination of the Aramaism טל and אורה (which appears elsewhere only in Ps 139 and Esth 8:16 – both probably late) might well lead to the conclusion that at least Isa 26:19c, if not more of the verse, is a late addition.

The matter hinges in part on the intertextual relationship between Isa 26 and

---

⁵⁷⁹ As with Hebrew צל and Akkadian ṣillu.
⁵⁸⁰ A fifth-century letter establishes that the Aramaic טלל could also be related to imagery of death. Although it occurs in a broken context, a writer adjures the recipient: וגרמיך לא יחתון שאול וטללך: "Your bones shall not go down to Sheol (or: "rest in Sheol"), and your shade ..." See A. E. Cowley, *Aramaic Papyri of the Fifth Century B.C.* (Oxford: Clarendon, 1923), no. 71, line 15. This might seem to refer to the ghost as a "shade," a sense attested nowhere else in classical Hebrew or Aramaic, to my knowledge. If so, it would lend credence to the suggestion that the title of CAT 1.161, *spr dbḥ ẓlm*, does indeed refer to the Rephaim as "shades."
⁵⁸¹ So already Duhm, *Das Buch Jesaja*, 165; also Archibald L.H.M. van Wieringen, " 'I' and 'We' Before 'Your' Face: A Communication Analysis of Isiah 26:7–21," in *Studies in Isaiah 24–27: The Isaiah Workshop* (ed. Hendrik Jan Bosman and Harm van Grol et al.; Leiden: Brill, 2000), 248.

Hos 13–14 that was argued by John Day, and is now widely noted.[582] The reference to the טל of YHWH as a blessing is one common feature of the two texts. The Hosea text is clearer: אהיה כטל לישראל, "I will be like טל to Israel, (and he will blossom like a lily, etc.)" – there is no odd construction like Isa 26:19's טל אורת. Therefore, Hos 14:6 might be perceived as an argument against the understanding of Isa 26:19 that I have just advanced. However, one should note that two verses later, in Hos 14:8, one reads ישבו ישבי בצלו יחיו [כ]דגן יפרח כגפן, "Dwellers shall again dwell in his shade; they shall flourish like the grain; they shall blossom like the vine." The shade of YHWH is one of the conditions of flourishing, which makes one wonder whether טל is a *double entendre* in both Hos 14:6 and Isa 26:19 – while in Hebrew, טל meant "dew/rain," perhaps an Israelite author could count on his audience to hear "shadow," in the sense of "protection." In the end, the question cannot be conclusively resolved.

The final line of v. 19, "you will bring down/cast down the Rephaim into the underworld," (or "cause the Rephaim to lay down in the underworld") contrasts the lot of YHWH's dead with that of the supposedly powerful divinized dead. To return again to v. 14, the whole rhetorical case here is that the cults of the dead are anti-Yahwistic practice that is powerless to save. The dead who are summoned for help do not rise; whereas the dead (or near-dead) who rely on YHWH will be saved and will rise and stand.

Isaiah's image of the dead rising and standing is, on the one hand, not a remarkable innovation. From many centuries before Isaiah come much more extensive descriptions of the dead rising, standing, and walking, from the Egyptian Book of the Dead.[583] These warrant mention not because they are likely to have exercised direct literary influence, but because they bear witness to the currency of the rhetoric of resurrection in the ancient Near East well before Isaiah's time.[584] For example, in Spell 68 the deceased says: "(I) lift myself from (my) right side and put myself in a sitting position, that (I) may stand and shake off my dust."[585] Or again in Spell 75, "I have ascended (from the netherworld; I

---

[582] John Day, "The Development of the Belief in Life after Death in Ancient Israel," in *After the Exile: Essays in Honor of Rex Mason* (ed. John Barton and David J. Reimer; Macon, Ga.: Mercer University Press, 1996), 243–48. Cf. Hibbard, *Intertextuality in Isaiah 24–27*, 148.

[583] Jan Assmann considers these Egyptian texts in light of later images of resurrection particularly explicitly in "Resurrection in Ancient Egypt," in *Resurrection: Theological and Scientific Assessments* (ed. T. Peters et al.; Grand Rapids: Eerdmans, 2002), 124–35.

[584] The idea that physical resurrection was imported from Zoroastrianism is not only unnecessary but relies on a highly contestable reconstruction of Zoroastrian resurrection beliefs in the sixth century BCE. The implausibility of this hypothesis is apparent when Bernhard Lang argues that Zoroastrianism somehow influenced Ezekiel in Babylon prior to the Persian conquest ("Life after Death in the Prophetic Promise," 154–55). The speculative nature of the case – there is no contemporaneous Zoroastrian evidence to support it – can seen also in Lang's "A Zoroastrian Prophecy of Resurrection" in *Hebrew Life and Literature: Selected Essays of Bernhard Lang* (Farnham, England: Ashgate, 2008), 83–91.

[585] Allen, *Book of the Dead*, 62.

have come) from the realm of earth."[586] As early as the Old Kingdom, the pharaoh Teti was instructed in a spell: "Raise yourself ... take your head, bind your bones, collect your members, wipe the earth off your flesh."[587] Now, whether these images of rising from the underworld were ever taken literally is a question for debate. It is increasingly apparent in later periods that Egyptians were aware that tombs and corpses were rarely left intact (see §§ 2.4.1; 2.4.3), and they had numerous other ways of speaking about hopes after death, many of them found in the same texts (§ 2.4.2). These considerations suggest that the expectation of physical resurrection was not central to Egyptian religion. The images of the happy afterlife in Mesopotamian and extrabiblical Syro-Palestinian texts never employ quite such explicit descriptions of rising from the dead (although the Hadad inscription and various Ugaritic *rpum* texts could be understood to refer to a similar phenomenon).

A number of biblical texts do attest to the physical raising of the dead. Although I have offered the possibility that the psalms that refer to salvation from death and Sheol are rhetorical conceits that referred to the speakers' near-death experiences (§ 4.6.2), it is harder to explain away an account such as that of 2 Kgs 4:18–37, in which a child who is flatly called "dead" (vv. 20, 32) awakens. Meanwhile, Ezek 37's baroque symphony of revivification, complete with descriptions of the restoration of sinew and skin to dry bones, could scarcely be more physical, even if it is ultimately symbolic of the revivification of the nation rather than individuals. With the caveat that we are not exactly talking about "doctrine" (if such a thing could be said to exist in ancient Israel), it has to be granted that ancient Israelite authors were quite capable of ascribing to YHWH the power to raise the dead, physically. It would have coexisted with a pessimistic strain of thought (cf. 2 Sam 12:23: "Now he is dead; why should I fast? Can I bring him back again? I shall go to him, but he will not return to me"), but it was certainly a rhetorical option that was available to express YHWH's power. Isaiah 26's imagery takes its place within this tradition of Israelite religious thought, along with Ezek 37 and Dan 12, but typologies of the development of religious thought alone are insufficient to determine the date of each of these manifestations, and Isa 24–27 in particular still awaits a definitive study.

The reprising of themes found elsewhere in chs. 1–33 continues in vv. 20–21. The image of hiding until the wrath passes by (עד־יעבור זעם) seems to allude to the prophecy of 10:5, 25: "the club in [Assyria's] hands is my fury (זעמי) ... [but] in a very little while my fury (זעם) will come to an end, and my anger will be directed to their destruction." The choice of the verb עבר further recalls the image of

---

[586] Allen, *Book of the Dead*, 66.
[587] Translation by Assmann, *Death and Salvation*, 241; cf. James P. Allen, *The Ancient Egyptian Pyramid Texts* (WAW 23; Atlanta: Society of Biblical Literature, 2005), 83. Compare also the text from the Book of Gates in Assmann, *Death and Salvation*, 346.

Assyria as a flood washing over the land in Isa 8:8; 28:15–19. In 26:21, the description of YHWH going forth in theophanic judgment uses language reminiscent of the theophany of ch. 30 (הנה), but not identical with it (יצא is not used of YHWH's going forth in battle in authentic Isaianic passages – see, however, 37:36 – but it has its own solid claim to antiquity in Divine Warrior imagery; cf. Judg 4:14; 2 Sam 5:24). The beginning of 26:21 and that of Mic 1:3 are identical.

Although the foregoing images and references might point to affinities between the outlook of 26:11–12 and that of authentically Isaianic passages, it must be granted that the image of hiding in one's room until the judgment passes (v. 20) does not sound quite like Isaiah; indeed, it sounds too similar to the passive behavior condemned in 22:13 and 28:15–20. The advice to hide makes sense in an environment in which Judah is no longer in a position to resist politically, another possible indicator of a seventh-century provenance. As I have remarked (§ 1.2), Judah must have been thoroughly pacified in order for Assyria to have free passage through Palestine en route to conquering Egypt. The events that brought about the end of the Neo-Assyrian Empire were distant from Judah, in Mesopotamia, and so indeed during the reign of Josiah it would have sufficed for Judeans to keep their heads down for the most part and watch as Assyria crumbled.

The verb פקד (v. 21) is used elsewhere of YHWH's revenge on Assyria (10:12, 28; 29:6), and "visiting (his) iniquity upon him" is very much in keeping with the *ius talionis* theme that runs through many of the earlier passages. It is possible that ישׁב הארץ is another reference to the Neo-Assyrian "ruler of the earth." However, פקד is also common in Isaianic texts usually attributed to later periods, e.g., 13:4, 11; 24:21–22; 26:14–16; 27:1–3. Blood (1:15; 4:4; 33:15; etc.) and the slain (10:4; 14:19; etc.) are also well-attested themes in Isaiah, although these elements are used differently here than elsewhere; they are intended not to horrify but to symbolize guilt. Here the earth's giving up of its dead expresses YHWH's unlimited reach in judgment (cf. Amos 9:2); those with blood on their hands will not be able to hide even in death. This may also be an image of healing; the earth cannot be at rest while it contains the unjustly slain (as perhaps reflected in Gen 4:11).

A brief summary of my conclusions is in order. Despite the significant intertextual affinities with presumably authentic Isaianic texts and other eighth-century prophets, the present study concurs with the assessment of H. L. Ginsberg: "[T]hough the language and the ideas are often Isaian, frequent divergences from Isaiah's style, spirit and outlook argue that the resemblances are due to imitation rather than Isaian authorship."[588] The most significant instances of divergence in the two passages under consideration here are the changed referent for "Death/covering" in 25:7–8 and the admonition to hide in 26:20. Ginsberg favors a

---

[588] Ginsberg, "Isaiah (First Isaiah)," 58.

terminus ad quem prior to the end of the exile (as Seitz rightly points out, the overthrow of the city in chs. 24–27 does not at all resemble the conquest of Babylon by Cyrus and the Persians, and thus is not likely to have been a response to that event). However, I have argued that at least these particular texts are more likely to reflect the situation in the latter half of the seventh century BCE, when the empires that had long dominated the land were thrown off. The joyous sense of restoration, coupled with the admonition to lay low, best fits that period. This accords with Matthijs de Jong's analysis of the ideology of Josiah's reign: "The collapse of Assyrian domination and regaining of independence were the ingredients of the portrayal of Josiah's reign as a glorious time ... a new and felicitous era."[589] This is in keeping with a common feature of ancient Near Eastern political discourse: "[t]he theme of a new and glorious time after a period of trouble is a prominent feature in royal ideology."[590] In this light, the extraordinary language of Isa 25 and 26 would be expressions of bright hopes: the anti-Assyrian plans of YHWH having been fulfilled, he celebrates with a victory banquet and extravagant promises of new life.

The banquet may further be identifiable as a celebration of covenant renewal. The language of restoration to life has deep resonance with ancient Near Eastern covenants, as J. Wingaards has shown; as far back at the Hittite treaties of the late Bronze Age and as late as the Persian Period, the deposition of a vassal king can be described as killing him, whereas his restoration to the throne can be described as restoring him to life.[591] Wingaards argued that this context explains the use of revivification language in Hos 6:2, which he took to reflect a renewal-of-covenant ceremony after the Syro-Emphraimitic crisis. He goes on: "The much disputed phrases 'after two days' – 'on the third day' ... may derive from the covenantal custom of celebrating the pact 'in the morning on the third day.' "[592] If one is indeed looking at a a seventh-century manifestation of this theme, then it is easy to associate it with the covenant renewal ordered by Josiah after the discovery of the book of the law, in 2 Kgs 23.

In that slightly later context, these passages reprise, and in some cases reshape, the themes of death and the underworld that were noted in earlier passages. They carry through the ideas that God has power over the realms of the living and the dead, while the dead have no power to help the living. The emphasis, however,

---

[589] De Jong, *Isaiah Among the Ancient Near Eastern Prophets*, 371–72.
[590] De Jong, *Isaiah Among the Ancient Near Eastern Prophets*, 392.
[591] Johannes N. M. Wijngaards, "Death and Resurrection in Covenantal Context (Hos. VI 2)," *VT* 17 (1967): 226–39.
[592] Wijngaards, "Death and Resurrection," 237; On the significance of the third day in covenant-making, see Exod 19:11, 16, and cf. Walter Brueggemann, "Amos iv 4–13 and Israel's Covenant Worship," *VT* 15 (1965): 9. Another later manifestation of the theme is in the Cyrus Cylinder, in which the people are said to be "like corpses" under incompetent native rule until the conquest of Cyrus, who "revives the dead."

has been reversed; in the earlier passages YHWH absorbed and redirected the power of death of Judah's enemies in order to punish them, and the promise of life is typically a faint whisper if it is there at all. In Isa 25 and 26, the promise of life comes to the fore, and the punishment of the wicked is pushed to the background. The nations are even offered a feast from God's bounty. Finally, there is a significant shift in the voice of the people; whereas in earlier texts the prophet's condemnations of the people's sinfulness and impotence had no discernible effect, the first person common plural forms in vv. 12–13, 17–18 confess faithlessness, apostasy, and powerlessness. Isa 25 and 26 therefore enact the faithful reaction for which the earlier passages call; well after the time of Isaiah of Jerusalem, they answer his question עד־מתי, "how long?" (6:9–11).

In order to keep the presentation of my thesis focused, I have thus far avoided interacting extensively with conflicting views about the historical context of Isa 26, but they are numerous. The majority of critical scholars would still hold to one of two differing opinions:

First, there is the view represented by John Collins, who associates 26:19 closely with Ezek 37 and Hosea 6:2 as instances of imagery of raising the dead that represent national restoration rather than physical resurrection, but generally associate it with the restoration from the Babylonian exile.[593] Collins states that the passage celebrates the fact that "the power of Babylon is broken" and although it "does not necessarily involve acual resurrection of dead Israelites," it did "[provide] language for the belief expressed in Daniel 12."[594] I agree with most of this, and I only ask whether it might not celebrate the breaking of *Assyria's* power instead of Babylon's. Collins writes that "Israel was dead in the Exile, and its restoration is as miraculous as resurrection"[595] – we have seen in the previous sections that Isaiah ben Amoz frequently portrayed the Israelites as dead long before the exile, so why should a later Josianic scribe not have seized on this image and use it in a more positive way? It is true that Isa 27:8 refers to exile; if that is indeed a reference to the Babylonian Exile, then it remains to be shown that 26 and 27 are of the same date; a similar pair of chapters, Isa 13 and 14, are regularly taken to refer to different periods – one to Babylon, the other to Assyria – and to have been joined together at a later stage. It may be that this sort of pairing of oracles was actually a compositional technique of the tradents who expanded the book.

Second, there is the view represented by Jon Levenson, who holds that the phrase "your dead (pl.) shall rise" suggests a partial salvation, not a complete national restoration like that of Ezek 37, and thus begins to sound like the dual judgment of Daniel 12:2 ("Many of those who sleep in the dust of the earth shall

---

[593] John J. Collins, *Daniel* (Hermeneia; Minneapolis: Fortress, 1993), 395.
[594] Collins, *Daniel*, 395.
[595] Collins, *Daniel*, 395.

awake, some to everlasting life, and some to shame and everlasting contempt"). Often it is assumed that those who are raised in v. 19 are contrasted with the dead of oppressive foreign nations in 26:13–14. But there is no explicit link in the text between the "other lords" in 26:13 and the dead who "do not rise" in 26:14.[596] Verse 14 instead appears to be a general statement of fact – albeit a rhetorical statement that the author goes on to contradict. To be sure, the foreign dead are subject to the general rule that "the dead do not rise," but YHWH's raising of the dead in v. 19 is an exception to a *general rule*, not an explicit contrast to some specific second group that has been judged negatively. Thus the passage shares in general prexilic ideas about resurrection (YHWH can raise the dead, though he doesn't always, or even typically), rather than being a small step away from Daniel's theology.

Levenson cites approvingly Robert Martin-Achard's comment, "The author of Isa 26:19 is not, like Ezekiel, envisaging the political revival of the nation; he is not even speaking about an event that would concern all Israel; he is thinking only of certain members of the Chosen People, of those to whom the words 'thy dead' refer."[597] This line of reasoning probably overinterprets the phrase in Ezek 37:11, "these bones are all the house of Israel (כל בית ישראל)," as a statement of national unity. It also assumes that prophets' views regarding the comprehensiveness of the nation's salvation evolved in a regular and consistent manner; in reality, the prophecies of Isaiah ben Amoz are already quite sectarian, *in addition to* being quite nationalistic; the two outlooks are not mutually exclusive. Isaiah may have literally led a kind of sect (8:16, 18), and certainly in the time of Josiah's controversial reform it would have been easy to view the nation as divided between the faithful adherents to the reform project on the one hand, and on the other hand those who, according to the old tradition, chose death. This is a different view from that of Ezekiel, but not necessarily a later one.[598]

---

[596] George Nickelsburg perceives a "contrast between the raising of the dead of Israel and the fact that their dead overlords will not rise" (*Resurrection, Immortality, and Eternal Life in Intertestamental Judaism* [Harvard Theological Studies 26; Cambridge: Harvard University Press, 1972], 18). It is even less clear why such a contrast would make a nationalistic interpretation "untenable." It seems to me that a contrast between the nation's dead and the dead of oppressive foreign empires would make for a *more* nationalistic reading

[597] Robert Martin-Achard, *De la mort à la résurrection: D'après l'Ancien Testament* (Neuchâtel: Delachaux & Niestlé, 1956), 131. Cited in Levenson, *Resurrection and the Restoration of Israel*, 199.

[598] If this were indeed a late text with sectarian tendencies, we might expect it to use familiar sectarian terminology from the postexilic portions of Isaiah – especially עבדים, "servants" (54:17; 56:6; 63:17, etc.), and perhaps חרדים, "those who tremble" (66:5). No such vocabulary appears in 24–27.

5.2.4.3 Isaiah 38:9–20: The Psalm of Hezekiah

This final passage elaborates and clarifies the theme of confession. The Psalm of Hezekiah, which might once have stood at the end of an earlier version of the book of Isaiah,[599] draws together the book's pervasive themes of death and new life. The psalm also presents the greatest text-critical and linguistic problems of all the pericopae covered so far. Unfortunately, one of the sections most significant to the present study, vv. 16–17a, is also one of the most difficult; Wildberger called it "an exegete's nightmare."[600] Nevertheless, although one must avoid laying too much weight on certain details, the overall structure and progression of the psalm are perceptible.

(9) A writing[601] of Hezekiah, king of Judah, when he was sick and lived through his sickness:
(10) I thought:
  On account of[602] the guilt[603] of my days I must depart;[604]
  I am consigned[605] to the gates of Sheol the rest of my years
(11) I said, "I shall not see the Lord;
  the Lord[606] is in the land of the living.
  "I shall no longer gaze on humankind,
  with the inhabitants of Decease."[607]

---

[599] Michael L. Barré, *The Lord Has Saved Me: A Study of the Psalm of Hezekiah (Isaiah 38:9–20)* (CBQMS 39; Washington, D.C.: Catholic Biblical Association of America, 2005), 256.
[600] Wildberger, *Isaiah 28–39*, 441.
[601] The suggestion to emend to מכתב (a term of uncertain meaning found in the superscriptions to Pss 16 and 56–60) carries no conviction. 1QIsaᵃ agrees with the MT, and the fact that the LXX reads προσευκή rather than στηλογραφία (as in every instance of מכתם) strongly suggests that the translator indeed had מכתב in his *Vorlage*, pace Barré, *Lord Has Saved Me*, 35–44. For similar views, see Sigmund Mowinckel, *The Psalms in Israel's Worship* (2 vols.; trans. D. R. Ap-Thomas; New York: Abingdon, 1962), 2:42; Blenkinsopp, *Isaiah 1–39*, 479; Sweeney, *Isaiah 1–39*, 490; Clements, *Isaiah 1–39*, 291.
[602] This is the causative ב; cf. Gen 18:28; Zech 9:11, etc. See Waltke and O'Connor, *Introduction to Biblical Hebrew Syntax*, 198 (11.2.5e).
[603] Read דְּמֵי. The common alternative theory that דמי can mean "half" is speculative, based purely on analogy with Akkadian *mašālu*. See further discussion below.
[604] For הלך="die," see Ps 39:14; 1 Kgs 2:2; 1 Chr 17:11; perhaps also Gen 15:2. Cf. Job 7:9, 10:21.
[605] This unusual meaning for פקד might be considered a calque of Akkadian *paqādu*, "hand over, assign" (Barré, *Lord Has Saved Me*, 62).
[606] Pace Wildberger (*Isaiah 28–39*, 438), there is no problem with the repetition of יה, nor should one be removed, nor should one read יה יה as יהוה (*pace* Clements, *Isaiah 1–39*, 291). It is likely to have been intended to resonate with the repeated חי חי in v. 19.
[607] I do not find good reason to emend חדל to חלד on the basis of Ps 49:2. (This might just as well be a wordplay on that very phrase.) The LXX and the Vulgate both read the root חדל in their *Vorlagen*; the Syriac reads "grave" (*ḥpr*ʾ), and the Targum "earth" (ʾrʿ:: Heb. ארץ). The English noun "decease" has not received much exercise in the past century, but it does happen to supply an example of a language that uses the root "cease" for death. Cf. Mitchell Dahood, "חֶדֶל Cessation in Isaiah 38,11," *Bib* 52 (1971): 215–16. A third option is espoused by Philip J. Calderone, who argues for a second root *ḥdl*, meaning "to be fat, full, prosperous" ("Supplemental Note on ḥdl-II," *CBQ* 24 [1962]: 412–19).

(12) My lifetime is plucked up
 and taken away from me like a shepherd's tent.
 My life is shrunk like a weaving;[608]
 he cuts me off from the thrum.
 Between daybreak and nightfall,
 you fulfill (your word) against me.[609]
(13) I cry out[610] until morning;
 Like a lion he crushes all my bones
 Between daybreak and nightfall,
 you fulfill (your word) against me.
(14) Like a swallow[611] I twitter;
 I moan like a dove
 My eyes are brought down[612] from[613] the heights
 O Lord, I am overwhelmed; support me!
(15) What should I say?
 For he has spoken to me,
 and he himself has done it.
 I will wander[614] all my years
 because of the bitterness of my soul.
(16) YHWH Most High is the one who gives life to every heart,
 who gives life to the spirit![615]
(17) See, he indeed exchanged my bitterness for wholeness.[616]

 You held back my life from the Pit of destruction
 You cast all my sins behind your back.

---

[608] Read אָרַג for אֹרְגִי and קִפַּדְתִּי (Qal passive) for קִפַּדְתִּי. For both readings, and the meaning "shrink," see Barré, *Lord Has Saved Me*, 88–107.

[609] שׁלם never has the meaning assumed by many translations, "bring (life) to an end." In the Hiphil, however, it can express the fulfillment of a plan or promise (Isa 44:26, 28; Job 23:14). Since this can only refer to the fulfillment of Isaiah's oracle in the prose section (38:1), it may suggest again a link between the psalm and the narrative.

[610] Read שִׁוַּעְתִּי for שִׁוִּיתִי; cf. Wildberger, *Isaiah 28–39*, 439.

[611] On the basis of Deir 'Alla I.7–8, it appears that סוּסעָגוּר should be understood as a single bird species. Cf. Barré, *Lord Has Saved Me*, 120–23.

[612] Not actually a passive verb; cf. the use of דלל in Pss 79:8; 116:6; 142:7. Wildberger (*Isaiah 28–39*, 440) points to the fact that the verb כלה ("fail, grow weak") is commonly used of the eyes, but this is precisely the reason not to make that emendation here: *lectio difficilior* strongly favors the MT.

[613] For ל = "away from," see Pss 85:9; 68:21; for other examples, see HALOT 508 (#5). The usage is equivalent to the "ventive" use of the Ugaritic preposition *l-*. Cf. DUL 477.

[614] Read אֶדַּדֶּה from נדד. Cf. 1QIsaᵃ אדודה. For discussion, see Barré, *Lord Has Saved Me*, 148–53.

[615] This translation of vv. 16–17a is based on the reconstruction of Barré: יהוה עלי המחיה כל לב המחיה רוח / תחלימני והחייני הנחל שלום / (*Lord Has Saved Me*, 153–68). For a summary of other significant suggestions, see also Wildberger, *Isaiah 28–39*, 441. See further discussion below.

[616] Read לְיָמֵר (שלום מר[י]), where לימר is the asseverative *lamed* plus the Hiphil imperfect third person masculine singular of מור.

(18) For Sheol does not give you thanks;
   Death does not praise you;
   Those who go down the pit
   do not hope for your faithfulness.
(19) The living, the living thank you, as I do today;
   Fathers will make known to sons, O God,[617] your faithfulness.
(20) YHWH has indeed saved me;[618] we will play my stringed instruments
   all the days of our lives before the house of the Lord.

The psalm opens with Hezekiah's account of his attitude upon receiving the news of his sentence (vv. 1–3); it might be said to pick up after he has received the oracle of his death from Isaiah. Hezekiah feared that he would "depart because of the bloodguilt of (his) days" (בדמי ימי אלכה). This translation not only avoids the need to propose a very unusual sense of דמי as "middle" (see translation note), it also undermines Kaiser's assertion that the first half of the psalm "does not display any awareness of sin or guilt."[619] On this revised understanding, the psalm falls into line with other psalms of thanksgiving; its structure is now akin to, for example, Ps 107's progression from sin (v. 12) to deliverance from the gates of death (v. 18) to praise in the sanctuary (v. 32).

A concern more precisely for *royal bloodguilt* is found in Psalm 51:16: "Deliver me from bloodshed (הצילני מדמים), O God, O God of my salvation, and my tongue will sing aloud of your deliverance." This turn of phrase encapsulates the whole movement of Hezekiah's psalm, which also ends with musical celebration of YHWH's deliverance. Psalm 51 also has a particularly royal feel, and is attributed to David. For examples of divine retribution for the "bloodguilt" of a king, see 2 Sam 21:1 and Hos 1:4.

One might wonder what this "bloodguilt" could refer to in Hezekiah's case; although he is generally presented positively in Dtr literature, he is condemned by Isaiah for his building practices, which apparently included what the prophet considered an unjust use of eminent domain (22:9–11). Indeed, there are other possible references that accuse Hezekiah specifically of bloodguilt: for example, Mic 3:10 condemns those who "build Zion with bloodguilt" (בנה ציון בדמים); and Hab 2:9–13 contains an oracle that is similar, if probably later: "*Hôy*, you who build a city with bloodshed!" (הוי בנה עיר בדמים).[620] It might appear that Hezekiah's psalm relates to an early and now mostly submerged tradition of his guilt

---

[617] Cf. אלוה in 1QIsaᵃ and אלה in 1QIsaᵇ.
[618] Read asseverative -ל, and הושיעני as a Hiphil perfect third person masculine plural with first common singular suffix. Cf. Barré, *Lord Has Saved Me*, 195–98.
[619] Kaiser, *Isaiah 13–39*, 404; cf. also Blenkinsopp, *Isaiah 1–39*, 482.
[620] Psalm 55:24 presents a specific reference to the divine shortening of life for bloodguilt: "bloodthirsty (דמים) and deceitful men will not live out half their days (לא יחצו ימיהם)." However, unless 28:10 contains a pun, one cannot preserve there both proposed senses of דמי (bloodguilt/half).

in matters of social justice. Thus, Hezekiah's sickness would have been a punishment, answering Wildberger's observation that "[w]hy Hezekiah was sick in the first place is never mentioned" (Wildberger, *Isaiah 28–39*, 466).

Whether or not the psalm was composed for this narrative context, it does seem to refer back to the prose account (vv. 1–8): the idea that he will "depart (הלך) in bloodguilt" finds a verbal echo in v. 3, where he protests his sentence, saying that he has "walked (הלך) before [YHWH] in faithfulness." The verb הלך must be understood differently in each case, but there seems to be a play on words; indeed, the meaning "depart, die" for הלך is unusual enough that it might not even have become clear until the second half of the verse, where the reference to Sheol clarifies the matter. The image of the "gates of Sheol," while strictly speaking a hapax legomenon, is similar to the "gates of death" (Ps 107:18) and the "gates of the shadow of death" (Job 38:17). The idea that the underworld was a city with gates is well attested in the ancient Near East, most famously in the Descent of Inanna / Ištar (§§ 1.4.3; 2.4.3; 3.3.3.3).

Verse 11 gives voice to Hezekiah's sense of abandonment, and it does so by playing with what must have been one traditional Israelite view of YHWH: that he had no commerce with the world of the dead. As in many psalms and ancient Near Eastern laments, the one praying likens himself (or herself) to the dead (§ 4.6.2). In the second half of the verse, the meaning of חדל has been a crux (see translation note on v. 11), but the force is the same whether one understands "I will no longer look on the living (when I am) with the inhabitants of (the underworld [חדל])" or emends to "I will no longer look on the living (as I did when I was) with the inhabitants of (this world [הלד])." I have chosen to follow Mitchell Dahood and understand חדל as a rare term for Sheol; apart from the linguistic and text-critical data usually cited, referring to the living three different ways would create an uneven and redundant verse. From a literary standpoint, it is more likely that "humankind" (אדם) is parallel with "the living" (החים), while ישבי חדל refers to a different group, creating an A:B::B:A pattern – I (dead) : the living :: (living) humankind : (dead) inhabitants of חדל.

The imagery in v. 12 of being "plucked up" as a metaphor for dying is uncommon, but not without parallel. The most obvious example Job 4:20–21:

מבקר לערב יכתו מבלי משים לנצח יאבדו
הלא־נסע יתרם בם ימותו ולא בחכמה

Between morning and evening they are destroyed;
   they perish forever without any regarding it.
Their tent-cord is plucked up within them,
   and they die devoid of wisdom.

Despite the similar collocation of tent imagery and the similar phrases "between morning and evening" and "between day and night," the only lexical link between the two passages is the verb נסע (Niphal). It seems quite possible that one is dealing here not with an instance of literary influence but with a common traditional image.⁶²¹

Verse 12b adds a second image from daily life, that of a weaving being cut off. God is elsewhere a potter who holds human fates in his hands (Isa 29:16; 41:25; 45:9; 64:8; Jer 18:6, 11), so this image, while original, is also quite comprehensible within the scope of traditional Judean theology. A person's life span was imagined as a thread or rope in the hands of the Fates or gods not only in Greco-Roman culture but also in the ancient Near East. The poet of the present text crafted a particularly erudite and complex expression of the motif. The repeated phrase מיום עד־לילה expresses not the time of day at which Hezekiah is suffering, but rather the suddenness of the fulfillment: it takes place within a single day.⁶²² (As in the phrase "Rome wasn't built in a day," here a day is taken to be a short span of time.)

Still other traditional lament terminology is found in vv. 13–14, portraying Hezekiah as one who is punished by God and draws near to death. The lion's attack is a common image of divine punishment (Job 10:16; Isa 15:19; 30:6; Jer 2:30; Hos 5:14; Dan 6:24, etc.) or demonic assault (Ps 17:12; 22:14; 35:17; 57:5, etc.)⁶²³ – two phenomena that are not neatly distinguished in the Hebrew Bible. YHWH may (more indirectly) be portrayed as a bone-crushing lion in Ps 50:10 and Lam 3:4. The images of doves and other songbirds are frequently used to symbolize human suffering, both in Mesopotamia (§ 1.4.2–3) and in Israelite literature (Ps 102:7). The choice of the Pilpael form of צפף (אצפצף) also clearly echoes the uses of the same root for sounds made by ghosts in 8:19 and 29:4. The "moaning" of a dove also evokes death: הגה is used of the sounds made by the spirits of the dead in 8:19; of moaning in lament for the dead in Isa 16:7 and Jer 48:31; and of the groans of suffering people in Isa 59:11. Thus, the comparison to a twittering bird portrays Hezekiah's approach to death. As Wildberger remarks, "whoever is sick finds himself in the realm of death already."⁶²⁴

In vv. 14d–15, Hezekiah, his hope gone, throws himself on the mercy of YHWH, the very one who has assaulted him. The basis for his trust is not immediately clear; as Michael Barré remarks, the entire first half of the psalm is "cast in extremely somber tones, overshadowed by death and the abandonment of a

---

⁶²¹ One might also mention Job 19:10 ("He breaks me down on every side, and I am gone, he has uprooted [ויסע] my hope like a tree"), and the well-known Neo-Assyrian lament of a husband for a wife, which mourns, "Your thwarts [are] in pieces, your mooring rope cut" – where the mooring rope is comparable to the tent-cord of Job 4:21. See Erica Reiner, *Your Thwarts in Pieces, Your Mooring Rope Cut: Poetry from Babylonia and Assyria* (Ann Arbor: University of Michigan Press, 1985), 86–87.
⁶²² Barré, *Lord Has Saved Me*, 107–11.
⁶²³ Lion imagery is used with similar language of military threats from Mesopotamian also in Jer 50:17 (cf. Isa 5:29). See Strawn, *What Is Stronger Than a Lion?*, esp. 336.
⁶²⁴ Wildberger, *Isaiah 28–39*, 462.

deity who has become the psalmist's tormentor."⁶²⁵ A final image that seems to compare Hezekiah to the dead is that of wandering in v. 15b. The fear of joining the wandering dead, those who were not buried or were otherwise unfortunate, was common in the ancient Near East (§§ 1.4.2; 2.4.2).⁶²⁶ Thus, even in his wandering Hezekiah is portrayed as one who approaches death.

Verse 16, with its hymnic declaration of praise, marks a shift. Hezekiah's proclamation that YHWH saves must be simultaneous with his experience of salvation, because v. 17 suddenly reflects backward on the event. The explanation of v. 16 is no simple matter, as a glance at the diverse translations demonstrates. The translation above, based on the text as reconstructed by Barré, finds support in a parallel from Isa 57:15, where one also finds Hiphil forms of חיה paired with רוח and לב:

> For thus says the high and lofty one
>   who inhabits eternity, whose name is Holy:
> "I dwell in the high and holy place,
>   and also with those who are contrite and humble in spirit,
> to revive the spirit of the humble (להחיות רוח שפלים),
>   and to revive the heart of the contrite (להחיות לב נדכאים).
> For I will not continually accuse,
>   nor will I always be angry;
> for then the spirits would grow faint before me,
>   even the souls that I have made.   (Isa 57:15–16)

In both passages (57:15–16 and 38:16–17), one sees a certain homology of psychological and physical states in psalmic rhetoric: at a first level, "giving life to the spirit/heart" means creating a shift in outlook or "mood." But in both cases an actual rescue from death lies just beneath the surface. In 57:16 one might perceive an echo of the judgment of the dead, since spirits and souls stand before YHWH. In 38:16–17 YHWH holds (or pulls) Hezekiah back from the brink of death, even after he has looked long and hard into the abyss.

The psalm's linguistic challenges ease considerably in its final section. The language is formulaic, with the appeal to YHWH that only the living can praise and give thanks (cf. Pss 6:5; 30:9). Both Death and Sheol are personified in v. 18, suggesting a lively sense of the underlying mythology on the author's part, as in 5:14; 25:8; or 28:15–18.

Verse 18 also reflects back on the hopelessness of the first half of the psalm: when Hezekiah felt himself to be in the pit, he did not hope for YHWH's faithfulness. Wildberger attributes this to a traditional Israelite view that YHWH had

---

[625] Barré, *Lord Has Saved Me*, 141. Cf. Wildberger, *Isaiah 28–39*, 452: "Though one would expect it, the text does not begin with praise to God."

[626] For example, in the hymn to Šamaš, "the wandering dead" and "the vagrant spirit" are beholden to the sun god. *COS* 1.117; Lambert, *Babylonian Wisdom Literature*, 134–35; Bottéro, "Les morts et l'au-delà," 201–2. See Akk. *murtappidu* (*CAD* M/2, 227–28).

no commerce with the underworld: "If Sheol was thought to be outside the territory that Yahweh ruled, the dying and those who had died already would not be in a position to hope any longer for Yahweh's grace and faithfulness."[627] But if the psalm shows an awareness of that belief, it does so precisely in disputing it: the psalm's most central claim is that *YHWH does save even from Death and Sheol*, and it proclaims it with great vigor. It takes the claims of a text like Ps 88:5–6 –

> I am counted among those who go down to the Pit;
> I am like *those who have no help*,
> like those forsaken among the dead,
> like the slain that lie in the grave,
> like *those whom you remember no more*,
> for *they are cut off from your hand*.

– and argues that they are mere pessimism, or perhaps the hyperbolic rhetoric of a supplicant seeking to invoke YHWH's help. Just as Amos 9:2 asserts YHWH's ability to seek out the underworld in wrath, Hezekiah's psalm affirms that he may do so in grace and mercy. Like other passages that refer to YHWH's power to save from death, the psalm might be seen as a testimony against the natural pessimism of human experience (as Assmann said of the Egyptian funerary cult; § 2.5). It is almost certain that these views coexisted historically, rather than that one replaced the other at some point in time.

Hezekiah's psalm both summarizes and caps many of the earlier passages surveyed in this chapter. Hezekiah is condemned by YHWH for wrongdoing; under divine judgment; he becomes like the dead; but he is pulled back from death. As Blenkinsopp observed, the end of the psalm is a most forceful "affirmation of life."[628]

Although it is not entirely explicit, one might conclude that it is Hezekiah's confession of guilt (vv. 10, 17) and his humility before YHWH (v. 14) that earn him a reprieve.[629] If the threat of punishment and promise of salvation mirror aspects of earlier passages, then the humbling of oneself before YHWH and the confession seem to express what the earlier sections are looking for: pride and refusal of YHWH's protection and counsel were sins that Isaiah repeatedly condemned. It carries the book's plot a step further, in that there is no sign that any of the objects of Isaiah's condemnation in the earlier sections repented at all. In fact, their refusal to hear him is one of the major themes of the book (e.g., 1:3; 6:9–13; 28:12; 30:9). Hezekiah, however, does hear and turn. This theological conclusion contrasts with his assertion of innocence in the prose account (v. 3) and fits better with the themes of Isa 1–39 as a whole.

---

[627] Wildberger, *Isaiah 28–39*, 463.
[628] Blenkinsopp, *Isaiah 1–39*, 485.
[629] For a discussion of the psalm as a confession, see P. A. H. de Boer, "Notes on the Text and Meaning of Isaiah XXXVIII, 9–20," *OTS* 9 (1951): 170–86.

One can and should distinguish between the psalm's composition and its placement in its present location. The psalm itself may be preexilic, as Barré argues. He demonstrates that the language is not late, as older exegetes thought, and its themes and images are consistent with cultic poetry of very early periods. William W. Hallo and H. L. Ginsberg have each pointed out ancient Near Eastern cognates in epistolary prayers in Sumerian, Akkadian, and Aramaic from earlier periods than that of Hezekiah,[630] with Ginsberg going so far as to theorize that the king would have originally had this text carved in stone.[631] Childs concluded on different grounds that the psalm must have existed in an "earlier form" that was adapted to the present context,[632] and Sweeney also believes that it might be Hezekiah's own work.[633] Nevertheless, critical scholarship can only establish the possibility, not prove the fact.

Thus, the text could stem from the period of Isaiah's prophetic career or from a more optimistic period in the seventh century. It stands in a tradition with texts such as Isa 9:1–6; 25:6–9; 26:11–21; and 29:5–8, emphasizing YHWH's power to save from a state of death. However, in its current position it reinforces Deuteronomistic theology, connecting the Isaianic themes of death and life to the well-known Deuteronomistic themes of repentance and "turning."[634] Hezekiah is spared in much the same way as Ahab was, when he repented of his own sins (1 Kgs 21:27–29). Isaiah's role in Isa 38 is almost identical to that of Elijah in 1 Kgs 21, announcing judgment only to see it mitigated by YHWH. It is also not an accident that the account of Hezekiah's restoration is juxtaposed directly with the story of Sennacherib's death (37:38). Sennacherib is destroyed because of his pride and because he challenged YHWH (rather like the attitude of the pharaoh in Exodus), while Hezekiah lives because of his praise for and faith in YHWH.[635] This confirms one final time YHWH's role as the dealer of death and the giver of life.

---

[630] Ginsberg compares the psalm of Hezekiah to the ninth/eighth-century Melqart Stele and Egyptian stelae dedicated to gods in thanks ("Psalms and Inscriptions of Petition and Acknowledgement...," in *Louis Ginzberg Jubilee Volume*, English Section [New York: American Academy for Jewish Research, 1945], 159–71). Hallo finds comparative material in Sumerian and Akkadian letter-prayers: "The Royal Correspondence of Larsa: I. A Sumerian Prototype for the Prayer of Hezekiah?" in *Kramer Anniversary Volume: Cuneiform Studies in Honor of Samuel Noah Kramer* (ed. B. L. Eichler et al.; AOAT 25; Kevelaer: Butzon & Bercker; Neukirchen-Vluyn: Neukirchener Verlag, 1976), 209–24.

[631] Ginsberg, "Psalms and Inscriptions," 169. The interpretation goes back at least to Hugo Grotius and C. B. Michaelis. On the practice of inscribing psalms, see Patrick D. Miller, "Psalms and Inscriptions," in *Congress Volume: Vienna 1980* (VTSup 32; Leiden: Brill, 1981), 312–14.

[632] Childs, *Isaiah*, 282.

[633] Sweeney, *Isaiah 1–39*, 502.

[634] H. W. Wolff, "The Kerygma of the Deuteronomistic Historical Work," in W. Brueggemann and H. W. Wolff, *The Vitality of Old Testament Traditions* (2nd ed.; Atlanta: John Knox, 1982), 83–100.

[635] See, e.g., Danna Fewell, "Sennacherib's Defeat: Words at War in 2 Kings 18:13–19:37," *JSOT* 34 (1986): 79–90.

Because of its significance as a cap for the Assyrian narratives, I hypothesize that the present arrangement of Isa 38 was created concurrently with the Josianic version of the Deuteronomistic History.[636] It both affirms Hezekiah as a king favored by YHWH, as is commonly observed,[637] and also brings into focus the rhetorical function of the imagery of death and life in earlier passages.

5.2.4.4 Isaiah 37:4, 17: "The living God"

The references in Isa 37 to "the living God" show the redactors' awareness of the contrast that earlier strata of the book make between YHWH's offer of life and the faithless behavior of those who refuse it – behavior that is consistently characterized as death-seeking.

"They said to him, 'Thus says Hezekiah, This day is a day of distress, of rebuke, and of disgrace; children have come to the birth, and there is no strength to bring them forth. It may be that YHWH your God heard the words of the Rabshakeh, whom his master the king of Assyria has sent to mock the living God (אלהים חי), and will rebuke the words that YHWH your God has heard; therefore lift up your prayer for the remnant that is left.' (Isa 37:3–4)

"O YHWH of hosts, God of Israel, who are enthroned above the cherubim, you are God, you alone, of all the kingdoms of the earth; you have made heaven and earth.

Incline your ear, O YHWH, and hear; open your eyes, O YHWH, and see; hear all the words of Sennacherib, which he has sent to mock the living God (אלהים חי)." (Isa 37:16–17)

The formula (אל(הים) חי(ים),[638] "living God," is not an invention of Isaiah or his tradents – the earliest attestation is probably Hos 2:1 (ET 1:10): "it shall be said to [the people], 'Children of the living God (אל חי)' "[639] – and in light of its use in Josh 3:10 the epithet might have great antiquity in a military context. It is partly true to say that calling YHWH "the living God" portrays him as "powerful, filled with vitality, [one who] works his will in the historical realm,"[640] but that is only part of the story. The epithet's use in Isaiah is almost certainly not incidental, in

---

[636] The observation that it could speak also to the postexilic restoration of Judah is accurate; indeed, it could speak to any number of periods in history.

[637] E.g., Wildberger, *Isaiah 28–39*, 466; Sweeney, *Isaiah 1–39*, 497; Clements, *Isaiah 1–39*, 289.

[638] The instances of the phrase אל חי are plausibly early (Hos 2:1, Pss 42:3; 84:3; Josh 3:10), whereas late texts use אלהים חיים (Jer 10:10; 23:36; Dan 6:21, 27). If a consistent typology could be established, then the Isaianic spelling אלהים חי would belong in the middle, thus plausibly in the seventh century. This remains less than certain, however.

[639] It has been theorized that the epithet is based on the oath formula חי אל, but I deem this uncertain, since the only biblical attestation is Job 27:2. See discussion and references in Baruch Halpern, "Sybil, or the Two Nations? Archaism, Kinship, Alienation, and the Elite Redefinition of Traditional Culture in Judah in the 8th–7th Centuries BCE," *The Study of the Ancient Near East in the Twenty-First Century* (eds. J. S. Cooper and G. M. Schwartz; Winona Lake, Ind.: Eisenbrauns, 1996), 327 n. 94.

[640] Wildberger, *Isaiah 28–39*, 402.

that it brings into sharper focus the consistent rhetorical contrast between YHWH as the source of life and other nominally divine powers as leading to death.

The epithet "the living God" frequently appears in literary strata that employ the "rhetoric of death." In Hosea it finds an echo in the promise of national resurrection in Hos 6:1–3 (יְחַיֵּנוּ: 6:2); in Ps 42:3 it is the name of the God who delivers the Psalmist's life (see v. 9: אֵל חָי); in Dan 6:21, 27, it is the living God who preserves Daniel's life in the lion's den and then send his adversaries to their deaths; and in Deut 5:26, the phrase is placed ironically on the lips of the nation to portray them as foolish: they fear that they will die of proximity to the "living God," when in reality that same God is the source of life, and *turning away* from God is death (Deut 30:15–19).[641]

There are specific, subtle markers of the theme of life and death within Isaiah 37. For example, the image of failed childbearing in 37:3 ("children have come to the birth, and there is no strength to bring them forth") resonates with the idea that YHWH is the god who brings about life, and that the people have failed to do so on their own.[642] The Assyrians threatened Judah with death, and some of those threatened sought out Judah's dead for advice and protection; but Isaiah portrays the living God as overcoming both of these groups in order to stake his own claim on his holy city and his people.

But the main context for the assertion of YHWH as "the living God" is the redactional context in which this passage functions: From the standpoint of the text's formation, the real antecedents to the use of "living God" in Isa 37 are *all* of the preceding passages. I have argued above (§ 5.2.1.4) that the account of Sennacherib's siege in Isa 36–37 reflects genuine Neo-Assyrian rhetoric, but it has certainly been recast and reframed by a Deuteronomistic author in a later period. Whether "the living God" is used here as a celebratory phrase in the time of Josiah, or as a promise of comfort at the end of the exile, it is an effort by a tradent who knew much of Isa 1–39 as we know it today to call attention again to the idea that YHWH is the God of life who overcomes death.

---

[641] Jeremiah uses the epithet differently – as part of polemics against idoltary (10:10) and false prophecy (23:36)

[642] The image of God as creator of heaven and earth (אֶרֶץ) in 37:17 both asserts that YHWH is creator of life, and that he is lord of the אֶרֶץ, which could have evoked the underworld for a contemporary audience – as I argued about Isa 7:10–13 (§ 5.2.3.1), claims of YHWH's mastery over the underworld can be understood as an implicit subversion of necromancy: *Why should one invoke the dead when one can invoke their Lord?*

6. Conclusions

This study began with the observation that rhetoric employing imagery of death and life plays a central role in Isa 1–39. It set out to explain how that rhetoric functioned in its ancient Near Eastern context.

6.1 Death in the ancient Near East during the Iron Age II

The opening four chapters laid out the historical, cultural, and religious contexts in which Isaiah and his earliest tradents composed the passages studied later in the book, analyzing the available data that bear on the ways inhabitants of the ancient Near East thought about death during Iron Age II.

Chapter 1 summarized the extensive interaction between the Neo-Assyrian empire and Judah during Isaiah's time. It concluded that although the Assyrians did not practice religious imposition *per se* in Judah, the near-identity of political and religious claims in the ancient Near East would still have caused Judeans to come into contact with the Assyrians' theopolitical rhetoric. In addition to the usual attractions of "elite emulation" of foreign cultures, the rise of Assyrian power in Syria-Palestine also likely brought a crisis of faith in YHWH in many quarters, making other forms of religious belief and practice more tempting.

Chapter 1 went on to analyze Mesopotamian beliefs and practices, investigating the observation of Thorkild Jacobsen that the first millennium in Mesopotamia saw an "increased interest in [the powers of death] and their domain." There is much to support Jacobsen's observation: The *kispu*-rite to care for and propitiate the spirits of dead ancestors attained great popularity under the later Sargonids; the period also seems to have been characterized by a rise in necromantic activity and the production of apotropaic texts against ghosts; and by increasingly detailed mythic portrayals of the underworld. Jacobsen associated this cultural shift with the death-dealing violence of the Neo-Assyrian and Babylonian empires, and that violence, too, had an impact on Israel and Judah, and on Isaiah.

Chapter 2 undertook a comparable study of Egypt. It demonstrated that the diplomatic relations between Egypt and Judah, which are attested in biblical and extrabiblical texts, became closer under the pressure of Neo-Assyrian expansion during the eighth and early seventh centuries. Furthermore, material culture showed significant Egyptian influence in Judean iconography during the same period. This is also the beginning of the same time frame in which Donald B. Redford advised scholars to look for Egyptian influence, because of the "cultural ... economic, and ... spiritual community of interests" among Eastern Mediterranean nations (§ 2.3).

In assessing Egyptian myths and rituals related to death, chapter 2 demonstrated that Egypt under the Twenty-fifth Kushite and Twenty-sixth Saite Dynasties saw a resurgence of cultural production in the funerary arts. Starting with the Napatan rulers, pharaohs looked to the models of the New Kingdom in building more elaborate tombs as part of a classicizing movement. This revival was also apparent in the rise in production of afterlife books. The later periods of Egyptian history also saw necromancy become an even more popular form of divination and supplication of the dead.

In sum, both of Judah's imperial neighbors in the late eighth century were experiencing significant increases in their cultural production surrounding death, which bears witness to a concomitant rise in interest in the subject. This fascination in Isaiah's historical moment helps to explain the prominence of the theme in the book.

Chapters 3 and 4 analyzed the beliefs and practices surrounding death in Syria-Palestine, through an analysis of the textual and archaeological evidence. In accordance with the available data, they focused primarily on Ugarit and Judah, respectively, but also made reference to other Bronze- and Iron-Age city-states in Syria and coastal Palestine.

Chapter 3 concluded that cults of the dead were a common feature of West Semitic religions in the Bronze Age, at least at the royal level. Specifically at Ugarit, it seems clear that dead kings were divinized, in that they received offerings and were thought to have the power to influence events. I also argued that the interpretation of the archaeological findings at Ugarit should not be considered settled; despite the influential and skeptical analysis of Wayne T. Pitard, the tomb architecture still allows for understanding certain features as reflecting mortuary cult usage. In the debate over Ugaritic cults of the dead that has run up to the present moment, I concluded that Gregorio del Olmo Lete's and Nick Wyatt's reconstructions of a more elaborate cult of the dead, including necromantic rites, are more likely than Dennis Pardee's minimalist view, although the latter has brought salutary cautions to the discussion.

Chapter 3 also discussed the significant methodological difficulties with correlating Ugaritic and Israelite religion, which are exacerbated by the scant corpus of Iron Age inscriptions from Palestine. However, it is notable that Ugaritic texts attest a number of distinctive terms – such as *rp'm* for the spirits of the dead, and *mrzḥ* as a cultic-feasting institution – that are found also in the Hebrew Bible. These are only the most prominent indicators that there may have been significant similarity between the Ugaritic and Israelite/Judean religions of the dead.

Chapter 4's analysis of Judean burial and mourning practices and religious ideas about death set the immediate context for Isaiah. It emphasized the complexity of the religious situation, concluding that not only were there competing theologies about the dead, but there were also different types of cults at the popular and elite levels. At a popular level, it seems likely that some long-standing tradition of family ancestor cults prevailed. Foreign influences from Mesopotamia and Egypt probably played a larger role at the elite and royal levels, though indigenous traditions would have formed a receptive matrix there as well. Burial practices were relatively consistent through the eighth and seventh centuries, with elite Judeans favoring family bench tombs. However, the period also saw an increase in wealthy tombs that showed greater individuation.

Regarding the crucial issue of cults of the dead, chapter 4 concluded that ancestor cults are subtly attested in a number of early texts, and that (as Mitchell Dahood thought) the Psalms may even reflect a hope for a divinized afterlife, akin to that expressed in the Hadad inscription. Although ancestor cults are largely obscured in the present form of the biblical texts, they probably coexisted with YHWH's cult in Jerusalem and elsewhere mostly without incident until the eighth century, when a combination of social and religious forces brought them into official disfavor. The Neo-Assyrians' destruction, first of Samaria and then of outlying Judean villages in 701 would have cut off families from their land and tombs – important aspects of traditional ancestor cults. Related to this, Hezekiah's national centralization program and an increased stridency on the part of the prophets regarding the primacy of Yahwistic divination over against other forms of mantic knowledge, notably necromancy, eventually led to the marginalization of ancestor cults.

6.2 The rhetoric of death in the Hebrew Bible

Chapter 4 also analyzed YHWH's interaction with death and its realm as it is described in the Hebrew Bible. While it is true that later texts emphasize YHWH's power over death more clearly, even in early texts there were clear assertions of his power to save from death and the extent of his reach over the underworld. YHWH was not necessarily a deity who kept his distance from the realm of death. In light of long-standing theological traditions of such rhetoric in the ancient Near East, these features were not surprising. Later Judaism and Christianity were distinguished primarily by their systematization of a doctrine of general resurrection.

The Hebrew Bible's employment of the rhetoric of death takes four primary forms:

(1) psalmic laments, in which the speaker uses imagery of death to describe his or her own state;
(2) legal punishment clauses, in which death is held up as a negative outcome;
(3) wisdom dichotomies/"two-path" theology, in which the hearer is exhorted to choose the way of life rather than the way of death; and
(4) prophetic judgment-speeches, which (akin to the legal texts) portray death, often in graphic ways, as the outcome of transgression of the will of God.

The analysis also noted a pessimistic tradition, a minority voice found primarily in Job and certain prophetic texts, that embraces death as a welcome respite from suffering.

6.3 Isaiah's rhetorical employment of death imagery

Chapter 5 compiled and analyzed fourteen passages in which death (and the overcoming of it) play a central role. If the conclusions about the provenance of the *hôy*-oracles as a mourning cry are correct, and one adds those into the tally, then the theme becomes not merely widespread but pervasive. At a minimum, the chapter demonstrated more comprehensively than ever the accuracy of Francis Landy's observation that "[d]eath is inscribed in many ways in the book of Isaiah. ... Death is the unseen, perhaps silent, dialogue partner, towards which all the words of the book are cast."[1]

The book of Isaiah consistently presents dichotomies and alternatives in which the negative or wrong side is portrayed as leading to death – and often to a miserable and lamentable death, at that. The motif of "death and life" merits inclusion in discussions of the book's primary theological themes, alongside such traditional *topoi* as "social justice" and "Royal Zion theology."

Isaiah's use of death imagery falls into a few major categories. The first is threats of unhappy afterlife. Both in 14:4–23, where a deceased Sargon II is taunted and cast out from his tomb, and in 30:27–33, where another (probably Assyrian) king is burned, the author subverts traditional afterlife expectations of Mesopotamian royalty by prescribing the worst possible death and (non-)burial for the king. These are also examples of *ius talionis*, in which the violent tactics of ancient Near Eastern monarchs are turned against them. Isaiah 22:15–19 shows that Isaiah could also curse his own countrymen to an unhappy afterlife. Shebna's wrongdoing, as Isaiah identified it, appears to have been a combination of social, political, and religious transgressions. Embracing styles and beliefs that we

---

[1] Francis Landy, "The Covenant with Death," in *Strange Fire: Reading the Bible after the Holocaust* (ed. Tod Linafelt; Sheffield: Sheffield Academic Press, 2000), 225. Landy's project, analyzing Isaiah in psychological and literary terms, was of course completely different from that undertaken here.

think of as Egyptian, Shebna hoped to rest in solitary peace and to be cared for by the living at a mortuary monument. Here too the expectations of the oracle's object are subverted; Isaiah prophesies that Shebna's hopes will be disappointed and he will be cast out from his elaborate tomb. Finally, the comment of the *rab šaqeh* (Isa 36:12) that the besieged Jerusalemites will eat dung and drink urine like the unhappy dead shows that the passage's author shared in a cultural *koine* in which such fears were widespread. Insofar as these threats may reflect the curses of actual Sargonid succession treaties, then one can see how Isaiah, when he employed similar rhetoric, was responding to the military and cultural threats of foreign empires with similar threats in the name of YHWH.

Isaiah's use of the rhetoric of death also extends to portraying the living as the dead when they reject his exhortations. This imagery takes various forms and responds to different types of wrongdoing. In 5:11–17, it is the debauched and greedy nobility of Jerusalem who are imagined as parading straight into the hungry gullet of Sheol. In 8:16–22, those who seek the dead for counsel instead of YHWH receive more than they bargained for; the advocates of necromancy are portrayed as being like the unhappy dead – hopeless, angry, hungry, and in the dark. The transgressions of the inhabitants of Jerusalem in Isa 29:1–4 are not specified, but they are reduced to whispering from the dust like the dead before YHWH miraculously saves them. Finally, the *hôy*-oracles that appear throughout the book have their roots in a cry of funerary lament and, in the eighth century, were still closely correlated with images and threats of death. They function as the prophets' proleptic lament over their fellow citizens.

Cults of the dead are subverted or condemned in other passages. In 7:10–13, the prophet subtly asserts to Ahaz that all worthwhile divinatory guidance is from YHWH, so there is no profit in seeking a different answer from Sheol. In 19:1–15, the necromancy of the Egyptians is portrayed as being just as futile as that of the Judeans. Egyptian cultic practices are also the subject of 28:1–22, in which the Judean king and nobility seek the protection of Egypt through a pact guaranteed by the national/mother goddess Mut. The covenant seems to have been ratified by participation in rites that are similar to hers, incorporating drunkenness, flowers, and a "strange" foreign language. Isaiah portrays those who seek Mut as helpless babies, borrowing a motif found in native Egyptian iconography and texts. He also takes Mut's underworld aspect and amplifies it so that the covenant with Mut becomes a "covenant with *death*," playing on the phonologically similar Hebrew word. He warns that YHWH will not abide this covenant but will use the Neo-Assyrians to wash it away and purify Judah of its sins.

In general, death and its associated phenomena are always portrayed negatively in Isaiah. There is no hint of death as welcome as in, say, Job 3:20–22; 7:13–19. Death and its manifestations are consistently invoked as the judgment upon the enemies of the prophet.

The rhetoric of death in Isaiah is frequently wrathful; it is unflinching and unequivocal in its condemnation of opposing views. However, the violent rhetoric had its point of origin prior to the prophet; Isaiah's condemnations are most often retaliatory in nature. In particular, they reflect the exceptionally graphic and violent propaganda of the Neo-Assyrian Empire. There is no doubt that Isaiah ben Amoz frequently employed "replacement theology," in which YHWH took on the characteristics of foreign rulers. As this chapter has shown, that tactic is both powerful and potentially dangerous, generating troubling images of God.

The forceful and disturbing nature of Isaiah's imagery should not distract the reader from the art and subtlety of its rhetoric in many places. Among the rhetorical devices the book most frequently employs are *ius talionis*, in which the punishment is a mirror image of the transgression. I have noted this particularly in the passages from Isa 5; 8; 22; 26; 28; and 30. Paronomasia (or *double entendre*) was another of the prophet's favorite devices. The text seems to play with multiple meanings and homophonous words in chs. 22; 29; 30; and in numerous instances in chs. 8 and 28. Finally, Isaiah's use of traditional ancient Near Eastern themes – especially images of the dead, the underworld, and its divinities – should not cause one to overlook the freshness and creativity of the ways in which he dramatized the destruction of a king (ch. 30); the violation of corpses (chs. 14 and 22); the oppression and salvation of a city (ch. 29); or the divine judgment of sinners and apostates (chs. 5; 8; 28). For all the instructive parallels adduced in this study, the ancient Near East knew nothing else quite like these texts. In the way that they view empire from below and subvert the rhetoric of the dominant cultures in a literary way, they supply a rare perspective.

6.4 The offer of life

Despite its emphasis on death, Isa 1–39 does not, finally, revolve around that topic, but rather uses the threat and horror of death to draw stark contrasts with YHWH's offer of life and hope. Uniting the themes just surveyed is the idea of a choice between life and death that confronts the hearer and/or reader. This "two-path" motif probably existed in Israelite and Judean wisdom literature prior to Isaiah's time (§ 4.6.2); it was found also in very ancient wisdom texts and political rhetoric in other nations. It is beyond the scope of this project to determine its ultimate roots, but I reiterate that Isaiah seems to have brought new prominence to the motif and could even have served as a model for the Deuteronomic proclamation, "I set before you life and death" (Deut 30:19).

Death does not have the final word in Isaiah. In the wake of the condemnations and warnings of 8:19–23 and 29:1–4, other passages such as 9:1–6 and 29:5–8 portray YHWH's overcoming of the state of death and his promise of life. Darkness turns to light and nightmares vanish. That power and that promise are developed even more clearly and extensively in 38:9–20; 25:6–8; and 26:11–21, and is alluded to by the epithet "the living God" in 37:4, 17. Hezekiah's psalm extols YHWH as one who saves from death; in 25:6–8 and 26:11–21, YHWH swallows up death, and his dead rise.

The research presented here suggests that warning those who were "seeking death" while presenting YHWH as a god who offered life both was one of the prominent themes of Isaiah ben Amoz's prophecies, and became a major emphasis of one of the book's first redactions, in the time of Josiah.

I have concluded that 38:9–20; 25:6–8; and 26:11–21 do not require a date after the seventh century. Most strikingly, I have reevaluated the usual conclusions about the date of Isa 25:6–8 and 26:11–21, in which YHWH is said to swallow up death and raise the dead. Subtle historical allusions and changes in the use of imagery compared to the oracles of Isaiah ben Amoz suggest that these passages were composed after his time. However, on the basis of their thematic consistency with older ancient Near Eastern texts and their historical and literary features, I have placed their composition in the reign of Josiah. They are consistent with the bright, optimistic, and nationalistic rhetoric of that period. As various parts of the book show, there is little reason to place themes such as YHWH's salvation from death, victory over death, or universal power in the postexilic period (see further below, § 6.5.2).

To step back and survey the matter in the broadest possible terms, the story of Isa 1–39, as we read it today, is of YHWH's victory over death. Death comes in various forms, such as the death-dealing power of the Assyrians and Babylonians and the death-seeking religious behavior of the advocates of necromancy – and YHWH triumphs over all of them.

6.5 Implications

Although the primary focus of this study has been on Isaiah's rhetoric, and it will not be mistaken for either a strictly religio-historical or a redaction-critical inquiry, its findings have broader implications. Further work would of course be required to confirm or rebut these arguments.

6.5.1 "Foreign" influences

The exegetical work in chapter 5 emphasizes how deeply Isaiah and his early tradents were enmeshed in the political events and cultural currents of their times. In general, Isaiah's repeated references to death may have been influenced by the growing (or resurgent) interest in the afterlife in Assyria and Egypt at that time. As I have shown, first-millennium Mesopotamia saw an increased interest in the dead, their powers, and their domain; and the Kushite pharaohs brought to

Egypt a renewed fascination with traditional underworld beliefs that resulted in vigorous new artistic and theological production surrounding underworld and afterlife. All of these influences intermingled in Isaiah's prophecies with long-standing Syro-Palestinian traditions about death and their manifestations in Judean culture, creating a fertile ground for literary and theological creativity.

The word "influence" must not be misunderstood to suggest that Isaiah was a passive recipient. If there is one theme that pervades the exegetical studies of chapter 5, it is that the text almost never presents opposing views "on the flat." Sometimes this is obvious, as when he puts damning words in the mouths of his opponents (8:19–20; 14:13–14; 28:15); but still more often his revisions and subversions are at the level of images, so that it is only in light of a reader's prior knowledge of the underlying traditions that Isaiah's own theological perspective makes sense (e.g., 5:14; 28:20). The subtlety of some of the prophet's formulations reinforces the conviction that not only would Isaiah himself (and his tradents) have been familiar with non-Yahwistic traditions, but so also would a significant portion of his audience have been.

One of the most striking results of this research was the large impact of Egyptian culture on Isaiah. If the reader accepts my conclusions about Isa 19; 22; and 28, in particular, then Isaiah becomes a much more significant locus of genuine Egyptian influence than has been thought heretofore. Those passages demonstrate knowledge of the Egyptians' necromantic rites, their burial practices, and one of their national deities. To those who have followed recent studies on iconography, the cultural and political influence of Egypt in Palestine during the Iron Age II will come as no surprise, since it is quite apparent in the material culture. These advances, however, do not yet seem to have infiltrated the study of Isaiah (or other prophetic books) in a very significant way; there is much room for further work in this area.

The Mesopotamian and Ugaritic comparative data have been far more extensively discussed in previous scholarship. Isaiah's appropriation of Mesopotamian themes is extensive, of course, from its myth of an assault on the high god's throne (Isa 14); to its violent rhetoric (36:12); its terrorizing military tactics (30:27–33); its imagery of the underworld (8:21–22); and its language of lament (38:9–20). As I (and others) have pointed out repeatedly, much of Isa 1–39 is in sharp reaction against Assyrian hegemony. Some will say that Isaiah has become the thing he hates by employing the imagery of his enemies. I would prefer to compare his rhetoric with that of Revelation's rider on the white horse.[2] That is, for the most part Isaiah recognizes that the overthrow of Assyria is no human task, but the task of the divine ruler, the true king of the universe, YHWH.

---

[2] On the rider on the white horse as a symbol of God's imposition of justice, see Miroslav Volf, *Exclusion and Embrace: A Theological Exploration of Identity, Otherness, and Reconciliation* (Nashville: Abingdon, 1996), 275–306.

Assyrian religion and myth were no doubt absorbed by Judeans, but I perceive no trace in Isaiah of their imposition. In contrast, I see numerous references to the *appeal* of foreign religions to Isaiah's Judean contemporaries. The Assyrians played a role in generating that appeal by seeking to humiliate the claims of nationalistic Yahwism, a phenomenon that is reflected both in the authentic oracles of Isaiah (e.g., Isa 10:8–14), and in the (Deuteronomistically redacted) account of Sennacherib's siege in Isa 36–37. The claim that the Assyrian monarch was the ruler of all the earth, and the ability to back up such a claim through military force, would have undermined the authority and appeal of Yahwistic worship in many quarters. From Isaiah, however, it elicited a furious reaction, foretelling the wrath of YHWH upon Assyria (30:27–33). During Isaiah's own time, there were only hints that these prophecies would come true (e.g., the death of Sargon reflected in Isa 14:4–21). When the Assyrian empire did finally crumble during Josiah's reign, the reaction from the book's tradents was a somewhat more joyful, serene, and lordly affirmation of YHWH's sovereignty and unlimited power (Isa 25–26).

Isaiah handles Syro-Palestinian themes as if they were native to him. There is no sense in which the "swallowing Death" (5:14, and its inversion in 25:8) or the Rephaim (14:9, etc.) appear as exotic or foreign entities in the text, even if they have various foreign manifestations as well. They are cultural phenomena that the prophet seems to assume are familiar to his audience. They fare differently in his handling, however. On the one hand, the references to a divinized Death look very much like the Mot that one knows from Ugarit: a demonic, threatening figure without a cult. On the other hand, Isaiah's portrayal of the Rephaim suggests a mild polemic: a phrase such as "Now even you are wasted away like us!" (14:10) would not likely be found on the lips of one who venerated the mighty dead. Thus, it would appear that Isaiah's concern is consistently for the worship of YHWH, that it should not be undermined. The belief that Death is divinized and demonic does nothing to undermine YHWH's cult (indeed it might have strengthened it, since the power of death would have made YHWH all the more necessary for salvation); therefore the prophet embraced it. However, reliance on the dead for mantic knowledge was a direct affront to YHWH's word as embodied in Isaiah's prophetic proclamation, and it became a central point of his message to subvert necromancy.

6.5.2 Death and life in the formation of Isaiah 1–39

While allowing for scribal additions as noted in various places, I have argued that there are two primary layers in the fourteen texts I have covered that relate to death and life in Isa 1–39:

5. (1) a darker layer of prophecies attributable to Isaiah ben Amoz in the late eighth century, in which imagery of death, as retaliation against enemies and

warnings against necromancy and other non-Yahwistic cultic practices, predominates; and

6. (2) a brighter layer, most likely added during Judah's flourishing under Josiah, which emphasizes YHWH's gracious salvation from death.

These two "movements" are not, of course, completely discrete; there are glimmers in the darkness (e.g., 29:5–8) and shadows in the light (e.g., 26:14). And of course, these few texts reflect only part of the long story of the book's formation.[3]

At the level of individual passages, I have argued that a full understanding of certain texts' ancient Near Eastern backgrounds supports compositional unity where it has often not been perceived. The recognition of the significance of the theme of death and life in Isaiah's rhetoric ought to give scholars more incentive to rethink the old assumptions that the salvation pericopae, and especially the references to resurrection, must be late additions. Death and life together were commonly joined in ancient Near Eastern rhetoric – for example, the sufferer who is near death is restored to life; the living are threatened with imminent death; and the audience is offered a choice between life and death – so it would seem most rhetorically effective for a prophet to *both* threaten death *and* hold out life.

Isaiah 28:1–22 is foremost among the individual texts that I have argued are more unified compositions than has usually been thought. The recognition that behind the "covenant with Death" lies a reference to the Egyptian goddess Mut reveals the coherence in the widely disparate imagery of the passage. Similarly, the proposed revisions of translations of terms in Isa 22:15–19 restore the passage's focus to the tomb and thereby obviate the need to propose that v. 19 was an expansion. The argument that the references to necromancy in Isa 19:1–15 may accurately reflect Egyptian religion in the Kushite and Saite periods strengthens the case for the unity of the whole pericope, since the reference to necromancy frames vv. 5–10, which are almost universally thought to be an accurate reflection of the Delta economy. Notably, each of these examples relies to some degree on a knowledge of Egyptian data that has not often been brought to bear.

In other cases, I have demonstrated that the presentation of an alternative to death, or salvation from death, is integral to Isaiah's rhetoric. Just as comparative ancient Near Eastern evidence leads one to expect, Isaiah ben Amoz was not only a prophet of judgment. Having studied the passages that hold out divine promises – especially 9:1–6; 29:5–8; 25:6–8; 26:11–21; and 38:9–20 – and found that the arguments for their lateness have largely been disproved, and that the eighth and seventh centuries offer very plausible historical contexts for all of them,[4] I

---

[3] I again refer the reader who is curious how these passages fit into the larger picture to my entry "Isaiah" in *The Encyclopedia of the Bible* (Oxford: Oxford University Press, forthcoming).

[4] I share J. J. M. Roberts's dissatisfaction with the tendency of some Isaiah scholars to "look

concluded that 29:5–8 originated with Isaiah, insofar as it is integral to the message of vv. 1–8. Although 9:1–6 and 38:9–20 are distinct and separate literary units within their present contexts, I found no particular reasons why they could not also derive from the prophet's own time.

In addition to the eighth-century layer, one can perceive an interest in death and life on the part of seventh-century redactors. Indeed, I find the idea of a "Life and Death Redaction" more illuminating for this layer than the commonly used "Anti-Assyrian Redaction." I have argued that the imagery of 25:6–8 and 26:11–21 seems more at home in the context of the reign of Josiah, a time of great national optimism and flourishing. Juxtaposed with the words of judgment by the book's redactors, these passages amplify the hopeful and salvific aspects of YHWH's rule. These findings fit well with the established hypothesis of a major Josianic redaction of Isaiah put forward by Hermann Barth and others, although it adjusts the contours (and to some extent the nature) of that redaction.

Let the reader understand that there is no theological agenda or imperative behind my emphasis on the unity of certain passages, or my openness to the authenticity of contested texts. The formation of the book of Isaiah, like that of the Bible, was a lengthy and complex process. But in the specific cases at hand, I confess that I have often come away unconvinced from the work of scholars who find these texts fragmentary and late.

6.5.3 Isaiah's role in the history of Judean religion

6.5.3.1 Isaiah's condemnation of religious practices

By far the practice most strongly condemned in the text is necromancy, which seems to have been an indigenous Judean practice. Although Isaiah's use of the Akkadian loanword אטים (19:3, from *eṭemmu*) could imply a knowledge of Mesopotamian ancestor cults, none of the passages surveyed actually attributes necromancy to the Mesopotamians. If anything, necromancy seems to have been advocated as a *response* to the Neo-Assyrian threat (e.g., 8:19–20). It *is* attributed to the *Egyptians* in Isa 19, but searching for the definitive foreign roots of necromancy would be in vain. No doubt its broad cultural currency was part of its allure among Jerusalem's intellectual and economic elites, but there is no way to correlate the references to necromancy in Isa 7 or 8 with any foreign practice. It was perceived as a threat not because it was foreign but because it was in competition with Yahwistic prophecy.

It is likely that the eighth-century prophets, especially Isaiah, were the first to condemn necromancy as inherently anti-Yahwistic (§ 4.4.2.3). It is of course possible that necromancy and cults of the dead were condemned earlier, and that

---

to late contexts for the work of redaction" (J. J. M. Roberts, "Isaiah 2 and the Prophet's Message to the North," *JQR* 75 [1985]: 291).

one simply has no record of it; but the legal texts in which such practices are banned are not likely to predate the eighth century.

There is probably no sharp distinction to be made between the royal and popular ancestor cults; both can be advanced as the "source" for Judean cults of the dead, since there is evidence for both. On the one hand, a royal cult of the dead finds strong cognates in every one of the major cultures surveyed (Mesopotamia, Egypt, Ugarit, Hatti). On the other hand, the idea that the ancestor cult was part of "family religion" apart from central sanctuaries of the national god not only finds archaeological and textual support, it is also logical – cults of the dead are not some elite innovation of a specific historical moment, but rather are of great extent and antiquity within human religious history. The only firm conclusion one can draw is that the condemnation of cults of the dead eventually came from the top of the society, for socioeconomic reasons related to the need to centralize political and religious authority. Although Isaiah surely had his own reasons for his critique that went beyond its pragmatic aspects, a Judean ruler such as Hezekiah would have been quite happy to have a theological rationale for his decision to centralize religious power in YHWH's sanctuary in Jerusalem.

Isaiah's own religious critique also went beyond necromancy and ancestor cults. His condemnation of Shebna's tomb suggests that he was sensitive to the social significance of burial practices. It would seem that, to him, the individuality of Shebna's tomb was a subversion of the familial structure of the traditional Judean afterlife. One should be gathered to one's kin, not rest alone in lordly solitude. Of course, the tomb may also have symbolized to him the unjustly gained wealth of the elite classes, and thus transgressed his sense of social justice as well.

Finally, Isaiah's condemnation of the covenant with Mut in 28:15, 18 strongly suggests that by his time there was a tradition of a covenant between YHWH and the ruling house of Jerusalem, by which the house of David thought to assure divine favor and protection. Without this assumption, the accusation of an illicit covenant loses some of its force. The condemnation of the covenant with Mut is thus part of the prophet's larger emphasis on allegiance and faithfulness to YHWH.

6.5.3.2 Isaiah and resurrection

Since this topic is already covered at some length in my discussions of Isa 25 and 26, I offer only a brief summary here. The ancient Near Eastern precedents for resurrection language – primarily the Syro-Palestinian tradition of feasting with a deity in the afterlife and the Egyptian expectation of bodily restoration in the afterlife – are well known and were literarily attested considerably earlier than any of the Hebrew Bible was written.

There is no doubt that Isaiah shared in the common Israelite belief in

YHWH's power over death and Sheol. However, the texts identified here as originating with Isaiah of Jerusalem, and which hold out the promise of life (primarily 9:1–6 and 29:5–8), do not speak of resurrection in the terms (קוּם, חיה) that later came to represent that belief. Hosea 6:2 is probably the earliest prophetic text that does so. (Because Hosea's language is already prefigured in earlier texts from all over the ancient Near East [§ 4.4.4], there is no reason to doubt its eighth-century provenance on thematic or theological grounds.) Isaiah probably knew of such traditions, but his own imagery of YHWH's salvation from death owes more to wisdom, and perhaps psalmic, traditions.

It was Isaiah's early redactors who first introduced *explicit* imagery of resurrection into the book. Even at that time, the imagery referred not to a belief in individual or universal resurrection but rather to the revivification of YHWH's people as a group. In other words, it referred first of all to a new age of freedom and prosperity for Judah. If the theory of a Josianic edition of the eighth-century prophets is correct,[5] then the oracles of both Isaiah and Hosea would have been collected at that time, a propitious moment for a cross-fertilization of ideas and images. In any case, it was probably only later, after Judah had ceased to be an independent nation, that such passages as Hos 6:2 and Isa 26:19 were understood as assertions about YHWH's resurrection of individual persons, as in Dan 12:2.

A Yahwistic prophet in the eighth century would not have phrased the question, "Can YHWH raise the dead?" The answer was obvious: Of course he could. The question, "*Will* YHWH raise the dead?" was another matter entirely. Because resurrection was primarily a political image in Hosea and Isaiah, the answer depended on whether historical events pointed to optimism or pessimism. Isaiah sometimes warned that there would be "no dawn" (8:20), but he might at another time promise that YHWH would blow the dust off the bodies of the near-dead Jerusalemites (29:4–5). By Josiah's time, it seemed obvious that YHWH had raised up his people (26:19) by freeing them from the murderous oppression of the Neo-Assyrian Empire, as Isaiah had promised.

6.6 Isaiah as Judah's "Book of the Dead"?

The book of Isaiah largely skips over the Babylonian exile. The period is portrayed elsewhere with imagery of death: "He has made me dwell in darkness like those long dead" (Lam 3:6). When Isaiah resumes, the so-called "Book of Com-

---

[5] In addition to the works cited in chapter 5 supporting a Josianic edition of Isaiah, see also Marvin A. Sweeney, *King Josiah of Judah: The Lost Messiah of Israel* (Oxford: Oxford University Press, 2001), 317. W. Schniedewind goes so far as to theorize a *Hezekian* edition of the eighth-century prophets that would have involved "collecting and editing" Isaiah and Micah along with Amos and Hosea (*How the Bible Became a Book: The Textualization of Ancient Israel* [Cambridge/New York: Cambridge University Press, 2004], 89).

fort" takes up again the old tradition of promising salvation from death: "'Do not fear; I will help you. Do not fear, worm of Jacob, dead of[6] Israel! I will help you,' says the Lord." (41:13b–14). Even a passage such as Isa 52:2 – "Shake yourself from the dust, rise up (קוּמִי), O captive Jerusalem!" – appears, in light of what has gone before, to be an image of the city's restoration as raising the dead.

Furthermore, Trito-Isaiah's condemnations of the people draw heavily on the earlier comparisons of transgressors to the dead. This is most clear in 59:10, where the prophet confesses on behalf of the people, "we stumble at noon as in the twilight, among the vigorous as though we were dead." And when the post-exilic prophet accuses the mockers, saying, "you open your mouth wide" (57:4), it is hard not to hear the echo of Sheol in 5:14 (both verses use רחב and פה).

In fact, there are likely numerous references to cult of the dead activities in Trito-Isaiah. Those who are described in Isa 65:3 as "provoking [YHWH] to [his] face continually" are specifically charged with "sitting in tombs and spending the night among rocks." Similar practices are probably in view in ch. 57, which refers to both child sacrifice (v. 5) and Molek (v. 9); particularly if the difficult word חלקי in v. 6 is related to the dead ("Your portion is with the *perished* (?) of the wadi…"), the passage is clearly condemning death cults.[7] Francesca Stavrakopoulou has further argued that the gardens condemned in Isa 65:3–5, 66:17 and 1:29–30 were mortuary gardens and thus also manifestations of cults of the dead.[8] And of course, the book ends with the unforgettable image of "the dead bodies of the people who have rebelled against [YHWH]; for their worm shall not die, their fire shall not be quenched, and they shall be an abhorrence to all flesh." This nascent image of hell is the apotheosis of the "aversion therapy" technique that was pioneered centuries earlier by Isaiah himself. The precise significance of many of these later instances of the tradition are contested; they deserve and have generated fairly extensive scholarship, which cannot be summarized here. It is clear enough that cults of the dead continued to be a major preoccupation in the postexilic period.[9]

---

[6] cf. 1QIsa[a]: מיתי. The word for "worm" used here (תועלה) is the same as that used in 66:24 ("their worm shall not die"), and apparently refers to the soul in both places.

[7] W. H. Irwin, "Smooth Stones of the Wady: Isaiah 57:6," *CBQ* 29 (1967): 31–40; T. J. Lewis, "Death Cult Imagery in Isaiah 57," *HAR* 11 (1987): 267–84; Lewis, *Cults of the Dead*, 143–58; Charles A. Kennedy, "Isaiah 57:5–6: Tombs in the Rocks," *BASOR* 275 (1989): 47–52; Susan Ackerman, *Under Every Green Tree: Popular Religion in Sixth-Century Judah* (HSM 46; Atlanta, Ga.: Scholars Press, 1992), 143–52. I would disagree with Ackerman that "the predominant image of Isa 57:3–13 is sexual" (152).

[8] Francesca Stavrakopoulou, "Exploring the Garden of Uzza: Death, Burial and Ideologies of Kingship," *Biblica* 87 (2006): 1–21. Cf. Ackerman, *Under Every Green Tree*, 165–212.

[9] Letter of Jeremiah 27: "Gifts are placed before [idols] just as before the dead"; Sirach 30:18: "Good things poured out upon a mouth that is closed are like offerings of food placed upon a grave"; Tobit 4:17: "Place your bread on the grave of the righteous, but give none to sinners." Note also Baruch 3:10–11: "Why is it, O Israel, why is it that you are in the land of your enemies, that you are growing old in a foreign country, that you are defiled with the dead, that you are counted among those in Hades?" Cf. 2:17.

At some point, the list of texts in Isaiah that relate to the theme of death and life grows to a point that it becomes arguably *the* dominant theme of the book, but to argue that Isaiah as a whole amounts to a Judean "Book of the Dead"[10] would be a project for another day.

---

[10] I of course mean this only playfully; as a whole, completed composition the book of Isaiah has practically nothing generic in common with the Egyptian books of the dead. I should probably thank (or blame) Massimo Baldacci for giving me the idea with his *Il Libro dei morti dell'antica Ugarit: Le più antiche testimonianze sull'Aldilà prima della Bibbia* (Casale Monferrato: Edizioni Piemme, 1998).

Bibliography

Abercrombie, J. R. "Palestinian Burial Practices from 1200 to 600 BCE." Ph.D. diss., University of Pennsylvania, 1979.
Ackerman, Susan. *Under Every Green Tree: Popular Religion in Sixth-Century Judah*. HSM 46; Atlanta, Ga.: Scholars Press, 1992.
Adams, Christina. "Shades of Meaning: The Significance of Manifestations of the Dead as Evidenced in Texts from the Old Kingdom to the Coptic Period." Pages 1–20 in *Current Research in Egyptology 2006: Proceedings of the Seventh Annual Symposium, University of Oxford, April 2006*. Edited by Maria Cannata. Oxford: Oxbow, 2007.
Aitken, K. T. "Hearing and Seeing: Metamorphoses of a Motif in Isaiah 1–39." Pages 12–41 in *Among the Prophets: Language, Image and Structure in the Prophetic Writings*. Edited by P. R. Davies and D. J. A. Clines. Sheffield: JSOT Press, 1993.
Akkermans, Peter M. M. G., and Glenn M. Schwartz. *The Archaeology of Syria: From Complex Hunter-Gatherers to Early Urban Societies (ca. 16,000–300 BC)*. Cambridge: Cambridge University Press, 2003.
al-Rawi, F. N. "Two Old Akkadian Letters Concerning the Offices of *kala'um* and *nârum*." *ZA* 82 (1992): 180–85.
Albert, Jean-Pierre. "Sacrifices humains et autres mises à mort rituelles: Une introduction." Pages 10–19 in *Le Sacrifice humain en Égypte ancienne et ailleurs*. Edited by Jean-Pierre Albert and Béatrix Midant-Reynes. Paris: Soleb, 2005.
Albertz, Rainer. *A History of Israelite Religion in the Old Testament Period*. Translated by J. Bowden. 2 vols. Louisville, Ky.: Westminster John Knox, 1994.
Albright, W. F. *Archaeology and the Religion of Israel*. 5th ed. Garden City, N.Y.: Doubleday, 1969.
– "The Babylonian Temple-Tower and the Altar of Burnt-Offering." *JBL* 39 (1920): 137–42.
– "The High Place in Ancient Palestine." Pages 242–58 in *Volume du Congrès: Strasbourg 1956*. VTSup 4. Leiden: Brill, 1957.
– "Mesopotamian Elements in Canaanite Eschatology." Pages 143–54 in *Oriental Studies (Paul Haupt Anniversary Volume)*. Baltimore: Johns Hopkins Press; Leipzig: Hinrichs, 1926.
– "The 'Natural Force' of Moses in the Light of Ugaritic." *BASOR* 94 (1944): 32–35.
– *The Vocalization of the Egyptian Syllabic Orthography*. New Haven: American Oriental Society, 1934.
– *Yahweh and the Gods of Canaan: A Historical Analysis of Two Contrasting Faiths*. Garden City, NY: Doubleday, 1968.
Alkier, Stefan. "Die Bibel im Dialog der Schriften und das Problem der Verstockung in Mk 4: Intertextualität im Rahmen einer kategorialen Semiotik biblischer Texte." Pages 1–22 in *Die Bibel im Dialog der Schriften: Konzepte Intertextueller Bibellektüre*. Tübingen: Francke, 2005.

Allen, James P. *The Ancient Egyptian Pyramid Texts*. Society of Biblical Literature Writings from the Ancient World 23. Atlanta: Society of Biblical Literature, 2005.
Allen, Thomas George, ed. *The Egyptian Book of the Dead: Documents in the Oriental Institute Museum at the University of Chicago*. Chicago: University of Chicago Press, 1960.
Alster, Bendt, ed. *Death in Mesopotamia: Papers Read at the XXVIe Rencontre Assyriologique Internationale*. Mesopotamia 8. Copenhagen: Akademisk Forlag, 1980.
Alter, Robert. *The David Story: A Translation with Commentary of 1 and 2 Samuel*. New York: W. W. Norton, 1999.
Amadasi Guzzo, M.G. "Une Empreinte de sceau de Tell Afis." *Orientalia* 70 (2003): 318–24.
Andersen, Francis I. Review of Mitchell J. Dahood, *Psalms* (Anchor Bible), *JBL* 88 (1969): 208–10.
Andersen, Francis I., and David Noel Freedman. *Amos: A New Translation with Introduction and Commentary*. Anchor Bible 24A. Garden City, N.Y.: Doubleday, 1989.
– *Hosea: A New Translation with Introduction and Commentary*. Anchor Bible 24. Garden City, N.Y.: 1980.
Anderson, Gary A. *A Time to Mourn, a Time to Dance: The Expression of Grief and Joy in Israelite Religion*. University Park, Pa.: Pennsylvania State University Press, 1991.
Andrae, Walter. *Stelenreihen in Aššur*. Leipzig: German Orient Society, 1913.
– *Das Wiedererstandene Assur*. Sendschrift der Deutschen Orientgesellschaft. Leipzig: Hinrichs, 1938.
Andrews, Carol A. R. "Amulets." Pages 75–82 in vol. 1 of *The Oxford Encyclopedia of Ancient Egypt*. Oxford: Oxford University Press, 2001.
– *Amulets of Ancient Egypt*. Austin, Tex.: University of Texas, 1994.
Archi, Alfonso. "Cult of Ancestors and Tutelary God at Ebla." Pages 103–11 in *Fucus: A Semitic/Afrasian Gathering in Remembrance of Albert Ehrman*. Edited by Yoël L. Arbeitman. Amsterdam: John Benjamins, 1988.
Arnaud, Daniel. "Prolégomènes à la rédaction d'une histoire d'Ougarit II: Les bordereaux des rois divinizés." *Studi Miceni ed Egeo-Anatolici* 41 (1998): 153–73.
– *Recherches au pays d'Aštata: Emar VI.3*. Paris: Éditions Recherche sur les Civilisations, 1986.
Arnold, Bill T. "Necromancy and Cleromancy in 1 and 2 Samuel." *CBQ* 66 (2004): 199–213.
– "Soul-Searching Questions about 1 Samuel 28." Pages 75–83 in *What about the Soul? Neuroscience and Christian Anthropology*. Edited by Joel B. Green. Nashville: Abingdon, 2004.
– and Brent A. Strawn, "$b^{e}y\bar{a}h$ $š^{e}mô$ in Psalm 68,5: A Hebrew Gloss on an Ugaritic Epithet?" *ZAW* 115 (2003): 428–32.
Asen, Bernhard. "The Garlands of Ephraim: Isaiah 28, 1–6 and the Marzeaḥ." *JSOT* 71 (1996): 71–87.
Ash, Paul S. *David, Solomon and Egypt: A Reassessment*. JSOTSup 297. Sheffield: Sheffield Academic Press, 1999.
Assmann, Jan. *Death and Salvation in Ancient Egypt*. Translated by David Lorton. Ithaca, N.Y.: Cornell University Press, 2005.
– "Resurrection in Ancient Egypt." Pages 124–35 in *Resurrection: Theological and Scientific Assessments*. Edited by T. Peters et al. Grand Rapids: Eerdmans, 2002.
– "Death and Initiation in the Funerary Religion of Ancient Egypt." Pages 135–59 in

Religion and Philosophy in Ancient Egypt. Edited by James P. Allen et al. Yale Egyptological Studies 3. New Haven, Conn.: Yale University, 1989.
Aster, Shawn Zelig. "The Image of Assyria in Isaiah 2:5–22: The Campaign Motif Revisited." *JAOS* 127 (2007): 249–78.
– "Isaiah 2:2–4 and Micah 4:1–5: The Vision of the End of Days as a Reaction to Assyrian Power." Paper delivered at the Annual Meeting of the Society of Biblical Literature, San Diego, 2007.
Astour, Michael C. "The Nether World and Its Denizens at Ugarit." Pages 227–38 in *Death in Mesopotamia: Papers Read at the XXVIe Rencontre Assyriologique Internationale*. Edited by Bendt Alster. Mesopotamia 8. Copenhagen: Akademisk Forlag, 1980.
Aubet, María Eugenia. "The Phoenician Cemetery of Tyre," *NEA* 73 (2010): 144–55.
Auret, A. "A Different Background for Isaiah 22:15–25 Presents an Alternative Paradigm: Disposing of Political and Religious Opposition?" *Old Testament Essays* 6 (1993): 46–56.
Auvray, Paul. *Isaïe 1–39*. Paris: J. Gabalda, 1972.
Avigad, N. "The Epitaph of a Royal Steward from Siloam Village." *IEJ* 8 (1953): 137–52.
Bahrani, Zainab. *The Graven Image: Representation in Babylonia and Assyria*. Archaeology, Culture, and Society. Philadelphia: University of Pennsylvania Press, 2003.
Barton, George Aaron. "Soul (Semitic and Egyptian)." Pages 749–753 in vol. 11 of *Encyclopedia of Religion*. Edited by James Hastings and John A. Selbie. 13 vols. Edinburgh: T&T Clark, 1908.
Baker, Heather. "Neo-Babylonian Burials Revisited." Pages 209–20 in *The Archaeology of Death in the Ancient Near East*. Edited by Stuart Campbell and Anthony Green. Oxbow Monographs 51. Oxford: Oxbow Books, 1995.
Bakhtin, Mikhail. *Rabelais and His World*. Translated by Helene Iswolsky. Cambridge, Mass.: MIT Press, 1968.
Baldacci, Massimo. *Il Libro dei morti dell'antica Ugarit: Le più antiche testimonianze sull'Aldilà prima della Bibbia*. Casale Monferrato: Edizioni Piemme, 1998.
Baldwin, Joyce G. *1 and 2 Samuel: An Introduction and Commentary*. Leicester: InterVarsity, 1988.
Barkay, Gabriel. "The Iron Age II–III." Pages 302–73 in *The Archaeology of Ancient Israel*. Edited by Amnon Ben-Tor. New Haven: Yale University Press, 1992.
– "The Cemeteries of Jerusalem in the Days of the First Temple Period." Pages 102–123 in *Jerusalem in the Days of the First Temple*. Edited by D. Amit and R. Goren. Jerusalem, 1990. (Hebrew)
Barré, Michael L. *The Lord Has Saved Me: A Study of the Psalm of Hezekiah (Isaiah 38:9–20)*. CBQMS 39. Washington, D.C.: Catholic Biblical Association of America, 2005.
Barrick, W. Boyd. "The Funerary Character of 'High Places' in Ancient Palestine: A Reassessment." *VT* 25 (1975): 265–95.
– *The King and the Cemeteries: Toward a New Understanding of Josiah's Reform*. Boston: Brill, 2001.
Barstad, Hans. "*Sic Dicit Dominus*: Mari Prophetic Texts and the Hebrew Bible." Pages 21–52 in *Essays on Ancient Israel in Its Near Eastern Context: A Tribute to Nadav Naaman*. Edited by Yairah Amit, Ehud Ben Zvi, Israel Finkelstein, and Oded Lipschits. Winona Lake, Ind.: Eisenbrauns, 2006.
– "What Prophets Do. Reflections on Past Reality in the Book of Jeremiah," *Prophecy in the Book of Jeremiah*. Edited by H. M. Barstad and R. G. Kratz. BZAW 388. Berlin: Walter de Gruyter, 2009.

Barth, Christoph. *Die Errettung vom Tode in den individuellen Klage- und Dankliedern des Alten Testaments*. Zollikon: Evangelischer Verlag, 1947.
Barth, Hermann. *Die Jesaja-Worte in der Josiazeit: Israel und Assur als Thema einer Produktiven Neuinterpretation der Jesajaüberlieferung*. WMANT 48. Neukirchen-Vluyn: Neukirchener Verlag, 1977.
Bates, Robert D. "Assyria and Rebellion in the Annals of Sennacherib: An Analysis of Sennacherib's Treatment of Hezekiah." *Near East Archaeological Society Bulletin* 44 (1999): 39–61.
Batto, Bernard F. *Slaying the Dragon: Mythmaking in the Biblical Tradition*. Louisville, Ky.: Westminster John Knox, 1992.
Baumgartner, W. "Miszelle zur Etymologie von 'Sche'ol.'" *TZ* 2 (1946): 233–35.
Bayliss, Miranda. "The Cult of Dead Kin in Assyria and Babylonia." *Iraq* 35 (1973): 115–25.
Becking, Bob. "Assyrian Evidence for Iconic Polytheism in Ancient Israel." Pages 157–71 in *The Image and the Book: Iconic Cults, Aniconism, and the Rise of Book Religion in Israel and the Ancient Near East*. Edited by Karel van der Toorn. Contributions to Biblical Exegesis and Theology 21. Leuven: Peeters, 1997.
— *The Fall of Samaria: An Historical and Archaeological Study*. Studies in the History of the Ancient Near East 2. Leiden/New York: Brill, 1992.
Beegle, Dewey. "Proper Names in the New Isaiah Scroll." *BASOR* 123 (1951): 26–30.
Bénédite, Georges. *Le temple de Philai*. Mémoires publiés par les Membres de la Mission Archéologique Française au Caire 13. Paris: Ernest Leroux, 1893.
Benicho-Safar, Hélène. *Les Tombes Puniques de Carthage: Topographie, structures, inscriptions et rites funéraires*. Etudes d'antiquités africaines. Paris: Editions du centre national de la recherche scientifique, 1982.
Ben Zvi, Ehud. "Who Wrote the Speech of Rabshakeh and When?" *JBL* 109 (1990): 79–92.
Berlandini, Jocelyne. "La Mout ḥnt-pr-Ptḥ sur un fragment memphite de Chabaka." *Bulletin de la Société d'Égyptologie de Genève* 9–10 (1984–85): 31–40.
Berlejung, Angelika. "Tod und Leben nach den Vorstellungen der Israeliten: Ein ausgewählter Aspekt zu einer Metapher im Spannungsfeld von Leben und Tod." Pages 465–502 in *Biblische Weltbild und seine altorientalischen Kontexte*. Edited by Bernd Janowski and Beate Ego. FAT 32. Tübingen: Mohr Siebeck, 2001.
Bernauer, James, S.J. "Foreword" to *Religion and Culture: Michel Foucault*. New York: Routledge, 1999.
Betz, Hans Dieter. *The Greek Magical Papyri in Translation, Including the Demotic Spells*. 2nd ed. Chicago: University of Chicago Press, 1996.
Beuken, Willem A. M. "Isaiah 30: A Prophetic Oracle Transmitted in Two Successive Paradigms." Pages 369–97 in *Writing and Reading the Scroll of Isaiah: Studies of an Interpretive Tradition*. Edited by Craig C. Boyles and Craig A. Evans. VTSup 70. Leiden/New York: Brill, 1997.
Bietak, Manfred. "Temple or 'Bêt Marzeaḥ'?" Pages 155–68 in *Symbiosis, Symbolism and Power of the Past: Canaan, Ancient Israel, and Their Neighbors from the Late Bronze Age through Roman Palaestina*. Edited by William G. Dever and Seymour Gitin. Winona Lake, Ind.: Eisenbrauns, 2003.
Biran, Avraham and Ram Gophna. "An Iron Age Burial Cave at Tel Ḥalif." *IEJ* 20 (1970): 151–169.
Bisson de la Roque, M. Fernand. "Complement de la stele d'Amenemhêt, fils d PN, Époux de Kyky." *BIFAO* 25 (1925): 47–49.

Blair, Judit M. *De-Demonizing the Old Testament: An Investigation of Azazel, Lilith, Deber, Qeteb and Reshef in the Hebrew Bible.* FAT II/37. Tübingen: Mohr Siebeck, 2009.
Blakely, Jeffrey A., and James W. Hardin. "Southwestern Judah in the Late Eighth Century B.C.E." *BASOR* 326 (2002): 11–64.
Bleibtreu, Erika. "Grisly Assyrian Record of Torture and Death." *BAR* 17 (1991): 52–61 75.
Blenkinsopp, Joseph. "Deuteronomy and the Politics of Post-Mortem Existence." *VT* 45 (1995): 1–16.
- *Isaiah 1–39: A New Translation with Introduction and Commentary.* AB 19. New York: Doubleday, 2000.
- *Isaiah 40–55: A New Translation with Introduction and Commentary.* AB 19A. New York: Doubleday, 2000.
- *Isaiah 56–66: A New Translation with Introduction and Commentary.* AB 19B. New York: Doubleday, 2003.
- "Judah's Covenant with Death (Isaiah XXVIII 14–22)." *VT* 50 (2000): 472–83.
- "Saul and the Mistress of the Spirits (1 Samuel 28.3–25)." Pages 49–62 in *Sense and Sensitivity*. Sheffield: Sheffield Academic Press, 2002.
Bloch-Smith, Elizabeth M. "The Cult of the Dead in Judah: Interpreting the Material Remains." *JBL* 111 (1992): 213–24.
- "Death in the Life of Israel." Pages 139–44 in *Sacred Time, Sacred Place: Archaeology and the Religion of Israel*. Edited by Barry M. Gittlen. Winona Lake, Ind.: Eisenbrauns, 2002.
- "Israelite Ethnicity in Iron I: Archaeology Preserves What Is Remembered and What Is Forgotten in Israel's History." *JBL* 122 (2003): 401–25.
- *Judahite Burial Practices and Beliefs about the Dead.* JSOTSup 123. Sheffield: JSOT Press, 1992.
- "Life in Judah from the Perspective of the Dead." *Near Eastern Archaeology* 65 (2002): 120–30.
- "Will the Real Massebot Please Stand Up: Cases of Real and Mistakenly Identified Standing Stones in Ancient Israel." Pages 64–79 in *Text, Artifact, Image: Revealing Ancient Israelite Religion.* Edited by Gary M. Beckman and Theodore J. Lewis. Brown Judaic Studies 346. Providence: Brown Judaic Studies, 2006.
Boccaccini, G. "I termini contrari come espressioni della totalita in Ebraico." *Biblica* 33 (1952): 173–90.
Boer, P. A. H. de. "Notes on the Text and Meaning of Isaiah XXXVIII, 9–20." *OTS* 9 (1951): 170–86.
Bolshrov, Audrey O. "Mut or Not? On the Meaning of a Vulture Sign on the Hermitage Statue of Amenemhat III." Pages 23–31 in *Servant of Mut: Studies in Honor of Richard A. Fazzini*. Edited by Sue H. D'Auria. Leiden: Brill, 2008.
Bonatz, Dominik. *Das syro-hethitische Grabdenkmal: Untersuchungen zur Entstehung einer neuen Bildgattung in der Eisenzeit im nordsyrisch-südostanatolischen Raum.* Mainz: von Zabern, 2000.
- "Syro-Hittite Funerary Monuments: A Phenomenon of Tradition or Innovation?" Pages 189–210 in *Essays on Syria in the Iron Age*. Edited by Guy Bunnens. Louvain: Peeters, 2000.
Bordreuil, Pierrea, and Dennis Pardee. "Textes ougaritiques oubliés et transfugés." *Semitica* 41–42 (1993): 23–58.
Borg, Barbara E. "The Dead as a Guest at Table? Continuity and Change in the Egyptian Cult of the Dead." Pages 26–32 in *Portraits and Masks: Burial Customs in Roman Egypt.* Edited by Morris L. Bierbrier. London: Published for the Trustees of the British Museum by British Museum Press, 1997.

Borger, Riekele. *Beiträge zum Inschriftenwerk Aššurbanipals: Die Prismenklassen A, B, C = K, D, E, F, G, H, J und T sowie andere Inschriften*. Wiesbaden: Harrassowitz, 1996.
Borghouts, J. F. *Ancient Egyptian Magical Texts*. Nisaba 9. Leiden: Brill, 1978.
Borowski, Oded. *Daily Life in Biblical Israel*. Atlanta: Society of Biblical Literature, 2003.
– "Hezekiah's Reforms and the Revolt against Assyria." *BA* 58 (1995): 148–55.
Bottéro, Jean. "La création de l'homme et sa nature dans le poeme d'Atrahasis." Pages 24–32 in *Societies and Languages of the Ancient Near East: Studies in Honour of I. M. Diakonoff*. Warminster: Aris & Phillips, 1982.
– "Les inscriptions cuneiforms funéraires." Pages 373–406 in *La Mort, les morts dans les sociétés anciennes*. Edited by G. Gnoli and J. P. Vernant. Cambridge/New York: Cambridge University Press, 1982.
– "Les morts et l'au-delà deans les rituels en accadien contre l'action des 'revenants.'" *ZA* 73 (1983): 153–203.
– "La mythologie de la mort en Mesopotamie ancienne." Pages 25–52 in *Death in Mesopotamia: Papers Read at the XXVIe Rencontre Assyriologique Internationale*. Edited by Bendt Alster. Mesopotamia 8. Copenhagen: Akademisk Forlag, 1980.
– *Religion in Ancient Mesopotamia*. Chicago: University of Chicago Press, 2001.
Walter Brueggemann, "Amos iv 4–13 and Israel's Covenant Worship," *VT* 15 (1965): 1–15.
Brichto, Herbert Chanan. "Kin, Cult, Land and Afterlife – A Biblical Complex." *HUCA* 44 (1973): 1–54.
Bright, John. *A History of Israel*. 4th ed. Louisville, Ky.: Westminster John Knox, 2000.
Brill's New Pauly: Encyclopedia of the Ancient World: Antiquity. Edited by Hubert Cancik and Helmuth Schneider. Leiden/Boston: Brill, 2002–7.
Brinkman, John A. "Unfolding the Drama of the Assyrian Empire." Pages 1–16 in *Assyria 1995: Proceedings of the 10th Anniversary Symposium of the New-Assyrian Text Corpus Project, Helsinki, September 7–11, 1995*. Edited by S. Parpola and R. M. Whiting. Helsinki: Neo-Assyrian Text Corpus Project, 1997.
Brovarski, Edward. "An Allegory of Death." *JEA* 63 (1977): 178.
Brown, Brian. "Kingship and Ancestral Cult in the Northwest Palace at Nimrud." *JANER* 10 (2010): 1–53.
Brown, M. L. "רפא." *TDOT* 13:593–602.
Brown, William P. *Seeing the Psalms: A Theology of Metaphor*. Louisville: Westminster John Knox, 2002.
– "An Update in the Search of Israel's History." Appendix in John Bright, *A History of Israel*. 4th ed. Louisville, Ky.: Westminster John Knox, 2000.
Brunsch, W. "Untersuchungen zu den griechischen Wiedergaben ägyptischer Personennamen." *Enchoria* 8 (1978): 123–28.
Bryan, Betsy M. "Making for Mut a Porch of Drunkenness: A Field Report on a Decade of Excavation at the Mut Temple." Lecture delivered at the Bowers Museum, Santa Ana, California, Dec. 11, 2010.
– "A Newly Discovered Statue of a Queen from the Reign of Amenhotep III." Pages 32–43 in *Servant of Mut: Studies in Honor of Richard A. Fazzini*. Edited by Sue H. D'Auria. Boston: Brill, 2008.
– "The Statue Program for the Mortuary Temple of Amenhotep III." Pages 57–81 in *The Temple in Ancient Egypt: New Discoveries and Recent Research*. London: British Museum Press, 1997.
– "The Temple of Mut: New Evidence on Hatshepsut's Building Activity." Pages 181–83 in *Hatshepsut: From Queen to Pharaoh*. New York: Metropolitan Museum of Art, 2005.

Budde, Karl. "Das hebräische Klagelied." *ZAW* 2 (1882): 1–52.
Budge, E. A. Wallis. *The Egyptian Heaven and Hell.* London: Kegan, Paul, Trench, Trübner, 1905.
Budge, E. A. Wallis, and L. W. King, *The Annals of the Kings of Assyria.* London: British Museum, 1902.
Budin, Stephanie Lynn. *Images of Woman and Child from the Bronze Age: Reconsidering Fertility, Maternity, and Gender in the Ancient World.* New York: Cambridge University Press, 2011.
Burkert, Walter. *The Orientalizing Revolution: Near Eastern Influence on Greek Culture in the Early Archaic Age.* Cambridge, Mass.: Harvard University Press, 1992.
Burkes, Shannon. *Death in Qohelet and Egyptian Biographies of the Late Period.* Society of Biblical Literature Dissertation Series 170. Atlanta: Society of Biblical Literature, 1999.
Burns, John Barclay. "Some Conceptions of the Afterlife in Ancient Egyptian Thought." *The Philosophical Journal, Glasgow* 9 (1972), 140–149.
Calderone, P. J. "The Rivers of 'Maṣor.'" *Biblica* 42 (1961): 423–32.
– "Supplemental Note on ḥdl-II." *CBQ* 24 (1962): 412–19.
Capart, Jean, et al. "New Light on the Ramesside Tomb-Robberies." *JEA* 22 (1936): 169–193.
Caplice, F. *Grundlagen der Ägyptische-Semitischen Vortvergleichung.* Vienna, 1936.
Caquot, André. "Anges et demons en Israël." Pages 113–52 in *Génies, anges et démons.* Sources orientales 8. Paris: Seuil, 1971.
– "Les Rephaim Ougaritiques." *Syria* 37 (1960): 72–93.
– *Textes Ougaritiques.* Vol. 2. Paris: Cerf, 1989.
Carroll, R. P. "Translation and Attribution in Isaiah 8.19f." *The Bible Translator* 31 (1980): 126–34.
Casanowicz, Immanuel M. "Paronomasia in the Old Testament." *JBL* 12 (1893): 105–67.
Cassin, Elena. "Le mort: Valeur et représentation en Mésopotamie Ancienne." Pages 355–72 in *La Mort, les Morts dans les Sociétés Anciennes.* Cambridge/New York: Cambridge University Press, 1982.
Cheyne, T. K. *The Prophecies of Isaiah: A New Translation with Commentary and Appendices.* 3rd ed. New York: Thomas Whitaker, 1884.
Childs, Brevard S. "Death and Dying in Old Testament Theology." Pages 89–91 in *Love & Death in the Ancient Near East: Essays in Honor of Marvin H. Pope.* Edited by J. H. Marks and R. M. Good. Guilford, Conn.: Four Quarters, 1987.
– *Isaiah.* OTL. Louisville, Ky.: Westminster John Knox, 2001.
– *Isaiah and the Assyrian Crisis.* SBT, 2nd series, 3. Naperville, Ill.: Alec R. Allenson, 1967.
– *Myth and Reality in the Old Testament.* 2nd ed. London: SCM, 1962.
Clements, R. E. "The Form and Character of Prophetic Woe Oracles." *Semitics* 8 (1982): 17–29.
– *Isaiah 1–39.* Grand Rapids: Eerdmans, 1980.
Clifford, Richard J. "The Use of Hôy in the Prophets." *CBQ* 28 (1966): 458–64.
– "The Prophecies of Isaiah and the Fall of Jerusalem." Pages 148–63 in *Prophecy in the Hebrew Bible: Selected Studies from Vetus Testamentum.* Leiden: Brill, 2000.
Cobb, William Henry. "The Ode in Isaiah XIV." *JBL* 15 (1896): 18–35.
Cogan, Mordechai [Morton]. "A Lamashtu Plaque from the Judaean Shephelah," *IEJ* 45 (1995): 155–61.
– *Imperialism and Religion: Assyria, Judah, and Israel in the Eighth and Seventh Centuries B.C.E.* SBL Monograph Series 19. Missoula, Mont.: Scholars Press, 1974.

- "Judah under Assyrian Hegemony: A Re-examination of *Imperialism and Religion*." *JBL* 112 (1993): 403–14.
- "The Other Egypt: A Welcome Asylum." Pages 65–70 in *Texts, Temples, and Traditions: A Tribute to Menahem Haran*. Edited by M. V. Fox et al. Winona Lake, Ind.: Eisenbrauns, 1996.

Cogan, Mordechai, and Hayim Tadmor. *II Kings: A New Translation with Introduction and Commentary*. Anchor Bible 11. Garden City, N.Y.: Doubleday, 1988.

Cohen, Andrew C. *Death Rituals, Ideology, and the Development of Early Mesopotamian Kingship: Toward a New Understanding of Iraq's Royal Cementery of Ur*. Studies in Ancient Magic and Divination 7. Leiden/Boston: Brill, 2005.

Cohen, Chaim. "Neo-Assyrian Elements in the Speech of the Rab-Šāqê." Pages 32–48 in *Israel Oriental Studies 9*. Tel Aviv: Tel Aviv University Press, 1979.

Cole, S. W. *Nippur in Late Assyrian Times (c. 755–512 BC)*. SAAS 4. Helsinki: Neo-Assyrian Text Corpus Project, 1996.

Collard, C., M. J. Cropp, and K. H. Lee. *Euripides: Selected Fragmentary Plays*. Vol. 1. Warminster: Aris & Phillips, 1995.

Collins, John J. *Daniel*. Hermeneia; Minneapolis: Fortress, 1993.

- "Death, the Afterlife and Other Last Things: Israel." Pages 480–83 in *Religions of the Ancient World: A Guide*. Edited by Sarah Iles Johnston. Cambridge, Mass.: Belknap Press of Harvard University Press, 2004.

Coogan, M. D., ed. *Stories from Ancient Canaan*. Philadelphia: Westminster, 1978.

Cook, Stephen L. "Funerary Practices and Afterlife Expectations in Ancient Israel." *Religion Compass* 1 (2007): 1–24.

Cooper, Alan. "Ps 24:7–19: Mythology and Exegesis." *JBL* 102 (1983): 37–60.

Cooper, Jerrold S. "The Fate of Mankind: Death and Afterlife in Ancient Mesopotamia." Pages 19–33 in *Death and Afterlife: Perspectives of World Religions*. Contributions to the Study of Religion 33. Westport, Conn: Greenwood, 1992.

Coulanges, Fustel de. *La cité antique*. Paris: Hachette, 1864.

Cowley, A. E. *Aramaic Papyri of the Fifth Century B. C.* Oxford: Clarendon, 1923.

Cox, Benjamin D. and Susan Ackerman. "Rachel's Tomb." *JBL* 128 (2009): 135–48.

Craig, James A. *Assyrian and Babylonian Religious Texts*. 2 vols. 1895–97. Reprint, Leipzig: Zentralantiquariat der Deutschen Demokratischen Republik, 1974.

Craigie, P. C. "Helel, Athtar and Phaeton (Jes 14:12–15)." *ZAW* 85 (1973): 223–25.

- "Ugarit, Canaan and Israel." *Tyndale Bulletin* 34 (1983): 145–67.

Cross, F. M., Jr. "The Cave Inscriptions from Khirbet Beit Lei." Pages 299–306 in *Near Eastern Archaeology in the Twentieth Century: Essays in Honor of Nelson Glueck*. Edited by J. A. Sanders. Garden City, N.Y.: Doubleday, 1970.

- *From Epic to Canon: History and Literature in Ancient Israel*. Baltimore: Johns Hopkins University Press, 1998.

Cross, F. M., and D. N. Freedman. "Josiah's Revolt against Assyria." *JNES* 12 (1953): 56–58.

- "The Song of Miriam." *JNES* 14 (1955): 237–50.

Currid, John D. *Ancient Egypt and the Old Testament*. Grand Rapids: Baker, 1997.

Cryer, Frederick H. *Divination in Ancient Israel and Its Near Eastern Environment: A Socio-Historical Investigation*. JSOTSup 142. Sheffield: Sheffield Academic Press, 1994.

Cuneiform Texts from Babylonian Tablets in the British Museum. Vol. 16. London: British Museum, 1903.

Dahood, Mitchell J. "חָדַל Cessation in Isaiah 38,11." *Biblica* 52 (1971): 215–16.

– *Psalms: Introduction, Translation, and Notes.* 3 vols. Anchor Bible 16, 17, 17A. Garden City, N.Y.: Doubleday, 1966–70.
– "The Value of Ugaritic for Textual Criticism." *Biblica* 40 (1959): 160–70.
Dalley, Stephanie. *Myths from Mesopotamia: Creation, the Flood, Gilgamesh, and Others.* Oxford: Oxford University Press, 1989.
– "Recent Evidence from Assyrian Sources for Judaean History from Uzziah to Manasseh." *JSOT* 28 (2004): 387–401.
Damerji, Muayad S. B. "Gräber Assyrischer Königinnen aus Nimrud." *Jahrbuch des Römisch-Germanischen Zentralmuseums* 45 (1998): 19–84.
Daumas, François. "Les objets sacrés de la déesse Hathor à Dendara." *Revue d'Égyptologie* 22 (1970): 7–18.
D'Auria, Sue, Peter Lacovara, and Catharine H. Roehrig. *Mummies & Magic: The Funerary Arts of Ancient Egypt.* Boston: Northeastern University Press, 1988.
David, Ann Rosalie. "Mummification." Pages 439–44 in vol. 2 of *The Oxford Encyclopedia of Ancient Egypt.* Oxford: Oxford University Press, 2001.
Davies, G. I. *Hosea.* OTG. Grand Rapids: Eerdmans, 1992.
Davies, Philip R. *In Search of Ancient Israel.* JSOTSup 148. Sheffield: Sheffield Academic Press, 1995.
Davis, Ellen F. "Exploding the Limits: Form and Function in Psalm 33." *JSOT* 53 (1992): 93–105.
Day, John. "The Development on the Belief in Life after Death in Ancient Israel." Pages 231–57 in *After the Exile: Essays in Honor of Rex Mason.* Edited by John Barton and David J. Reimer. Macon, Ga.: Mercer University Press, 1996.
– *Molech: A God of Human Sacrifice in the Old Testament.* Cambridge: Cambridge University Press, 1989.
– *Yahweh and the Gods and Goddesses of Canaan.* JSOTSup 265. Sheffield: Sheffield Academic Press, 2000.
De Buck, Adrian, "La Fleur au Front du Grand-Prêtre. Pages 18–29 in *Oudtestamentische studiën*, vol. 9. Edited by P. A. H. de Boer. Leiden: E. J. Brill, 1951.
De Hulster, Izaak J. *Iconographic Exegesis and Third Isaiah.* FAT II/36; Tübingen, Germany: Mohr Siebeck, 2009.
Dearman, J. Andrew. *Religion and Culture in Ancient Israel.* Peabody, Mass: Hendrickson, 1992.
– "The Tophet in Jerusalem: Archaeology and Cultural Profile." *JNSL* 22 (1996): 59–71.
– *The Book of Hosea.* NICOT; Grand Rapids, Mich.: Eerdmans, 2010.
Dekker, Jaap. *Zion's Rock-Solid Foundations: An Exegetical Study of the Zion Text in Isaiah 28:16.* Leiden: Brill, 2007.
Deck, Scholastika. *Die Gerichtsbotschaft Jesajas: Charakter und Begründung.* Forschung zur Bibel 67. Würzburg: Echter, 1991.
Deller, K. Review of R. de Vaux, *Les sacrifices de l'Ancien Testament.* Orientalia n.s. 34 (1965): 382–86.
Demarée, R. J. *The ꜣḫ iḳr n Rʿ–Stelae: On Ancestor Worship in Ancient Egypt.* Leiden: Nederlands Instituut voor het Nabije Oosten, 1983.
Devaud, Eugène. "Sur l'étymologie de שְׁאוֹל *šᵉʾôl*." *Sphinx* 13 (1909): 120–21.
Dever, William G. "Iron Age Epigraphic Material from the Area of Khirbet el-Kôm." *HUCA* 40–41 (1970); 139–204.
– "Khirbet el-Qôm." Page 976 in vol. 4 of *The Encyclopedia of Archaeological Excavations in the Holy Land.* Edited by Michael Avi-Yonah. Englewood Cliffs, N.J.: Prentice-Hall, 1978.

Dever, William G., and Seymour Gitin, editors. *Symbiosis, Symbolism and Power of the Past: Canaan, Ancient Israel, and Their Neighbors from the Late Bronze Age through Roman Palaestina: Proceedings of the Centennial Symposium W. F. Albright Institute of Archaeological Research and American Schools of Oriental Research, Jerusalem, May 29–31, 2000.* Winona Lake, Ind.: Eisenbrauns, 2003.

Dhorme, Eduard. *A Commentary on the Book of Job.* Translated by H. Knight. London: Nelson & Sons, 1967. French original *Le Livre de Job,* 1927.

Dhorme, Paul. "Le séjour des morts chez les Babyloniens et les Hébreux." *RB* 4 (1907): 59–78.

Dietrich, M., O. Loretz, and J. Sanmartin. "Ugaritisch *ILIB* und hebräisch *'(W)B* 'Totengeist.'" *UF* 6 (1974): 450–51.

– "Zur ugaritischen Lexicographie (XII)." *UF* 6 (1974): 41–44.

Dietrich, Walter. *Jesaja und die Politik.* Beiträge zur evangelischen Theologie: Theologische Abhandlungen 74. Munich: Kaiser, 1976.

Dinsmoor, William Bell. *The Architecture of Ancient Greece: An Account of Its Historic Development.* 3rd rev. ed. London: B. T. Batsford, 1950.

Dodson, Aidan. "Third Intermediate Period." Pages 388–94 in *The Oxford Encyclopedia of Ancient Egypt.* Oxford: Oxford University Press, 2001.

– "Death After Death in the Valley of the Kings." Pages 53–59 in *Death and Taxes in the Ancient Near East.* Edited by Sara E. Orel. Lewiston, N.Y.: Edwin Mellen Press, 1992.

Donner, Herbert. *Israel unter den Völkern: Die Stellung der klassischen Propheten des 8. Jahrhunderts v. Chr. zur Aussenpolitik der Könige von Israel und Juda.* Leiden: Brill, 1964.

Douglas, Mary. "One God, No Ancestors, in a World Renewed." Pages 176–95 in *Jacob's Tears: The Priestly Work of Reconciliation.* Oxford: Oxford University Press, 2004.

Doxey, Denise M. "Priesthood." Pages 68–73 in vol. 3 of *The Oxford Encyclopedia of Ancient Egypt.* Oxford: Oxford University Press, 2001.

Doyle, Brian. *The Apocalypse of Isaiah Metaphorically Speaking: A Study of the Use, Function, and Significance of Metaphors in Isaiah 27–27.* BETL 161. Leuven: Peeters, 2000.

Dozeman, Thomas B. "OT Rhetorical Criticism." Pages 712–15 in vol. 5 of *Anchor Bible Dictionary.* Edited by David Noel Freedman. 6 vols. New York: Doubleday, 1992.

Driver, G. R. "Another Little Drink – Isa 28:1–22." Pages 47–67 in *Words and Meanings: Essays Presented to David Winton Thomas on His Retirement from the Regius Professorship of Hebrew in the University of Cambridge, 1968.* Edited by P. R. Ackroyd and B. Lindars. London: Cambridge University Press, 1968.

– *Canaanite Myths and Legends.* Edinburgh: T&T Clark, 1956.

– "Hebrew Notes on Prophets and Proverbs." *JTS* 41 (1940): 162–75.

– "Isaianic Problems." Pages 43–49 in *Festschrift für Wilhelm Eilers.* Wiesbaden: Harrassowitz, 1967.

– "Lilith." *PEQ* 91 (1959): 55–57.

Driver, S. R. *Isaiah: His Life and Times.* New York: Fleming H. Revell, 1888.

Dubovský, Peter. *Hezekiah and the Assyrian Spies: Reconstruction of the Neo-Assyrian Intelligence Services and Its Significance for 2 Kings 18–19.* BO 49. Rome: Editrice Pontificio Istituto Biblico, 2006.

Duhm, Bernhard. *Das Buch Jesaja.* 4th ed. Göttingen: Vandenhoeck & Ruprecht, 1922.

Dunand, Françoise, and Roger Lichtenberg. *Les Momies et la Mort en Egypte.* Paris: Errance, 1998.

Dunham, Dows. *The Royal Cemeteries of Kush.* Vol. 1. Cambridge, Mass.: Harvard University Press, 1950.

Durkheim, Emile. *The Elementary Forms of the Religious Life: A Study in Religious Sociology.* Translated by J. W. Swain. London: G. Allen & Unwin, 1915.
Dussaud, René. "Deux steles de Ras Shamra portent une dédicace au dieu Dagon." *Syria* 16 (1935): 177–80.
Eaton, J.H. "The Origin of the Book of Isaiah," *VT* 9 (1959): 138–57.
Ebach, J. H. "PGR = (Toten-)opfer? Ein Vorschlag zum Verständnis von Ez. 43,7.9." *UF* 3 (1971): 365–368.
Ebeling, Erich. *Literarische Keilschrifttexte aus Assur.* Berlin: Akademie-Verlag, 1953.
— *Tod und Leben nach den Vorstellungen der Babylionier. I. Teil.* Berlin: De Gruyter, 1931.
Eberhardt, Gönke. *JHWH und die Unterwelt: Spuren einer Kompetenzausweitung JHWHS im Alten Testament.* FAT II/23. Tübingen: Mohr Siebeck, 2007.
Eisling, H. "יאר." Pages 539–63 in vol. 5 of *Theological Dictionary of the Old Testament.* Edited by G. J. Botterweck. Grand Rapids: Eerdmans, 1977.
Eissfeldt, Otto. *Molk als Opferbegriff im Punischen und Hebräischen und das Ende des Gottes Moloch.* Beiträge zur Religionsgeschichte des Altertums 3. Halle: Max Niemeyer, 1935.
Eitan, I. "An Egyptian Loan Word in Isa 19." *Jewish Quarterly Review* 15 (1924–25): 419–22.
El-Leithy, Hisham. "Letters to the Dead in Ancient and Modern Egypt." Pages 304–313 in *Egyptology at the Dawn of the Twenty-first Century: Proceedings of the Eighth International Congress of Egyptologists, Cairo, 2000.* Edited by Zahi Hawass and Lyla Pinch Brock. New York: American University in Cairo Press, 2003.
Elat, Moshe. "The Economic Relations of the Neo-Assyrian Empire with Egypt." *Journal of the American Oriental Society* 98 (1978): 20–34.
Emerton, J. A. "Some Difficult Words in Isaiah 28:10 and 13." Pages 39–56 in *Biblical Hebrew, Biblical Texts: Essays in Memory of Michael P. Weitzman.* Edited by Ada Rapoport-Albert and Gillian Greenberg. JSOTSup. 333. Sheffield, England: Sheffield Academic, 2001.
— "Some Linguistic and Historical Problems in Isaiah VIII.23." *Journal of Semitic Studies* 14 (1969): 151–75.
— "The Textual Problems of Isaiah v 14." *VT* 17 (1967): 135–42.
Engelbach, R. "Notes of Inspection, April 1921." *ASAE* 21 (1921): 188–96.
Erlandsson, Seth. *The Burden of Babylon: A Study of Isaiah 13:2–14:23.* ConBOT 4. Lund: Gleerup, 1970.
Eshel, Hanan. "Isaiah VIII.23: An Historical-Geographical Analogy." *VT* 40 (1990): 104–8.
Evans, Paul S. *The Invasion of Sennacherib in the Book of Kings: A Source-Critical and Rhetorical Study of 2 Kings 18–19.* Leiden: Brill, 2009.
Exum, J. Cheryl. "Of Broken Pots, Fluttering Birds and Visions in the Night: Extended Simile and Poetic Technique in Isaiah." *CBQ* 43 (1981): 331–52.
— "'Whom Will He Teach Knowledge?' A Literary Approach to Isaiah 28." Pages 108–39 in *Art and Meaning: Rhetoric in Biblical Literature.* Edited by David J. A. Clines, David M. Gunn, and Alan J. Hauser. Sheffield: JSOT Press, 1982.
Fabry, H.-J. "מות." Pages 205–9 in vol. 8 of *Theological Dictionary of the Old Testament.* Edited by G. J. Botterweck. Grand Rapids: Eerdmans, 1977.
Fales, Frederick Mario. "On *Pax Assyriaca* in the Eighth-Seventh Centuries BCE and Its Implications," pages 17–35 in *Isaiah's Vision of Peace in Biblical and Modern International Relations: Swords Into Plowshares.* Edited by Raymond Cohen and Raymond Westbrook. New York: Palgrave Macmillan, 2008.

— *Guerre et paix en Assyrie: Religion et imperialism*. Paris: Editions du Cerf, 2010.
Fales, Frederick Mario, and J. N. Postgate. "Introduction," in *Imperial Administrative Records*, part 2. SAA 11. Helsinki: Helsinki University Press, 1995.
Fantalkin, Alexander. "The Appearance of Rock-Cut Bench Tombs in Iron Age Judah as a Reflection of State Formation." Pages 17–44 in *Bene Israel: Studies in the Archaeology of Israel and the Levant during the Bronze and Iron Ages in Honour of Israel Finkelstein*. Edited by A. Fantalkin and A. Yassur-Landau. Culture and History of the Ancient Near East Series 31. Leiden: Brill, 2008.
Farber, Walter. *Schlaf, Kindchen, Schlaf! Mesopotamische Baby-Beschwörungen und -Rituale*. Mesopotamian Civilizations 2. Winona Lake, Ind.: Eisenbrauns, 1989.
— "Witchcraft, Magic and Divination in Ancient Mesopotamia." Pages 1895–1909 in vol. 3 of *Civilizations of the Ancient Near East*. Edited by Jack M. Sasson et al. New York: Scribner, 1995.
Faulkner, Raymond O. *The Ancient Egyptian Book of the Dead: The Book of Going Forth by Day*. San Francisco: Chronicle Books, 1994.
— *The Ancient Egyptian Coffin Texts*. London: Aris & Phillips, 2004.
Faust, Avraham, and Shlomo Bunimovitz. "The Judahite Rock-Cut Tomb: Family Response at a Time of Change." *Israel Exploration Journal* 58 (2008): 150–70.
Faust, Avraham, and Ehud Weiss. "Judah, Philistia, and the Mediterranean World: Reconstructing the Economic System of the Seventh Century BCE." *BASOR* 338 (May 2005): 71–92.
Fazzini, Richard A. "Standard Bearing Statue of Queen." Pages 114–15 in *Mistress of the House, Mistress of Heaven: Women in Ancient Egypt*. Edited by A. K. Capel and G. E. Markoe. Cincinnati: Cincinnati Art Museum, 1996.
— "A Monument in the Precinct of Mut with the Name of the God's Wife Nitocris I." Pages 51–62 in *Artibus Aegypti: Studia in Honorem Bernardi V. Bothmer a Collegis Amicis Discipulis Conscripta*. Edited by Herman de Meulenaere and L. Limme. Brussels: Musées Royaux d'Art et d'Histoire, 1983.
— "A Sculpture of King Taharqa (?) in the Precinct of the Goddess Mut at South Karnak." Pages 293–306 in *Mélanges Gamal Eddin Mokhtar* 1. Edited by Paule Posener-Kriéger. Cairo: Le Caire Institut Français d'Archéologie Orientale, 1985.
Fazzini, Richard, and William Peck. "The Precinct of Mut during Dynasty XXV and Early Dynasty XXVI: A Growing Picture." *Society for the Study of Egyptian Antiquities Journal* 11 (1981): 115–26.
Feigin, Samuel. "The Meaning of Ariel." *JBL* 39 (1920): 131–37.
Fewell, Danna. "Sennacherib's Defeat: Words at War in 2 Kings 18:13–19:37." *JSOT* 34 (1986): 79–90.
Fey, Reinhard. *Amos and Jesaja: Abhängigkeit und Eigenständigkeit des Jesaja*. Neukirchen-Vluyn: Neukirchener Verlag, 1963.
Fichtner, J. "Jesaja unter den Weisen." *TL* 74 (1949): cols. 75–80.
Finkel, Irving R. "Necromancy in Ancient Mesopotamia." *AfO* 29 (1984): 1–17.
Finkelstein, Jacob J. "Early Mesopotamia, 2500–1000 BC." Pages 50–110 in *The Symbolic Instrument in Early Times*. Edited by Harold D. Lasswell et al. Propaganda and Communication in World History 1. Honolulu: University of Hawaii Press, 1979.
— "The Genealogy of the Hammurapi Dynasty." *Journal of Cuneiform Studies* 20 (1966): 97–103, 116–17.
Fischer, Johann. *Das Buch Jesaja*, Teil I. Bonn: Peter Hanstein, 1937.
Fisher, Amy M. "Pour Forth the Sparkling Chalice: An Examination of Libation Practices in the Levant." Honors thesis, Macalester College, 2007.

Fisher, Loren R. and Stan Rummel, eds. *Ras Shamra Parallels*. 3 vols. Analecta Orientalia 49–51. Rome: Pontificium Institutum Biblicum, 1972–81.
Fitzenreiter, Martin. "Zum Ahnenkult in Ägypten." *Göttinger Miszellen* 143 (1994): 51–72.
Foster, Benjamin R. *Before the Muses: An Anthology of Akkadian Literature*. 3rd ed. Baltimore: CDL, 2005.
– , ed. and trans. *The Epic of Gilgamesh*. New York: W. W. Norton, 2001.
– *From Distant Days: Myths, Tales, and Poetry of Ancient Mesopotamia*. Bethesda, Md.: CDL, 1995.
Frahm, Eckart. "Images of Assyria in Nineteenth- and Twentieth-Century Western Scholarship." Pages 74–94 in *Orientalism, Assyriology and the Bible*. Edited by Steven W. Holloway. Hebrew Bible Monographs 10. Sheffield: Sheffield Phoenix, 2006.
Frandsen, Paul J. "On Fear of Death and the Three 3bwts Connected with Hathor." Pages 131–48 in *Gold of Praise: Studies on Ancient Egypt in Honor of Edward F. Wente*. Edited by Emily Teeter and John Larson. Studies in Ancient Oriental Civilization 58. Chicago: Oriental Institute of the University of Chicago, 1999.
Franklin, Norma. "Lost Tombs of the Israelite Kings: Century-Old Excavation Report Yields Startling New Discovery." *BAR* 33:4 (2007): 26–35.
– "Don't Be So Quick to Be Disappointed, David Ussishkin." *BAR* 34:2 (2008): 70–71.
Frazer, J. G. *Pausanius' Description of Greece*. London: Macmillan, 1898.
Freedman, David Noel, ed.. *The Anchor Bible Dictionary*. New York: Doubleday, 1996.
Fretheim, Terence E. "God and Violence in the Old Testament." *Word and World* 24 (2004): 18–28.
Friedman, R. E., and S. D. Overton, "Death and Afterlife: The Biblical Silence," Pages 35–59 in *Judaism in Late Antiquity*, part 4, *Death, Life-after-Death, Resurrection and the World to Come in the Judaisms of Antiquity*. Edited by Alan J. Avery-Peck and Jacob Neusner. Handbuch der Orientalistik 55. Leiden/New York: Brill, 2000.
Froidefond, Christian, ed. *Isis et Osiris. Plutarque: Oeuvres Morales, Tome V, 2e partie*. Paris: Belles Lettres, 1988.
Gadd, C. J. "The Harran Inscriptions of Nabonidus." *Anatolian Studies* 8 (1958): 35–92.
Gallagher, W. R. "On the Identity of Hêlēl Ben Šaḥar." *UF* 26 (1994): 131–46.
Galling, Kurt. *Biblisches Reallexikon*. HAT 1. Tübingen: Mohr Siebeck, 1937.
Gallou, Chrysanthi. *The Myceanean Cult of the Dead*. BAR International Series 1372. Oxford: Archaeopress, 2005.
Galpaz-Feller, Pnina. "'And the Physicians Embalmed Him' (Gen 50,2)." *ZAW* 118 (2006): 209–17.
– "Is That So? (2 Kings XVII 4)." *Revue Biblique* 107 (2000): 338–47.
– "The Victory Stela of King Piye: The Biblical Perspective on War and Peace." *Revue Biblique* 100 (1993): 399–414.
Gandhi, Leela. *Postcolonial Theory: A Critical Introduction*. New York: Columbia University Press, 1998.
Gardiner, Alan H. *The Attitude of the Ancient Egyptians to Death and the Dead*. Frazer Lecture for 1935. Cambridge: Cambridge University Press, 1935.
– "A New Letter to the Dead." *JEA* 16 (1930): 19–22.
Gardiner, Alan H., and Kurt Sethe. *Egyptian Letters to the Dead, Mainly from the Old and Middle Kingdoms*. London: Egypt Exploration Society, 1928.
Garnier, John. *The Worship of the Dead; or, The Origin and Nature of Pagan Idolatry and its Bearing upon the Early History of Egypt and Babylonia*. London: Chapman & Hall, Limited, 1909.

Garr, W. Randall. *Dialect Geography of Syria-Palestine, 1000–586 B.C.E.* Philadelphia: University of Pennsylvania Press, 1985.
- "The *qinah*: A Study of Poetic Meter, Syntax and Style." *ZAW* 95 (1983): 54–75.
Gee, John. "The Use of the Daily Temple Liturgy in the Book of the Dead." Pages 73–86 in *Totenbuch-Forschungen: Gesammelte Beiträge des 2. Internationalen Totenbuch-Symposiums, Bonn, 25. bis 29. September 2005.* Edited by Burkhard Backes, Irmtraut Munro and Simone Stöhr. Studien zum altägyptischen Totenbuch 11. Wiesbaden: Harrassowitz, 2006.
Geller, Markham J. *Evil Demons: Canonical Utukkū Lemnūtu Incantations.* State Archives of Assyria Cuneiform Texts 5. Helsinki, Finland: Helsinki University Press, 2007.
George, A. R. "Sennacherib and the Tablet of Destinies." *Iraq* 48 (1986): 133–46.
- *The Babylonian Gilgamesh Epic: Introduction, Critical Edition, and Cuneiform Texts.* 2 vols. Oxford: Oxford University Press, 2003.
George, Mark K. "Foucault." Pages 91–98 in *Handbook of Postmodern Biblical Interpretation.* Edited by A. K. M. Adam. St. Louis: Chalice, 2000.
Germer, Renate. "Flowers." Pages 541–44 in vol. 1 of *Oxford Encyclopedia of Ancient Egypt.* Oxford: Oxford University Press, 2001.
Gerstenberger, Erhard S. *Theologies in the Old Testament.* Translated J. Bowden. Minneapolis: Fortress, 2002.
- "The Woe-Oracles of the Prophets." *JBL* 81 (1962): 249–63.
Gese, Hartmut. "Die Stromende Geissel des Hadad un Jesaja 28:15–18." Pages 127–34 in *Archäologie und Altes Testament. Festschrift für Kurt Galling.* Edited by Arnulf Kuschke and Ernst Kutsch. Tubingen: Mohr-Siebeck, 1970.
Ginsberg, H. L. "Gleanings in First Isaiah." Pages 245–59 in *Mordecai M. Kaplan Jubilee Volume on the Occasion of His Seventieth Birthday.* Edited by Moshe Davis. New York: Jewish Theological Seminary, 1953.
- "Isaiah (First Isaiah)." Pages 50–60 in vol. 9 of *Encyclopaedia Judaica.* New York: Macmillan, 1971–72.
- "An Obscure Hebrew Word." *JQR* 22 (1931–32): 143–45.
- "Psalms and Inscriptions of Petition and Acknowledgement." Pages 159–71 in *Louis Ginzberg Jubilee Volume*, English Section. New York: American Academy for Jewish Research, 1945.
- "Reflexes of Sargon in Isaiah after 715 BCE." *JAOS* 88 (1968): 47–53.
- "The Ugaritic Texts and Textual Criticism." *JBL* 62 (1943): 109–15.
- "An Unrecognized Allusion to Kings Pekah and Hoshea of Israel." *Eretz Israel* 5 (1958): 61*–65*.
Goedicke, Hans. "The Death of Amenemhet I and Other Royal Demises." Pages 137–143 in *Es werde niedergelegt als Schriftstück: Festschrift für Hartwig Altenmüller zum 65. Geburtstag.* Edited by Nicole Kloth, Karl Martin und Eva Pardey. Hamburg: Buske, 2003.
- "The Egyptian Idea of Passing from Life to Death (An Interpretation)." *Orientalia* 24 (1955): 225–239.
Gogel, Sandra Landis. *A Grammar of Epigraphic Hebrew.* SBL Resources for Biblical Study 23. Atlanta: Scholars Press, 1998.
Good, Edwin M. *Irony in the Old Testament.* 2nd ed. Sheffield: Almond, 1981.
Good, Robert M. "The Ugaritic Steward." *ZAW* 95 (1983): 110–111.
- "The Israelite Royal Steward in the Light of Ugaritic '*l bt.*" *RB* 86 (1979): 580–582.
Gordon, Andrew A. "The *ka* as an Animating Force." *Journal of the American Research Center in Egypt* 33 (1996): 31–35.

Gordon, C. H. *Before the Bible: The Common Background of Greek and Hebrew Civilisations.* New York: Harper & Row, 1962.
- "The Marriage and Death of Sinuhe." Pages 43–44 in *Love & Death in the Ancient Near East: Essays in Honor of Marvin H. Pope.* Edited by John H. Marks and Robert M. Good, Guilford, Conn.: Four Quarters, 1987.
Gordon, Robert P. "Introducing the God of Israel." Pages 3–19 in *The God of Israel.* Edited by Robert P. Gordon. Cambridge: Cambridge University Press, 2007.
Görg, Manfred. "Der Spiegeldienst der Frauen (Ex 38,8)." *BN* 23 (1984): 9–13.
Gosse, Bernard. *Isaïe 13,1.14,23 dans les traditions littéraires du livre d'Isaïe et dans la tradition des oracles contre les nations.* OBO 78. Göttingen: Vandenhoeck & Ruprecht, 1988.
Gowan, Donald E. *When Man Becomes God: Humanism and Hybris in the Old Testament.* Pittsburgh Theological Monographs 6. Pittsburgh: Pickwick, 1975.
Goyon, Jean-Claude. "Rituels de l'embaumement et des funérailles." *Les Dossiers d'Archéologie* 257 (2000): 14–25.
Graesser, Carl F. "Standing Stones in Ancient Palestine." *BA* 35 (1972): 34–63.
Grajetzki, Wolfram. *Burial Customs in Ancient Egypt: Life in Death for Rich and Poor.* London: Duckworth, 2003.
Grandet, Pierre. *Le papyrus Harris I (BM 9999).* 2 vols. Bibliothèque d'Étude 109/1–2. Cairo: Imprimerie de l'Institut français d'archéologie orientale du Caire, 1994.
Gray, G. B. *A Critical and Exegetical Commentary on the Book of Isaiah, I–XXXIX.* ICC. New York: Charles Scribner's Sons, 1912.
Gray, John. "DTN and RP'UM in Ancient Ugarit." *PEQ* 84 (1952): 39–41.
- "The Rephaim." *PEQ* 81 (1949): 127–39.
Grayson, A. K. *Assyrian and Babylonian Chronicles.* Texts from Cuneiform Sources. Locust Valley, N.Y.: J. J. Augustin, 1975.
- *Assyrian Royal Inscriptions II: From Tiglath-Pileser I to Ashur-nasir-apli II.* Wiesbaden: Harrassowitz, 1976.
- "Assyrian Rule of Conquered Territory in Ancient West Asia." Pages 959–68 in vol. 1 of *Civilizations of the Ancient Near East.* Edited by Jack M. Sasson et al. New York: Scribner, 1995.
- *Assyrian Rulers of the Early First Millennium BC.* Royal Inscriptions of Mesopotamia, Assyrian Periods 2. Toronto: University of Toronto Press, 1991.
- "History and Culture of Assyria." Pages 732–55 in vol. 4 of *Anchor Bible Dictionary.* Edited by David Noel Freedman. 6 vols. New York: Doubleday, 1992.
Green, A. R. W. *The Role of Human Sacrifice in the Ancient Near East.* SBLDS 1. Missoula, Mont.: Scholars Press, 1975.
Green, Alberto R. "Esarhaddon, Sanduarri, and the Adon Papyrus." Pages 88–97 in *Inspired Speech: Prophecy in the Ancient Near East, Essays in Honor of Herbert B. Huffmon.* Edited by J. Kaltner and Louis Stulman. Edinburgh: T & T Clark, 2004.
Greenfield, J. C. "Un rite religieux araméen et ses parallèles." *RB* 80 (1973): 46–52.
- "Two Proverbs of Aḥiqar." Pages 194–201 in *Lingering over Words: Studies in Ancient Near Eastern Literature in Honor of William L. Moran.* Atlanta: Scholars Press, 1990.
- "The Zakir Inscription and the *Danklied*." Pages 174–91 in *Proceedings of the Fifth World Congress of Jewish Studies, 1969.* Jerusalem: Magnes, 1971.
Gressmann, Hugo. *The Tower of Babel.* New York: Jewish Institute of Religion Press, 1928.
- *Israels Spruchweisheit im Zusammenhang der Weltliteratur.* Berlin: K. Curtius, 1925.
Griffiths, J. Gwyn. *The Divine Verdict: A Study of Divine Judgement in the Ancient Religions.* Leiden: Brill, 1991.

- "Human Sacrifice in Egypt: The Classical Evidence." *ASAE* 48 (1948): 409–23.
Grøndahl, Frauke. *Die Personennamen der Texte aus Ugarit.* Studia Pohl 1. Rome: Pontifical Biblical Institute, 1967.
Gulde, Stefanie Ulrike. *Der Tod als Herrscher in Ugarit und Israel.* FAT II/22. Tübingen: Mohr Siebeck, 2007.
Gunkel, Hermann. *Creation and Chaos in the Primeval Era and the Eschaton: A Religio-Historical Study of Genesis 1 and Revelation 12.* Translated by K. W. Whitney. Grand Rapids: Eerdmans, 2006. German original, 1895.
- "The Prophets: Oral and Written." Pages 85–133 in *Water for a Thirsty Land: Israelite Literature and Religion.* Edited by K. C. Hanson. Fortress Classics in Biblical Studies. Minneapolis: Fortress, 2001.
Hadley, Judith. "The Khirbet el-Qom Inscription." *VT* 37 (1987): 50–62.
Halevi, B. "*'qbwt nwspym lpwlḥn ʾbwt*" (in Hebrew). *Beth Mikra* 64 (1975): 101–17.
Haller, Arndt. *Die Gräber und Grüfte von Assur.* Wissenschaftliche Veröffentlichung der Deutschen-Orient Gesellschaft in Assur 65. Berlin: Gebr. Mann, 1954.
Hallo, William W. "Royal Ancestor Worship in the Biblical World." Pages 381–401 in *Sha'arei Talmon: Studies in the Bible, Qumran, and the Ancient Near East Presented to Shemaryahu Talmon.* Edited by Michael Fishbane and Emanuel Tov. Winona Lake, Ind.: Eisenbrauns, 1992.
- "The Royal Correspondence of Larsa: I. A Sumerian Prototype for the Prayer of Hezekiah?" Pages 209–24 in *Kramer Anniversary Volume: Cuneiform Studies in Honor of Samuel Noah Kramer.* Edited by B. L. Eichler et al. Alter Orient und Altes Testament 25. Kevelaer: Butzon & Bercker; Neukirchen-Vluyn: Neukirchener Verlag, 1976.
- "Isa 28:9–13 and the Ugaritic Abecedaries," *JBL* 77 (1958): 324–338.
Hallo, William W., and William Kelly Simpson. *The Ancient Near East: A History.* New York: Harcourt Brace Jovanovich, 1971.
Hallote, Rachel S. *Death, Burial, and Afterlife in the Biblical World: How the Israelites and Their Neighbors Treated the Dead.* Chicago: Ivan R. Dee, 2001.
Halpern, Baruch. "'The Excremental Vision': The Doomed Priests of Doom in Isaiah 28." *Hebrew Annual Review* 10 (1986): 109–21.
- *The First Historians: The Hebrew Bible and History.* San Francisco: Harper & Row, 1988.
- "The Plaster Texts from Deir 'Alla." Pages 58–72 in *The Balaam Text from Deir 'Alla Re-Evaluated: Proceedings of the International Symposium Held at Leiden, 21–24 August 1989.* Edited by J. Hoftijzer and G. van der Kooij. Leiden: Brill, 1991.
- "Sybil, or the Two Nations? Archaism, Kinship, Alienation, and the Elite Redefinition of Traditional Culture in Judah in the 8th–7th Centuries BCE" Pages 291–338 in *The Study of the Ancient Near East in the Twenty-First Century: The William Foxwell Albright Centennial Conference.* Edited by J. S. Cooper and G. M. Schwartz. Winona Lake, Ind.: Eisenbrauns, 1996.
Halpern, Baruch, and David S. Vanderhooft, "The Editions of Kings in the 7th–6th Centuries. B.C.E.," *Hebrew Union College Annual* 62 (1991): 179–244.
Handy, Lowell K. "Josiah in a New Light: Assyriology Touches the Reforming King." Pages 415–35 in *Orientalism, Assyriology and the Bible.* Edited by Steven W. Holloway. Hebrew Bible Monographs 10: Sheffield: Sheffield Phoenix, 2006.
- "Lilith." Pages 324–25 in vol. 4 of *Anchor Bible Dictionary.* Edited by David Noel Freedman. 6 vols. New York: Doubleday, 1992.
Haran, Menahem. *Temples and Temple-Service in Ancient Israel: An Inquiry into the Character of Cult Phenomena and the Historical Setting of the Priestly School.* Winona Lake, Ind.: Eisenbrauns, 1985.

Harer, W. Benson, Jr. "Lotus." Pages 304–5 in vol. 2 of *Oxford Encyclopedia of Ancient Egypt*. Oxford: Oxford University Press, 2001.
Harper Collins Bible Dictionary. San Francisco: HarperOne, 1996.
Harrington, Nicola. "Children and the Dead in New Kingdom Egypt." Pages 52–65 in *Current Research in Egyptology 2006: Proceedings of the Seventh Annual Symposium, University of Oxford, April 2006*. Edited by Maria Cannata. Oxford: Oxbow, 2007.
Hasel, Gerhard F. "Resurrection in the Theology of Old Testament Apocalyptic." *ZAW* 92 (1980): 267–84.
Hasel, Michael G. *Domination and Resistance: Egyptian Military Activity in the Southern Levant, ca. 1300–1185 B. C.* Leiden: Brill, 1998.
Haussig, H. W. *Wörterbuch der Mythologie*. Vol. 1. Stuttgart: E. Klett, 1965.
Hawkins, J. David. "The Neo-Hittite States in Syria and Anatolia." Pages 372–441 in vol. 3, part 1, of *The Cambridge Ancient History*. 2nd ed. Cambridge: Cambridge University Press, 1982.
- "Late Hittite Funerary Monuments." Pages 213–26 in *Death in Mesopotamia: Papers Read at the XXVIe Rencontre Assyriologique Internationale*, ed. B. Alster. Mesopotamia 8. Copenhagen: Akademisk Forlag, 1980.
- "More Late Hittite Funerary Monuments." Pages 189–97 in *Anatolia and the Ancient Near East. Studies in Honor of Tahşin Özgüç*. Ankara, 1989.
Hayes, John H., and Stuart A. Irvine. *Isaiah, the Eighth Century Prophet: His Times and His Preaching*. Nashville: Abingdon, 1987.
Hays, Christopher B. "Chirps from the Dust: The Affliction of Nebuchadnezzar in Daniel 4:30 in Its Ancient Near Eastern Context." *JBL* 126 (2007): 305–25.
- "The Covenant with Mut: A New Interpretation of Isaiah 28:1–22." *VT* 60 (2010): 212–40.
- "Damming Egypt/Damning Egypt: The Paronomasia of *skr* and the Unity of Isa 19:1–15." *ZAW* 120 (2008): 612–16.
- "Echoes of the Ancient Near East?: Intertextuality and the Comparative Study of the Old Testament." Pages 20–43 in *The Word Leaps the Gap: Essays on Scripture and Theology in Honor of Richard B. Hays*. Edited by J. Ross Wagner, C. Kavin Rowe, and A. Katherine Grieb. Winona Lake, Ind.: Eerdmans, 2009.
- "The Egyptian Goddess Mut in Iron-Age Palestine: Further Data From Amulets and Onomastics." *JNES*, forthcoming.
- "Isaiah" in *The Encyclopedia of the Bible*. Oxford: Oxford University Press, forthcoming.
- "Kirtu and the 'Yoke of the Poor': A New Interpretation of an Old Crux (KTU 1.16 VI:48)." *UF* 37 (2005): 361–70.
- "Refocusing Shebna's Tomb: A New Reading of Isa 22:15–19 in its Ancient Near Eastern Context," *ZAW* 122 (2010): 558–75.
- "Religio-Historical Approaches: Monotheism, Method, and Mortality," Pages 169–93 in *Method Matters: Essays on the Interpretation of the Hebrew Bible in Honor of David L. Petersen*. Edited by Joel M. LeMon and Kent Harold Richards. Atlanta: SBL, 2009.
Hays, Christopher B. and Joel M. LeMon. "The Dead and Their Images: An Egyptian Etymology for Hebrew *ʾôb*." *Journal of Ancient Egyptian Interconnections* 1 (2009): 1–4.
Healey, John F. "The Immortality of the King: Ugarit and the Psalms." *Orientalia* n.s. 53 (1984): 245–54.
- "Das Land ohne Wiederkehr: Die Unterwelt im antiken Ugarit und im Alten Testament." Translated by Herbert Niehr. *Theologische Quartalschrift* 177 (1997): 94–104.
- "Malkū : MLKM : Anunnaki." *UF* 7 (1975): 235–38.

- "MLKM/RPUM and the Kispum." *UF* 10 (1978): 89–91.
- "Mot." Pages 599–600 in *Dictionary of Deities and Demons in the Bible*. 2nd edition. Edited by Karel van der Toorn, B. Becking, and P. W. van der Horst. Leiden: Brill, 1995.
- *The Religion of the Nabataeans: A Conspectus*. Leiden/Boston: Brill, 2001.
- "The Sun Deity and the Underworld in Mesopotamia and Ugarit." Pages 239–42 in *Death in Mesopotamia: Papers Read at the XXVIe Rencontre Assyriologique Internationale*. Edited by Bendt Alster. Mesopotamia 8. Copenhagen: Akademisk Forlag, 1980.
- "The Ugaritic Dead: Some Live Issues." *UF* 18 (1986): 27–32.

Hegenbarth-Reichardt, Ina. *Der Raum der Zeit: Eine Untersuchung zu den Altägyptischen Vorstellungen und Konzeptionen von Zeit und Raum Anhand des Unterweltbuches Amduat*. Wiesbaden: Harrassowitz, 2006.

Heidel, Alexander. *The Gilgamesh Epic and Old Testament Parallels*. Chicago: University of Chicago Press, 1946.

Heider, George C. *The Cult of Molek: A Reassessment*. JSOTSup 43. Sheffield: JSOT Press, 1985.

- "Molech." Pages 581–85 in *Dictionary of Deities and Demons in the Bible*. 2nd edition. Edited by Karel van der Toorn, B. Becking, and P. W. van der Horst. Leiden: Brill, 1995.

Heidorn, Lisa A. "The Horses of Kush." *JNES* 56 (1997): 105–14.

Heiser, M. S. "The Mythological Provenance of Isa. XIV 12–15: A Reconsideration of the Ugaritic Material." *VT* 51 (2001): 354–69.

Helck, Wolfgang. *Die Prophezeihung des Nfr.tj*. Wiesbaden: Harrassowitz, 1970.

Herrmann, Christian. *Ägyptische Amulette aus Palästina/Israel: Mit einem Ausblick auf ihre Rezeption durch das Alte Testament*. Freiburg, Schweiz: Universitätsverlag; Göttingen: Vandenhoeck & Ruprecht, 1994.

Hibbard, J. Todd. *Intertextuality in Isaiah 24–27: The Reuse and Evocation of Earlier Texts and Traditions*. FAT II/16. Tübingen: Mohr Siebeck, 2006.

Hiebert, Theodore. "Theophany in the OT." Pages 505–11 in vol. 6 of *Anchor Bible Dictionary*. Edited by David Noel Freedman. 6 vols. New York: Doubleday, 1992.

Higginbotham, Carolyn R. *Egyptianization and Elite Emulation in Ramesside Palestine: Governance and Accommodation on the Imperial Periphery*. Leiden: Brill, 2000.

Hillers, Delbert R. "Hôy and Hôy-Oracles: A Neglected Syntactic Aspect." Pages 155–58 in *The Word of the Lord Shall Go Forth: Essays in Honor of David Noel Freedman in Celebration of His Sixtieth Birthday*. Edited by Carol L. Meyers and M. O'Connor. Winona Lake, Ind.: Eisenbrauns: 1983.

- *Treaty-Curses and the Old Testament Prophets*. Rome: Pontifical Biblical Institute, 1964.

Hodder, Ian, and Scott Hutson. *Reading the Past: Current Approaches to Interpretation in Archaeology*. 3rd ed. Cambridge: Cambridge University Press, 2003.

Hoffmeier, James K. "Egypt's Role in the Events of 701 B.C. in Jerusalem." Pages 219–34 in *Jerusalem in Bible and Archaeology: The First Temple Period*. Edited by Andrew G. Vaughn and Ann E. Killebrew. SBL Symposium Series 18. Atlanta: Society of Biblical Literature, 2003.

- "Egypt's Role in the Events of 701 B.C.E.: A Rejoinder to J. J. M. Roberts." Pages 285–90 in *Jerusalem in Bible and Archaeology: The First Temple Period*. Edited by Andrew G. Vaughn and Ann E. Killebrew. SBL Symposium Series 18. Atlanta: Society of Biblical Literature, 2003.

Hoffner, H. A. "אוֹב" Pages 130–34 in vol. 1 of *Theological Dictionary of the Old Testament*. Edited by G. J. Botterweck. Grand Rapids: Eerdmans, 1977.

- "The Royal Cult in Hatti." Pages 132–51 in *Text, Artifact, Image: Revealing Ancient*

Israelite Religion. Edited by Gary M. Beckman and Theodore J. Lewis. Brown Judaic Studies 346. Providence: Brown Judaic Studies, 2006.
- "Second Millennium Antecedents to the Hebrew 'Ôb." *JBL* 86 (1967): 385–401.
- *Hittite Myths*. Second edition. SBLWAW 2; Atlanta, Ga.: SBL, 1998.

Høgenhaven, Jesper. "On the Structure and Meaning of Isa VIII.23b." *VT* 37 (1987): 218–21.

Holladay, John S. "Assyrian Statecraft and the Prophets of Israel." *HTR* 63 (1970): 29–51.
- "Hezekiah's Tribute, Long-Distance Trade, and the Wealth of Nations ca. 1000–600 BCE: A New Perspective" Pages 309–31 in *Confronting the Past: Archaeological and Historical Essays on Ancient Israel in Honor of William G. Dever*. Edited by Seymour Gitin et al. Winona Lake, Ind.: Eisenbrauns, 2006.
- "Judeans (and Phoenicians) in Egypt in the Late Seventh to Sixth Centuries B.C." Pages 405–38 in *Egypt, Israel, and the Ancient Mediterranean World: Studies in Honor of Donald B. Redford*. Edited by G. N. Knoppers and A. Hirsch. Leiden: Brill, 2004.

Holladay, William L. *Isaiah: Scroll of a Prophetic Heritage*. Grand Rapids: Eerdmans, 1978.
- "Text, Structure, and Irony in the Poem on the Fall of the Tyrant, Isaiah 14." *CBQ* 61 (1999): 633–45.

Holloway, Steven W. *Aššur is King! Aššur is King! Religion in the Exercise of Power in the Neo-Assyrian Empire*. Culture and History of the Ancient Near East 10; Leiden: Brill, 2002.

Hölzl, Regina. "Stela." Pages 319–24 in vol. 3 of *Oxford Encyclopedia of Ancient Egypt*. Oxford: Oxford University Press, 2001.

Hornung, Erik. *The Ancient Egyptian Books of the Afterlife*. Translated by David Lorton. Ithaca, N.Y.: Cornell University Press, 1999.
- "Black Holes Viewed From Within: Hell in Ancient Egyptian Thought." *Diogenes* 42 (1994): 133–56.
- *Conceptions of God in Ancient Egypt: The One and the Many*. Translated by J. Baines. Ithaca, N.Y.: Cornell University Press, 1982.

Horowitz, Wayne. *Mesopotamian Cosmic Geography*. Winona Lake, Ind.: Eisenbrauns, 1998.

Horowitz, Wayne, Takayoshi Oshima, and Seth Sanders. *Cuneiform in Canaan: Cuneiform Sources from the Land of Israel in Ancient Times*. Jerusalem: Israel Exploration Society and the Hebrew University of Jerusalem, 2006.
- "A Bibliographical List of Cuneiform Inscriptions from Canaan, Palestine/Philistia, and the Land of Israel." *JAOS* 122 (2002): 753–66.

Horwitz, William J. "The Significance of the Rephaim," *JNSL* 7 (1979): 37–43.

Hout, Theo P. J. van den "Death as a Privilege: The Hittite Royal Funerary Ritual." Pages 37–76 in *Hidden Futures: Death and Immortality in Ancient Egypt, Anatolia, the Classical, Biblical and Arabic-Islamic World*. Edited by J. M. Bremmer, Th. P. J. van den Hout, and R. Peters. Amsterdam: Amsterdam University Press, 1994.
- *The Purity of Kingship: An Edition of CHT 569 and Related Hittite Oracle Inquiries of Tuthaliya IV*. Leiden: Brill, 1998.
- "Death, the Afterlife and Other Last Things: Anatolia." Pages 483–85 in *Religions of the Ancient World: A Guide*. Edited by Sarah Iles Johnston. Cambridge, Mass.: Belknap Press of Harvard University Press, 2004.
- "The (Divine) Stone House and Ḫegur Reconsidered." Pages 73–91 in *Recent Developments in Hittite Archaeology and History: Papers in Memory of Hans G. Güterbock*. Edited by K. Aslihan Yener and Harry A. Hoffner, Jr. Winona Lake: Eisenbrauns, 2002.

Huehnergard, John. "Biblical Notes on Some New Akkadian Texts from Emar (Syria)." *CBQ* 47 (1985): 428–34.
- *Ugaritic Vocabulary in Syllabic Transcription.* HSS 32. Atlanta: Scholars Press, 1987.

Huffmon, H. B. "Shalem." Pages 755–57 in *Dictionary of Deities and Demons in the Bible.* Edited by Karel van der Toorn, B. Becking, and P. W. van der Horst. Leiden: Brill, 1995.

Hussein, Mahmoud I. "Anatomy of the Egyptian Tomb,'The Egyptian Tomb as a Womb.'" *Discussions in Egyptology* 49 (2001): 25–33.

Hutter, Manfred. "Lilith." Pages 520–21 in *Dictionary of Deities and Demons in the Bible.* 2nd edition. Edited by Karel van der Toorn, B. Becking, and P. W. van der Horst. Leiden: Brill, 1995.

Ikram, Salima. "Afterlife Beliefs and Burial Customs." Pages 340–51 in *The Egyptian World.* Edited by Toby Wilkinson. New York: Routledge, 2007.
- *Death and Burial in Ancient Egypt.* Harlow, England: Longman, 2003.

Ikram, Salima and Aidan Dodson. *The Mummy in Ancient Egypt: Equipping the Dead for Eternity.* New York: Thames & Hudson, 1998.

Illman, K. J. *Old Testament Formulas About Death.* RIAAF 48. Åbo, Finland: Åbo Akademi, 1979.

Irwin, Brian P. "Molek Imagery and the Slaughter of Gog in Ezekiel 38 and 39." *JSOT* 65 (1995): 93–112.

Irwin, William H. "Job's Redeemer." *JBL* 81 (1963): 217–29.
- "Smooth Stones of the Wady: Isaiah 57:6." *CBQ* 29 (1967): 31–40.

Israelit-Groll, Sarah. "The Egyptian Background to Isaiah 19:18." Pages 300–303 in *Boundaries of the Ancient Near Eastern World: A Tribute to Cyrus H. Gordon.* Edited by Meir Lubetski et al. JSOTSup 273. Sheffield: JSOT Press, 1998.

Jacobsen, Thorkild. "Abstruse Sumerian." Pages 279–91 in *Ah, Assyria...: Studies in Assyrian History and Ancient Near Eastern Historiography Presented to Hayim Tadmor.* Edited by Mordechai Cogan and Israel Eph'al. Jerusalem: Magnes Press, 1991.
- "Death in Ancient Mesopotamia." Pages 19–24 in *Death in Mesopotamia: Papers Read at the XXVIe Rencontre Assyriologique Internationale.* Edited by Bendt Alster. Mesopotamia 8. Copenhagen: Akademisk Forlag, 1980.
- *The Treasures of Darkness: A History of Mesopotamian Religion.* New Haven: Yale University Press, 1976.

Jacobson, Rolf A. "A Rose by Any Other Name: Iconography and the Interpretation of Isaiah 28:1–6." Pages 125–46 in *Images and Prophecy in the Ancient Eastern Mediterranean.* Edited by Martti Nissinen and Charles E. Carter. Göttingen: Vandenhoeck & Ruprecht, 2009.

Janowski, Bernd. *Konfliktgespräche mit Gott: Eine Anthropologie der Psalmen.* Neukirchen-Vluyn: Neukirchener Verlag, 2003.

Janzen, Waldemar. *Mourning Cry and Woe-Oracle.* BZAW 125. Berlin/New York: De Gruyter, 1972.

Jarick, John. "Questioning Sheol." Pages 22–32 in *Resurrection.* Edited by Stanley E. Porter et al. JSNTSup 186. Sheffield: Sheffield Academic Press, 1999.

Jastrow, Marcus. *A Dictionary of the Targumim, the Talmud Babli and Yerushalmi, and the Midrashic Literature.* 2 vols. New York: Pardes, 1903.

Jellicoe, Sidney. "Hebrew-Greek Equivalents for the Nether World, Its Milieu and Inhabitants, in the Old Testament." *Textus* 8 (1973): 1–19.

Jensen, Hans J. L. "The Fall of the King." *SJOT* 1 (1990): 121–47.

Jensen, Joseph. "Helel ben Shahar (Isaiah 14:12–15) in Bible and Tradition." Pages 339–56

in *Writing and Reading the Scroll of Isaiah: Studies of an Interpretive Tradition*. Edited by C. C. Broyles and C. A. Evans; Leiden: Brill, 1997.
Jensen, P. "Akkadisch *mudū*." *ZA* 35 (1924): 124–32.
Jenson, Philip Peter. *Graded Holiness: A Key to the Priestly Conception of the World*. Sheffield: JSOT Press, 1992.
Jeppesen, Knud. "Call and Frustration: A New Understanding of Isaiah viii 21–22." *VT* 32 (1982): 145–57.
– "The Cornerstone (Isa 28:16) in Deutero-Isaianic Re-Reading of the Message of Isaiah." *Studia Theologica* 38 (1984): 93–99.
Jeremias, Alfred. *Hölle und Paradies bei den Babyloniern*. 2nd ed. Leipzig: Hinrichs, 1903.
Jeremias, Jörg. *The Book of Amos*. OTL. Louisville, Ky.: Westminster John Knox, 1998.
Johnson, A. R. *The Vitality of the Individual in the Thought of Ancient Israel*. Cardiff: University of Wales Press, 1949.
Johnson, Dan G. *From Chaos to Restoration: An Integrative Reading of Isaiah 24–27*. JSOTSup 61. Sheffield: Sheffield Academic Press, 1988.
Johnson, W. Raymond, and J. Brett McClain. "A Fragmentary Scene of Ptolemy XII Worshiping the Goddess Mut and Her Divine Entourage." Pages 134–39 in *Servant of Mut: Studies in Honor of Richard A. Fazzini*. Edited by Sue H. D'Auria. Boston: Brill, 2008.
Johnston, Philip S. *Shades of Sheol: Death and Afterlife in the Old Testament*. Downer's Grove, Ill.: InterVarsity, 2002.
Jong, Matthijs J. de. *Isaiah Among the Ancient Near Eastern Prophets: A Comparative Study of the Earliest Stages of the Isaiah Tradition and the Neo-Assyrian Prophecies*. VTSup 117. Leiden: Brill, 2007.
Joüon, Paul, S.J., and Takamitsu Muraoka. *A Grammar of Biblical Hebrew*. SubBi 14. Rome: Pontificio Istituto Biblico, 2000.
Junker, Hermann. *Das Götterdekret über das Abaton*. Vienna: Alfred Hölder, 1913.
Kaiser, Otto. *Isaiah 1–12: A Commentary*. Translated by John Bowden. 2nd ed. OTL. Philadelphia: Westminster, 1983.
– *Isaiah 13–39: A Commentary*. Translated by R. A. Wilson. OTL. Philadelphia: Westminster, 1973.
Kaiser, Werner. "Zur Buste als einer Darstellungsform ägyptischer Rundplastik." *Mitteilungen des Deutschen Archäologischen Instituts Kairo* 46 (1990), 269–85.
Kalmanofsky, Amy. *Terror All Around: The Rhetoric of Horror in the Book of Jeremiah*. London: Continuum, 2008.
Kanawati, Naguib. *The Tomb and Beyond: Burial Customs of Egyptian Officials*. Warminster, England: Aris & Phillips, 2001.
Kassian, Alexei, Andrej Korolëv, and Andrej Sidel'tsev. *Hittite Funerary Ritual: šalliš waštaiš*. Münster: Ugarit-Verlag, 2002.
Kaufmann, Yehezkel. *The Religion of Israel, from Its Beginnings to the Babylonian Exile*. Translated by Moshe Greenberg. Chicago: University of Chicago Press, 1960.
Kawai, Nozomu. "Royal Tombs of the Third Intermediate and Late Periods: Some Considerations." *Orient* 33 (1998): 33–45.
Keel, Othmar. *The Symbolism of the Biblical World: Ancient Near Eastern Iconography and the Book of Psalms*. Translated by Timothy J. Hallett. New York: Seabury Press, 1978.
– "Das Vergraben der 'fremden Götter' in Genesis XXXV 4b." *VT* 23 (1973): 305–36.
Keel, Othmar, and Christoph Uehlinger. *Gods, Goddesses and Images of God in Ancient Israel*. Translated by Thomas H. Trapp. Minneapolis: Fortress, 1998.
Kelle, Brad E. *Hosea 2: Metaphor and Rhetoric in Historical Perspective*. Academia Biblica 20. Atlanta: Society of Biblical Literature, 2005.

Keller, Sharon Ruth. "Egyptian Letters to the Dead in Relation to the Old Testament and Other Near Eastern Sources." Ph.D. dissertation, New York University, 1989.
Kennedy, Charles A. "Dead, Cult of the." Pages 105–8 in vol. 2 of *Anchor Bible Dictionary*. Edited by David Noel Freedman. 6 vols. New York: Doubleday, 1992.
– "Isaiah 57:5–6: Tombs in the Rocks," *BASOR* 275 (1989): 47–52.
Kennedy, George. *Comparative Rhetoric: An Historical and Cross-Cultural Introduction*. New York/Oxford: Oxford University Press, 1998.
Kenyon, Kathleen. "Palestine in the Middle Bronze Age." Pages 77–116 in vol. II/3 of *Cambridge Ancient History*. Rev. ed. Cambridge: Cambridge University Press, 1966.
Kienast, Burkhart. "Igigū und Anunnakū nach den Akkadischen Quellen." *Assyriological Studies* 16 (1965): 141–58.
Killebrew, Ann E. *Biblical Peoples and Ethnicity: An Archaeological Study of Egyptians, Canaanites, Philistines, and Early Israel (ca. 1300–1100 BCE)*. Archaeology and Biblical Studies 9. Atlanta: Society of Biblical Literature, 2005.
King, Philip J. "The Eighth, the Greatest of Centuries?" *JBL* 108 (1989): 3–15.
– Review of Elizabeth Bloch-Smith, *Judaihite Burial Practices*. *CBQ* 56 (1994): 748–49.
King, Philip J., and Lawrence E. Stager. *Life in Biblical Israel*. Library of Ancient Israel. Louisville, Ky.: Westminster John Knox, 2001.
Kinney, Lesley. "The Funerary Procession." Pages 157–70 in *Egyptian Art: Principles and Themes in Wall Scenes*. Edited by Leonie Donovan and Kim McCorquodale. Prism Archaeological Series 6. Guizeh, Egypt: Prism, 2000.
Kissane, Edward J. *The Book of Isaiah*. Vol. 1. Dublin: Browne & Nolan, 1941.
Kitchen, K. A. "High Society and Lower Ranks in Ramesside Egypt at Home and Abroad." *British Museum Studies in Ancient Egypt and Sudan* 6 (2006): 31–36.
– *On the Reliability of the Old Testament*. Grand Rapids: Eerdmans, 2003.
– *The Third Intermediate Period in Egypt, 1100–650 B.C.* 3rd ed. Warminster: Aris & Phillips, 1996.
Klawans, Jonathan. "Pure Violence: Sacrifice and Defilement in Ancient Israel." *HTR* 94 (2001): 133–55.
Klein, George L. "The 'Prophetic Perfect.' " *JNSL* 16 (1990): 45–60.
Kletter, Raz. "People without Burials? The Lack of Iron I Burials in the Central Highlands of Palestine." *IEJ* 52 (2002): 28–48.
Kloner, Amos. "Iron Age Burial Caves in Jerusalem and Its Vicinity." *Bulletin of the Anglo-Israel Archaeological Society* 19–20 (2004): 95–118.
Knohl, Israel. *The Sanctuary of Silence: The Priestly Torah and the Holiness School*. Minneapolis: Fortress, 1994.
Köhler, Ludwig. *Hebrew Man*. Translated by Peter R. Ackroyd. New York: Abingdon, 1956.
Korpel, Marjo C. A. *A Rift in the Clouds: Ugaritic and Hebrew Descriptions of the Divine*. Münster: Ugarit-Verlag, 1990.
Köszeghy, Miklós. "Hybris und Prophetie: Erwägungen zum Hintergrund von Jesaja XIV 12–15." *VT* 44 (1994): 549–54.
Kramer, Samuel N. "The Death of Ur-Nammu and His Descent to the Netherworld." *Journal of Cuneiform Studies* 21 (1969): 104–25.
Krause, H. J. "Hôj als Prophetische Leichenklage über das eigene Volk im 8. Jahrhundert." *ZAW* 85 (1973): 15–46.
Kristensen, William Brede. *Life out of Death: Studies in the Religions of Egypt and of Ancient Greece*. Translated by H. J. Franken and G. R. H. Wright. Louvain: Peeters Press, 1992.
Kristeva, Julia. *Revolution du langage poétique: L'avant-garde à la fin du XIXe siècle: Lautréamont et Mallarmé*. Paris: Seuil, 1974.

Kuan, Jeffrey K. *Neo-Assyrian Historical Inscriptions and Syria-Palestine: Israelite/Judean-Tyrian-Damascene Political and Commercial Relations in the Ninth-Eighth Centuries B.C.E.* Hong Kong: Alliance Bible Seminary, 1995.
Kuhrt, Amélie. *The Ancient Near East.* Vol. 1, *From c. 3000 B.C. to c. 1200 B.C.* Vol. 2, *From c. 1200 B.C. to c. 330 B.C.* Routledge History of the Ancient World. London: Routledge, 1995.
Kuschke, Arnulf, and Martin Metzger. "Kumudi und die Ausgrabungen auf Tell Kāmid el-Loz." Pages 142–73 in *Congress Volume: Uppsala, 1971.* VTSup 22. Leiden: Brill, 1972.
Kutsch, Ernst. "Sehen und Bestimmen: Die Egymologie von בְּרִית." Pages 165–78 in *Archäologie und Altes Testament: Festschrift für Kurt Galling.* Edited by Arnulf Kuschke and Ernst Kutsch. Tübingen: Mohr Siebeck, 1970.
Kutscher, E. Y. *The Language and Linguistic Background of the Isaiah Scroll (1 Q Isa^a).* Leiden: Brill, 1974.
Laberge, Leo. "The Woe-Oracles of Isaiah 28–33." *Église et Théologie* 13 (1982): 157–90.
Lambdin, Thomas. "Egyptian Loan Words in the Old Testament." *JAOS* 73 (1953): 145–55.
Lambert, W. G. *Babylonian Wisdom Literature.* Oxford: Clarendon, 1960.
– "DINGIR.ŠÀ.DIB.BA Incantations." *JNES* 33 (1974): 267–322.
– "Mesopotamian Sources and Pre-Exilic Israel," Pages 352–65 in *In Search of Pre-Exilic Israel: Proceedings of the Oxford Old Testament Seminar.* Edited by John Day. London: T & T Clark International, 2004.
Landy, Francis. "The Covenant with Death." Pages 220–32 in *Strange Fire: Reading the Bible after the Holocaust.* Edited by Tod Linafelt. Sheffield: Sheffield Academic Press, 2000.
– "Tracing the Voice of the Other: Isaiah 28 and the Covenant with Death." Pages 140–62 in *The New Literary Criticism and the Hebrew Bible.* Edited by J. Cheryl Exum. JSOTSup 143. Sheffield: JSOT Press, 1993.
Lang, Bernhard. "A Zoroastrian Prophecy of Resurrection." Pages 83–91 in *Hebrew Life and Literature: Selected Essays of Bernhard Lang.* Farnham, England: Ashgate, 2008.
– "Life after Death in the Prophetic Promise." Pages 144–56 in *Congress Volume: Jerusalem 1986.* Edited by J. A. Emerton. VTSup 40. Leiden: Brill, 1988.
Lapinkivi, Pirjo. *The Neo-Assyrian Myth of Ištar's Descent and Resurrection.* Helsinki: Neo-Assyrian Text Corpus Project, 2010.
Lateiner, Donald. *The Historical Method of Herodotus.* Journal of the Classical Association of Canada Supplementary Volume 23. Toronto: University of Toronto Press, 1989.
Layton, Scott C. "The Steward in Ancient Israel: A Study of Hebrew (*ʾašer*) *ʿal-habbayit* in Its Near Eastern Setting." *JBL* 109 (1990): 633–49.
Leahy, Anthony. "Death by Fire in Ancient Egypt." *Journal of the Economic and Social History of the Orient* 27 (1984): 199–206.
Leeuwen, Raymond C. Van. "Isa 14:12, *ḥôlēs ʿal gwym* and Gilgamesh XI, 6." *JBL* 99 (1980): 173–84.
Leibovici, Marcel. "Génies et démons en Babylonie." Pages 85–111 in *Génies, anges, et démons, Égypte, Babylone, Israel, Islam.* Sources orientales 8. Paris: Seuil, 1971.
Lemaire, André. "Déesses et dieux de Syrie-Palestine d'après les Inscriptions (c. 1000–500 av. n. é.)." Pages 127–58 in Walter Dietrich and Martin A. Klopfenstein, eds., *Gott Allein? JHWH-Verehrung und biblischer Monotheismus im Kontext der israelitischen und altorientalische Religionsgeschichte.* Orbis biblicus et orientalis 139. Göttingen: Vandenhoeck & Ruprecht, 1994.

- Review of Brian R. Schmidt, *Israel's Beneficent Dead: Ancestor Cult and Necromancy in Ancient Israelite Religion and Tradition.* JNES 58 (1999): 217–19.
- "Les inscriptions de Khirbet el-Qôm et l'Ashérah de YHWH." *RB 84* (1977): 595–608.

Lesko, Barbara. *The Great Goddesses of Egypt.* Norman: University of Oklahoma, 1999.

Lesko, Leonard H. "Death and Afterlife in Ancient Egyptian Thought." Pages 1763–74 in *Civilizations of the Ancient Near East.* Edited by Jack M. Sasson. Peabody, Mass.: Hendrickson, 2000.

Levenson, Jon D. *The Death and Resurrection of the Beloved Son: The Transformation of Child Sacrifice in Judaism and Christianity.* New Haven: Yale University Press, 1993.
- *Resurrection and the Restoration of Israel.* New Haven: Yale University Press, 2006.

Levine, Baruch. "Assyrian Ideology and Israelite Monotheism." *Iraq* 67 (2005): 411–427.

Levine, B. A. and J. M. de Tarragon, "Dead Kings and Rephaim: The Patrons of the Ugaritic Dynasty," *JAOS* 104 (l984): 649–59.

Lewis, Theodore J. *Cults of the Dead in Ancient Israel and Ugarit.* HSM 39. Atlanta: Scholars Press, 1989.
- "Dead." Pages 223–31 in *Dictionary of Deities and Demons in the Bible.* 2nd edition. Edited by Karel van der Toorn, B. Becking, and P. W. van der Horst. Leiden: Brill, 1995.
- "Death Cult Imagery in Isaiah 57." *HAR* 11 (1987): 267–84.
- "How Far Can Texts Take Us? Evaluating Textual Sources for Reconstructing Ancient Israelite Beliefs about the Dead." Pages 169–217 in *Sacred Time, Sacred Place: Archaeology and the Religion of Israel.* Edited by Barry M. Gittlen. Winona Lake, Ind.: Eisenbrauns, 2002.
- "Mot (deity)." Pages 922–24 in vol. 4 of *Anchor Bible Dictionary.* Edited by David Noel Freedman. 6 vols. New York: Doubleday, 1992.
- "Toward a Literary Translation of the Rapiuma Texts." Pages 115–23 in *Ugarit, Religion and Culture: Essays Presented in Honour of Professor John C. L. Gibson.* Edited by N. Wyatt, W. G. E. Watson, and J. B. Lloyd. Ugaritisch-biblische Literatur 12. Münster: Ugarit-Verlag, 1996.
- "You Have Heard What the Kings of Assyria Have Done": Disarmament Passages vis-à-vis Assyrian Rhetoric of Intimidation." Pages 75–100 in eds. R. Cohen and R. Westbrook, *Isaiah's Vision of Peace in Biblical and Modern International Relations: Swords Into Plowshares.* New York: Palgrave Macmillan, 2008.

L'Heureux, Conrad. *Rank Among the Canaanite Gods: El, Baʻal, and the Repha'im.* Missoula, Mont.: Scholars Press, 1979.
- "The Ugaritic and Biblical Rephaim." *HTR* 67 (1974): 263–74.

Lichtheim, Miriam. *Ancient Egyptian Literature: A Book of Readings.* 3 vols. Berkeley: University of California Press, 1973–80.

Lipiński, Edward. "Phoenician Cult Expressions in the Persian Period." Pages 297–308 in *Symbiosis, Symbolism and Power of the Past: Canaan, Ancient Israel, and Their Neighbors from the Late Bronze Age through Roman Palaestina.* Edited by William G. Dever and Seymour Gitin. Winona Lake, Ind.: Eisenbrauns, 2003.
- *On the Skirts of Canaan in the Iron Age: Historical and Topographical Researches.* OLA 153. Leuven: Peeters, 2006.

Lipschits, Oded. *The Fall and Rise of Jerusalem: Judah under Babylonian Rule.* Winona Lake, Ind.: Eisenbrauns, 2005.

Littauer, M. A. "New Light on the Assyrian Chariot." Pages 246–57 in *Selected Writings on Chariots and Other Early Vehicles, Riding and Harness.* Culture and History of the Ancient Near East 6. Leiden/Boston: Brill, 2002.

Littauer, M. A., and J. H. Crouwel. *Chariots and Related Equipment from the Tomb of Tutʿankhamūn.* Tutʿankhamūn's Tomb Series 8. Oxford: Griffith Institute, 1985.
– "The Origin of the True Chariot." Pages 45–52 in *Selected Writings on Chariots and Other Early Vehicles, Riding and Harness.* Culture and History of the Ancient Near East 6. Leiden/Boston: Brill, 2002.
Livingstone, Alasdair. *Court Poetry and Literary Miscellanea.* SAA 3. Helsinki: Helsinki University Press, 1989.
– *Mystical and Mythological Explanatory Works of Assyrian and Babylonian Scholars.* Oxford: Clarendon, 1986.
– "The Underworld Vision of an Assyrian Prince." Pages 68–76 in *Court Poetry and Literary Miscellanea.* Edited by Alasdair Livingstone. SAS 3. Helsinki: Helsinki University Press, 1989.
Lloyd, Alan B. "Psychology and Society in the Ancient Egyptian Cult of the Dead." Pages 117–33 in *Religion and Philosophy in Ancient Egypt.* Edited by James P. Allen et al. Yale Egyptological Studies 3. New Haven, Conn.: Yale University, 1989.
– *Herodotus, Book II. Vol. 1, Introduction.* Leiden: Brill, 1975.
Lods, Adolphe. *La croyance à la vie future et le culte des morts dans l'antiquité Israélite.* Paris: Fischbacher, 1906.
Loffreda, Stanislao. "Iron Age Rock-Cut Tombs in Palestine." *SBFLA* 18 (1968): 244–87.
– "The Late Chronology of Some Rock-Cut Tombs of the Selwan Necropolis, Jerusalem." *SBFLA* 23 (1973): 7–36.
Lohwasser, Angelika. *The Kushite Cemetery of Sanam: A Non-Royal Burial Ground of the Nubian Capital, ca. 800–600 BC.* London: Golden House Publications, 2010.
Longman, Tremper, III. *Proverbs.* Grand Rapids: Baker Academic, 2006.
Lord, Albert B. *The Singer of Tales.* Cambridge, Mass.: Harvard University Press, 1964.
Loretz, Oswald. "Die Teraphim als 'Ahnen-Götter-Figur(in)en im Lichte der Texte aus Nuzi, Emar, und Ugarit: Anmerkungen zu *ilānū/ilh, ilhm/ʾihym* und DINGIR.ERÍN.MEŠ/*ins ilm.*" *UF* 24 (1992): 152–67.
– "Der ugaritische Topos *bʿl rkb* und die 'Sprache Kanaans' in Jes 19,1–25." *UF* 19 (1987): 101–12.
Lowery, R. H. *The Reforming Kings: Cults and Society in First Temple Judah.* JSOTSup 120. Sheffield: JSOT Press, 1991.
Lust, J. "On Wizards and Prophets." Pages 133–42 in *Studies on Prophecy: A Collection of Twelve Papers.* VTSup 26. Leiden: Brill, 1974.
Lucarelli, Rita. "Demons (Benevolent and Malevolent)." In *UCLA Encyclopedia of Egyptology.* Edited by Jacco Dieleman and Willeke Wendrich. Los Angeles, 2010. (Accessed online: *http://escholarship.org/uc/item/1r72q9vv*)
– "Demons in the Book of the Dead." Pages 203–12 in *Totenbuch-Forschungen: Gesammelte Beiträge des 2. Internationalen Totenbuch-Symposiums, Bonn, 25. bis 29. September 2005.* Edited by Burkhard Backes, Irmtraut Munro und Simone Stöhr. Studien zum altägyptischen Totenbuch 11. Wiesbaden: Harrassowitz, 2006.
Luckenbill, D. D. *The Annals of Sennacherib.* Oriental Institute Publications 2. Chicago: University of Chicago Press, 1924.
Lüddeckens, Erich. *Untersuchungen über religiösen Gehalt, Sprache und Form der ägyptischen Totenklage.* MDAIK 11. Berlin: 1943.
Luukko, Mikko, and Greta van Buylaere. *The Political Correspondence of Esarhaddon.* SAA 16. Helsinki: Helsinki University Press, 2002.
Machinist, Peter. "Assyria and Its Image in First Isaiah." *JAOS* 103 (1983): 719–37.

– "Literature as Politics: The Tukulti-Ninurta Epic and the Bible." *CBQ* 38 (1976): 455–82.
– "The Rab Šāqēh at the Wall of Jerusalem: Israelite Identity in the Face of the Assyrian 'Other.'" *Hebrew Studies* 41 (2000): 151–68.
Majerick, Ruth. "Rhetoric and Rhetorical Criticism." Pages 710–12 in vol. 5 of *Anchor Bible Dictionary*. Edited by David Noel Freedman. 6 vols. New York: Doubleday, 1992.
Malul, Meir. "Eating and Drinking (One's) Refuse." *Nouvelles Assyriologiques Brèves et Utilitaires* (1993): 82–83.
Mankowski, Paul V. *Akkadian Loanwords in Biblical Hebrew*. Winona Lake, IN: Eisenbrauns, 2000.
Mann, Michael. *The Sources of Social Power: Volume 1, A History of Power from the Beginning to AD 1760*. Cambridge: Cambridge University Press, 1986.
March, Eugene. "Prophecy." Pages 159–62 in *Old Testament Form Criticism*. Edited by John H. Hayes. TUMSR 2. San Antonio: Trinity University Press, 1977.
Margalit, Baruch. *A Matter of "Life" and "Death": A Study of the Baal-Mot Epic (CTA 4–5–6)*. Alter Orient und Altes Testament 206. Kevelaer: Butzon & Bercker, 1980.
Margueron, Jean-Claude. "Babylon." Pages 563–65 in vol. 1 of *Anchor Bible Dictionary*. Edited by David Noel Freedman. 6 vols. New York: Doubleday, 1992.
Markoe, Glenn. "The Emergence of Orientalizing in Greek Art: Some Observations on the Interchange between Greeks and Phoenicians in the Eighth and Seventh Centuries B.C." *BASOR* 301 (1996): 47–67.
– "The Emergence of Phoenician Art." *BASOR* 279 (1990): 13–26.
Marlow, Hilary. "The Lament Over the River Nile – Isaiah xix 5–10 in its Wider Context," *VT* 57 (2007): 229–242.
Marsham, John. *Canon Chronicus Aegyptiacus, Ebraicus, Graecus & Disquisitiones*. London, 1672.
Marti, D. Karl. *Das Buch Jesaja*. KHC 10. Tübingen: Mohr Siebeck, 1900.
Martin, Karl. "Stele." Pages 1–6 in vol. 6 of *Lexikon der Ägyptologie*. Wiesbaden: Harrasowitz, 1986.
Martin-Achard, Robert. *De la mort à la résurrection: D'après l'Ancien Testament*. Neuchâtel: Delachaux & Niestlé, 1956.
– *From Death to Life: A Study of the Development of the Doctrine of the Resurrection in the Old Testament*. Translated by John Penney Smith. Edinburgh: Oliver & Boyd, 1960.
Matthiae, Paolo. "Princely Cemetery and Ancestors Cult at Ebla during Middle Bronze II: A Proposal of Interpretation." *UF* 11 (1979): 563–69.
– "New Discoveries at Ebla: The Excavations of the Western Palace and the Royal Necropolis of the Amorite Period," *BA* 47 (1984): 18–32.
Mauchline, John. *Isaiah 1–39: Introduction and Commentary*. London: SCM, 1962.
May, Herbert G. "Ephod and Ariel." *AJSL* 56 (1939): 44–69.
Mayer, Walter. "Sennacherib's Campaign of 701: The Assyrian View." Translated by Julia Assante. Pages 168–200 in *"Like a Bird in Cage": The Invasion of Sennacherib in 701 BCE*. Edited by Lester L. Grabbe. JSOTSup 363. London: Sheffield Academic Press, 2003.
Mays, James L. *Hosea*. OTL. London: SCM, 1969.
Mazar, Amihai. *Archaeology of the Land of the Bible, 10,000–586 B.C.E.* Anchor Bible Reference Library. New York: Doubleday, 1990.
McCarter, P. Kyle. "The Religious Reforms of Hezekiah and Josiah." Pages 57–80 in *Aspects of Monotheism: How God Is One: Symposium at the Smithsonian Institution, October 19, 1996, sponsored by the Resident Associate Program*. Edited by Hershel Shanks and Jack Meinhardt. Washington, D.C.: Biblical Archaeology Society, 1997.

McEvenue, S. "A Source-Critical Problem in Nm 14, 26–38." *Biblica* 50 (1969): 453–65.
McGinnis, John. "A Neo-Assyrian Text Describing a Royal Funeral." *SAAB* 1 (1987): 1–12.
McKane, William. *Proverbs: A New Approach.* Philadelphia: Westminster, 1970.
McKay, John W. *Religion in Judah under the Assyrians, 732–609 BC.* SBT, 2nd series, 26. Naperville, Ill.: Alec R. Allenson, 1973.
McKenzie, John L. Review of Mitchell J. Dahood, *Psalms* (Anchor Bible), *CBQ* 31 (1969): 80–81.
McLaughlin, John L. *The Marzēaḥ in the Prophetic Literature: References and Allusions in Light of the Extra-Biblical Evidence.* VTSup 86. Leiden: Brill, 2001.
Medina, Richard W. "Life and Death Viewed as Physical and Lived Spaces: Some Preliminary Thoughts from Proverbs." *ZAW* 122 (2010): 199–211.
Meeks, Dmitri. "Demons." Pages 375–78 in *The Oxford Encyclopedia of Ancient Egypt.* Edited by Donald B. Redford. New York: Oxford University Press, 2001.
– "Notes de Lexicographie." *Revue d'Égyptologie* 26 (1974): 52–65.
Mendenhall, George E. "From Witchcraft to Justice: Death and Afterlife in the Old Testament." Pages 67–81 in *Death and Afterlife.* Westport, Conn.: Greenwood, 1992.
Menu, Bernadette. "Mise à mort cérémonielle et prélèvements royaux sous la Ire dynastie." Pages 122–135 in *Le Sacrifice humain en Égypte ancienne et ailleurs.* Edited by Jean-Pierre Albert and Béatrix Midant-Reynes. Paris: Soleb, 2005.
Mettinger, Tryggve N. D. *The Riddle of Resurrection: "Dying and Rising Gods" in the Ancient Near East.* Stockholm: Almqvist & Wiksell International, 2001.
– *No Graven Image? Israelite Aniconism in Its Ancient Near Eastern Context.* ConBOT 42. Stockholm: Almqvist & Wiksell International, 1995.
– *Solomonic State Officials: A Study of the Civil Government Officials of the Israelite Monarchy.* ConBOT 5. Lund: Gleerup, 1971.
Michalowski, Piotr. "The Death of Šulgi." *Orientalia* 46 (1977): 220–25.
Mieroop, Marc Van de. *A History of the Ancient Near East, ca. 3000–323 BC.* 2nd ed. Blackwell History of the Ancient World. Malden, Mass.: Blackwell, 2007.
Milde, Henk. "Going out into the Day." Pages 15–34 in *Hidden Futures. Death and Immortality in Ancient Egypt, Anatolia, the Classical, Biblical and Arabic-Islamic World.* Edited by Jan Maarten Bremer, Theo P.J. van den Hout, and Rudolph Peters. Amsterdam: Amsterdam University Press, 1994.
Milgrom, Jacob. "Were the Firstborn Sacrificed to YHWH? To Molek? Popular Practice or Divine Demand?" Pages 49–55. Edited by A. I. Baumgarten. *Sacrifice in Religious Experience.* Leiden: Brill, 2002.
Millar, William R. *Isaiah 24–27 and the Origin of Apocalyptic.* HSM 11. Missoula, Mont.: Scholars Press, 1976.
Millard, A. R. "Sennacherib's Attack on Hezekiah." *Tyndale Bulletin* 36 (1985): 61–77.
Miller, J. Maxwell. "Moab." Pages 882–93 in vol. 4 of *Anchor Bible Dictionary.* Edited by David Noel Freedman. 6 vols. New York: Doubleday, 1992.
Miller, J. Maxwell, and John H. Hayes. *A History of Ancient Israel and Judah.* 2nd ed. Louisville, Ky.: Westminster John Knox, 2006.
Miller, Patrick D. "The Mrzḥ Text." Pages 37–48 in *The Claremont Ras Shamra Tablets.* Edited by L. R. Fisher. AnOr 48. Rome: Pontifical Biblical Institute, 1971.
– "Psalms and Inscriptions." Pages 311–32 in *Congress Volume: Vienna 1980.* VTSup 32. Leiden: Brill, 1981.
– *The Religion of Ancient Israel.* Library of Ancient Israel. Louisville, Ky.: Westminster John Knox, 2000.

– *Sin and Judgment in the Prophets: A Stylistic and Theological Analysis.* SBLMS 27. Chico, Calif.: Scholars Press, 1982.
– "Vocative Lamed in the Psalter: A Reconsideration." *UF* 11 (1979): 617–37.
Miralles Maciá, Lorena. *Marzeah y Thíasos: Una Institución Convival en el Oriente Próximo Antiguo y el Mediterráneo.* Anejos 20. Madrid: Publicaciones Universidad Complutense de Madrid, 2007.
Mittman, S. "Die Grabinschrift des Sängers Uriahu." *Zeitschrift der deutschen Palästina-Vereins* 97 (1981): 139–52.
Moor, J. C. de. *A Cuneiform Anthology of Religious Texts from Ugarit.* Leiden: Brill, 1987.
– "Demons in Canaan." *JEOL* 27 (1981–82): 106–19.
– *New Year with Canaanites and Israelites.* Kampen: Kok, 1972.
– "Rapi'uma – Rephaim," *ZAW* 88 (1976): 323–45.
Moor, J. C. de, and P. van der Lugt. "The Spectre of Pan-Ugaritism." *BO* 31 (1974): 3–26.
Moor, J. C. de, and Klaas Spronk. "More on Demons in Ugarit (KTU 1.82)." *UF* 16 (1984): 237–50.
Moorey, P. R. S. *Ur 'of the Chaldees': A Revised and Updated Edition of Sir Leonard Woolley's Excavations at Ur.* Ithaca, N.Y.: Cornell University Press, 1982.
– "Where Did They Bury the Kings of the Third Dynasty of Ur?" *Iraq* 46 (1984): 1–18.
Morenz, Siegfried. *Egyptian Religion.* Translated by Ann E. Keep. Ithaca, N.Y.: Cornell University Press, 1973.
Morrow, William. "Cuneiform Literacy and Deuteronomic Composition." *BO* 62 (2005): 204–13.
– "Resistance and Hybridity in Late Bronze Age Canaan," *RB* 115 (2008), 321–39.
– "'To Set the Name' in the Deuteronomic Centralization Formula: A Case of Cultural Hybridity." *JSS* 55 (2010): 365–83.
Mowinckel, Sigmund. *The Psalms in Israel's Worship.* Translated by D. R. Ap-Thomas. 2 vols. Oxford: Basil Blackwell, 1962. Reprint, Grand Rapids: Eerdmans, 2004.
Muchiki, Yoshiyuki. *Egyptian Proper Names and Loanwords in North-West Semitic.* SBLDS 173. Atlanta, Ga.: Society of Biblical Literature, 1999.
Muilenburg, James. "Form Criticism and Beyond." *JBL* 88 (1969): 1–18.
Müller, Hans-Peter. "Das Wort von Totengeistern (Jes 8,19f.)." *WO* 8 (1975–76): 65–76.
– "Malik," Pages 538–42 in *Dictionary of Deities and Demons in the Bible.* Edited by Karel van der Toorn, B. Becking, and P. W. van der Horst. Leiden: Brill, 1995.
Müller, Maya. "Afterlife." Pages 32–37 in the *The Oxford Encyclopedia of Ancient Egypt.* Edited by Donald B. Redford. New York: Oxford University Press, 2001.
Munro, Peter. *Die spätägyptischen Totenstelen.* Glückstadt: J. J. Augustin, 1973.
Na'aman, Nadav. "An Assyrian Residence at Ramat Rahel?" *Tel Aviv* 28 (2001): 260–280.
– "Death Formulae and the Burial Place of the Kings of the House of David." *Biblica* 85 (2004): 245–54.
– "'Let Other Kingdoms Struggle with the Great Powers – You, Judah, Pay the Tribute and Hope for the Best': The Foreign Policy of the Kings of Judah in the Ninth-Eighth Centuries BCE." Pages 55–73 in *Isaiah's Vision of Peace in Biblical and Modern International Relations: Swords Into Plowshares.* Edited by R. Cohen and R. Westbrook. New York: Palgrave Macmillan, 2008.
– "The Brook of Egypt and Assyrian Policy on the Border of Egypt." *Tel Aviv* 6 (1979): 68–90.
Naveh, J. "Graffiti and Dedications." *BASOR* 235 (1979): 27–30.
Neiman, David. "PGR: A Canaanite Cult-Object in the Old Testament," *JBL* 67 (1948): 55–60.

Nelson, Harold Hayden. *Reliefs and Inscriptions at Karnak.* Chicago: University of Chicago Press, 1936.
Nelson, Richard D. "The Double Redaction of the Deuteronomistic History: The Case is Still Compelling," *JSOT* 29 (2005): 319–37.
Nemet-Najat, Karen Rhea. *Daily Life in Ancient Mesopotamia.* Peabody, Mass.: Hendrickson, 2002.
Niccacci, Alviero. "Isaiah XVIII–XX from an Egyptological Perspective," *VT* 48 (1998): 214–238.
Nickelsburg, George W. E. *Resurrection, Immortality, and Eternal Life in Intertestamental Judaism.* Harvard Theological Studies 26. Cambridge: Harvard University Press, 1972.
Niditch, Susan. *Oral World and Written Word.* Louisville, Ky.: Westminster John Knox, 1996.
Nissinen, Martti. "Prophecy against the King in Neo-Assyrian Sources." Pages 157–70 in *'Lasset uns Brücken bauen ...': Collected Communications to the XVth Congress of the International Organization for the Study of the Old Testament.* Beiträge zur Erforschung des Alten Testaments und des Antiken Judentums 42. Frankfurt am Main: Lang, 1998.
– ed. *Prophecy in Its Ancient Near Eastern Context: Mesopotamian, Biblical, and Arabian Perspectives.* SBL Symposium Series 13. Atlanta: Society of Biblical Literature, 2000.
– *Prophets and Prophecy in the Ancient Near East.* Edited by Peter Machinist. Writings from the Ancient World 12. Atlanta: Society of Biblical Literature, 2003.
Noth, Martin *Die israelitischen Personennamen im Rahmen der gemeinsemitischen Namengebung.* Beiträge zur Wissenschaft vom Alten und Neuen Testament 3. Folge, Heft 10. Hildesheim: Georg Olms, 1966.
Nutkowicz, Hélène. *L'Homme face à la mort au royaume de Juda: Rites, pratiques, et représentations.* Paris: Cerf, 2006.
O'Connell, R. H. "Isaiah XIV 4B–23: Ironic Reversal Through Concentric Structure and Mythic Allusion." *VT* 38 (1988): 407–18.
O'Connor, M. P. "The Poetic Inscription from Khirbet el-Qôm." *VT* 37 (1987): 224–30.
O'Donoghue, Michael. "The 'Letters to the Dead' and Ancient Egyptian Religion." *Bulletin of the Australian Centre for Egyptology* 10 (1999): 87–104.
Oded, Bustenay. "Observations on Methods of Assyrian Rule in Transjordania after the Palestinian Campaign of Tiglath-Pileser III." *JNES* 29 (1970): 177–86.
– *War, Peace, and Empire: Justification for War in Assyrian Royal Inscriptions.* Wiesbaden: Dr. Ludwig Reichert Verlag, 1992.
Ogdon, Jorge R. "A Hitherto Unrecognized Metaphor of Death in Papyrus Berlin 3024." *Göttinger Miszellen* 100 (1987): 73–80.
Oldenburg, Ulf. "Above the Stars of El: El in Ancient South Arabic Religion." *ZAW* 82 (1970): 187–208.
Olmo Lete, G. del. *Canaanite Religion: According to the Liturgical Texts of Ugarit.* Translated by W. G. E. Watson. Winona Lake, Ind.: Eisenbrauns, 2004.
– "GN, el cementerio regio de Ugarit," *SEL* 3 (1986): 62–64.
– *Mitos y Leyendas de Canaan: Según la Tradición de Ugarit.* Madrid: Ediciones Cristiandad; Valencia: Institución San Jerónimo, 1981.
– "The Ugaritic Ritual Texts: A New Edition and Commentary; A Critical Assessment." *UF* 36 (2004): 539–648.
Olyan, Saul M. *Biblical Mourning: Ritual and Social Dimensions.* Oxford: Oxford University Press, 2004.
– "Some Neglected Aspects of Israelite Interment Ideology." *JBL* 124 (2005): 601–16.

- "Was the 'King of Babylon' Buried Before His Corpse Was Exposed? Some Thoughts on Isa 14,19." *ZAW* 118 (2006): 423–26.
Oppenheim, A. Leo. *Ancient Mesopotamia: Portrait of a Dead Civilization*. Chicago: University of Chicago Press, 1964. Rev. ed. by Erica Reiner. Chicago: University of Chicago Press, 1977.
- "The Interpretation of Dreams in the Ancient Near East: With a Translation of an Assyrian Dream-Book." *Transactions of the American Philosophical Society* n.s. 46/3 (1956): 179–373.
- "Neo-Assyrian and Neo-Babylonian Empires." Pages 111–44 in *The Symbolic Instrument in Early Times*. Edited by Harold D. Lasswell et al. Propaganda and Communication in World History 1. Honolulu: University of Hawaii Press, 1979.
Orthmann, W. "Grab." Pages 581–605 in *Reallexikon der Assyriologie*. Edited by Erich Ebeling et al. Berlin: De Gruyter, 1928.
Otto, Eckart. *Das Deuteronomium: Politische Theologie und Rechtsform in Juda und Assyrien*. BZAW 284. Berlin: De Gruyter, 1999.
Otzen, Benedikt. "Israel under the Assyrians." Pages 251–61 in *Power and Propaganda: A Symposium on Ancient Empires*. Edited by Mogens Trolk Larsen. Mesopotamia 7. Copenhagen: Akademisk Forlag, 1979.
Page, H. R. *The Myth of Cosmic Rebellion: A Study of Its Reflexes in Ugaritic and Biblical Literature*. VTSup 65. Leiden: Brill, 1996.
Pardee, Dennis. "A New Datum for the Meaning of the Divine Name Milkashtart," Pages 55–68 in *Ascribe to the Lord: Biblical and Other Studies in Memory of Peter C. Craigie*. Edited by L. Eslinger and G. Taylor. JSOTSup 67. Sheffield: Sheffield Academic Press, 1988.
- "As Strong as Death." Pages 65–69 in *Love & Death in the Ancient Near East*. Edited by J. H. Marks and R. M. Good. Guilford, Conn.: Four Quarters, 1987.
- Review of George C. Heider, *Cult of Molek*. *JNES* 49 (1990): 372.
- "*Marzihu, Kispu*, and the Ugaritic Funerary Cult: A Minimalist View." Pages 273–87 in *Ugarit, Religion and Culture: Essays Presented in Honour of Professor John C. L. Gibson*. Edited by N. Wyatt, W. G. E. Watson and J. B. Lloyd. Ugaritisch-biblische Literatur 12. Münster: Ugarit-Verlag, 1996.
- *Ritual and Cult at Ugarit*. SBL Writings from the Ancient World 10. Atlanta: Society of Biblical Literature, 2002.
- "G. del Olmo Lete's Views on Ugaritic Epigraphy and Religion." *UF* 37 (2005): 767–816.
- "A New Aramaic Inscription From Zincirli," *BASOR* 356 (2009): 51–71
Parker, Bradley J. *The Mechanics of Empire: The Northern Frontier of Assyria as a Case Study in Imperial Dynamics*. Helsinki: Neo-Assyrian Text Corpus Project, 2001.
Parker, Simon B. "The Ugaritic Deity Rapi'u." *UF* 4 (1972): 97–104.
- , ed. *Ugaritic Narrative Poetry*. SBL Writings from the Ancient World 9. Atlanta: Scholars Press, 1997.
Parpola, Simo. *Assyrian Prophecies*. SAA 9. Helsinki: Helsinki University Press, 1997.
- , ed. *The Correspondence of Sargon II. Part I, Letters from Assyria and the West*. SAA 1. Helsinki: Helsinki University Press, 1987.
- *Letters from Assyrian and Babylonian Scholars*. SAA 10. Helsinki: Helsinki University Press, 1993.
- "Assyria's Expansion in the 8th and 7th Centuries and Its Long-Term Repercussions in the West." Pages 99–111 in *Symbiosis, Symbolism and Power of the Past: Canaan, Ancient*

Israel, and Their Neighbors from the Late Bronze Age through Roman Palaestina. Edited by William G. Dever and Seymour Gitin. Winona Lake, Ind.: Eisenbrauns, 2003.

Parpola, Simo, and Kazuko Watanabe, eds. *Neo-Assyrian Treaties and Loyalty Oaths.* SAA 2. Helsinki: Helsinki University Press, 1988.

Parry, Donald W. and Elisha Qimron. *The Great Isaiah Scroll (1QIsaᵃ): A New Edition.* Leiden: Brill, 1999.

Patton, L. B. *Spiritism and the Cult of the Dead in Antiquity.* New York: Macmillan, 1921.

Pedersen, Johannes. *Israel: Its Life and Culture.* London: Oxford University Press, 1926–40.

Peet, T. Eric. *The Great Tomb-Robberies of the Twentieth Egyptian Dynasty.* Oxford: Clarendon, 1930.

Pernot, Laurent. *Rhetoric in Antiquity.* Translated by W. E. Higgins. Washington, D.C.: Catholic University of America Press, 2005.

Petersen, David L. "The Ambiguous Role of Moses as Prophet." Pages 311–24 in *Israel's Prophets and Israel's Past: Essays on the Relationship of Prophetic Texts and Israelite History in Honor of John H. Hayes.* Edited by B. E. Kelle and M. B. Moore. New York: T&T Clark, 2006.

– "Isaiah 28: A Redaction-Critical Study." Pages 101–22 in vol. 2 of *SBL Seminar Papers, 1979.* Edited by P. J. Achtemeier. Atlanta: Scholars Press, 1979.

– *The Prophetic Literature: An Introduction.* Louisville, Ky.: Westminster John Knox, 2002.

Petersen, David L., and Kent Harold Richards. *Interpreting Hebrew Poetry.* Minneapolis: Fortress, 1992.

Piepkorn, A. C. *Historical Prism Inscriptions of Ashurbanipal.* Vol. 1, Assyriological Studies 5. Chicago: University of Chicago Press, 1933.

Pitard, Wayne T. "Care of the Dead at Emar." Pages 123–40 in *Emar: The History, Religion and Culture of a Syrian Town in the Late Bronze Age.* Edited by M. Chavalas. Bethesda, Md.: CDL, 1996.

– "The 'Libation Installations' of the Tombs of Ugarit." *BA* 57 (1994): 20–37.

– "A New Edition of the Rapi'uma Texts." *BASOR* 285 (1992): 33–77.

– "Tombs and Offerings: Archaeological Data and Comparative Methodology in the Study of Death in Israel." Pages 145–68 in *Sacred Time, Sacred Place: Archaeology and the Religion of Israel.* Edited by Barry M. Gittlen. Winona Lake, Ind.: Eisenbrauns, 2002.

– "The Ugaritic Funerary Text RS 34.126." *BASOR* 232 (1978): 65–75.

Poirier, J. C. "An Illuminating Parallel to Isaiah XIV 12." *VT* 49 (1999): 371–89.

Polzin, Robert. *Late Biblical Hebrew: Toward an Historical Typology of Biblical Hebrew Prose.* HSM 12. Missoula, Mont.: Scholars Press for the Harvard Semitic Museum, 1976.

Pope, Marvin. "The Cult of the Dead at Ugarit." Pages 225–50 in *Probative Pontificating in Ugaritic and Biblical Literature: Collected Essays.* Edited by Mark S. Smith. Münster: Ugarit-Verlag, 1994.

– *Job: Introduction, Translation, and Notes.* Anchor Bible 15. 2nd ed. Garden City, N.Y.: Doubleday, 1965.

– "Le *mrzḥ* à Ougarit et ailleurs." *Annales Archéologiques Arabes Syriennes* 29–30 (1979–80): 141–43.

– "Mot." Pages 607–8 in the *Supplement to The Interpreter's Dictionary of the Bible.* Edited by George Arthur Buttrick, et al. New York: Abingdon Press, 1976.

– "Notes on the Rephaim Texts from Ugarit." Pages 163–82 in *Essays on the Ancient Near East in Memory of Jacob Joel Finkelstein.* Edited by M. de Jong Ellis. Memoirs of the Connecticut Academy of Arts and Sciences 19. Hamden, CT: Archon Books, 1977.

- Review of Brian B. Schmidt, *Israel's Beneficent Dead: Ancestor Cult and Necromancy in Ancient Israelite Religion and Tradition*. Jewish Quarterly Review 88 (1997): 91–93.
- *Song of Songs: A New Translation with Introduction and Commentary*. Anchor Bible 7C. Garden City, N.Y.: Doubleday, 1977.

Porter, Barbara Nevling. "Language, Audience and Impact in Imperial Assyria." Pages 51–72 in *Language and Culture in the Near East*. Edited by Shlomo Izre'el. Israel Oriental Studies 15. Leiden: Brill, 1995.

Posener, Georges. "Une nouvelle histoire de revenant." *RdE* 12 (1960): 75–82.

Postgate, J. N. "Archaeology and the Texts – Bridging the Gap." *ZA* 80 (1990): 228–40.
- *Early Mesopotamia: Society and Economy at the Dawn of History*. London: Routledge, 1994.
- "The Land of Assur and the Yoke of Assur." *World Archaeology* 23 (1992): 247–63.
- "Royal Ideology in Sumer and Akkad." Pages 409–10 in vol. 1 of *Civilizations of the Ancient Near East*. Edited by Jack M. Sasson. New York: Scribner, 1995.

Prinsloo, W. S. "Isaiah 14 12–15: Humiliation, Hubris, Humiliation." *ZAW* 93 (1981): 432–38.

Puech, Émile. *La croyance des Esséniens en la vie future: Immortalité, résurrection, vie éternelle? Histoire d'une croyance dans le Judaïsme ancien*. Paris: Librairie Lecoffre, 1993.

Quirke, Stephen G. J. "Judgment of the Dead." Pages 211–14 in vol. 2 of *Oxford Encyclopedia of Ancient Egypt*. Edited by Donald B. Redford. Oxford: Oxford University Press, 2001.

Quirke, Stephen G. J., and Jeffrey Spencer, eds. *The British Museum Book of Ancient Egypt*. London: Trustees of the British Museum by British Museum Press, 1992.

Rad, Gerhard von. *Old Testament Theology. Vol. 1, The Theology of Israel's Historical Traditions*. Louisville, Ky.: Westminster John Knox, 2001.

Radner, Karen. "Assyriche *ṭuppi adê* als Vorbild für Deuteronomium 28,20–44?" Pages 351–378 in *Die deuteronomistischen Geschichtswerke: Redaktions- und religionsgeschichtliche Perspektiven zur "Deuteronomismus"-Diskussion in Tora und Vorderen Propheten*. Edited by Markus Witte, Konrad Schmid, Doris Prechel and Jan Christian Gertz. Berlin: De Gruyter, 2006.

Rahmani, L. Y. "Ancient Jerusalem's Funerary Customs and Tombs, Part Two." *BA* 44 (1981): 229–35.

Rainey, Anson F. "The Fate of Lachish during the Campaigns of Sennacherib and Nebuchadrezzar," Pages 45–60 in *Investigations at Lachish, The Sanctuary and the Residency (Lachish V)*. Edited by Y. Aharoni. Tel Aviv: Institute of Archaeology, Tel Aviv University, 1975.

Ranke, Hermann. *Die Ägyptischen Personennamen*. Glückstadt: J. J. Augustin, 1935.

Ray, John D. "The Late Period: An Overview." Pages 267–72 in vol. 2 of *Oxford Encyclopedia of Ancient Egypt*. Oxford: Oxford University Press, 2001.

Reade, Julian. "Ideology and Propaganda in Assyrian Art." Pages 329–43 in *Power and Propaganda: A Symposium on Ancient Empires*. Edited by Mogens Trolle Larsen. Mesopotamia 7. Copenhagen: Akademisk Forlag, 1979.

Redford, Donald B. *Akhenaten: The Heretic King*. Princeton: Princeton University Press, 1984.
- *Egypt, Canaan, and Israel in Ancient Times*. Princeton: Princeton University Press, 1992.
- "History and Egyptology," Pages 23–35 in *Egyptology Today*. Edited by Richard H. Wilkinson. Cambridge: Cambridge University Press, 2008.
- "The Relations between Egypt and Israel from El-Amarna to the Babylonian Conquest."

Pages 192–205 in *Biblical Archaeology Today: Proceedings of the International Congress on Biblical Archaeology, Jerusalem, April 1984*. Jerusalem: Israel Exploration Society, 1985.
- "Studies in Relations between Palestine and Egypt during the First Millennium B.C.: II. The Twenty-Second Dynasty." *JAOS* 93 (1973): 3–17.
- *A Study of the Biblical Story of Joseph (Genesis 37–50)*. Leiden: Brill, 1970.

Reiner, Erica. "First-Millennium Babylonian Literature." Pages 293–321 in *The Cambridge Ancient History. Part 2, The Assyrian and Babylonian Empires and Other States of the Near East, from the Eighth to the Sixth Centuries BC*. 2nd ed. Cambridge: Cambridge University Press, 1991.
- *Your Thwarts in Pieces, Your Mooring Rope Cut: Poetry from Babylonia and Assyria*. Ann Arbor: University of Michigan Press, 1985.

Renan, Ernest. *History of the People Israel*. London: Chapman & Hall, 1891.

Rendsburg, Gary A. "Bilingual Worplay in the Bible," *VT* 38 (1988): 354–56.
- "A Comprehensive Guide to Israelian Hebrew: Grammar and Lexicon." *Orient* 38 (2003): 5–35

Ribar, J. W. "Death Cult Practices in Ancient Palestine." Ph.D. dissertation, University of Michigan, 1973.

Richards, Janet E. *Society and Death in Ancient Egypt: Mortuary Landscapes of the Middle Kingdom*. New York: Cambridge University Press, 2005.

Richardson, Seth. "An Assyrian Garden of Ancestors: Room I, Northwest Palace, Kalḫu." *SAAB* 13 (1999–2001): 145–216.
- "Death and Dismemberment in Mesopotamia: Discorporation between the Body and the Body Politic." Pages 189–208 in *Performing Death: Social Analyses of Funerary Traditions in the Ancient Near East and Mediterranean*. Edited by N. Lanieri. Chicago: University of Chicago Press, 2007.

Riede, Peter. *Im Netz des Jägers: Studien zur Feindmetaphorik der Individualpsalmen*. Neukirchen-Vluyn: Neukirchener Verlag, 2000.

Ritner, Robert K. "Magic." Pages 321–36 in *The Oxford Dictionary of Ancient Egypt*. Edited by Donald B. Redford. New York: Oxford University Press, 2001.
- "Necromancy in Ancient Egypt." Pages 89–96 in *Magic and Divination in the Ancient World*. Edited by Leda Ciraolo and Jonathan Seidel. Ancient Magic and Divination 2. Leiden: Brill, 2002.
- *The Libyan Anarchy: Inscriptions from Egypt's Third Intermediate Period*. SBLWAW 21. Society of Biblical Literature: Atlanta, 2009.

Roberts, J. J. M. "Amos 6:1–7." Pages 155–66 in *Understanding the Word: Essays in Honour of Bernhard W. Anderson*. Edited by James T. Butler et al. JSOTSup 37. Sheffield: JSOT Press, 1985.
- *The Bible and the Ancient Near East*. Winona Lake, Ind.: Eisenbrauns, 2002.
- "The Davidic Origin of the Zion Tradition." *JBL* 92 (1973): 329–44.
- "Double Entendre in First Isaiah." *CBQ* 54 (1992): 39–48.
- *The Earliest Semitic Pantheon: A Study of the Semitic Deities Attested in Mesopotamia before Ur III*. Baltimore: Johns Hopkins University Press, 1972.
- "Egypt, Assyria, Isaiah, and the Ashdod Affair: An Alternative Proposal." Pages 265–83 in *Jerusalem in Bible and Archaeology: The First Temple Period*. Edited by Andrew G. Vaughn and Ann E. Killebrew. SBL Symposium Series 18. Atlanta: Society of Biblical Literature, 2003.
- "Form, Syntax and Redaction in Isaiah 1:2–20." *Princeton Seminary Bulletin* 3 (1982): 293–306.

- "In Defense of the Monarchy: The Contribution of Israelite Kingship to Biblical Theology." Pages 377–96 in *Ancient Israelite Religion: Essays in Honor of Frank Moore Cross*. Edited by P. D. Miller, Jr., P. D. Hanson, and S. D. McBride. Philadelphia: Fortress, 1987.
- "Isaiah 2 and the Prophet's Message to the North." *Jewish Quarterly Review* 75 (1985): 290–308.
- "Isaiah's Egyptian and Nubian Oracles." Pages 201–9 in *Israel's Prophets and Israel's Past: Essays on the Relationship of Prophetic Texts and Israelite History in Honor of John H. Hayes*. Edited by B. E. Kelle and M. B. Moore. Library of Hebrew Bible/Old Testament Studies 446. New York: T&T Clark, 2006.
- *Nahum, Habakkuk, and Zephaniah: A Commentary*. Louisville, Ky.: Westminster John Knox, 1991.
- "The Relations between Egypt and Israel from El-Amarna to the Babylonian Conquest." Pages 192–205 in *Biblical Archaeology Today: Proceedings of the International Congress on Biblical Archaeology, Jerusalem, April 1984*. Jerusalem: Israel Exploration Society, 1985.
- "Yahweh's Foundation in Zion (Isa 28:16)." *JBL* 106 (1987): 27–45.

Roberts, J. J. M., et al. *Hebrew Inscriptions: Texts from the Period of the Monarchy*. New Haven: Yale University Press, 2003.

Robertson, D. A. Review of Mitchell J. Dahood, *Psalms* (Anchor Bible), *JBL* 85 (1966): 484–86.

Röllig, Wolfgang. *Neue Ephemeris für semitische Epigraphik*. Vol. 2. Edited by Rainer Degen, Walter Wilhelm Müller, and Wolfgang Röllig. Wiesbaden: Harrassowitz, 1974.

Rosenberg, Ruth. "The Concept of Biblical Sheol within the Context of Ancient Near Eastern Beliefs: A Thesis." Ph.D. dissertation, Harvard University, 1981.

Rouillard, Hedwige, and Josep Tropper. "*Trpym*, rituels de guérison et culte de ancêtres d'après 1 Samuel XIX 11–17 et les textes parallèles d'Assur et de Nuzi." *VT* 37 (1987): 340–61.

Routledge, Robin L. "The Siege and Deliverance of the City of David in Isaiah 29:1–8." *Tyndale Bulletin* 43 (1992): 181–90.

Routledge Dictionary of Egyptian Gods and Goddesses. London: Routledge, 2005.

Rowley, H. H. "Hezekiah's Reform and Rebellion," *Bulletin of the John Rylands Library* 44 (1962): 395–431.

Rubio, Gonzalo. "Inanna and Dumuzi: A Sumerian Love Story." *JAOS* 121 (2001): 268–74.

Rudman, Dominic. "The Use of Water Imagery in Descriptions of Sheol." *ZAW* 113 (2001): 240–44.

Rudolph, Wilhelm. *Hosea*. KAT 13/1. Gütersloh: G. Mohn, 1966.
- *Jesaja 27–27*. BWANT 62. Stuttgart: W. Kohlhammer, 1933.

Rykwert, Joseph. *The Dancing Column: On Order in Architecture*. Cambridge, Mass.: MIT Press, 1996.

Sabottka, Liudger. "Is 30,27–33: Ein Übersetzungsvorschlag." *BZ* 12 (1968): 241–45.

Saenz-Badillos, Angel. *A History of the Hebrew Language*. Translated by John Elwolde. Cambridge: Cambridge University Press, 1993.

Saggs, H. W. F. "Assyrian Warfare in the Sargonid Period." *Iraq* 25 (1963): 165–70.
- "'External Souls' in the Old Testament." *JSS* 19 (1974): 1–12.
- *The Might That Was Assyria*. London: Sidgwick & Jackson, 1984.
- *The Nimrud Letters*. Cuneiform Texts from Nimrud 5; British Institute for the Study of Iraq, 2001.

Salles, Jean-François. "Rituel mortuaire et rituel social à Ras Shamra/Ougarit." Pages 171–84 in *The Archaeology of Death in the Ancient Near East*. Edited by Stuart Campbell and Anthony Green. Oxbow Monographs 51. Oxford: Oxbow Books, 1995.
Sanders, Seth L. *The Invention of Hebrew*. Urbana: University of Illinois Press, 2009.
— "The First Tour of Hell: From Neo-Assyrian Propaganda to Early Jewish Revelation." *JANER* 9 (2009): 151–69.
Sandmel, Samuel. "Parallelomania." *JBL* 81 (1962): 1–13.
Sarna, Nahum. "The Mythological Background of Job 18." *JBL* 82 (1963): 315–18.
— *Understanding Genesis*. Heritage of Biblical Israel 1. New York: Jewish Theological Seminary, 1966.
Sasson, Jack M. "Literary Criticism, Folklore Scholarship, and Ugaritic Literature." Pages 81–98 in *Ugarit in Retrospect: Fifty Years of Ugarit and Ugaritic*. Edited by Gordon D. Young. Winona Lake, Ind.: Eisenbrauns, 1981.
Sasson, Victor. "An Unrecognized 'Smoke-Signal' in Isaiah XXX 27." *VT* 33 (1983): 90–95.
Sayce, A. H. *The Life and Times of Isaiah: As Illustrated by Contemporary Monuments*. Oxford: Horace Hart, 1889.
Schaeffer, Claude F. A. *The Cuneiform Texts of Ras Shamra-Ugarit*. Schweich Lectures 1936. London: Oxford University Press, 1939.
— "Les fouilles de Ras Shamra." *Syria* 16 (1935): 141–76.
— *Ugaritica: Études Relatives aux Découvertes de Ras Shamra*. Première série. Mission de Ras Shamra 1. Paris: P. Guethner, 1939.
Schearing, L. S., and S. L. McKenzie, eds. *Those Elusive Deuteronomists: The Phenomenon of Pan-Deuteronomism*. JSOTSup 268. Sheffield: Sheffield Academic Press, 1999.
Schipper, Jeremy. *Parables and Conflict in the Hebrew Bible*. Cambridge: Cambridge University Press, 2009.
Schloen, J. David. *The House of the Father as Fact and Symbol: Patrimonialism in Ugarit and the Ancient Near East*. Winona Lake, Ind.: Eisenbrauns, 2001.
Schmidt, Brian B. "Afterlife Beliefs: Memory as Immortality." *Near Eastern Archaeology* 63 (2000): 236–39.
— *Israel's Beneficent Dead: Ancestor Cult and Necromancy in Ancient Israelite Religion and Tradition*. FAT 11. Tübingen: Mohr Siebeck, 1994.
— "Memory as Immortality: Countering the Dreaded 'Death After Death' in Ancient Israelite Society." Pages 87–100 in *Judaism in Late Antiquity* part 4, *Death, Life-after-Death, Resurrection and the World to Come in the Judaisms of Antiquity*. Edited by Alan J. Avery-Peck and Jacob Neusner. Handbuch der Orientalistik 55. Leiden/New York: Brill, 2000.
Schmidt, H. "âwb." Pages 253–54 in *Vom Alten Testament: Festschrift K. Marti*. BZAW 41. Giessen: Töpelmann, 1925.
Schmitz, Philip C. "The Grammar of Resurrection in Isaiah 26:19a–c." *JBL* 122 (2003): 145–55.
Schniedewind, William M. *How the Bible Became a Book: The Textualization of Ancient Israel*. Cambridge/New York: Cambridge University Press, 2004.
— "Aramaic, the Death of Written Hebrew, and Language Shift in the Persian Period." Pages 137–47 in *Margins of Writing, Origins of Culture*. Edited by S. L. Sanders; Oriental Institute Seminars 2. Oriental Institute: Chicago, 2006.
Schorch, Stefan. "Between Science and Magic: The Function and Roots of Paronomasia in the Prophetic Books of the Hebrew Bible." Pages 205–22 in *Puns and Pundits: Word Play*

in the Hebrew Bible and Ancient Near Eastern Literature. Edited by Scott B. Noegel. Bethesda, Md.: CDL, 2000.

Schulman, Alan R. "Some Observations About the ȝḥ ỉkr n Rʿ Stelae," *BO* 43 (1986): 302–48.

Schwartz, Jeffrey H., et al. "Skeletal Remains from Punic Carthage Do Not Support Systematic Sacrifice of Infants." *PLoS ONE* 5 (2010): e9177.

Scott, Gerry D., III. *Temple, Tomb, and Dwelling: Egyptian Antiquities from the Harer Family Trust Collection.* San Bernardino, Calif.: University Art Gallery, California State University, San Bernardino, 1992.

Scott, R. B. Y. *Proverbs, Ecclesiastes: Introduction, Translation, and Notes.* Anchor Bible 18. Garden City, N.Y.: Doubleday, 1965.

Scrolls from Qumran Cave I: The Great Isaiah Scroll, the Order of the Community, the Pesher to Habakkuk. From the photographs by John C. Trever. Jerusalem: Albright Institute of Archaeological Research and the Shrine of the Book, 1974.

Scurlock, Jo Ann. "Death and the Afterlife in Ancient Mesopotamian Thought." Pages 1883–93 in vol. 3 of *Civilizations of the Ancient Near East.* Edited by Jack M. Sasson. New York: Scribner, 1995.

– "Ghosts in the Ancient Near East: Weak or Powerful?" *HUCA* 68 (1997): 77–96.

– "Magical Means of Dealing with Ghosts in Ancient Mesopotamia." Ph.D. dissertation, University of Chicago, 1988.

– *Magico-Medical Means of Treating Ghost-Induced Illnesses in Ancient Mesopotamia.* Ancient Magic and Divination 3. Leiden: Brill/Styx, 2006.

– "Soul Emplacements in Ancient Mesopotamian Funerary Rituals." Pages 1–6 in *Magic and Divination in the Ancient World.* Edited by Leda Ciraolo and Jonathan Seidel. Ancient Magic and Divinations 2. Leiden: Brill, 2002.

Scurlock, Jo Ann, and Burton Andersen. *Diagnoses in Assyrian and Babylonian Medicine: Ancient Sources, Translations, and Modern Medical Analyses.* Urbana and Chicago: University of Illinois Press, 2005.

Seibert, Peter. *Die Charakteristik: Untersuchungen zu einer altägyptischen Sprechsitte und ihren Ausprägungen in Folklore und Literatur.* Ägyptologische Abhandlungen 17. Wiesbaden: Harrassowitz, 1967.

Seitz, Christopher R. *Isaiah 1–39.* IBC. Louisville: Westminster John Knox, 1993.

Selms, A. van. "Isaiah 28:9–13: An Attempt to Give a New Interpretation." *ZAW* 85 (1973): 332–39.

Shea, William H. "The Khirbet el-Qom Tomb Inscription Again." *VT* 40 (1990): 110–16.

Sheppard, Gerald T. "The Anti-Assyrian Redaction and the Canonical Context of Isaiah 1–39." *JBL* 104 (1985): 193–216.

Sherratt, Susan, and Andrew Sherratt. "The Growth of the Mediterranean Economy in the Early First Millennium BC." *World Archaeology* 24 (1993): 361–78.

Shih, Shang-Ying. "Death in Deir el-Medina: A Psychological Assessment." *The Journal of the Society for the Study of Egyptian Antiquities* 27 (2000): 62–78.

Shipp, R. Mark. *Of Dead Kings and Dirges: Myth and Meaning in Isaiah 14:4b–21.* Academia Biblica 11. Leiden: Brill, 2002.

Shore, Arthur F. "Human and Divine Mummification." Pages 226–35 in *Studies in Pharaonic Religion and Society in Honour of J. Gwyn Griffiths.* Edited by Alan B. Lloyd. London: Egypt Exploration Society, 1992.

Simons, J. *Jerusalem in the Old Testament: Researches and Theories.* Leiden: Brill, 1952.

Simpson, W. K., editor. *The Literature of Ancient Egypt,* 3rd edition. New Haven & London: Yale University Press, 2003.

Singer, Itamar. " 'The Thousand Gods of Hatti': The Limits of an Expanding Pantheon." Pages 81–102 in *Concepts of the Other in Near Eastern Religions*. Edited by I. Alon, I. Gruenwald and I. Singer. Israel Oriental Studies 14. Leiden: Brill, 1994.
Skehan, Patrick W. "Some Textual Problems in Isaia." *CBQ* 22 (1960): 47–55.
Skinner, John. *The Book of the Prophet Isaiah, Chapters I–XXXIX*. 2nd ed. Cambridge: Cambridge University Press, 1915.
Smith, Mark S. "Death in Jeremiah ix, 20." *UF* 19 (1987): 289–93.
– "The God Athtar in the Ancient Near East and His Place in KTU 1.6 I." Pages 627–40 in *Solving Riddles and Untying Knots: Biblical, Epigraphic, and Semitic Studies in Honor of Jonas C. Greenfield*. Edited by Ziony Zevit, Seymour Gitin, Michael Sokoloff. Winona Lake, Ind.: Eisenbrauns, 1995.
– Review of Brian R. Schmidt, *Israel's Beneficent Dead: Ancestor Cult and Necromancy in Ancient Israelite Religion and Tradition*. *CBQ* 58 (1996): 724–25.
– "Yahweh, El, and the Divine Astral Family in Iron Age II Judah." Pages 265–77 in *Symbiosis, Symbolism and Power of the Past: Canaan, Ancient Israel, and Their Neighbors from the Late Bronze Age through Roman Palaestina*. Edited by William G. Dever and Seymour Gitin. Winona Lake, Ind.: Eisenbrauns, 2003.
– *The Origins of Biblical Monotheism: Israel's Polytheistic Background and the Ugaritic Texts*. Oxford: Oxford University Press, 2001.
– *The Early History of God: Yahweh and the Other Deities in Ancient Israel*. 2nd ed. Biblical Resource Series. Grand Rapids: Eerdmans, 2002.
– *The Rituals and Myths of the Feast of the Goodly Gods of KTU/CAT 1.23: Royal Constructions of Opposition, Intersection, Integration, and Domination*. Resources for Biblical Study 51. Leiden/Boston: Brill, 2006.
– "Recent Study of Israelite Religion in Light of the Ugaritic Texts." Pages 1–25 in *Ugarit at Seventy-Five*. Edited by K. Lawson Younger Jr. Winona Lake, IN: Eisenbrauns, 2007.
– "Rephaim," Pages 674–76 in vol. 5 of *Anchor Bible Dictionary*. Edited by David Noel Freedman. 6 vols. New York: Doubleday, 1992.
– *God in Translation: Deities in Cross-Cultural Discourse in the Biblical World*. FAT I/57; Tübingen: Mohr Siebeck, 2008.
Smith, Mark S., and Elizabeth Bloch-Smith. "Death and Afterlife in Ugarit and Israel." *JAOS* 108 (1988): 277–84.
Smith, Morton. "The Common Theology of the Ancient Near East." *JBL* 71 (1952): 135–47.
– "A Note on Burning Babies." *JAOS* 95 (1975): 477–79.
Smith, W. Stevenson. *The Art and Architecture of Ancient Egypt*. Revised edition with additions by W. K. Simpson. New Haven: Yale University Press, 1998.
– *Interconnections in the Ancient Near East: A Study of the Relationships between the Arts of Egypt, the Aegean, and Western Asia*. New Haven: Yale University Press, 1965.
Smith-Christopher, Daniel L. *A Biblical Theology of Exile*. Overtures to Biblical Theology. Minneapolis: Fortress, 2002.
Sokoloff, Michael. *A Dictionary of Judean Aramaic*. Ramat-Gan: Bar Ilan University Press, 2003.
Soncino, Rifat. "Law (Forms of Biblical Law)." Pages 252–54 in vol. 4 of *Anchor Bible Dictionary*. Edited by David Noel Freedman. 6 vols. New York: Doubleday, 1992.
Spalinger, Anthony. "A Religious Calendar Year in the Mut Temple at Karnak." *RdE* 44 (1993): 161–84.
Speiser, E. A. "'People' and 'Nation' of Israel." *JBL* 79 (1960): 157–63.

Spencer, A. J. *Death in Ancient Egypt*. London: Penguin, 1982.
Spieckermann, Hermann. *Juda unter Assur in der Sargonidenzeit*. FRLANT 129. Göttingen: Vandenhoeck & Ruprecht, 1982.
Spronk, Klaas. *Beatific Afterlife in Ancient Israel and in the Ancient Near East*. Alter Orient und Altes Testament 219. Neukirchen-Vluyn: Neukirchener Verlag, 1986.
– "'Down with Hêlēl!' The Assumed Mythological Background of Isa. 14:12." Pages 717–26 in *"Und Mose schrieb dieses Lied auf": Studien zum Alten Testament und zum Alten Orient*. Festschrift O. Loretz. Edited by M. Dietrich and I. Kottsieper. Alter Orient und Altes Testament 250. Münster: Ugarit-Verlag, 1998.
Stade, Bernhard. "Miscellen 16. Anmerkungen zu 2 Kö 15–21," *ZAW* 6 (1886): 156–92.
Stansell, Gary. "Blest Be the Tie That Binds (Isaiah Together)." Pages 68–103 in *New Visions of Isaiah*. Edited by R. Melugin. JSOTSup 214. Sheffield: Sheffield Academic Press, 1996.
Starodoub-Scharr, Ksenia. "The Royal Garden in the Great Royal Palace of Ugarit: To the Interpretation of the Sacral Aspect of the Royalty in the Ancient Palestine and Syria." Pages 253*–268* in *Proceedings of the Twelfth World Congress of Jewish Studies. Division A: The Bible and Its World*. Edited by R. Margolin. Jerusalem: World Union of Jewish Studies, 1999.
Starr, Ivan, ed. *Queries to the Sungod: Divination and Politics in Sargonid Assyria*. SAA 4. Helsinki: Helsinki University Press, 1990.
Stede, Véronique van der. *Mourir au pays de deux fleuves: L'au delà Mésopotamien d'après les sources Sumériennes et Akkadiennes*. Lettres Orientales 12. Leuven: Peeters, 2007.
Steinmann, Jean. *Le Prophète Isaïe: Sa vie, son oeuvre et son temps*. 2nd ed. Lectio divina 5. Paris: Cerf, 1955.
Stern, Ephraim. *Archaeology of the Land of the Bible. Vol. 2, The Assyrian, Babylonian and Persian Periods, 732–332 BCE*. Anchor Bible Reference Library. New York: Doubleday, 2001.
– "The Phoenician Source of the Palestinian Cults at the End of the Iron Age." Pages 309–22 in *Symbiosis, Symbolism and Power of the Past: Canaan, Ancient Israel, and Their Neighbors from the Late Bronze Age through Roman Palaestina*. Edited by William G. Dever and Seymour Gitin. Winona Lake, Ind.: Eisenbrauns, 2003.
Sternberg, Meir. *The Poetics of Biblical Narrative: Ideological Literature and the Drama of Reading*. Bloomington, Ind.: Indiana University Press, 1985.
Stewart, Alistair C. "The Covenant with Death in Isaiah 28," *Expository Times* 100 (1989): 375–377.
Stewart, H. M. "A Crossword Hymn to Mut." *Journal of Egyptian Archaeology* 57 (1971): 87–104.
Stieglitz, Robert R. "The Deified Kings of Ebla." Pages 215–22 in *Eblaitica 4*. Edited by C. H. Gordon and G. A. Rendsburg. Winona Lake, Ind.: Eisenbrauns, 2002.
Strange, John. "The Idea of the Afterlife in Ancient Israel: Some Remarks on the Iconography of Solomon's Temple." *PEQ* 117 (1985): 35–40.
– "Some Notes on Biblical and Egyptian Theology." Pages 345–58 in *Egypt, Israel, and the Ancient Mediterranean World*. Leiden: Brill, 2004.
Stavrakopoulou, Francesca. "Exploring the Garden of Uzza: Death, Burial and Ideologies of Kingship." *Biblica* 87 (2006): 1–21.
– *King Manasseh and Child Sacrifice: Biblical Distortions of Historical Realities*. BZAW 338. Berlin: Walter de Gruyter, 2004.
– *Land of Our Fathers The Roles of Ancestor Veneration in Biblical Land Claims*. LHBOTS 473. London: T & T Clark, 2010.

Strawn, Brent A. "Herodotus' *Histories* 1.141 and the Deliverance of Jerusalem: On Parallels, Sources, and Histories of Ancient Israel." Pages 210–38 in *Israel's Prophets and Israel's Past: Essays on the Relationship of Prophetic Texts and Israelite History in Honor of John H. Hayes*. LHBOTS 446. New York: T&T Clark, 2006.
- "Psalm 11:17b: More Guessing." *JBL* 119 (2000): 439–51.
- *What Is Stronger Than a Lion? Leonine Image and Metaphor in the Hebrew Bible and the Ancient Near East.* OBO 212. Fribourg: Academic Press; Göttingen: Vandenhoeck & Ruprecht, 2005.

Streck, Maximilian. *Assurbanipal und die letzten assyrischen Könige bis zum Untergange Ninevehs*. 1916. Reprint, Leipzig: Zentralantiquariat, 1975.

Struble, Eudora J., and Virginia Rimmer Herrmann, "An Eternal Feast at Sam'al: The New Iron Age Mortuary Stele from Zincirli in Context," *BASOR* 356 (2009) 15–49.

Sugirtharajah, R. S. *The Bible and the Third World: Precolonial, Colonial and Postcolonial Encounters.* Cambridge/New York: Cambridge University Press, 2001.

Sweeney, Marvin A. "Dating Prophetic Texts." *Hebrew Studies* 48 (2007): 55–73.
- *King Josiah of Judah: The Lost Messiah of Israel.* Oxford: Oxford University Press, 2001.
- *Isaiah 1–39, with an Introduction to Prophetic Literature.* Forms of the Old Testament Literature 16. Grand Rapids: Eerdmans, 1996.
- "A Philological and Form-Critical Reevaluation of Isaiah 8:16–9:6." *Hebrew Annual Review* 14 (1994): 215–31.

Szpakowska, Kasia. "Demons in Ancient Egypt," *Religion Compass* 3 (2009): 799–805.

Tadmor, Hayim. "The Campaigns of Sargon II of Assur: A Chronological-Historical Study. *Journal of Cuneiform Studies* 12 (1958): 22–40, 77–100.
- *The Inscriptions of Tiglath-Pileser III, King of Assyria: Critical Edition, with Introductions, Translations, and Commentary.* Publications of the Israel Academy of Sciences and Humanities, Section of Humanities. Jerusalem: Israel Academy of Sciences and Humanities, 1994.
- "On the Role of Aramaic in the Assyrian Empire." Pages 419–26 in *Near Eastern Studies Dedicated to H. I. H. Prince Takahito Mikasa on the Occasion of His Seventy-Fifth Birthday*. Bulletin of the Middle Eastern Culture Center in Japan 5. Wiesbaden: Harrassowitz, 1991.
- "Some Aspects of the History of Samaria during the Biblical Period." Pages 1–10 in *The Jerusalem Cathedra*. 3 vols. Jerusalem: Yad Izhak Ben Zvi Institute; Detroit: Wayne State University Press, 1983–85.

Tadmor, Hayim, Benno Landsberger, and Simo Parpola. "The Sin of Sargon and Sennacherib's Last Will." *SAAB* 3 (1989): 3–51.

Talmon, Shemaryahu. "The 'Comparative' Method in Biblical Interpretation: Principles and Problems." Pages 320–56 in *Congress Volume: Gottingen, 1977.* VTSup 29. Leiden: Brill, 1978.

Tanghe, Vincent. "Lilit in Edom." *ETL* 69 (1993): 125–33.

Tarler, David, and Jane M. Cahill. "David, City of." Pages 64–65 in vol. 2 of *Anchor Bible Dictionary*. Edited by David Noel Freedman. 6 vols. New York: Doubleday, 1992.

Taylor, J. Glenn. "A First and Last Thing to Do in Mourning: KTU 1.161 and Some Parallels." Pages 151–77 in *Ascribe to the Lord: Biblical and Other Studies in Memory of Peter C. Craigie.* Edited by Lyle Eslinger and J. Glen Taylor. JSOTSup 67. Sheffield: JSOT Press, 1988.

Taylor, John H. *Death and the Afterlife in Ancient Egypt.* Chicago: University of Chicago Press, 2001.

Terrien, Samuel. "Amos and Wisdom." Pages 110–11 in *Israel's Prophetic Heritage: Essays in Honor of James Muilenburg*. Edited by B. W. Anderson and W. Harrelson. New York: Harper & Bros., 1962.
Thériault, Carolyn. "The Literary Ghosts of Pharaonic Egypt." Pages 193–211 in *Death and Taxes in the Ancient Near East*. Edited by Sara E. Orel. Lewiston, N.Y.: Edwin Mellen Press, 1992.
Thiong'o, Ngugi wa. *Decolonising the Mind: The Politics of Language in African Literature*. London: J. Currey, 1986.
Thomason, Allison Karmel. *Luxury and Legitimation: Royal Collecting in Ancient Mesopotamia*. London: Ashgate, 2005.
Thompson, R. Campbell. "Assyrian Prescriptions for the 'Hand of the Ghost.'" *Journal of the Royal Asiatic Society of Great Britain and Ireland* (1929): 801–19.
– *The Devils and Evil Spirits of Babylonia*. 2 vols. London: Luzac, 1903–4.
Tigay, Jeffrey H. "On Evaluating Claims of Literary Borrowing." Pags 250–55 in *The Tablet and the Scroll: Near Eastern Studies in Honor of William W. Hallo*. Edited by M. E. Cohen, D. C. Snell and D. B. Weisberg. Bethesda, Md.: CDL Press, 1993.
– *You Shall Have No Other Gods: Israelite Religion in the Light of Hebrew Inscriptions*. HSS 31. Atlanta: Scholars Press, 1986.
Tobin, Vincent. "Amarna and Biblical Religion." Pages 231–77 in *Pharaonic Egypt: The Bible and Christianity*. Edited by Sarah Israelit-Groll. Jerusalem: The Magnes Press, 1985.
Toorn, Karel van der. "Echoes of Judean Necromancy in Isaiah 28,7–22." *ZAW* 100 (1988): 199–217.
– *Family Religion in Babylonia, Syria and Israel: Continuity and Change in the Forms of Religious Life*. Leiden: Brill, 1996.
– "Funerary Rituals and Beatific Afterlife in Ugaritic Texts and the Bible." *BO* 48 (1991): 40–66.
– "Israelite Figurines: A View from the Texts." Pages 45–62 in *Sacred Time, Sacred Place: Archaeology and the Religion of Israel*. Edited by Barry M. Gittlen. Winona Lake, Ind.: Eisenbrauns, 2000.
Toorn, Karel van der, and Theodore Lewis. "תרפים." Pages 777–89 in vol. 15 of *Theological Dictionary of the Old Testament*. Edited by G. Johannes Botterweck and Helmer Ringgren. Grand Rapids: Eerdmans, 1974–.
Török, László. *The Image of the Ordered World in Ancient Nubian Art: The Construction of the Kushite Mind (800 BC–300 AD)*. Probleme der Ägyptologie 18. Leiden: Brill, 2002.
– *The Kingdom of Kush: Handbook of the Napatan-Meroitic Civilization*. Leiden: Brill, 1997.
Tov, Emanuel. "The Literary History of the Book of Jeremiah in Light of Its Textual History. Pages 211–37 in *Empirical Models for Biblical Criticism*. Edited by Jeffrey H. Tigay. Philadelphia: University of Pennsylvania Press, 1985.
Tromp, Nicholas J. *Primitive Conceptions of Death and the Nether World in the Old Testament*. Biblica et Orientalia 21. Rome: Pontifical Biblical Institute, 1969.
Tropper, Josef. *Nekromantie: Totenbefragung im Alten Orient und im Alten Testament*. Alter Orient und Altes Testament 223. Kevelaer: Butzon & Bercker; Neukirchen-Vluyn: Neukirchener Verlag, 1989.
Troy, Lana. "Mut Enthroned." Pages 301–15 in *Essays on Ancient Egypt in Honour of Herman te Velde*. Edited by Jacobus van Dijk. Egyptological Memoirs 1. Groningen: Styx, 1997.

Tsukimoto, Akio. *Untersuchungen zur Totenflege (kispum) im alten Mesopotamien*. Alter Orient und Altes Testament 216. Neukirchen-Vluyn: Neukirchener Verlag, 1985.
Tucker, Gene M. "Isaiah 1–39." Pages 25–306 in vol. 6 of *The New Interpreter's Bible*. Edited by Leander E. Keck. Nashville: Abingdon, 1994–2004.
Uehlinger, Christoph. *Weltreich und "Eine Rede": Eine neue Deutung der sogenannten Turmbauerzählung (Gen 11, 1–0)*. OBO 101. Freiburg, Schweiz: Universitätsverlag, 1990.
Ussishkin, David. "Answers at Lachish," *BAR* 5 (1979): 16–39
— "Megiddo and Samaria: A Rejoinder to Norma Franklin." *BASOR* 348 (2007): 49–70.
— "Sennacherib's Campaign to Philistia and Judah: Ekron, Lachish, and Jerusalem." Pages 339–57 in *Essays on Ancient Israel in its Near Eastern Context: A Tribute to Nadav Na'aman*. Edited by Yairah Amit et al. Winona Lake, Ind.: Eisenbrauns, 2006.
— "The Necropolis from the Time of the Kingdom of Judah at Silwan, Jerusalem." *BA* 33 (1970): 33–46.
— "The Disappearance of Two Royal Burials." *BAR* 33:6 (2007): 68–70.
— *The Village of Silwan: The Necropolis from the Period of the Judean Kingdom*. Jerusalem: Yad Ben-Tzvi and the Society for the Exploration of the Land of Israel and Her Antiquities, 1986.
Vanderhooft, D. S. *The Neo-Babylonian Empire and the Latter Prophets*. HSM 59. Atlanta: Scholars Press, 1999.
Vaux, Roland de, O.P. *Ancient Israel: Its Life and Institutions*. Translated by John McHugh. New York: McGraw-Hill, 1961.
— *Les institutions de l'Ancien Testament*. Vol. 1. Paris: Cerf, 1958.
Vawter, Bruce. "Intimations of Immortality and the Old Testament." *JBL* 91 (1972): 158–71.
Velde, Herman te. "The Goddess Mut and the Vulture." Pages 242–45 in *Servant of Mut: Studies in Honor of Richard A. Fazzini*. Edited by Sue H. D'Auria. Boston: Brill, 2008.
— "Mut and Other Ancient Egyptian Goddesses." Pages 455–62 in vol. 2 of *Ancient Egypt, the Aegean, and the Near East: Studies in Honor of Martha Rhoads Bell*. San Antonio, Tex.: Van Siclen Books, 1997.
— "Mut, the Eye of Re." *Studien zur Altägyptischen Kultur Beihefte* 3 (1988): 395–403.
— "The Cat as Sacred Animal of the Goddess Mut." Pages 127–137 in *Studies in Egyptian Religion: Dedicated to Professor Jan Zandee*. Edited by M. Heerma van Voss et al. Leiden: E. J. Brill, 1982.
— "Commemoration in Ancient Egypt." Pages 135–46 in *Visible Religion: Annual for Religious Iconography, 1982, Volume I – Commemorative Figures: Papers Presented to Dr. Th. P. Van Baaren on the Occasion of His Seventieth Birthday, May 13, 1982*. Edited by H. G. Kippenberg, L. P. van den Bosch et al. E. J. Brill: Leiden, 1982.
— "Toward a Minimal Definition of the Goddess Mut." *JEOL* 26 (1979–80): 3–9.
Veldhuis, Niek. "Entering the Netherworld." *CDL Bulletin* 2003:6. Accessed electronically at *http://cdli.ucla.edu/pubs/cdlb/2003/cdlb20030006.html*
Vergote, J. *Joseph en Égypte: Genèse Chap. 37–50 à la lumière des études égyptologiques récentes*. Louvain: University of Louvain, 1959.
Vermeylen, Jacques. *Du prophète Isaïe à l'apocalyptique: Isaïe, I–XXXV, miroir d'un demi-millénaire d'expérience religieuse en Israël*. 2 vols. Paris: J. Gabalda, 1977–78.
— "L'Unité du Livre d'Isaïe." Pages 11–53 in *The Book of Isaiah/Le Livre d'Isaïe: Les Oracles et Leurs Relectures, Unité et Complexité de l'Ouvrage*. Edited by Jacques Vermeylen. Leuven: Leuven University Press, 1989.

Vernus, Pascal. "Les inscriptions de SA-Mut Surnommé KYKY." *Révue d'Égyptologie* 30 (1978): 115–46.
Vieyra, Maurice. "Les Noms du 'Mundus' en Hittite et en Assyrien et la Pythonisse d'Endor." *Revue Hittite et Asianique* 19 (1961): 47–55.
Virolleaud, Charles. *Légendes de Babylone et de Canaan*. Orient ancien illustré 1. Paris, Dépôt: A. Maisonneuve, 1949.
Volf, Miroslav. *Exclusion and Embrace: A Theological Exploration of Identity, Otherness, and Reconciliation*. Nashville: Abingdon, 1996.
Von Beckerath, Jürgen. "Zur Geschichte von Chonsemhab und dem Geist." *Zeitschrift für ägyptische Sprache und Altertumskunde* 119 (1992): 90–107.
Wächter, Ludwig. *Der Tod im Alten Testament*. Stuttgart: Calwer, 1967.
Waltke, B. K. Review of Mitchell J. Dahood, *Psalms* (Anchor Bible). *Bibliotheca Sacra* 123 (1966): 175–77.
Waltke, Bruce, and M. O'Connor. *Introduction to Biblical Hebrew Syntax*. Winona Lake, Ind.: Eisenbrauns, 1990.
Wanke, Gunther. "אוֹי und הוֹי." *ZAW* 78 (1966): 215–18.
Ward, W. A. "The Semitic Biconsonantal Root SP and the Common Origin of Egyptian CWP and Hebrew SÛP: Marsh(-Plant)." *VT* 24 (1974): 339–49.
Watanabe, Chikako E. *Animal Symbolism in Mesopotamia: A Contextual Approach*. Vienna: Institut für Orientalistik der Universität Wien, 2002.
Watson, Duane F. "Hinnom Valley (Place)." Pages 202–3 in vol. 3 of *Anchor Bible Dictionary*. Edited by David Noel Freedman. 6 vols. New York: Doubleday, 1992.
Watson, S.J. "Death and Cosmology in Ancient Egypt." *JNSL* 17 (1991): 151–71.
Watson, Paul Layton. "Mot, the God of Death, at Ugarit and in the Old Testament." Ph.D. dissertation, Yale University, 1970.
Watts, J. D. W. *Isaiah 1–33*. Word Biblical Commentary 24. Waco, Tex.: Word Books, 1985. Rev. ed., Nashville: Thomas Nelson, 2005.
Weber, Max. "Judaism: The Psychology of the Prophets." Pages 299–328 in *The Symbolic Instrument in Early Times*. Edited by Harold D. Lasswell et al. Propaganda and Communication in World History 1. Honolulu: University of Hawaii Press, 1979.
Wegner, Paul D. "Another Look at Isa VIII 23B." *VT* 41 (1991): 481–84.
Weidner, E. F. "Ein astrologischer Sammeltext aus der Sargonidenzeit." *AfO* 19 (1959/60): 105–13.
Weill, Raymond. *Cité de David: Campagne de 1913–14*. Paris: Geuthner, 1920.
Weinfeld, Moshe. "Ancient Near Eastern Patterns in Prophetic Literature." Pages 84–101 in *Prophecy in the Hebrew Bible: Selected Studies from Vetus Testamentum*. Compiled by David E. Orton. Leiden: Brill, 2000.
– *Deuteronomy 1–11*. AB 5. New York 1991.
– "The Moloch Cult in Israel and Its Background." Pages 37–61 in *Proceedings of the 5th World Congress of Jewish Studies*. Vol. 1, *Hebrew University, Jerusalem, 1969*. Jerusalem: World Union of Jewish Studies, 1973.
– *The Place of the Law in the Religion of Ancient Israel*. Leiden: Brill, 2004.
– "The Worship of Molech and the Queen of Heaven and Its Background." *UF* 4 (1972): 133–54.
Weisman, Ze'ev. *Political Satire in the Bible*. Atlanta: Scholars Press, 1998.
Wente, Edward. *Letters from Ancient Egypt*. Edited by Edmund S. Meltzer. Writings from the Ancient World 1. Atlanta: Scholars Press, 1990.
– "Funerary Beliefs of the Ancient Egyptians. An Interpretation of the Burials and the Texts." *Expedition* 24 (1982), 17–26.

Werlitz, Jürgen. *Studien zur literarkritischen Methode: Gericht und Heil in Jesaja 7,1–17 und 29,1–8*. BZAW 204. Berlin/New York: De Gruyter, 1992.
Werner, Wolfgang. *Eschatologische Texte in Jesaja 1–39: Messias, Heiliger Rest, Völker*. Würzburg: Echter Verlag, 1982.
Westermann, Claus. *Basic Forms of Prophetic Speech*. Translated by Hugh Clayton White. Louisville, Ky.: Westminster John Knox, 1991.
Whedbee, J. William. *Isaiah and Wisdom*. Nashville: Abingdon, 1971.
Whitehouse, Helen. "Roman in Life, Egyptian in Death." Pages 254–270 in *Life on the Fringe: Living in the Southern Egyptian Deserts during the Roman and Early-Byzantine Periods*. Edited by Olaf E. Kaper. CNWS Publications 7. Leiden: Research School CNWS, School of Asian, African, and Amerindian Studies, 1998.
Whitley, C. F. "The Language and Exegesis of Isaiah 8 16–23." *ZAW* 90 (1978): 28–43.
Whybray, R. N. "The Sage in the Israelite Court." Pages 133–39 in *The Sage in Israel and the Ancient Near East*. Edited by J. G. Gammie and Leo G. Perdue. Winona Lake, Ind.: Eisenbrauns, 1990.
Wieringen, Archibald L.H.M. van. " 'I' and 'We' Before 'Your' Face: A Communication Analysis of Isiah 26:7–21," in *Studies in Isaiah 24–27: The Isaiah Workshop*. Edited by Hendrik Jan Bosman and Harm van Grol et al. Leiden: Brill, 2000.
Wiggins, Steve A. "Shapsh, Lamp of the Gods." Pages 327–350 in *Ugarit, Religion and Culture: Proceedings of the International Colloquium on Ugarit, Religion and Culture: Edinburgh, July 1994: Essays Presented in Honour of Professor John C. L. Gibson*. Edited by N. Wyatt, W. G. E. Watson and J. B. Lloyd. Ugaritisch-Biblische Literatur, Band 12. Munster: Ugarit Verlag.
Wijngaards, Johannes N. M. "Death and Resurrection in Covenantal Context (Hos. VI 2)." *VT* 17 (1967): 226–39.
Wilford, John Noble. "Found: An Ancient Monument to the Soul," *The New York Times*, Nov. 18, 2008.
Wildberger, Hans. *Isaiah 1–12: A Commentary*. CC. Minneapolis: Fortress, 1991.
- *Isaiah 13–27: A Commentary*. CC. Minneapolis: Fortress, 1997.
- *Isaiah 28–39: A Commentary*. CC. Minneapolis: Fortress, 2002.
Wilkinson, Richard H. *The Complete Gods and Goddesses of Ancient Egypt*. London: Thames & Hudson, 2003.
Williams, James G. "The Alas-Oracles of the Eighth Century Prophets." *HUCA* 38 (1967): 75–91.
Williams, Patrick, and Laura Chrisman, eds. *Colonial Discourse and Postcolonial Theory: A Reader*. New York: Columbia University Press, 1994.
Williams, Ronald J. "The Sage in Egyptian Literature." Pages 19–30 in *The Sage in Israel and the Ancient Near East*. Edited by John G. Gammie and Leo G. Perdue. Winona Lake, Ind.: Eisenbrauns, 1990.
Williamson, H. G. M. *The Book Called Isaiah: Deutero-Isaiah's Role in Composition and Redaction*. Oxford: Oxford University Press, 1994.
- "First and Last in Isaiah." Pages 95–108 in *Of Prophets' Visions and the Wisdom of Sages: Essays in Honour of R. Norman Whybray on his Seventieth Birthday*. Edited by Heather A. McKay and David J. A. Clines. Sheffield: JSOT Press, 1993.
- "Isaiah 8:21 and a New Inscription from Ekron." *Bulletin of the Anglo-Israel Archaeological Society* 18 (2000): 51–55.
Willis, J. T. "'ab as an Official Term." *SJOT* 10 (1996): 115–36.
- "Historical Issues in Isaiah 22,15–25." *Biblica* 74 (1993): 60–70.

- "Song of Hannah and Psalm 113." *CBQ* 35 (1973): 139–54.
- "Textual and Linguistic Issues in Isaiah 22,15–25." *ZAW* 105 (1993): 377–99.
Wilson, J. A. "The Theban Tomb (No. 409) of Si-Mut, Called Kiki." *JNES* 29 (1970): 187–92.
Wilson, Nigel, ed. *Encyclopedia of Ancient Greece*. London: Routledge, 2005.
Wilson, R. R. *Genealogy and History in the Biblical World*. New Haven: Yale University Press, 1977.
- *Prophecy and Society in Ancient Israel*. Philadelphia: Fortress, 1980.
Winkler, Hugo. *Alttestamentliche Untersuchungen*. Leipzig: E. Pfeiffer, 1892.
Wiseman, Donald J. "Medicine in the Old Testament World." Pages 13–42 in Bernard Palmer, ed., *Medicine and the Bible*. Exeter: Paternoster, 1986.
- *Nebuchadrezzar and Babylon*. Schweich Lectures. Oxford: Oxford University Press, 1985.
- *The Vassal-Treaties of Esarhaddon*. Iraq 20, pt. 1. London: British School of Archaeology in Iraq, 1958.
Wolff, Hans Walter. *Anthropology of the Old Testament*. Translated by Margaret Kohl. Philadelphia: Fortress, 1974.
- *Hosea*. Philadelphia: Fortress, 1974.
- *Joel and Amos*. Philadelphia: Fortress, 1977.
- "The Kerygma of the Deuteronomistic Historical Work." Pages 83–100 in *The Vitality of Old Testament Traditions*. 2nd ed. Edited by Walter Brueggemann and Hans Walter Wolff. Atlanta: John Knox, 1982.
Wolff, Samuel R. "Mortuary Practices in the Persian Period of the Levant." *Near Eastern Archaeology* 65 (2002): 131–37.
Wolkstein, Diane, and Samuel Noah Kramer. *Inanna: Queen of Heaven and Earth*. New York: Harper & Row, 1983.
Wong, G. C. I. "On 'Visits' and 'Visions' in Isaiah XXIX 6–7." *VT* 45 (1995): 370–76.
Woude, Adam S. van der. "Jesaja 8,19–23a als literarische Einheit." Pages 129–36 in *Studies in the Book of Isaiah: Festschrift Willem A. M. Beuken*. Edited by J. van Ruiten and M. Verbenne. Leuven: Leuven University Press, 1997.
Wright, David P. *Inventing God's Law: How the Covenant Code of the Bible Used and Revised the Laws of Hammurabi*. Oxford: Oxford University Press, 2009.
- *The Disposal of Impurity: Elimination Rites in the Bible and in Hittite and Mesopotamian Literature*. Atlanta: Scholars Press, 1987.
Wright, George Ernest. *The Old Testament Against Its Environment*. SBT 2. London: SCM, 1957.
Wyatt, Nicolas (Nick). "The Concept and Purpose of Hell: Its Nature and Development in West Semitic Thought." *Numen* 56 (2009): 161–84.
- "The Hollow Crown: Ambivalent Elements in West Semitic Royal Ideology." *UF* 18 (1986): 421–36.
- "The Religion of Ugarit: An Overview." Pages 560–62 in *Handbook of Ugaritic Studies*. Edited by W. G. E. Watson and N. Wyatt. Leiden: Brill, 1999.
- "The Religious Role of the King at Ugarit." *UF* 37 (2005): 695–727.
- *Religious Texts from Ugarit*. 2nd ed. Sheffield: Sheffield Academic Press, 2002.
Xella, Paolo. "Aspekte Religiöser Vorstellungen in Syrien nach den Ebla- und Ugarit-Texte." *UF* 15 (1983): 279–290.
- "Culto Dinastico Tradizioni Amoree nei Rituali Ugaritici." *SEL* 5 (1988): 219–25.
- "Death and the Afterlife in Canaanite and Hebrew Thought." Pages 2059–70 in vol. 3 of

Civilizations of the Ancient Near East. Edited by Jack M. Sasson. New York: Scribner, 1995.
- "Gunu(m)⁽ᵏⁱ⁾ dans les texts d'Ebla," *Nouvelles Assyriologiques brèves et utilitaires* 89 (1995): 80–81.
- "Resheph." Pages 700–703 in *Dictionary of Deities and Demons in the Bible.* 2nd edition. Edited by Karel van der Toorn, B. Becking, and P. W. van der Horst. Leiden: Brill, 1995.
- "Sur la Nourriture des Morts." Pages 151–60 in *Death in Mesopotamia: Papers Read at the XXVIe Rencontre Assyriologique Internationale.* Edited by Bendt Alster. Mesopotamia 8. Copenhagen: Akademisk Forlag, 1980.
Yaron, R. "The Meaning of ZANAH." *VT* 13 (1963): 237–39.
Yee, Gale A. "The Anatomy of Biblical Parody: The Dirge Form in 2 Samuel 1 and Isaiah 14." *CBQ* 50 (1988): 565–86.
Yeivin, S. "The Sepulchers of the Kings of the House of David." *JNES* 7 (1948): 30–45.
Youngblood, Ronald. "Ariel, 'City of God.'" Pages 457–62 in *Essays on the Occasion of the Seventieth Anniversary of the Dropsie University.* Philadelphia: Dropsie University, 1979.
Younger, K. Lawson, Jr. *Ancient Conquest Accounts: A Study in Ancient Near Eastern and Biblical History Writing.* JSOTSup 98. Sheffield: JSOT Press, 1990.
- "Assyrian Involvement in the Southern Levant at the End of the Eighth Century B.C.E." Pages 235–63 in *Jerusalem in Bible and Archaeology: The First Temple Period.* Edited by Andrew G. Vaughn and Ann E. Killebrew. SBL Symposium Series 18. Atlanta: Society of Biblical Literature, 2003.
- "The Fall of Samaria in Light of Recent Research." *CBQ* 61 (1999): 461–82.
- "Recent Study on Sargon II, King of Assyria: Implications for Biblical Studies." Pages 288–329 in *Mesopotamia and the Bible: Comparative Explorations.* Edited by Mark W. Chavalas and K. Lawson Younger, Jr. Grand Rapids: Baker, 2002.
- "Some of What's New in Old Aramaic Epigraphy," *Near Eastern Archaeology* 70 (2007): 139–46.
Yoyotte, Jean. "Hera d'Heliopolis et le sacrifice humain." *École Pratiques des Hautes Études Ve section, Annuaire Résumés des Conférences et Travaux* 89 (1980–81): 31–102.
Zevit, Ziony. "The Khirbet el-Qom Inscription Mentioning a Goddess." *BASOR* 255 (1984): 39–47.
- *The Religions of Ancient Israel: A Synthesis of Parallactic Approaches.* London: Continuum, 2001.
Zimmerli, Walther. *Ezekiel.* Translated by J. D. Martin. Philadelphia: Fortress, 1979.
Zorn, Jeffrey R. "The Burials of the Judean Kings: Sociohistorical Considerations and Suggestions." Pages 801–20 in *"I Will Speak of the Riddles of Ancient Times": Archaeological and Historical Studies in Honor of Amihai Mazar on the Occasion of His Sixtieth Birthday.* Edited by A. M. Maier and P. de Miroschedji. Winona Lake, Ind.: Eisenbrauns, 2006.

Index of Sources

I. Ancient Near Eastern Sources

Akkadian and Sumerian

Amarna Letters	4, 23, 264, 265n
Assyrian administrative texts	
SAA 11	13n
Cuneiform in Canaan	24n
Assyrian and Babylonian Chronicles	
I.ii.1–5	217n
Assyrian and Babylonian Letters	
	283n
LAS 132 (Esarhaddon)	48n
Ašakki Marṣûti	46n

Babylonian Theodicy
181–87   254n
Bilgamesh and the Netherworld 228

Curse of Agade   209n

Descent of Inanna   51, 187, 214, 340
Descent of Ištar   44, 45n, 48n, 49n,
                        50n 214, 255n, 340
Descent of Ur–Nammu   50n, 54n
Dialogue Between a Man and His God 122
DINGIR.ŠA.DIB.BA (Appeasing the Heart
  of an Angry God)   86

Ebla
TM.75.G.2403
  obv. I:16–II:5.   96
TM.75.G.2398   96
TM.75.G.10088   96
Elegy for a Woman Dead in Childbirth
                        46n
Emar
Emar 6, 452   96
Emar 6, 359   96
Enuma Eliš   215n, 220n
Erra   214, 269n,
IV.13   283n

Etana   214
Evil Demons (*Utukkū Lemnūtu*) 45–47,
                        271n

Gilgamesh   40, 44, 122, 160,
                        187, 205n
I:642–43   46n
V:291–97   209
VII   51
VII:3   40n
VIII:2–91   40n
X:3   40n
XI:3–4   214
XII:87   44n
XII:90–116   50
XII:96–99   210n
XII:113–16   55
Gilgamesh, Enkidu, and the Netherworld
                        50, 51
Hymn to Šamaš   53–54, 342n
Lamaštu Series   46n
Lu professions list   47
Ludlul bēl Nēmeqi
II.114–15   41
IV.4, 33, 35   54–55

Maqlû Incantation Series
                        201n
Mari   96, 125n
ARM I 65:5   96
ARM II 90:18, 22   96
ARM III 40:16   96
ARM III 40, II 90   125n
ARM X 63:15   96, 125n

Nabonidus' Ḫarran Inscription
                        38n, 40n, 209–10
Neo-Assyrian annals   255n

Adad-nirari II	215n	KAI 222A:31	204n
Aššurnasirpal II	209n, 228n	KAI 225 (Sinzeribni)	130n
Aššurbanipal	38n, 39n, 262, 270n	KAI 226 (Si'gabbar)	130n
Esarhaddon	20n, 209n	KAI 267:1	153n
Sargon II	13n, 60n	KAI 269:1	153n
Sennacherib	16n, 18n, 61, 226n, 262, 264–65	KTMW Stele	128
Tiglath-Pileser III	13n	Melqart Stele	344n
Neo-Assyrian funerary inscriptions	277n	Zakkur Stele	152, 269

Neo-Assyrian prophecies
   194–95

Neo-Assyrian Text Describing a Royal Funeral 37n, 38n, 54n

Neo-Assyrian Treaties and Loyalty-Oaths
  AfO 8 25 iv.15 251n
  SAA 2 2.I:21–27 15n
  Vassal Treaty of Esarhaddon
  (SAA 2 #6) 251–52n
  SAA 2 6.524–25 228n
  SAA 2 6.534–39 228n
Nergal and Ereškigal 45n

Prayer of Lamentation to Ištar
  46n

Substitute King Ritual 47–48

Ti'i (Headache) Series 45n, 47n
The Sin of Sargon 37n, 48n, 217n
Tukulti-Ninurta Epic
  ii 30 244

Underworld Vision of an Assyrian Prince
  52–53, 83, 258, 268n, 269

Ammonite

CAI 44	293n

Aramaic

Cowley no. 71:15	131n, 330n
Cowley no. 71:29–31	131n
Deir 'Alla	183, 205, 338n
KAI 214 (Hadad)	114, 116, 130n, 146n, 320, 332, 349
KAI 215 (Panammuwa)	130

Egyptian

Able Spirit of Re (3ḥ iḳr n Rʿ) Stelae
  73, 78n
Admonitions of Ipuwer
  210–11n

Amduat	84, 255
Amherst Papyrus	73n
Book of Caverns	84, 200n
Book of Gates	84, 255, 332

Book of the Dead (Book of Going Forth by Day) 78, 80n, 88, 179, 302, 331

Spells 51–52	87n
Spell 53	251
Spell 68	331
Spell 75	331
Spell 125	86
Spell 137A	299n
Spell 164	298–99
Spell 175	72, 87, 245n
Book of Nut	84
Books of Sky and Earth	84
Book of the Night	84

Coffin Texts	68n, 74, 84, 88, 110
Spell 147	172n
Spell 149	172
Spell 411	78

Crossword Hymn to Mut
  295, 299, 301

Dispute Between a Man and His Ba
  77, 79, 122

Edfu Stele	300–01
Harper's Songs	87, 122, 303
Harris Papyrus	82

I. Ancient Near Eastern Sources

Instruction of Amenemhet I
   81–82
Instruction of Amenemope
   65n
Instruction of Any   67, 78–79
Khonsemhab and the Ghost
   82–3
Lament of Isis   88
Letters to the Dead   80–82, 120, 172, 277
The Levitating Ghost   82
Litany of Re   84
Magical Texts   79, 251n
Memphite Theology (Shabaka Stone)
   63–64, 69
Papyrus Chester Beatty IV
   74
Passage (game)   86
Piye Victory Stele   251n, 254n, 296, 307
Prophecy of Neferti   254n
Pyramid Texts   74, 76n, 78, 185, 332
Report of Wenamun   64n
Ritual to Repulse the Aggressor
   229n
Sinuhe   248n
Song from the Tomb of King Intef
   70
Stela of the Sealbearer Meri
   115n, 320
Stela of Sheshonq I   312n
Taharqa Building Inscription
   308
Temple of Philae Inscription
   230n
Theban Tomb 83   79n
Tomb Curse of Ankmahor
   80
Tomb of Kiki/Samut Inscription (Theban Tomb 409)   297–98
Tomb of Mentuemet   295
Tomb of Nefersekheru   87–88, 210n

Hittite

Hittite Royal Funerary Ritual
   96–98, 109n, 124, 129
KBo XV 2 rev 14'–19'   97
KUB 22.35   98n
KUB 43.60 i 26–28   98n

(for Neo-Hittite, see Aramaic)

Hebrew

Inscriptions
Khirbet Beit Lei   151
Khirbet el-Qom
   No. 3   151–53
Kuntillet 'Ajrud   152
Lachish Letters
   4:10   222
Nimrud Ivory   239n
Seals   304n
Silwan Tomb 34   151n
Silwan Tomb 35   151n
Tomb of the Royal Steward Inscription
   151, 235–36

Dead Sea Scrolls
4Q385 (pseudo-Ezekiel)
   189n
4Q184:9–11   198n

Hurrian

Kumarbi Myths   122, 123n

Moabite

Mesha Stele
   ll. 12–13   265–66
   ll. 17–18   265–66

Phoenician

KAI 1 (Ahiram)   129–130
KAI 13 (Tabnit)   131, 236n
   13:4–7   208
KAI 14 (Eshmunazor)   131

Syriac

Ahiqar
no. 10 — 174

Ugaritic

CAT/KTU²
1.1 ii:19–25 — 104n
1.3–6 (Baal Cycle) — 105, 113, 114, 122, 123, 124, 126, 162, 179, 215n
1.3 ii:5–6 — 244–45
1.3 ii:9–11 — 244–45
1.3 iii:5–22 — 104
1.3 iii:16 — 105n
1.3 iii:23 — 327n
1.3 iv:8–14 — 104n
1.3 iv:28–31 — 104n
1.4 v:58–vi:15 — 179
1.4 vii:46 — 123
1.4 vii:55 — 109n, 127
1.4 viii 1–14 — 126
1.5 — 255
1.5 i:7–8 — 126n
1.5 i:18–22 — 122n
1.5 ii:2–3 — 122n
1.5 vi:6–7 — 127
1.5 vi:6 — 179
1.5 vi:10 — 127, 183
1.5 vi:14–1.6 i:7 — 105
1.6 i:13–18 — 124
1.6 i:42 — 183
1.6 i:43–65 — 213
1.6 i:65 — 213n
1.6 ii:30–35 — 122
1.6 ii:30–34 — 230n
1.6 vi:17–20 — 179
1.6 vi:26–27 — 123
1.6 vi:45–46 — 124n
1.6 vi:45–47 — 107
1.6 vi.46–47 — 115
1.14–16 (Kirta) — 105, 122, 127
1.14 i:26–35 — 105
1.14 ii:19–24 — 105
1.15 iii:4 — 112, 113n
1.15 iii:15 — 112, 113n
1.16 vi 13 — 304n
1.17–19 (Aqhat) — 112, 113–15, 127
1.17 i:26–34 (Duties of an Ideal Son) — 106n, 110–11, 129
1.17 i:26 — 108n, 111
1.17 i:28 — 111–12
1.17 ii:1–8 — 110–11
1.17 ii:16–23 — 110–11
1.17 ii 26–27 — 219n
1.17 vi:27–29 — 139
1.17 vi:26–33 — 113–114
1.17 vi:30–33 — 114, 187
1.17 vi 30–31 — 320
1.17 vi:34–38 — 122
1.19 iv:24 — 112
1.20–22 (*Rpum* Texts) — 105, 111–12, 332
1.20 — 111–12
1.20 i:1–3 — 111
1.20 i:1 — 112
1.20 i:2 — 113n
1.21 — 116
1.21:1 — 119n
1.21:1 — 116n
1.21:9 — 116n
1.21:3–9 — 112n
1.21:4 — 113n
1.22 i:5 — 112
1.22 i:6–7 — 114n
1.22 i:7 — 112
1.22 i:8 — 113n
1.22 i:10 — 112
1.22 i:15 — 112
1.23 — 214
1.23:8–9 — 123
1.23:9–11 — 124
1.24:6 — 219n
1.24:15 — 219n
1.24:41–42 — 219n
1.39 — 119n, 121n
1.39:22 — 115n
1.41:5 — 115n
1.41:27 — 115n
1.41:40 — 115n
1.41:46 — 121n
1.47:2 — 108n
1.41:48 — 112
1.43:2–3 — 112
1.43:9 — 112
1.43:17 — 112

1.46:8	115n	1.132:24	115n		
1.78:3–4	126n	1.134:4	115n		
1.82:5	124n, 304n	1.161 (Royal Funerary Text)			
1.87:49–50	121n		105, 106n, 108–10,		
1.87:52	112		118, 120, 124, 127,		
1.100	125n, 126		129, 209, 277, 330n		
1.100:5	327n	1.161:2–12	211		
1.102:12	126	1.161:2–3	113n		
1.105	121n	1.161:7	112		
1.105:26	115n	1.161:13–14	105		
1.106	121n	1.161:18	124n		
1.106:2	115n	1.161:20	109n		
1.106:3	121n	1.161:23–26	109		
1.106:7	115n	1.161:21	127		
1.106:23–33	158	1.161:27–30	109		
1.107	125n, 126	1.171:5	115n		
1.108:1	113n	2.10	124, 179		
1.108:2	113n	3.9	116		
1.108:8	112	3.9:4, 5	116		
1.108:17	113	4.232:8	107n		
1.112	121n	4.232:33	107n		
1.112:5	115n	4.642:3	116		
1.113 (Ugaritic King List)		6.13–14	(Dagan Stelae)		
	106n, 108, 111n, 120		106n, 125, 239		
1.114	112n, 116–17	RS			
1.114:15	117	14.14	116n		
1.114:21–22	116–17	15.70	119n		
1.114:28	107n,	15.80	119n		
1.118:1	108n	18.01:5	116		
1.124	113n, 121n	24.257	106n		
1.127:29	123	34.126	106n		
1.132:14–15	115n	94.2158	108, 111n, 118, 120		
1.132:21	115n	1986.2235:17	126		

II. Classical Sources

Diodorus Siculus
1.88   229–30n

Euripides
Phaeton   212

Eusebius of Caesarea
Praeparatio Evangelica
1.10.34   292n

Herodotus
Histories   70–71, 250n, 266n
2.141   18–19
2.60   300n

Hesiod   212n

Homer   195
Odyssey XI.34   326n

Index of Sources

Manetho	229n, 296	Plutarch	
Ovid		*De Iside et Osiride*	
Metamorphoses		374 B	292n
Book 2	212n	Thucydides	
Plato		*History of the Peloponnesian War*	
Phaedrus	195	1.22	250n

III. Biblical Texts

Hebrew Bible / Old Testament

Genesis	160	40:19	122
4:11	333	40:11–13	164
5:24	177	41:25	268
10:26	293	42:38	177
11	33	44:29–31	177
12:2–3	319	49:9	264
14:5	167	49:29–33	154
15:2	337	50:2	57, 155
15:20	167	50:2–3	154
18:28	337	50:3	155
19:2	235	50:10	110, 162, 163
19:24	160	50:25	166
20:3	268	50:26	154, 155
22	182	Exodus	269
22:1	280	4:22–23	224
23	154	13:19	166
27:28	329	14:4	326
27:39	329	14:13–14	325
27:41	163	15:14–15	328
28:17–18	154	15:25	280
28:18	241	17:2	280
28:22	241	19:3	274
29:2	222	20:5	191
31	173	20:12	140, 174
31:13	241	20:20	280
31:19–35	173	21:12	197
31:45	241	21:15–17	197
31:51	241	21:28–29	197
31:52	241	22:2	197
33:8	235	22:19	197
35:2–4	174	22:27	276
35:20	154, 241	22:28–29	182
37:34	162, 163	23:24	241
38:24	160	24:4	154, 241

24:9–11	321	12:3	241
34:9	182	12:31	180, 181
34:13	241	13	268
38:8	293	13:4	280
Leviticus		14:1	162, 163
10:3	326	16:22	241
11:31	165	18:9–22	273
16:4	244	18:10–13	273
18:21	142, 180	18:11	137, 169
18:21–27	181	18:21–22	273
19:11–16	165	21:23	154
19:28	162	23:4–9	61
19:31	169	26:13–14	86
20:2–5	142, 180	26:14	140–41, 174
20:5	180	28:26	161
20:6	169	28:43	290
20:14	160	30:4	271
20:18	325	30:15	251, 253
20:27	169, 170	30:15–19	198, 346
21:1–2	165	30:19	352
21:9	160	32:8	319
21:10–11	165	32:22	176
24:17	174	32:39	168, 186
24:22	174	34:5–6	155
26:1	241	34:10	199
26:30	157	34:8	162, 163
31:19	165	Joshua	
Numbers		3:10	345
11:15	197	6	223, 226
12:6	268	6:20	226
16:28–34	178	22:16	271
16:35	160	22:22	271
20:29	162, 163	23:13	317
25	174	24:29	156
25:11	324	24:31	325
31:22	165	Judges	
Deuteronomy	192, 269	1:6–7	224
2:11	167	2:7	325
3:11	167	2:8	156
3:11–14	107	2:10	325
4:29	275	2:11	270
4:34	280	2:22	280
5:16	140, 174	4:3	241
5:26	346	4:9	241
6:16	242, 280	4:14	333
7:5	241	5:26	289
8:2	280	8:33	311

9:4	311	17:23	160
10:11–12	314–15	18:18	241
11:29–40	182	19:38	160
11:39–40	163	21:1	339
17:5	173	21:12–14	166
18:14–20	173	21:14	156
		21:20	167
1 Samuel		21:22	167
1:21	174	22:6	198
2:6	186	22:28	328
2:6–8	329	23:14	241
2:19	154, 174	23:20	265
4–6	266	23:31	293
5:20	315	26:6	178
8:11	246		
9:9	275	1 Kings	
12:23	189	1:2	238
13–14	241	1:4	238
15	143	2:2	337
15:23	174	2:10	156
15:27	154	2:34	160
15:36	222	3	268
17:44	122	3:1	61
18	161	5:10	286
19	173	5:31	291
20:6	174	6:18	302
25:1	162	6:18–35	63
28	141, 169, 171, 192	6:29	302
28:6	268	6:32	302
28:6–7	273	6:34	302
28:13	137, 271	7:9–11	291
28:14	154, 243	7:19	302
28:15	208, 268	9:16	61
31:13	110	10:28–29	61
31:11–13	160	11:4–8	150
		11:5	180
2 Samuel		11:7	180
1:11	162	11:17–18	61
1:19–27	208	11:33	180
1:23–25	210	11:40	61
3	161	11:43	156
3:32	160	13	161
4:12	160	13:22	161
5	262	13:30	258
5:24	333	14:2	222
12:23	332	14:11–13	161
12:33	163	14:18	162
13:37	163	14:23	241
14:2	162	14:25	61

III. Biblical Texts

14:26	57	18:13	17
15:18–21	278	18:13–16	249
16:28	156	18:14	322
17:4	59	18:14–16	18
17:10	222, 241	18:17–19:9	249
19:4	197	19:9–35	249
19:9	234	18:21	60
19:13	234	18:22	158
21	344	18:26–27	249
21:13	276	18:36–37	249
21:24	122	19:7	60
21:27–29	344	19:9	60, 61
22:6	269	19:11–17	173
23:14	241	19:23	209
		19:35	18
2 Kings		20:12–21	220
2:10	177	21:1–18	159
2:11	177	21:2	181
3:2	241	21:3–5	27
3:27	181	21:6	169, 181
4:18–37	332	21:18	142, 158
4:20	332	21:26	142, 158
4:32	332	22:1	20
4:32–37	187	22:8–13	64
4:39	329	23	334
5:7	187	23:3	242
7:6	61	23:4	27
8:5	187	23:6	148
9:10	161	23:10	180, 227
9:28	156	23:13	180
9:33–37	161	23:15–18	157
10:26	241	23:16–20	161
10:27	241	23:20	142
11:14	242	23:21–23	231
13:21	165	23:24	141, 170, 171, 174
13:30	165	23:29	20
15:7	159	23:30	156, 159
15:11	160	23:31	330
15:16	265	24:48	330
15:23	160	25:4	158
16	27		
16:3	181	1 Chronicles	
16:10–18	28	6:10	293
16:17–18	32	7:22	163
17:4	61	9:1	271
17:16	27	10:12	110
17:17	181	10:13–14	169
17:24–28	29	11:33	293
18:4	158	12:3	293

12:33	274	2:8	162
17:11	337	3:11	197
20:4	167	3:16	327
20:6	167	3:20–22	351
20:8	167	4:20–21	340–41
23:28	242	4:21	341
27:35	293	5:8	275
		5:11	328
2 Chronicles		7:9	189, 337
2:2–12	57	7:13–19	351
11:22	265	10:16	341
14:2	241	10:21	337
16	278	10:22	186
16:10	160	11:17	176
16:12	160	12:22	186
16:14	159	14:12	188
21:1	183	14:14	188
21:19	160	17:13	176, 205
21:20	159	17:16	176, 178
23:11	159	18:13–14	183
26:23	159	18:18	242
29:6	271	19	66
28:27	159	19:10	341
29:19	271	21:33	183
31:1	241	23:12	86
32:1–22	249	23:14	338
32:33	157	24:19–20	176
33:19	271	26:5	167
34:3	20	26:6	189
34:3–7	26	26:12	215
35:15	242	27:2	345
35:20–23	20	27:13	162
35:24	162	28:4	183
35:24–25	163	28:22	179
35:25	162	31:6	178
		31:22–26	178–79
Ezra		31:27	179
5:13	216	31:30	86
9:2	271	33:15–18	268
9:4	271	33:18	178
10:6	271	34:2	274
		34:11	224
Nehemiah		38:17	176, 178, 189, 224, 340
3:15	158	38:17–18	245
Esther			
8:16	330	Psalms	
Job	1, 122, 141, 184, 192, 219	1	1, 139, 349
		6:5	197
1–2	183		342

III. Biblical Texts

9:13	178	51:16	339		
9:14	186, 224	55:3	275		
10:18	213	55:5	183		
13:3	186	55:24	339		
14:2	275	56–60	337		
16	337	56:14	186		
16:3	142	57:5	341		
16:9–10	166	58:9	327		
16:10	177	63:2	275		
17:12	341	68:5	191		
18:5	178, 198	68:21	338		
18:5–6	197	69:3	242		
18:7–15	266	69:15	178		
18:20	245	69:23	317		
21:3–5	146	69:33	275		
21:4	166	71:5	177		
21:5	139	73:17–20	268–69		
22:13–19	184	73:27–28	177		
22:14	341	75:8	328		
22:16	176	75:9	164		
22:30	66, 176, 177, 188	77:3	275		
23:4	176	77:19	266		
23:6	139, 157	78:34	275		
24:7–10	185	78:48–49	183		
25:5	317	78:56	280		
26:2	280	78:64	162		
28:1	177, 186	79:3	161		
30:3	186	79:8	338		
30:9	342	82:8	319		
30:9–13	186	83:13–15	266		
30:10	166	84:3	345		
31:9	245	85:9	338		
31:13	176	88:5	176		
33:10	319	88:5–6	343		
35:13	162, 163	88:6	176		
35:17	341	88:10	107, 167		
39:14	337	88:13	186		
40:10–11	86	88:16	183		
42:3	345, 346	89:11	215		
42:6	346	89:46	244		
44:24–25	273	89:48	177		
47:11	275	91:6	183		
47:15	275	94:17	328		
49:2	337	102:7	341		
49:14	179	103:4	186		
49:15	186	104:29	273		
50:10	341	106:28	142, 174		
51	339	107:12	339		

107:18	224, 339, 340	23:30	257
107:32	339	24:12	178
109:19	244	24:20	140
109:29	244	24:21	276
110:3	329	28:18	197
115:17	166, 328	30:11	140
116:3	178	Ecclesiastes	1, 71, 122, 192
116:6	338	3:21	177
116:13	164	6:3	161, 327
118:5	245	7:2	163
118:15	325	7:4	163, 164
137:8–9	232	7:26	198
139	330	9:5	166
139:6–7	189	9:10	166, 176
139:8	185, 314	9:11	274
139:11–12	330	12:5	205
140:6	317		
141:9	317	Song of Songs	141
142:7	338	1:3	289
143:3	176	4:10	289
143:7	186, 273	8:6	179
Proverbs	139	Isaiah	
1:11–12	257	1–33	1, 259, 262, 279, 286, 332
2:18	167, 198	1	262
5:5	198	1:3	288, 343
7:27	198	1:4	259
8:35–36	198	1:5–6	259
9:1	198	1:10	234, 275
9:13	257	1:15	333
9:18	257	1:21–26	259
11:27	275	1:24	259
12:28	197	1:29–30	360
13:14	198	2–39	3
14:12	197	2:1–12	328
14:27	198	2:3	275
15:11	186	2:3–4	318
15:24	197	2:5–22	226
16:2	178	2:6	286
16:25	197	2:8	282
20:2	317	2:17	328
20:20	140	2:18	282
21:2	178	2:19	213
21:6	198	2:21	213
21:16	197	3–33	3
22:17–24:22	65	3:3	327
23:14	198, 257, 270	3:8	328
23:16	257	3:12	234
23:20–21	257		

III. Biblical Texts

3:13	319	7:11	279, 280
3:20	327	7:17	291
4:4	333	7:18	204
5–38	1	8	274, 286, 357
5	307, 325, 352	8:2	282, 284
5:5	226	8:7–8	274, 288
5:7	254	8:8	224, 333
5:8	232, 234, 254, 259	8:10	291
5:8–22	254	8:13	213
5:8–24	254	8:14	47, 317
5:11	255, 257, 283, 287	8:14–15	312
5:11–12	232	8:15	328
5:11–13	164, 255	8:16	275, 336
5:11–14	256	8:16–20	273, 280
5:11–17	8, 253–57, 351	8:16–22	8, 351
5:12	255	8:16–23	272, 273, 279
5:13	255, 256, 288	8:16–9:6	270–79
5:13–14	234, 257	8:17	273, 274, 317
5:14	178, 179, 255, 256, 259, 262, 323, 342, 354, 355, 360	8:18	336
		8:19	137, 160, 263, 273, 275, 277, 279, 341
5:14–17	256	8:19–20	243, 272, 274, 275, 276, 354, 357
5:15–16	256		
5:16	254	8:19–22	272
5:17	256	8:19–23	273, 352
5:18	258, 260	8:20	330, 359
5:20	258, 260	8:21–22	276, 354
5:20–21	275	8:22	273, 276, 277–78, 311
5:21	258, 260		
5:22	258, 260	8:23	272, 277–78
5:23	254	9:1–6	8, 272, 273, 278–79, 315, 321, 344, 352, 356–57, 358
5:24	275		
5:24–25	260		
5:25–30	256	9:2	330
5:26–30	256	9:3	279
5:29	341	9:4	279
6	199	9:6	324
6:1–7	226	9:13	282
6:5	325	9:14	282
6:9	132, 288	10	227, 230, 270
6:9–10	308, 311	10:1	232, 260
6:9–11	335	10:3–4	260
6:9–13	343	10:4	328, 333
7	357	10:5	224, 260, 279, 315, 332
7:3	241		
7:3–9	280	10:5–22	226
7:10–13	8, 279–81, 346, 351	10:6	306
7:10–17	279–80	10:8	25, 292

10:8–14	355	14:19	210, 216–17, 333
10:10–11	282	14:19–20	161, 221
10:12	233, 333	14:20	211, 216
10:12–15	207	14:20–21	211, 221
10:12–19	268	14:21	321
10:13	328	14:22–23	207, 209, 211
10:15	224, 279	14:23	221
10:16–18	260	14:24	291
10:24	224	14:24–27	207, 276, 322
10:25	332	14:25	279
10:28	333	14:29	224, 279
10:28–34	226	14:30	233
10:34	328	15:19	341
11:15	246	16:7	341
13–23	207	16:9	25
13:1–14:23	207	17:2	206
13	207, 211, 335	17:12	260
13:4	333	17:12–14	266
13:11	333	17:14	260
13:15	328	18–20	65, 284
14	20, 33, 141, 192, 203–207, 262, 325, 328, 335, 352, 354	18	59
		18:1	260
		18:2	311
14:1–4	207–08	18:4	330
14:3–21	260	18:5–6	260
14:4	208, 215, 217, 221, 288	18:7	311
		19	255, 286, 287, 354
14:4–21	194, 207, 208, 230, 355	19:1	191, 231
		19:1–4	282, 283, 284, 285–86
14:4–23	7, 203–22, 350		
14:5	224, 279	19:1–10	283, 284
14:5–6	208	19:1–15	8, 9, 246, 281–88, 351, 356
14:6	319		
14:7–11	208	19:3	160, 170, 171, 283, 284, 286, 357
14:9	107, 167, 208, 221, 277, 355		
		19:4	321
14:10	208, 210, 221, 355	19:5	285
14:11	207, 210, 221, 314	19:6	285
14:12	208, 209, 210, 212, 221, 328	19:7	285
		19:5–10	65, 282–83, 285–86
14:12–15	215, 218	19:11	284
14:13	213, 218	19:11–14	283, 286
14:13–14	354	19:11–15	282, 285
14:15	221	19:13	284, 312
14:16	208	19:13–14	287
14:16–17	208, 210	19:14	283, 287
14:18	210, 221, 277	19:15	282
14:18–21	208	19:19	242

19:20	246	25:7–8	333
19:22	270	25:8	319, 322, 323, 342, 355
19:23–24	16		
20	195	25:9	318
20:1	61	25:9–10	317
20:1–6	294	25:9–12	318
21:9	328	25:10	322
22	292, 352, 354	25:12	226
22:3	234	26	189, 193, 325, 329, 330–32, 352
22:5	226		
22:9–11	339	26:5	328
22:12–14	236	26:9	275
22:13	71, 283, 287, 333	26:11	325
22:15	238–39, 240–41, 243	26:11–12	329
		26:11–19	318, 325
22:15–19	7, 232–249, 350, 356	26:11–21	8, 323–36, 344, 352–53, 356–57
22:16	205, 234–35, 248	26:12–13	325–26, 335
22:17	248	26:12–19	325
22:17–18	243	26:13	326, 336
22:18	246–48	26:13–14	326, 336
22:19	233, 238, 241–43	26:14	188, 326, 328, 329, 331, 336, 356
22:20–25	233		
22:25	328	26:14–16	333
24–27	279, 315–18, 320–21, 332–33	26:15–16	326–27
		26:15	326
24:11	255	26:16	328
24:18	328	26:17	327
24:17–18	317	26:17–18	328, 335
24:20	328	26:18	327
24:21–22	333	26:18–19	328
24:23	321	26:19	66, 188, 328–31, 335–36, 359
25–26	334–35, 355, 358		
25	193, 321	26:20	333
25:1–5	318	26:20–21	325, 332
25:1–8	322	26:21	333
25:2	206, 320, 321	26:30	333
25:2–3	321	27	335
25:4–5	330	27:1–3	333
25:5	320	27:7	322
25:6	318–19, 320, 321–22	27:8	335
		28	255, 287, 300, 303, 322, 326, 328, 352, 354
25:6–7	319		
25:6–8	8, 318–23, 352–53, 356		
		28:1	260, 289, 302, 303
25:6–9	344	28:1–4	164, 305, 306
25:6–12	322	28:1–22	8, 86, 288–305, 305–15, 318, 351, 356
25:7	314, 319		

424 Index of Sources

28:2	224, 305, 306, 315	29:5–6	266
28:3	289, 306	29:5–8	8, 266, 269, 315,
28:3–4	307		321, 344, 352,
28:4	302		356–57, 358
28:5–6	305, 307	29:6	266, 333
28:7	283, 311	29:7	225, 263, 267–68
28:7–8	164, 287	29:7–8	266, 267, 268–69
28:7–13	305	29:8	263, 267
28:7–22	288	29:9	283, 287
28:8	302, 308	29:15	261, 330
28:9	288	29:16	341
28:10	302, 308–11, 339	29:23	213
28:11	308, 309	29:24	288
28:12	307, 308, 343	30	262, 263, 325, 352
28:13	302, 308–11, 312	30:1	322
28:14	305, 311	30:1–7	246, 294
28:14–21	260	30:2–8	184
28:14–22	305	30:5	322
28:15	289, 303, 304, 306,	30:6	341
	311, 323, 354, 358	30:7	204
28:15–18	224, 342	30:9	343
28:15–19	333	30:10–11	275
28:15–20	333	30:16	227
28:16	312	30:25	328
28:16–17	312	30:27	230–31
28:17	315	30:27–28	224
28:17–18	306, 313	30:27–33	7, 222–232, 260,
28:17–19	312		350, 354, 355
28:18	289, 290, 304, 313,	30:28	224, 230
	323, 358	30:29	224, 230, 231
28:19	305	30:30	224
28:20	313, 322, 354	30:30–31	224
28:21	309, 314–15	30:31	224, 226
28:22	164, 305	30:32	224, 230, 231
28:24	135	30:33	160, 161, 223, 224,
29	327, 328, 352		227–28, 230
29:1	260	31:1	261
29:1–2	263	31:3	261, 328
29:1–4	260, 269, 270, 351,	31:4	225
	352	31:7	282
29:1–7	267	31:8	328
29:1–8	8, 262–270, 328,	33:1	261
	357	33:2	317
29:2	264, 266	33:7	265
29:3	226, 263	33:15	333
29:4	47, 264, 328, 341	34:14	184
29:4–5	359	36–37	233, 234, 251, 253,
29:5	266, 321		263, 346, 355

36:1–37:9	249	44:28	338
36	3	45:5–6	189
36:10	315	45:9	341
36:11–12	249–253	45:23	189
36:11–17	253	46:10	291
36:12	7, 250, 256, 351, 354	47:5	177
		47:12	213
36:16–17	252	49	317
37	3, 345, 346	49:22–23	317
37:3	345–46	51	317
37:3–4	345	51:3–4	318
37:4	8, 345–46, 352	51:5	317
37:7	328	51:9	215
37:9	60, 61	52:2	360
37:9–35	249	55:1	261
37:16–17	345–46	56:7	318
37:17	346, 352	56:9–57:13	164
37:24–25	209	57	360
37:32	324	57:4	360
37:33–36	253	57:5	360
37:36	260, 333	57:5–6	182
37:38	344	57:6	360
38	344–45	57:9	180, 360
38:1	338	57:15–16	342
38:1–3	339	58:5	314
38:1–8	340	59:10	360
38:3	340, 343	59:11	341
38:9–20	8, 337–345, 352, 353, 354, 356–57	59:18	224
		60:20	163
38:10	224, 343	61:10	243
38:11	340	65:3	360
38:12	340–41	65:3–5	360
38:13–14	341	65:4	314
38:14	343	66:17	360
38:14–15	341–42	66:24	359
38:16	342		
38:16–17	337, 338, 342	Jeremiah	269, 316
38:17	342, 343	2:30	341
38:18	342–43	2:35	86
38:19	337	3:14	326
39	220	4:8	162
40–66	317	6:26	162
40:6–8	302	7	294
40:8	291	7:31–32	227
40:30–31	271	7:32	158, 228
41:13–14	359–60	7:33–8:2	200
41:25	341	7:33	122, 161
44:26	338	8:1–2	161
		8:3	271

9:16–17	162	46:28	271
9:20	179	48:2	177
9:21	183	48:31	341
9:22	161, 200	48:43–44	317
10:10	345, 346	49:1	180
14:16	161	49:3	180
15:7	224	50:15	226
16:4	161, 162	50:17	278, 341
16:4–7	163–64	51:7	164
16:5–7	116	52:1	330
16:7	164	52:7	158
16:8	164	58:8	123
16:15	271		
17:13	177	**Lamentations**	
18:6	341	3:4	341
18:11	341	3:6	166, 176, 359
19:5	180	3:47	317
19:7	161	3:55–58	186
19:10–13	105	4:12	328
19:11	228	4:21	164
20:7–18	197		
21:8	198	**Ezekiel**	269, 331, 336
21:8–10	251	3:23	222
22:18	161, 162, 258	6:5	157, 165
22:26	243, 248	6:5–7	200
23:8	271	8:4	222
23:36	345, 346	8:7–13	164
24:9	271	8:14	222
25:14	224	13:14	226
25:15	164	16:20	181
25:33	162	18:23	199
26:23	148	18:32	199
27:10	271	19:14	162
27:15	271	21:26	173
29:14	271	20:25–26	182
29:18	271	23:22–23	164
31:15	259	23:37–39	181
31:32	326	23:42–43	301–2
31:39–40	148	26:3–14	226
32:35	142, 180, 182	26:11	242
32:37	271	27:2	162
34:5	160, 162	27:31	162
36:12	222	27:32	162
36:30	161	28:8	176
37:5–7	60	28:12	162
39:4	158	28:13	314
43:12	243	29:5	161, 200
44	293	30:12	65
		31:15	178

III. Biblical Texts

32	326	Joel	
32:2	162	1:8	162
32:16	162	2:12	162
32:17–32	168		
33:11	199	Amos	316
37	66, 189, 332, 335	1:5	328
37:11	336	1:8	328
39:13	326	2:1	161
39:17	320	2:2	160
39:17–20	164	2:5	160
43	157, 158	2:7–8	164
43:7–8	142	3:15	265
43:15–16	265–66	4:1	164
44:25	165	4:11–12	164
46:19	222	5:1	162
		5:8	186
Daniel		5:16	162, 259
2	268	5:16–20	259
4:30	113	5:18–20	307
6:21	345, 346	5:18–24	164
6:24	341	5:20	271
6:27	345, 346	6:1–7	255
10:6	205	6:6	289
12	189, 332, 335	6:7	164
12:2	176, 335, 359	6:9	164
12:3	177	6:9–10	160
		6:11	265
Hosea	189, 224, 316, 326	7:2	291
1:4	339	7:11	243
2:1	345	8:1–2	292
3:4	241	8:9	162, 307
4:16–19	164	9:1–2	185
5:14	341	9:1–4	185
5:15	275	9:2	281, 333, 343
6	188		
6:2	334, 335, 346, 359	Obadiah	
6:1–2	187	15	224
6:1–3	187, 346		
9:1–6	164	Jonah	
9:4	174	2:2	186
10:1	241	2:7	177, 178
10:2	241		
11:2–3	168	Micah	316, 359
12:3	224	1:3	333
13–14	330–31	2:1	259
13:14	179, 186, 187	2:1–11	307
14:6	331	2:2	307
14:8	331	2:4	259
		2:10	307
		3:9	274

3:10	339	10:2	173		
4:1–5	227	10:11	65		
4:6	271	12:12	162		
5:6	329				
5:12	241	1 Maccabees			
		1:33–35	206		
Nahum		6:18–27	206		
1:6	291	9:20	163		
1:8	224, 288	11:20–23	206		
3:1–3	200	13:26	163		
		13:49–52	206		
Habbakuk		13:51–52	321–22		
2:5	179				
2:6–8	232	Judith			
2:9–10	232	16:24	110		
2:9–13	339				
2:15–17	232	Sirach	219		
2:16	164	22:12	110, 163		
3:5	183	30:17	174		
		38:17	163		
Zephaniah		Tobit			
1:5	180	4:17	174		
1:7	320				
Haggai					
2:13–14	165	*New Testament*			
Zechariah		Romans			
1:14	324	14:10–11	189		
2:10–11	261				
3:1–2	183	1 Corinthians			
7:3–5	163	15:54	323		
8:12	329				
8:22	319	Revelation	354		
9:11	337	21:4	323		

IV. Biblical textual witnesses

Dead Sea Scrolls

1QIsa^a	316n	1QIsa^a 29:1–2	263–65
1QIsa^a 5:15	253n	1QIsa^a 29:7	263–65
1QIsa^a 14:4	204n	1QIsa^a 30:28	222n
1QIsa^a 14:11–12	205n	1QIsa^a 30:32	223n
1QIsa^a 22:15	232n	1QIsa^a 30:33	223n
1QIsa^a 22:17	243	1QIsa^a 38:9	337n
1QIsa^a 26:11–21	323	1QIsa^a 38:15	338n
1QIsa^a 28:1	289n	1QIsa^a 38:19	339n
1QIsa^a 28:10	290n	1QIsa^a 41:13–14	359n
1QIsa^a 28:20	291n	1QIsa^b 38:19	339n

LXX

2 Sam 23:20	265n
Isa 7:10	280n
Isa 8:16ff	270
Isa 14:4	204n
Isa 14:19	206n
Isa 19:3	281n
Isa 22:15	232n
Isa 22:17	243
Isa 28:10	291n
Isa 38:9	337n
Isa 38:11	337n
Jer 31:43–44	317

Aquila

Isa 7:10	280n

Symmachus

Isa 7:10	280n

Theodotion

Isa 7:10	280n
Isa 28:10	291n

Peshitta

Isa 14:4	204n
Isa 38:11	337n

Targums

2 Sam 23:20	265n
Isa 14:4	204n
Isa 22:15	232n
Isa 38:11	337n

Vulgate

2 Sam 23:20	265n
Isa 22:15	232n
Isa 38:11	337n

Index of Authors

Abercrombie, J. R. 147
Abusch, T. 45
Ackerman, S. 154, 314, 360
Adams, C. 82, 83
Akkermans, P. M. M. G. 127
al-Rawi, F. N. 40
Albertz, R. 133, 145, 147, 180
Albright, W. F. 26, 111, 126, 138–140, 155, 170, 176, 191, 215, 239, 264, 285
Alkier, S. 196
Allen, J. P. 78, 84, 185, 332
Allen, T. G. 299, 331, 332
Alster, B. 39
Alter, R. 154
Andersen, B. 44
Andersen, F. I. 140, 185, 187, 188, 292
Anderson, G. A. 186
Andrae, W. 37, 38, 41
Andrews, C. A. R. 293
Archi, A. 96
Arnaud, D. 108, 176
Arnold, B. T. 169, 191
Asen, B. 283, 287, 302
Ash, P. S. 63
Assmann, J. 5, 57, 66, 68, 69, 70, 71, 72, 73, 74, 75, 76, 77, 78, 79, 83, 84, 86, 87, 88, 89, 90, 111, 115, 141, 173, 177, 184, 198, 210, 248, 254, 285, 287, 299, 313, 320, 328, 331, 332, 343
Aster, S. Z. 23, 226, 320
Astour, M. C. 106, 116, 123, 126
Aubet, M. E. 130, 131, 240
Auret, A. 246
Auvray, P. 288, 303
Avigad, N. 235, 236, 239

Baker, H. 36
Bakhtin, M. 209
Baldacci, M. 106, 361
Baldwin, J. G. 170

Barkay, G. 21, 148
Barré, M. L. 337, 338, 339, 341, 342, 344
Barrick, W. B. 155, 243
Barth, C. 136, 186
Barth, H. 3, 231, 267, 357
Barstad, H. 1, 2, 267
Baumgarten, A. I. 182
Baumgartner, W. 176
Bates, R. D. 19
Bayliss, M. 35, 42
Beegle, D. 264
Bénédite, G. 230
Benicho-Safar, H. 181
Ben Zvi, E. 250–251
Berlandini, J. 295
Beuken, W. A. M. 228, 231
Bietak, M. 117, 163
Biran, A. 237
Bisson de la Roque, M. F. 301
Blair, J. M. 183
Blakely, J. A. 13, 306
Bleibtreu, E. 14
Blenkinsopp, J. 135, 145, 169, 170, 175, 207, 208, 227, 233, 234, 241, 243, 244, 245, 257, 264, 266, 267, 270, 272, 274, 278, 279, 280, 281, 282, 286, 288, 304, 307, 311, 315, 316, 318, 319, 323, 329, 337, 339, 343
Bloch-Smith, E. 16, 104, 106, 114, 117, 118, 130, 134, 135, 143, 146, 147–149, 150, 153, 154, 155, 156, 157, 158, 160, 161, 168, 169, 174, 175, 192, 239, 273, 320
Boccaccini, G. 281
Boer, P. A. H. de 343
Bolsharov, A. O. 294
Bonatz, D. 97, 128
Borg, B. E. 71
Borghouts, J. F. 79, 87, 251
Borowski, O. 147
Bottéro, J. 35, 37, 41, 43, 44, 45, 46, 49, 52, 54, 55, 109, 120, 227, 277, 342

Brichto, H. C. 140–141, 174, 200, 217, 245
Bright, J. 11, 13, 26, 28
Brinkman, J. A. 20, 26
Brown, B. 37, 41, 43
Brown, M. L. 168
Brown, W. P. 197
Brueggemann, W. 334
Brunsch, W. 292
Bryan, B. M. 294, 297, 300, 301, 302
Budde, K. 162, 208
Budge, E. A. W. 84, 255
Bunimovitz, S. 149
Burkert, W. 101
Burkes, S. 89, 91, 122
Burney, C. A. 98

Cahill, J. M. 156
Calderone, P. J. 285, 337
Capart, J. 73
Capel, A. K. 308
Caplice, F. 285
Caquot, A. 107, 116, 183, 184, 304
Carroll, R. P. 270
Casanowicz, I. M. 242
Cassin, E. 39
Cheyne T. K. 283
Childs, B. S. 136, 189, 207, 218, 249, 250, 252, 267, 274, 280, 283, 321, 323, 344
Clements, R. E. 244, 249, 261, 262, 266, 272, 288, 321, 324, 337, 345
Clermont-Ganneau, C. 156
Clifford, R. J. 258, 261
Cobb, W. H. 264
Cogan, M. 26–30, 32, 46, 61, 226, 252, 262
Cohen, A. C. 34
Cohen, C. 23, 250
Cole, S. W. 39
Collard, C. 212
Collins, J. J. 166, 335
Coogan, M. D. 99
Cook, S. L. 141, 235
Cooper, A. 185
Cooper, J. S. 35, 45, 48
Cowley, A. E. 131, 330
Cox, B. D. 154
Craig, J. A. 44
Craigie, P. C. 100, 212, 214
Cropp, M. J. 212

Cross, F. M. 3, 26, 151, 169, 328
Crouwel, J. H. 246, 247
Cryer, F. H. 47
Currid, J. D. 62, 65, 285

Dahood, M. J. 99, 139–140, 146, 166, 224, 245, 337, 349
Daiches, S. 309
Dalley, S. 14, 16–17, 33, 40, 45, 46, 51, 216, 262
Damerji, M. S. B. 37
D'Auria, S. 69
David, A R. 155
Davies. G. I. 187
Davies, P. R. 118
Davis, E. F. 188
Day, J. 54, 123, 126, 140, 167, 176, 177, 179, 180, 181, 182, 183, 187, 188, 224, 276, 288, 304, 331
De Buck, A. 111, 302
De Hulster, I. J. 241
Dearman, J. A. 181, 187, 188
Deck, S. 22
Deller, K. 228
Demarée, R. J. 73, 78
Dever, W. G. 151
Dhorme, E. 178
Dietrich, M. 170, 171
Dietrich, W. 22
Dinsmoor, W. B. 104
Dobbs-Allsopp, F. W. 234
Dodson, A. 58, 80, 248
Donner, H. 22
Dornemann, R. 102
Douglas, M. 145, 175
Doxey, D. M. 287
Doyle, B. 315
Dozeman, T. B. 196
Driver, G. R. 99, 156, 184, 271, 272, 275, 276, 278, 283, 287, 289, 290, 291, 308
Driver, S. R. 22
Dubberstein, W. H. 26
Dubovský P. 21
Duhm, B. 303, 315, 330
Dunand, F. 68, 69
Dunham, D. 247
Durand, J.-M. 96
Durkheim, E. 94–95

Dussaud, R. 125

Eaton, J. H. 316, 322
Ebach, J. H. 125
Ebeling, E. 41, 326
Eberhardt, G. 185, 186, 189
Eisling, H. 285
Eissfeldt, O. 138, 180
Eitan, I. 285
Elat, M. 4
Emerton, J. A. 257, 278
Engelbach, R. 301
Erlandsson, S. 207, 218, 220
Eshel, H. 278
Evans, P. S. 18
Exum, J. C. 306, 308

Fales, F. M. 13, 14, 22
Fantalkin, A. 150
Farber, W. 45, 46, 184
Faulkner, R. O. 86, 172
Faust, A. 16, 22, 62, 149
Fazzini, R. A. 294, 295, 300
Feigin, S. 264, 265, 266
Fewell, D. 344
Fey, R. 255
Fichtner, J. 256
Finkel, I. R. 47, 54
Finkelstein, I. 267
Finkelstein, J. J. 42
Fischer, J. 303
Fisher, L. R. 99, 104
Fitzenreiter, M. 83
Franklin, N. 134
Frazer, J. G. 104
Foster, B. R. 41, 46, 50, 51
Frahm, E. 15, 34
Freedman, D. N. 26, 185, 187, 188, 292, 328
Fretheim, T. E. 270
Friedman, R. E. 102, 174, 192, 200
Froidefond, C. 292

Gadd, C. J. 38, 40
Gallagher, W. R. 17, 218, 219, 220, 249
Galling, K. 244
Gallou, C. 101, 104
Galpaz-Feller, P. 59, 60, 155
Gardiner, A. H. 67, 78, 80, 81

Garr, W. R. 162, 292
Geller, M. J. 45, 46, 47
George, A. R. 39, 40, 44, 46, 48, 50, 55, 228
Germer, R. 301, 302
Gerstenberger, E. S. 133, 258
Ginsberg, H. L. 33, 99, 114, 217, 222, 232, 278, 316, 322, 333, 344
Goedicke, H. 74
Gogel, S. L. 152, 153, 277
Good, E. M. 242, 275
Good, R. M. 233
Gophna, R. 237
Gordon, A. A. 77
Gordon, C. H. 67, 101, 213
Gordon, R. P. 191
Görg, M. 294, 307
Gosse, B. 205, 207
Gowan, D. E. 214
Graesser, C. F. 154
Grandet, P. 82
Gray, G. B. 272
Gray, J. 115, 167
Grayson, A. K. 11, 13, 14, 16, 33, 215, 217, 218, 228, 231
Green, A. R. W. 181, 216
Greenfield, J.C. 42, 106, 116, 130, 174, 269
Gressman, H. 26, 178, 269, 319
Griffiths, J. G. 178, 230
Grøndahl, F. 108
Guilmot, M. 81
Gulde, S. U. 306
Gunkel, H. 194, 195, 212, 215, 261
Guzzo, M. G. A. 114

Hackett, J. 206
Hadley, J. 151, 152
Halevi, B. 168
Haller, A. 36
Hallo, W. W. 18, 344
Hallote, R. S. 147, 150, 160
Halpern, B. 19, 150, 156, 206, 250, 308, 309, 311, 345
Handy, L. K. 26, 184
Haran, M. 165
Hardin, J. W. 13, 306
Harer, W. B., Jr. 302
Harrington, N. 73, 75
Hasel, G. F. 315, 316, 325, 328

Index of Authors

Hasel, M. G. 230
Haussig, H. W. 212
Hawkins, J. D. 128, 218
Hayes, J. H. 11, 12, 13, 20, 22, 59, 65, 94, 194, 206, 217, 274, 316, 321, 322
Hays, C. B. 2, 64, 113, 133, 170, 184, 203, 206, 222, 279, 282, 284
Healey, J. F. 17, 52, 54, 112, 117, 122, 123, 124, 125, 126, 143, 167, 304
Heidel, A. 54, 160, 169, 176, 187
Heider, G. C. 142, 143, 180, 227, 276
Heidorn, L. A. 4, 247
Heiser, M. S. 213, 215
Helck, W. 254
Herrmann, C. 64, 128, 293
Hibbard, J. T. 315, 316, 317, 331
Hiebert, T. 266
Higginbotham, C. R. 61
Hillers, D. R. 201
Hodder, I. 153
Hoffmeier, J. K. 18
Hoffner, H. A. 97, 123, 171
Høgenhaven, J. 278, 279
Holladay, J. S., Jr. 16, 62, 208
Holladay, W. L. 267, 306
Holloway, S. W. 18, 19, 26, 29–31, 47, 48
Hölzl, R. 73, 239
Hornung, E. 77, 78, 84, 87, 200, 238, 255
Horowitz, W. J. 23, 48, 168, 312
Hout, T. P. J. van den 96, 97, 98
Huehnergard, J. 96, 119
Huffmon, H. B. 265
Hussein, M. I. 313
Hutson, S. 153
Hutter, M. 184

Ikram, S. 71, 72, 74, 77
Illman, K. J. 156
Irvine, S. A. 22, 194, 206, 217, 316, 321, 322
Irwin, W. 183, 227, 360
Israelit-Groll, S. 17, 64, 286

Jacobsen, T. 34, 50, 51, 91, 127, 196, 347
Jacobson, R. A. 301
Janowski, B. 186
Janzen, W. 162, 258, 259, 261
Jarick, J. 144, 166, 177
Jastrow, M. 160, 289, 329

Jellicoe S. 177, 328
Jensen, H. J. L. 214
Jensen, J. 214
Jensen, P. 171
Jenson, P. P. 165
Jeppesen, K. 272, 313
Jeremias, A. 89
Jeremias, J. 185
Johnson, A. R. 136
Johnson, D. G. 315, 316
Johnson, W. R. 295
Johnston, P. S. 5, 143–144, 313
Jong, M. J. de 193, 194, 195, 196, 267, 305, 334
Joüon, P. 280
Junker, H. 177

Kaiser, O. 215, 231, 234, 246, 266, 271, 275, 282, 283, 304–305, 319, 323, 325, 339
Kaiser, W. 71
Kalmanofsky, A. 200
Kanawati, N. 67, 69, 74, 75, 77, 78, 81, 85, 89, 209
Kassian, A. 97
Katz, D. 48
Kaufmann, Y. 26, 136
Keel, O. 32, 63, 77, 100, 173, 174, 302
Kelle, B. E. 1, 195, 196
Keller, S. R. 80, 81
Kennedy, C. A. 95, 182, 183, 192, 360
Kennedy, G. 193, 194, 199
Kenyon, K. 99
Kienast, B. 51
Killebrew, A. E. 190
King, L. W. 255
King, P. J. 94, 104, 147, 154, 181
Kissane, E. J. 288
Kitchen, K. A. 18, 58, 61, 154
Klawans, J. 165
Klein, G. L. 261
Kletter, R. 148
Kloner, A. 149
Knohl, I. 169, 200
Köhler, L. 136, 176
Korolëv, A. 97
Korpel, M. C. A. 127, 176
Köszeghy, M. 218, 220, 221
Kramer, S. N. 36, 50, 209

Kristeva, J. 203
Kuhrt, A. 11, 18, 21, 65, 252
Kuschke, A. 242
Kutsch, E. 290
Kutscher, E. Y. 264, 291, 316

Lacovara, P. 69
Lambdin, T. 171, 285, 312
Lambert, M. 36
Lambert, W. G. 41, 54, 55, 86, 250, 254, 342
Landsberger, B. 37, 48, 217, 250
Landy, F. 350
Lang, B. 140, 255, 331
Lapinkivi, P. 35, 44, 45, 48, 49, 50, 266
Lateiner, D. 250
Layton, S. C. 233
Leahy, A. 229
Lee, K. H. 212
Leeuwen, R. C. Van 205, 209, 214
Leibovici, M. 46
Lemaire, A. 99, 120, 151
LeMon, J. M. 64, 170
Lesko, L. H. 72, 76, 80, 296, 297, 299
Lesley, K. 87
Levenson, J. D. 5, 144, 182, 187, 189, 322, 327, 335–336
Levine, B. A. 23, 24, 109, 227, 319, 320
Levinson, B. M. 23, 24
Lewis, T. J. 14, 22, 101, 102, 106, 107, 108, 109, 110, 111, 112, 114, 115, 120. 124, 125, 142, 143, 144, 146, 155, 169, 171, 173, 271, 272, 281, 284, 304, 360
L'Heureux, C. L. 112, 167
Lichtenberg, R. 68, 69
Lichtheim, M. 64, 65, 67, 68, 70, 77, 79, 82, 211, 248, 251, 254, 295, 296
Lipinński, E. 58, 131
Lipschits, O. 21, 267
Littauer, M. A. 246, 247
Livingstone, A. 30, 34, 48, 52, 53, 218, 219, 220, 258
Lloyd, A. B. 70, 71, 76, 77
Lods, A. 135, 170
Loffreda, S. 147
Longman, T., III 65
Lord, A. B. 195
Loretz, O. 43, 96, 115, 170, 171, 239, 284
Lowery, R.H. 32

Lucarelli, R. 79, 80, 85
Luckenbill, D. D. 13, 14, 226
Lüddeckens, E. 209, 303
Lugt, P. van der 99
Lust, J. 170, 171

Machinist, P. 23, 33, 220, 249, 250, 292
Majerick, R. 193
Malul, M. 251, 252
Mankowski, P. V. 24, 327
Mann, M. 12
March, E. 199
Marchegay, S. 102
Margalit, B. 127
Margueron, J.-C. 220
Markoe, G. 101, 246
Marlow, H. 282, 284
Marsham, J. 140
Marti, D. K. 288
Martin, K. 73, 239
Martin-Achard, R. 136, 188, 336
Matthiae, P. 95, 96, 158, 246
Mauchline, J. 316
May, H. G. 264
Mayer, W. 14, 18
Mazar, A. 61, 62, 148
McCarter, P. K. 63, 64
McClain, J. B. 295
McEvenue, S. 155
McGinnis, J. 37, 38, 54
McKane, W. 65
McKay, J. W. 26, 28
McKenzie, J. L. 139
McLaughlin, J. L. 164, 255, 304
Medina, R. W. 197
Meeks, D. 79, 85, 172
Melchert, C. 98
Mendenhall, G. E. 5, 169
Menu, B. 297
Merola, M. 96
Mettinger, T. N. D. 155, 188, 233, 236, 238, 239
Metzger, M. 242
Mieroop, M. Van de 11, 12, 62
Milgrom, J. 182
Millar, W. R. 316, 320, 321
Millard, A. R. 19
Miller, J. M. 11, 12, 13, 20, 59, 65, 94, 274, 322

Miller, P. D. 99, 116, 133, 147, 151, 152, 153, 191, 224, 344
Miralles Maciá, L. 165
Mittman, S. 153
Moor, J. C. de 99, 105–106, 107, 111, 114, 117, 121, 123, 124, 167, 168, 304
Moorey, P. R. S. 36, 38
Morenz, S. 67, 70, 72
Morrow, W. 23, 25
Mowinckel, S. 167, 184, 337
Muchiki, Y. 293
Muilenburg, J. 2, 196
Müller, H.-P. 170
Müller, M. 89
Munro, P. 237
Muraoka, T. 280

Na'aman, N. 4, 36, 37, 149, 158, 206
Naveh, J. 151
Neiman, D. 157
Nelson, R. D. 3
Nemet-Najat, K. R. 35
Neyrey, 135
Niccacci, A. 17, 65, 282, 284
Nickelsburg, G. 336
Niditch, S. 194
Nissinen, M. 194, 195
Noth, M. 26
Nutkowicz, H. 150, 162

O'Connell, R. H. 214
O'Connor, M. P. 152, 153, 261, 306, 337
O'Donoghue, M. 81
Obayashi, H. 5
Oded, B. 12, 21
Oldenburg, U. 212, 213
Olmo Lete, G. del 99, 101, 111, 112, 119, 120–121, 158, 304, 348
Olmstead, A. T. 26
Olyan, S. M. 161–162, 163, 216
Oppenheim, A. L. 14, 26, 33, 35, 38, 247, 268
Orthmann, W. 36
Oshima, T. 23, 312
Otto, E. 22, 23, 253
Overton, S. D. 102, 174, 192, 200

Page, H. R. 205

Pardee, D. 96, 108, 111, 114, 115, 117, 118–121, 123, 126, 128, 180, 348
Parker, B. J. 12, 14, 19, 21, 31, 250
Parker, S. B. 113, 114, 167
Parpola, S. 14–16, 20, 21, 22, 28, 32, 35, 37, 48, 195, 217, 218, 228, 250
Parry, D. W. 205, 243, 264
Patton, L. B. 104
Peck, W. 295
Pedersen, J. 136
Peet, T. E. 73
Pernot, L. 2, 194
Petersen, D. L. 11, 187, 194, 199, 232, 305, 312
Piepkorn, A. C. 39, 229
Pitard, W. T. 95, 96, 100, 101–104, 110, 114, 118, 119–120, 124, 348
Poirier, J. C. 212, 213
Polzin, R. 160
Pope, M. H. 106, 110–111, 116, 117, 118, 141, 142, 165, 178, 255, 283, 287, 307
Posener, G. 82
Postgate, J. N. 13, 28, 30, 31, 32, 33, 36, 247
Prinsloo, W. S. 215
Puech, E. 166

Qimron, E. 205, 243, 264
Quirke, S. G. J. 85, 297

Rad, G. von 137
Radner, K. 29
Rahmani, L. Y. 156, 157
Rainey, A. F. 210
Ranke, H. 234
Ray, J. D. 294
Redford, D. B. 18, 58, 59, 62, 63, 68, 69, 79, 156, 195, 284, 286, 348
Reiner, E. 40, 46, 47, 341
Renan, E. 26
Rendsburg, G. A. 134, 292
Ribar, J. W. 101, 103, 104, 135, 138, 147
Richards, J. E. 57, 66, 68, 69, 75, 151
Richards, K. H. 232
Richardson, S. 15, 37, 39, 158, 159, 201, 229, 231, 246
Riede, P. 198
Ritner, R. K. 71, 73, 74, 79, 80, 81, 82, 85
Roaf, M. 41

Roberts, J. J. M. 17, 18, 59, 61, 125, 126, 151, 152, 191, 230, 242, 253, 261, 274, 285, 289, 290, 291, 306, 311, 312, 356
Robertson, D. A. 140
Roehrig, C. H. 69
Röllig, W. 239
Rosenberg, A. J. 276
Rosenberg, R. 176
Rouillard, H. 43, 170, 174
Routledge, R. L. 267
Rowley, H. H. 19
Rubio, G. 40
Rudman, D. 178
Rudolph, W. 160, 187, 316
Rummel, S. 99
Rykwert, J. 104

Sabottka, L. 222
Saggs, H. W. F. 8, 11, 12, 14, 225, 250
Salles, J.-F. 100, 103
Sanders, S. 23, 52, 53, 269, 312
Sandmel, S. 99
Sanmartin, J. 170, 171, 239
Sarna, N. 33, 183
Sasson, J. M. 105, 106
Sasson, V. 222
Sayce, A. H. 22
Schaeffer, C. F. 100–101, 103, 105, 125
Schipper, J. 204
Schloen, J. D. 103, 115, 128
Schmidt, B. B. 5, 44, 95, 96, 98, 107, 108, 109, 119–120, 143–145, 158, 166, 171, 211, 270, 272, 273, 281, 283, 284, 287
Schmitz, P. C. 324
Schniedewind, W. M. 13, 17, 24, 359
Schorch, S. 243
Schroer, S. 306
Schulman, A. R. 73, 76, 241
Schwartz, G. M. 127
Schwartz, J. H. 181
Scott, G. D., III 297
Scott, R. B. Y. 178
Scurlock, J. 34, 35, 43, 44, 45, 49, 51, 119, 120
Segal, A. F. 5
Seibert, P. 210
Seitz, C. R. 17, 256, 278, 334
Selms, A. van 308

Sethe, K. 81
Shea, W. H. 152
Sheppard, G. T. 3
Sherratt, A. 16
Sherratt, S. 16
Shipp, R. M. 214, 218, 220
Shore, A. F. 71, 83
Sidel'tsev, A. 97
Simons, J. 156, 157
Simpson, W. K. 83
Singer, I. 4
Skehan, P. W. 276
Skinner, J. 303
Smith, G. 26
Smith, Mark S. 4, 99, 100, 105, 106, 114, 117, 118, 120, 123, 124, 130, 146, 167, 179, 185, 191, 213, 219, 273, 320
Smith, Morton 15, 90, 181, 228
Smith, W. S. 23, 62, 64, 247
Soden, W. von 52, 53
Sonsino, R. 197
Spalinger, A. 300, 301
Speiser, E. A. 319
Spencer, A. J. 66, 68, 78
Spencer, J. 297
Spieckermann, H. 28–29
Spronk, K. 7, 66, 101, 106, 107, 109–111, 112–119, 121, 124, 126, 127, 135, 138, 142, 143, 146, 151, 152, 170, 191, 213, 220, 304
Stade, B. 249
Stager, L. E. 104, 154, 181
Stansell, G. 288, 305
Starodoub-Scharr, K. 158
Starr, I. 47, 48
Stavrakapoulou, F. 140, 158–159, 183, 227, 360
Steinmann, J. 22
Stede, V. van der 6–7, 34, 41, 43, 49, 50, 52, 326
Stern, E. 12, 17, 20, 21, 22, 32, 62, 65, 76, 93
Stewart, H. M. 295, 299, 301
Stieglitz, R. R. 96
Strange, J. 63, 302
Strawn, B. A. 19, 184, 191, 264, 265, 341
Streck, M. 38, 262
Struble, E. J. 128
Sweeney, M. A. 208, 214, 224, 227, 231, 256,

267, 270, 271, 275, 282, 283, 288, 305, 315, 316, 317–318, 325, 337, 344, 345, 359
Szpakowska, K. 80, 85

Tadmor, H. 13, 15, 18, 24, 37, 39, 48, 217, 218, 250, 252
Talmon, S. 93
Tanghe, V. 184
Tarler, D. 156
Tarragon, J. M. de 109
Tawil, H. ben Yosef 327
Taylor, J. Glen 209
Taylor, John H. 69, 70, 71, 74, 155
Terrien, S. 199, 256
Thériault, C. 82
Thiong'o, Ngugi wa, 31
Thomason, A. K. 252
Thompson, R. C. 44, 45, 46, 47
Tigay, J. H. 4, 236, 294, 304
Toorn, K. van der 43, 114, 140, 146, 150, 155, 169, 173, 174, 239, 272, 280, 283, 287, 304, 307, 308–309
Török, L. 69, 73, 295, 308
Tov, E. 317
Trever, J. C. 264
Tromp, N. J. 107, 139–140, 176, 178, 184, 224, 245
Tropper, J. 43, 170, 174, 273
Troy, L. 296, 299, 314
Tsevat, M. 312
Tsukimoto, A. 34, 35, 37, 41, 42, 43
Tucker, G. M. 229

Uehlinger, C. 32, 33, 63, 100, 173, 302, 319
Ussishkin, D. 12, 134, 150, 151, 210, 235, 236, 237, 238

Van Seters, J. 23
Vanderhooft, D. S. 21, 156
Vaux, R. de 137, 160, 228
Vawter, B. 139
Velde, H. te 72, 83, 294, 295, 296, 297, 298
Velduis, N. 49
Vergote, J. 155
Vermeylen, J. 258, 266, 272, 282, 283, 285, 304, 316, 319, 321
Vernus, P. 298

Vieyra, M. 171
Virolleaud, C. 99
Volf, M. 354

Wächter, L. 136, 156
Waldemar, J. 162
Waltke, B. K. 140, 261, 306, 337
Wanke, G. 258
Ward, W. A. 285
Watanabe, C. E. 46
Watanabe, K. 15–16, 228
Watson, D. F. 181
Watson, P. L. 123
Watson, S. J. 84, 238, 302
Watts, J. D. W. 236, 245, 270
Wegner, P. D. 278
Weidner, E. F. 219
Weill, R. 157
Weinfeld, M . 23, 180, 181, 200, 228, 268
Weisman, Z. 261
Weiss, E. 16, 22, 62
Wente, E. 67
Werner, W. 278
Westermann, C. 197, 258
Whedbee, J. W. 256
Whitley, C. F. 270, 278
Whybray, R. N. 65
Wieringen, A. L. H. M. van 330
Wiggins, S. A. 125
Wijngaards, J. N. M. 334
Wildberger, H. 16, 205, 206, 207, 215, 224, 227, 228, 231, 233, 234, 235, 241, 244, 246, 254, 256, 267, 270, 275, 282, 283, 285, 286, 301, 304, 305, 311, 312, 316, 319, 321, 323, 324, 337, 338, 340, 341, 342, 343, 345
Wilford, J. N. 128
Wilkinson, R. H. 297
Williams, J. G. 256, 258, 261
Williams, R. J. 287
Williamson, H. G. M. 272, 274, 276, 277, 279
Willis, J. T. 186, 232, 233, 234, 238, 239, 245
Wilson, J. A. 298
Wilson, R. R. 110, 195
Winckler, H. 285
Wiseman, D. J. 18, 38, 40, 252
Wolff, H. W. 136, 185, 187, 344

Wolkstein, D. 51
Wong, G. C. I 267
Woude A. S. van der 272, 279
Wright, D. P. 23, 165
Wright, G. E. 136
Wyatt, N. 108, 112, 114, 121, 123, 189, 220, 229, 348

Xella, P. 87, 95, 124, 126, 158, 251

Yee, G. A. 208, 222
Yeivin, S. 156
Youngblood, R. 264–265
Younger, K. L., Jr. 13, 14, 18, 69, 114, 220
Yoyotte, J. 172, 229, 230

Zevit, Z. 152, 153, 184, 304
Zimmerli, W. 157
Zorn, J. R. 157, 159

Index of Subjects

Anatolia 6, 98, 128 (*see also* Hatti)
afterlife 5, 7, 34, 38, 41, 42, 49, 55, 57, 63n, 66, 67n, 73–78, 80, 81, 84, 86–91, 94, 97–98, 118, 122, 124, 128–132, 138–41, 151–53, 166–67, 172, 176n, 177–79, 185, 190–92, 199, 203, 210–11, 229, 231, 232, 243, 246, 248, 251–53, 298, 298–302, 308, 332, 348–50, 353–54, 358
- beatific 7, 55, 114–15, 139–40, 146n, 166–67
- happy 71–72, 74, 88–90, 94, 211, 243, 297–98, 299, 332
- judgment in 41, 66n, 83, 85–87, 139, 178–79, 189, 255, 299, 335, 336, 342
- lack of food and drink in 45, 50–51, 72, 97, 251–52

Akkadian language (outside ch. 1) 64, 96, 104n, 107n, 108, 109n, 114n, 116n, 119n, 125, 126n, 171, 178, 204n, 211, 218, 226, 228n, 238n, 239n, 244, 245, 258n, 262, 264–65, 275n, 279n, 282n, 284, 287, 290n, 291n, 308, 327n, 330n, 337n, 342n, 357
- knowledge of in Judah 24–25

Anat 105, 113, 117, 122, 230n, 245
ancestors 1, 71, 73, 94–95, 103, 104, 115n, 116, 119, 121, 131–32, 135, 138, 140–41, 144–45, 155, 168n, 169–75, 191–92, 209, 235, 271, 274, 278, 284, 349, 357–58
- royal 35, 37–39, 42n, 93, 97, 107–11, 113n, 158–59, 287, 314, 347
apocalyptic 231n, 283, 307, 315–16, 323
Aram(eans) 11, 27, 29, 154, 274
Aramaic 24, 117, 130, 131, 132, 153n, 181, 204n, 216, 249, 269n, 329–30, 344
Asherah 28, 150n, 151–53, 173
Assyria 5, 7, 11–56, 58–63, 65, 91, 119, 127–29, 145–47, 161, 168, 173n, 175, 191, 201, 204n, 206n, 207, 210, 215–221, 221–32, 246n, 247, 249–53, 256, 260n, 262n, 265, 267, 270, 274, 276n, 278–79, 285n, 287–88, 296, 300, 303–07, 308n, 313–15, 319–23, 325–26, 332–35, 345–46, 347, 349–55, 357, 359
- (Neo-)Assyrian prophecy 193–95
Aššurbanipal 20, 26n, 37, 38–39, 42–43, 44, 47, 48, 52–53, 60, 201, 262n, 319
Aššurnasirpal II 11, 14, 36, 37, 158, 228, 231
"aversion therapy" 199–201, 314, 360

Baal 16n, 28, 99n, 105, 107, 110–11, 113–15, 122–24, 126–27, 139, 142, 168, 174, 179, 187–88, 190–91, 213, 218n, 224, 226n, 284, 304, 311n, 320
Babylon 5, 6, 11, 12, 20–21, 29, 33, 56, 60, 62, 65, 99, 159, 162, 179, 185n, 198, 204, 206, 207, 211, 215–221, 231, 250, 256n, 277n, 319, 322, 325, 331n, 334, 347, 353
Babylonian exile 2–3, 23, 33, 198, 243, 245–46, 256n, 334–35, 359
birds 46–47, 51–53, 74, 77, 113, 122n, 206, 243, 260, 309n, 338n, 341
- as symbols of wastelands and consumers of carrion 161, 163, 200
bones 38–39, 66n, 97, 130, 131n, 150, 151, 157, 165–66, 177, 235, 236, 299, 330n, 332, 336, 338, 341
Bronze Age 6, 23, 61, 64, 76, 93, 95–127, 132–32, 138, 157, 163n, 334, 348
burial /grave /tomb 1, 6, 8, 35–41, 43–44, 49–50, 54–55, 57, 66–77, 80, 82, 86–88, 94–98, 100–5, 115n, 118, 124, 127, 130–32, 134, 138, 140, 142–43, 146–166, 174n, 177–78, 182–83, 186, 189–91, 205n, 206, 208, 210–11, 216, 217n, 228, 230n, 232–49, 253, 254n, 258, 275, 277n, 293, 297–300, 302, 308, 313–14, 332, 337n, 342–43, 348–51, 354, 356, 358, 360 (*see also* graves)
- hierarchy of burial types 161

- nonburial / anti-burial 38, 45, 161, 184, 206n, 253, 342 (*see also* corpse violation)
burning 212n, 272
- in the afterlife 49, 85, 360
- of sacrifices 36, 264, 266
- of the dead (cremation) 39, 96–98, 127, 130, 147, 160–61
- of the living 23n, 39n, 160n, 161, 181, 222–32, 260, 263, 296–97, 303, 324–25, 350

child sacrifice 15n, 142, 180–83, 190, 192, 227–28, 304, 360 (*see also* burning, Molek)
choice of life or death / "two-paths" theology 167, 197–99, 251–53, 257, 350, 352, 356,
chops, mutton 11, 133, 187, 194, 199, 232, 305, 312
client states (*see* provinces)
common people 36, 74–76, 77, 80, 100, 115, 133, 142–43, 148, 160, 210, 348–49, 358,
corpse 35–39, 43, 67–68, 77, 83, 90, 125, 131, 142, 154, 157, 165–66, 173, 184, 293, 299, 324, 329, 332, 334n
- violation / exposure 38–39, 56, 73, 77, 80, 138n, 161, 165, 168n, 199–201, 204–6, 210, 216, 221, 243–45, 260, 352
- impurity 158, 159, 160n, 165, 184, 200, 314
cults of the dead (*see* mortuary cults)
curse
- Nile 65, 282
- prophetic 161, 198, 210, 244, 271, 276–77, 308, 350–51
- tomb 80, 131, 151, 236
- treaty/contract 15, 180n, 201, 228–29, 244, 251, 258, 296, 351

Dagan 96, 106n, 123, 125–26, 239
darkness 46, 49–51, 53, 54, 72, 82, 87–89, 109n, 127, 166, 176, 183, 186, 190, 233, 244, 245n, 259, 261, 270–79, 311, 330, 351, 352, 359
death cults (*see* mortuary cults)
deities, underworld 38, 42, 51–55, 83–86, 107–8, 112n, 113n, 122–26, 134, 179–83, 188n, 219, 268n, 271, 277, 281, 288n, 352

"democratization of death" 74–76, 78–79, 115, 128, 167, 297
demons 34, 44–47, 49, 51n, 79–80, 84–85, 112n, 113, 123–24, 153, 179, 183–84, 185, 190–92, 200n, 244n, 255, 271n, 341, 355
Deuteronomic Code 147, 165, 169
Deuteronomism / Deuteronomistic History 3, 19n, 27, 29, 62, 138, 144–45, 156–59, 169–70, 171, 198, 241, 249–50, 252, 272n, 284, 306, 339, 344–45, 346, 352, 355
diplomacy 4, 22, 24, 29, 60, 61, 76, 220, 252n, 347
divination / omina / mantic practices 27n, 35, 41, 47–48, 81–82, 96, 168–74, 255, 261n, 268–70, 273–75, 280–81, 287–88, 304, 307, 311, 331, 348–49, 351, 355 (see also *necromancy*)
divinization /deification of the dead 45, 55–56, 73, 76–78, 93–97, 101n, 107–116, 119–21, 130–32, 145, 167–69, 172, 210, 235, 277, 348–49 (*see also* Rephaim, rpum)
double entendre (*see* paronomasia)
dreams 50, 52, 81, 263, 267–69, 273, 289n, 314 (*see also* divination)
drunkenness 110–11, 116–17, 254–57, 282–83, 287–91, 300–3, 307, 312, 315, 351

economy 4, 11, 16, 19–23, 31–32, 58, 62–63, 65, 94, 283n, 285, 348, 356, 357, 358
Egypt(ians) (notable instances only) 7, 17, 57–91, 115, 156, 170–73, 176, 177, 178–79, 190, 198, 210, 218, 223, 229, 236–39, 244–49, 251–52, 254, 255, 281–288, 288–315, 320, 322, 326–326, 331–32, 347–48, 349, 350–51, 353–54, 356, 357, 358
El 105, 110, 112n, 133, 114n, 116–17, 123, 169, 205, 230
elites
- Assyrian 39, 247n
- Egyptian 66, 67n, 69n, 71–72, 74, 75–76, 79, 246, 297,
- Israelite and Judean 4, 17, 22, 23, 25, 32–33, 56, 64, 133, 148–50, 235, 240,

244, 251–52, 254, 302n, 311, 323, 349, 357–58
- Syro-Hittite 128–29
- Ugaritic 115
empire / imperial rule 3–4, 11–21, 24–34, 40, 48, 56, 58, 60–61, 91, 94, 97–98, 128–29, 168, 175, 208, 211n, 217, 220–21, 227n, 230, 231n, 252–53, 279, 286n, 287, 319–20, 322–23, 325, 333–34, 336n, 347, 351–52, 355, 359
emulation, elite 32, 55, 61, 115, 128, 133, 347
- cross cultural 69, 101, 159, 160n (see also influence)
enemies, of Isaiah 262, 330, 351, 354, 355
- political 19n, 27, 38, 39n, 44, 56, 151–53, 168, 200, 208n, 219n, 224, 227–32, 246n, 248, 259, 263, 265, 297, 303, 321, 324–27, 335, 354, 360n
- personal / supernatural 172, 244, 268–69, 304, 320
Esarhaddon 20, 43n, 47–48, 60, 216n, 217n, 228, 252n, 312n, 319

family religion 41–43, 55, 71, 90, 95n, 105, 116, 136n, 165, 169, 171–74, 271n, 286, 349, 358
- family tomb / burial 75, 140–41, 145, 148–50, 154–56, 160–61, 166, 206n, 235, 246, 349
- in mourning 35, 40, 162
feasting 40, 42–43, 70–71, 87, 111–12, 114–17, 128n, 130, 163–65, 174, 236, 253, 255, 300–2, 307, 318–21, 323, 335, 348, 358

ghost / spirit 34n, 35, 38, 39n, 41–54, 70, 72–73, 76, 78–83, 96, 97n, 103, 105, 109, 112, 115–16, 120, 125, 135n, 137, 142–43, 154n, 160, 162, 169–71, 207n, 209, 227n, 228, 239, 260, 263, 269n, 271, 274, 277, 281–82, 299, 313, 324, 326, 330n, 338, 341–42, 347
gods see *deities*
graves (*see* burial)
grave goods (*see* provisioning, tomb)
grave robbery 68, 73, 80, 151, 247
Greek culture, texts 19n, 70, 79n, 87, 91, 101, 105, 117, 127, 165, 174n, 177, 193, 212–14, 218, 229n, 292, 296, 311, 315, 326, 328n,
Greek textual witnesses (LXX, etc.) 180n, 204n, 206n, 232n, 243, 264n, 265n, 270, 280n, 281n, 291n, 317, 337n

Hatti / Hittites (see also: *Anatolia*) 4–5, 94, 96–98, 105, 109n, 122–23n, 124, 128, 129, 144, 167, 171, 334, 358
- knowledge of foreign pantheons 4
hegemony 11, 20, 27–32, 60–61, 253 (*see also* influence, imposition)
hell 49n, 52–53, 88–89, 200n, 229, 253, 280n, 313, 360
heterodoxy (*see* orthodoxy and heterodoxy)
Hezekiah 17–19, 24, 60, 63, 226, 252, 286, 322, 337–45, 352
- and the formation of the book of Isaiah 2, 65, 193, 279, 359n
- prosperity of his reign 16, 235, 248
- centralization and religious reforms 26, 28, 129, 133, 142, 158, 175, 192, 349, 358
- death and burial 157–59
hôy-oracles 1n1, 8, 162, 258–262
Hoshea 13, 59, 278n
hybridity 6–7, 221, 238

imperialism (*see* empire)
imposition, religious 25–34, 69n, 175, 347, 354
influence, cultural 7, 55–56, 83, 89, 91, 94, 101n, 119, 128, 131, 133, 140, 181, 190–91, 193, 212–14, 221, 236–38, 246, 284, 287, 307, 331, 348–49, 353–55
- mechanisms of 3–4, 7, 21–34, 60–66, 159, 196
influence, literary 7, 165, 199n, 207n, 223n, 248n, 265n, 327, 331, 341
inscriptions, mortuary 6, 55, 74n, 75, 80, 114, 120n, 125, 128–32, 151–53, 172, 177n, 208, 235–37, 240, 248, 277, 297–98, 313, 320, 332, 344n, 349 (*see also* stelae)
- historical and other 13–15, 17–18, 20, 24n, 27, 30, 37–39, 42, 58, 61, 64, 93, 168, 180, 209n, 215, 224–26, 228, 230n, 239,

241–42, 251, 265–66, 269–70, 293–94, 300, 308, 312n, 319, 348
intertextuality 23n, 196n, 203n, 312, 316–317, 330–31, 333,
Iron Age 4–6, 11, 23, 24, 46n, 57, 58n, 61, 63–64, 76, 93, 98, 130, 132, 135, 138, 146–51, 156–58, 190, 192, 230n, 235–39, 246n, 247n, 252, 284, 292–93, 312, 327n, 347, 348, 354
Isaiah
- "First Isaiah" 1, 2, 267
- formation of the book 2–3, 194–95, 346, 355–56
- of Jerusalem (Isaiah ben Amoz) 3, 8, 22, 65, 149, 175, 193, 267n, 284, 313, 315, 319, 323, 335, 336, 352, 353, 355, 356, 357, 358,
- Second Isaiah (Deutero-Isaiah) 2, 189, 207
Israel (northern kingdom) 13, 26n, 134, 146, 148n, 160n, 164, 169, 175, 181, 207, 252n, 256, 274, 278n, 288, 292, 305–6 (see also Samaria)
ius talionis 80, 131, 164n, 168n, 224, 227, 229, 253n, 256, 315, 325, 333, 350, 352

Jerusalem 2, 16–19, 22, 24, 25, 29, 32n, 33, 60–61, 142, 146–47, 148–49, 156–58, 175, 181, 183, 206n, 220, 224, 226, 227, 228, 230, 235–36, 249, 256, 262–67, 270, 274, 276, 286, 315, 319, 321–23, 358, 360
- as religiously diverse 192, 349
- destruction of 21, 163
- leaders of 234, 239–40, 288–89, 305–9, 311, 315, 351
Josiah 3, 17, 20, 142, 231, 242n, 279
- death and burial 20n, 156, 159, 163
- reforms 26, 28, 63, 133, 141, 170–71, 174–75, 192
- and the formation of the book of Isaiah 193, 250, 273n, 279n, 322, 333–36, 345–46, 353, 355–57, 359

Kalḫu 12, 37, 158
kings (see royal)
kispu(m) 37, 41–43, 56, 74, 94, 95n, 96, 108–10, 115, 116, 118, 120, 131, 172, 192, 209, 277, 347

Kush(ites)/Nubia(ns) 6n, 18n, 57, 59–61, 63, 69, 73, 85, 156, 218, 229n, 238, 247, 251, 254, 284, 285n, 287–88, 294–95, 303, 308, 311, 348, 353, 356

Lachish 12, 46n, 148, 161, 163n, 210, 222n, 225–26
life 1, 7, 8, 9, 54–55, 67–68, 72, 74n, 77, 113–15, 117, 122, 135n, 136, 139, 178, 186–87, 196, 197–99, 237, 251, 267, 270, 285n, 300, 301n, 315, 323, 328–29, 334–38, 342–46, 347, 350, 352–53, 355–58, 360 (see also choice of life or death)
- eternal 139, 166–67
- after death (see afterlife)
loanwords / calques
- Akkadian 24, 108n, 279n, 282n, 327n, 337n, 357
- Egyptian 64, 155n, 170–73, 233n, 284, 285, 287, 293n, 312n,
- West Semitic 238n

Marduk 54–55, 185, 190, 219–20, 250
marzēaḥ 134, 141, 163–65, 255, 307
marziḥu 106n, 115–17, 119, 131, 165, 190, 348
mercenaries 12, 225, 231n, 263, 266
Molek 27n, 126, 142, 180–83, 227, 276–77, 304, 360
mortuary cults /cults of the dead 6, 8, 34, 36n, 37, 41–43, 56, 68–74, 86, 89, 91, 94–98, 100–4, 106, 110–12, 114, 117n, 118–19, 121, 125, 128, 132, 134–35, 138–40, 143, 145–46, 149–50, 157–59, 165, 169n, 172–73, 177, 185n, 191–92, 211, 221, 238–41, 255, 273n, 279–283, 286–88, 293, 300, 302n, 304, 331, 348–49, 351, 357–58, 360 (see also kispu)
- definitions 94–95
Mot 122–24, 126–27, 141, 179–80. 183, 213, 230n, 255, 288n, 292, 304, 355
mourning / lamentation 35, 40–41, 44, 48, 50, 52n, 53n, 67, 69–71, 83, 88, 105, 109–10, 116, 118, 129, 154–55, 161–64, 174, 179, 186n, 190–91, 197, 208–9, 210, 214n, 258–262, 264, 274, 282n, 303, 314, 329, 340–41, 349–51, 354
- in mockery 207–11

Index of Subjects 443

mummification 57, 70–71, 74, 77, 82–83, 87, 90, 155, 172, 244, 302
Mut 8, 86, 229n, 288–315, 322, 351, 356, 358
mythology 35, 43–44, 46, 49–56, 66, 83–87, 90, 93, 105–7, 116–17, 122–24, 127, 132, 134, 139, 143, 167, 178, 180, 185, 198, 204n, 209, 211–15, 218–22, 229–30, 251–52, 255–56, 269n, 276, 295, 300, 302n, 303–4, 320, 326, 342, 347–48, 354

name, invocation of (*see* remembrance of the dead)
necromancy 9, 47, 54, 56, 81–82, 97, 121, 130, 131, 132, 134, 141, 142–43, 146, 165, 168–74, 176, 190, 192, 255–56, 261n, 270, 273–88, 307, 311, 312, 326, 330, 346n, 347–49, 351, 353–58
Neo-Assyrian Empire (*see* Assyria)
Nineveh 17n, 20, 22, 32, 37n, 39, 47, 216, 219, 226

offerings, mortuary 35–38, 42–43, 45, 50, 54n, 56, 70, 72–74, 78, 87, 95–97, 101–4, 108–10, 115, 118, 120n, 121n, 123–27, 129, 131, 138, 141, 174n, 211, 221, 239, 302, 320, 348, 360n (*see also* kispu)
orthodoxy and heterodoxy 27, 133, 138, 150n, 182–83, 192, 327

paronomasia/*double entendre* 194, 204n, 205n, 242, 245, 248, 265, 274, 290n, 291n, 292, 311, 312, 313, 314n, 331, 352
Persia 2n, 3, 91, 140, 174n, 207, 216, 331n, 334
pessimism 49, 72, 87–90, 122, 166, 197, 332, 343, 350, 359
politics 2–3, 6, 9, 11–13, 16, 20–23, 28–33, 48, 55, 59, 61n, 63, 65, 80–81, 89, 91, 94, 133, 144, 149, 161, 175, 194, 196, 203, 211, 216, 218n, 220–21, 229–30, 246, 248–49, 274, 278, 284, 287, 307, 331n, 321–23, 325, 333–34, 336, 347, 350, 352–54, 358–59
propaganda 14–15, 30, 33, 42n, 53, 56, 181n, 209, 215, 220, 352
prophets / prophecy 1–2, 43, 65, 138, 143, 145, 147, 160n, 165, 181, 187n, 190–201,

255, 258, 261, 267, 269n, 273, 275, 280, 282n, 287, 306, 307, 311n, 333, 336, 349–51, 354, 357, 359 (*see also* divination)
provinces / vassals / client states 13, 15, 16,19, 20–33, 56, 58, 60, 206n, 228, 229, 238, 296, 313, 334 (*see also* empire, treaties)
provisioning, tomb 36–41, 43, 49, 68, 71–74, 87, 90, 97, 131, 147, 149–50, 154, 190, 237, 246–49

remembrance of the dead / invocation of the name 41–42, 45, 48, 55, 73–74, 76–77, 81, 109–10, 113n, 132, 141, 206, 209n, 211, 221, 228, 237, 277, 300, 324, 326, 343, 346n (*see also* second death)
Rephaim (post-Ugarit) 107n, 131, 160, 167–68, 204, 209, 221, 257, 277, 324, 326, 330–31, 355 (*see also* rpum)
"replacement theology" 226, 320, 352
rpum (Ugaritic) 107–20, 124n, 141, 326, 332
resurrection / revivification / raising the dead 45, 55, 63n, 66n, 84n, 113–15, 117, 139–40, 165, 186–90, 191, 255n, 302, 320–21, 324n, 328–29, 331–32, 335–36, 342, 346, 349, 353, 356, 358–60
rhetoric 210, 220, 230n, 267, 269–70, 275, 279, 312, 343
  – of death 1–2, 7–9, 91, 179, 189, 193–201, 203, 204n, 215, 246, 251–52, 256, 261–62, 281, 302, 318, 323, 329, 331–32, 336, 342, 345–46, 347, 349–54, 356
  – Neo-Assyrian 23n, 25, 33, 56, 209n, 224, 226, 229–30, 249–53, 256, 319,
ritual / rites 8, 15, 27, 32, 35, 40–44, 47, 54, 70, 84, 87–88, 90, 93–98, 103–19, 121, 126, 129–32, 137, 138n, 140–41, 147, 158–59, 165, 174, 181–82, 186, 209, 211, 214n, 218, 227, 229n, 232, 256, 296–97, 299, 301–4, 307–8, 312, 315, 347–48, 351, 354
royal
  – ancestor cults 35, 37, 42, 48, 56, 70, 73–74, 82, 94, 96–98, 101n, 107–9, 118–19, 121, 129, 131–32, 142, 166, 172, 192n, 208–11, 277, 287, 348, 349, 357–58

Index of Subjects

- tombs 36–38, 41, 71–72, 74–76, 95, 97, 121, 131, 134, 142, 156–60, 210, 247, 287, 314

Saites/Libyans 6n, 57, 59, 60, 69, 74, 85, 156, 229n, 251n, 288, 294–96, 303, 348, 356
sacrifice 36, 41, 54, 70, 83, 95–96, 105, 108–11, 116, 119n, 121n, 125–26, 130, 138, 168, 172, 174, 206n, 229–30, 266, 297, 320n (see also child sacrifice, ritual)
Šalmaneser III 12, 201
Šalmaneser V 13, 217n
Samaria 13, 29, 59, 103, 134, 156, 207, 217n, 301n, 305–6, 349
Sargon II 13, 17, 20, 24, 33, 37, 39, 48, 61, 201, 208, 214n, 216–18, 312n, 319, 322, 350, 355
scribes and scribal practices 4, 6, 20n, 23–25, 51, 52, 65, 74, 81, 112, 144, 170, 173n, 175, 180, 190, 194n, 196n, 205n, 206n, 232n, 233, 243n, 245, 264, 265n, 272n, 277, 280, 297, 308n, 335, 344n, 355
"second death" 80, 211, 248
Sennacherib 14, 15, 17–19, 37, 39, 48, 59–61, 210n, 216n, 217n, 220, 249, 264, 266, 279, 322, 344–45
Sheol 131n, 134, 135, 176–79, 185–86, 189–90, 197, 198, 203–5, 209, 221, 224n, 253, 256, 257, 260, 276, 279–81, 288, 290, 291, 303n, 304, 311, 313–14, 326, 329, 330n, 332, 337, 339, 340, 342, 343, 351, 358, 360 (see also underworld)
Sidon 6, 80, 94, 131, 168, 208, 236n
SPAAC 12
stelae / memorial monuments 37, 41, 58n, 59, 60, 72–75, 78, 97n, 98, 110–11, 115, 125, 127–28, 131, 138, 152, 154–55, 157n, 173, 232–33, 239–42, 248, 251n, 266, 269, 296, 300–1, 307n, 308, 312–13, 320, 344n, 350
subversion / inversion 7, 25, 58, 192, 208, 209n, 210, 211n, 231, 275, 314, 320, 346n, 350, 352, 354, 355, 358
sun gods 50n, 53–54, 68, 73, 84, 87n, 90, 97, 109, 124–25, 132, 185n, 200n, 212n, 219, 238n, 269n, 342n
swallowing / devouring Death 45, 84–85, 122, 126n, 178–79, 253, 255–57, 318, 320, 323, 351, 353, 355

Syria 4n, 6, 11, 12,37, 93–96, 98–128, 130–32, 138, 143, 181, 218, 278, 347, 348
Syro-Ephraimite War 12–13, 274, 276, 306n, 334

Tayinat 4n, 29, 30
temple 4, 27, 30, 69, 86, 97, 110, 138n, 163, 230, 294–95, 298, 300, 301n, 308
- Jerusalem 18, 28, 32, 63n, 142, 146–47, 157–59, 231, 302, 313
teraphim 141, 173–74
Tiglath-Pileser III 12–13, 14, 17, 18, 19, 22, 28, 44n, 217n, 250, 278
tombs (see burial)
trade 4, 16, 19–23, 60, 62, 64, 76, 129, 149
tradents 190, 223
- Isaianic 1, 2, 7, 9, 156, 191, 221, 227, 231, 279, 322–23, 335, 345–46, 347, 353, 354, 355
transposition 203
treaties 4n, 8, 15–16, 22n, 27, 29, 228, 229n, 251–52, 288, 296, 304, 306, 311, 334, 351
tribute and taxation 12, 13, 16–19, 27, 30n, 33n, 59, 129, 322
Tyre 12, 130–31, 238–40

underworld / netherworld 1, 34–35, 38, 41, 44–46, 48–56, 68–69, 74, 80, 83–89, 103, 107, 110, 112n, 113, 122–27, 138–39, 176–80, 184–191, 198, 199n, 207n, 209–10, 213n, 214, 215n, 219, 221, 224, 228, 245, 254–57, 262–264, 266, 268n, 269, 271, 273, 276–77, 279, 280n, 281, 288, 292, 299, 301n, 303–5, 314, 324–26, 328, 331–32, 334, 340, 343, 346n, 347, 349, 351–54 (see also Sheol, afterlife)
- as dusty 49–51, 66n, 69, 105, 109–11, 162, 176, 178n, 186n, 190, 251–52, 263–64, 273, 314, 324, 328, 331, 335, 351, 359–60
- as muddy 110, 127, 207, 209, 221, 251
Ugarit 5–7, 53, 90, 93–132, 134, 136, 139, 141–43, 146, 152, 157–58, 163–64, 166–71, 176–77, 180, 189, 190, 209, 211, 213–14, 218, 220, 238, 255, 277, 284, 304, 320, 326, 332, 338n, 348, 354, 355, 358, 361n
Ugaritic language (outside ch. 3) 207, 215n, 219n, 233n, 238n, 239, 262n, 291n, 327n

wisdom 41, 54, 55, 65, 77, 141, 178, 197–99, 256–58, 282n, 287n, 288, 307, 340, 350, 352, 359
women 46n, 78, 79, 187, 294, 301, 308, 324
– in ancestor cults 41, 73, 96–97, 109, 140, 172
– in necromancy 48, 170, 273

– burial 37–38, 40, 154n, 160, 162, 208
– figurines 150
– mourning 40, 69, 129, 162, 164
– "wicked woman" 198n, 256–57

Zion 230–31, 257n, 263–64, 267, 269, 271, 290, 311–12, 321, 323, 339, 350

www.ingramcontent.com/pod-product-compliance
Lightning Source LLC
Chambersburg PA
CBHW021350290426
44108CB00010B/180